MW00909640

Windows .NET Server 2003
Domains & Active Directory

Windows .NET Server 2003 DOMAINS & ACTIVE DIRECTORY

Alex Tchekmarev

alist

A-LIST, LLC
295 East Swedesford Rd.
PMB #285
Wayne, PA 19087
702-977-5377 (FAX)
mail@alistpublishing.com
http://www.alistpublishing.com

This book is printed on acid-free paper.

Windows .NET Server 2003 Domains & Active Directory
By Alex Tchekmarev

ISBN: 1-931769-00-1

Printed in the United States of America

03 04 7 6 5 4 3 2 1

A-LIST, LLC titles are distributed by Independent Publishers Group and are available for site license or bulk purchase by institutions, user groups, corporations, etc.

Book Editor: Rizwati Freeman

Contents

INTRODUCTION

This book is based on *Windows 2000 Domain & Active Directory* published in March 2001. It has been totally revised and adapted to conform to the Windows .NET Server 2003 environment and over 100 pages have been added. (From now on, all products of the Windows .NET Server 2003 family will be referred to as Windows .NET for short.) As a result, this book will be useful for those administrators who currently work with Windows 2000 domains and for those who are planning to deploy Active Directory on Windows .NET servers. For an administrator, the new version of Active Directory does not have any new principle features, and all options that are only available on Windows .NET servers are specifically described in the book. Therefore, an administrator can deal with any version of Active Directory domains and compare the working environment's features with those that were on the old platform.

Many books have already been published which cover Active Directory's goals, its advantages and disadvantages, strategies for developing Active Directory in a large corporate network, and other important questions that have not changed with the advent of Windows .NET. (However, this does not mean that the new version of Active Directory is not more mature, effective, and convenient for administrators than the initial version that appeared in Windows 2000!) In this book, the author has tried to take a look at the more practical problems that come up while *using* Active Directory. Even though the book may not offer an answer to *all* the problems that might arise, you will at least learn how to approach them.

One probably would not even consider repairing a defective car or a complex electronic device without special additional tools and facilities. Nonetheless, administrators who work with Active Directory often forget that the problems which come up in the process of working with Active Directory are also impossible to eliminate without the help of the appropriate tools and utilities. Most of the tools that you need for working with Active Directory (and that are looked at in this book) are furnished along with the system, and are found in the *Windows Support Tools* pack. This book is dedicated, to a large extent, to working with exactly these tools. A few tools and scripts from the *Windows 2000 Server Resource Kit* are also considered, since they work properly in the Windows .NET environment.

Besides, the author would like to turn administrators' attention to methods of program access to Active Directory, and in part to scripts that use the *Active Directory*

Service Interfaces (ADSI). Scripts can be used to solve many administrative tasks, and you may use already written scripts after a minimal number of modifications to fit your needs. Creating scripts does not require you to be a highly qualified programmer — a fact which the author tried to get across in the last two chapters of the book.

This book is geared towards a relatively prepared reader, one who has already had some experience working with Windows 2000, and is familiar with the basic work methods and components of the system (e.g., with Microsoft Management Console snap-ins). However, information on these questions can easily be found in the Help system.

Below is a summary of each chapter.

Part I: Active Directory Fundamentals and Standards

- *Chapter 1, "LDAP Basics,"* covers one of the standards that make up the basis of Active Directory — the Lightweight Directory Access Protocol (LDAP).
- In *Chapter 2, "Active Directory Terminology and Concepts,"* relates the essential Active Directory concepts. The terms and concepts described in *Chapter 1* and in this chapter will be widely used in the rest of this book; therefore, their knowledge will affect how the reader understands Active Directory operating mechanisms and topics described later in the other chapters. New Active Directory features offered by domain controllers running Windows .NET are also reviewed.
- *Chapter 3, "Domain Name System (DNS) as Main Naming Service,"* comprises Active Directory requirements of mandatory DNS service, as well as new DNS features introduced in Windows .NET.

Part II: Deploying Active Directory Domains

- In *Chapter 4, "Windows .NET DNS Server,"* the essential operations of installing, configuring, and verifying Windows 2000/.NET DNS Servers are considered. An example of interoperation between Active Directory and a legacy DNS infrastructure is discussed.
- *Chapter 5, "Installing Active Directory,"* tells you what you need to pay attention to before and during installation of Active Directory. Certain typical problems that you may encounter when deploying Active Directory forests (on Windows 2000 and Windows .NET domain controllers) are also examined.
- *Chapter 6, "Configuring and Troubleshooting Active Directory Domains,"* gives recommendations that you need to consider when deploying and troubleshooting Active Directory domains.

Part III: Administering Active Directory

- In *Chapter 7, "Domain Manipulation Tools,"* we will look at all standard snap-ins intended for administering Active Directory. To use them effectively (especially in the new, Windows .NET Server 2003, environment), the administrator must be aware of certain features and methods of working with them.

- In *Chapter 8, "Common Administrative Tasks,"* we will examine both typical administrative tasks — like working with user and network resources — and tasks specific to Active Directory domains, like delegating administrative control, managing FSMO roles, refreshing group policies, searching and recovering Active Directory, and others.

Part IV: Using System Utilities and Support Tools

- The main task of *Chapter 9, "General Characteristics and Purpose of System Tools,"* is to give the administrator an idea of what a certain utility is used for, and to help in choosing the tool to use for a specific task.
- Described in *Chapter 10, "Diagnosing and Maintaining Domain Controllers,"* are utilities that allow you to determine the health of a single domain controller and the integrity of the Active Directory database replica stored on it.
- *Chapter 11, "Verifying Network and Distributed Services,"* covers the utilities that allow you to diagnose problems that arise due to the fact that Active Directory is a distributed network database, that is, problems of connectivity between domain controllers, authentication, and replication.
- *Chapter 12, "Manipulating Active Directory Objects,"* looks at the utilities used for work with Active Directory logical objects — tools for searching directory for objects of various types and editing their attributes, utilities for exporting and importing objects, and tools used for manipulating workstations, domain controllers and trust relationships.
- In *Chapter 13, "Migration and Directory Reorganization Tools,"* those utilities intended for reorganizing domain trees and migration of objects between forests are examined.
- The tools that allow you to view and manage access permissions on Active Directory objects are looked at in *Chapter 14, "Security Tools".*
- *Chapter 15, "Group Policy Tools"* offers an examination of those utilities that allow you to test Group Policy Objects (GPOs) and determine the resulting security settings defined by group policies.

Part V: Program Access to Active Directory

- *Chapter 16, "Active Directory Service Interfaces (ADSI),"* will acquaint administrators with ways to manage Active Directory programmatically. The difficult thing about working with the documentation on ADSI is that it is tough for a novice to find what he/she needs in the midst of such a huge amount of unfamiliar information. This chapter gives the reader an understanding of the basic concepts, which will be illustrated in the following chapter with examples.
- *Chapter 17, "Scripting Administrative Tasks,"* consists almost completely of program examples. It seems to me that the principles of programming with ADSI are easier to master when you have a specially designed example with commentary. After having understood these basic concepts, it will be much easier to work with documentation that describes in detail all of the interfaces and their methods and properties.

Part VI: Appendixes

- The *Appendixes* include "must-see" and simply useful references to web resources; a list of registry keys and directory objects that allow you to "fine tune" Active Directory or manage its internal mechanisms; a table of ADSI interfaces supported by the main system providers and a list of all the functions implemented by the IADsTools ActiveX object, which are useful for developing administrative scripts.

The *Glossary* will help you find a short description of an unfamiliar term quickly, or to verify your understanding of this term.

The *"How to...?"* section is set up like a typical FAQ. In this section, you may find the solution you need for a specific problem faster than if you were to simply look through the table of contents or the *Index*.

For finding references to a certain utility or tool in the *Index*, use its *file name*. You can also find references to interfaces, methods, properties, attributes, enumerations, etc., the same way — under their names.

The author can be reached at **ATchekmarev@msn.com**. The listings included in this book can be found at **http://www.alistpublishing.com**.

Conventions

Here are the conventions used in the book:

- Names of administrative snap-ins and UI elements (such as menu, commands, pop-up windows, etc.) are in bold, for example, "the **Active Directory Users and Computers** snap-in" or "the **Delegate Control** command on the **Action** menu".
- Names of Active Directory object attributes, ASDI interfaces, methods, and properties, are shown in italics, for example, *objectSid*.
- Certain important words or new terms are also marked in *italics*.
- If a long command or string displayed on the screen does not fit on one line in the book, the ↳ symbol will be used. For example:

```
createusers LDAP://OU=Staff,DC=w2k,DC=dom cn:"User User01"
↳ samAccountName:user-ldap01 password:psw1
```

This means that the line shown should be considered as one, unbreakable line.

- As you can see from the previous example, the mandatory elements of a command line — the command name and the parameters — are in bold in order to be more visible. The other elements of the command are specific to your environment and you should determine them.

PART I

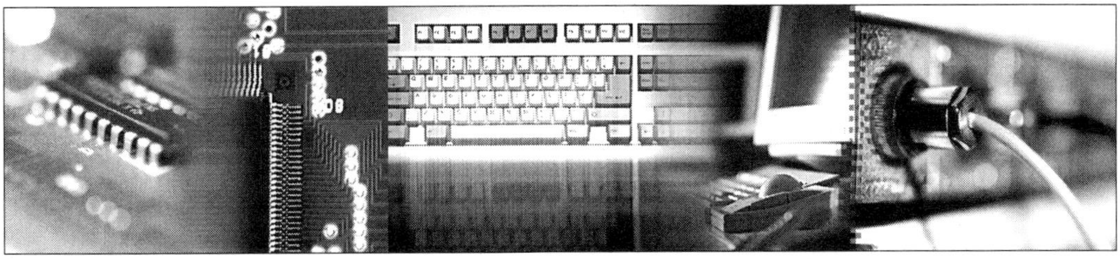

Active Directory Fundamentals and Standards

CHAPTER 1: **LDAP Basics**

CHAPTER 2: **Active Directory Terminology and Concepts**

CHAPTER 3: **Domain Name System (DNS) as Main Naming Service**

Chapter 1: LDAP Basics

The purpose, advantages, organization, and role of Active Directory for Windows 2000-based domains have already been described extensively in many books and articles. If you are not familiar with Active Directory basics at this point, comprehensive information on it can be easily found. The Windows .NET version of Active Directory is a rather evolutionary step in the architecture of Windows domains. (The Windows 2000 version of Active Directory was, indeed, a revolution if one compares it with "flat" NT Directory Service (NTDS) domains.) Therefore, an administrator deploying Active Directory on computers running Windows .NET will face the same problems that are peculiar to the Active Directory in general. In addition, most requirements for installing Active Directory and the methods of administering the Windows .NET-based domains have not been changed in the new version of Active Directory.

There are two Internet standards that appeared long before Active Directory, but which are very closely related to it. These standards are *Lightweight Directory Access Protocol* (LDAP v3) and *Domain Name System* (DNS). It is impossible to speak about Active Directory without using the terms stated by these standards. That is why in the first three chapters of the book, we will discuss the terminology and concepts that are widely used in the remaining chapters.

LDAP as a Cornerstone of Active Directory

Use of the Active Directory service (both on Windows 2000 and Windows .NET operating systems) requires a good understanding of the LDAP protocol basics since this protocol is used everywhere for accessing directory information. Familiarity with and knowledge of LDAP are also necessary for working with many tools and utilities, such as the *Active Directory Administrative Tool* (Ldp.exe), **ADSI Edit** snap-in, *Search.vbs* script, *LDIF Directory Exchange* utility (LDIFDE.exe), and others, and are needed for scripting as well. This concerns all four LDAP models discussed below. Therefore, before we begin to discuss the Active Directory installation, administrative snap-ins, system tools, and other topics, let us first review the LDAP concepts. Then, some Active Directory specific terms and technologies will be considered in the next chapter.

Note

All main features of LDAP v3 are described in RFC 2251 through RFC 2256. Refer to these RFCs for more information, or check out the *Q221606* article in the *Microsoft Knowledge Base*. You may also find links to other related standards there.

Informational Model

The *informational (data) model* of the LDAP protocol, and therefore, of Active Directory as well, is based on X.500 — the International Standards Organization (ISO) special standard defining elements of a distributed directory service. This standard proposes an object-oriented data model; therefore, it uses such terms as *class*, *instance*, and *inheritance*.

Schema

The *schema* defines classes and attributes, from which all directory objects can be derived. The schema itself is stored in the directory as a set of objects.

Directory Entry (Object)

Entry is an instance of a specific structural class and in Active Directory is usually called an *object.* An object can either be a *container* or a *leaf.* It is uniquely identified by its *relative distinguished name* (RDN) and *distinguished name* (DN).

Classes

Each directory object is an instance of one or more *classes* defined in the schema. In general, every object inherits from at least one structural object class and zero or more auxiliary object classes. There are three types of classes:

- *Abstract classes* serve as templates for deriving new abstract, auxiliary, and structural classes. Abstract classes cannot be instantiated in Active Directory, i.e., you cannot create a directory object of an abstract class. The definition of an abstract class can include any number of auxiliary classes.
- Structural classes are derived from abstract or structural classes and inherit all attributes of all parent classes. Active Directory objects can only be instances of structural classes. The definition of a structural class can include any number of auxiliary classes.
- An auxiliary class is derived from an abstract or auxiliary class and can be included in the definition of a structural, abstract, or auxiliary class. The defined class inherits all attributes of the auxiliary class listed in the *mustContain*, *systemMustContain*, *mayContain*, and *systemMayContain* properties. Auxiliary classes cannot be instantiated in Active Directory. The definition of an auxiliary class can include any number of auxiliary classes.

Attributes

Attributes contain the data used to describe properties of the defined classes. Attributes may be mandatory or optional, single- or multi-valued. An attribute is defined in the schema by a name and an *object identifier* (OID). Attributes are defined in RFC 2252 and RFC 2256. Here are the examples of attributes (these are the values of the *lDAPDisplayName* and *attributeID* attributes of the *attributeSchema* objects in the Schema container):

- nTSecurityDescriptor (1.2.840.113556.1.2.281)
- distinguishedName (2.5.4.49)

Attribute Syntax

The *attribute syntax* (see RFC 2252) defines the type of an attribute (e.g., a Unicode string, a number, an octet string, etc.), byte ordering, and the matching rules for comparisons of property types. The syntax of LDAP attributes is represented by *object identifier* (OID). For example:

- Distinguished Name (1.3.6.1.4.1.1466.115.121.1.12)
- UTC time (1.3.6.1.4.1.1466.115.121.1.53)

RootDSE Object

Every LDAP v3-complaint server has an individual DSA-Specific Entry object — *RootDSE* — defined in RFC 2251. This object is the root of the *Directory Information Tree* (DIT), but is not a part of any naming context (partition). It defines a directory server's configuration and capabilities.

Note

Directory System Agent (DSA) is the system process that provides clients with access to directory information physically stored on a hard disk of a domain controller, or directory server. In Active Directory servers running on Windows 2000 or Windows .NET, the DSA is a part of the *Local System Authority* (LSA) subsystem.

RootDSE has properties that can be retrieved programmatically (see *Listing 17.2*) or by using a query tool (such as Ldp.exe or the **ADSI Edit** snap-in). To query a RootDSE from Ldp.exe, specify the empty base DN, the *base* scope, and the filter `objectClass=*`. (Search operations will be considered a bit later.) It is possible to bind to a specific server, or to use a server-less query. In the latter case, the first available LDAP server (a Windows 2000- or Windows .NET-based domain controller) will respond. Here is an example of the RootDSE data:

```
    1> currentTime: 6/12/2002 9:29:2 Central Standard Time Central Standard Time;
    1> subschemaSubentry:
CN=Aggregate,CN=Schema,CN=Configuration,DC=net,DC=dom;
    1> dsServiceName: CN=NTDS Settings,CN=NETDC2,CN=Servers,CN=NET-Site,
CN=Sites,CN=Configuration,DC=net,DC=dom;
    5> namingContexts: CN=Configuration,DC=net,DC=dom;
CN=Schema,CN=Configuration,DC=net,DC=dom; DC=subdom,DC=net,DC=dom;
DC=DomainDnsZones,DC=net,DC=dom; DC=ForestDnsZones,DC=net,DC=dom;
    1> defaultNamingContext: DC=subdom,DC=net,DC=dom;
    1> schemaNamingContext: CN=Schema,CN=Configuration,DC=net,DC=dom;
    1> configurationNamingContext: CN=Configuration,DC=net,DC=dom;
```

```
    1> rootDomainNamingContext: DC=net,DC=dom;
    20> supportedControl: 1.2.840.113556.1.4.319; 1.2.840.113556.1.4.801;
1.2.840.113556.1.4.473; 1.2.840.113556.1.4.528; 1.2.840.113556.1.4.417;
1.2.840.113556.1.4.619; 1.2.840.113556.1.4.841; 1.2.840.113556.1.4.529;
1.2.840.113556.1.4.805; 1.2.840.113556.1.4.521; 1.2.840.113556.1.4.970;
1.2.840.113556.1.4.1338; 1.2.840.113556.1.4.474; 1.2.840.113556.1.4.1339;
1.2.840.113556.1.4.1340; 1.2.840.113556.1.4.1413; 2.16.840.1.113730.3.4.9;
2.16.840.1.113730.3.4.10; 1.2.840.113556.1.4.1504; 1.2.840.113556.1.4.802;
    2> supportedLDAPVersion: 3; 2;
    11> supportedLDAPPolicies: MaxPoolThreads; MaxDatagramRecv;
MaxReceiveBuffer; InitRecvTimeout; MaxConnections; MaxConnIdleTime;
MaxPageSize; MaxQueryDuration; MaxTempTableSize; MaxResultSetSize;
MaxNotificationPerConn;
    1> highestCommittedUSN: 124992;
    4> supportedSASLMechanisms: GSSAPI; GSS-SPNEGO; EXTERNAL; DIGEST-MD5;
    1> dnsHostName: netdc2.subdom.net.dom;
    1> ldapServiceName: net.dom:netdc2$@SUBDOM.NET.DOM;
    1> serverName: CN=NETDC2,CN=Servers,CN=NET-Site,
CN=Sites,CN=Configuration,DC=net,DC=dom;
    3> supportedCapabilities: 1.2.840.113556.1.4.800;
1.2.840.113556.1.4.1670; 1.2.840.113556.1.4.1791;
    1> isSynchronized: TRUE;
    1> isGlobalCatalogReady: TRUE;
    1> domainFunctionality: 2;
    1> forestFunctionality: 2;
    1> domainControllerFunctionality: 2;
```

(Notice the numbers at the beginning of the lines — they indicate the number of values within an attribute.)

RootDSE contains the following standard attributes (refer to RFC 2251 and 2252):

- `altServer` — references to other servers that can be used when this server becomes unavailable. By default, this attribute is absent on Active Directory servers.
- `namingContexts` — the list of naming contexts stored on the server. Notice that in our example, the domain naming context (directory partition) refers to the *subdom.net.dom* domain, but two other contexts, the Schema and Configuration, refer to the forest root domain — *net.dom*. These contexts should be used when searching the directory. Windows .NET-based domain controllers can also store application directory partitions, and this attribute lists their names, too. In the example, you can see the distinguished names of two application partitions: *domainDnsZones.net.dom* and *forestDnsZones.net.dom*.

- `subschemaSubentry` — the name of the *subschema* entry (or the *abstract schema*; see *Chapter 16, "Active Directory Service Interfaces (ADSI)"*). This object contains definitions of available attributes and classes.
- `supportedControl` — the object identifiers (OID) of the LDAP controls that the server supports. This attribute may be absent. In comparison with Windows 2000, Windows .NET-based domain controllers support four new controls.
- `supportedExtension` — the object identifiers (OIDs) of the extended LDAP operations that the server supports. By default, this attribute is absent on Active Directory servers.
- `supportedLDAPVersion` — the LDAP versions supported by the server.
- `supportedSASLMechanisms` — the *Simple Authentication and Security Layer* (SASL) mechanisms supported by the server. This attribute may be absent. In comparison with Windows 2000, Windows .NET-based domain controllers support two new controls.

In addition, Active Directory supports the following attributes:

- `configurationNamingContext` — the *Configuration* context.
- `currentTime` — the current time.
- `defaultNamingContext` — the default context for the server. By default, this is the distinguished name of the domain where the server is located.
- `dnsHostName` — the server's DNS name.
- `dsServiceName` — the name of the directory service (NTDS).
- `highestCommittedUSN` — the highest USN committed to the database on this server.
- `ldapServiceName` — the *Service Principal Name* (SPN) for the server; used for mutual authentication.
- `rootDomainNamingContext` — the name of the forest where the server is located.
- `schemaNamingContext` — the *Schema* context.
- `serverName` — the distinguished name of the server object.
- `supportedCapabilities` — the object identifiers (OID) of the capabilities that the server supports. In comparison with Windows 2000, Windows .NET-based domain controllers support two new capabilities.
- `supportedLDAPPolicies` — supported LDAP management policies.

There are also two important operational attributes:

- `isSynchronized` — `TRUE`, if initial synchronization of this Active Directory replica with its partners has been completed (i.e., a newly promoted server can advertise itself as a domain controller).

- `isGlobalCatalogReady` — `TRUE`, if the domain controller has not simply been *promoted to be* a Global Catalog (GC) server, but has already advertised itself as a GC server.

Windows .NET-based domain controllers support three additional operational attributes, which represent domain and forest *functional levels* (see the next chapter for details):

- `domainFunctionality` — either `0` (both Windows 2000 mixed and Windows 2000 native levels) or `2` (Windows .NET level).
- `forestFunctionality` — either `0` (Windows 2000 level) or `2` (Windows .NET level).
- `domainControllerFunctionality` — is equal to `2` for any Windows .NET-based domain controller.

Naming Model

The naming model defines how directory objects can be uniquely specified. The OSI directory model uses distinguished names for that purpose.

Distinguished Name (DN)

A *distinguished name* is unique within a forest or *Directory Information Tree* (DIT) that it is placed in, and serves as a primary key for a directory object. DN consists of *relative distinguished names* (RDN), which represent branches in the directory information tree.

Here is an example of an object's distinguished name (CN stands for *Common Name*, OU means *Organizational Unit*, and DC means *Domain Component*):

CN=John Smith,OU=Staff,DC=net,DC=dom

Relative Distinguished Name (RDN)

A *relative distinguished name* uniquely identifies objects in a container. The RDNs consist of an *attribute naming specifier* (DC, CN, and OU; other specifiers are not usually used in Active Directory) and a value, for example:

- CN=Domain Controllers
- OU=Staff
- DC=net

Other Name Types Used in Active Directory

- *SAM (Pre-Windows 2000) Account Names.* SAM account names are required for compatibility with down-level clients. A SAM name must be unique within a domain.
- *Globally Unique Identifiers* – the Globally Unique Identifier (GUID) is a 128-bit number, which uniquely identifies the object when it is created. It never changes and ensures that the object will be addressed — even if it has been renamed or moved.
- *Fully Qualified Domain Name (FQDN)* is also known as the *full computer name*; this is a concatenation of the host name (the NetBIOS name) and the primary DNS suffix, for example:

  ```
  netdc2.subdom.net.dom
  ```

- *User Principal Names* – the User Principal Name (UPN) consists of the user logon name and a UPN suffix (the current or root DNS domain name, or a specially created shortened name), for example, `JohnS@net` or `John@net.dom`. UPN is intended for simplified logon and can be used for logging on to the network on a computer that can belong to any domain within the forest.
- *LDAP Uniform Resource Locator (URL).* LDAP URLs are used by LDAP-enabled clients for accessing Active Directory objects. LDAP URLs can also be used as binding strings in scripts and applications, for example (the server name is optional):

  ```
  LDAP://netdc4.net.dom/CN=John Smith,OU=Staff,DC=net,DC=dom
  ```

- *Active Directory Canonical Name.* Canonical names are used in the administrative snap-in's user interface for displaying object names. A canonical name is similar to the distinguished name without the naming attribute specifiers (DC, CN, etc.). For example, the canonical name for the LDAP URL shown above is:

  ```
  net.dom/Staff/John Smith
  ```

Referrals

In a multi-domain forest, complete directory information is not available on a single domain controller (DC). (You can only obtain a subset of attributes of all objects from a Global Catalog server.) You need to have a mechanism that will redirect the query from a DC to the DC that stores the requested object. This mechanism may also be required if the object is located in another naming partition on the same server (for example, if you specify the domain naming context as the search base and want to find objects that can be stored in either Schema or Configuration partitions).

To inform a client that the server does not have a copy of the requested object, the requested server uses an LDAP *referral* in accordance with RFC 2251. Ideally, the referral indicates the DC that stores the necessary object. The server can generate referrals to other DCs according to the *cross-reference* objects stored in the directory. Cross-references give every DC the opportunity to be aware of all directory partitions in the forest. The references are stored in the Configuration container, and are therefore replicated to every DC in the forest. Hence, any DC can generate referrals to any other domain in the forest, as well as to the Schema and Configuration partitions. Cross-references can be created either automatically or manually by an administrator.

Functional Model

The *functional model* describes the operations that can be conducted with information stored in a directory using the LDAP protocol. You need to be able to access information, and read and update it as well. These operations are implemented in somewhat different ways for various system tools that use the LDAP protocol, but the main concepts and parameters remain the same.

Authentication

Authentication operations allow a user to establish a connection with a Directory System Agent (DSA) and to get the right to access the stored information.

- **Open** — this command creates and initializes a connection block, and then opens a connection to the DSA.
- **Bind** — this command initiates a protocol session to the DSA and authenticates the client to the DSA.
- **Unbind** — this command terminates a session, frees all resources associated with the session, and closes a connection.

Interrogation

Interrogation methods describe ways of retrieving information.

Search

The widely used *search* operations retrieve information based on user criteria. Search operations have the following parameters:

- **Search base** — the distinguished name of a directory object (called the *base* object) from which the search begins (e.g., `DC=net,DC=dom` or `OU=Stuff, DC=net,DC=dom`).

Note

All search parameters are mandatory. Many LDAP-compatible tools and utilities, such as DsQuery, LDIFDE, Search.vbs, and so on, do not require that users specify some parameters. However, this only means that these tools themselves substitute some default values instead of the missed parameters.

Note

The search base can also have the "<GUID=...>" format (the angle brackets are included!) (e.g., "<GUID=0855ae368790cb4b8726cf37cb2222a5>").

- **Search scope** — defines the depth of searching relative to the search base (Fig. 1.1 shows various scopes for the domain object). There are three options:
  - **Base**. Only the base object is searched (i.e., you will work with properties of the base object only).
  - **One level**. The *children* of the base object are searched; the base object itself and *grandchildren* are excluded.
  - **Subtree**. The entire subtree is searched, beginning with and including the base object (i.e., all "visible" objects in the subtree).

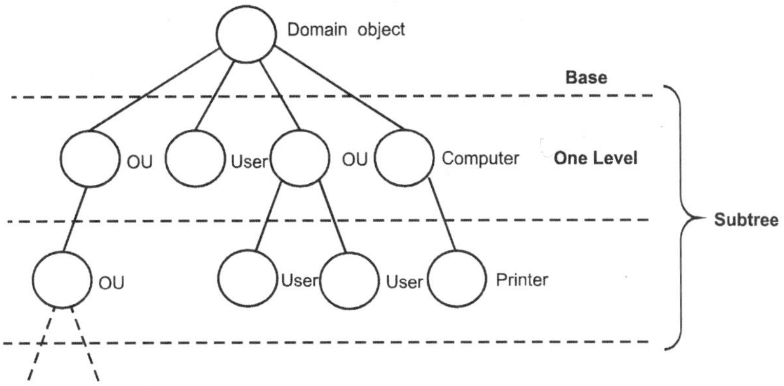

Fig. 1.1. Search scopes for a domain object (which is the *search base*)

- **Filter**. A rule (see RFC 2254) for selecting objects from a subtree (e.g., `(cn=*)` or `&(objectCategory=Person)(cn=d*)`).
- **Selection**. A list of attributes returned from the selected objects that match the filter.
- **Optional controls**. LDAP functions that extend or modify a LDAP operation; for example, you may ask the LDAP server to sort the results or return a large result set in small pages. (See examples of using some LDAP controls in *Chapter 12, "Manipulating Active Directory Objects."*)

Types of Filters

The following table shows a few examples of search filters:

Condition	Filter
Equality match	`(sAMAccountName=jsmith)`
Partial match	`(name=s*)` or `(name=*s*)`
Comparing with a value	`(uSNChanged>=10000)` or `(CN<=Sales)`
Presence of object	`(objectClass=*)`
Logical AND of two conditions (users with names that begin with "H")	`(&(objectClass=user)(cn>=h))`
Logical OR of two conditions (objects with names that begin with "A" OR "H")	`(|(cn=a*)(cn=h*))`
Logical NOT (all users with name that begin with "A" except "Administrators")	`(&(objectClass=user)(cn=a*)(!(cn=adm*)))`
Binary (attributes with syntax 2.5.4.1)	`(attributeSyntax=\32\2e\35\2e\34\2e\31)`

Selection Options

Usually, you provide the list of object attributes returned by a query. There are, however, a few special cases:

- If you only need the objects' DNs rather than their attributes, specify OID `1.1` as the selection.
- It is possible to specify the attribute OID instead of its name; for example, you can replace `objectClass` with `2.5.4.0`.

Example. Listing Attributes replicated to Global Catalog

As an example of a search operation, let us consider how to view all attributes replicated to Global Catalog. You may use any search tool, such as the Search.vbs script or the Ldp.exe utility. (For more information, see *Chapter 12.*) Here is a sample command:

```
search "LDAP://CN=Schema,CN=Configuration,DC=net,DC=dom"
  ↳ /C:"(&(objectClass=attributeSchema)
```

```
↳ (isMemberOfPartialAttributeSet=*))"
↳ /P:ADsPath,attributeID,attributeSyntax,isSingleValued,
↳ lDAPDisplayName,oMSyntax
```

The query produces a result similar to the following (only one entry from the list is shown):

```
...
ADsPAth 140 = LDAP://CN=User-Principal-Name,CN=Schema,
↳ CN=Configuration,DC=net,DC=dom
attributeID 140 = 1.2.840.113556.1.4.656
attributeSyntax 140 = 2.5.5.12
isSingleValued 140 = True
lDAPDisplayName 140 = userPrincipalName
oMSyntax 140 = 64
...
```

The same results can be obtained with the DsQuery utility:

```
C:\>dsquery * "CN=Schema,CN=Configuration,DC=net,DC=dom"
↳ -filter
↳ "(&(objectClass=attributeSchema)(isMemberOfPartialAttributeSet=*))"
↳ -attr ADsPath attributeID attributeSyntax isSingleValued
↳ lDAPDisplayName oMSyntax -l -limit 1000 | more
```

Compare

The *compare* operation returns a Boolean result (TRUE or FALSE) based on the comparison of an attribute value with a specified value.

Administrative Limits and Query Policy

The LDAP server resources, which are available to clients that make LDAP queries and request paged or sorted result sets, are limited by the *Default Query Policy*. *Administrative limits* constitute the query policy objects which are stored in the container CN=Query-Policies,CN=Directory Service,CN=Windows NT,CN=Services in the Configuration partition.

If there are no *assigned* policies, all domain controllers use the default query policy. A site policy can also be assigned. However, if a specific policy has been assigned to a domain controller, this policy overrides all others. There is no UI for assigning a policy to a site. You can do this by manually editing the *queryPolicyObject* attribute of the *NTDS Site Settings* object of the *nTDSSiteSettings* class object. Use the **ADSI Edit** snap-in. It is also possible to use the ModifyLDAP.vbs script (see below).

Query policy applies to the following LDAP query-related operations:

- **Search**. By default, you cannot obtain a result set whose size exceeds 1000 rows. You need to use a paged search to perform operations that generate a significant amount of information. Also, you may exceed the default timeout set for search operations.
- **Paged search**. The client may ask the server to hold the result set and return it in pages. In this case, the query policy defines the page size. (See also comments to *Listing 16.1*.)
- **Search with Sorted Results**. The requested result set can be sorted in a particular order. This operation can significantly overload the LDAP server.
- **Search with Replication**. The client can specify the maximum number of attribute values that can be returned per request.
- **Change Notify**. The client can request change notification in an asynchronous LDAP query. The query policy can limit the number of simultaneous asynchronous requests.

Tools for Manipulating LDAP Query Policies

There are two standard tools that allow you to work with LDAP query policies (see *Chapter 10, "Diagnosing and Maintaining Domain Controllers"*):

- The NTDSutil.exe tool. This tool can only be used with the Default Query Policy object. It allows you to view or modify the query policy of a domain controller.
- The ModifyLDAP.vbs script from the *Windows 2000 Server Resource Kit*. This script can create, delete, assign, or modify the query policy objects.

Update

The *update* operations perform modifications of the stored information.

- **Add** allows user to create an object, which must meet the schema requirements for the object class.
- **Modify** creates, modifies, and deletes attributes of an object.
- **Modify RDN** is actually an operation of renaming or moving an object to another location.
- **Delete** deletes an object (if it is possible and the user has the appropriate rights to the object).

Security Model

To provide secure access to an LDAP server, the LDAP v.3 protocol allows the use of *Simple Authentication and Security Layer* (SASL) mechanisms. Active Directory confirms the LDAP v.3 requirements and, therefore, supports SASL mechanisms, which include Kerberos version 5 and MS Negotiate (on Windows 2000). The *supportedSASLMechanisms* attribute of the RootDSE object stored on every Active Directory server (a domain controller running on Windows 2000 or Windows .NET) contains two values: GSSAPI and GSS-SPNEGO. GSSAPI means *Kerberos*, and GSS-SPNEGO stands for *NT Negotiate* (Kerberos, NT LAN Manager (NTLM), etc.). Windows .NET-based domain controllers also support two other SASL mechanisms: EXTERNAL and DIGEST-MD5.

LDAP Ports

The connections via the LDAP protocol between a client and DSA use either a Transmission Control Protocol (TCP) or User Datagram Protocol (UDP). The table below lists the protocol sockets used in different access modes:

Function	Port
LDAP	389
LDAP Secure Sockets Layer (SSL)	636
Global Catalog (GC)	3268
Global Catalog Secure Sockets Layer	3269

Chapter 2: Active Directory Terminology and Concepts

This chapter relates to basic Active Directory elements, features, and requirements that will be mentioned repeatedly in the other chapters of the book. You should have a solid understanding of all these concepts and ideas before you go any further. If a term is not clear to you, you can easily find detailed information in other sources. For example, you can use the search function and quickly find an exhaustive description of any term (including its relation to other Active Directory elements) in the *Help and Support Center*. Thus, it is not necessary to place such information here.

Active Directory Essentials and Components

Let us first consider what essential information is necessary to comprehend in order to deploy and manage both Windows 2000 and Windows .NET domains. (You may skip this section, if you are familiar with Active Directory basics, and go to the new features' description.) The Active Directory elements considered in this section will be addressed later, in subsequent chapters. If you find that you are not completely grasping the meaning of a particular word, just search for it in *Help and Support Center*. (It would take up too much space to put everything here.)

Logical Organization

The Active Directory service is the foundation for *domains* managed by *domain controllers* (that are also called Active Directory servers) running Windows 2000 or/and Windows .NET. A domain is a group of logically linked computers and users who work on them and are united by an idea of centralized management.

All "housekeeping" tasks are performed on domain controllers that hold the *Active Directory database* which contains information about managed objects such as users, computers, groups, and so on. This information is stored as directory objects of corresponding types. User, group, and computer (and InetOrgPerson — in Windows .NET) objects (so-called *accounts*) represent *security principles* that can be granted privileges to perform certain computer-, domain, or forest-wide tasks or permissions for access to shared network resources (such as files, folders, and printers). Thus, a domain client being logged on to the domain once using an account can access all allowed resources without needing to log on repeatedly to each server holding a resource. A domain administrator can change Active Directory objects on any domain controller and, thus, control all options permitted to domain members. Therefore, a domain is a boundary of administrative power.

In short, to deploy an Active Directory domain, you need to first plan it, install domain controller(s), add domain client computers, and create user (and group) accounts. Then you can share resources on domain members and assign necessary privileges and permissions to users (and groups). (All required operations and tools used to perform them will be described in this book in *Chapters 3* through *Chapter 8*. The remaining chapters consider problems that occur during *exploitation* of Active Directory domains as well as all necessary system utilities.)

An Active Directory domain can contain sets of directory objects that are called *organizational units* (OU), and that usually contain user or computer accounts. Each OU can have its own administrator and a *Group Policy Object* (GPO)(s) linked to OU object. The group policy technology is intended for centralized configuration of user environment and computer system settings. GPOs can be local or linked to site, domain, or OU objects.

Active Directory domains form a *forest* (a forest can comprise one or more domains), where all domains are linked by two-way, transitive *trusts*. Trusts allow users logged on to a domain to access resources located in any location in the forest, or to have privileges in any domain. Administrator-created trusts can be established with foreign Active Directory forests or Windows NT 4.0 domains.

Physical Organization

The entire Active Directory database is logically divided into *directory partitions*, which are units of replication (i.e., each partition is replicated independently, although the replication mechanisms, such as scheduled replication or notification procedure, may affect all partitions). Since Active Directory is a distributed network database, any domain controller holds a *replica* of the entire database.

Each replica counts at least three partitions: the *Schema* and *Configuration* partitions that are shared by all domains in a forest and stored on every domain controller; and *domain partition* that contains objects of a specific domain and is stored on domain controllers that belong to that domain. Each forest has one more partition called *Global Catalog* (GC), which contains a *limited* set of attributes of *all* Active Directory objects. GC allows users to quickly find any directory object in the forest. GC is a part of the Active Directory database and can be stored on any domain controller.

Active Directory can take into account the fact that a large enterprise network (a forest) usually contains a number of *subnets* linked by fast and slow channels. A set of subnets connected with fast channels can be referred to as a *site*. Sites, in turn, are connected with slow (dial-up) channels. By default, all domains are placed in the same *Default-First-Site* (which can be safely renamed).

Directory partition requirements as well as site infrastructure will determine the *replication topology* that, by default, is automatically generated by the *Knowledge Consistency Checker* (KCC) service running on every domain controller. This service manages *replication connections* between domain controllers depending on which directory partitions they store. Replication is performed in accordance with rules, intervals, and schedules defined for *inter*- and *intra-site* replication types.

Active Directory Clients

Pre-Windows 2000 clients (running Windows 9*x*/ME and Windows NT 4.0) regard an Active Directory domain (operating in any mode or at any functional level) as a Windows NT domain, i.e., they can be authenticated in the domain and access the shared domain resources (see also later the *"Domain Modes and Functional Levels"* section).

Active Directory Client Extension allows pre-Windows 2000 clients to use some Active Directory features, such as Active Directory Service Interfaces (ADSI), site awareness, DFS fault tolerance, search options, and NTLM version 2 authentication (see the Web or the *Help and Support Center* for a detailed description). Active Directory Client Extension is available on the Windows 2000 Server CD or the Microsoft website (the links are in *Appendix A*). Certainly, all of the listed features as well as many others are available on Windows 2000/XP/.NET-based clients.

Active Directory Client Extension ***does not support*** some important Active Directory options, such as Group Policy functionality, Kerberos V5 protocol, IPSec and L2TP, nor does it allow users to browse through the Active Directory organizational units (OU) and containers (thus, the only visual options that appear when the extension has been installed on a computer are the **For Printers** and **For People** commands on the **Start | Search** menu).

New Active Directory Features on Windows .NET Servers

This section covers the most important, and up-to-date Active Directory features that are available on the Windows .NET Server family domain controllers and may allow administrators to manage Windows .NET domains more efficiently (certainly, this will not be a complete list of features).

Domain Modes and Functional Levels

Let us first discuss certain general domain and forest functionalities that, to some degree, are common for both Windows 2000 and Windows .NET domains.

Windows 2000 domains can operate in either default *mixed mode* (when a domain can contain Windows 4.0 Backup Domain Controllers, BDC) or *native mode* (when a domain contains only Windows 2000-based domain controllers).

When a domain's mode is changed to native, the following considerations should be taken into account:

- Domain controllers (DC) no longer support NTLM replication; as a result, the domain's PDC Emulator (a DC that performs the role of Windows NT 4.0

Primary Domain Controller, PDC) cannot replicate data to Windows NT 4.0 BDCs, and Windows NT 4.0-based DCs cannot be added to the domain.

- Domain controllers provide *pass-through* authentication that allows users and computers using pre-Windows 2000 systems to be authenticated in any domain in the forest (notwithstanding the fact that these systems do not support the Kerberos V5 protocol). Thus, they can use transitive trusts existing in an Active Directory forest and access resources in any domain.

In Windows .NET domains, a new term, *functional level*, is introduced. Functional levels are defined for a domain as well as for the forest.

The following table lists three available *domain functional levels* and DC types supported (or that can be introduced into the domain) at these levels:

Domain functional level	Domain controllers supported
Windows 2000 mixed (default)	Windows NT 4.0, Windows 2000, and Windows .NET
Windows 2000 native	Windows 2000 and Windows .NET
Windows .NET	Windows .NET only

Two first levels correspond to the Windows 2000 modes, and aforementioned considerations for the native mode domains are applicable to the *Windows 2000 native* functional level, too.

Among features that require the *Windows .NET* domain functional level is the Domain Controller Rename option (see later). Native mode Windows 2000 domains as well as Windows .NET domains at the *Windows 2000 native* or *Windows .NET* domain functional level support the following features: universal groups; group nesting; converting group types, and the SID History option (discussed in *Chapter 13, "Migration and Directory Reorganization Tools"*).

Forest functional levels define features available across all domains within a forest. The following table lists two available forest functional levels and DC types supported at these levels:

Forest functional level	Domain controllers supported	Domain functional levels permitted for existing or new domains
Windows 2000 (default)	Windows NT 4.0, Windows 2000, and Windows .NET	Any level
Windows .NET	Windows .NET only	Windows .NET only

There is also a special *Windows .NET Interim* forest functional level that is only available when a Windows NT 4.0 domain is upgraded to a new Windows .NET forest, which does not contain domain controllers running Windows 2000. (When upgrading a Windows NT 4.0 domain, you might also be interested in the *Q284937* and *Q298713* articles from the *Microsoft Knowledge Base*.)

The forest-wide features available at the Windows .NET forest functional level are listed later in this chapter.

Keep in mind the following information regarding the domain modes or forest/domain functional levels:

- It is *impossible to change* a domain mode from native to mixed mode or *to lower* a functional level without re-installing Active Directory in this domain or in the entire forest.
- Domains in a forest are *not required* to operate in the *same* mode or at the *same* functional level.
- The native mode or a functional level higher then *Windows 2000 mixed* level has *no impact* (except the pass-trough authentication ability) on down-level clients such as Windows 9*x*/ME or Windows NT (with or without the Active Directory Client extension). This is also the case with trusts between the local domain and any external domains (Windows NT 4.0, Windows 2000 or Windows .NET). However, remember that any external trust is always explicit, unidirectional (one-way), and non-transitive (except for forest trusts).

To learn how to change a domain mode or to raise a domain/forest functional level, see *Chapter 5, "Installing Active Directory"*.

New Features for Windows .NET Domain Controllers

Any domain controller running Windows .NET provides new features described below.

Enhancements in the Administrative Tools

In Windows .NET, the standard administrative snap-ins available in Windows 2000 provide additional options that allow administrators to manage domains more effectively. Among these options are the following:

- Saved directory queries in the **Active Directory Users and Computers** snap-in
- Selection and modification of multiple of directory objects
- Drag-and-drop operations
- Efficient search capabilities that include new filter and find options

For detailed information, see *Chapter 7, "Domain Manipulation Tools"*.

Active Directory Command-Line Tools

New LDAP-compliant tools, such as *DsQuery.exe*, *DsAdd.exe*, *DsMod.exe*, etc., allow administrators to perform batch and routine operations with directory objects. You can find the tools' descriptions in *Chapter 12, "Manipulating Active Directory Objects."*

Adding Domain Controllers from Backup Files

An additional domain controller in a domain can be installed from the files restored from a backup of an existing domain controller. This reduces the promotion time, as well as network replication traffic. This installation type will be described in *Chapter 5, "Installing Active Directory."*

Universal Group Membership Caching

All user authentication attempts are verified on a Global Catalog server to check user membership in the universal groups. This process will generate additional traffic across a WAN to a remote GC server. To eliminate the need to have a GC server in every site, you can designate a DC to cache universal group membership and update that information from a specified site. To learn how to enable caching, see *Chapter 7, "Domain Manipulation Tools."*

Application Directory Partitions

An *application directory partition* can be created by an application or administrator, who also defines the partition replication scope. This is the main distinction between this partition type and other Active Directory partitions (whose replication topology, as a rule, is generated automatically by the *Knowledge Consistency Checker*, KCC). The replication scope for an application partition can include any set of domain controllers in the forest.

An application partition can store any directory objects (except security principals) defined in the schema (including *dynamic objects*). Objects in application partitions are not replicated to Global Catalog. There are two built-in application partitions that can be used by the Windows .NET DNS servers running on domain controllers (see the next chapter for details).

To view the contents of application partitions, you can use the **ADSI Edit** snap-in (see *Chapter 7, "Domain Manipulation Tools"*). To learn how to manage application directory partitions, see *Chapter 10, "Diagnosing and Maintaining Domain Controllers."*

InetOrgPerson Object Class

The *inetOrgPerson* object class defined in RFC 2798 has been added to the Active Directory schema to make migration from third party LDAP directories to Active Directory more efficient. The objects of that class are the security principals and can be used as standard user objects.

New Features for Pure Windows .NET Domains and Forests

This section describes new features that are only available when the domain/forest functional level has been raised to *Windows .NET*.

Rename Options

You can rename a domain controller without first demoting it or change the DNS or NetBIOS name of any domain. Renaming a domain may result in moving it to other location in the forest infrastructure. Detailed descriptions are provided later in this chapter.

Forest Trusts

Forest trust is established between the forest root domains that operate at the *Windows .NET* functional level and can have a one-way as well as a two-way direction. Unlike usual external trusts, the forest trusts are transitive, i.e., they allow a user authenticated in one forest to access resources located in any domain in another forest.

Forest trusts are discussed in detail in *Chapter 5, "Installing Active Directory."*

Defunct Objects

Active Directory does not allow you to delete a directory object class or attribute: you can only deactivate it. A deactivated class or attribute is called *defunct*. It is possible to activate a deactivated class or attribute and redefine it, if there was an error when the class or attribute was initially created.

Replication Enhancements

Some replication related problems existing in Windows 2000 have been addressed in Windows .NET. Primarily, this concerns the enhanced linked value and Global Catalog replication as well as algorithms used by the *Knowledge Consistency Checker* (KCC) for generating replication topology in forests with large number of sites.

Linked value replication reduces network traffic when group membership is changed: only new or deleted group members are replicated instead of the entire list of group members stored in the *member* attribute. This is essential for groups with a large number of members.

In Windows 2000, when a new attribute is added to Global Catalog, a full synchronization of partial replicas is required, and this process affects all domains in the forest. In a Windows .NET, only the new attribute is replicated to Global Catalog servers.

Dynamic Auxiliary Classes and Dynamic Objects

It is possible to dynamically link or remove auxiliary classes to object *instances* as well as to object *classes.*

Dynamic objects are instantiated from an object class that has the auxiliary class *dynamicObject.* This class can also be added to an object instance by using a program or script. As a result, a dynamic object exists during the time defined by a *Time-to-Live* (TTL) value that is assigned at the object creation and can be renewed by a client or an application (see also *Appendix B*).

Renaming Domains

The Windows .NET version of Active Directory allows administrators to change domain names and, thus, reconstruct the forest. This procedure is not intended to be a *routine operation* and is ***only possible*** when the forest functional level has been raised to Windows .NET. The rename procedure is not simple and includes a step-by-step process that requires use of the RenDom.exe utility (see the link in *Appendix A*) and depends on the kind of rename operation.

The simplest case is when you rename a domain and do not change the forest parent-child structure. A more complex case is when you change the domain position in a forest tree, e.g., make a child domain a tree root domain or change the parent for a child domain. The rename procedure may require many supplementary operations, such as pre-creating additional inter-domain trusts, preparing DNS zones, configuring member computers, and so on.

The rename procedure allows you to:

- Change the DNS or/and NetBIOS names of any domain without affecting the forest structure. This includes renaming a root domain, which results in changing names of all child domains.
- Change the parent domain for a child domain (the new parent can be in the same or another domain tree).
- Rename a child domain to be a new tree-root domain.

None of the listed operations ***is possible*** in a Windows 2000 forest.

The following rename operations are not possible:

- You cannot redefine the forest root domain (i.e., the forest root will always be the same domain). However, you can change its DNS or/and NetBIOS name.
- One cannot delete or add a domain: the total number of domains in a forest must remain the same. A usual promotion/demotion procedure should be used in such cases.

You cannot rename two domains in a single operation and give a domain the name of another domain. The rename procedure requires quite a long, detailed description — and so, it is inappropriate to include one here. You can find two comprehensive operation guides (about 90 pages in total) on the Microsoft website (see the link in *Appendix A*) if you are interested in learning more about this topic.

Renaming Domain Controllers

In a Windows .NET domain, you may rename a domain controller (i.e., change its FQDN and NetBIOS names). To rename a domain controller from the local console:

1. Open the **System Properties** window. (Press the <Win>+<Pause/Break> keys, or click **System** in **Control Panel**.)
2. On the **Computer Name** tab, click **Change**.
3. Click **OK** to continue renaming.
4. Enter a new computer name and click **OK**.
5. Enter a domain administrator's credentials if required.
6. Restart the domain controller. Wait until the DNS information and Active Directory replication topology is renewed. After that, the clients and replication partners will be able to locate the renamed DC and be authenticated on it. Verify the DC with the `dcdiag` and `repadmin /showreps` commands.

Important

To rename domain controllers, you must first raise the *domain* functional level to Windows .NET. This is because only Windows .NET-based domain controllers support the *msDS-AdditionalDnsHostName*, *msDS-AdditionalSamAccountName*, and some other attributes necessary to perform renaming. This means that it is ***not possible*** to rename a DC in a Windows 2000 domain.

The rename operation does not change the domain membership of the controller, i.e., it does not allow you to move a DC to another domain (even if you change the primary DNS suffix). To do so, you must first demote the DC and promote it with a new domain name.

To rename a remote domain controller, it is necessary to use the NetDom.exe utility. The renaming procedure is not complicated and is described in the *Help and Support Center* (search for the "rename controller" words).

Windows Time Service

Windows Time service provides computer clock synchronization for domain clients and domain controllers. This is especially important on client computers running Windows/XP/.NET and domain controllers since all of them rely on authentication procedure that use Kerberos V5 protocol, which by default requires clock synchronization with a delta of 5 minutes. The service operation is defined by registry settings located in the `HKLM\SYSTEM\CurrentControlSet\Services\W32Time` key. (This key will be the reference for all registry values mentioned in this section.)

Domain clients running Windows XP/.NET will automatically synchronize their clocks with the PDC Emulator time upon their startup and authentication in the domain. A domain's PDC Emulator, in turn, synchronizes its clock with the clock of the PDC Emulator of a parent or forest root domain. The forest root domain's PDC Emulator should synchronize its clock with an external timeserver(s) or you can leave it "as is".

To specify an external timeserver, use the `net time /SETSNTP:timeSrvName` command. On Windows .NET DCs, you can also use the command

```
C:\>w32tm /config /manualpeerlist:timeSrvName /update
```

By default, all computers running Windows XP/.NET use the *time.windows.com* site as the timeserver.

On a Windows .NET DC, to disable synchronization with an external timeserver, you may set the registry value `Parameters\Type` to `NoSync`, clear the `Parameters\NtpServer` value, and stop the NTP Client by setting the `TimeProviders\NtpClient\Enabled` value to zero). On a Windows 2000 DC, you may use the following command:

```
C:\>net time /SETSNTP:w2kdc2.w2k.dom,
```

where `w2kdc2.w2k.dom` is the PDC Emulator name.

Note

Each time you change the settings of the Windows Time service, restart it by using the **Service** snap-in or from the command prompt (with the `net stop w32time` and `net start w32time` commands).

When a client running Windows XP/.NET joins a domain, the `Parameters\Type` value is automatically changed from default `NTP` to `NT5DS`. The same change is performed on Windows .NET servers when they are promoted to domain controllers. On clients and domain controllers running Windows 2000, you may either manually set the `Parameters\Type` value or use the `net time /SETSNTP` command.

On computers running Windows XP/.NET, the following sample command allows you to view the timeserver (marked as `PDC`) as well as the time offsets for computers in the *net.dom* domain (if this parameter is omitted, the current domain is tested):

```
C:\>w32tm /monitor /domain:net.dom
netdc1.net.dom *** PDC *** [192.168.1.2]:
    ICMP: 0ms delay.
    NTP: +0.0000000s offset from netdc1.net.dom
        RefID: 'LOCL' [76.79.67.76]
netdc4.net.dom [192.168.1.103]:
    ICMP: 0ms delay.
    NTP: -0.0100835s offset from netdc1.net.dom
        RefID: netdc1.net.dom [192.168.1.2]
```

Chapter 3: Domain Name System (DNS) as Main Naming Service

Domain Name System (DNS) is one of the "cornerstone" services of an Active Directory domain (both Windows 2000 and Windows .NET), and you *must* use it in any domain structure based on Active Directory even if the forest root domain is not registered in the Internet DNS namespace. It is possible to exploit other DNS servers besides Microsoft DNS Server, but these servers must conform to specific requirements. You need not become a DNS *guru*, but you *have to* be familiar with all DNS essentials and its interoperation with the Active Directory.

Be careful! The system (even Windows .NET) *permits* promotion of a server to domain controller (i.e., installation of the Active Directory and creation of a domain) without specifying *any* DNS servers. However, this does not guarantee that your domain will work correctly. Quite the contrary! Nevertheless, such an approach can be useful in some cases (as a prelude to domain deployment) if you thoroughly understand all the details of DNS configuring and its interoperation with Active Directory.

You could, for example, first promote a server to DC, and then prepare a DNS server for dynamic updating of the appropriate zones. Enter the DNS server's IP address in the DC's TCP/IP properties, and reboot the DC (or restart the Netlogon service and execute the `ipconfig /registerdns` command). The result will be a fully operable configuration! The same procedure is used when you select another authoritative DNS server for a domain and want to re-register all necessary DNS records.

This chapter covers some general aspects of Active Directory and DNS interoperation, as well as basic features of Microsoft DNS servers. In *Chapter 4, "Windows .NET DNS Server"*, operations with native Microsoft DNS servers will be considered, and the DNS issues related to Active Directory deployment and maintenance will be considered in *Chapter 5, "Installing Active Directory."*

Note

Name-resolving systems, such as DNS and WINS, are a vast, complex topic. There are plenty of good specialized books on TCP/IP, DNS, and Windows 2000 DNS Server in particular, and you may wish to read them to obtain a deeper understanding of the DNS system in general and its realization in Windows 2000. This information applies to Windows .NET DNS Server, too.

In this chapter and the entire book, *"Microsoft DNS Server"* refers to both Windows 2000 DNS Server and Windows .NET DNS Server. The differences between these products, if such exist, are specifically indicated when necessary.

What Active Directory Requires from the DNS Service

There are no "secret relations" between Active Directory and DNS. All that Active Directory requires from DNS is a standard resolving of DNS names (including some system names) into IP addresses. The following two postulates are related to Active Directory and DNS:

- Active Directory ***requires*** a DNS infrastructure. Active Directory uses DNS as a locator service, and thus uses the DNS hierarchical name for naming domains, computers, and many other Active Directory objects. (*Windows Internet Naming Service*, WINS, used in Window NT domains, is now regarded as supplementary and can be used in mixed environments comprising pre-Windows 2000 computers. This is why WINS will not be considered in this book.)
- Active Directory ***does not necessary require*** a Microsoft DNS Server (on either Windows 2000 or Windows .NET platforms).

To meet Active Directory requirements, a DNS server ***must*** have two of the following features:

- The server must support resource records of the *SRV* type according to RFC 2052 ("A DNS RR for specifying the location of services (DNS SRV)"), since SRV records are widely used by domain clients and domain controllers for locating various directory resources, such as domain controllers, Global Catalog servers, Kerberos servers, and so on.
- The server must permit use of underscores ("_") in the DNS names, since this character is used in the reserved system DNS names (e.g., _gc._tcp.*domain.com*). (See examples of system DNS names in the last section of this chapter.)

One more feature is eagerly required for deploying Active Directory; however, it ***is not mandatory***:

The server should support dynamic updates of resource records according to RFC 2136 ("Dynamic Updates in the Domain Name System (DNS UPDATE)"). By default, all Active Directory domain controllers and clients automatically register and update the appropriate records of SRV, CNAME, and A types. If dynamic updates are not supported, an administrator must manually manage all records, which is a difficult task in a large network.

Any DNS server that meets at least the first two requirements can be used in an Active Directory environment (e.g., Windows NT 4.0 DNS Server with SP 4 or higher; however, that server does not support dynamic updates). For example, according to many sources, the DNS BIND 8.2.2 server or later is suitable for work with Active Directory.

Note

Reverse zones are not necessary for Active Directory to work; and Active Directory Installation Wizard will not create them. However, it is recommended that you create the applicable reverse zones so that various DNS utilities and tools (e.g., Nslookup or Ping) can work well.

As a rule, on both client computers and domain controllers running Windows 2000 or later systems, the IP address(es) of the same preferred DNS server(s) that holds the authoritative zone for a domain should be entered into the TCP/IP properties on the **DNS** tab in the **Advanced TCP/IP Settings** window. This address must not be the *Internet Service Provider* (ISP) DNS server's address. If necessary, the preferred server should forward clients' queries for external domains to the ISP's DNS servers.

Active Directory allows administrators to change IP addresses of DNS servers and domain controllers, since the Active Directory infrastructure is linked to LDAP, DNS, or GUID names. If the IP address of a DNS server is changed (or if another server is selected), you need to specify the new address in the preferred DNS server settings on all client computers and domain controllers, and re-register the appropriate resource records on the DNS server. If the IP address of a domain controller is changed, you need to re-register its A and SRV records on the preferred server. Keep in mind that the DNS client (resolver) on Windows 2000/XP/.NET systems caches both successful and failed DNS query responses, and this caching may affect name resolving (for example, a domain controller can hold the outdated IP address of its replication partner, which may result in replication errors).

Microsoft DNS Server Features

In addition to the above-mentioned options, the DNS service running on Windows 2000 or Windows .NET servers provides many other features; among them:

- **Integration with other network services**, such as WINS and DHCP. (For example, pre-Windows 2000 computers can neither register nor update their DNS names directly; they can perform that operation through WINS, which acts as an intermediary to DNS).
- **Interoperability with third party DNS servers**. (For example, the Windows .NET DNS development team has tested interoperability with the BIND DNS server version 4.9.7, 8.1.2, 8.2, and 9.1.0.)
- **Support for secure dynamic updates** that allows only domain-authenticated clients to re-register DNS names.
- **Incremental zone transfers** between DNS servers (zone transfers are only required for non-Active Directory-integrated zones).
- **Support for Active Directory-integrated zones**, i.e., zones that store their data in the directory. These zones can only be created on DNS servers running on domain controllers and, therefore, can benefit from Active Directory multi-master replication.

The replication scope for a zone depends on the directory partition where it is stored. On Windows 2000 DNS Servers, a zone can only be stored in a domain partition that is replicated among domain controllers that belong to that domain. Even if you create a zone with the same name in *another* domain, there will be *two different* zones, which results in a big mess for the entire DNS infrastructure. If two DNS servers belong to different domains, one server must be primary for the other one. On Windows .NET DNS Servers, the situation is simpler since these DNS servers can store their data in *application directory partitions* whose replication scope is defined by administrators (see details in the *"Domain Management"* section in *Chapter 10, "Diagnosing and Maintaining Domain Controllers"*).

- **Event logging and debug options**.

As any typical DNS server, Microsoft DNS Servers can operate in the following modes:

- **Caching sever** — as a rule, a standalone DNS server that does not host any authoritative zones after its installation, and therefore only caches the clients' queries. A caching Windows .NET Server can also hold *stub zones.*
- **Primary server** — the server that hosts an updatable, authoritative zone(s) for some domain(s), i.e., it is permitted to resolve client queries. Resource records from such a server may be transferred to the secondary servers.
- **Secondary server** — the server that hosts a read-only replica(s) of zone(s) transferred from a primary (authoritative) server. However, if both the primary and secondary DNS servers hold an *Active Directory-integrated* zone(s), these servers can be regarded as *peers* that are able to accept updates. Active Directory-integrated zones require a DNS server running on a Windows 2000-based domain controller.

Certainly, any DNS server can combine any of these modes; however, you need to thoroughly plan operation modes of all DNS servers in your network, as well as interoperations between these DNS servers and "external" servers, e.g., your ISP's DNS servers.

Two main tools that can be used for administering local and remote Microsoft DNS Servers are:

- The **DNS** snap-in (DNS console)
- The *DnsCmd.exe* command-line utility

New DNS Features in Windows .NET

In comparison to Windows 2000, the Windows .NET Server family offers a few new DNS related features that are implemented either in the system itself or in the Windows .NET DNS Server. Let us consider features that are the most important for administering both DNS servers and Active Directory domains:

- **Enhanced domain joining procedures**. When a client computer is added to a domain or a new domain controller is created in an existing or a new domain, the appropriate procedures verify the DNS infrastructure and explain possible failures and how to fix them.
- **New group policies** for managing DNS client settings on computers running Windows XP/.NET (look at the **Computer Configuration | Administrative Templates | Network | DNS Client** node of a Group Policy Object) and policies that control DNS registration of SRV records by domain controllers running Windows .NET.
- **Active Directory-integrated zones** that can be stored in *application* directory partitions. A DNS server installed on a domain controller running Windows .NET can use two built-in application directory partitions for storing DNS information. These partitions, ForestDnsZones.*domainName* and DomainDnsZones.*domainName*, are replicated to all DNS servers in the forest or in the domain, respectively. In addition, DNS server can store data in *user created* application partitions with their own replication scopes. In both cases, it is the administrator who defines the set of domain controllers that store application partition replicas. (Keep in mind that DNS data stored in application partitions is not replicated to Global Catalog.)
- **Stub zones and conditional forwarding**. *Stub zones* only contain resource records (of type SOA, NS, and A) that specify the authoritative DNS server(s) (primary and secondary) for the zone, and therefore simply redirect a client queries to the DNS server(s) that holds the authoritative zone and is able to resolve these requests. Look, for example, at Fig. 4.1. If there are DNS servers that are authoritative for the child domain (*subdom.net.dom*), you can convert the child zone into a stub zone; as a result, the root DNS server will remain aware of the DNS servers authoritative for the delegated child zone and will only cache the answers to queries for the child zone names.

  Conditional forwarders redirect client queries to other DNS servers depending on the domain name contained in these queries. Conditional forwarders can be useful, for example, when you establish trusts between different forests, which have their own DNS servers, and do not want to query the Internet DNS servers. To provide name resolving, you can specify the other side's DNS server as a conditional forwarder for foreign forest DNS names.

DNS Records Registered by Active Directory Domain Controllers

All SRV and A resource records (20 in total, if the domain controller is a Global Catalog server; 15 if it is not) that each Active Directory domain controller must register on a DNS server, are contained in the *%SystemRoot%*\system32\config\netlogon.dns file. (If your DNS server does not support dynamic records update, you need to manually manage these records.) An example of such a file is presented below.

Note

It is possible to set a group policy that will prohibit registration of some or all SRV records by Windows .NET domain controllers. This policy, *DC Locator DNS records not registered by the DCs*, is located in the **Computer Configuration** | **Administrative Templates** | **System** | Net **Logon** | **DC Locator DNS Records** node of a Group Policy Object (GPO).

In this example: server name — *netdc2.subdom.net.dom*, domain name — *subdom.net.dom*, root domain name — *net.dom*, site name — *NET-Site*. The records are sorted for clarity. The real order will differ, but this does not matter. The records for a global catalog server are shown in bold. You can verify resource records with the **DNS** snap-in.

```
subdom.net.dom. 600 IN A 192.168.1.102
1affcd49-c47f-4499-82b8-48721ed1c799._msdcs.net.dom.
 ↳           600 IN CNAME netdc2.subdom.net.dom.
_ldap._tcp.subdom.net.dom. 600 IN SRV 0 100 389 netdc2.subdom.net.dom.
_ldap._tcp.dc._msdcs.subdom.net.dom. 600 IN SRV 0 100 389
 ↳           netdc2.subdom.net.dom.
_ldap._tcp.pdc._msdcs.subdom.net.dom. 600 IN SRV 0 100 389
 ↳           netdc2.subdom.net.dom.
_ldap._tcp.gc._msdcs.net.dom. 600 IN SRV 0 100 3268
 ↳           netdc2.subdom.net.dom.
_ldap._tcp. 729173d2-f48b-4655-ac5c-
 ↳           5f1c0c93cbdd.domains._msdcs.net.dom. 600 IN SRV
 ↳           0 100 389 netdc2.subdom.net.dom.
_ldap._tcp.NET-Site._sites.subdom.net.dom. 600 IN SRV 0 100 389
 ↳           netdc2.subdom.net.dom.
_ldap._tcp.NET-Site._sites.dc._msdcs.subdom.net.dom.
 ↳           600 IN SRV 0 100 389 netdc2.subdom.net.dom.
_ldap._tcp.NET-Site._sites.gc._msdcs.net.dom.
```

```
↳           600 IN SRV 0 100 3268 netdc2.subdom.net.dom.
gc._msdcs.net.dom. 600 IN A 192.168.1.102
_gc._tcp.net.dom. 600 IN SRV 0 100 3268 netdc2.subdom.net.dom.
_gc._tcp.NET-Site._sites.net.dom. 600 IN SRV 0 100 3268
↳           netdc2.subdom.net.dom.
_kerberos._tcp.subdom.net.dom. 600 IN SRV 0 100 88
↳           netdc2.subdom.net.dom.
_kerberos._udp.subdom.net.dom. 600 IN SRV 0 100 88
↳           netdc2.subdom.net.dom.
_kerberos._tcp.dc._msdcs.subdom.net.dom. 600 IN SRV 0 100 88
↳           netdc2.subdom.net.dom.
_kerberos._tcp.NET-Site._sites.dc._msdcs.subdom.net.dom.
↳           600 IN SRV 0 100 88 netdc2.subdom.net.dom.
_kerberos._tcp.NET-Site._sites.subdom.net.dom.
↳           600 IN SRV 0 100 88 netdc2.subdom.net.dom.
_kpasswd._tcp.subdom.net.dom. 600 IN SRV 0 100 464
↳           netdc2.subdom.net.dom.
_kpasswd._udp.subdom.net.dom. 600 IN SRV 0 100 464
↳           netdc2.subdom.net.dom.
```

As you can see, the first two records are of the A (host) and CNAME (alias) types, respectively; the other records are of the SRV (service location) type. Let us discuss the purpose of every record in the order that they are presented in the listing above. *DNSDomainName* is the name of the current domain, e.g., `subdom.net.dom`. *DNSRootName* is the name of the forest root domain (it can be also a *tree* root domain name if there is only one tree in the domain structure), e.g., `net.dom`.

Important

Do not confuse a *tree* root domain name (there may be a few in the forest) with the *forest* root domain name (only one). For example, a forest may include two domain trees with the root domains *net.dom* and *net2.dom*. Only the first created domain — net.dom — will be the forest root domain. Therefore, if the Global Catalog servers appear in the net2.dom domain (or in any child domains), they will still register the appropriate records in the net.dom DNS zone.

<DNSDomainName> — a client can use this A record to find a domain controller in the domain by using a normal host record lookup.

<NTDSSettingsGUID>._msdcs.<DNSRootName> — each domain controller registers this CNAME record for its child object (Directory System Agent, DSA), CN=NTDS Settings,CN=<DCName>,CN=Servers,CN=<SiteName>,CN=Sites,CN=Configuration, DC=<DomainName>, which uniquely identifies this controller in the Active Directory replication topology. A client can use this CNAME record to find a specific DC in the forest.

_ldap._tcp.<DNSDomainName> — a client can use this record to find a LDAP server in the specified domain. Each domain controller registers this record.

_ldap._tcp.dc._msdcs.<DNSDomainName> — allows a client to find a DC in the specified domain. Each domain controller registers this record. This record (with appropriate domain names) is used for joining a domain, a tree, or a forest; the current, parent, or root domain name is specified, respectively.

_ldap._tcp.pdc._msdcs.<DNSDomainName> — a client can use this record to find the Primary Domain Controller (PDC) Emulator in a mixed-mode domain. Only the PDC masters register this record.

_ldap._tcp.gc._msdcs.<DNSRootName> — a client can use this record to locate a Global Catalog (GC) server in the forest. Only GC servers register this record.

_ldap._tcp.<DomainGUID>.domains._msdcs.<DNSRootName> — a client can use this record to locate a domain controller in the domain specified by the domain GUID. Each domain controller registers this record.

_ldap._tcp.<SiteName>._sites.<DNSDomainName> — a client can use this record to find an LDAP server (not necessarily a DC) in the specified domain and site. Each Active Directory DC registers this record for its site.

_ldap._tcp.<SiteName>.sites.dc._msdcs.<DNSDomainName> — a client can use this record to locate a domain controller in the specified domain and site. Each domain controller registers this record.

_ldap._tcp.<SiteName>.sites.gc._msdcs.<DNSRootName> — allows a client to find a GC server for the forest in the specified site. Only GC servers register this record for their site.

gc._msdcs.<DNSRootName> — allows a non-SRV-aware client to find a GC server for the forest.

_gc._tcp.<DNSRootName> — a client can use this record to locate a GC server (not necessarily a DC) in the forest. Only an LDAP server that is the GC server registers this record.

_gc._tcp.<SiteName>._sites.<DNSRootName> — allows a client to find a GC server (not necessarily a DC) for the forest in the specified site.

_ldap._tcp.<SiteName>._sites.<DNSRootName> — a client can use this record to find a LDAP server (not necessarily a DC) in the forest.

_kerberos._tcp.<DNSDomanName> — a client can use this record to locate a server (not necessarily a DC) that is running the Kerberos Key Distribution Center (KDC) service in the specified domain. Each Active Directory DC registers this record.

_kerberos._udp.<DNSDomanName> — the same as above, but for the UDP protocol.

_kerberos._tcp.dc._msdcs.<DNSDomanName> — a client can use this record to locate a server (not necessarily a DC) that is running the Kerberos KDC service in the specified domain and site. Each DC registers this record.

_kerberos._tcp.<SiteName>._sites.dc._msdcs.<DNSDomanName> — a client can use this record to locate Active Directory DC that is running the Kerberos KDC service in the specified domain. Each DC registers this record.

_kerberos._tcp.<SiteName>._sites.<DNSDomanName> — a client can use this record to locate an Active Directory DC that is running the Kerberos KDC service in the specified domain and site. Each DC registers this record.

_kpasswd._tcp.<DNSDomanName> — a client can use this record to locate a server (not necessarily a DC) that is running the Kerberos Password Change service in the specified domain. Each Active Directory DC that is running the Kerberos KDC service registers this record.

_kpasswd._udp.<DNSDomanName> — the same as above, but for the UDP protocol.

> ***Note***
>
> Notice that all records for global catalog servers refer to the *forest root* domain name.

Resource Records for Application Partitions

If a Windows .NET domain controller holds one or more application directory partitions, it registers two SRV records and an A record for each partition in DNS. These records are not currently used by Active Directory; however, they allow other applications to find a server for a specific partition by using a DNS lookup operation. For example, if the DC *netdc2.subdom.net.dom* stores replicas of two built-in DNS application partitions, it will register the following records on the preferred DNS server:

```
DomainDnsZones.net.dom. 600 IN A 192.168.1.102
ForestDnsZones.net.dom. 600 IN A 192.168.1.102
_ldap._tcp.DomainDnsZones.net.dom. 600 IN SRV 0 100 389
↳ netdc2.subdom.net.dom.
_ldap._tcp.NET-Site._sites.DomainDnsZones.net.dom. 600 IN SRV
↳ 0 100 389 netdc2.subdom.net.dom.
_ldap._tcp.ForestDnsZones.net.dom. 600 IN SRV 0 100 389
↳ netdc2.subdom.net.dom.
_ldap._tcp.NET-Site._sites.ForestDnsZones.net.dom. 600 IN SRV
↳ 0 100 389 netdc2.subdom.net.dom.
```

Verifying and Updating DNS Registration

To test the DNS configuration for the entire forest, use the *Nslookup* command. The following sample dialog illustrates how to query the DNS server for the records registered by the Global Catalog servers. (Input commands are in bold.)

```
C:\>nslookup
Default Server:  netdc1.net.dom
Address:  192.168.1.2
> set type=SRV
> _gc._tcp.net.dom
```

```
Server:  netdc1.net.dom
Address:  192.168.1.2
_gc._tcp.net.dom        SRV service location:
          priority       = 0
          weight         = 100
          port           = 3268
          svr hostname   = netdc2.subdom.net.dom
_gc._tcp.net.dom        SRV service location:
          priority       = 0
          weight         = 100
          port           = 3268
          svr hostname   = netdc1.net.dom
netdc2.subdom.net.dom   internet address = 192.168.1.102
netdc1.net.dom  internet address = 192.168.1.2
>
```

The *DCdiag* command verifies DNS settings of a domain controller's replication partners and connectivity with them.

To verify DNS records registered by a specific domain controller, you can use on that DC the following commands:

- `netdiag /test:DNS` (or `netdiag /test:DNS /v`) — a very powerful and trustworthy tool.
- `nltest /DSQUERYDNS` — available on Windows .NET-based DCs; this command does not test SRV records for application partitions.

To re-register the register records on a DNS server (provided that it implements dynamic updating), one of the following methods can be used:

- Run the `ipconfig /registerdns` or `netdiag /fix` command
- Restart the Netlogon service in the **Services** snap-in
- Enter `net stop netlogon`, then `net start netlogon` at the command prompt
- On Windows .NET-based DCs, run the `nltest /DSREGDNS` command

For a Windows .NET domain controller, it is also possible to de-register (e.g., for the test purpose) all SRV records with the command

```
C:\>nltest /DSDEREGDNS:netdc1.net.dom
The command completed successfully
```

Important

When you are testing DNS, remember the cache of the DNS server as well as local DNS resolver. Its stale data can affect your test results. You might want to flush the cache after some DNS settings have been updated.

PART II

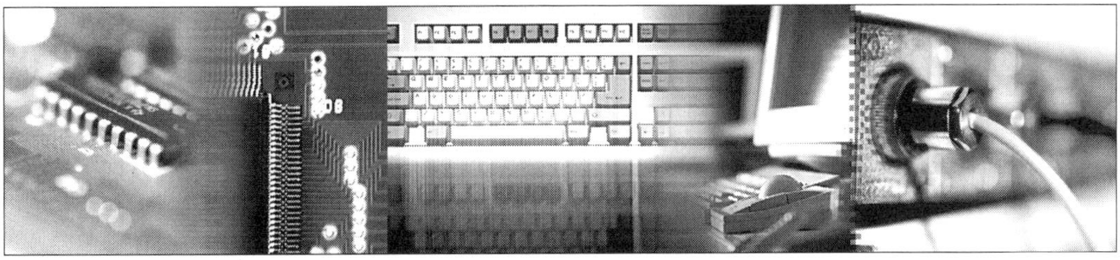

Deploying Active Directory Domains

Chapter 4: Windows .NET DNS Server

This chapter deals with various aspects of Microsoft DNS Server installation and configuration and covers two product versions: Windows 2000 DNS Server and Windows .NET DNS Server. Most of the things considered can be applied to both products (in such a case, we will call them the *Microsoft DNS Server*); the differences, if they exist, are explicitly stated. (Windows NT 4.0 DNS Server is only mentioned in the section *"Configuring Windows 2000/.NET DNS Server for Use with Legacy DNS."*)

The DNS service is mandatory for Active Directory, and you should be familiar with all DNS requirements within an Active Directory environment, which have been discussed in detail in *Chapter 3, "Domain Name System (DNS) as Main Naming Service"*. You can skip this section if DNS service has already been deployed in your network and configured accordingly. Some DNS specific problems will also be considered in *Chapter 5, "Installing Active Directory."*

This chapter also contains an example of using a legacy DNS system (that, for example, does not support SRV resource records and updatable DNS zones) for deploying Active Directory.

Prerequisites

To install a Microsoft DNS Server successfully, you have to consider some issues listed below.

IP Address

The server providing the DNS Service *must* have a *static* IP address. You should not use the address assigned by a DHCP Server.

Important

This IP address can be changed if needed, even if the DNS server is running on a domain controller. (However, this is not a normal practice!) In such a case, you also have to change the preferred DNS settings on all domain clients and domain controllers and update registration of all DNS resource records.

Primary DNS Suffix

Before installing DNS service, you must check the primary DNS suffix for the server (see *"Setting the DNS Suffix"* section). This is especially important if this server is also going to be a domain controller. In that case, you can either set the DNS suffix to be the same as the DNS name of the domain that the domain controller will belong to, or first promote the server and then install the DNS service. In any configuration, you must be sure that all names — the computer name (that includes the primary DNS suffix), the domain name of a member server or domain controller, and the name(s) of authoritative zone(s) stored on the DNS server — are consistent.

Planning DNS

Microsoft DNS Server can operate as:

- Caching server
- Primary server
- Secondary server

A DNS server can perform all listed roles at the same time (for example, it can be the primary server for one zone and the secondary server for another zone). In addition, each zone can be stored in a standard text file or in Active Directory. Therefore, you need first to carefully plan the DNS namespace and any questions related to DNS (see details in the previous chapter).

Installing a Microsoft DNS Server

To install and start the DNS service on a computer running Windows 2000/.NET Server, use the standard Windows Component Wizard that can be found in the Add/Remove Programs applet in the Control Panel. Select **Network Services** and click **Details**. Check the **Domain Name System (DNS)** box and click **OK** and then **Next**.

After the system files have been copied (the Windows 2000/.NET Server installation CD will be required) and the service started, you will see a new **DNS** snap-in in the **Administrative Tools** group. The DNS service is now installed on the computer and needs to be configured.

At first, the new DNS server running on a normal server will work as a caching server and will not be authoritative for any zones. Look up the DNS Server log in the Event Viewer to be sure that the service was started successfully. (If you have installed the DNS server on a domain controller, its behavior will be different; see the next sections of this chapter.)

To configure and manage a Microsoft DNS Server, run the **DNS** command from the **Administrative Tools** menu. In the **DNS** snap-in's main window (see Fig. 4.1), you can use a convenient wizard — *New Zone Wizard* that will help you to create forward and reverse zones.

Installing a DNS Server on the First Domain Controller

When you simultaneously install Active Directory and the DNS service on a server that is the *first* domain controller in the network, the Active Directory Installation Wizard (DCpromo.exe) automatically creates an authoritative zone for the forest root domain on the DNS server. (If a DNS server already exists, you must first manually create a zone for the new forest and enable dynamic updates of the zone.)

When a *child domain* in an existing forest is created, the zone of the forest root domain is used, and the wizard itself will create an authoritative zone for that child. (You may change this behavior; see later in this chapter.) However, if you add a *tree* to a forest, you must manually create an authoritative zone for the new DNS namespace. Therefore, you always need to create the authoritative zones for every new domain tree manually (or new forest), except with simultaneous installation of Active Directory and DNS service on the same server.

Caution

The Dcpromo utility does not create any *reverse* zones on the DNS server. Therefore, to make the DNS server configuration fully operational, it is recommended that you: manually create an appropriate reverse zone (because some utilities and applications use it), enable dynamic updates for it, and re-register the domain controller address with the `ipconfig /registerdns` command.

Secure updates are only enabled for *Active Directory-integrated* zones. These zones are available if only the DNS server is installed on a domain controller.

When a text file zone becomes Active Directory-integrated, the appropriate zone file is moved from the *%SystemRoot%*\system32\dns folder to the nested \backup folder. At the same time, new objects (of *dnsZone* and *dnsNode* types) for the zone are created in the Active Directory in the System/MicrosoftDNS container in the domain partition (if zones are stored on domain controllers) or within the appropriate application partition (on a Windows .NET Server). The reverse transformation of a zone (from Active Directory-integrated zone to text file zone) is also possible.

Important

Remember that Windows 2000 does not support application directory partitions. Therefore, to enable a DNS server running on a Windows 2000 DC to replicate Active Directory-integrated zones from a Windows .NET DNS server running on a Windows .NET DC, you must select the appropriate *zone replication scope*.

A Windows 2000 Environment

By default, the forward forest root domain authoritative zone (that includes the *_msdcs* subdomain, or node) and the root zone (".") are created as *Active Directory-integrated* and allow *Only secure updates*. This means that only authenticated users can update records. Sometimes, the **Yes** option in the **Allow dynamic updates?** list appears to be a better choice.

The "." zone, configured by default, makes the DNS server the *root* server, which prevents clients' queries from being sent — forwarded — to an external DNS namespace, e.g., to the Internet. To enable forwarders, you can just delete the "." zone. By default, the DNS server's IP address is specified on the **Root Hints** tab in the server's **Properties** window. If you have deleted the "." zone, make sure the server name has also been deleted from that tab.

A Windows .NET Environment

The root zone (".") is not created by default on Windows .NET DNS servers. As a result, the DNS server can "natively" resolve DNS queries for external names (e.g., the Internet names) provided that the default gateway has been configured for the server and network connectivity has been established. In that case, *root hints* are used. To resolve external queries more efficiently, you may specify a DNS server's IP address (e.g., the server of your Internet Service Provider, ISP) on the **Forwarders** tab in the server's **Properties** window.

By default, the Dcpromo utility creates two authoritative zones: the forest zone and the domain system zone *_msdcs* (see Fig. 4.1). Both zones are *Active Directory-integrated* and allow *Only secure updates.* The former zone is stored in the *DomainDnsZones* application partition that is replicated to all DNS servers in the forest root domain. The latter zone is stored in the *ForestDnsZones* application partition that is replicated to all DNS servers in the entire forest. Therefore, to enable a Windows 2000 DNS server running on a Windows 2000 DC to support these zones, you should change the replication scope of these zones.

Installing a Secondary DNS Server

You can increase the reliability of your network and install an additional (backup) DNS server. This task will be very simple if all the zones are Active Directory-integrated and the DNS server is installed on a domain controller. In that case, all DNS servers will be *peers,* and the term "secondary server" is not applicable since the authoritative zone(s) can be updated on any server.

In a Windows 2000 environment, every DC in the domain contains full DNS information. In a Windows .NET environment, you should first enable the DC to store replicas of the appropriate application partitions that hold DNS information. (Otherwise, the new DNS server will act as a simple caching server.) In either case, when you install a new DNS server, it will automatically load zone(s) from Active Directory and you need not create any zones. (For more information on managing application partitions, see the NTDSutil description in *Chapter 10, "Diagnosing and Maintaining Domain Controllers."*)

If the new DNS server is installed on a normal server, or if Active Directory-integrated zones are not used, you must create the zones manually and maintain the *zone transfers*. In that case, the new DNS server will act, most likely, as a secondary server, and the zones must be created as *secondary*.

When an additional DNS server has been installed, you may add the server's IP address to the list of DNS servers on every domain client computer or domain controller.

Configuring Zones

All operations on managing Microsoft DNS Server can be performed by using a GUI tool — the **DNS** snap-in, or from the command prompt — with the *DnsCmd.exe* utility. This utility is standard in Windows .NET, and has been included in the *Windows 2000 Support Tools* pack. The Windows .NET version of the utility has many new commands, since it allows users to work with application directory partitions. (However, you need to use the *NTDSutil.exe* tool to manage the partition replicas.)

Note

The DNS snap-in allows you to manage a local as well as one or more remote DNS servers.

Let us consider some aspects of managing zones on a Windows .NET DNS Server. Most of the issues discussed are also applicable to Windows 2000 DNS server.

Fig. 4.1 shows the main window of the **DNS** snap-in that contains authoritative zones (and their subdomains, or nodes) created by default for a sample forest. Let us discuss these zones in more detail.

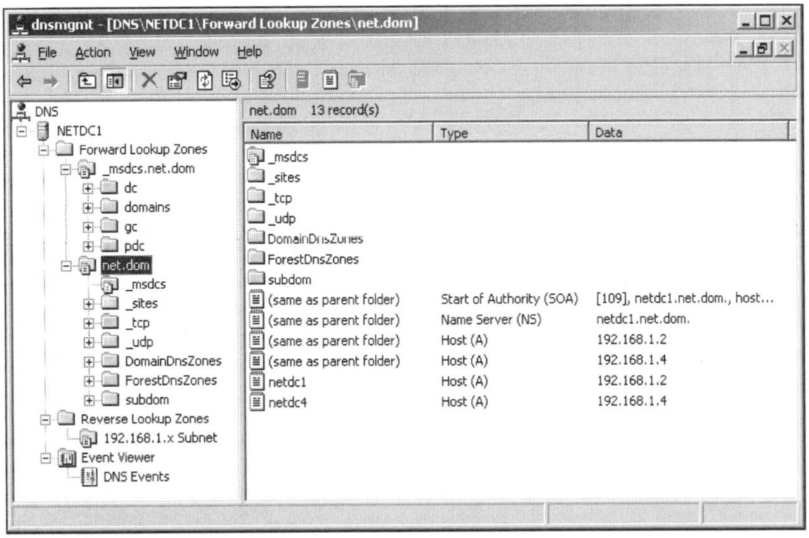

Fig. 4.1. The **DNS** snap-in's main window containing a few authoritative zones

A primary updatable reverse zone *192.168.1.x* (with the real name *1.168.192.in-addr.arpa*) has been created manually and requires no comments.

There are two authoritative zones for the forest root domain (*net.dom*): *net.dom* and *_msdcs.net.dom* (called the *domain system zone*). The former zone is stored in the *DomainDnsZones* application partition, whereas the latter one is stored in the ForestDnsZones application partition. As you can see, the corresponding DNS subdomains for these zones have been created within the main authoritative zone. In a similar way, any application partition with the *net.dom* suffix will have appropriate subdomains within that zone.

An authoritative zone for the *subdom.net.dom* domain has been automatically created within the main net.dom zone after the first domain controller for the child domain has been created and rebooted. As you might notice, this zone is also stored in the DomainDnsZones application partition and, therefore, will be replicated to all DNS servers in the net.dom domain. If such default behavior does not meet your requirements, you can rebuild it at any moment or create all necessary zones manually from scratch (after the first domain controller's installation).

Fig. 4.2 illustrates the same DNS configuration that is shown in Fig. 4.1, i.e., the clients performing DNS queries will not notice any differences in these configurations. However, in fact, there are many important distinctions that concern the child domain zones. Two independent zones — *subdom.net.dom* and *_msdcs.subdom.net.dom* — have been created. Since these are authoritative zones, you can manage their storage method as well as their replication scope. You may use built-in application partitions or create your own partition scheme that will store DNS information for the entire forest.

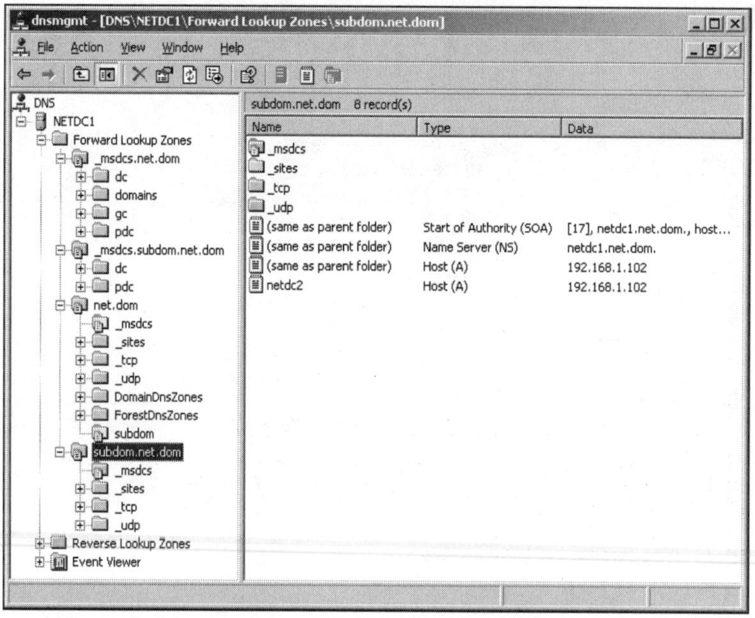

Fig. 4.2. An example of manually created zones

It is possible to safely change DNS configuration (the zones themselves as well as their properties) at any time. However, you must be sure that all necessary resource records have been re-registered after any changes have been made and all clients will be able to resolve DNS queries without interruption.

In Fig. 4.3, you can see a zone property window. (Note that the **Security** tab appears for Active Directory-integrated zones only.) Let us discuss a few important zone property features that have been added to Windows .NET DNS Server. These features can be selected when a zone is created as well as changed for an existing zone.

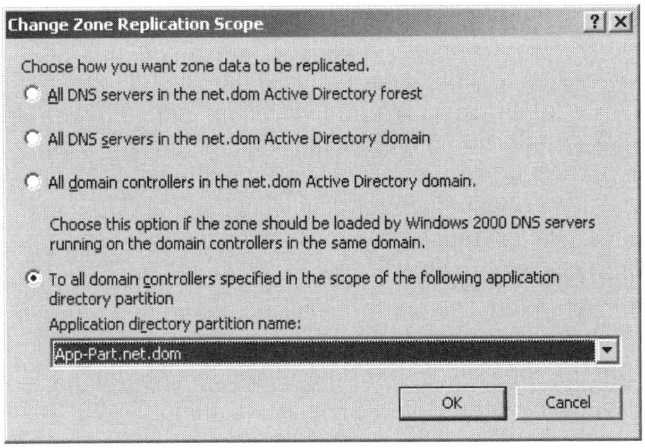

Fig. 4.3. Properties of a DNS zone on a Windows .NET DNS Server

As you might notice in Fig. 4.4, Windows .NET DNS Server supports a new zone type — *stub zone*. Stub zones allow the root DNS server (that holds the forest authoritative zone, e.g., *net.dom*) to remain aware of the DNS servers authoritative for a delegated child zone (e.g., *subdom.net.dom*).

In Fig. 4.5, you can see all zone replication scopes supported by Windows .NET DNS Server. To change the replication scope for a zone, it is also possible to use the DnsCmd command-line utility. To view the contents of an application partition, use the **ADSI Edit** snap-in or the `dnscmd /ZonePrint` command. The following sample command allows you to quickly view all replicas of an application partition:

```
C:\>dnscmd netdc1.net.dom /DirectoryPartitionInfo ForestDnsZones.net.dom
Directory partition info:
  DNS root:    ForestDnsZones.net.dom
  Flags:       0x19 Enlisted Auto Forest
  State:       0
  Zone count:  4
  DP head:     DC=ForestDnsZones,DC=net,DC=dom
  Crossref:    CN=4579c777-4ff0-46ec-9ef5-b825de36f677,CN=Partitions,CN=Con...
```

```
Replicas:   2
   CN=NTDS Settings,CN=NETDC2,CN=Servers,CN=NET-Site,CN=Sites,CN=Configur...
   CN=NTDS Settings,CN=NETDC1,CN=Servers,CN=NET-Site,CN=Sites,CN=Configur...
Command completed successfully.
```

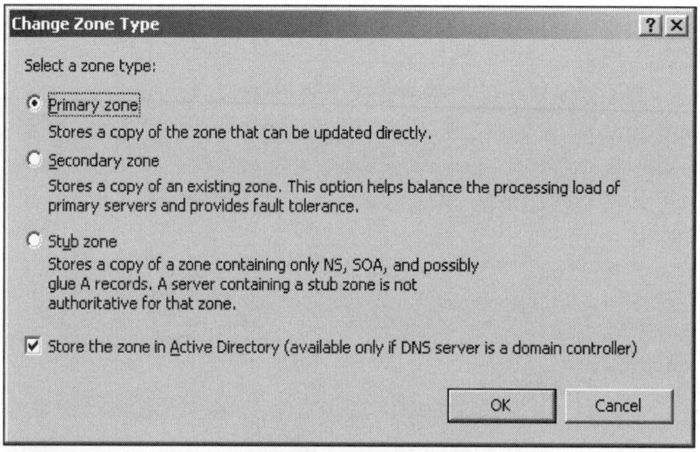

Fig. 4.4. Zone types

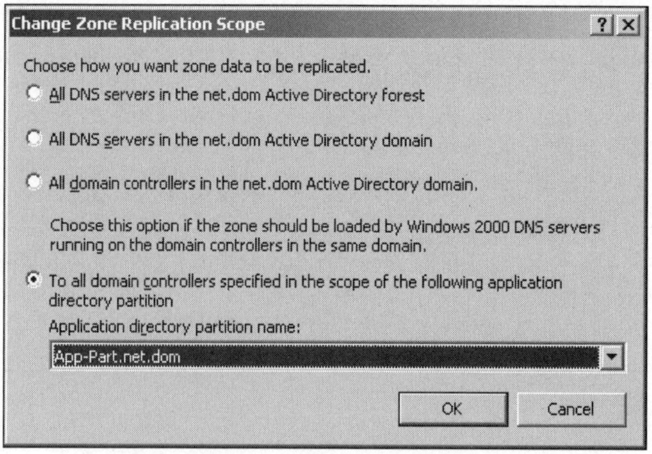

Fig. 4.5. Zone replication scopes

The first scope option corresponds to the *DomainDnsZones* application partition. To change the scope, or to move a zone to a new partition, you can use the command:

```
C:\>dnscmd netdc1.net.dom /ZoneChangeDirectoryPartition net.dom /domain
```

```
DNS Server netdc1.net.dom moved zone net.dom to new directory partition
Command completed successfully.
```

The DNS server name (`netdc1.net.dom`) is not required if the command is run on the DNS server. As you might notice, one can only move the entire zone, not a subdomain of a zone.

The second scope option corresponds to the ForestDnsZones application partition. To move a zone to the forest new partition, use the command:

```
C:\>dnscmd netdc1.net.dom /ZoneChangeDirectoryPartition net.dom /forest
```

The third scope option enables the zone to be stored in the domain partition (in the System/MicrosoftDNS container). This is a storage method supported for Active Directory-integrated zones in Windows 2000. The following command is used in this case:

```
C:\>dnscmd netdc1.net.dom /ZoneChangeDirectoryPartition net.dom /legacy
```

The last option allows you to store the zone in a user-created application directory partition that can be replicated between DNS servers running on any domain controllers that belong to any domains. Remember that you are fully responsible for managing such partitions and should create application replicas to provide DNS fault tolerance and distribute workload on DNS servers. To move a zone to a user created partition, use the command:

```
C:\>dnscmd netdc1.net.dom /ZoneChangeDirectoryPartition
↳ net.dom App-Part.net.dom,
```

where `App-Part.net.dom` is the DNS name of the application partition.

Configuring Windows 2000/.NET DNS Server for Use with Legacy DNS

If Active Directory is deployed in an existing network which already uses DNS service, an interoperation problem may arise if the legacy DNS service does not conform to Windows 2000/.NET DNS requirements. This is a neither rare, nor hopeless situation; there is a way to achieve a compromise. We shall use the adjective *legacy* for any DNS servers that support neither dynamic records update, nor SRV records (this can be, for example, an NT 4.0 DNS Server or a UNIX DNS server). In addition, the configuration shown below can serve as an example of heterogeneous DNS service deployment and DNS zone delegation (which may be helpful in various cases).

You can easily diagnose the problem by looking up the System log after creating the first domain controller. (It is strongly recommended that you check all logs when *each* DC is created!) After the domain controller boots, the warning (ID 5773) from

Netlogon may appear in the System log; Windows .NET systems provide a clear issue explication:

```
The following DNS server that is authoritative for the DNS domain controller
locator records of this domain controller does not support dynamic DNS updates:
DNS server IP address: 192.168.1.155
Returned Response Code (RCODE): 4
Returned Status Code: 9004

USER ACTION
Configure the DNS server to allow dynamic DNS updates or manually add
the DNS records from the file
'%SystemRoot%\System32\Config\Netlogon.dns' to the DNS database.
```

Let us take a specific scenario and discuss in detail how to solve the problem. To simplify the situation, we will use a minimal number of computers.

Suppose we have an existing Windows NT 4.0 DNS server authoritative for the *net.dom* domain. The server stores the forward and reverse zones: *net.dom* and *1.168.192.in-addr.arpa*. All domain controllers and clients (including Windows 2000/XP/.NET computers) have to use this server as preferred.

Note

Remember that reverse zones are not necessary for Active Directory, but rather provide a fully operational DNS configuration.

The second DNS server (based on a Windows 2000 or Windows .NET server) has to be configured to support all updateable resource records for an Active Directory domain. Computer names and addresses are shown in the table below:

Computer's name and role	FQDN	IP address
NT4SRV5 (NT 4.0 DNS server)	nt4srv5.net.dom	192.168.1.155
NETDC1 (Windows .NET DNS server)	netdc1.net.dom	192.168.1.2
NETDC4 (Windows .NET domain controller)	netdc4.net.dom	192.168.1.4

By default, the dynamic registration of a host's name and address on the preferred DNS server is enabled; so, in our scenario we need to disable registration on all Windows 2000/XP/.NET computers to avoid error messages in the computers' System logs. To do this, reset the **Register this connection's addresses in DNS** flag on the **DNS** tab in the **Advanced TCP/IP Setting** window. Then, you have to manually create a host record (type A) for each domain controller and computer on the preferred server.

Creating Authoritative Zones

On the Windows .NET DNS server, we need to create four dynamic authoritative zones necessary for domain functioning. These zones will answer the DNS queries for specific IP addresses that could not be resolved by the preferred server. In our scenario, all these zones' names have the *net.dom* suffix. (In general, these zones can be either standard or Active Directory-integrated.)

The zones created will be the following:

- _msdcs.net.dom
- _sites.net.dom
- _tcp.net.dom
- _udp.net.dom

Furthermore, we also have to allow dynamic updates of these zones. Fig. 4.6 illustrates the result obtained in this preliminary step. Notice that each zone has SOA and NS records. This means that the server that supports such a record can resolve DNS queries stored in that zone.

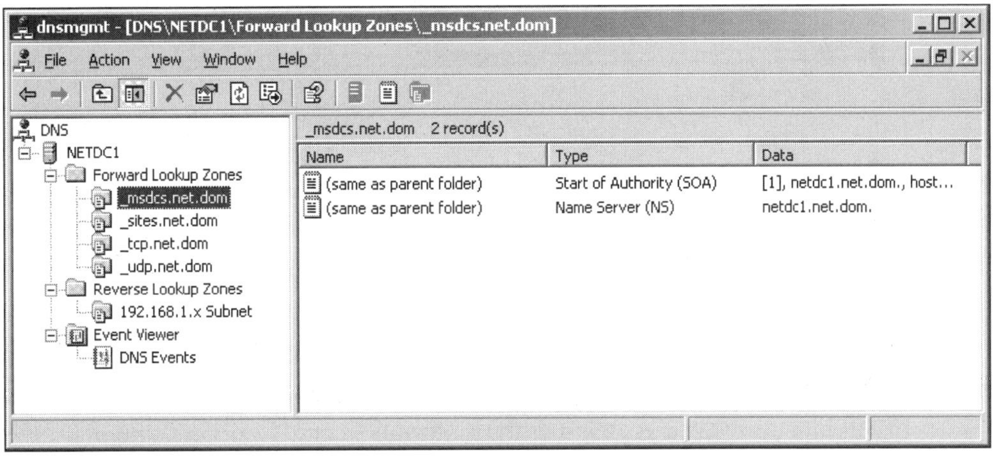

Fig. 4.6. Creating dynamically updatable authoritative zones on a Windows .NET DNS server

Delegating Names from the Main Authoritative Zone

It is now necessary to create the dynamic zone names in the domain authoritative zone and delegate them to the Windows .NET DNS server, where the zones will be stored and updated. All zone names are created as *domains* within the main authoritative zone net.dom. (The procedure described below will also help you to create a zone on any type of DNS server and delegate the zone to another DNS server.) The following operations have to be carried out:

1. Right click the main zone name and select the **New Domain** command from the context menu. Create four necessary domains.
2. Right click a created domain (e.g., *_msdcs.net.dom*) and select the **New Record** command the context menu. Then you must select the *NS Record* type and specify the DNS name of the server that stores the authoritative zone with the same name. Repeat this step for each created domain.

The result that should be obtained is illustrated in Fig. 4.7. (A Windows NT 4.0 Server SP6a was used.) All DNS queries for records that belong to the zones shown will be addressed to the DNS server *NETDC1* (that is authoritative *to resolve* these queries).

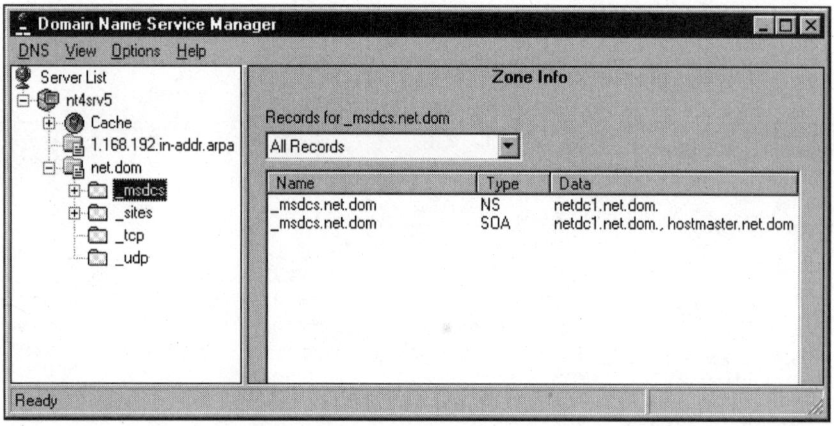

Fig. 4.7. Authoritative DNS server for domain net.dom and the zones delegated to the dynamic DNS server NETDC1

In addition, we need to register the following records on the Windows NT 4.0 DNS server in the domain authoritative zone:

- Two *type A* (host) records (with corresponding *PTR* records) for the Windows .NET computers: NETDC1 and NETDC4. (Such records will be necessary for each domain computer.)
- A *type A* (host) record for the net.dom name (this record is needed for finding a domain controller using a simple name lookup). To create such a record, select a usual *A Record*, leave out its name, and specify the IP address of a domain con-

troller (NETDC4). (This record must be created for *each* domain controller in the net.dom domain.)

The latter *type A* record requires additional attention. By design, this record is dynamically updatable. The domain controllers' Netlogon service re-registers it after each system boot. In our case, an update is impossible, so an error message will be periodically generated in the System log. You may get rid of the problem by adding the `RegisterDNSARecords` DWORD value (set the value to 0x0) to the registry subkey `HKLM\SYSTEM\CurrentControlSet\Services\Netlogon\Parameters`.

If you disable registration of A records using the `RegisterDNSARecords` subkey equal to 0, two records will be deleted from the netlogon.dns file on the domain controller NETDC4:

```
net.dom. IN A 192.168.1.4
```

and

```
gc._msdcs.net.dom. IN A 192.168.1.4
```

If a domain controller stores an application partition, a corresponding A record will also be deleted, for example:

```
ForestDnsZones.net.dom. 600 IN A 192.168.1.4
```

Caution

The `RegisterDNSARecords` value (being set to 0x0) also prevents the Netlogon service from updating the host (type A) record for the gc._msdcs.net.dom name. You must manually add this record, and re-register it if a Global Catalog server's location is changed.

Resulting Configuration

Thus, we have covered the preliminary steps and now the domain controller NETDC4 is able to update (or first to create) all necessary SRV records. You need to restart the Netlogon service or, preferably, reboot the system. (You can also use the `nltest /DSREGDNS` command.) After this, you will get all updatable records on the Windows .NET DNS server (NETDC1) (Fig. 4.8).

Now you can (and *should*) check all DNS logs and test the domain controller to be sure that all records have been registered correctly.

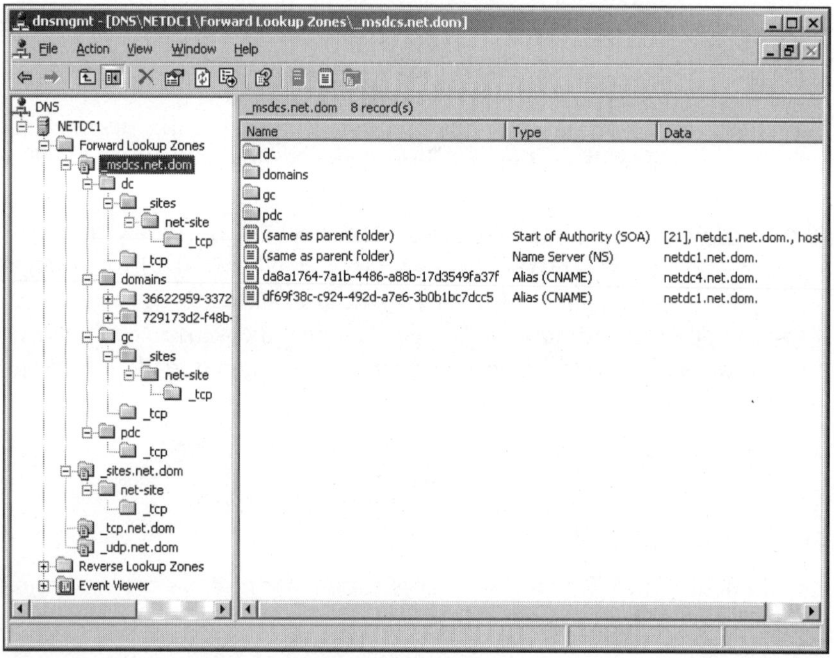

Fig. 4.8. The name structure of all needed SRV records, shown on a dynamic DNS server

Verifying the DNS Service

After you have installed DNS service on a Windows 2000/.NET Server, or if you already have a functioning Microsoft DNS server (or a third party DNS server), you may wish (or rather, *need*) to verify the DNS configuration. This is especially important if you use an "outside" DNS server (a server running on a remote computer or even in another organization). It is not enough that you yourself think that all DNS parameters are properly set; rather, it is the system and program tests that should confirm that everything is working fine.

You must check that the DNS server holds the correct forward and reverse zones and that these zones allow dynamic record updates. For testing Microsoft DNS Servers, it is helpful to use a general-purpose command-line *DnsCmd.exe* utility (that is standard in Windows .NET, or has been included in the *Windows 2000 Support Tools* pack). You can start it from any computer that has access to the inspected DNS server. This utility can perform all operations necessary for remote maintenance of a Microsoft DNS server.

Note

In *Chapter 5, "Installing Active Directory"*, we will discuss how to use specialized utilities that also help to verify DNS configuration, such as DCdiag.exe and NetDiag.exe.

To verify a zone, use the /enumzones command. You will get an output similar to the following (which is the output for the simplest configuration):

```
C:\>dnscmd netdc1.net.dom /EnumZones
Enumerated zone list:

        Zone count = 8

 Zone name                      Type       Storage          Properties

 .                              Cache      AD-Domain
 _msdcs.net.dom                 Primary    AD-Forest        Update
 1.168.192.in-addr.arpa         Primary    AD-Forest        Update Rev
 net.dom                        Primary    AD-Domain        Update

Command completed successfully.
```

In this case, netdc1.net.dom is the Microsoft DNS Server name, "." corresponds to the cached lookups, net.dom is an authoritative zone name and the DNS name of the future domain, and 1.168.192.in-addr.arpa is a manually created reverse zone for the private network 192.168.1.0 (255.255.255.0 mask; the address and mask depend on your network configuration).

The Update parameter indicates whether or not the zone is dynamically updatable. You can also check this property of zones (e.g., the net.dom zone) using the following command. (Be careful; in the Windows 2000 version of DnsCmd, the AllowUpdate and other zone properties are case-sensitive!):

```
C:\>dnscmd netdc1.net.dom /ZoneInfo net.dom AllowUpdate
Zone query result:
Dword:  1 (00000001)
Command completed successfully.
```

The value 1 indicates that this zone can be dynamically updated.

You must also verify DNS server responsiveness. It is recommended that you do this before any DC creation in a Windows 2000 environment (in Windows .NET, similar tests are built-in), in order to avoid serious domain problems in the future. Enter the following command on the inspected computer (a client, or a server to be promoted):

```
C:\>nslookup 192.168.1.2
```

192.168.1.2 is the DNS server's IP address, specified in the TCP/IP properties of that computer. The result will be similar to the following output:

```
Server:  netdc1.net.dom
```

```
Address:  192.168.1.2

Name:     netdc1.net.dom
Address:  192.168.1.2
```

Here, the `Server` reply contains the DNS server name, and `Name` is the name resolved from the specified IP address. In this case, the names are the same (because we have asked the DNS server for its own name), but you may want to resolve any other IP addresses if their corresponding host names are registered on the DNS server. You may also verify resolving DNS computer names into IP addresses, for example: `nslookup net.dom`.

Note

In contrast to DnsCmd.exe, the Nslookup command can be used with any type of DNS servers.

If you receive any different outputs or error messages, like "Can't find server name for address" or "Default servers are not available," you need to check all TCP/IP properties, the connectivity and the existence of forward and reverse zones. The DNS server may reply with the aforementioned messages, if, for example, the server is operational but the reverse zone is absent or corrupted.

After a domain controller is created (and especially when the first DC in the forest is created), it is strongly recommended that you verify the registration of all necessary SRV records (see *Chapter 3, "Domain Name System (DNS) as Main Naming Service"*). You can check an SRV record with the DNSCmd.exe utility by entering, for example, the command (asking the SRV record registered by the PDC operations master):

```
C:\>dnscmd netdc1.net.dom /EnumRecords _msdcs.net.dom _tcp.pdc /Type SRV
Returned records:
_ldap [Aging:3519689] 600 SRV   0 100 389 netdc1.net.dom.
Command completed successfully.
```

(Here, `_msdcs.net.dom` is the authoritative zone name.)

In conclusion, it is worth repeating that the best command for testing domain controllers is the *DcDiag.exe* utility that reliably verifies DNS issues for a specified computer. For example, if the following command returns no information, you may be sure that the selected DC is "healthy":

```
C:\>dcdiag /s:netdc4.net.dom /q
```

All described procedures will help you to avoid some pitfalls of domain functioning. Do not forget to set aside at least a half an hour for DNS testing. Take your time and be thorough, or you could spend days trying to resolve potential problems, such as "why is network reaction so slow?" or "why doesn't the new domain controller replicate data?"

Setting the DNS Suffix

To set the *primary DNS suffix* on a computer running Windows 2000/XP/.NET, open the **System Properties** window (press <Win>+<Break>, or right click **My computer** on the **Start** menu or the desktop, and click **Properties**). Then, click **Properties** on the **Computer Name** tab (in Windows 2000 — **Network Identification**), click **Change**, and **More**. In the pop-up window (Fig. 4.9), enter the DNS name of the domain to which the computer will belong.

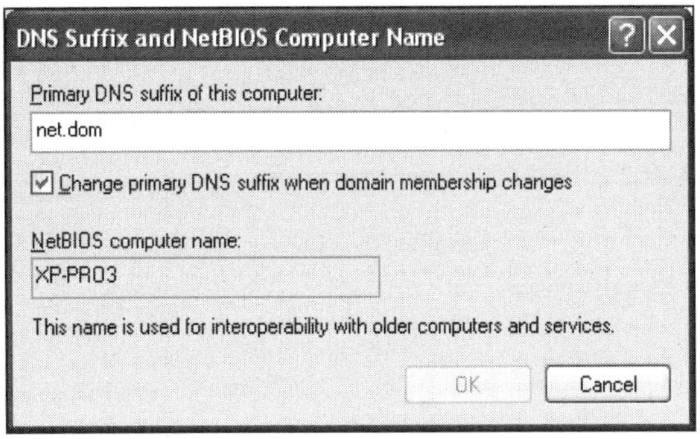

Fig. 4.9. Setting the DNS suffix of the computer

Note

Note that the **Change primary DNS suffix when domain membership changes** checkbox must be normally set. This is especially important for servers that have to be promoted.

You can manage the primary DNS suffix by using a group policy. See the *Primary DNS Suffix* policy at the node **Computer Configuration** | **Administrative Templates** | **Network** | **DNS Client**.

Chapter 5: Installing Active Directory

An administrator who is not yet closely acquainted with Active Directory must be aware of the two following postulates:

- The terms "creating a domain controller", "installing Active Directory", and "promoting a server" are, in a sense, synonymous because they describe the same process. You cannot install Active Directory without creating a domain controller and vice versa.
- Active Directory-based (Windows 2000 and Windows .NET) domains simply do not work without DNS.

Administrators, even those who are quite experienced, should always remember that the DNS is the "heart" of Active Directory domains, and *many, many* faults, all very different by nature (e.g., issues related to the authentication process, or applying group policies to users and computers), can derive from an improperly configured DNS system. That is why troubleshooting practically every domain-level problem should begin with verifying the DNS configuration. And that is why the DNS related issues are mentioned in this chapter again.

This chapter does not contain step-by-step descriptions of *all* typical operations; instead, it deals with only the most important issues.

Note

In this chapter, "Windows DNS Server" means either a Windows 2000 DNS Server or Windows .NET DNS Server, depending on the platform used.

Installing Domain Controllers

Active Directory can only be installed on an existing Windows 2000/.NET Server. Active Directory installation is a process independent from installing/upgrading the operating system itself. Moreover, you can *demote* a domain controller (or uninstall Active Directory) to a member (or standalone) server (and promote it again if you wish). The *Active Directory Installation Wizard* is used in both operations. This behavior differs principally from the Windows NT 4.0 "rules", where the role of a server (member server, Primary Domain Controller (PDC), or Backup Domain Controller (BDC)) is specified during installation, and typically cannot be changed without full system re-installation.

Therefore, you can create an Active Directory domain controller (DC) in the following ways:

- Start the Active Directory Installation Wizard on a Windows 2000/.NET Server (standalone or member server) that has already been installed. The DCpromo.exe utility is used in such cases. You can work with it either interactively or in unattended mode (discussed later in this chapter). The result will be a DC in a new domain or an additional DC in an existing domain.

- Upgrade a Windows NT 4.0-based domain controller (PDC or BDC). You can also upgrade a Windows 2000-based DC to Windows .NET. The DCpromo.exe utility will start automatically after the upgrade to Windows 2000/.NET Server has been completed and the computer has been rebooted.
  - A Windows NT 4.0 PDC can only be upgraded to a DC in a new domain.
  - A Windows NT 4.0 BDC can be upgraded to an additional DC in an existing domain, or to a member server (if one chooses not to install Active Directory).

Upgrading from a Windows NT/2000 Domain

We will not discuss this topic in detail, since all the necessary information pertaining to it can be found quite easily in the *Help and Support Center*. Let us note the most important aspects only.

To upgrade a Windows NT domain to Windows 2000/.NET, you ***must*** upgrade the Primary Domain Controller (PDC) first. This ensures that you will keep all existing users and groups. If the DNS service was not used in the Windows NT environment, you ***must*** plan a DNS namespace and install a DNS server (of any type). It is also possible to use a legacy DNS with the Windows 2000/.NET DNS Server (see an example in *Chapter 4, "Windows .NET DNS Server"*). Provide a recovery plan in case of an unsuccessful upgrade.

To upgrade a Windows 2000 domain to Windows .NET, or to install a Windows .NET-based domain controller within a Windows 2000 domain, you ***must*** upgrade the schema first, or in other words, *prepare* the forest and domains.

At first, you need to prepare the forest with the `adprep /forestprep` command that should be run on the Schema Master. All changes must be replicated within the forest. If the command has run without errors, continue the procedure.

During your second step, you will need to prepare ***each*** domain with the `adprep /domainprep` command that should be run on the Infrastructure Masters separately.

You may also consider migrating Windows NT or Windows 2000 domains to a pristine Active Directory domain by using such tools as Active Directory Migration Tool (ADMT) and ClonePrincipal (see *Chapter 13, "Migration and Directory Reorganization Tools"*).

Adding Windows 2000 Domain Controllers to a Windows .NET Domain

You can promote a Windows 2000 server to be a domain controller in a Windows .NET domain running at the *Windows 2000 mixed* or *Windows 2000 native* functional levels only. Keep in mind that in this case, the new Windows 2000 DC will support the Windows .NET schema version (26 or higher) rather than the schema version 13 designated for pure Windows 2000 domains.

If you try to add a Windows 2000 DC to a *Windows .NET (version 2002)* level domain, or to create a Windows 2000 domain within a *Windows .NET (version 2002)* level forest, the Active Directory installation will fail. The system reports "An error with no description has occurred" in the former case, or "Indicates two revision levels are incompatible" in the latter.

Adding Windows .NET Domain Controllers to a Windows 2000 Domain

A Windows .NET server can be promoted to be a domain controller only in a forest (domain) that supports the Windows .NET schema version. You can upgrade the schema by using the `adprep /forest` and `adprep /domain` commands, and create a Windows .NET domain controller; however in such a case, one should speak about a Windows .NET forest (running at the *Windows 2000 mixed* functional level) rather than a pure Windows 2000 forest (domain).

Note

See also the section entitled *"Adding a Windows NT 4.0 BDC to a Windows 2000/.NET Domain."*

Requirements and Restrictions

The Active Directory can be installed only if several critical conditions are met. The *Active Directory Installation Wizard* (DCpromo.exe) will check different parameters depending on the type of DC that is being created. Among these conditions are the following:

- Active Directory can be installed only on a NTFS 5.0 formatted disk partition.
- This partition must have at least 250 MB of free space. (This does not mean that all that space will be employed at once; the default size of the Active Directory database including the log files is about 40 Mbytes. However, the system must have reserved space for normal work.)
- If the server is a standalone computer, only a user that is a member of the local Administrators group can start DCpromo.exe. If the server is a member of a domain, members of the Domain Admins and Enterprise Admins groups can also initiate promotion.

Important

Remember that you cannot add a Windows NT 4.0 BDC to a *native mode* Windows 2000 domain or create a Windows 2000-based domain controller in a Windows .NET domain running at the *Windows .NET (version 2002)* domain functional level. It is also not possible to create a Windows 2000 domain in a Windows .NET forest running at the *Windows .NET (version 2002)* forest functional level (see details in *Chapter 2, "Active Directory Terminology and Concepts"*).

If you create a new Windows .NET domain in a forest running at the *Windows .NET (version 2002)* forest functional level, the domain functional level of the new domain will automatically be raised to the same level.

- When a new DC is created in an existing forest, any user that is not logged on as a domain or enterprise administrator must provide sufficient credentials (a pre-Windows 2000 logon name and a password; names in UPN form, e.g., `admin@net.dom`, are not acceptable):
  - Only members of the Enterprise Admins group can create new domains (child domains or new trees). It is possible to have a pre-created new domain in the forest (see the description of NTDSutil.exe in *Chapter 10, "Diagnosing and Maintaining Domain Controllers"*).
  - The members of the Domain Admins and the Enterprise Admins groups are permitted to add a DC to an existing domain. The privileges to join a computer to the domain and create the appropriate replication objects can also be given to some user accounts.
- TCP/IP protocol must be installed and configured on the computer. Typically, domain controllers have static IP addresses (however, conceptually this does not necessarily have to be the case).

Important

- It is possible to safely change the IP address of a domain controller and then re-register all SRV records (see the previous chapter). Sometimes, this change can affect directory replication, since the controller's replication partners have to learn the new IP address. However, this is not a crucial issue. Remember also that the caching of DNS requests on the preferred DNS server and clients can prevent the new address from "propagating" in a moment.

- The computer should have the primary DNS suffix (see the previous chapter). This is a *critical* requirement if the computer is also going to act as a DNS server. For an ordinary domain controller, the **Change primary DNS suffix when domain membership changes** checkbox must at least be set. The suffix will be properly set if the computer is a member of a domain, and you need not change anything.
- An already deployed DNS service must be available. If a legacy or third party DNS server is used, it should meet the Active Directory requirements and be properly configured. If the promoted server is the first DC and there is no DNS

server in the network, you *must* allow the Active Directory Installation Wizard to install and configure the Windows DNS server.

Important

If you create the first DC and enable the DNS installation and configuration on the same computer, you ***must assign*** an applicable IP address (e.g., 192.168.1.1) to the computer and ***specify*** that address as the preferred DNS server address. The Active Directory Installation Wizard will not do this itself, and as a result, the new domain (forest) will not be operational!

Note

A reverse DNS zone is not *required* for Active Directory. Nevertheless, it is recommended that you configure one for the other applications that use it.

- The server NetBIOS name must be unique in the domain. The NetBIOS (pre-Windows 2000) name of new domain must be unique in the forest.
- If a child domain (or a new tree) is created, the parent and forest root domains must exist and be accessible. This means that you cannot create a child domain — e.g., *subdom.net.dom* — if the *net.dom* domain does not exist.
- Without going into detail and in order to considerably simplify the situation, it is possible to say that *all* FSMO masters should be available for starting and successfully completing server promotion. Otherwise, you should always know and remember which FSMO masters are required for each specific type of domain controller created (an additional DC, a new tree, and so on).

Note

By default, all domain controllers will be created in the *Domain Controllers* OU in the domain partition.

Note

The computer SID remains the same after the Active Directory installation or removal.

Note

Let us suppose a server was previously a domain controller and has been demoted, and that you wish to install the Active Directory on to it again. It may be useful to make sure that the folders where the Active Directory files (the database and logs) were stored have been deleted (by default, the *%SystemRoot%*\NTDS folder is used). Moreover, if the Distributed File System (DFS) is not used on this computer, stop the File Replication Service by using the `net stop ntfrs` command and delete the contents of the *%SystemRoot%*\ntfrs\jet folder. Then restart the service: `net start ntfrs`.

Important

- During one of the preliminary steps, the Active Directory Installation Wizard asks for your "Directory Services Restore Mode Administrator Password". This password is only used in the logon process after you have pressed the <F8> key in the boot menu and selected the *Directory Services Restore Mode*. The password is not used often, so try not to forget it (this does happen!).

Verifying DNS Configuration

DNS testing is one of the most important steps in preparing a server for promotion. Any undetected errors in DNS configuration may result in an inoperable domain controller. The following DNS related faults are possible:

- The computer has no settings for the preferred DNS server.
- The specified DNS server does not host the specified authoritative zone (domain name).
- The authoritative zone exists, but is not updatable.

Microsoft has done a great job in extending the initial functionality of the DCdiag and NetDiag utilities from the *Support Tools* to allow an administrator to verify the DNS configuration in a few seconds. (For a Windows 2000 environment, you can download updated versions from the Microsoft website. For additional information on these tools, see *Chapter 10, "Diagnosing and Maintaining Domain Controllers"* and *Chapter 11, "Verifying Network and Distributed Services."*)

A further step has been taken in the Windows .NET Server family: the Active Directory Installation Wizard diagnoses DNS-related and forest configuration issues and stops server promotion if any problems exist. Nevertheless, you can use the DCdiag and NetDiag utilities on computers running Windows .NET, too.

Important

- All tests described below verify DNS only; connectivity with existing domain controllers is not checked. The Active Directory Installation Wizard verifies both DNS and connectivity (including authentication) issues.

If a preferred DNS server's IP address is not specified on the tested computer in the **TCP/IP Properties** window, the `dcdiag /test:DcPromo` or `dcdiag /test:RegisterInDNS` command outputs a message with the error 9852, which means "No DNS servers configured for local system."

The following command reports that you can safely create an additional domain controller in an existing Windows 2000 or Windows .NET domain (*net.dom* in this example):

```
C:\>dcdiag /test:DcPromo /DnsDomain:net.dom /ReplicaDC
   Starting test: DcPromo
      The DNS configuration is sufficient to allow this computer to be
      promoted as a replica domain controller in the net.dom domain.

...
      DNS configuration is sufficient to allow this domain controller to
      dynamically register the domain controller Locator records in DNS.

      The DNS configuration is sufficient to allow this computer to
      dynamically register the A record corresponding to its DNS name.

      ......................... netdc4 passed test DcPromo
```

In such a case, you can begin to promote the server. (For compactness, some lines are skipped in this output. When the Windows 2000 version of the tool is used, all tests executed (both successful and failed) end with the same "passed test" line. The Windows .NET version reports results more correctly.)

The following output indicates that the authoritative zone (*w2000.dom*) exists, but there are no SRV records registered by the existing domain controller(s):

```
C:\>dcdiag /test:DcPromo /DnsDomain:w2000.dom /ReplicaDC
   Starting test: DcPromo
      This computer cannot be promoted as a domain controller of the
      w2000.dom domain. This is because either the DNS SRV record for
      _ldap._tcp.dc._msdcs.w2000.dom is not registered in DNS, or some
      zone from the following list of DNS zones doesn't include
      delegation to its child zone: w2000.dom, dom and the root zone.
      Ask your network/DNS administrator to perform the following
      actions: To find out why the SRV record for
      _ldap._tcp.dc._msdcs.w2000.dom is not registered in DNS, run the
      dcdiag command prompt tool with the command RegisterInDNS on the
      domain controller that did not perform the registration.
...
      DNS configuration is sufficient to allow this domain controller to
      dynamically register the domain controller Locator records in DNS.

      The DNS configuration is sufficient to allow this computer to
      dynamically register the A record corresponding to its DNS name.

      ......................... netdc4 failed test DcPromo
```

This might be a serious problem: the existing DC for the specified domain could be promoted incorrectly. You should verify the DNS configuration and make the DC re-register all its SRV records. Then run DCdiag on that DC.

In all cases when updating of an authoritative zone is not enabled on the DNS server (or the server does not support dynamic updates), the command output will be similar to the following:

```
C:\>dcdiag /test:DcPromo /DnsDomain:dotnet.dom /ReplicaDC
   Starting test: DcPromo
      The DNS configuration is sufficient to allow this computer to be
      promoted as a replica domain controller in the dotnet.dom domain.

      Messages logged below this line indicate whether this domain
      controller will be able to dynamically register DNS records
      required for the location of this DC by other devices on the
      network. If any misconfiguration is detected, it might prevent
      dynamic DNS registration of some records, but does not prevent
      successful completion of the Active Directory Installation Wizard.
      However, we recommend fixing the reported problems now, unless you
      plan to manually update the DNS database.

      This domain controller cannot register domain controller Locator
      DNS records. This is because either the DNS server with IP address
      192.168.1.2 does not support dynamic updates or the zone
      dotnet.dom is configured to prevent dynamic updates.
...
      ......................... netdc4 failed test DcPromo
```

Detailed instructions on configuring the DNS server are also displayed. You must follow them. To check whether a zone is updatable, it is also possible to use the command

```
dcdiag /test:RegisterInDNS /DnsDomain:dotnet.dom
```

which produces a similar output.

Other parameters of the `dcdiag /test:DcPromo` command allow you to test whether you can create a child domain, new tree, or new forest in the current domain structure. The command's messages are clear, and it is not necessary to place them all here.

If the preferred DNS server is specified incorrectly or not accessible, or if the authoritative zone did not configure on the server, the following command will discover the problem and instruct you on what to do:

```
C:\>dcdiag /test:RegisterInDNS /DnsDomain:net2.dom
   Starting test: RegisterInDNS
      Please verify that the network connections of this computer are
      configured with correct IP addresses of the DNS servers to be used
```

```
for name resolution. If the DNS resolver is configured with its
own IP address and the DNS server is not running locally, the
DcPromo will be able to install and configure local DNS server,
but it will be isolated from the existing DNS infrastructure (if
any). To prevent this, either configure local DNS resolver to
point to existing DNS server or manually configure the local DNS
server (when running) with correct root hints.

If the DNS resolver is configured with its own IP address and the
DNS server is not running locally, the Active Directory
Installation Wizard can install and configure the local DNS
server. However, if this server is not connected to the network
during domain controller promotion then admin needs to
appropriately configure root hints of the local DNS server after
the completion of the domain controller promotion.

DnsUpdateTest returned 1460. The A record test is thus
inconclusive.

......................... netdc4 passed test RegisterInDNS
```

Do not forget that you should also test the DNS configuration (registration of the SRV records) *after* the server promotion has been completed.

Running the Active Directory Installation Wizard

There are two ways to start the Active Directory Installation Wizard in interactive mode:

- Choose the **Start** | **All Programs** | **Administrative Tools** | **Configure Your Server Wizard** command, and then assign the domain controller role to the server.
- Open the **Run** window and enter `dcpromo.exe`.

In general, you have four options for installing the Active Directory; these are graphically represented in Fig. 5.1. (Installation from a backup media is described later in this chapter.) The selections, which you should consequently make on the wizard's pages[1], are listed below for each option:

1. The first Active Directory installation in the network, or creating a new forest:
    - **Domain controller for a new domain**
    - **Domain in a new forest**

[1] The Active Directory Installation Wizard pages in Windows .NET are slightly differ from the wizard's pages in Windows 2000; however, all operations' general concepts are the same in both versions.

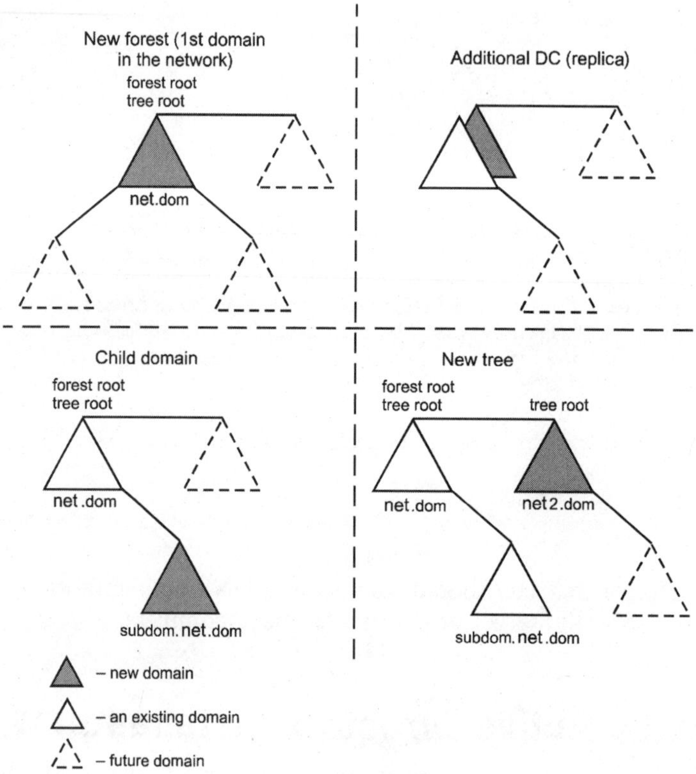

Fig. 5.1. Four scenarios for creating a new domain controller

Note

Creating a new forest is the only option that does not require any existing domain (or domain controller). In all other cases, the *Schema* and the *Configuration* partitions are replicated from a source domain controller located in either an existing domain (for an additional DC), the parent (for a child domain), or the root domain (for a new tree). Even if you are installing a Windows .NET-based DC from backup media, some other domain controllers must be accessible (dealt with later in this chapter).

2. Additional DC in any existing domain:
   - **Additional domain controller for an existing domain**
3. Creating a new child domain:
   - **Domain controller for a new domain**
   - **Child domain in an existing domain tree**

4. Creating a new tree (a root domain with a non-contiguous DNS name) in an existing forest:
   - **Domain controller for a new domain**
   - **Domain tree in an existing forest**

Depending on the selected option, the wizard will ask you to enter a domain name. It can be the name of an existing domain, parent domain, or forest root domain. In Windows 2000, it is always recommended that you specify a *DNS* name because DNS name resolving must already be operational at this stage. (Although the wizard can sometimes accept NetBIOS domain names, this does not guarantee successful execution of the subsequent Active Directory installation steps.) In Windows .NET, you simply have no alternatives.

> ***Caution***
>
> During the next step, you must specify the domain NetBIOS name. You can choose a name different from the one offered by default if you like (e.g., if the DNS domain name is net.dom, then the default NetBIOS name will be NET). If Service Pack 1 or later is not installed on a server running Windows 2000, you will get an error when publishing a printer in Active Directory (see *Chapter 8, "Common Administrative Tasks"*).

> ***Note***
>
> During Active Directory installation, synchronization with existing domain controllers is carried out. It is possible to stop that process by clicking the **Finish Replication Later** button in the wizard window. The domain controller will be advertised when the replication is completed (after the computer has been rebooted).

DNS Issues

In Windows .NET, the Active Directory Installation Wizard will stop if a preferred DNS server address is not configured on the computer and you simply will not be able to continue with Active Directory installation.

In Windows 2000, the message shown in Fig. 5.2 may appear at a certain moment during the execution of Active Directory Installation Wizard. It means one of the following:

- There is no DNS server in the network (you are going to install the DNS server and the domain controller on the same server).
- No address or an incorrect preferred DNS server address has been entered in the computer's **TCP/IP Properties** window. (This is a configuration error that the system identifies as the absence of a DNS server.)
- There is no authoritative zone for the new domain on the specified DNS server.

Fig. 5.2. This window displays warnings about potential problems with the preferred DNS server

The warning window will not appear if a DNS server address has been entered correctly and the authoritative zone has been configured on this server. However, this zone may not allow dynamic updates. In such a case, the wizard page "Configure DNS" (Fig. 5.3) will be next. A similar window will appear on a Windows .NET server that has no preferred DNS server and is promoted to be the first forest domain controller.

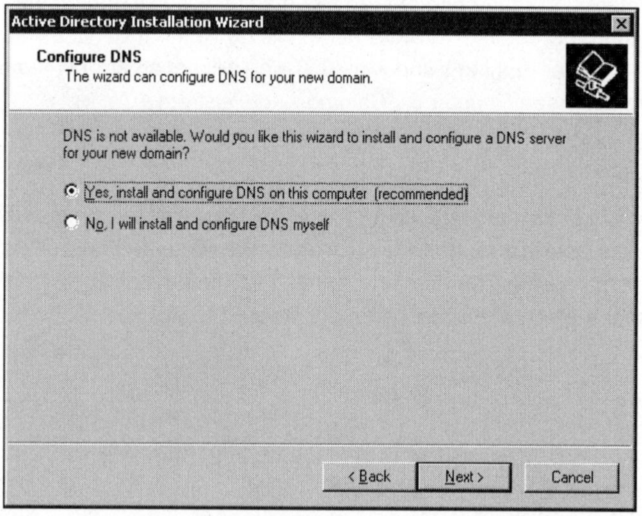

Fig. 5.3. At this point, you must decide whether or not to install the DNS server

This step is a critical point in the installation process, because whether the new domain configuration will work or not depends on what you do here. You only have three options:

- Click **Cancel**, which will terminate the wizard, and verify the DNS configuration. You *must* select this option if the promoted server is not the first controller in the domain (forest). If you do not, the Active Directory installation on this server will definitely be unsuccessful: the server will not be able to locate other domain controllers and replicate the Active Directory information from them.

- Agree with the default option and install the DNS server and domain controller on the same computer.
- If you are using a legacy DNS service and have the required sub-zones delegated to a DNS server that allows dynamic updates, select the **No, I will install and configure DNS myself** option and continue the Active Directory installation.

You may also refuse the default option and continue the installation process if the promoting server is *the only* DC in the network and if for some reason, you are planning to connect it to a fully configured DNS server only after installing Active Directory and *before* the first DC reboot. This approach may not seem very logical, but is technically quite possible. When the domain controller boots for the first time, it will register all necessary resource records on the DNS server (but in the forward zone only, since the wizard does not create a reverse zone).

And only if the DNS configuration fully meets all the necessary requirements, you will not see any of the wizard pages described above, and the wizard will go onto the subsequent steps.

The Active Directory Installation Wizard on a Windows .NET server provides an exhaustive DNS diagnostic that allows an administrator to easily locate possible problems. Basically, problem origins and an administrator's actions are the same as those described above. For example, if the wizard cannot find the authoritative zone for a new specified domain, you will see results of DNS queries performed (Fig. 5.4). Depending on the situation, you can verify the DNS configuration and re-run the DNS test, or install the DNS server.

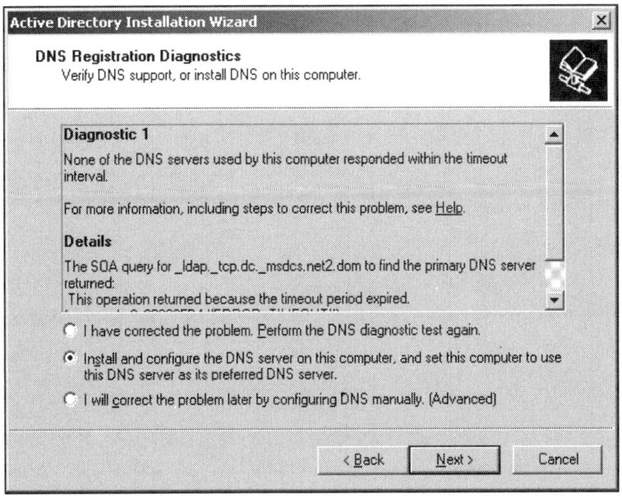

Fig. 5.4. DNS diagnostics reveal name resolution problems for a future domain controller

If you add a DC to an existing domain and the wizard could not get the DNS name of a DC located in that domain, you will see a window similar to the one shown in Fig. 5.5. The domain name (*net.dom*) as well as the preferred DNS server address (*192.168.1.2*) are displayed here, and should be verified.

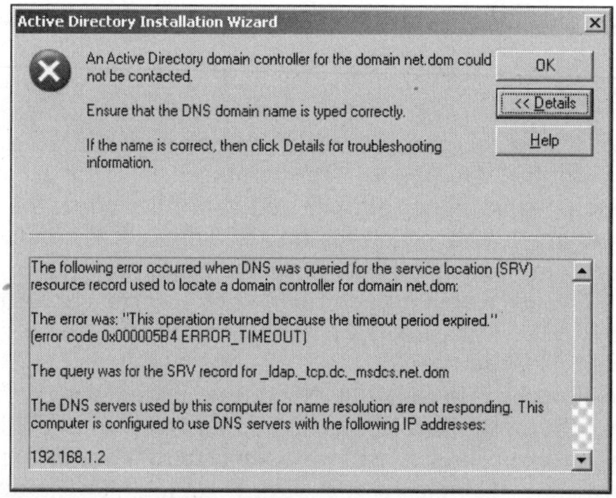

Fig. 5.5. Failed DNS diagnostics for a server promoted to be an additional domain controller

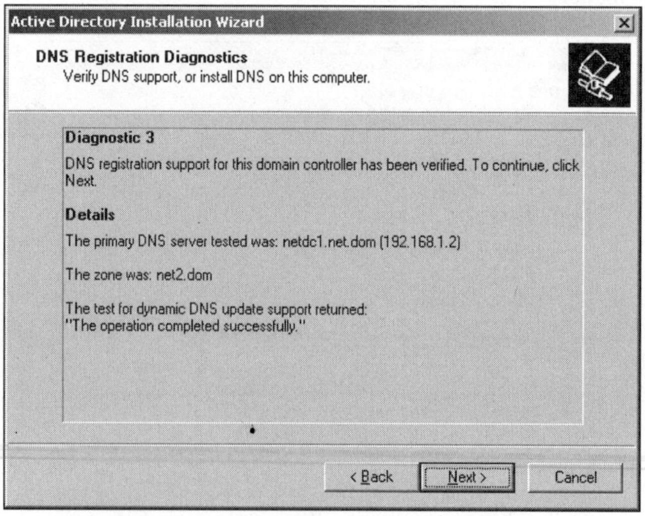

Fig. 5.6. An example of a successful DNS test

Fig. 5.5 illustrates an example of a successful DNS test. Normally, every promotion operation should be completed with a similar result. In such a case, you can be sure that the new domain controller will not have name resolution problems.

Completing and Testing the Installation

After completing the Active Directory installation, the system automatically installs and configures the Windows DNS Server if this operation has been requested.

After system restart, you can logon to the created domain with the local administrator credentials. The local administrator of the server that has been promoted to the first domain controller in a new forest will become a member of the following groups:

- Administrators (built-in local group)
- Domain Admins (is a member of the Administrators group)
- Domain Users (is a member of the built-in local Users group)
- Enterprise Admins (is a member of the Administrators group)
- Group Policy Creator Owners
- Schema Admins

Note

Sometimes, while working on domain controllers in the test environments, administrators attempt to logon to a domain using a domain user account, and encounter the "The local policy of this system does not permit you to logon interactively" message. Open the *Default Domain Controllers Policy* GPO, and click the **Computer Configuration | Windows Settings | Security Setting | Local Policies | User Rights Assignment** node. Find the *Log on locally* policy. This policy is *defined* by default, and only the following groups can logon locally: *Account Operators*, *Administrators*, *Backup Operators*, *Print Operators*, and *Server Operators*. Therefore, "normal" users cannot logon on domain controllers. If you wish (and if security requirements permit), add the *Authenticated Users* or *Everyone* group to this list, and you will be able to logon locally using any account.

If any applications are running on a Windows NT 4.0-based server that is a member of an Active Directory domain, verify that the *Everyone* group has been included in the *Pre-Windows 2000 Compatible Access* group with the `net localgroup "Pre-Windows 2000 Compatible Access"` command. If not, type `net localgroup "Pre-Windows 2000 Compatible Access" everyone /add` at the command prompt on a domain controller computer and then restart the domain controller computer. Do not perform this operation by using the **Active Directory Users and Groups** snap-in!

On Windows .NET domain controllers, the Everyone group does not include the *NT AUTHORITY\ANONYMOUS LOGON* group. Therefore, if backward compatibility is required, add both security groups to the Pre-Windows 2000 Compatible Access group.

You can manage backward compatibility during a server promotion (by selecting the appropriate permissions option), as well as at any moment (manually, by using the `net localgroup` command).

Log Files

The events that have taken place during Active Directory installation are written in the logs located in the *%SystemRoot%*\Debug folder (and are especially useful if the installation has crashed):

- csv.log
- DCPROMO.LOG
- dcpromohelp.log
- dcpromoui.log
- NetSetup.LOG
- NtFrs_xxxx.log
- NtFrsApi.log

Installation from a Backup Media

A Windows .NET server can be promoted using the System State data from an existing Windows .NET domain controller. (Such a feature is absent in Windows 2000 domains.) This approach considerably reduces the initial replication time if slow dial-up lines are used or the Active Directory database is large enough. However, the promotion process still requires network connectivity with the existing domain!

The only restriction of this approach is that the replicas of any application partitions existing on the backed up domain controller will not be created automatically on the new DC. You should manage the application partitions manually (see the NTDSutil description in *Chapter 10, "Diagnosing and Maintaining Domain Controllers"*).

To install an additional DC in an existing domain:

1. Backup the System State of a DC located in the domain where you are creating an additional DC. Make sure that the **Automatically backup System Protected Files with the System State** box is cleared (you do not need the system files!). (See additional information on system backup in *Chapter 8, "Common Administrative Tasks."*)
2. Copy the backup file to the server that is to be promoted.
3. Restore the System State data to any empty folder on the target server.

4. To do so, start the NTBackup utility, click **Catalog a backup file** on the **Tools** menu, and enter the backup file name. Check the **System State** box, select **Alternate location** from the **Restore files to** list, and enter the target folder name (Fig. 5.7). Click **Start Restore**. In the **Confirm Restore** window, click **OK**.

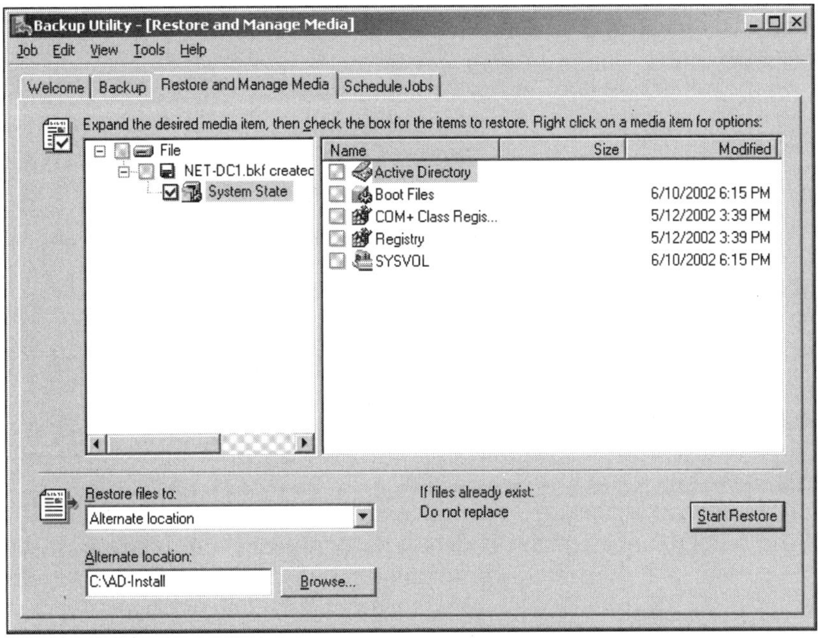

Fig. 5.7. Restoring the System State to an *alternate location*

5. When the restore operation is completed, enter `dcpromo /adv` in the **Run** window (click **Start | Run**). The Active Directory Installation Wizard will start.
6. On the "Domain Controller Type" wizard page, select the **Additional domain controller for an existing domain** option and click **Next**. If you select the other option, a normal DC creation procedure will begin.
7. On the "Copying Domain Information" page, select the **From these restored backup files** option, enter the backup file name, and click **Next**.
8. If the System State was backed up from a DC that was a Global Catalog server, the wizard will ask you whether to configure the new DC as a GC server ("No" by default).

Then, the installation process will proceed as a usual server promotion.

Deleting a Domain Controller

You cannot *simply* remove a domain controller (DC) from an existing domain structure, since the information about it will remain in the Active Directory. The process known as *demotion* allows you to properly remove Active Directory from a DC and automatically update all relative directory information (if this DC is not the last one in the forest). If the DC is corrupted or has failed, and you cannot successfully perform this operation, you must *manually* cleanup the Active Directory (see *Chapter 10, "Diagnosing and Maintaining Domain Controllers"*).

After removing Active Directory, the last DC in *any* domain becomes a standalone server that belongs to the *WORKGROUP* workgroup. If a DC is not the last controller, it will become a member server in the same domain. The DNS suffix of the computer will not be changed in either case.

Requirements

As during Active Directory installation, the other domains (parent or root) must be accessible (otherwise, the demotion will not start). The Active Directory cannot be removed if replication of directory partitions from the demoted server to other DCs fails. If the demoted DC is an operations master, you will also need to consider transferring the FSMO roles to other servers. Otherwise, the system itself will try to find the appropriate candidates for these roles.

If the last DC in a domain is demoted, this means the removal of the entire domain. You can only delete a *leaf* domain, i.e., a domain that has no child domains and is not the forest root domain (which can only be deleted last).

A Windows .NET domain controller cannot be demoted if it stores the last replica of one or more application directory partitions. You should first either delete these partitions manually or allow the Active Directory Installation Wizard to remove them.

Running the Active Directory Installation Wizard

To remove Active Directory from a DC, start the Active Directory Installation Wizard.

You may get the message shown in Fig. 5.8.

Make sure that another GC server exists in the forest. If necessary, designate a new GC server, wait until it will be advertised, and only then continue the demotion process.

On the next step of Active Directory Installation Wizard you must set or reset the **This server is the last domain controller in the domain** flag. To delete the last DC in a child domain (i.e., to delete this child domain) or in a tree root domain (i.e., to delete the tree), you must provide the credentials of a member of the Enterprise Admin group. To delete the last DC in a forest (i.e., to destroy the entire forest), you must be logged on as the local administrator or as a member of the Domain Admins group. To delete an additional DC, it is sufficient to be logged on as a member of the Domain Admins group.

If the demoted DC runs Windows .NET and stores the *last* replica of one or more application directory partitions, you need to manually delete these partitions (by using the NTDSutil.exe or DnsCmd.exe utilities). If the DC holds one or more last partition replicas, you will see a window similar to that shown in Fig. 5.9. In such a case, the system itself can completely remove all partitions if you set the **Delete all application directory partitions on this domain controller** checkbox on the next wizard's page. Otherwise, the demotion will be stopped.

Fig. 5.8. Do not delete the last Global Catalog server without creating another GC server

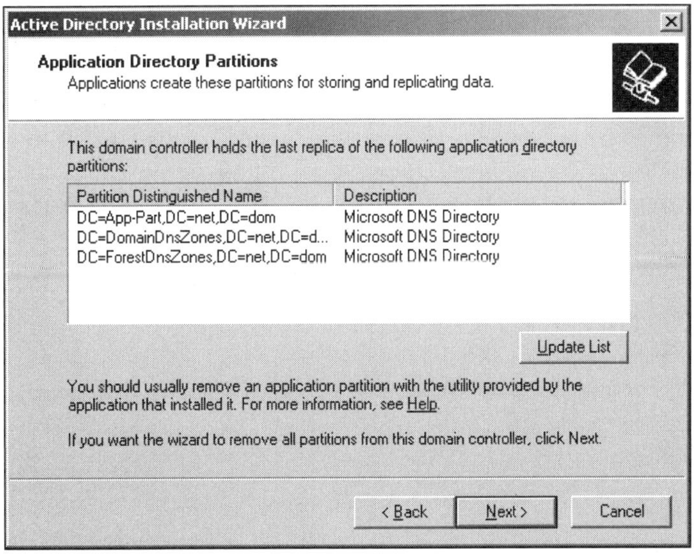

Fig. 5.9. Deleting application directory partitions

When the Active Directory has been deleted from a DC, and the demotion process has been completed (after the server reboot), all appropriate DNS records (a domain controller's records, sub-domains with names starting with "_", or an entire authoritative zone) will be deleted from the preferred DNS server (obviously, if the server allows dynamic registration) and the netlogon.dns file will be cleared.

Unattended Installing and Removing of Active Directory

Besides the interactive mode (described above), the Active Directory Installation Wizard has an unattended mode similar to the unattended setup of the operating system. All parameters needed for the wizard to operate are written in an answer file that is launched from the command prompt by entering the following string:

```
dcpromo /answer:<answerFile>
```

As in the case of the interactive mode, the wizard's window will display all ongoing operations having to do with promoting/demoting the server. If a parameter is missing or incorrect, the wizard will ask the operator for the required or correct value. You may then enter the value and continue the process.

The description of keys used in the answer file for installing Active Directory (the `[DCInstall]` section) can be found in the *"Microsoft Windows 2000 Guide to Unattended Setup"* (see the Resource Kit links in *Appendix A*, or the *Q223757* and *Q224390* articles in the *Microsoft Knowledge Base*). This file (unattend.doc) is copied to the folder where the *Windows 2000 Resource Kit* is installed, or can be manually extracted from the Windows 2000 operating system CD. In the Windows Explorer, open the \Support\Tools\Deploy.cab file and copy unattend.doc to any location.

The Active Directory can be installed in unattended mode immediately after a Windows 2000/.NET Server setup, or independently at any moment.

For example, to demote a DC (not the last DC in the domain!) to a member server, you need only specify the following parameters (enter the values appropriate to your installation) in the answer file:

```
[DCInstall]

UserName              = DomAdmin
Password              = dadm123
UserDomain            = net.dom

AdministratorPassword = locAdmin123
RebootOnSuccess       = Yes
```

where the first three parameters are the credentials of a domain administrator, and `AdministratorPassword` is the local administrator password. The last parameter indicates that the computer must reboot after successful demotion.

Note

After the wizard completes the requested operation, all specified passwords will be deleted from the answer file. Therefore, you must enter them again if you want to repeat the operation.

To create an additional domain controller in a domain (*net.dom*), the following parameters are necessary:

```
[DCInstall]
UserName                = DomAdmin
Password                = dadm123
UserDomain              = net.dom
ReplicaDomainDNSName    = net.dom
SiteName                = NET-Site
RebootOnSuccess         = Yes
```

`SiteName` is not a required parameter. It is used here because the domain is located in a site that has a non-default name (the default site name is *`Default-First-Site`*).

The following answer file will create the child domain *subdom* of the parent domain *net.dom* (notice that an enterprise administrator's credentials are necessary in this case):

```
[DCInstall]
UserName                = EntAdmin
Password                = eadm12345
UserDomain              = net.dom
ReplicaOrNewDomain      = Domain
ChildName               = subdom
DomainNetBiosName       = SUBDOM
ParentDomainDNSName     = net.dom
SiteName                = NET-Site
RebootOnSuccess         = Yes
```

Adding Domain Client Computers

When a computer running Windows NT/2000/XP/.NET system joins an Active Directory domain, a corresponding computer account is *always* created in the *Computers* container. You can then move this account to any desired OU or container. There is, however, an alternative way. It is possible to create an account *before* actually adding the computer to the domain (manually, or with the `netdom ADD` command). Pre-create the account in any container, and then add the computer using this account.

There are two main problem sources that can prevent domain members running Windows 2000/XP/.NET from correctly joining or working with a domain:

- DNS
- Windows Time service

Verifying the Preferred DNS Server

To add a client computer (a workstation running Windows 2000/XP or a member server running Windows 2000/.NET) to an Active Directory domain, you should first verify the client's DNS settings and the availability of a DC that belongs to that domain. The updated version of the NetDiag.exe utility is the best instrument for that purpose. The test command and successful sample output are shown below:

```
C:\>netdiag /test:DsGetDc /d:net.dom /v
...
DC discovery test. . . . . . . . . : Passed

    Find DC in domain 'NET':
    Found this DC in domain 'NET':
        DC. . . . . . . . . . . . : \\netdc1.net.dom
        Address . . . . . . . . . : \\192.168.1.2
        Domain Guid . . . . . . . : {36622959-3372-43E6-BBBA-
                                    8D77CAA1FC46}
        Domain Name . . . . . . . : net.dom
        Forest Name . . . . . . . : net.dom
        DC Site Name. . . . . . . : NET-Site
        Our Site Name . . . . . . : NET-Site
        Flags . . . . . . . . . . : PDC emulator GC DS KDC TIMESERV GTIMESERV WRIT
ABLE DNS_DC DNS_DOMAIN DNS_FOREST CLOSE_SITE 0x8

    Find PDC emulator in domain 'NET':
    Found this PDC emulator in domain 'NET':
        DC. . . . . . . . . . . . : \\netdc1.net.dom
...

    Find Windows 2000 DC in domain 'NET':
    Found this Windows 2000 DC in domain 'NET':
        DC. . . . . . . . . . . . : \\netdc1.net.dom
...

The command completed successfully
```

This result indicates that you can add the tested computer to the specified domain.

When a client computer is already added to a domain, you may verify that this operation has been successfully completed. *Both* command — `netdiag /test:DsGetDc` and `netdiag /test:DcList` — should run successfully. The following example indicates that problems exist: the command reports that for some reason the client cannot access the DC:

```
C:\>netdiag /test:DcList /d:net.dom /v
...
DC list test . . . . . . . . . . . : Failed

    Find DC in domain 'NET':
    Found this DC in domain 'NET':
        DC. . . . . . . . . . . : \\netdc1.net.dom
...
    You don't have access to DsBind to netdc1 (192.168.1.2).
    [ERROR_ACCESS_DENIED]
    List of DCs in Domain 'NET':
        netdc1.net.dom

The command completed successfully
```

DNS Settings and Domain Name

Make sure that the *primary DNS suffix* is properly set. (It is enough if the **Change primary DNS suffix when domain membership changes** checkbox is always set; in that case, the suffix is changed automatically and you need not worry about it.) An improper value may affect DNS registration of the computer name, which results in various errors, such as a failed secure channel, authentication problems, etc.

When a Window XP/.NET client computer is deleted from a domain, its primary DNS suffix will be cleared, and as a result, its name is de-registered from the domain's authoritative zone. The primary DNS suffix will remain on clients running Windows 2000 and therefore, the computer name will still be present in the domain zone, whereas the computer itself no longer belongs to that domain.

If a computer running Windows 2000/XP/.NET is added to a domain, it is strongly recommended that you specify the DNS name of the domain rather than its NetBIOS name. (Nevertheless, the latter case is also possible, especially if you perform the operation on a remote computer.) In any case, when a computer has been added to a domain, verify that a secure channel has been established between the computer and a domain controller. On a local computer, it is possible to use the commands `nltest /query` and `nltest /sc_query` (see details in *Chapter 11, "Verifying*

Network and Distributed Services"). On a remote computer, use the following command parameters:

```
C:\>netdom VERIFY xp-pro3 /D:net.dom
```

or

```
C:\>nltest /sc_query:net.dom /server:xp-pro3
```

When the TCP/IP settings are incorrect on a Windows XP/.NET computer, or the specified domain is not accessible, you will see a pop-up window similar to the one shown in Fig. 5.5. A Windows 2000 computer will report, "The specified domain either does not exist or could not be contacted". If this happens, you will need to check the computer network configuration and accessibility of domain controllers (see later *"Verifying DNS and Availability of Domain Controllers"*).

While adding a client computer running Windows 2000/XP/.NET to a domain, you may specify the NetBIOS name of the domain. If, nevertheless, the computer can find a domain controller belonging to that domain, it will be added to the domain. However, if the computer's TCP/IP settings are incorrect, the following NetDiag tests may fail (the Windows 2000 and Windows .NET version of NetDiag may produce slightly different results):

- DC discovery test
- DC list test
- Trust relationship test
- Kerberos test (skipped with a diagnostic message "Cannot find DC")
- LDAP test

Therefore, it is always recommended that you verify the computer's DNS settings if the computer experiences problems such as slow system startup or access to shared resources; improper group policies applied; failed start of domain administrative tools, and so on.

Windows Time Service

When you add a Windows XP/.NET client to a domain, the client computer will then periodically synchronize its clock with the PDC Emulator of that domain. The register value `Parameters\Type` that controls the Windows Time service and is set by default to `NTP`, will be changed to `NT5DS` (see details in *Chapter 2, "Active Directory Terminology and Concepts"*). The following command will help you to see the computer time offset and the name and IP address of a domain controller that serves as the timeserver:

```
C:\>w32tm /monitor /domain:net.dom
```

A domain client running Windows 2000 does not automatically synchronize its clock with the domain. You may manually set both registry values — `Parameters\ServerType` and `Parameters\Type` — to `NT5DS` and thus enable time synchronization with the PDC Emulator. The following command will display the name and IP address of the timeserver:

```
C:\>w32tm -source -v
```

Note

Windows 2000 and Windows .NET systems have different versions of the W32tm utility. Therefore, you need to select the appropriate parameters for the version that you happen to be using.

Adding a Windows NT 4.0 BDC to a Windows 2000/.NET Domain

You may, for some reason, need to have the Windows NT 4.0-based Backup Domain Controllers (BDC) in a Windows 2000/.NET domain. The only problem that may (or rather, *will*) arise during the BDC installation is that the Windows NT 4.0 Setup program creates the wrong type of account. A pop-up window with the following error message will appear:

```
The Machine Account for This Computer either does not exist or is
inaccessible.
```

If, for example, the account *NT4BDC5* was used when installing BDC, the following error will be registered in the System log on the Windows 2000- or Windows .NET-based domain controller that owns the PDC Emulator FSMO role:

```
...
Event Source:   SAM
...
Event ID:       12298
...
Description:
The account NT4BDC5$ cannot be converted to be a domain controller
account as its object class attribute in the directory is not computer
or is not derived from computer. If this is caused by an attempt to
install a pre Windows 2000 domain controller in a Windows 2000 domain or
later, then you should precreate the account for the domain controller
with the correct object class.
```

As a result, you will not be able to proceed with the BDC installation. See the instructions below.

Windows 2000 Domain Scenario

To pre-create a computer account for a Windows NT 4.0 BDC, log on to the domain using an administrative account on any Windows 2000 domain member, and perform the following operations:

1. Start the Server Manager (enter `srvmgr` at the command prompt), which is supported with Windows 2000. (Do not use the Server Manager from the Windows NT 4.0 installation!)
2. Select **Add to Domain** from the **Computer** menu.
3. Select **Windows NT Backup Domain Controller**, enter the BDC computer name, and click **Add,** then **Close**. A "Windows NT Backup" type account will appear in the computer list. The account will be created in the "default" *Domain Controllers* OU.

Then you can install a Windows NT 4.0 server as BDC. Or, if the BDC was already installed, it may be necessary to use NetDom.exe to reset the computer account password.

The following operations will yield the same result as described above:

1. Open the **Active Directory Users and Computers** snap-in and create a computer object in any container.
2. Start the **ADSI Edit** snap-in, find the *userAccountControl* property (decimal INTEGER type; see ADS_USER_FLAG_ENUM in the ADSI SDK) for the new computer object, and change the value from 4128 (0x1020 — WORKSTATION_TRUST_ACCOUNT) to 8192 (0x2000 — SERVER_TRUST_ACCOUNT).

The third way to create a computer account for a BDC is to install the *Support Tools* pack and enter the following string at the command prompt (this command does not work on Windows .NET domains!):

```
netdom ADD <BDC-computer-name> /D:<domain-name> /DC
```

The account will be created in the "default" *Domain Controllers* OU.

Windows .NET Domain Scenario

To add a Windows NT 4.0 BDC to a Windows .NET domain (that should run at the *Windows 2000 mixed* functional level!), use the following operations:

1. Open the **Active Directory Users and Computers** snap-in and select any applicable container.

2. Select the **New | Computer** command from the **Action** menu.
3. Enter the computer name and set the **Assign this computer account as a pre-Windows 2000 computer** and **Assign this computer account as a backup domain controller** checkboxes. Click **OK**.
4. Install a Windows NT 4.0 server as BDC or continue a failed installation.

Raising Functional Levels. Switching to Native Mode

If there isn't a Windows NT 4.0 BDC in a Windows 2000 domain, this domain can be switched from the default *mixed mode* to *native mode.* In Windows .NET domains, the "functional level" term is used in such a case. You can *raise* the domain functional level to a level that depends on the types of domain controllers used in the domain. If there are no Windows NT 4.0- or Windows 2000-based domain controllers in the entire Windows .NET forest, it is also possible to raise the *forest* functional level (see details in *Chapter 2, "Active Directory Terminology and Concepts"*).

Remember that only the type of controllers located in a domain affect the domain mode or level; the domain clients (*with* or *without* Active Directory client software) will "see" this level of functionality of an Active Directory domain (see *Chapter 2, "Active Directory Terminology and Concepts"* for just about the only exception.)

To change a domain mode or functional level, use either snap-in:

- **Active Directory Users and Computers**
- **Active Directory Domains and Trusts**

In the Windows 2000 environment, select a domain and open its **Properties** window. Click the **Change Mode** button on the **General** tab and wait 15 minutes for replication of the changes to all DCs in the domain. Operations in the Windows .NET environment will be described in the *"Raising Functional Level"* section in *Chapter 7, "Domain Manipulation Tools."*

To check that the domain is now in the native mode (or at a higher level), you may try to create a universal group or to add a domain local group to another local group.

To view a domain's mode or level, it is convenient to use the **Active Directory Domains and Trusts** snap-in. You can quickly select any domain and see its mode (level).

Establishing Domain Trusts

Creating inter-domain trusts is a rather simple operation if one understands the trusts mechanism used in Active Directory. The **Active Directory Domains and Trusts** snap-in is used for all work with any trusts in Active Directory domains. You can easily select domains in the snap-in's tree window and look up existing trusts. However, to verify, create, or remove trusts, you must provide the credentials of a user that has privileges to modify trusts.

Let us discuss various trust types by using a sample domain structure shown in Fig. 5.10.

These are the domains and trusts shown in Fig. 5.10:

- *net.dom* — the forest root domain that has a *Child* relationship with its child domain.
- *subdom.net.dom* — a child domain that has a *Parent* relationship with the root domain.
- *net2.dom* — a tree root domain that is connected with the *Tree Root* relationships with the forest root domain.

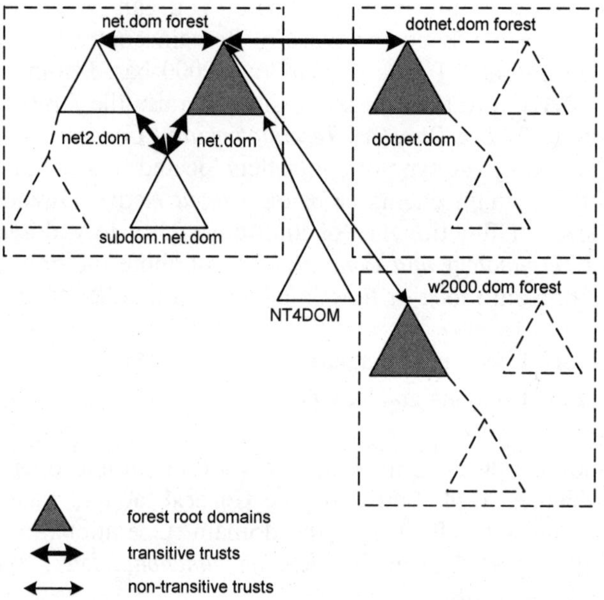

Fig. 5.10. A sample domain structure that illustrates various trust types

All of the above-mentioned trusts have been created automatically; they are transitive and two-way. You can, for example, logon to the *subdom.net.dom* domain (i.e., you can specify a user account located in that domain) on a computer that belongs to the *net2.dom* domain. To speed up the authentication process, you may want to create an explicit one-way or two-way trust between these domains:

- The *subdom.net.dom* and *net2.dom* domains are also connected with a trust marked as *Shortcut* (shown only for the *net2.dom* domain).

You are also able to establish trust relationships (one- or two-way) with other Active Directory forests or Windows 4.0-based domains:

- *w2000.dom* — the root domain of a foreign Windows 2000-based forest.
- *NT4DOM* — an independent Windows 4.0-based domain. The relationships with such domains, as well as with other Active Directory forests, are marked as *External*.

In addition, Windows .NET-based forests that operate at the *Windows .NET (version 2002)* functional level can be linked with the *Forest* transitive relationships:

- *dotnet.dom* — a forest root domain that has two-way forest trusts with the *net.dom* forest

Figs. 5.11 and 5.12 illustrate all listed trust types as they are represented in the **Active Directory Domains and Trusts** snap-in.

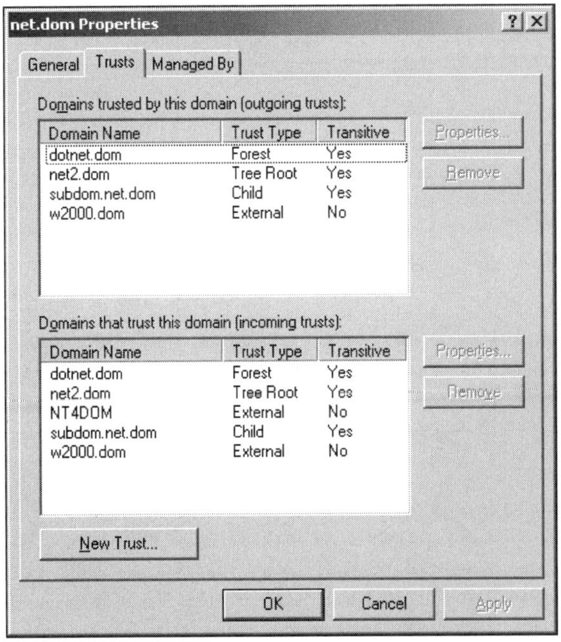

Fig. 5.11. Various types of trusts existing in Active Directory forests

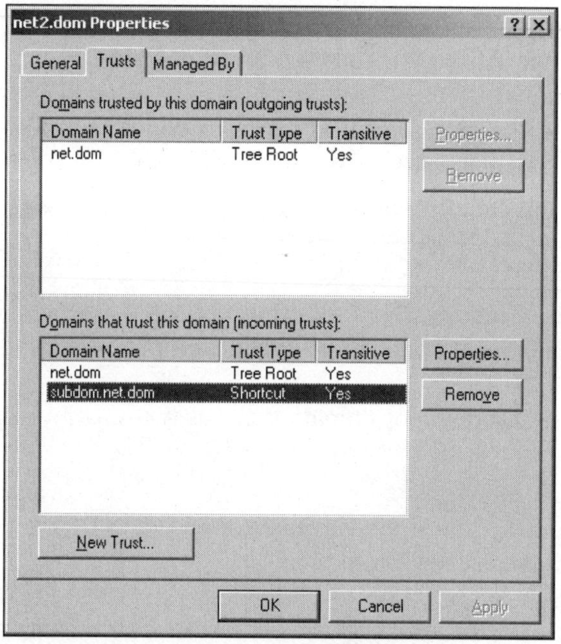

Fig. 5.12. The shortcut trust between two domains within the same forest

Note

Keep in mind that any trusts are always possible between Windows NT 4.0, Windows 2000, and Windows .NET domains, regardless of the mode in which the Active Directory domains are working.

Only shortcut, external, or forest trusts can be removed. You cannot delete "default" (Parent-Child and Tree Root) trusts by using the **Active Directory Domains and Trusts** snap-in or other tools. This can only be done by removing the appropriate domain or tree.

Verifying the Trust State

The state of all existing trusts can be verified. Select the desired trust on the **Trusts** tab (see Fig. 5.11); click **Properties**, and then **Validate**[1]. Normally, you will get the message: "The trust has been verified. It is in place and active". You may be asked for additional credentials in another domain (e.g., if you test the "parent-child" trust from a child domain, you will be asked for credentials in the parent domain).

---

[1] In Windows 2000, the corresponding buttons are named **Edit** (funny enough, you cannot *edit* anything in the appropriate window) and **Verify**.

Creating and Deleting the Shortcut and External Trusts

Basically, the trust creation process is the same on all platforms: for a one-way trust, you should first create an outgoing trust in the trusting domain, and then create the corresponding ingoing trust in the trusted domain. For a two-way trust, this process should be executed twice: it is necessary to create both outgoing and ingoing trusts in each domain. For the sake of simplicity, we will discuss trust creation in a Windows .NET domain only.

For a Windows .NET domain, the trust creation process is simplified, since the wizard allows you to create any trusts in both domains simultaneously (in that case, you must specify the appropriate credentials in both trusting and trusted domains).

To discuss the trust creation in detail, let us use a sample domain structure shown in Fig. 5.10. In this structure, you may create a shortcut to speed up the access from the *net2.dom* to the resources located in the *subdom.net.dom* domain. The *subdom.net.dom* domain (the *trusting* domain) will then trust the *net2.dom* (the *trusted* domain).

Within a forest, users can log on to any forest domain on computers that can belong to any domain in the same forest. This is possible due to transitive Kerberos trusts existing within the entire forest. However, before a shortcut trust is created, there is no direct trust between the *net2.dom* and *subdom.net.dom* domains, and the authentication process should run over all domains that have direct trusts and connect these two domains. A shortcut trust can speed up this process.

All direct trusts can be verified with the *NLtest* command. Initially, this command fails on a DC in the *subdom.net.dom* domain (because there is no direct connection between the current and specified domains, and there are no trusted servers in the *net2.dom* domain):

```
C:\>nltest /sc_query:net2.dom
I_NetLogonControl failed: Status = 1355 0x54b ERROR_NO_SUCH_DOMAIN
```

To create a shortcut trust:

1. Open the **Active Directory Domains and Trusts** snap-in, select the trusted domain (*net2.dom*), and open the **Properties** window.
2. Click **New Trust**. The *New Trust Wizard* will help you to do all preliminary work to create trusts of any type. Click **Next**.
3. Enter the name of the trusting (or *target*) domain (*subdom.net.dom*) and click **Next**.
4. On the next wizard page (Fig. 5.13), you should select the trust direction. By default, the wizard suggests that you create a two-way trust (therefore, the domain selected earlier will be both a *trusting* and *trusted* domain). However, in our case, it is necessary to choose the second option — **One way: incoming**. Then click **Next**.

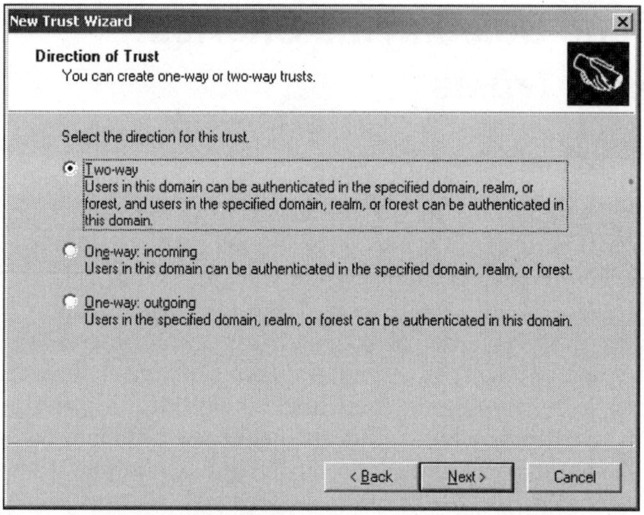

Fig. 5.13. Selecting the direction of the trust

5. The next wizard page (Fig. 5.14) will appear on Windows .NET-based DCs only. If the target domain is based on domain controllers running Windows 2000 or Windows .NET, you can create the trust in both domains at the same time. You should only provide the appropriate credentials for the target domain.

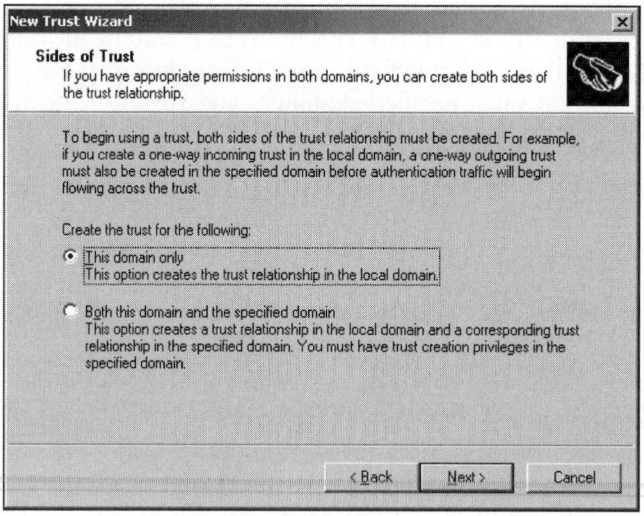

Fig. 5.14. You can create a trust in either the local domain only or both domains at the same time

If the other "half" of a trust is a Windows NT 4.0 domain, you can create it in the local domain only; the other side of the trust must be created on a DC in the trusting domain by an administrator or a user that has trust creation privileges in that domain. (Windows NT 4.0 does not support system calls necessary for the "remote" trust creation.)

If you leave the default option, the wizard will ask you for the trust password on the next step. This password is an arbitrary character sequence, which you must reproduce when the other side of the trust is created on the target domain.

In our case, we can select the lower option and go further.

6. On the next wizard page, you need to enter the credentials of a user with appropriate privileges in the trusting (target) domain and click **Next**.
7. All selections are complete now. Click **Next**.
8. If the selections have been made properly, you will see the "Trust Creation Complete" wizard page. Click **Next**.
9. On the next wizard pages, you may *confirm* the creation of outgoing and incoming trusts. This is only necessary if you have selected the trust creation in both domains. Otherwise, the trust must be created first in the trusting (target) domain. Skip the confirmation steps if the other side(s) of the trust has not been created yet.
10. On the last wizard page — "Completing the New Trust Wizard", you will see the report on operations performed. Close the wizard by clicking **Finish**.

That is all. A one-way transitive trust has been created. (The trusts with *foreign* forests or domains will not be transitive!) You can check it by using the NLtest command. After the trust has been created, you should see:

```
C:\>nltest /sc_query:net2.dom
 Flags: 30 HAS_IP  HAS_TIMESERV
Trusted DC Name \\netdc4.net2.dom
Trusted DC Connection Status Status = 0 0x0 NERR_Success
The command completed successfully
```

This means that the displayed DC in the trusting domain will authenticate the requests from DCs in the net2.dom domain.

You may also establish a two-way trust, in which both domains will trust each other. To create the trust in the reverse direction, repeat the procedure described above, but this time start from the other domain in the pair (in our example it would be the *subdom.net.dom* domain). It does not matter from which domain — trusted or trusting — one begins to create a trust. The main thing to remember is that every trust has to be created on *both* sides of a domain pair, and you must use the *same* trust password.

To delete a trust in a Windows .NET domain:

1. Select a trust on the **Trusts** tab and click **Remove**.
2. Select the necessary option in the pop-up window (Fig. 5.15) and click **OK**.
3. Confirm the deletion.

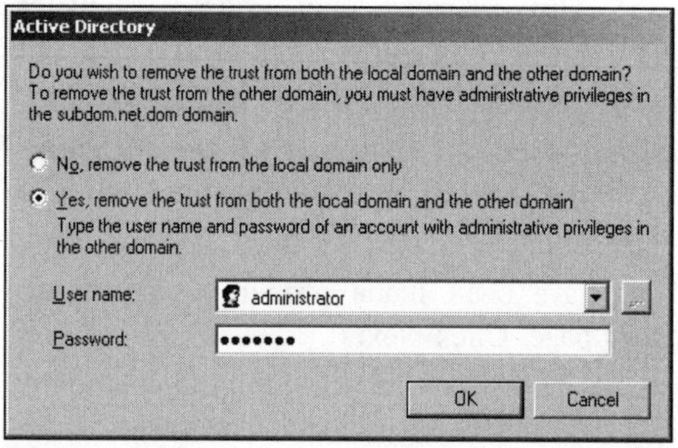

Fig. 5.15. You can delete a trust from either local domain only or from both domains at the same time

If you have deleted the trust in the local domain only, do not forget to delete it from the other domain, too.

Establishing Trusts with Windows NT 4.0-Based Domains

If the trusting domain in the example discussed in the previous section were a Windows NT 4.0-based domain (named, let us say, *NT4DOM*), the necessary steps would look like this:

1. Start the User Manager for Domains, and select the **Policies | Trust Relationships** command.
2. Click **Add** (to the right of the **Trusted domains** panel).
3. Enter the NetBIOS (pre-Windows 2000) name of the trusted domain (*NET2*) and the trust password entered in Step 5 (see above). Click **OK**.
4. Normally, you will get the message: "Trusted Relationship with ("NET2" for our example) successfully established".

Note

You must establish two-way trusts between domains for migrating from a Windows NT 4.0/2000/.NET domain to an Active Directory domain (which must be in the ***native*** mode or higher) by using the *Active Directory Migration Tool (ADMT)*, *ClonePrincipal*, or similar (third-party) tools.

Creating Forest Trust

The forest trusts are always transitive and can have a one-way as well as two-way direction. Remember that the forest functional levels of both forests must be raised to *Windows .NET (version 2002)*! If this condition has not been met, you may create a usual *external* trust only. Make sure that domain controllers of each forest can resolve the DNS name of another forest.

To create a forest trust:

1. Open the **Active Directory Domains and Trusts** snap-in on any DC in the forest root domain of either forest that participates in the forest trust. (The forest root domain is preferred, because you should run this snap-in with the administrative privileges in that domain.)
2. Open the **Trusts** tab in the **Properties** window of the ***forest root*** domain (*net.dom* in our example) and click **New Trust**.
3. On the "Trust Name" wizard page, enter the DNS name of another forest's ***root*** domain (*dotnet.dom*). (If you select any other domain names, the page shown in Fig. 5.16, will never appear!)
4. If you leave the default option on the "Trust Type" wizard page (Fig. 5.16), you will be able to create a usual external trust only. Therefore, select the lower option (**Forest trust**) and click **Next**.
5. On the next page (see an example in Fig. 5.13), select the direction of the trust and click **Next**.
6. Then, select the sides of the trust (see Fig. 5.14). Click **Next**. Enter credentials of a user with appropriate privileges, if necessary.
7. A very important selection should be made on the next wizard page (Fig. 5.17). (The good news is that it is possible to change this selection at any moment in the future.) By default, all users from the target forest will be able to access those shared resources in the local forest that are available for the Everyone group. Otherwise, you should grant the permissions manually.

   If the created trust is two-way, a similar page will appear for the target forest, too.

   For an already created forest trust, you can open its **Properties** window and manage the authentication scope on the **Authentication** tab.

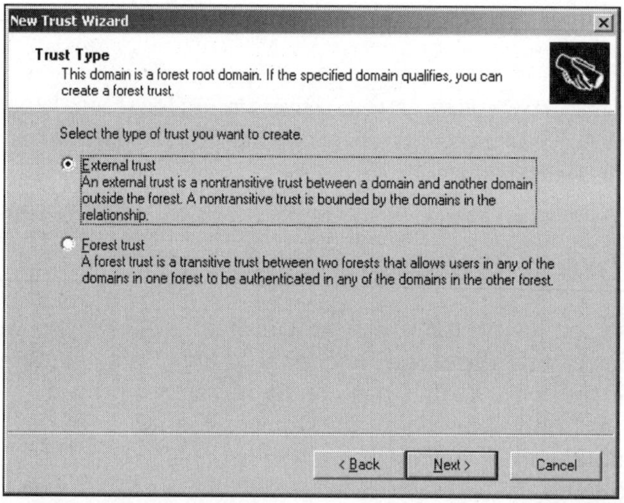

Fig. 5.16. This page allows you to create a transitive forest trust

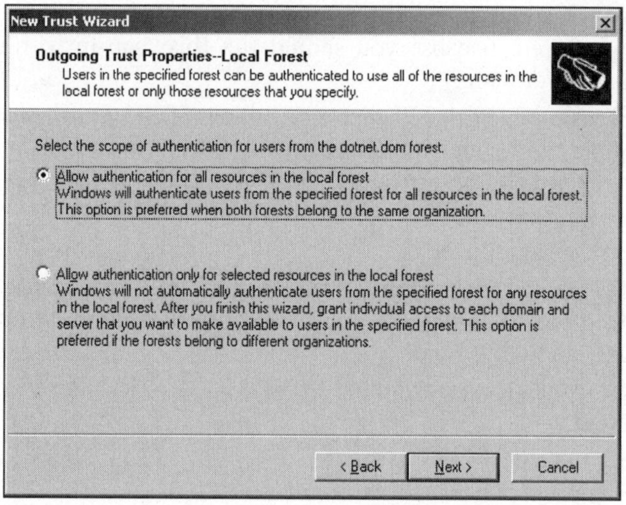

Fig. 5.17. On this page, you will select the authentication scope for users from the target forest

8. On the consequent wizard pages, confirm the trust creation if necessary.
9. Then, you can confirm the name suffix routing parameters offered by the system; in the future, you can change them (if necessary) on the **Name Suffix Routing** tab in the trust's **Properties** window.
10. Close the wizard by clicking **Finish**.

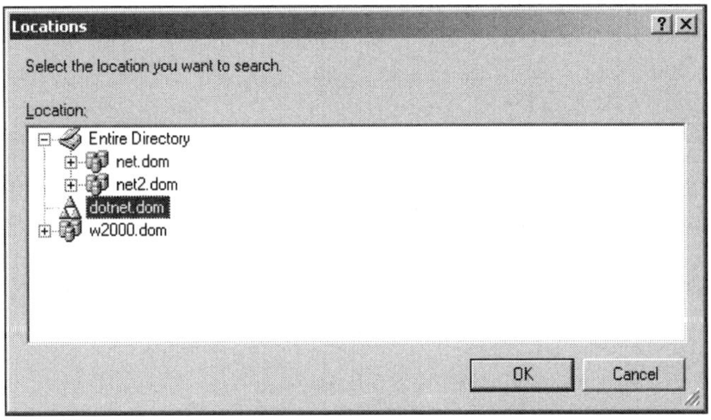

Fig. 5.18. This window displays all external forests

Now, it is possible to grant permissions and privileges to any user within either forest. For example, if you want to select an applicable user account and will open the **Locations** window (Fig. 5.18), you will see any domains and forests that trust the current domain. However, an external forest *w2000.dom* connected with non-transitive trusts is shown as a usual domain, whereas the *dotnet.dom* forest is shown as a domain tree, which means that it is possible to choose accounts from the entire forest.

Chapter 6: Configuring and Troubleshooting Active Directory Domains

Certainly, the title of this chapter encompasses a broad topic that cannot be fully covered even in a dozen books. We will discuss only certain issues here, ones that you inevitably encounter in your practice, and that you should not forget about. See also *Chapter 9, "General Characteristics and Purpose of System Tools"*, that will help you to select the necessary tools and utilities for your work, and simplify the troubleshooting process. Do not neglect these very useful tools! (Though alas, in practice, quite often many indeed do neglect them.)

In this chapter, all considerations of Active Directory domains cover both Windows 2000 and Windows .NET domains unless otherwise noted.

Placing Flexible Single-Master Operation (FSMO) Roles

Every Active Directory beginner first gets a piece of good news: all Active Directory domain controllers (running either Windows 2000 or Windows .NET) are peers; write operations are permitted on every domain controller (DC); and all changes are replicated from the originating DC to others (so-called *multi-master replication* is used). These features are quite advantageous when compared to the rules accepted in Windows NT-based domains.

Some time later, the beginner gets some bad news: there are operations when some DCs perform additional functions (i.e., in comparison with other DCs), and instead of the one role available for a DC in Windows NT-based domains — either Primary Domain Controller (PDC) or Backup Domain Controller (BDC) — an Active Directory domain controller can simultaneously perform up to five different roles[1]. These roles are known as *Flexible Single-Master Operation* (FSMO) roles. (You can easily find a description of each role in the *Help and Support Center*. Open the **Index** tab and enter `FSMO` as the keyword, or use the **Search** tab. See also the *"Managing FSMO Roles in the Forest"* section in *Chapter 8, "Common Administrative Tasks"* and the *"How to Find an FSMO Master?"* section in *Chapter 17, "Scripting Administrative Tasks."*)

Fig. 6.1 illustrates the default placement of FSMO roles within a forest. As you can notice, every first DC created in a domain holds three *domain-wide* roles; and in addition, the first DC located in the forest root domain holds two *forest-wide* roles.

There are many guidelines for placing FSMO roles; we will consider only a few rules that you should not violate:

- Notwithstanding the fact that the *Primary Domain Controller (PDC) Emulator* in Active Directory domains does not play as important a role as the PDC plays

[1] In fact, this number may even increase if one takes into consideration the fact that the Infrastructure Master role also exists for each created application directory partition.

in Windows NT domains, you must carefully assign this role. Even in the *native mode* Windows 2000 domains or *Windows .NET (version 2002)* level Windows .NET domains, the PDC Emulator is used as a primary authority for updating user passwords and controlling failed authentication requests.

By default, the PDC Emulator is selected by the **Group Policy Object Editor** snap-in, and you may have trouble editing group policies if the PDC Emulator is inaccessible.

Keep the PDC Emulator and *Relative Identifier (RID) Master* role on the same DC. However, keep in mind that these two roles can produce a considerable workload on that DC.

All DCs in a domain will synchronize the clock with the PDC Emulator. In a multiple-domain forest, the PDC Emulator from each domain will synchronize the clock with the PDC Emulator located in the forest root domain. The forest root PDC Emulator should synchronize its clock with an external time source.

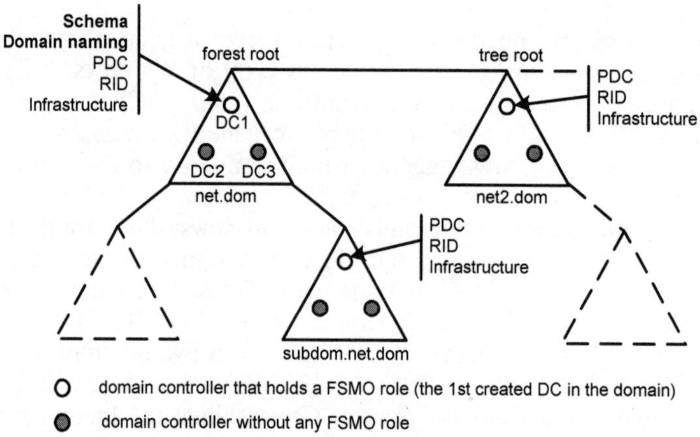

Fig. 6.1. Default placement of FSMO role owners in a forest

- If a domain has two or more DCs, the *Infrastructure Master* and a *Global Catalog* (GC) server must not be placed on the same DC; however, they need to be connected by a high-speed link to reduce network traffic. (You can ignore this requirement if there is only one DC in a domain, or if each DC in a domain is the GC server.) It is advisable to deploy at least one GC per site. (You may also consider *universal group membership caching* available in Windows .NET domains.) However, it is not typically recommended that you designate all DCs in the domain as GC servers, since this produces additional network traffic.
- Place both per-forest roles — *Schema Master* and *Domain Naming Master* on the same DC. In Windows 2000, assign this DC as a GC server; this is not required, if Domain Naming Master runs on a Windows .NET-based DC. This is mandatory to guarantee the uniqueness of names in the forest.

- By default, the first DC installed into a domain owns all of the domain operations master roles. If you remove Active Directory from this domain controller, all roles are automatically transferred to another available DC. If the demotion process fails, you must manually seize the operations master roles. As a "best practices" rule, you might consider manual transferring of any roles before demotion of a DC. (See the description of the NTDSutil tool in *Chapter 10, "Diagnosing and Maintaining Domain Controllers."*) If the demoting DC is a GC server, you must first be sure that there are other GC servers in the forest, and then designate a new GC server if necessary.
- If you restore a DC that owns some FSMO roles, these roles will be also restored. Therefore, you may need to review all current role owners after the restore is completed.

Replication Issues

The Active Directory service is a distributed network database, and synchronization of its replicas stored on different domain controllers is vital in order for the whole service to work. Replication issues are one of the main sources of trouble for an administrator; that is why we will consider some replication-related topics in more detail.

Intra- and Inter-Site Replication

The concept of the *site* that has appeared in Active Directory domains significantly affects the methods of replicating directory partitions (within a site and between sites) as well as the replication *transports* (protocols).

Replication Transports

The following table lists the rules applicable to the various transports used for different types of replication:

Directory partitions	**Within a site**	**Between sites**	
		The same domain	**Different domains**
Domain Naming context	RPC over IP	"IP" (RPC over IP)	—
Configuration Schema Global Catalog		"IP" (RPC over IP)	"IP" (RPC over IP) *or* SMTP over IP
	Uncompressed	Compressed (by default)	

"RPC over IP" enables high-speed, synchronous replication.

"IP" (as accepted in the **Active Directory Sites and Services** snap-in) enables a low-speed, point-to-point, synchronous replication for all directory partitions.

"SMTP over IP" provides low-speed, asynchronous replication between sites and supports only Configuration, Schema, and Global Catalog replication; requires installation of an enterprise *Certification Authority* (CA).

Important

It is not possible to change the default replication transport for connections generated automatically by the directory system. You may either agree with the protocol used or mark the connection as manually created (in the **Active Directory Sites and Services** snap-in, such connections will have GUID names, whereas for the user created connections you can specify any name).

Normal Replication Intervals

There are two default methods of replicating object changes in Active Directory forests:

- *Change notification* is usually used between DCs within a site. If a DC updates an object attribute, it will send notification to its first replication partner within a specified time interval (5 minutes by default). Then, the partner "pulls" the changes from the originating DC. You can change the default interval (300 seconds) by modifying the `Replicator notify pause after modify (secs)` value under the `HKLM\SYSTEM\CurrentControlSet\Services\NTDS\Parameters` registry key. The originating DC will notify the next replication partner within the time specified by the `Replicator notify pause between DSAs (secs)` registry value (30 seconds by default). On Windows .NET domain controllers, these values are not defined, and the defaults are used. Therefore, you should first create the key values.
- Changes are replicated between sites according to a *schedule* (configured for site links and connections). You can configure change notifications between sites too. (Microsoft, however, does not generally recommend such a practice.) To do so, point to the **Sites | Inter-Sites Transports | IP** node in the **Active Directory Sites and Services** snap-in, open the **Properties** window, and check the **Ignore schedules** box on the **General** tab.

Tip

Use ReplMon.exe for monitoring various replication parameters. Select a monitored server and run the **Generate Status Report** command from the context menu.

If you experience unrecoverable problems after modification of the replication structure, you can delete all disturbing connections in the **Active Directory Sites and Services** snap-in and re-create them by starting the Knowledge Consistency Checker (KCC) for each affected server. To do so, right click an **NTDS Settings** object and select the **All Tasks | Check Replication Topology** command from the context menu.

See also the *"Replication Issues"* section in *Appendix B*.

Urgent Replication

Certain events on DCs are replicated immediately rather than at predefined intervals. This is known as urgent replication. The following events on any domain controller trigger urgent replication between DCs in the same site:

- Setting an account lockout after a certain number of failed user logon attempts
- Changing a Local Security Authority (LSA) secret
- Changing the RID Master FSMO role owner

(If a change notification is configured between sites, the urgent replication can be propagated to other sites.)

Urgent replication in Active Directory domains is not initiated by the following events:

- Changing the Account Lockout Policy
- Changing the domain Password Policy
- Changing the password on a machine account
- Changing inter-domain trust passwords

If a user changes the password at a specific DC, that DC attempts to urgently replicate the changes to the PDC Emulator. The updated password is then normally replicated to other DCs located in the same site. If the user is repeatedly authenticated by a DC that has not yet received the updated password, this DC refers to the PDC Emulator to check the user credentials.

Replication of Group Policy Objects

A Group Policy Object (GPO) consists of two parts. One part is located in Active Directory (the *DS part*), and the other part is stored on the hard disk in the SYSVOL volume (the *Sysvol part*). Hence, GPOs are replicated in two ways: by normal Active Directory replication and by File Replication Service (FRS). If one replication completes successfully, this does not mean that there are no problems with the other replication. That is why you should monitor the consistency of GPOs. For that purpose, use such tools as *Active Directory Replication Monitor* (ReplMon.exe) (see a server's Status Report) or *GPOTool.exe* that display the DS version and the Sysvol version separately for each GPO. (See detailed description of GPOTool.exe in *Chapter 15, "Group Policy Tools."*)

Monitoring Replication

You may wish to monitor replication events both in a test and a field environment. (The only difference may be in the level of detail given for registering events.) To fulfill this task, it is possible to use the event logs and performance counters.

Logging Replication Events

You can use the *Directory Service* event log for monitoring such events as the moments of replication request completion, the number, total size, and names of replicated attributes, and so on. The granularity level of logged events is set through the system registry (see below).

Set the `5 Replication Events` value at the `HKLM\SYSTEM\CurrentControlSet\Services\NTDS\Diagnostics` registry key equal to 3 or 4 (the difference between the cases will be discussed later). This will help you to see all replication requests, the sequence of replicated directory partitions, and the result of the requests. (Two domain controllers from the same domain — *NETDC3* and *NETDC4* — are used in the following examples.) The following two events are logged after each directory partition has been successfully replicated (NETDC4 asks NETDC3 for the changes):

```
Event Type:     Information
Event Source:   NTDS Replication
Event Category: Replication
Event ID:       1060
...
User:           Everyone
Computer:       NETDC4
Description:
Internal event: The directory replication agent (DRA) call completed
successfully.
- - - - -
Event Type:     Information
Event Source:   NTDS Replication
Event Category: Replication
```

```
Event ID:         1488
...
User:             NETDOM\administrator
Computer:         NETDC4
Description:
Internal event: The Directory Service completed the sync request with
status code 0.
```

Any replicated information is logged as an event similar to the following (NETDC3 asks NETDC4 for the outbound changes):

```
Event Type:       Information
Event Source:     NTDS Replication
Event Category:   Replication
Event ID:         1073
...
User:             NETDOM\NETDC3$
Computer:         NETDC4
Description:
Internal event: The directory replication agent (DRA) got changes
returning 2 objects, 2448 bytes total and entries up to update sequence
number (USN) 100225, with extended return 0.
- - - - -
Event Type:       Information
Event Source:     NTDS Replication
Event Category:   Replication
Event ID:         1490
...
User:             NETDOM\NETDC3$
Computer:         NETDC4
Description:
Internal event: The Directory Service finished gathering outbound
changes with the following results:

 Object Update USN: 100225
 Attribute Filter USN: 100225
 Object Count: 2
 Byte Count: 2448
 Extended Operation Result: 0
 Status: 0
```

To see replication events, set the registry value to at least level 3. Level 4 allows you to track replication of each changed attribute. (Use this level for debugging only!

If many objects are replicated, the number of events in the Directory Service log may be huge. This also significantly affects the performance of the DC.) You can easily find all replicated data by the Event ID. A message (ID 1239) similar to the following is written in the log for all *unchanged* attributes of the replicated objects:

```
Event Type:     Information
Event Source:   NTDS Replication
Event Category: Replication
Event ID:       1239
...
User:           NETDOM\NETDC3$
Computer:       NETDC4
Description:
Property 20002 (whenCreated) of object CN=John
Smith,OU=Staff,DC=net,DC=dom (GUID 3b2653cf-76e6-4d35-abf5-ec4c78fad8ee)
is not being sent to DSA a9d28d8e-e681-449f-b1be-38dadf6f4c06 because
its up-to-date vector implies the change is redundant.
```

If an attribute was changed, it is replicated to another DC, and a message with the ID 1240 will appear in the log:

```
Event Type:     Information
Event Source:   NTDS Replication
Event Category: Replication
Event ID:       1240
...
User:           NETDOM\NETDC3$
Computer:       NETDC4
Description:
Property d (description) of object CN=John Smith,OU=Staff,DC=net,DC=dom
(GUID 3b2653cf-76e6-4d35-abf5-ec4c78fad8ee) is being sent to DSA
a9d28d8e-e681-449f-b1be-38dadf6f4c06.
```

You can filter out events that do not have ID 1240, and quickly check all replicated objects and changed attributes.

Using the Performance Counters

Performance counters are very useful to monitor replication events, especially the replication traffic. To start monitoring, run the **Performance** snap-in (from the Administrative Tools group). Select **System Monitor** and click the **Add** button on the taskpad. Select **NTDS** in the **Performance object** list and add the counters shown in Fig. 6.1.

(The *Report View* seems to be the most useful in this case.) All counters have zero values immediately after startup of the DC. (The NTDS performance object has a great number of counters, and I have selected only some of them that are related to replication.)

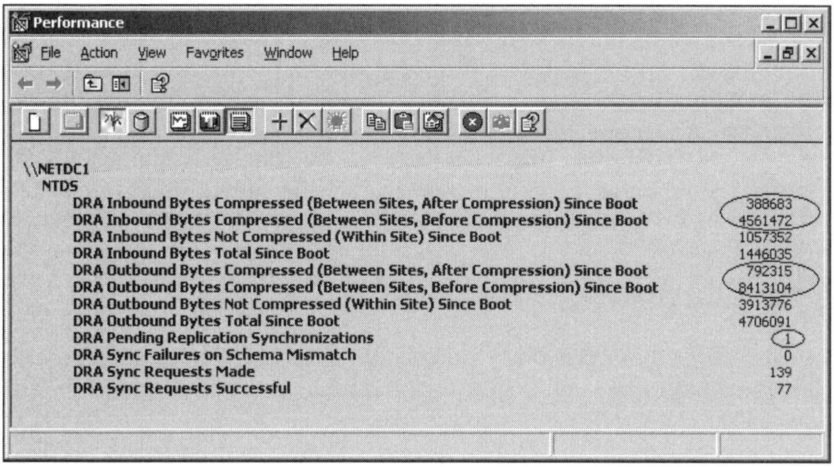

Fig. 6.2. Some of the performance counters important for monitoring replication

Note

As you can see in Fig. 6.1, compression of replication traffic (both inbound and outbound) can reach a ratio 12 to 1 (ratios up to 20 to 1 are also possible). If the replicated block of information is not large enough (less than 32 Kbytes), compression of inter-site traffic is not carried out.

You can also create a custom MMC console that will contain a copy of the System Monitor Control for each selected domain controller. (Start an MMC console, select **ActiveX Control** in the **Add Standalone Snap-in** window, and find the *System Monitor Control* in the **Control type** list. Repeat this procedure for each desired DC. Then, select the performance counters from different DCs and add them to the appropriate ActiveX controls.) See also the *"Managing Replication"* section in *Chapter 11, "Verifying Network and Distributed Services."*

The *DRA Sync Requests Successful* value must normally be equal to the *DRA Sync Request Made* value. However, these values usually differ on the DC(s) booted first, when its replication partners may yet be non-operational. Remember the values when all DCs in the network are online and replicated. From that moment on, the difference between these values must not increase.

The *DRA Pending Synchronizations* counter displays the number of replication requests that have not been completed yet (any result — a success or a failure — is possible).

The *DRA Inbound/Outbound Bytes Not Compressed (Within Site) Since Boot* counters register both intra- and inter-domain replication traffic, provided this traffic has not been compressed (i.e., replication block size does not exceed 32 KB).

Some General Troubleshooting Tips

It is not possible to answer each question related to troubleshooting Active Directory. (It is *Microsoft Knowledge Base* that tries to solve these problems, and usually, it does so with success!) I'd rather like to consider a few relatively simple tips here, which, nevertheless, could be very useful in various real-life situations. (Do not let the brevity of the tips fool you; this information is quite profound. Try it for yourself.)

Logging Diagnostic Events

On Active Directory domain controllers, the `HKLM\SYSTEM\CurrentControlSet\Services\NTDS\Diagnostics` registry key contains diagnostic entries (total 19 on Windows 2000, and 24 on Windows .NET) that represent the events that Active Directory can register in the Directory Service log. Each entry has a REG_DWORD value ranging from 0 to 5, which corresponds to the level of granularity of logged events.

When the default level 0 is set, only critical events are logged. This is the normal value for most entries. "Super-verbose" level 5 should be used with care, since it causes all events to be logged and is only used for debugging specific problems. If you have encountered an Active Directory-related problem, try to slightly increase the value of the appropriate registry value and to reproduce the problem. Do not forget to restore the default value after the problem has been solved.

There are no strict rules for selecting an entry value. You can do this in an experimental way. Use of the Replication Events entry has been discussed above. If, for example, the value of the Garbage Collection entry is set to 3, you can see when the garbage collection starts and completes, as well as the volume of free space in the directory database file. When the value is set to 5, each object deletion will also be logged.

Internal Errors During Replication

There is a kind of replication error that happens when a specific object "prevents" a replication request from being completed. (Remember that you cannot simply delete this object, since deleted objects are also replicated.) The *Q265090* article from the *Microsoft Knowledge Base* describes troubleshooting similar errors that may appear during the replication phase of the server promotion process. A similar approach can also be used for other cases of internal errors related to replication. (You can also consider this article as an example of troubleshooting replication issues.) To solve the problem, you should delete the interfering object, decrease the tombstone lifetime to the lowest value possible (2 days), and wait until the garbage collection entirely deletes the object. In Windows 2000, this trick has saved my network a few times, when all other means did not help at all. Windows .NET systems seem to be more proof against similar problems.

Verifying an Active Directory Server Status

As you know, a server running Windows 2000 or Windows .NET systems can advertise itself as a *domain controller* (if it has been promoted to perform such a role), and an Active Directory domain controller can also advertise itself as a *Global Catalog (GC) server*. There are quite a few cases when you may wish to be sure that this process has been successfully completed.

For example, if the File Replication Service (FRS) encounters some trouble, it does not initialize the system volume, and the Netlogon service thus cannot share the SYSVOL volume. (The NETLOGON volume also cannot be shared in that case.) This results in problems with applying group policies, as well as many other replication and authentication problems.

Here is another situation. The promotion of a DC to a GC server is normally delayed for 5 minutes. However, due to replication problems this process can last longer.

In both cases, before you begin to locate connectivity, authentication, or other potential problems, you need to be sure that your server *really acts* as a domain controller or a GC server.

Advertising a Server as a Domain Controller

Here are the methods that will allow you to identify whether a Windows 2000- or Windows .NET-based server is a domain controller after its promotion or normal reboot:

- The `HKEY_LOCAL_MACHINE\SYSTEM\CurrentControlSet\Services` registry key must contain the `NTDS` subkey.
- Enter `net accounts` at the command prompt. The "Computer role" of a domain controller is "PRIMARY", while standalone servers identify themselves as "SERVERS".
- Enter `net start` at the command prompt. The list of running services must contain the Kerberos Key Distribution Center (KDC) service.

- Enter `nbtstat -n` at the command prompt. The domain name with the <1C> type must be registered.
- Enter `net share` at the command prompt. The SYSVOL (*%SystemRoot%*\SYSVOL\sysvol) and NETLOGON (*%SystemRoot%*\SYSVOL\sysvol\<DomainDNSName>\scripts) shares must exist.
- Use Ldp.exe to view the *isSynchronized* attribute of the RootDSE object. (For additional information, see *Chapter 1, "LDAP Basics"* and *Chapter 12, "Manipulating Active Directory Objects".*) After a server promotion, the system must perform a full synchronization of all directory partitions. When this process is completed, the *isSynchronized* attribute is set to TRUE.
- Use NLtest.exe. (More details are in *Chapter 11, "Verifying Network and Distributed Services".*)
- Use NTDSutil.exe to connect to the domain controller and verify its responding to LDAP queries. (For more information, see *Chapter 10, "Diagnosing and Maintaining Domain Controllers".*) You can also use this tool to verify whether the DC knows about the FSMO roles in its domain.

Advertising a Domain Controller as a Global Catalog Server

Assigning a domain controller as a Global Catalog server (for example, in the **Active Directory Sites and Services** snap-in) and *advertising* this DC as a GC server are not the same things. A domain controller can advertise itself as a Global Catalog server only after it has *replicated in* all domain partitions existing in the forest at the moment.

You can use the following methods to verify advertising of a DC in the role of Global Catalog server:

- After a DC has been promoted to a GC server, the event with ID 1110 (Event Source: `NTDS General`; Event Category: `Replication`) appears in the Directory Service log. The advertising process completes with the ID 1119 event: "This domain controller is now a global catalog."
- The `Global Catalog Promotion Complete` registry value under the `HKEY_LOCAL_MACHINE\SYSTEM\CurrentControlSet\Services\NTDS\Parameters` key must be equal to 1.
- Use Ldp.exe to view the *isGlobalCatalogReady* attribute of the RootDSE object. (For more information, see *Chapter 1* and *Chapter 12.*)
- Use NLtest.exe. (More details are in *Chapter 11.*)

PART III

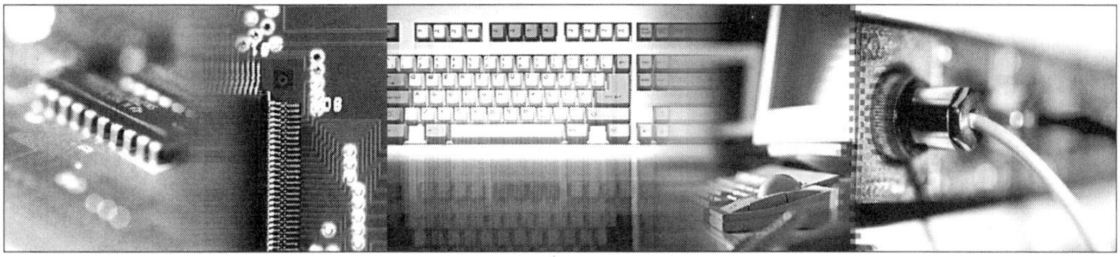

Administering Active Directory

Chapter 7: Domain Manipulation Tools

This chapter has perhaps more illustrations than any other in the whole book. No wonder! A picture is worth a thousand words! This is not a formal reference to all administrative snap-ins' screens, menus, commands, features, or to the operations that they implement. Neither are all snap-ins discussed. I wound like to make the reader focus his or her attention on certain details and options that are unapparent or which might not be noticed upon first acquaintance with snap-ins intended to manage Active Directory. Using this "know-how" will allow you to organize your workplace more efficiently. The differences between the Windows 2000 and Windows .NET versions of the snap-ins are also considered.

This chapter unveils certain aspects involved in using the features of the administrative tools for managing Active Directory. Other typical administrative tasks carried out by these and other tools will be discussed in *Chapter 8, "Common Administrative Tasks,"* and in other chapters, where specific tasks are described in detail.

Basic Active Directory Administrative Snap-ins

Both Windows 2000 and Windows .NET systems use the same set of snap-ins for administering Active Directory. For the most part, these tools have not changed in the new version; they perform the same functions (although in Windows .NET, all of them have some additional features). Therefore, an administrator acquainted with Windows 2000-based domains can easily master commonly used operations in the Windows .NET environment.

After a Windows .NET Server has been promoted to a domain controller, new tools (listed in Table 7.1) will appear in the **Administrative Tools** group on the **Start** menu.

Table 7.1. Standard Tools for Administering Active Directory

Icon	Tool name	Main operations performed by the tool
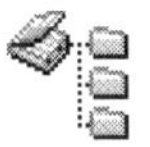	Active Directory Domains and Trusts	Selecting a domain for management in large forests. Managing domain functional levels. Creating, verifying, and deleting trusts between domains
	Active Directory Sites and Services	Creating and manipulating sites, transports, and subnets. Managing replication schedules and links. Triggering replication between domain controllers. Setting permissions on objects. Linking GPOs to sites. Enabling DCs to act as global catalog servers
	Active Directory Users and Computers	Creating and manipulating AD objects (users, groups, OUs, etc.). Setting permissions for objects. Linking GPOs to domains and OUs. Managing domain functional levels. Transferring FSMO roles

continues

Table 7.1 Continued

Icon	Tool name	Main operations performed by the tool
	Domain Controller Security Policy	*In Windows 2000-based domains*: Editing the **Security Settings** node of the GPO linked to the *Domain Controllers* OU. *In Windows .NET-based domains*: Editing any settings in the GPO linked to the *Domain Controllers* OU.
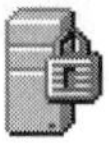	Domain Security Policy	*In Windows 2000-based domains*: Editing the **Security Settings** node of the GPO linked to a domain container. *In Windows .NET-based domains*: Editing any settings in the GPO linked to a domain container.
	Group Policy Object Editor[1]	Editing GPOs linked to an Active Directory container (site, domain, OU) or stored on a local computer. This snap-in is not shown on the **Start** menu, but is accessible from other administrative snap-ins or can be added to a custom MMC console.

These tools can be installed as a part of the *Administration Tools Pack* (see *"Remote Administration"* in *Chapter 8*, *"Common Administrative Tasks"*) onto any client computer with Windows XP Professional or a member server with Windows .NET. The **Security Policy** snap-ins will not appear on the **Start** menu in that case.

Note

The **Active Directory Schema Manager** snap-in included in the *Administration Tools Pack* is also installed on domain client computers and appears on the **Start** menu.

Important

- It is not possible to install Windows .NET administrative snap-ins onto Windows 2000-based computers.

Some other important tools (Table 7.2) for administering Active Directory are included in the *Support Tools* pack. These tools might be regarded as mandatory for an administrator, and are discussed later in this book.

---

[1] In Windows 2000, this snap-in is called **Group Policy**.

Table 7.2. Some Additional Tools for Maintaining Active Directory (from *Support Tools*)

Icon	Tool name	Main operations performed by the tool
	ADSI Edit (adsiedit.msc)	"Low-level" editing of the Active Directory objects that belong to any directory partition (application, domain, configuration, and schema). (The *RootDSE* object is also accessible.) Setting permissions on objects.
	Active Directory Administration Tool (Ldp.exe)	Searching Active Directory and modifying directory objects using LDAP queries.
	Active Directory Replication Monitor (replmon.exe)	Monitoring replication status and topology. Triggering replication. Monitoring FSMO roles and flags of domain controllers.

Common Topics

Since most Active Directory administrative tools have been realized as MMC snap-ins, all of them have similar interfaces and basic features. Knowing these features allows you to use all of these tools in the most effective way possible, and to optimize them to fit your specific tasks. Sometimes, a snap-in's design and features may even affect some aspects of deploying Active Directory in an enterprise (see a bit later in this chapter *"Choosing Columns for Displaying"*). Let us start by discussing administrative snap-ins, taking into consideration some common features of snap-ins.

Making a Custom MMC Console

Most standard administrative tools can be started from the **Start | Administrative Tools** menu, or can be added to a custom MMC console. Such tools as the **Active Directory Schema Manager** snap-in or the **Group Policy Object Editor** snap-in should always be initially added to an MMC document:

1. Enter `mmc` in the **Start | Run** window.
2. Press <Ctrl>+<M>, or select the **Console | Add/Remove Snap-in** command. Click **Add** in the window that is open.
3. Select the desired snap-in in the **Add Standalone Snap-in** window, and click **Add**. You can repeat this step for all the snap-ins you need. Then in turn click **Close** and **OK**.
4. Save the resulting console with any name.

Making your own administrative console may have some valuable advantages:

- You will have on hand all the instruments you want, which will be configured to your discretion. For example, you may have snap-ins connected to different domains, or **Group Policy Object Editor** snap-ins linked to various GPOs.
- There will be more options for configuring and customizing snap-ins (see in this chapter *"Customizing Snap-ins"*).
- The computer's memory is used more efficiently. A number of tools started separately allocate considerably more memory than the same tools added to a single MMC console.

Note

On Windows .NET-based domain controllers (unlike those in Windows 2000), all administrative snap-ins can be opened in the "Author" mode (right click on a snap-in's name and select **Author** in the context menu), which allows you to reconfigure these tools (add new snap-ins in the same MMC document, etc.).

Browsing the *Tree* Pane in a Snap-in's Window

While working in a snap-in window, don't forget about such simple but timesaving web-style features on the *Standard* toolbar as the **Forward** and **Back** buttons, the **Up one level** button, and the **Refresh** button. When pointing to an object, you can view its properties either by selecting the **Properties** command in the context menu, or — to do it faster — by clicking the **Properties** button.

Choosing Columns for Displaying

When working with different Active Directory objects, it is possible (and may be very helpful) to display more fields than just the three default ones, or to delete unnecessary ones. Select the **Add/Remove Columns** (in Windows 2000 — **Choose Columns**) command in the **View** menu, and add or delete the necessary columns in the **Add/Remove Columns** window (Fig. 7.1). Each object will have its own set of fields.

In Fig. 7.1, note that in MMC v.2.0 you can move any item to the beginning of the **Displayed columns** list. In Windows 2000, the **Name** item is always at the top.

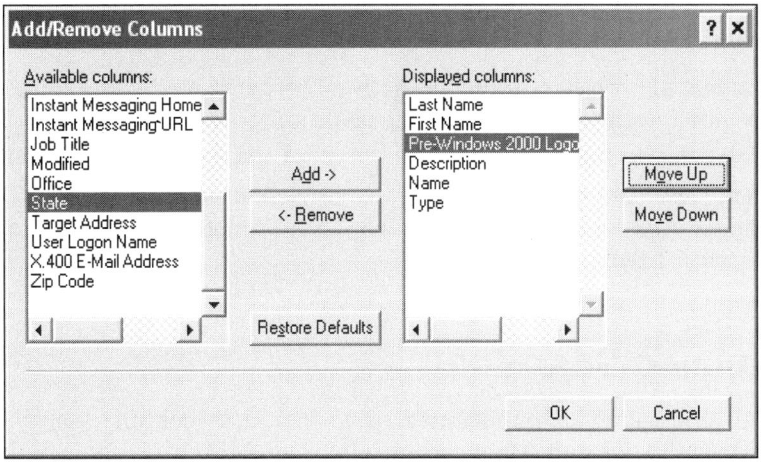

Fig. 7.1. Choosing necessary object attributes to be displayed

Note

When the **Active Directory Users and Computers** snap-in is used for creating new users, the **Full Name** field is generated as a concatenation of the **First name** and **Last Name** fields. The **Full name** field, in turn, determines the value of the *cn* attribute. (You can, however, change this order, if you like — see articles *Q250455* and *Q277717* in the *Microsoft Knowledge Base*.) You may want, for some reason, to use proprietary naming conventions in your organization. (This can be easily organized by using scripts or batch tools, such as LDIFDE or CSVDE. Manual manipulations are also possible.) For instance, you may wish for the *cn* attribute (i.e., the **Full name** field) to have the same value as the *sAMAccountName* attribute (the **Pre-Windows 2000 Logon Name** field) or as a proprietary ID code.

Note

Sometimes, the Windows 2000 version of the **Active Directory Users and Computers** snap-in does not sort a container contents on some columns. (In Windows .NET, this is not an issue.) You can use the **Find Users, Contacts, and Groups** window rather than the main snap-in's window. This window allows you to sort rows according to the contents of *any* column. "Hide" the **Name** column from view and rearrange the columns in the order most useful for you. (It is not possible to remove this column in the main window. Moreover, in Windows 2000, this column must always be first.) Click **Browse** to view the forest tree and go to any location (then click **Find Now**). You can select the most appropriate of the two windows depending on your requirements.

Exporting the List of Objects

To document the objects stored in Active Directory, you can export any currently displayed list into a file for processing or printing from the Word or Excel applications. Point to a container or an object and click the **Export List** button, or select the **Export List** command in the context or **Action** menu. You can choose between tab-separated (.txt) and comma-separated (.csv) formats. CSV files are easily imported into Microsoft Excel documents.

Customizing Snap-ins

Standard configured administrative snap-ins lack certain useful features that are realized in Microsoft Management Console (MMC) technology. These features are common for all MMC consoles, and there are many reasons why using them in the *administrative tools* allows an administrator to save a lot of time and effort.

Favorites

In Windows .NET, this feature is implemented in a slightly different way than it is in Windows 2000. (Keep in mind that the Windows 2000 systems use the MMC version 1.2, whereas the Windows XP/.NET systems use the MMC version 2.0.)

In a custom MMC v.1.2 console, the **Favorites** tab will appear near the usual **Tree** tab. A MMC v.2.0 console has the **Favorites** command on the main console menu. You can browse Active Directory in a web-like style, and save the pages you'd like to access later. Point to any container in the **Tree** pane, and select **Add to Favorites** in the **Favorites** menu. This feature can be very helpful in large domains that contain many OUs and other objects.

Notice also that any container in Active Directory that can be viewed in *different* snap-ins can be designated as a favorite; it will be placed in the *same* list of favorites. You can, for instance, simultaneously have main OUs from different domains, authoritative DNS zones, DHCP scopes, site connections, etc., all on the **Favorites** tab (or on the **Favorite** menu — in MMC v.2.0). Do not forget about traditional browsing features, such as the **Back**, **Forward**, **Up one level**, and **Refresh** buttons.

Creating Custom Taskpads

An administrator may create specialized taskpads for him- or herself (for some routine tasks) as well as for users that need to carry out certain (limited) tasks, or for subordinate administrators to whom control of some OUs or objects is delegated.

Let us discuss an example of how to create a taskpad for administering organizational units. This taskpad will allow us to view all accounts in an OU and perform three predefined operations: create a computer, user, and group.

Select an OU in the **Active Directory Users and Computers** snap-in, and click **New Taskpad View** from the **Action** menu. The *New Taskpad View Wizard* will be started, which will guide you through all necessary steps. At any step of wizard working, you can go back and change the selected options or entered information.

Leave the default options in the *Taskpad Display* and *Taskpad Target* steps unchanged. This means that the tab of the created taskpad will appear for each OU in the domain (but not for other domain containers!). Enter the necessary information at the *Name and Description* step. When the wizard has finished (i.e., the view without task buttons has been generated), check the **Start New Task wizard** box in the last window and click **Finish**. The *New Task Wizard* will start.

The default *Command Type* is **Menu command**. In the *Shortcut Menu Command* step, select **Tree item task** in the **Command source** list (Fig. 7.2). In this case, we will be able to choose the commands for the entire OU. First, select **New->Computer**.

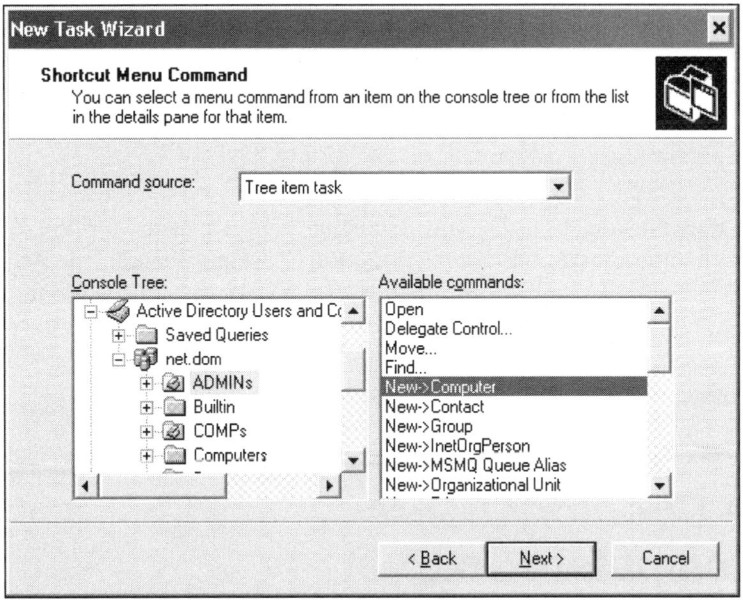

Fig. 7.2. Selecting the source of the commands for the new taskpad

At the next step, enter a relevant task name, and a description for this task. Then you can choose a graphical representation (icon) for the task. A new task has now been created. To add the other two commands, check the **Run this wizard again** box in the last window of the wizard, and click **Finish**. The wizard will start again. Repeat the necessary steps, the first time selecting **New->User**, and the second time — **New->Group**. Fig. 7.3 shows an example of a taskpad created according to the described procedure.

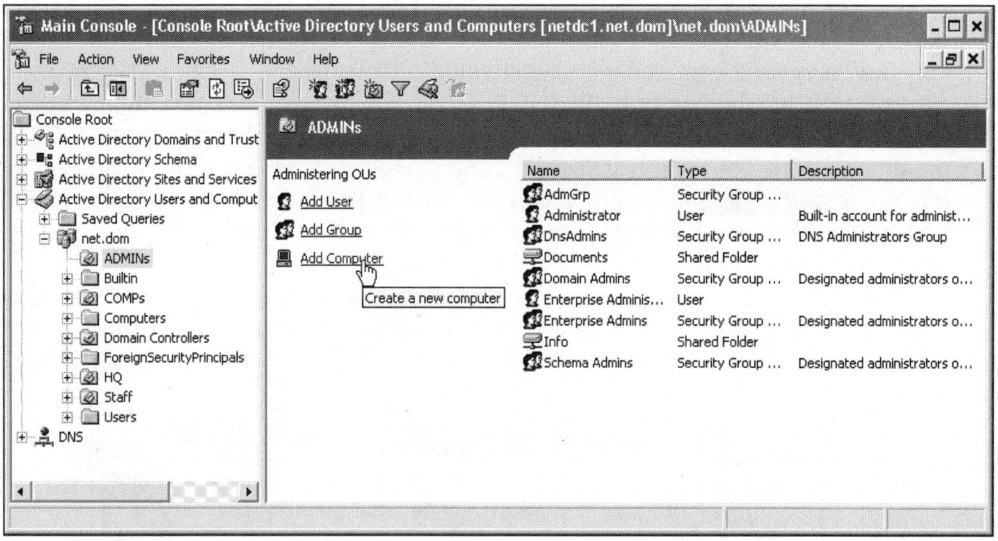

Fig. 7.3. An example of a taskpad

You may add/delete tasks, and/or change the properties (options) of a taskpad by selecting the appropriate tab and clicking **Edit Taskpad View** in the **Action** menu.

It is possible to define commands (tasks) for an entire container as well as for an individual (selected) object in a container. While browsing the object tree, only those commands that are acceptable for the selected object will be enabled in a taskpad.

Active Directory Users and Computers Snap-in

The **Active Directory Users and Computers** snap-in is perhaps one of the tools that an administrator will use most often. That is why it is advisable to learn all of the features that this snap-in provides for an administrator. This is especially true if a domain contains thousands of objects, which complicates viewing and manipulating them.

New Features

The Windows .NET version of the **Active Directory Users and Computers** snap-in offers some new features:

- Multiple selection of directory objects
- Drag-and-prop option for move operations of various type and adding member(s) to a group
- Saved Queries

Connecting to Domain or Domain Controller

The **Active Directory Users and Computers** snap-in operates with only one DC — and, therefore, one domain — at a time. By default, this is your current logon domain and DC (unless you have changed the domain or DC and checked the **Save this domain setting for the current console** box, Fig. 7.4).

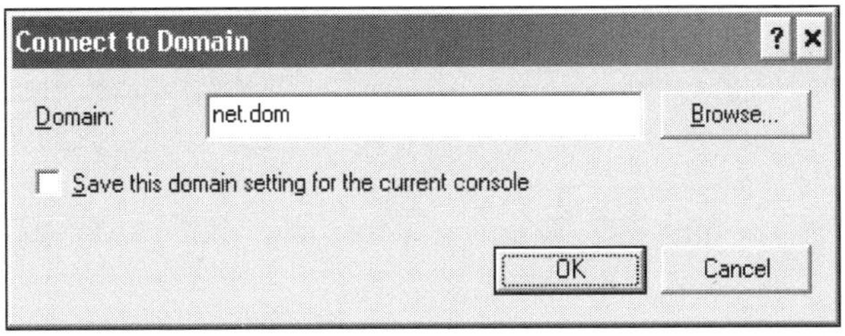

Fig. 7.4. You may choose any domain in the forest to administer

You can choose a domain that you wish to investigate by pointing to the root of the snap-in (or by selecting the domain object from the tree pane) and then selecting the **Connect to Domain** command in the **Action** menu. In the **Connect to Domain** window enter the domain name in the **Domain** field, or click the **Browse** button and select the domain from the expanding domain tree. Notice the **Save this domain setting for the current console** box, which allows you to have a few saved snap-ins configured for different domains.

Similarly, you can select any domain controller in the current domain with the **Connect to Domain Controller** command in the **Action** menu. It makes sense to do this when, for some reason (e.g., regarding a replication issue), you need to administer a Global Catalog server, or a DC performing a specific FSMO role, such as PDC Emulator. In the **Connect to Domain Controller** window (Fig. 7.5) you can see your current DC's name and the list of available controllers.

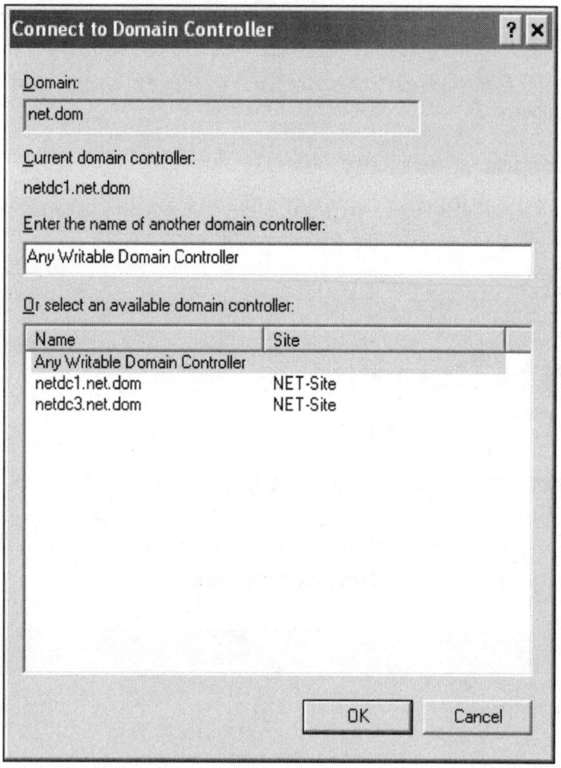

Fig. 7.5. Selecting a controller within a domain

Contents Displaying Options

The **Active Directory Users and Computers** snap-in has a few specific features, which don't change the administrative options of the snap-in essentially, but significantly affect the scope of objects available for manipulating. These features are discussed below.

Saved Queries

This is a new feature available in Windows .NET only.

An administrator can create one or more queries using the LDAP filters and save them in the snap-in for subsequent use. These queries will allow him or her to quickly select the necessary objects only, which simplifies work with large number of directory objects of a specific type (user, group, computer, etc.). All queries are stored in the **Saved Queries** folder in the snap-in's tree pane and can be organized in a folder structure (see an example in Fig. 7.6).

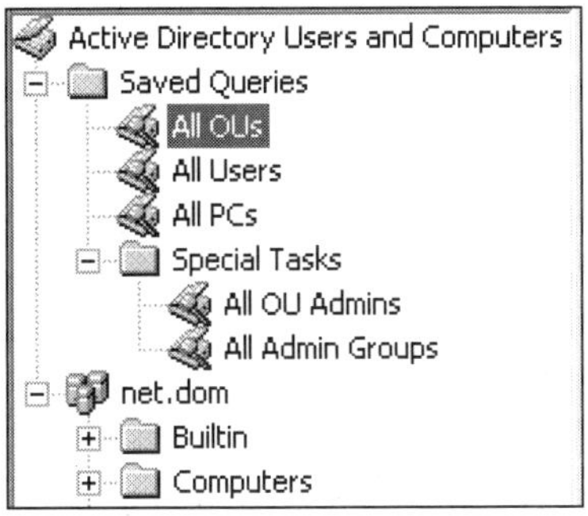

Fig. 7.6. A sample structure of saved queries

You can either immediately create a new query on a computer or import query definition of an already existing query.

To create a query:

1. Select the **Saved Queries** folder and right click it.
2. Select **New | Query** in the context menu.
3. In the **New Query** window (Fig. 7.7), fill in the **Name** and **Description** (optional) fields.

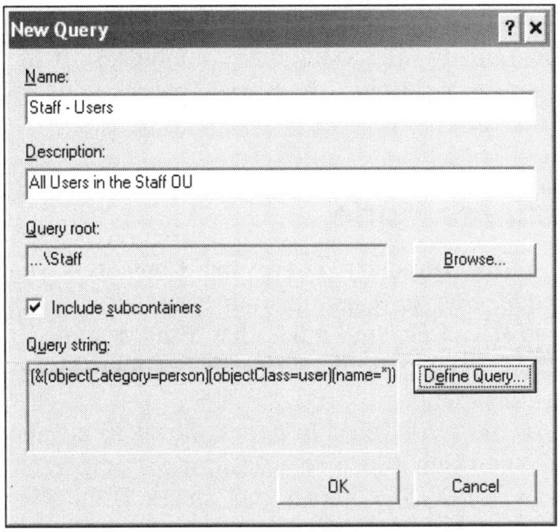

Fig. 7.7. An example of a new saved query

4. Click **Browse** and select the query root — a container in the domain structure (by default, the entire domain container will be looked through). Make sure that the **Include subdirectories** box is properly set.

5. Click **Define Query** and compose a necessary query string. For detailed information on that operation, see the *"Filter Options"* section.
6. Click **OK**. The query is ready.

The saved queries are not sorted and are placed in the query structure in the order that they are created.

Saved queries are stored on the computer where they have been created. (These queries are included in the roaming user profile if the user has such a profile.) To distribute saved queries, the *Help and Support Center* proposes to copy the dsa.msc file to other domain controllers (located in the same domain). However, this statement most likely needs clarification.

In Windows .NET, some administrative snap-ins save the user settings in XML files located in the "Documents and Settings\<*UserName*>\Application Data\Microsoft\MMC folder. The name of such a file correlates with the snap-in's file name (see details in the next chapter, section *"File Names of Administrative Snap-ins"*). I have found in my own experience that you can safely copy the *dsa* file from that folder to another computer (to a similar folder in the user profile). Remember, however, that *all* snap-in's settings (including *all* saved queries) are copied with this operation.

There is a legitimate and proven way to distribute saved queries. You can simply export a *query definition* (in XML format) and import it to every computer where it is necessary. Right click a query name and select **Export Query Definition**. Save the definition to a file, copy the file to another computer, start the **Active Directory Users and Computers** snap-in, right click the **Saved Queries** folder, and select **Import Query Definition**.

Advanced Features Mode

By default, the **Active Directory Users and Computers** snap-in only displays five nodes in basic mode. For some administrative tasks this is not enough, and you need to switch to the *Advanced Features* mode that displays some important "invisible" containers and has additional options. This can be done using the **Advanced Features** command in the **View** menu.

Perhaps one of the most valuable nodes shown in advanced mode is the **System** container (Fig. 7.8), which provides access to a number of system objects, for instance, to the *MicrosoftDNS* container that stores DNS zone information if a zone (zones) is (are) Active Directory-integrated and is replicated on all DCs in the current domain. (This is the only option in Windows 2000-based domains and one of four possible options in Windows .NET-based domains.)

Even more important is that only in the Advanced Features mode will you have the **Object** and **Security** tabs in the **Properties** window of any Active Directory object. All changes related to delegation of control over some object are displayed in the

Security tab. For example, if you want to revoke an administrative right from a user or a group, you need to open this tab for the object and delete the appropriate permissions.

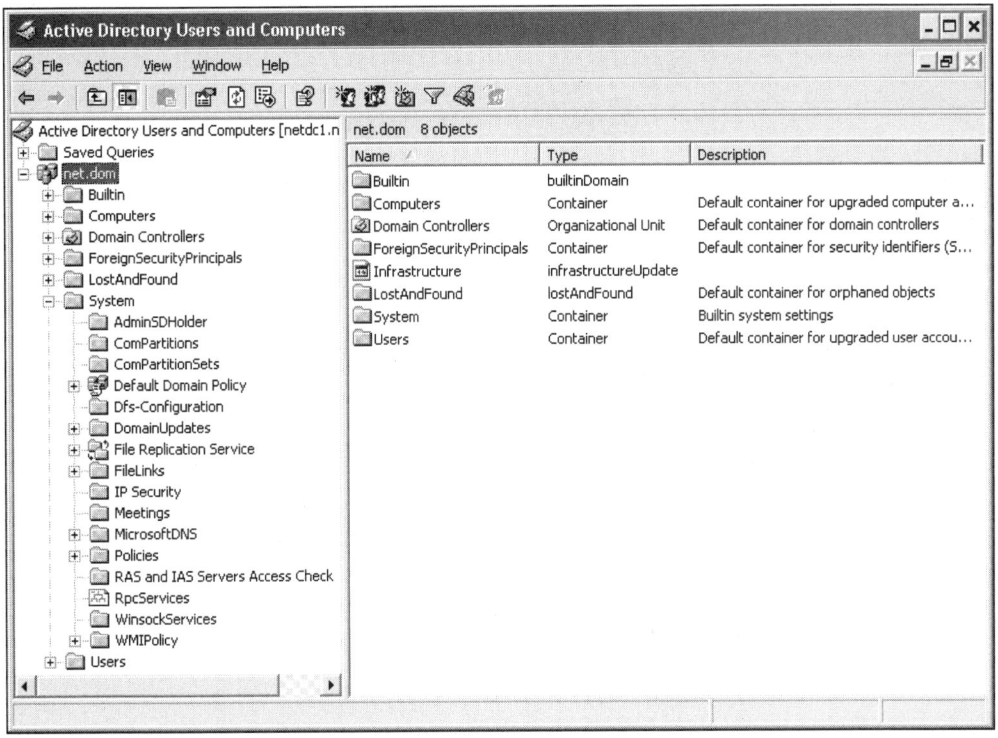

Fig. 7.8. The advanced view of a domain objects tree

There is also one remarkable possibility related to this mode. You might notice that five "default" nodes (plus the possible subdomains) are visible while browsing the **Directory** node in the **My Network Places** folder from Windows 2000-based domain clients (see Fig. 7.9 where a root and a child domains are shown). Sometimes this information will annoy *end users*, while at other times *you* may not want end users to be able to access these nodes.

You can control the "visibility" of any Active Directory container or object by using an optional Boolean attribute *showInAdvancedViewOnly* (it can be set to FALSE or TRUE, the case of the letters doesn't matter). The majority of Active Directory objects have this attribute, and you can change its value as needed with the **ADSI Edit** tool (see the *"ADSI Edit Snap-in"* section in this chapter). If an object (container) has this attribute set to TRUE, the object will not be displayed during domain browsing

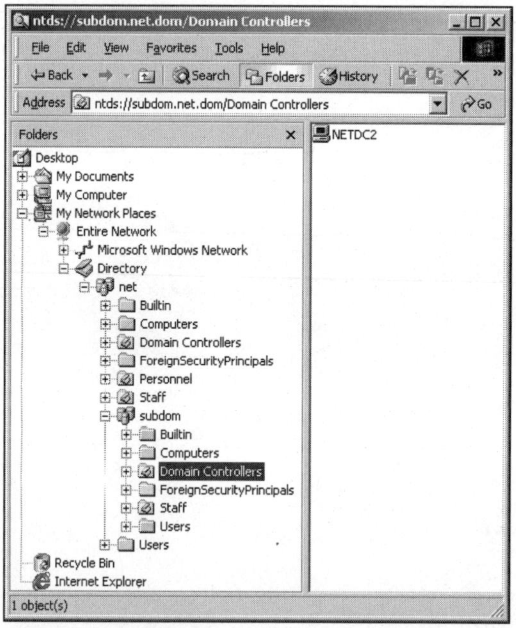

Fig. 7.9. Browsing the entire domain tree may be tiresome or undesirable

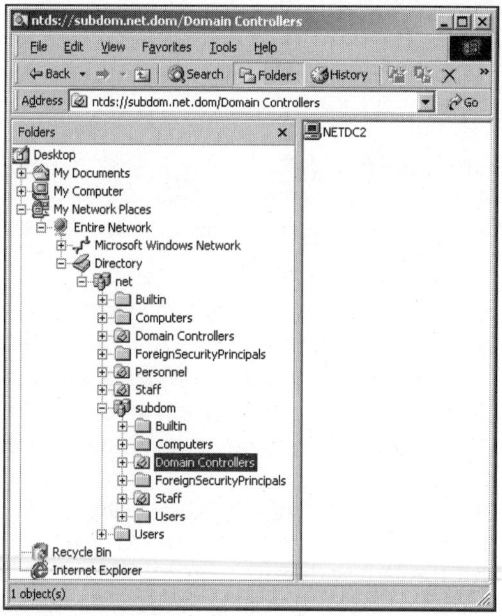

Fig. 7.10. You can restrict browsing of both parent and child domains for clients and "hide" unnecessary objects from viewing

or in the base mode in the **Active Directory Users and Computers** snap-in. This has no affect on the general behavior of the domain.

Fig. 7.10 shows the same domain structure that is represented in Fig. 7.9, but the *showInAdvancedViewOnly* attribute has been set to TRUE for some domain objects, so none of the users in the forest will be able to see the contents of these domains. (In an actual situation, this might be too strict a limit, but do not forget that this is only an example!)

Important

Windows 2000-based client computers can browse any Active Directory domains (Windows 2000- and Windows .NET-based). This feature has not been included in Windows XP/.NET, and the **Directory** node is not present in the **My Network Places** folder.

Note

It is also possible to control the "visibility" of Active Directory objects using access permissions. Both methods have their own *pros* and *cons*; therefore, select the most convenient method, depending on your requirements. For example, permissions allow for more comprehensive control, but if you use them, rather than have the ability to make selected object invisible (or visible), you will have to accept that all objects will become invisible (or visible) with your selection.

Users, Groups, and Computers as Containers Mode

Some Active Directory objects act as containers for other objects. By default, this fact has no visible representation in the **Active Directory Users and Computers** snap-in. Nevertheless, there are situations when you may wish to see all object relations. For example, compare the two screenshots shown in Fig. 7.11 and Fig. 7.12. The first one is a default view of the *Domain Controllers* OU and the *NETDC1* domain controller; the second one shows the same controller as a container.

As you can see in Fig. 7.12, the domain controller has child objects; in particular, a published printer. You might want to move the printer object to any other OU. This will not affect the printer's behavior.

Note

All printers are initially published in Active Directory as child objects of relative computers. You may want to gather them in a single OU for users' or administrators' convenience, although the **Search** option is a more convenient way to work with printers.

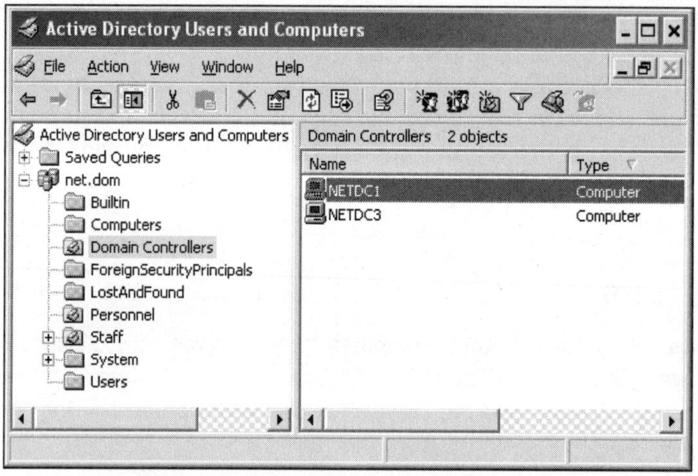

Fig. 7.11. The default view of a domain controller

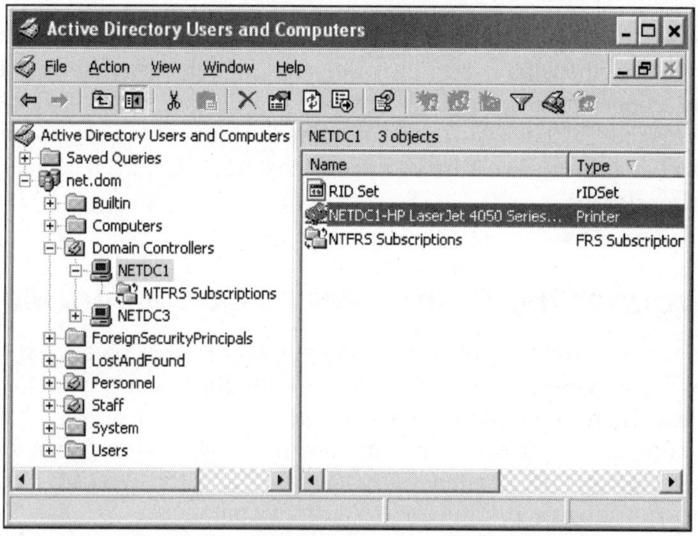

Fig. 7.12. Using the *Users, Groups, and Computers as containers* mode for locating a published printer connected to the selected domain controller

Filter Options

As the number of objects in Active Directory considerably increases, the length of time it takes to find specific objects may become unbearable. However, you can set *a filter* and look up only the desired objects. Select the **Filter Options** command in the

View menu or click the **Set Filtering Options**  button on the Standard toolbar. You can set the types of objects to be displayed from a predefined list, or create your own *custom* filter. The process of creating a filter is intuitively simple. Fig. 7.13 shows how to create a filter for selecting user accounts with names starting with the letter "a". To activate the filter, you must click the **Add** button and place the criteria onto the list.

Caution

- Using a filter may present a potential danger when working with containers (OUs). Suppose you have set a filter that displays only computer accounts. You may decide that an OU is empty or holds only unnecessary computer accounts (since it seems it does not contain any computers). You might just forget that this OU can contain other objects and inadvertently delete the *entire* OU rather than only the necessary accounts... Therefore, do not forget to turn off any filters when doing such operations as deleting or moving container objects!

Note

Many Active Directory objects have the *Name* attribute. Regretfully, the *object* name isn't displayed in the **Fine Custom Search** window in any form. Therefore, you must remember all parameters of any added criteria.

Note

Since two or more added criteria are AND-combined, an object is displayed in the snap-in window only if *all* specified conditions are true. OR-combined criteria are not available. Use the LDAP query if you need a complicated filter condition.

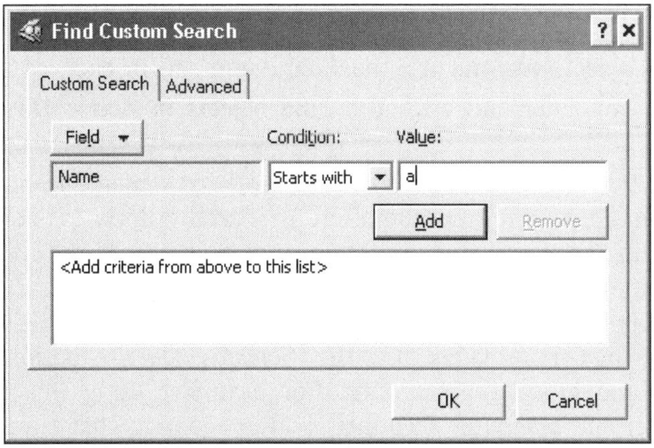

Fig. 7.13. An example of a custom filter

Caution

Filters, especially complex ones, may considerably slow down object display in the snap-in window.

In addition, you can use LDAP queries. Click the **Advanced** tab in the **Find Custom Search** window and enter a query (LDAP filter string) in text format. For example, the following query fetches only non-default user accounts:

```
(&(objectCategory=Person)(objectClass=user)(displayName=*))
```

Caution

All defined custom search filters along with the LDAP query are connected by a logical AND. This means that you may, for instance, define the first filter condition as "Name + Starts with + **a**", and view all user accounts whose names start with "a". If you add the second filter condition defined as "Name + Starts with + **d**" (or add an LDAP query such as `(cn=d*)`), you won't see user accounts beginning with "a" *or* "d". (You must instead specify an OR-condition in a *single* filter!) You'll see no accounts at all, because there are no accounts whose names start with "a" *and* "d". Therefore, the combination of filter conditions and LDAP queries has to be regarded as a chain of sub-queries within other queries, i.e., as an *intersection of sets*.

Finding Active Directory Objects

Another option that helps to process large numbers of Active Directory objects is the *Find* feature. In a sense, it works as a filter, but has a wider scope: you can find objects in the entire directory (forest), in any domain, or in a selected container. To find an object, you can use the **Find** command in each container's context menu or select a container and click the **Find objects in Active Directory** button on the toolbar.

Search (and advanced search) fields can vary, depending on the type of directory objects (users, computers, printers, etc.). Search criteria for advanced operations are composed in the same way as filters and have the same constraints. The *Custom Search* option is the most flexible; it allows you to specify practically any attribute of any directory object. The Windows .NET version of the **Active Directory Users and Computers** snap-in provides also the *Common Queries* option that finds the user, computer, and group objects only. For example, using this option, you can find disabled user and computer accounts, or user accounts that have not been used during a specified number of days.

Note

When you find users in the **Find Users, Contacts, and Groups** window, the string entered in the **Name** field is verified for matches with *all* user-naming attributes — *cn*, *First name*, *Last name*, and *Display name*.

Note

The **In** list comprises the names of containers (OUs) you've already visited.

In the window of the objects found, you can select all context menu commands that are available for these objects in the usual snap-in window.

An example of the **Find** window and a sample result is shown in Fig. 7.14. This search query finds all groups in the entire directory with names starting with the letter "s". The example shown might not be particularly useful, but note that you can search the *whole domain forest* (two domains in this case) as well as a selected domain or container. In addition, it demonstrates that such a group as *Server Operators* is present in either domain, but only one (root) domain has the *Schema Admins* group.

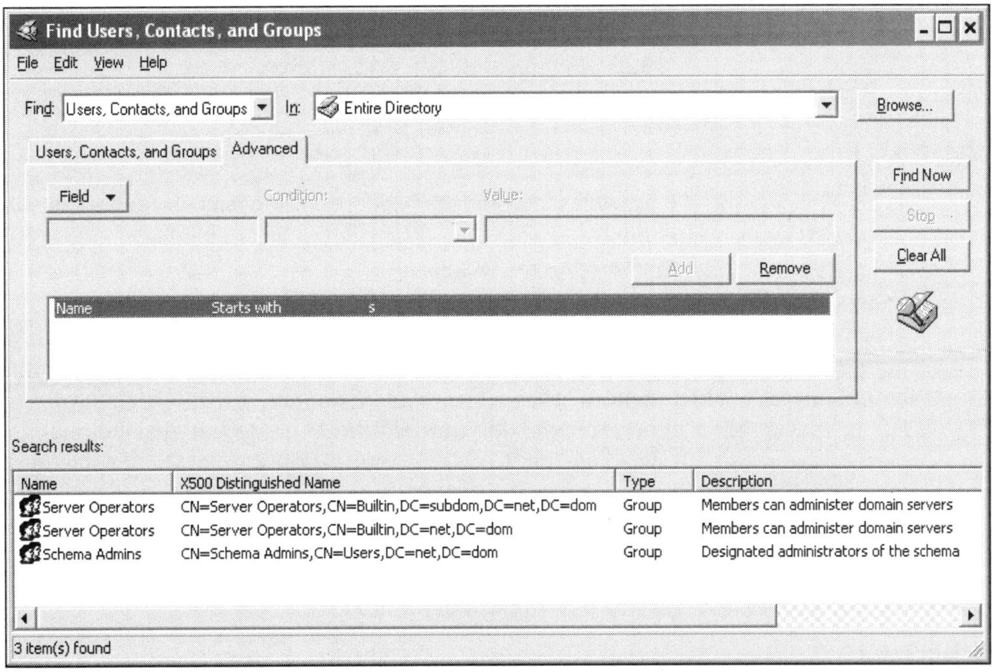

Fig. 7.14. Finding objects in Active Directory

Fine Tuning the *Find* Window

The display mode shown in Fig. 7.14 is not the default. To see the distinguished names (i.e., all RDNs of the parent objects) of found objects, click **Choose Columns** in the **View** menu, select the **X500 Distinguished Name** item and add it to **Columns shown**.

To further filter the result of a find operation, click **Filter** in the **View** menu. The filter bar will appear at the top of the result pane in the **Find** window. How to filter out some groups and users among a number of similar objects is shown in Fig. 7.15.

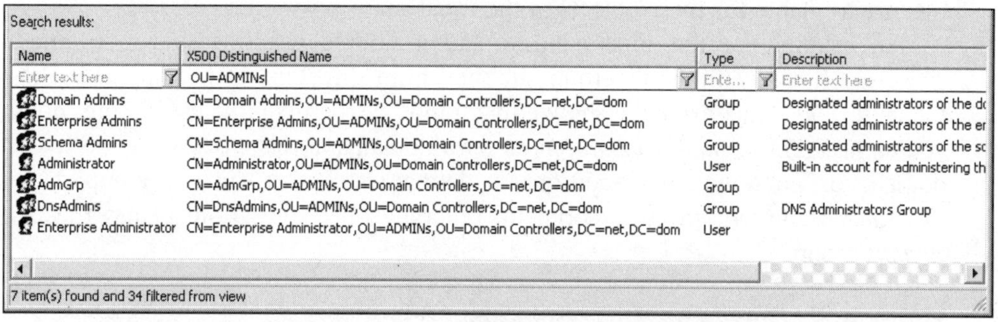
Search results:
Name
X500 Distinguished Name
Type
Description
Enter text here
OU=ADMINs
Ente...
Enter text here
Domain Admins
CN=Domain Admins,OU=ADMINs,OU=Domain Controllers,DC=net,DC=dom
Group
Designated administrators of the d
Enterprise Admins
CN=Enterprise Admins,OU=ADMINs,OU=Domain Controllers,DC=net,DC=dom
Group
Designated administrators of the e
Schema Admins
CN=Schema Admins,OU=ADMINs,OU=Domain Controllers,DC=net,DC=dom
Group
Designated administrators of the sc
Administrator
CN=Administrator,OU=ADMINs,OU=Domain Controllers,DC=net,DC=dom
User
Built-in account for administering th
AdmGrp
CN=AdmGrp,OU=ADMINs,OU=Domain Controllers,DC=net,DC=dom
Group
DnsAdmins
CN=DnsAdmins,OU=ADMINs,OU=Domain Controllers,DC=net,DC=dom
Group
DNS Administrators Group
Enterprise Administrator
CN=Enterprise Administrator,OU=ADMINs,OU=Domain Controllers,DC=net,DC=dom
User
7 item(s) found and 34 filtered from view

Fig. 7.15. Filtering the search results: among all administrators, we have selected those that belong to the ADMINs OU

Note

In the **Find** window, it is possible to turn on the filter option for clients (by default, the filter is set to off) by using the *Enable filter in Find dialog box* policy in the user's administrative templates (sub-node **Desktop | Active Directory**).

It so happens that it is not possible to see some directory objects' (computers, printers, etc.) distinguished names. In that case, you can add the **Published At** column to the default view of the **Find** window. The *canonical names* of the objects will be displayed in that column. For example, for the *XP-PRO3* computer that belongs to the *net.dom* domain and is placed in the *COMPs* organizational unit, the displayed string will be `ntds://net.dom/COMPs/XP-PRO3`.

Multiple Selection of Directory Objects

One of the most troublesome disadvantages of the **Active Directory Users and Computers** snap-in in Windows 2000 is its inability to manipulate a number of directory objects, primarily, and user objects. Windows .NET offers a pleasant improvement in that area.

For the most of directory objects (e.g., computers, groups, OUs, and etc.), you can change the description only. However, in user objects, over 30 attributes can be changed simultaneously. You select the objects as usual — using the <Shift> and <Ctrl> keys. Then, you select the **Properties** command on the context or **Action** menu. The set of allowed commands will be determined by the type of the objects selected. When two or more objects are selected, the modified **Properties** window opens. An example of that window for user objects is shown in Fig. 7.16.

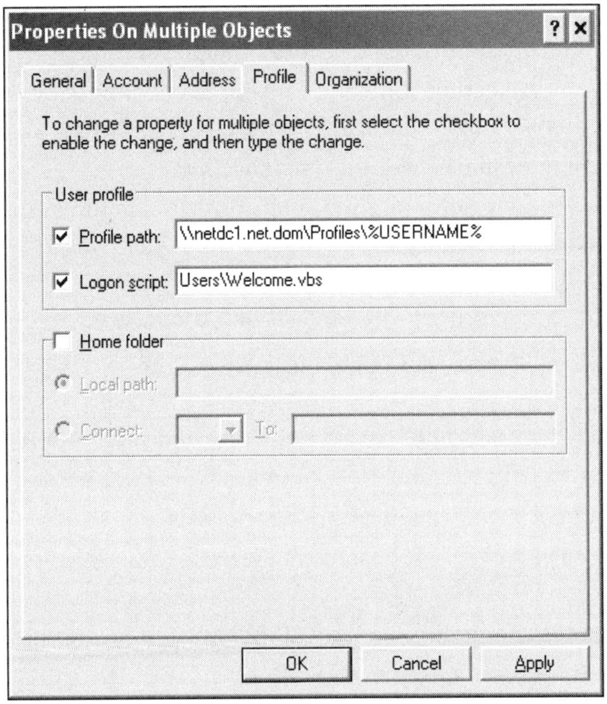

Fig. 7.16. Appointing a profile and logon script to a number of users

On the **Profile** tab, it is possible to set all the same properties that are available in the usual user's properties window. If you set a box, you define the value entered in the appropriate field. If the field is empty, the existing attribute value will be cleared. If a box is not checked (the appropriate field is grey), the existing value will be retained without changes.

Active Directory Sites and Services Snap-in

The **Active Directory Sites and Services** snap-in is the main GUI tool that allows an administrator to configure Active Directory as a distributed network service. (Other administrative tools consider Active Directory as a whole, at a logical level.) You might almost forget about this snap-in in a small, single-site network with just a few domain controllers. However, in large networks with many sites, this snap-in becomes one of the essential administrative tools.

The **Active Directory Sites and Services** snap-in allows you to perform the following operations:

- Designate domain controllers as Global Catalog servers.
- Modify forest replication topology (create/delete sites, subnets, links, link bridges, and connections); view replication contexts.
- Enable caching of universal group membership.
- Design a location scheme used by the printer, computer, site, and subnet objects (for detailed information, search in the *Help and Support Center* for "Enabling printer location tracking").
- Trigger intra-site and inter-site replication events.
- Trigger the Knowledge Consistency Checker (KCC) to re-generate replication topology.
- Change schedules and intervals for intra-site and inter-site replications.
- Assign costs to links.
- Designate domain controllers as bridgehead servers.
- Delegate control over sites, subnets, servers, and other containers to users or groups.
- Define security and auditing settings for various replication topology objects.
- Select Group Policy Objects (GPO), link GPOs to sites, and start the **Group Policy Object Editor** snap-in for editing GPO.
- Select LDAP query policies.

In Fig. 7.17, you can see the main window of the **Active Directory Sites and Services** snap-in, which displays practically all major elements of network configuration: sites, subnets, inter-site links, connections, and servers (domain controllers). Use and configuration of these elements is discussed in other chapters of the book, since it is more advantageous to describe these questions in the context of specific administrative tasks rather than in isolation.

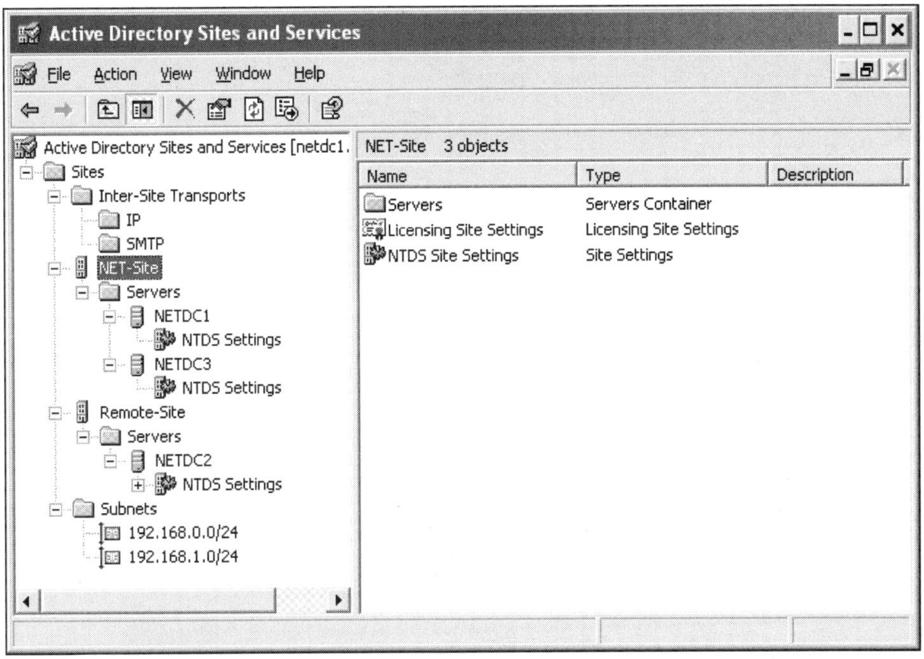

Fig. 7.17. An example of a simple network with two sites

Caching Universal Group Membership

Domain controllers running Windows .NET can store universal group membership information locally, and refresh it periodically (by default, every 8 hours). This diminishes the necessity to have a Global Catalog server in branch office locations; as well, it reduces network traffic that occurs when users are authenticated in a forest.

To enable that option:

1. In the tree pane, select a site where GC server is not designated.
2. Right click the corresponding *NTDS Site Settings* object (of the *nTDSSiteSettings* type) and select the **Properties** command on the context menu.
3. On the Site Settings tab of the Properties window, check the **Enable Universal Group Membership Caching** box and select a site from the **Refresh cache from** list (Fig. 7.18).
4. Click **Apply** and **OK**.

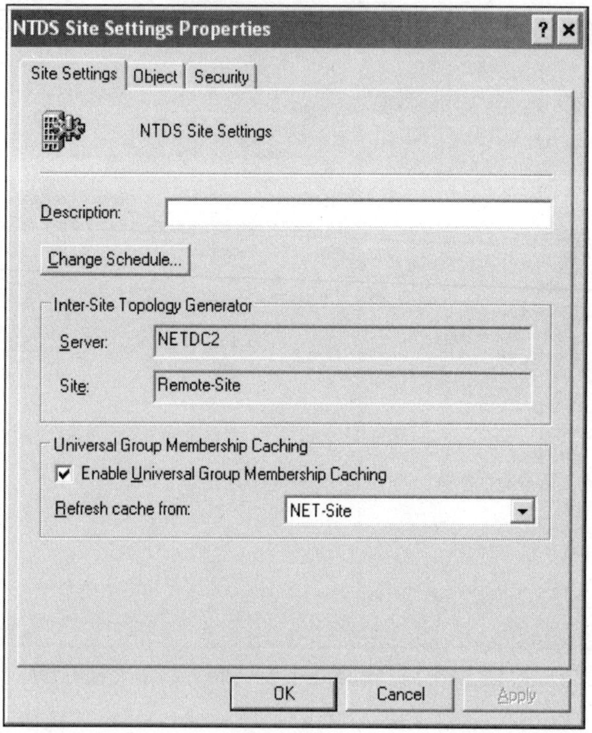

Fig. 7.18. Enabling universal group caching

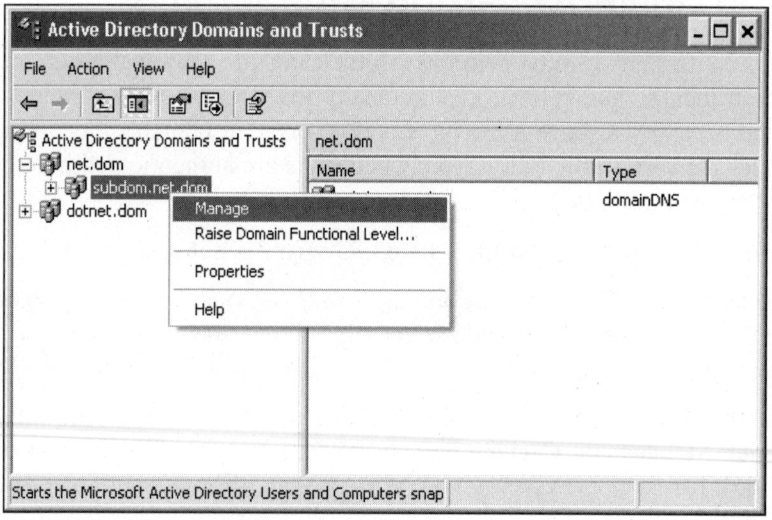

Fig. 7.19. Selecting a domain for management in the enterprise (domain forest)

Active Directory Domains and Trusts Snap-in

The **Active Directory Domains and Trusts** snap-in is an enterprise administrator's tool that allows you to look up the forest easily and select a domain for administering. Other purposes of the **Active Directory Domains and Trusts** snap-in are discussed below in detail.

An example of a forest (which contains two non-adjacent trees — *net.dom* and *dotnet.dom*) represented in the snap-in's main window is shown in Fig. 7.19. If you point to a domain in the tree and select the **Manage** command on the context or **Action** menus, the **Active Directory Users and Computer** snap-in will be started for this domain.

Raising Functional Level

Using the **Active Directory Domains and Trusts** snap-in, you can raise the domain as well as the forest functional level. In Windows 2000, a similar operation is called *changing mode* (mixed mode or native mode). Right click a domain in the domain tree and select the **Raise Domain Functional Level** command on the context menu (see Fig. 7.19). You will see a window (Fig. 7.20) that informs you about the current domain level and possible levels (if available).

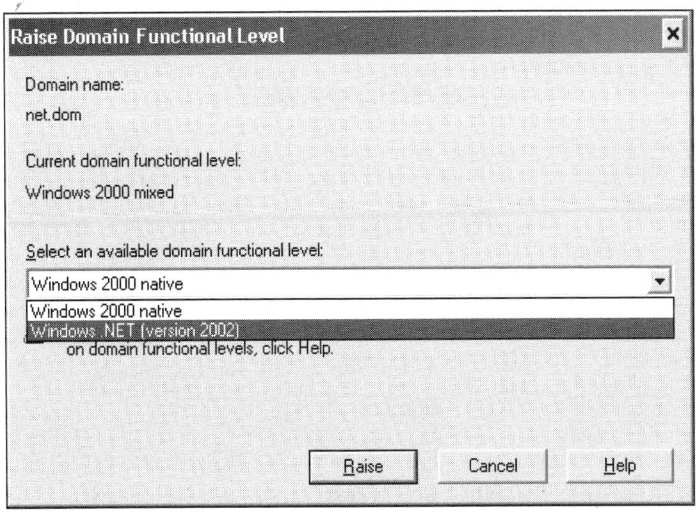

Fig. 7.20. Selecting functional level of a domain

If the domain consists of Windows .NET-based domain controllers only, you can raise the domain level to *Windows .NET (version 2002)* right away. Select a level and click **Raise**. If there are domain controllers on other platforms (Windows NT 4.0 or Windows 2000), then the operation will fail. The system will report the controllers that prevent raising the functional level. Such a report will contain lines similar to the following:

```
The following domains include domain controllers that are running earlier
versions of windows:
Domain Name Domain Controller    Version of Windows
subdom.net.dom w2kdc3.subdom.net.dom   Windows 2000 Server 5.0 (2195)
```

Otherwise, the operation will be replicated over other controllers in the same domain. Wait until replication has been completed. Then, you can verify functional levels by querying the *RootDSE* object on domain controllers (see *Chapter 1, "LDAP Basics"*).

To raise the forest level, point to the root in the tree pane (Fig. 7.21) and select the **Raise Forest Functional Level** command on the context menu. Again, all errors that have occurred will be reported.

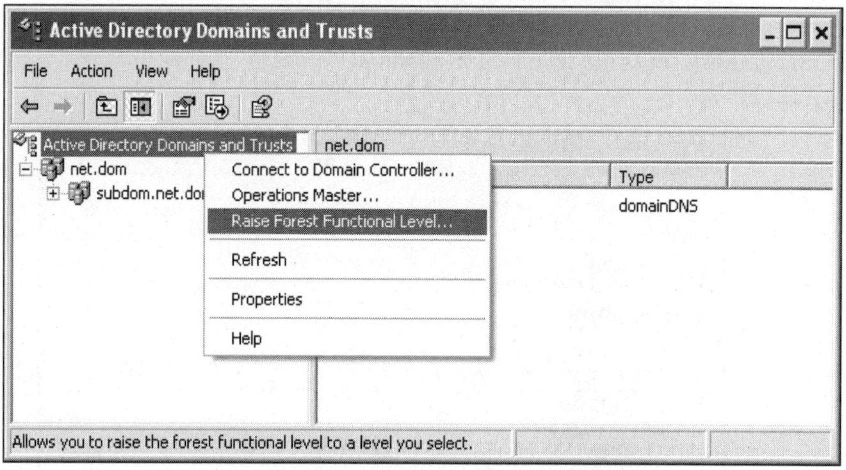

Fig. 7.21. Raising forest functional level

If two domain forests have the *Windows .NET (version 2002)* functional level, then the **Active Directory Domains and Trusts** snap-in will allow you to establish forest trusts between root domains of those forests.

Using User Principal Names (UPN)

The concept of *user principal names* can considerably simplify the logon process in large domain trees. While logging on, the domain users can use one of two methods for specifying their names. They can:

- Enter a UPN name, such as `user@DNSdomainName` (in this case, the domain list becomes unavailable).
- Enter a pre-Windows 2000 (SAM account) user name (without the "@" symbol) and then select a domain from the list.

Each method has certain advantages. It may be inconvenient to enter long domain names, such as *dom1.comp1.ent1.com*. The first method is, in fact, just a particular instance of a general format: userName@UPNSuffix. The default UPN suffix is the DNS name of that domain where a user account is located. It is possible to add alternative suffixes that can be used *by all users of a domain forest.*

To add a UPN suffix, open the **Active Directory Domain and Trusts** snap-in, point to the root in the tree pane, and select **Properties** from the context menu. Enter a suffix in the **Alternative UPN suffixes** field and click **Add** and **Apply**. The entered suffix (`net` in Fig. 7.22) will appear in the dialog box during new user creation.

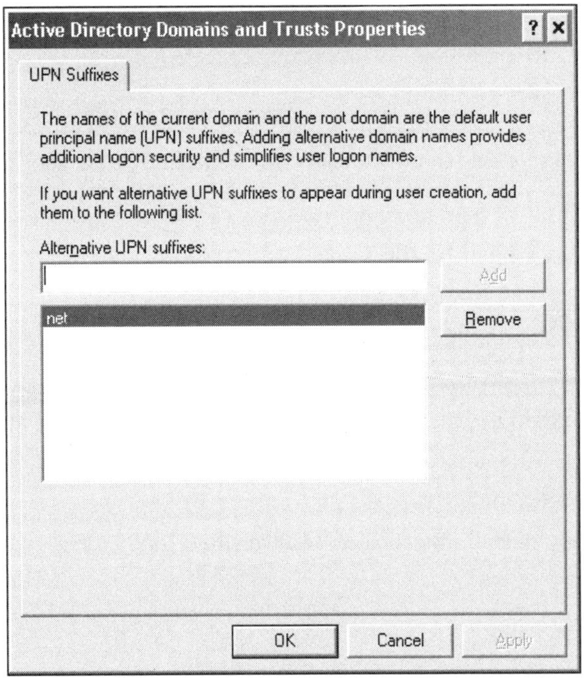

Fig. 7.22. Adding an alternative UPN suffix

Now you can choose any UPN suffix for a new user (the current domain, parent domain and alternative UPN suffixes) or change the UPN name for an existing user. Let us create, for example, a user with the logon parameters shown in Fig. 7.23. Initially, the *logon* name and the *pre-Windows 2000* name are the same, but you can specify any name you like.

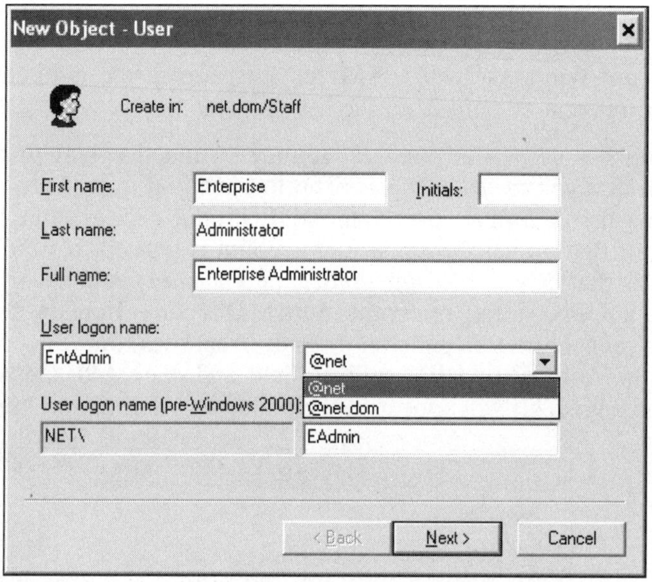

Fig. 7.23. Choosing UPN suffixes during new user creation

The created user will be able to log onto the domain tree with the following names (the password will be the same for both logon names):

- `EntAdmin@net` — UPN name
- `EAdmin` (and a domain name selected from the list) — SAM account name

You can also check these names using the **ADSI Edit** snap-in (*sAMAccountName* is a mandatory attribute, and *userPrincipalName* is an optional attribute).

Note

Notice that, by default, the "built-in" Administrator and Guest accounts do not have UPN names.

Attention

- UPN names are not supported by Windows 9*x*/ME clients.

Understandably, all account names must be unique. SAM account (pre-Windows 2000) names in the same domain cannot be repeated. A *full name* must not be used more than once in an OU. However, the same full name *can* be used for accounts in *different* OUs (because the canonical names of objects will differ, e.g., `domain.com/OU1/John Smith` and `domain.com/OU2/John Smith`), provided that the UPN and SAM account names are different (e.g., `jsmith@domain.com` and `johnSmith@domain.com; JSMITH` and `JOHNS`).

Verifying Trusts

A domain administrator can use the **Active Directory Domains and Trusts** snap-in for verifying trusts between domains and for creating new trusts. This process primarily concerns trusts with Windows NT 4.0 domains. Such trusts must be *manually* created (see *Chapter 5, "Installing Active Directory"*).

However, you may also want to create explicit, unidirectional trusts between AD-based domains that belong to different domain trees (or forests — if the forest trusts are established) or even to the same tree. This, for instance, may be required in order to reduce logon time into a *"remote"* domain. Here, "remote" is related to the "distance" between domains in a tree structure. (All considerations stated are even applicable to *transitive* Kerberos trusts.)

For example, the *dom1.comp1.ent1.com* and *dom2.comp2.ent2.com* domains (Fig. 7.24) can be regarded as "remote", because trusts between trees in a forest are established through the root domains.

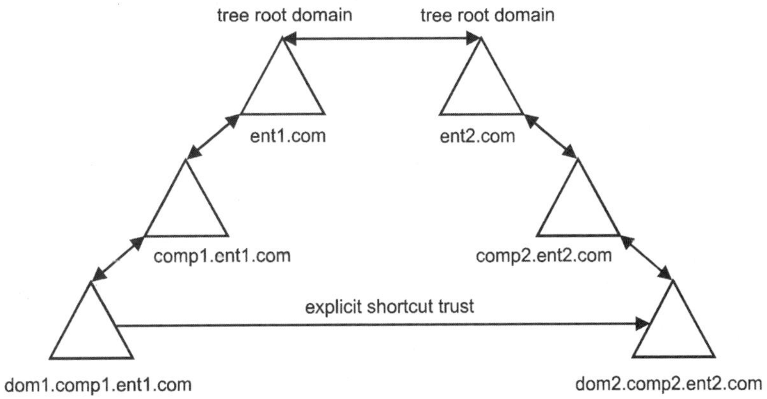

Fig. 7.24. A shortcut trust between two "remote" domains

To check a trust between domains:

1. Open the **Properties** window for a domain.
2. Select a trust on the **Trusts** tab and click **Properties** (in Windows 2000 — **Edit**).

3. In the next window, click **Validate** (in Windows 2000 — **Verify**). If the trust is operational, you should see the message: "The trust has been verified. It is in place and active." If the system reports an error and proposes that you reset the trust, confirm the operation. Usually, the trusts will be reset successfully. In Windows .NET, you can simultaneously verify both sides of two-way trusts if you know a domain administrator's credentials in the second domain.

   You can also use the *NetDom* tool for verifying and resetting trusts.

ADSI Edit Snap-in

The **ADSI Edit** snap-in, which is included in the *Support Tools* pack, is a tool that provides "low-level" access to Active Directory. It allows you to perform the following operations:

- Connect to any directory partitions (including application partitions).
- Connect directly to any Active Directory object using its distinguished name.
- View, move, rename, and modify any attribute of any object.
- Tune security settings down to a single attribute.
- Perform a query through a whole domain tree and save it.
- Create and delete objects of any type.
- Connect to Global Catalog servers.

Connecting to Namespaces

The newly installed **ADSI Edit** snap-in is configured for work with three Active Directory namespaces (contexts, or partitions):

- Domain (*DC=domainName, DC=com*)
- Configuration (CN=Configuration, *DC=domainName, DC=com*)
- Schema (CN=Schema, CN=Configuration, *DC=domainName, DC=com*)

The first namespace is replicated among all DCs that belong to the same domain. The other two are replicated over every DC in the domain tree.

The **ADSI Edit** snap-in allows you to connect to any application directory partitions. There are two default (built-in) application partitions that can be created on a DC and used by the DNS server installed on the same DC (see *Chapter 3, "Domain Name System (DNS) as Main Naming Service"*):

- ForestDnsZones (DN=ForestDnsZones, *DC=domainName, DC=com*)
- DomainDnsZones (DN=Schema, CN=Configuration, *DC=domainName, C=com*)

There is one more object, which the **ADSI Edit** snap-in can be connected to: RootDSE

Note

Note that the Windows 2000 version of **ADSI Edit** only shows the informational (LDAP) attributes of the RootDSE object. Operational (system specific) attributes, such as *isSynchronized* or *isGlobalCatalogReady* are not accessible. The Windows .NET version of the tools displays all RootDSE's attributes.

You can also add the standalone **ADSI Edit** snap-in to any MMC console opened in the author mode. In this case, it is added without any connection. If you create your own MMC console, you have a feature such as the **Favorites** tab, which can be very helpful for working with multilevel tree structures and various Active Directory objects (which all have very long LDAP names).

To make a new connection, point the root node in the tree pane and select the **Connect to** command from the context menu. Enter any string you want in the **Name** field and specify the distinguished name of an object, or select a predefined namespace from the **Naming Context** list (Fig. 7.25). You may also enter a domain or server name different from the default one.

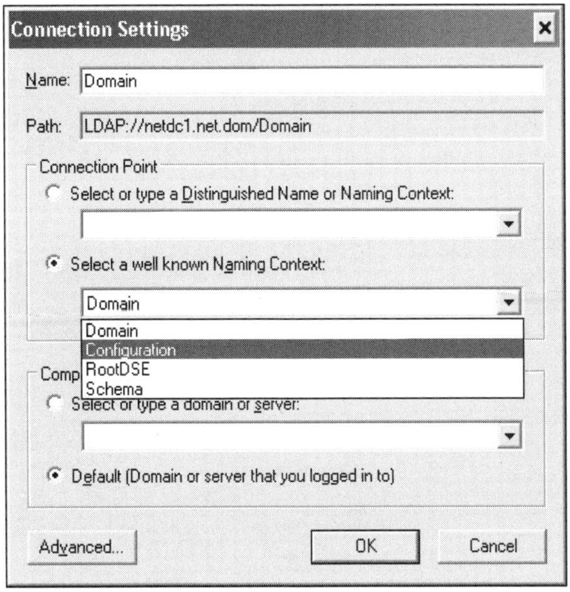

Fig. 7.25. Connecting to a namespace

You can also create a connection to any object while browsing through the object tree. Point to an object and select **New Connection from here** in the context menu. All new connections are saved upon exit from the snap-in.

In the **Advanced** window (click **Advanced** in the **Connection** window) you can specify alternative credentials, a port number, or choose the protocol: LDAP or Global Catalog. To view or modify the current properties of a connection, select the **Settings** command from the context menu for this connection. Any connection may be deleted with the **Remove** command.

Editing Attributes of Active Directory Objects

Let us see how to work with the **ADSI Edit** snap-in in the two following examples that contain some tips which may be useful for an administrator.

Example 1. Hiding Directory Objects from Browsing

Using the example of the `showInAdvancedViewOnly` attribute (see the *"Advanced Features Mode"* section), let us discuss how to locate attributes of an Active Directory object and modify their values.

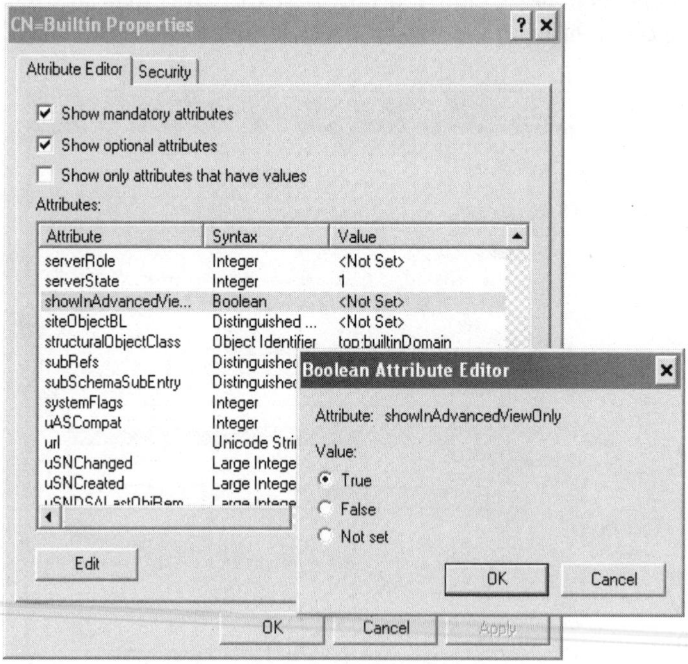

Fig. 7.26. Finding and editing an attribute of an Active Directory object

Suppose we would like to hide the *Builtin* container from browsing. Point to it in the tree pane of the **ADSI Edit** snap-in and click **Properties** on the toolbar. In the opened window, the Attributes pane (in Windows 2000 — the **Select a property to view** drop-down list) contains all attributes of the selected object. You can quickly locate an attribute in the list by typing in the first few characters of the attribute's name (Fig. 7.26).

When the attribute has been selected, select **True** in the **Boolean Attribute Editor** window and click **OK,** then **Apply**. (In Windows 2000, enter the new value `TRUE`, or `true` — it does not matter — into the **Edit Attribute** field and click **Set,** then **Apply**.) To delete the value of an attribute, click either **Clear** or **Non set**. If the attribute is multi-valued, select a value, and click **Remove**.

Example 2. Enabling Creation of Containers through User Interface

This example shows how to modify the schema by using **ADSI Edit**.

By default, you cannot create a new object of the *Container* type using the **Active Directory Users and Computers** snap-in. Sometimes it may be useful to have such an option for organizing directory objects. (You might also wish to enable the creation of any other object types.) To create this option, it is necessary to modify the schema.

1. If you have not yet connected to the schema name context, do so now.
2. Open the schema folder and find the container class (`CN=Container`).
3. In the **Properties** window, select the optional *defaultHidingValue* attribute (the default value is `TRUE`).
4. Set value to `False`, then click **Apply** and **OK**.
5. Point to the **Schema** node and select **Update Schema Now** from the context menu.

If the schema cache has been updated successfully, open the **Active Directory Users and Computers** snap-in (restart it, if it has been already opened) and check that the container object has appeared in the **Action** | **New** menu.

Creating a Custom Query

A *query* in the **ADSI Edit** snap-in is a custom template for displaying only desired objects in the tree pane. (This is an analog to saved queries in the **Active Directory Users and Computers** snap-in.) This makes working with large numbers of objects or objects related to different Active Directory containers simpler. The queries can be created in any Active Directory namespace (partitions), but remember that since a namespace belongs to a specific domain, the queries work within the borders of one domain only.

Let us create a query for all published folders. Point to the node related to the domain context and select the **New | Query** command in the context menu. Give the new query any name you like (Fig. 7.27) and click **Browse** to define a container — the root of the search. In our case, it will be the root domain (*net.dom*).

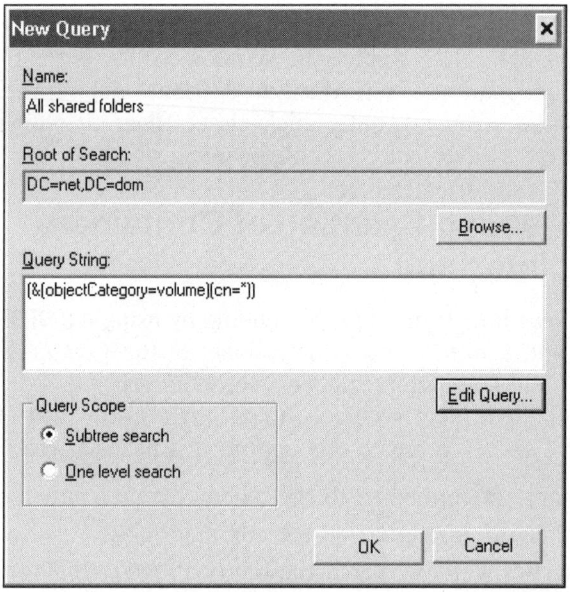

Fig. 7.27. This window contains the parameters necessary for creating a custom query

The next step is to define the query itself. You can either directly enter a query in the **Query String** field or click **Edit Query** and start the wizard that helps to create a custom filter (see the "*Filter Options*" section, Fig. 7.13). The generated string is displayed in the **Query String** field. (Remember the limitations of custom filters!)

To see *all* folders, you must specify the **Is present** option (the "*" character) for the folder name. Select the appropriate query scope — **Subtree Search** or **One Level Search**.

An example of the resulting display is shown in Fig. 7.28. Notice (in the **Distinguished Name** column) that the selected folders are related to *different* OUs in the same domain. This means that you have really searched the entire domain.

All queries are saved upon snap-in closing, and refreshed upon its loading. You can refresh the contents of a query at any time. To edit a query, select **Setting** from the query's context menu.

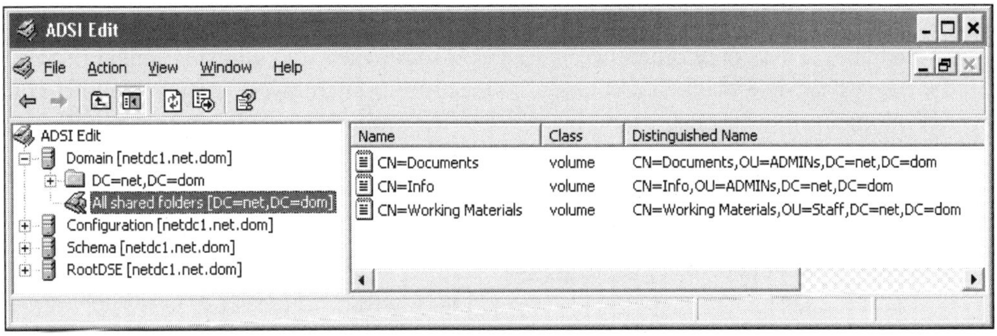

Fig. 7.28. The query that allows you to work with all published folders in the whole domain forest

Creating Active Directory Objects

Using the **ADSI Edit** snap-in, you can create Active Directory objects of any type. However, it can hardly be recommended that you do so, because of a high probability of errors with object attributes: you must be familiar with the meaning of all mandatory and optional attributes and their valid values. Using the "standard" administrative snap-ins and tools is much more preferable.

If, nevertheless, you do decide to create an object manually, point to the desired object in the tree pane and select the **New | Object** command. The wizard will start and ask you for all required values. The list of possible new objects depends on the type of object selected initially. (See also *"Extending the Schema"* in *Chapter 16, "Active Directory Service Interfaces (ADSI)."*)

Working with Global Catalog

Being able to work directly with a global catalog (GC) server may be helpful while troubleshooting the problems related to GC replication. You can connect to different GC servers and compare the values of stored attributes (see also the description of *DsaStat.exe* in *Chapter 11, "Verifying Network and Distributed Services"*). You can also verify the representation of attributes in a GC. (This process can be controlled via the **Active Directory Schema Manager** snap-in, see the next section.)

Note

Only some of Active Directory object's attributes are presented in Global Catalog. When you have enabled/disabled replication of an attribute to Global Catalog, you may wish to use the **ADSI Edit** snap-in to verify the presence of this attribute on a GC server.

In general, the procedures for working with Global Catalog are the same as described above. The only difference is that you must select the **Global Catalog** protocol in the **Advanced** window when creating a connection to an Active Directory naming context (partition). It must be clear that it is impossible to *create* new objects in Global Catalog.

Active Directory Schema Manager Snap-in

The **Active Directory Schema Manager** snap-in is the preferred GUI tool (the other one is the **ADSI Edit** snap-in; its usage requires that you have a more advanced familiarity with Active Directory's interiors) that allows viewing and modifying of Active Directory classes and the attributes the classes contain. (Two other ways to extend the schema are scripting and using command-line tools, such as LDIFDE and CSVDE.) This snap-in allows an administrator to view X.500 OIDs of classes and attributes, a range of values for attributes, mandatory and optional attributes for classes, and other meta-information on attributes and classes.

Installation

The **Active Directory Schema Manager** snap-in is installed by default on domain controllers. This snap-in is also included in the *Windows Administration Tools* pack, and can be installed onto any computer with Windows XP/.NET. (Windows 2000 has its own version of that tool.) It appears neither on the **Start** menu nor in the Control Panel, and should be manually added to an MMC console. (If the snap-in is installed as a part of Windows Administration Tools, it does appear on the **Start** menu as well as other administrative snap-ins.) You only need to first register the DLL by entering the following command at the command prompt:

```
regsvr32 schmmgmt.dll
```

You should get the message shown in Fig. 7.29.

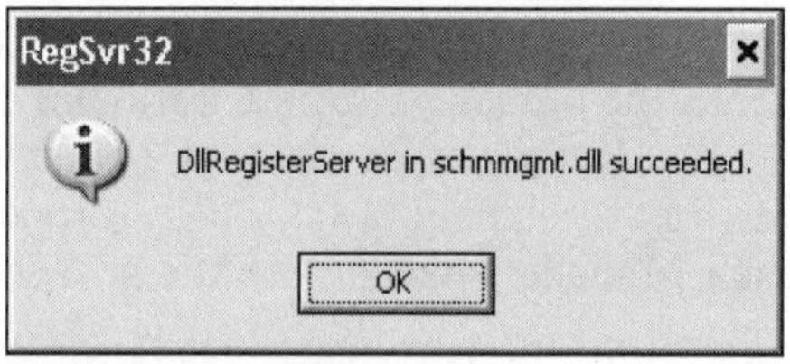

Fig. 7.29. This message will appear if the DLL-file is registered successfully

If you install *Windows Administrative Tools* on a computer (see *Chapter 8, "Common Administrative Tasks"*), the appropriate DLL is registered automatically.

After schmmgmt.dll is registered on a computer, you can create an MMC document (which is a console saved with any name you like) containing the **Active Directory Schema Manager** snap-in, or add the snap-in to an existing custom console.

Modifying the Schema

All modifications of the schema are only permitted on the DC that possesses the Schema Master FSMO role. It is highly recommended that you adhere to this requirement.

Note

To find the Schema Master in a forest, use the following command: `dsquery server -hasfsmo schema`.

In Windows 2000, by default, the modification of the schema is disabled. Therefore, to modify the schema, start the **Active Directory Schema Manager** snap-in (which by default is targeted to the Schema Master) and set first the flag **The Schema may be modified on this Domain Controller** in the **Change Schema Master** window. After this, you can change the schema itself and schema access permissions. In Windows .NET, this flag is absent.

Attention

- By default, only members of the Schema Admins group can modify the schema. It is, however, also possible to grant this permission to other people.

  The schema's updates are dumped from cache to disk every 5 minutes. You can manually reload the schema to force this process.

Modification and, in particular, extension of the schema, require a profound understanding of Active Directory concepts and classes structure, and this could be the theme of a separate book. (Some basic information on this question is given in *Chapter 16, "Active Directory Service Interfaces (ADSI)."*) However, in routine work an administrator may want to perform the following operations (these are the names of checkboxes at the **General** tab in the **Properties** window of an attribute or a class; see Fig. 7.31):

- **Attribute (class) is active** (in Windows 2000, a similar flag **Deactivate this attribute (class)** has an opposite meaning). If a newly created (e.g., a test) attribute or class is not yet used (i.e., there are no new objects of that class, or that attribute has not been added to a class) in Active Directory, you may "disable" it. (You cannot *delete* attributes and classes in Active Directory.) Such an attribute or class is considered to be *defunct.* In Windows .NET, it is possible to *redefine* and *reactivate* it.

- **Index this attribute in the Active Directory.** Indexing of an attribute speeds up the frequently used query operations that include the attribute.
- **Replicate this attribute to the Global Catalog.** If an attribute is included in Global Catalog, you can get the attribute's values when performing forest-wide queries.
- **Show objects of this class while browsing.** This flag controls the state of the *showInAdvancedViewOnly* attribute (see above *"Hiding Directory Objects from Browsing"*). If this flag is set, the attribute's value is `FALSE`. The flag possibly affects the custom (newly created) classes only.

To carry out these operations, expand the **Attributes** or **Classes** node in the tree pane and find the desired attribute or class. Open the **Properties** window and set the appropriate flag on the **General** tab.

Caution

After a new attribute has been added to the global catalog, a forest-wide replication is triggered. (This is the case regarding *all schema modification* operations.) This can result in significant network traffic. Therefore, this operation should not be performed often and should be well planned.

Extending the Schema

Extension of the schema is not a particularly complicated operation, but nonetheless, it is a very crucial one. You must always remember that all extensions of the schema are not reversible (even if you restore Active Directory from a backup copy!) and may result in significant forest-wide replication traffic.

Let us discuss how to create a new attribute and class on a few examples. (See also about extending the schema in *Chapter 16, "Active Directory Service Interfaces (ADSI)"* and *Chapter 17, "Scripting Administrative Tasks."*)

Creating an Attribute

Before creating an attribute, you must carry out the following operations:

- Choose the attribute's common and LDAP display names according to Microsoft recommendations.
- Obtain the base X.500 OID (see *Chapter 16*) and add your specific attribute ID to it.
- Select the attribute's syntax.
- Choose the minimum and maximum values for the attribute (optional).

Attention

- The base X.500 OIDs — one for classes and one for attributes — are obtained only *once* for your organization. Then you can add your own increasing IDs to the base OIDs.

When you have gathered all this information, point to the **Attributes** node in the tree pane and click **Create Attribute** in the context menu. Click **Continue** in the warning window. Fill in the fields in the **Create New Attribute** window. (All fields except **Minimum** and **Maximum** are mandatory.) Click **OK**. Fig. 7.30 displays sample information necessary for the creation of a string attribute.

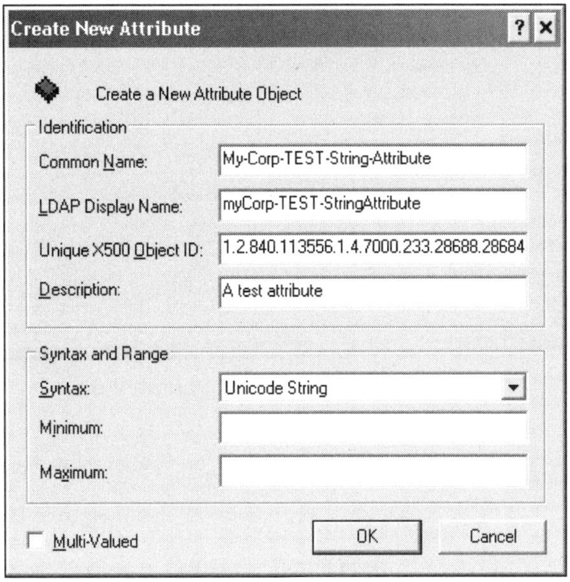

Fig. 7.30. An example of creating a new string attribute

Attention

- In Windows 2000, if you receive the "Schema update failed in recalculating validation cache" error, verify the selected OID. Windows .NET provides more specific diagnostic messages.

Now you can find the new attribute on the list, view the attribute's properties (Fig. 7.31), give a description to it, and set the necessary flags (checkboxes). At this point, you can use the created attribute, i.e., add it to an existing class(es) (see below and in *Chapter 17, "Scripting Administrative Tasks"*).

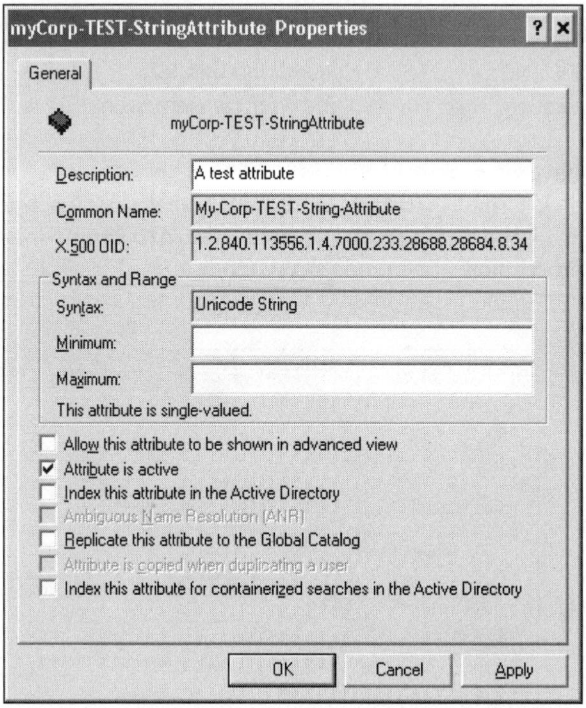

Fig. 7.31. Properties of an attribute

Creating a Class

To create a class, you must gather the following information:

- The class's common and LDAP display names according to Microsoft recommendations
- The base X.500 OID (and add your specific class ID to it)
- The type of class (commonly, *structural*) and the parent class (optional; *top* by default)
- The lists of mandatory and optional attributes of the class (if a structural or auxiliary class inherits only the attributes from the parent and does not have its own attributes, why create such a class?)
- The possible superior(s) — the container(s), in which creation of the class's objects is permitted

Point to the **Classes** node in the tree pane and click **Create Class** in the context menu. Click **Continue** in the warning window. Fill in the fields in the **Create New Schema Class** window. Fig. 7.32 illustrates this step. Click **Next**.

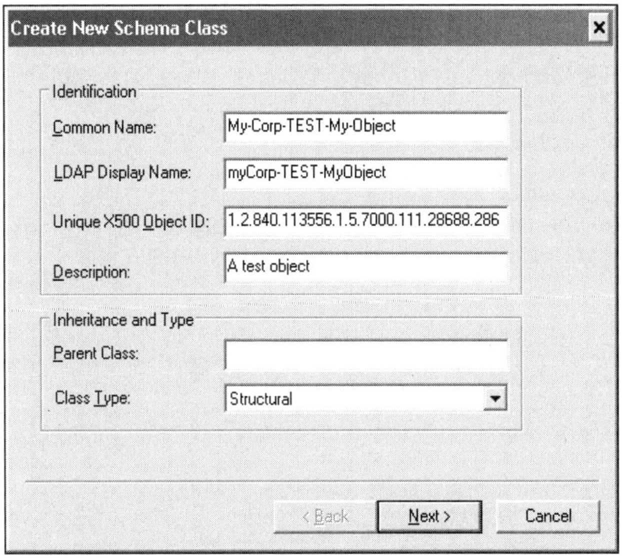

Fig. 7.32. The first step in creating a new object class

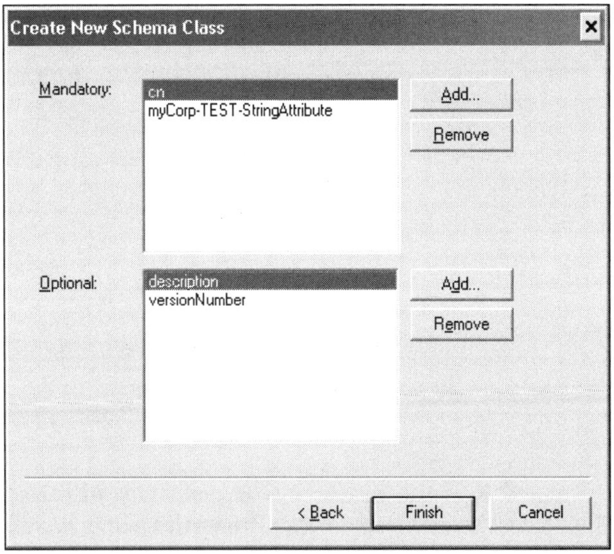

Fig. 7.33. In this window, you can add mandatory and optional attributes

In the next window (Fig. 7.33), you can add mandatory and optional attributes to the class. If you leave both lists empty, the new class will have only the attributes of the parent class. You can add and remove attributes until you click **Finish**.

Attention

- It is possible to add optional attributes to a class at any time, but the mandatory attributes are added only at the class's creation.

To define a *possible superior* for the new class, select the class from the list, open the **Properties** window, and click the **Relationship** tab (Fig. 7.34). Add the necessary class, click **Apply**, and close the window. You have now created a new class.

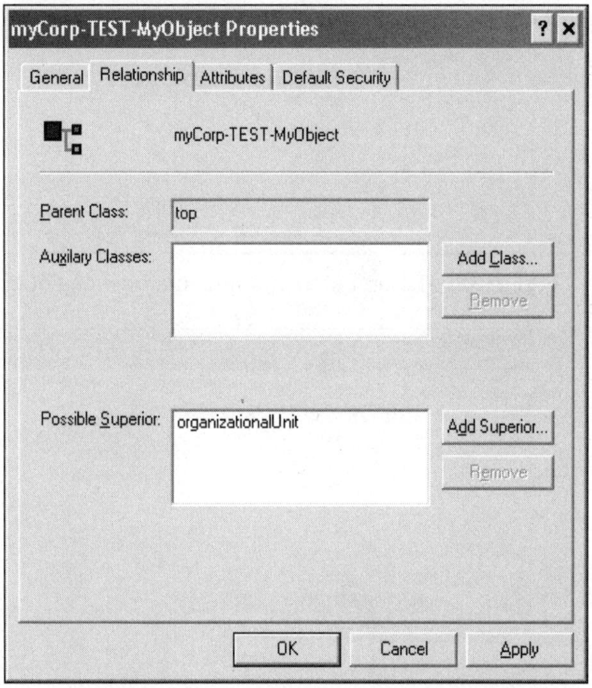

Fig. 7.34. This window allows you to add auxiliary classes to a class and to define containers (possible superiors), in which objects of that class can be created

If the class created is of the *auxiliary* type, you may wish to add it to an existing class. To do this, select a class, open the **Properties** window, click the **Relationship** tab, and add the new class to the **Auxiliary Classes** list (Fig. 7.34).

Adding Attributes to Existing Classes

It is possible to add newly created or existing attributes to classes — new or standard ones. Select the applicable class from the list and open the **Properties** window.

You can add necessary attributes to the **Optional** tab on the **Attributes** tab: click **Add** and choose an attribute from the **Select Schema Object** list. Click **Apply** and close the window. Reload the schema or wait until the schema's updates are written to disk. Then the new attributes of the class will be "visible" in other administrative tools.

Group Policy Object Editor Snap-in

The main purpose of the **Group Policy Object Editor**[1] snap-in is the editing of a group policy object (GPO) stored locally on a computer or in Active Directory, and linked (in the second case) to an Active Directory container: a site, a domain, or an OU.

In Windows 2000, you should have a solid understanding of the difference between the **Group Policy Object Editor** snap-in and the **Security Policy** — **Local**, **Domain Controller**, or **Domain** — snap-ins. (These last three snap-ins are configured by default on every DC; the **Local Security Policy** snap-in is also configured on every client Windows 2000 system.)

The **Group Policy Object Editor** snap-in works with an *entire* GPO, and can be run from certain administrative snap-ins or from a custom MMC console. It contains both computer and user policies (the **Computer Configuration** and **User Configuration** nodes of GPO).

The **Security Policy** snap-ins deal *only* with the **Security Setting** sub-node of the corresponding GPO, and can be run from the **Start** menu (the **Administrative Tools** submenu). These snap-ins allow you to configure computer policies only.

In Windows .NET, the **Security Policy** snap-ins are always configured to work with entire GPOs.

Note

Do not forget about two other important snap-ins — **Security Configuration and Analysis** and **Security Templates** — that also help an administrator to deploy Active Directory security in an enterprise. Due to space limitations and other reasons, these snap-ins are not discussed in this book.

Note

See *Chapter 8, "Common Administrative Tasks,"* about refreshing your computer (machine) and/or user policies after editing a GPO's parameters.

---

[1] In Windows 2000, this snap-in is called **Group Policy**.

Linking to a Group Policy Object (GPO)

A running **Group Policy Object Editor** snap-in is always linked to a GPO. Therefore, you need to learn two things: how to start the snap-in itself, and how to link it to a GPO.

There are three ways to start the **Group Policy Object Editor** snap-in:

- From the **Active Directory Users and Computers** snap-in — select the domain or an OU, open the **Properties** window, and click the **Group Policy** tab (Fig. 7.35).

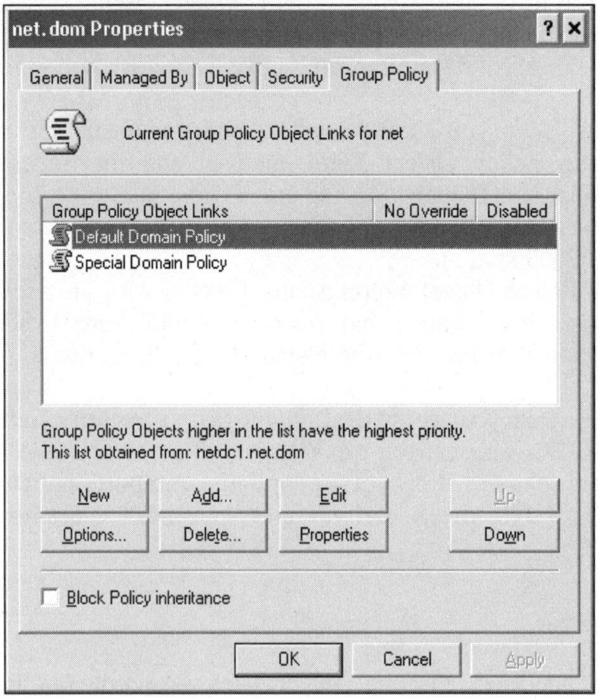

Fig. 7.35. A sample list of GPOs linked to a domain container

- From the **Active Directory Sites and Services** snap-in — select a site, open the **Properties** window, and click the **Group Policy** tab.
- From Microsoft Management Console (MMC) — start MMC (enter `mmc` in the **Run** window) or open a custom console, and add the **Group Policy Object Editor** snap-in. The **Select Group Policy Object** window allows you to link to the local GPO (default option) on the local computer (it is also possible to select another computer). An alternative option is to open the **Browse for a Group Policy Object** window (by clicking **Browse)** (see Fig. 7.36).

In two first cases, you have three options:

- *Select* an existing GPO (i.e., already linked) in the list and edit it by using the **Group Policy Object Editor** snap-in
- *Create* a new GPO that will be linked to the selected container
- *Add* (link) an existing GPO to the container

From a MMC console, you can only *select* an existing GPO.

Let us discuss the last case (use of MMC). If you click **Add** on the **Group Policy** tab, the **Browse for a Group Policy Object** window will open. An example of the default view of such a window is shown in Fig. 7.36. (You may click the circled icon and create a new GPO.)

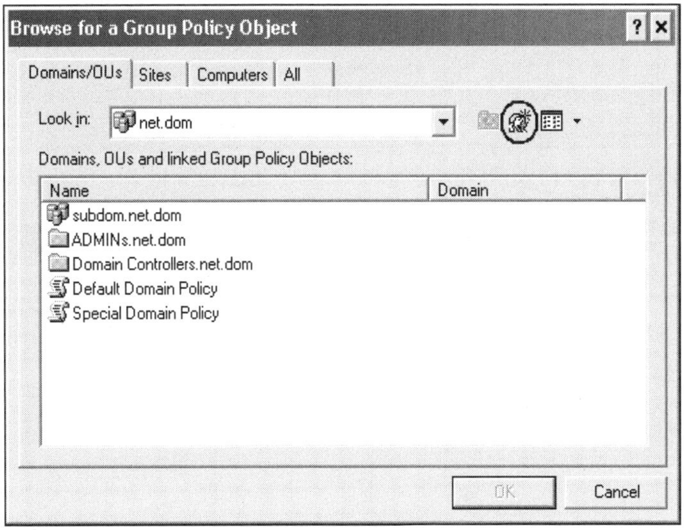

Fig. 7.36. In this window, you can see the entire structure of OUs in a domain as well as the GPOs linked to them

As shown in Fig. 7.37, all GPOs that exist in a domain are listed in the **All** tab, so you can quickly find the necessary GPO.

Important

- When the **Group Policy Object Editor** snap-in is opened or a custom MMC console is created, it is not possible to *re-link* the snap-in to another GPO.

You *cannot change* the DC with which the **Group Policy Object Editor** snap-in works (therefore, the default **Security Policy** snap-ins, too) (see later *"Selecting a Domain Controller"*, and it is not possible to connect to a local GPO stored on another computer.

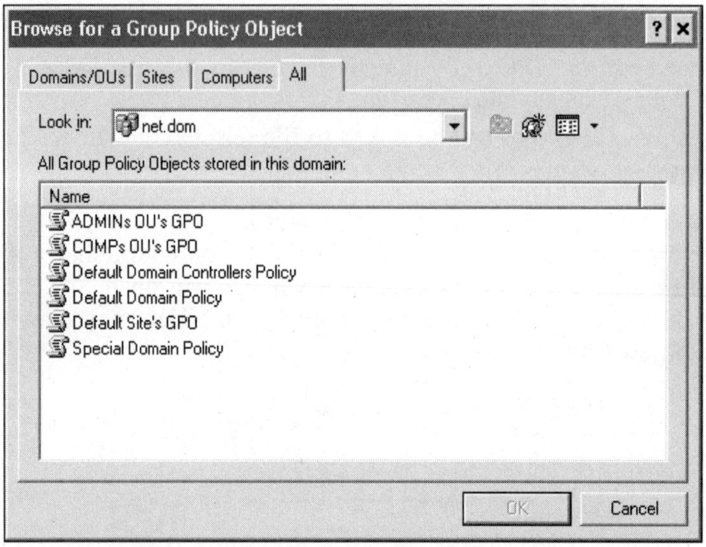

Fig. 7.37. Use this tab to quickly find a GPO that you want to link to the current container

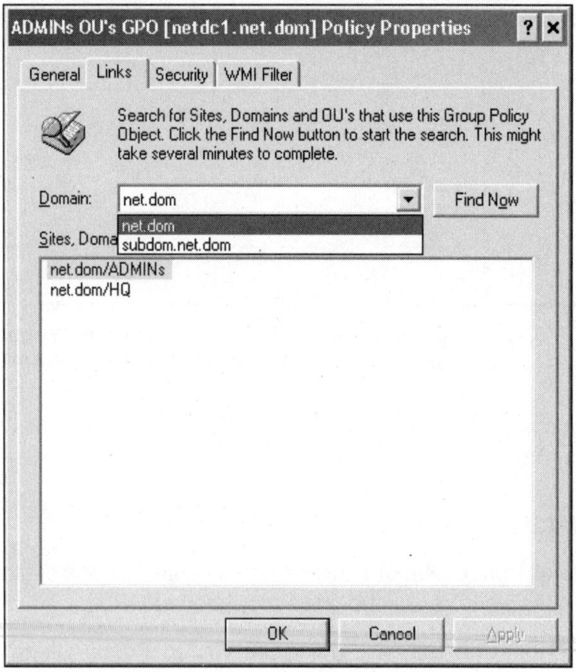

Fig. 7.38. You can quickly verify whether the selected GPO is linked to other containers besides the current one

You can check which containers the selected GPO is currently linked to. In the **Group Policy Object Editor** snap-in's window, point to the root node in the tree pane and open the **Properties** window for the GPO. Click **Links** tab (Fig. 7.38). Select an applicable domain and click **Find Now**. If the GPO is linked to other containers, you will see their names on the list in addition to the name of the current container.

Attention

- Due to possible security and administrative conflicts, it is not advisable to link GPOs stored in a domain to containers from another domain.

Creating and Deleting a GPO

To create a GPO, it is sufficient to click **New** on the **Group Policy** tab in a container's **Properties** window (see Fig. 7.35), or to click the button in the **Browse for a Group Policy Object** window (see Fig. 7.36). Name the new GPO, and you may then begin editing it.

When you are going to delete a GPO, you have two options:

- **Remove the link from the list.** When selecting this option, you break only the link between the selected GPO and the current container. The GPO remains intact, and you can use it later.
- **Remove the link and delete the Group Policy Object permanently.** As the message indicates, this is a more decisive option, since you not only break the link, but entirely delete the GPO. (Remember that this GPO can be used by other containers!)

WMI Filters

In Windows .NET-based domains, you are able to "link" a GPO to a specific property of client computer. Let me explain this in the following example.

Suppose we want to assign some group policy settings (a GPO) to users (or computers) that work on Windows 2000 Professional systems only, and that GPO will in no way affect the other users (or computers). The following procedure will permit us to carry out this task:

1. Create a new GPO. (You can select an existing GPO. However, it would be better to use a new GPO and link it to a container only when all configuration operations are completed.)
2. Configure al necessary policies.
3. Open the GPO's **Properties** window and click the **WMI Filter** tab (Fig. 7.39).

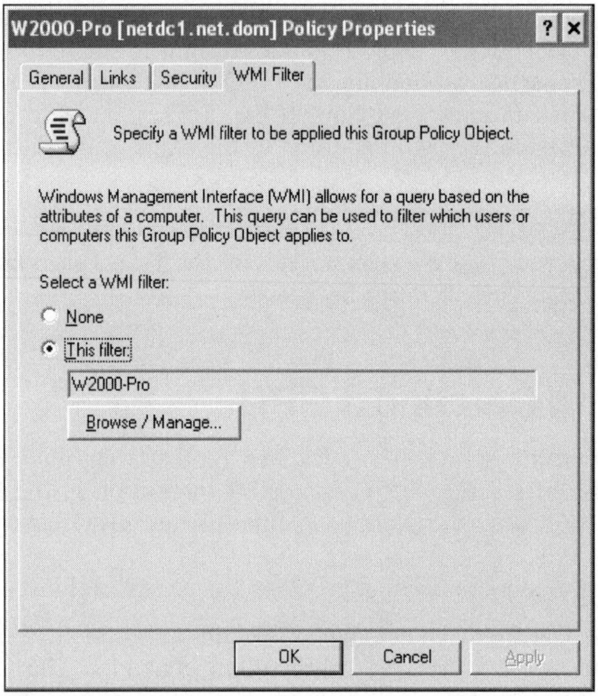

Fig. 7.39. This tab allows you to select a WMI filter and link it to the GPO selected

4. Click **This filter** and **Browse/Manage**.
5. The **Manage WMI Filters** window will allow you to create, delete, and edit WMI filters as well as to perform other operations. To create a filter, click **Advanced** and **New**.
6. Fill in the **Name** and **Description** (optional) fields and enter a WMI query string in the **Queries** pane (Fig. 7.40). (See information on WMI in *Chapter 17*, "*Scripting Administrative Tasks*".) For our task, we shall use the following string:

```
SELECT * FROM Win32_OperationSystem WHERE
↳ caption="Microsoft Windows 2000 Professional"
```

7. Click **Save** and **OK**.
8. In the **Properties** window, click **Apply** and **OK**.
9. Link the GPO to a necessary container (domain, OU).

From the **Manage WMI Filters** window you can manipulate (edit, export, etc.) all WMI filters stored in the system. Many examples of WMI filters can be found in the *Help and Support Center*.

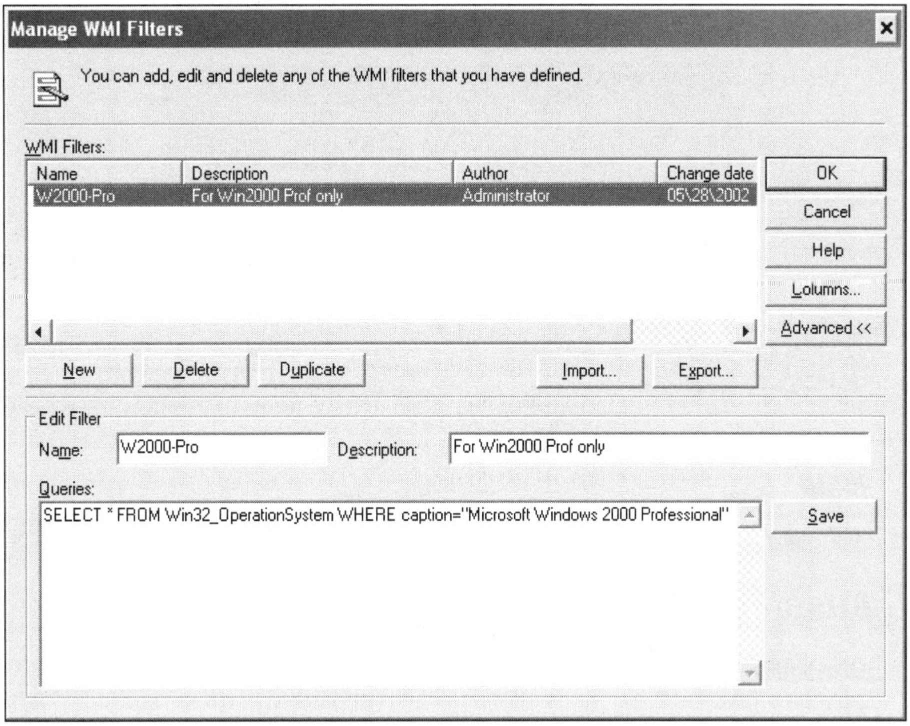

Fig. 7.40. Managing WMI filters

Selecting a Domain Controller

A **Group Policy Object Editor** snap-in is always targeted to a specific —"preferred"— domain controller. (Notice the **This list obtained from...** line in Fig. 7.35. By default, all **Group Policy Object Editor** snap-ins started on computers that belong to the sample domain *net.dom* will select the same DC.) There are some rules that define this behavior of the snap-in. To verify or change the default settings of a **Group Policy Object Editor** snap-in, point to the root node in the tree pane and click **View | DC Options** in the context menu. You can select one of the options shown in Fig. 7.41. (This selection may be overridden by a group policy; see later.)

It is necessary to comment only the second option. You can start the **Group Policy Object Editor** snap-in from either the **Active Directory Users and Computers** or the **Active Directory Sites and Services** snap-in, which is targeted to a DC (any DC in the forest) at that moment. If you select the second option, the **Group Policy Object Editor** snap-in will obtain a group policy setting from a GPO stored on *that* DC.

The selected option is saved and used when the snap-in runs the next time.

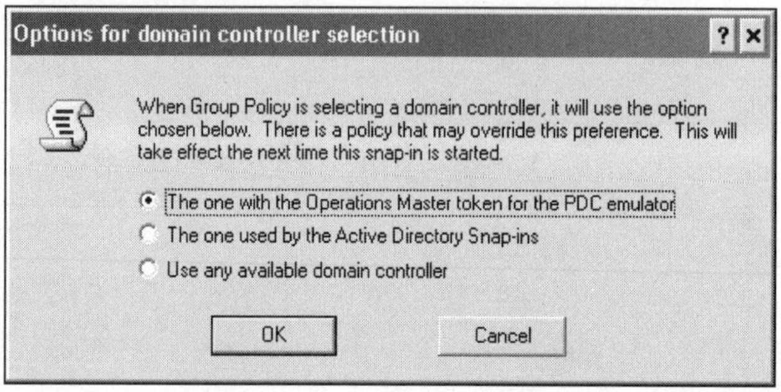

Fig. 7.41. These options determine which DC the **Group Policy Object Editor** snap-in selects at its startup

Note

In Windows 2000, you cannot define the "preferred" DC for the **Security Policy** snap-ins.

Attention

If the selected DC is not accessible at the snap-in's startup, an error will be reported. Verify the setting (and the policy if defined), and select another option if necessary.

A window similar to shown in Fig. 7.41 will appear when you start the **Group Policy Object Editor** snap-in from an administrative snap-in and the PDC Emulator is not accessible at the moment. In that case, you can select any option except the first one and obtain a GPO from another DC.

Because the DNS is used for locating GPOs, the errors at the **Group Policy Object Editor** snap-in's startup are very often related to the malfunctioning of DNS. Therefore, always verify the DNS configuration when you encounter such errors. Remember that DNS is a dynamic system, and the registered records periodically expire.

There is a group policy that allows an administrator to define the strategy of selecting a "preferred" DC. Open the *Default Domain Policy* GPO (or other applicable GPO) and select the **User Configuration | Administrative Templates | System | Group Policy** node. Double click the **Group Policy domain controller selection** policy. Click **Enable** and select one of the following options:

- Use the Primary Domain Controller
- Inherit from the Active Directory Snap-ins
- Use any available domain controller

If this policy is disabled or not configured, the **Group Policy Object Editor** snap-in will always select the PDC Operation Master (PDC Emulator) for the domain. When defined, the policy overrides the option selected in the **Group Policy Object Editor** snap-in.

Note

How to run the **Group Policy Object Editor** snap-in from the command prompt, see the *"Running GPO Editor"* section in the next chapter.

Configuring Group Policy Objects

In Windows .NET, the user interface of the **Group Policy Object Editor** snap-in has been enhanced. As you can see in Fig. 7.42, all nodes (primarily, the **Administrative Templates**) comprise two tabs — **Extended** and **Standard**. If you select a policy on the **Extended** tab, you can view the policy description and OS requirements. This information is a good substitute for many pages of documentation and makes learning the policy purpose and selection of a proper policy considerably simpler. In Windows 2000, the policy description is only available on the **Explain** tab in the policy's **Properties** window.

There are some common recommendations and tips for using and configuring GPOs. Let us discuss them.

- Disable unused settings in a GPO. This improves performance when a computer or user is logged onto the domain. Open the **Properties** window of the GPO (see Fig. 7.38 where the **Links** tab of this window is shown) and click the **General** tab. Check the appropriate box: **Disable Computer Configuration settings** or **Disable User Configuration settings**. When both boxes are disabled, it means that the GPO is linked to the container, but does not affect it.
- In Windows 2000, for the **Administrative Templates** nodes, you can set the **Show Configured Policies Only** flag (point to a node and set the flag in the **View** menu). This prevents you from viewing not-configured policies. This flag is set for the **Computer Configuration** and **User Configuration** node separately.
- In Windows .NET, the policy filtration feature is much more powerful (see Fig. 7.43). To open this window, point to an **Administrative Templates** node and select **Filtering** on the **View** menu.
- If your system was upgraded from Windows NT 4.0 and/or you use the older ADM-files, pay attention to the value of the **Show Policies Only** flag in the **View** menu for the **Administrative Templates** nodes. When set, this flag prevents Windows NT 4.0-style system policy settings from applying to Windows 2000/XP/.NET systems.

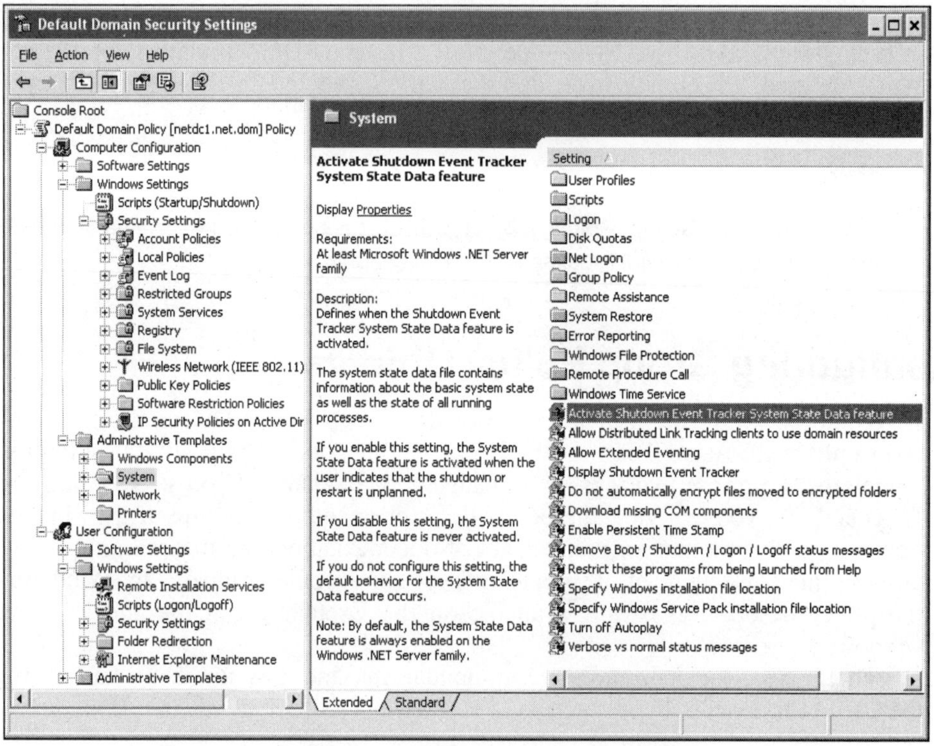

Fig. 7.42. The main window of new version of the **Group Policy Object Editor** snap-in

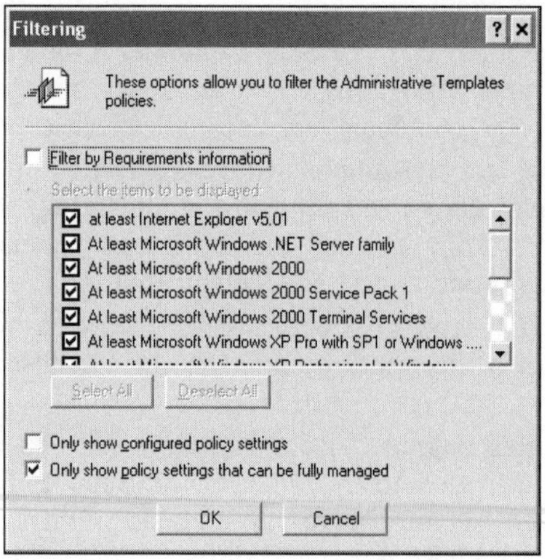

Fig. 7.43. Filtering group policies in Windows .NET (default settings)

Chapter 8: Common Administrative Tasks

This chapter deals with some typical administrative tasks related to Active Directory (some operations have already been considered in the previous chapter). These tasks in no way cover *all* the objectives which an administrator accomplishes every day.

The tasks discussed below are carried out using administrative snap-ins or different utilities from the *Windows .NET Support Tools* or the *Windows 2000 Resource Kit.*

Using the *RunAs* Command

Due to security requirements, it is not recommended that you be permanently logged on to the system (domain) with a user account that has full administrative privileges. Windows 2000/XP/.NET offers a very helpful command — *RunAs*. This command allows a system administrator to carry out common tasks using an account with restricted (or "normal" user) rights, and to start a specific command on behalf of a "power" user (this can be an administrator account or an account with some additional rights). Thus, it is not necessary to repeatedly re-register into the system.

Let us consider how to use this command with the administrative snap-ins.

> ***Note***
>
> If the RunAs command fails, make sure that the *Secondary Logon* service (seclogon; in Windows 2000, it is called *RunAs Service*) is running on the computer (run the **Services** snap-in and check the status of the service).

Running Administrative Tools from the Context Menu

You can select an administrative tool in one of the following ways:

- Select the tool in the **Start** | **Programs** | **Administrative Tools** menu (or **Start** | **All Programs** | **Administrative Tools**).
- Open the window that contains all the tools. Click **Start** | **All Programs** | **Administrative Tools**, and select either **Open** or **Open All Users** in the context menu. (The former command will open the window that only contains the tools created by the user, while the latter opens the window that contains all tools installed by default.) Select the tool in the open window.
- Copy (drag and drop) icons of the necessary tools to the desktop. (You may also create one or more folders on the desktop, and copy the icons to them.)

Then, for any administrative snap-in, you can open the context menu and select the **Run as** command. (There are some limitations on computers running Windows 2000.) You will see a window similar to the one shown in Fig. 8.1.

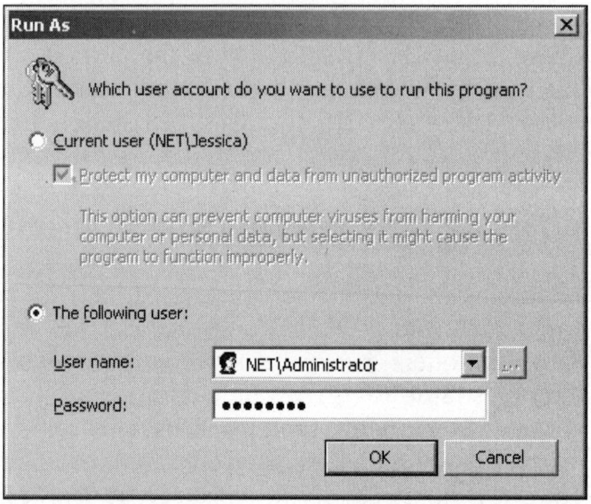

Fig. 8.1. By entering proper credentials in this window, you can start a program on behalf of another user

The upper (default) switch allows you to start the tool on behalf of your current account (i.e., with your current privileges). The other option (shown) — **The following user** — will allow you to enter an administrator's credentials, and start the tool in the "privileged" mode. Both the domain and user names should be used in this window (this covers Windows 2000 domains, too): you can specify either a full SAM account (pre-Windows 2000) name (as shown on the screenshot) or, in Windows .NET, a UPN name (e.g., `JSmith@net`).

Note

The procedure described above can be used with *any* EXE- or MSC-file, and not only with administrative tools. (See the next section.)

In addition, you can open any administrative tool's **Properties** window, click **Advanced** on the **Shortcut** tab, and set the **Run with different credentials** flag. In Windows 2000, you should check the **Run as different user** box on the **Shortcut** tab. After this operation is performed, the system will *always* propose that you start the tool as another user.

Note

Notice also the **Author** command on the context menu of administrative tools. This command allows you to start a snap-in in author mode and then to modify it. By default, all tools are saved in **User mode — full access**, and the **Do not save changes in this console** box is not checked. To prevent users from changing the administrative snap-ins, you may use the user administrative templates in the **Group Policy Object Editor** snap-in.

Starting a Tool from the Command Prompt

Using the RunAs command, it is possible to start any executable file — EXE, COM, CMD, BAT, MSC; shortcuts to programs (LNK); and Control Panel items (CPL) — on behalf of a different user. Let us discuss some examples. (You can get complete information on RunAs in the *Help and Support Center* or by running `runas /?`)

Note

RunAs cannot be used with some items, such as Windows Explorer, the **Printers** folder, and desktop items.

Note

Usually, it is much more convenient to start MMC tools with RunAs from the command prompt rather than from the **Run** window, because in the first case, you will be able to see possible errors. For frequently used commands, you may want to create shortcuts on the desktop.

Example 1. Work in the Same Domain

Suppose you are currently logged on to the *net.dom* domain with a "normal" user account, and want to configure the domain controller security settings, which requires administrative privileges (see Table 8.1). In the **Run** window or at the command prompt enter the command:

```
runas /user:administrator@net.dom "mmc dcpol.msc"
```

`Administrator` is the name of a user that is a member of the Domain Admins group. Enter the administrator's password when prompted.

Example 2. Administering Another Domain

Now you want to create a user in the *subdom.net.dom* domain using the **Active Directory Users and Computers** snap-in (i.e., you would like to work in a domain, other then the domain where you are logged on). Enter the following string:

```
runas /netonly /user:SUBDOM\administrator "mmc dsa.msc"
```

Note

As you can see, it is possible to use two formats for representing a user account: a UPN format, and a standard SAM format — `DOMAIN\USER`. Both formats are acceptable, but in the last case, you must use the SAM format, or the snap-in will be running for the domain in which you are currently logged on.

Example 3. Verifying User Permissions

RunAs can be very helpful for setting up user permissions on a file or Active Directory objects. To set the necessary permissions for a user, you may start a tool using administrative privileges. At the same time, it is possible to open the command prompt or start a program on behalf of this user and check the resulting permissions. You need not either repeatedly log on to the system using different accounts or use several computers.

File Names of Administrative Snap-ins

To use administrative tools with RunAs, you should know the names of the corresponding snap-ins. Also, some tools can only be used with administrative privileges. Table 8.1 contains information on some important tools.

Note

All installed snap-ins can be found in the *%SystemRoot%*\system32 folder.

Table 8.1. Some Administrative Tools and the Privileges Necessary to Use Them

Tool name	Snap-in's name	Necessary privileges
Active Directory Domains and Trusts	domain.msc	User
Active Directory Schema	*userCreatedName*.msc	User
Active Directory Sites and Services	dssite.msc	User
Active Directory Users and Computers	dsa.msc	User
Computer Management	compmgmt.msc	User
Distributed File System	dfsgui.msc	User
DNS	dnsmgmt.msc	User
Domain Controller Security Settings	dcpol.msc	Administrator
Domain Security Settings	dompol.msc	Administrator
Group Policy (see below)	gpedit.msc	Administrator
Local Security Settings	secpol.msc	Administrator
Routing and Remote Access	rrasmgmt.msc	Administrator
Services	services.msc	User

continues

Table 8.1 Continued

Tool name	Snap-in's name	Necessary privileges
Snap-ins that aren't displayed on the *Administrative Tools* menu		
Device Manager	devmgmt.msc	User
Disk Management	diskmgmt.msc	User
Local Users and Groups	lusrmgr.msc	User
Shared Folders	fsmgmt.msc	Administrator

Running GPO Editor

By default (when started without any parameters), the **Group Policy Object Editor** snap-in is focused on the local GPO stored on computer. Generally, you have two options:

- Run this snap-in with a preconfigured GPO. You can use either the standard snap-ins (gpedit.msc, dompol.msc, and dcpol.msc) or custom MMC consoles with the **Group Policy Object Editor** snap-in.
- Specify a GPO when the snap-in runs.

In the first case, you can create a custom MMC console, add the **Group Policy Object Editor** snap-in to it, link the snap-in to a necessary GPO (stored on a remote computer or in Active Directory), and save the console with any name you like. Then you can start the console by its name. This is the "static" approach.

By using the second method, you are exploiting the fact that the **Group Policy Object Editor** snap-in (the gpedit.msc file) allows you to change its focus (the "dynamic" approach). For example, the following command allows you to open a GPO stored on a *remote* computer (even the local computer specified with the `/gpcomputer` parameter is considered to be a "remote" one!):

```
C:\>gpedit.msc /gpcomputer:"netdc1.net.dom"
```

Attention

- You cannot view and manage the **Security Settings** extension (except for the **IP Security Policies**) of a *remote* computer's GPO. The **Software Installation** and **Folder Redirection** extensions are never displayed for *local* GPOs.

You can also run gpedit.msc and specify the distinguished name of any GPO stored in Active Directory. The following approach will help the user to do this most effectively.

At the command prompt, carry out a search operation by using the Search.vbs script (Ldp.exe and DsQuery.exe can also be used) with parameters similar to:

```
C:\>search "LDAP://DC=net,DC=dom"
↳ /C:(objectCategory=GroupPolicyContainer)
↳ /S:subtree /P:AdsPath,displayName
```

On the screen, you will see the list of all GPOs stored in the domain, for instance:

```
<LDAP://DC=net,DC=dom>;((objectCategory=GroupPolicyContainer));
AdsPath,displayName;subtree
Finished the query.
Found 5 objects.
AdsPath 1 = LDAP://CN={31B2F340-016D-11D2-945F-00C04FB984F9},
↳CN=Policies,CN=System,DC=net,DC=dom
displayName 1 = Default Domain Policy
AdsPath 2 = LDAP://CN={6AC1786C-016F-11D2-945F-00C04fB984F9},
↳CN=Policies,CN=System,DC=net,DC=dom
displayName 2 = Default Domain Controllers Policy
...
```

The DsQuery command shown below will produce the same result:

```
C:\>dsquery * -filter (objectCategory=GroupPolicyContainer) -attr
distinguishedName displayName
```

You can easily select a necessary policy by its friendly name and use its DN as the parameter. (Don't forget about the *copy-and-paste* feature of the command prompt window.) For example, to open the *Default Domain Policy* shown above, use the following command (the quotes are mandatory):

```
C:\>gpedit.msc /gpobject:"LDAP://
↳CN={31B2F340-016D-11D2-945F-00C04FB984F9},
↳CN=Policies,CN=System,DC=net,DC=dom"
```

This command used with the RunAs will have the following syntax:

```
C:\>runas /user:net\administrator "mmc gpedit.msc
↳ /gpobject:\"LDAP://CN={31B2F340-016D-11D2-945F-00C04FB984F9},
↳CN=Policies,CN=System,DC=net,DC=dom\""
```

Remote Administration

To administer Active Directory from a domain client computer, you have the following standard options (the order is not important):

- *Terminal Services* allow an administrator to work on a client computer in the same way as he or she can at the domain controller's console. This is the only standard option for down-level client computers (Windows NT, Windows 9*x*) to run the administrative tools, and the only option for low-speed (dial-up) connections. Although many administrative command-line tools can connect directly to remote computers, you will need the Terminal Services to get the full functionality of the command prompt on a DC.

On Windows .NET-based computers, the Terminal Services are installed by default. These computers have a built-in feature, *Remote Desktop*, that is enabled on the **Remote** tab in the **System Properties** window and provides an administrator with single-user access to the desktop of the computer.

Note

There is no *Terminal Service Connection* option configured on computers running Windows .NET. You can enter `mstsc /console` at the command prompt or use the **Remote Desktops** command on the **Start | Administrative Tools** menu.

- The *Windows .NET Administration Tools Pack* contains practically all administrative snap-ins (see Table 8.2). This pack is installed from the *%SystemRoot%*\system32\adminpak.msi file available on every Windows .NET-based domain controller. You can install the Administration Tools on any computer with Windows XP/.NET, but to use them, you must be logged on as a user with domain administrative rights.

Caution

- The Windows .NET Administration Tools Pack cannot be installed on computers running Windows 2000! In general, Windows 2000 Administration Tools could be used for administering Windows .NET-based domains; however, some limitations exist in that case. A better choice would be to install the Windows .NET Administration Tools Pack and use it for managing domain controllers running both Windows 2000 and Windows .NET systems.

- You can manually install the selected administrative snap-ins on a client computer (see the next section).

Table 8.2. Snap-ins Included in the Windows .NET Administration Tools Pack

Active Directory Domains and Trusts	Internet Information Services
Active Directory Schema Manager	Network Load Balancing Manager
Active Directory Sites and Services	Remote Desktops
Active Directory Users and Computers	Remote Storage
Certification Authority	Routing and Remote Access

continues

Table 8.2 Continued

Cluster Administrator	Server Extensions Administrator
Connection Manger Administration Kit	Telephony
DHCP	Terminal Services Licensing
Distributed File System	Terminal Services Manager
DNS	WINS

Installing Administrative Snap-ins Selectively

For some reason, you might want to install only one or just a few separate administrative tools on a client computer instead of the entire *Administration Tools* pack. This can be done quite easily. (But don't forget about security requirements!) You will have to carry out the following steps:

1. Copy the necessary snap-ins (files with MSC extension) from the *%SystemRoot%*\system32 folder on a DC to any local folder you wish.
2. Copy the appropriate DLL(s) to the local *%SystemRoot%*\system32 folder or to any local folder.
3. If the DLL has been copied to a folder other than *%SystemRoot%*\system32, you must first change the folder as necessary. To register the DLL, enter the following string at the command prompt:

```
regsvr32 <DLLname>
```

4. For example, to register the DLL for the **Active Directory Users and Computers** snap-in, enter `regsvr32 dsadmin.dll`.

Now you may create shortcuts for new snap-ins, and then run them. Of course, you have to be logged on to the domain with appropriate (administrative) privileges.

The following table contains DLL names for some administrative snap-ins.

Tool name	Snap-in's name	DLL's name
Active Directory Domain and Trusts	domain.msc	domadmin.dll
Active Directory Sites and Services	dssite.msc	dsadmin.dll
Active Directory Schema	*userCreatedName*.msc	schmmgmt.dll
Active Directory Users and Computers	dsa.msc	dsadmin.dll

Note

After schmmgmt.dll has been copied to a local computer, you will be able to add the snap-in to any custom MMC console (since there is no schema snap-in configured by default).

By default, the **Group Policy Object Editor** snap-in is present on any computer running Windows 2000/XP/.NET. Therefore, to use this tool and link it to any domain GPO, you need only to have administrator's privileges in the domain.

Noticc that both the **Active Directory Users and Computers** and **Active Directory Sites and Services** snap-ins use the same dsadmin.dll file. Both snap-ins actually provide similar operations (browsing and editing properties) with directory objects. The former enables you to work with the entire domain naming partition of Active Directory. The latter provides access to two containers in the Configuration partition, namely, *Sites* and *Services* (you can also view them with the **ADSI Edit** snap-in).

Querying Active Directory

Querying is a commonly used operation in network directories, and Active Directory is not an exception. Active Directory may contain a huge number of objects, whose precise locations are frequently unknown. Querying the directory rather than browsing the directory tree is preferable for both users and administrators. Users of AD-based domains have the following instruments (some of them are available to all clients, including down-level systems, and others only work on Windows 2000/XP/.NET systems) which assist the user in finding one or more objects in Active Directory:

- *Built-in search features* (see the next section) — the most convenient way for a user to find a shared folder or printer, user, group, or other common directory object. All other tools are intended for administrators.
- *DsQuery.exe* and *Dsget.exe* — the standard Windows .NET command-line search utilities (see *Chapter 12, "Manipulating Active Directory Objects"*).
- The **ADSI Edit** snap-in (from the *Support Tools*) — using this tool, an administrator can create powerful queries and modify objects in all directory partitions (see *Chapter 7, "Domain Manipulation Tools"*).
- The *Search.vbs* script (from the *Support Tools*) — the simplest query tool that uses the LDAP protocol. Can be used on any Windows platforms (see *Chapter 12*).
- *Active Directory Administration Tool* (Ldp.exe from the *Support Tools*) and *Active Directory Browser* (AdsVw.exe from *ADSI SDK*) — complicated administrative tools that also allow an administrator to browse through the directory tree and modify objects. Ldp.exe uses the LDAP protocol and is the only tool that can retrieve deleted objects. AdsVw.exe uses both LDAP and WinNT protocols,

and works with AD-based (Windows 2000 and Windows .NET) and Window NT domains (see *Chapter 12*).

- The *Guid2obj.exe* utility (from the *Windows 2000 Resource Kit*) — a specialized tool that can determine the distinguished name of an object from its GUID.

Most of the listed tools require a good understanding of LDAP filter syntax. Only then will you be able to quickly and precisely find or choose the necessary objects.

Configuring *Search* Option on the Client Computers

By default, users — those who are aware of this option — can search Active Directory for various objects by using the **Find** command from the context menu of a domain displayed in the **Directory** folder (in **My Network Places**). This option is available on computers running Windows 2000 and has been removed from Windows XP/.NET. (One can also use the **Active Directory Users and Computer** snap-in installed on a client computer.) There are two specialized commands called from the **Start | Search** menu: **For Printers** and **For People**.

It is possible to provide users with powerful search features and add a shortcut for these operations to the desktop or any folder. You need to perform the following steps:

1. Right click the desktop and select **New | Shortcut** from the context menu.
2. Enter the following string (case sensitive!) in the **Type the location of the item** field, and click **Next**:

```
rundll32.exe dsquery,OpenQueryWindow
```

3. In the next window, enter a name for the shortcut and click **Finish**.
4. You might also wish to move the created shortcut to some folder or menu.

After clicking the shortcut, the user will see the search window similar to the one shown in Fig. 7.14. From that window, it is possible to find users, contacts, groups, printers, OUs, etc.

Note

This feature works fine on all Windows systems (from Windows 95 to Windows NT 4.0) provided that the *Active Directory Client Extension* (DSClient.exe from the Windows 2000 Server CD; see also links in *Appendix A*). (Windows 2000/XP/.NET systems have that client as a built-in feature.) Just keep in mind that you must not enter a space between the `dsquery` and `OpenQueryWindow` parameters.

Modifying Directory Objects. Export and Import

There are, in fact, quite a number of tools that allow an administrator to create, delete, and modify one or more Active Directory objects. You should be familiar with all (or at least most) of them to be able to choose the most effective tool for a specific task. Let us list all of the main facilities provided on Windows 2000 and Windows .NET platforms:

- Standard snap-ins installed by default (see *Chapter 7, "Domain Manipulation Tools")* — universal GUI tools that work with one object only, and in Windows 2000, have modest support for group operations.
  - The **Active Directory Users and Computers** snap-in creates users, contacts, groups, computers, printers, shared folders, and OUs.
  - The **Active Directory Sites and Services** snap-in creates sites, subnets, links, and connections.
  - The **Active Directory Domains and Trusts** snap-in creates inter-domain trusts.
- Standard Windows .NET command-line utilities that perform specialized operations and can be used for managing Active Directory objects from the command prompt.
  - DsAdd.exe (see below) creates specific types of objects.
  - DsMod.exe (see *Chapter 12, "Manipulating Active Directory Objects"*) modifies properties of specific object types.
  - DsRm.exe removes any objects.
  - DsMove.exe moves any objects to another container as well as renames them.

Note

Pay attention to the fact that the DsMod.exe utility can pipe in results from DsQuery.exe, which significantly enhances the utility's flexibility and effectiveness.

- Specialized administrative GUI tools (see *Chapter 7* and *Chapter 12*) used for specific operations and for fine-tuning and troubleshooting Active Directory.
  - The **Active Directory Schema** snap-in creates attributes and classes.
  - The **ADSI Edit** snap-in, Ldp.exe and AdsVw.exe create objects of any type (including objects which cannot be created by any other tools), but are primarily useful for editing attributes.
- Tools for import/export (see *Chapter 12*) — command-line utilities that could (and should) serve as powerful tools for administering large-scale Active Directory installation. LDIFDE can also be used for changing the attributes

of a number of similar objects. On computers running Windows .NET, utilities from the Ds*.exe "family" might be a better choice in many cases.

- LDIFDE
- CSVDE

- Utilities intended for specific tasks (see later in this chapter and the *Remote Administration Scripts* in the *Windows 2000 Server Resource Kit*).
  - AddUsers.exe, CreateUsers.vbs, and others (e.g., NetDom.exe can be used for creating machine accounts in domains)

- ADSI scripts (see *Chapter 16, "Active Directory Service Interfaces (ADSI)"* and *Chapter 17, "Scripting Administrative Tasks"*) — the most flexible of the options and, in fact, a quite simple way to manipulate Active Directory objects (especially for periodic routine tasks and when a large number of objects are to be processed).

Using the *Active Directory Users and Computers* Snap-in

The **Active Directory Users and Computers** snap-in is, maybe, the main tool that an administrator will use daily to manage various domain resources. The procedure of creating and deleting Active Directory objects is basically the same for all types of objects. There are buttons on the *Standard* toolbar for some of the most used objects:

- **Create a new user in the current container** 
- **Create a new group in the current container** 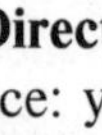
- **Create a new organizational unit in the current container** 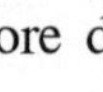

You can select one, several, or all created objects and move them into any container or OU in the current domain. As usual in Windows, use the <Shift> or <Ctrl> keys for selecting multiple objects.

The Windows .NET version of the **Active Directory Users and Computers** snap-in offers some improvements in the user interface: you can use drag-and-drop operations, and modify properties of several objects selected (for more details, see *Chapter 7, "Domain Manipulation Tools"*).

It is possible to choose a user account as a template, and create users with the same properties (group memberships, profile settings, etc.) To start this process, select a "template" user and click **Copy** on its context menu.

Note

Organizational units can only be created in the OU or domain containers.

Note

If you want to move objects between *different* domains in the same tree or non-adjacent trees, you need to use the MoveTree utility from the *Support Tools* (see *Chapter 13, "Migration Tools"*).

Caution

Built-in domain local groups cannot be deleted or moved from the *Builtin* container.

Adding Users and Groups to Domain

There are a few utilities (besides the batch import tools LDIFDE and CSVDE and custom scripts) that simplify the creation of a number of user accounts in a field or test environments.

Windows .NET Utility — DsAdd

A brand-new Windows .NET utility, *DsAdd.exe*, can create single computer, contact, group, OU, and user objects in AD-based domains. It uses the LDAP protocol only.

With DsAdd, you can create a local, global, or universal (if it is allowed) group and add specified members to it at the same time (not later!). For example:

```
C:\>dsadd group CN=Admins,OU=Staff,DC=net,DC=dom -members
↳ "CN=John,OU=Staff,DC=net,DC=dom" "CN=Tim,OU=Personnel,DC=net,DC=dom"
```

Here is an example of how to use DsAdd to create a user and add it to the specified groups:

```
C:\>dsadd user CN=Alice,OU=Staff,DC=net,DC=dom -memberof
↳ "CN=Admins,OU=Staff,DC=net,DC=dom"
↳ "CN=Account Operators,CN=Builtin,DC=net,DC=dom"
```

CreateUsers.vbs Script (RK)

This script can only create users. It operates with both the WinNT and LDAP providers. The created accounts will be enabled. The following attributes are required (the minimal set of attributes):

- WinNT — *name* and *password*
- LDAP — *cn*, *samAccountName*, and *password*

Note

You can specify many other attributes, too; however, not *any* attribute available for an user object is permitted. Carefully test your command (and the input file, if present). Be sure that all specified attributes are consistent; otherwise, you could easily get an error message similar to:

```
Error 0X80072035 occurred in settings properties for user cn=...
```

This error (8245) means that "The server is unwilling to process the request". One of the possible sources of this error is the incorrect "naming" attributes: *cn*, *name*, *sn*, *distinguishedName*, etc. Do not forget to enclose any attributes' values containing spaces in double quotes.

Here is the simplest example of how to create a user with CreateUsers.vbs:

```
C:\>createusers WinNT://NET name:user01 password:psw1
```

The script must output the following:

```
Working ...
Getting domain WinNT://NET...
Creating user user01
Succeeded in creating user user01 in NET.
```

To disable output of informative messages, use the `/q` parameter.

New users will always be created in the *Users* container. You could move them to other containers (most probably, organizational units), but a better way would be to use the "LDAP-version" of the CreateUsers.vbs, which "understands" the Active Directory structure:

```
C:\>createusers LDAP://OU=Staff,DC=net,DC=dom cn:"User User01"
↳ samAccountName:user-ldap01 password:psw1
```

Maybe the most intriguing issue is how to create a number of users *at once*. It is actually very easy. Create a file with the desired user properties and use the appropriate provider (WinNT or LDAP). For example, the following command will create users specified in a file in the Staff OU:

```
createusers LDAP://OU=Staff,DC=net,DC=dom /i:newUsers.txt
```

The file of descriptions may be similar to the following:

```
cn:"User01" samAccountName:user01 password:psw1
cn:"User02" samAccountName:user02 password:psw2
...
```

AddUsers.exe (RK)

In comparison to CreateUsers.vbs, AddUsers.exe has a few additional features. Besides adding users and groups to a domain, it allows you to:

- Dump account information (users and groups) to a file.
- Specify the control account-creation options. By default, a new user must change his or her password at logon.
- Delete users or groups. Account names can only be specified in the input file.
- Create an input file in a spreadsheet program, such as Microsoft Excel, and save it in comma-delimited format, which the tool can use. A separator character other than a comma can be specified.

One negative aspect of AddUsers.exe is that the tool doesn't "see" the Active Directory structure.

Note

Using AddUsers.exe, you can successfully *add* users to existing groups, despite the "Group already exists" error message. The groups may be located in any container in Active Directory, not only in the "default" *Users* container.

A sample dump file produced by AddUsers.exe is placed below (the attributes' names are in bold braces and are not really included in the file). Such a file can easily be imported to a spreadsheet.

```
[User]
{samAccountName, name, password, description, homeDrive, homeDirectory,
profilePath, scriptPath}
Administrator,,,Built-in account for administering the
↳ computer/domain,,,,
Guest,,,Built-in account for guest access to the computer/domain,,,,
JSmith,John Smith,,A test user,Z:,\\netdc1\UserData\JSmith,
↳\\netdc1\Profiles\JSmith,Users\Welcome.vbs...
[Global]
{samAccountName, description, member's account names...}
Domain Admins,Designated administrators of the domain,Administrator,
Domain Controllers,All domain controllers in the
↳ domain,NETDC1$,NETDC4$,
Domain Users,All domain users,Administrator,HelpAssistant_67861b,
SUPPORT_388945a0,krbtgt,SUBDOM$,Bob,John,Pam,...
```

```
...
[Local]
{samAccountName, description, member's account names...}
Administrators,Administrators have complete and unrestricted
↳ access to the computer/domain,NET\Administrator,NET\Enterprise
↳ Admins,NET\Domain Admins,
DC1LocalGroup,NET\John,NET\Lee,NET\Jessica,NET\GlobalGr1,NET\UniGr2,
↳NET\DC1LocGr1,
...
```

Notice in the last line that groups may contain other groups (the group names are shown in bold) including local groups (at the *native* and *Windows .NET (version 2002)* functional levels of a domain).

Caution

It is possible that this tool has problems displaying memberships in global and universal (placed in the [Global] section) groups. Test this in your environment before you do any real work!

As you can see, the dump file contains three sections: *User*, *Global*, and *Local*. The same format can be used for creating new users and groups. The irrelevant trailing commas, as well as unused sections, can be omitted in the input file. New groups may either be empty or contain the names of their members.

Modifying Group Membership

The **Active Directory Users and Computers** snap-in has a feature for "bulk" operations that permits you to add a number of selected users and contacts to a group. Point to an account (or choose a few accounts) and select the **Add to a group** command from the context or **Action** menu, or click the **Add the selected objects to a group you specify** button on the toolbar. Then specify a group in the **Select Group** window. In Windows .NET, you can also carry out *drag-and-drop* operations.

If you initially select an OU, the system asks whether you want to add all users and contacts from this container to the specified group. This feature is very helpful for administering OUs (but in Windows .NET, it is lacking).

To populate groups, you can use the LDIFDE and CSVDE tools, as well as the AddUsers.exe utility. LDIFDE is also able to delete members from groups.

On computers running Windows .NET, you can use the standard DsMod.exe utility that performs all modifications of groups. For example, the following command adds two new members to the Schema Admins group:

```
C:\>dsmod group "CN=Schema Admins,CN=Users,DC=net,DC=dom" -addmbr
↳ "CN=John Smith,OU=Staff,DC=net,DC=dom"
↳ "CN=Pamela,OU=Staff,DC=net,DC=dom"
```

The `-rmmbr` parameter removes the specified members, and the `-chmbr` parameter replaces all group members.

Publishing Folders and Printers

Active Directory considerably simplifies work with shared network resources in comparison with the traditional method of browsing domains. If a resource has been *published* in Active Directory, users can easily locate it (see, for example, the **Search | For Printers** command in the **Start** menu) and connect to it (see Fig. 8.2). Furthermore, to simplify the process of locating resources, you might want to publish all of them in one OU.

Publishing a folder or a printer in Active Directory means, in other words, creating a new directory object — *Shared Folder* or *Printer*, respectively.

Shared folders in Active Directory have a feature that helps users to search for information according to its characteristics. Select a published folder from the **Active Directory Users and Computers** snap-in's tree pane, open its **Properties** window, and click **Keywords**. You can add words that are logically related to the folder's contents to the list. Then, if a user begins a search for shared folders in the **Find** window, he or she can specify keywords and find resources based on their contents rather than their names.

Printers (more precisely — *printer devices*) connected to Windows 2000/XP/.NET computers can be published only from a printer's **Properties** window (the **List in the Directory** flag on the **Sharing** tab). In other cases, you can use the Pubprn.vbs script.

By default, the local printer on a domain client computer is not published during its installation if you do not share it at once. If a printer is installed as shared, it is immediately published in Active Directory in the computer's container (see "*Users, Groups, and Computers as Containers Mode*" in *Chapter 7*). You can clear the **List in the Directory** flag at any moment, and the printer object will be deleted from Active Directory.

Caution

- When publishing a folder, you must be cautious, because the system will not verify the entered folder name, and, as a result, you may run into an error in the future, but only when you open the folder or map to it.

If the RDN and NetBIOS names of a Windows 2000 domain are different, you will get the error — "The system cannot find the file specified" — when publishing a printer (see the *Microsoft Knowledge Base article Q255496*). To resolve the problem, you must install the latest Windows 2000 Service Pack (at least, SP 1).

You can configure the process of publishing and pruning printers in the domain by using group policies (see the **Computer Configuration | Administrative Templates | Printers** node in the **Group Policy Object Editor** snap-in).

Both in Windows 2000 and Windows .NET domain, it is possible to enable *Location Tracking*, a feature that allows users to find printers accordingly to their physical locations. (See a remark in the "*Active Directory Sites and Services snap-in*" section of the previous chapter.)

Pubprn.vbs Script

You can execute the system Pubprn.vbs script without parameters and get the help information. The following command, for example, publishes the *HP6MP* printer connected to the *WKS10* computer in the *Staff* OU of the *net.dom* domain:

```
pubprn \\wks10\hp6mp "LDAP://OU=Staff,DC=net,DC=dom"
```

The system verifies the printer name and the existence of the object that is specified by the LDAP name. If the printer has been published successfully, you will see a message displaying the LDAP name of the printer in Active Directory.

Connecting to Shared Resources

Search operations are the preferred way for locating shared network resources in AD-based domains. A user can find the necessary printer or shared folder easily and perform any operation available while browsing through the domain tree.

The scope of the search can vary from a specific container (OU) in a domain to the entire forest. (The **Entire Directory** option is equivalent to searching Global Catalog.) In addition, users can specify various search criteria such as printer speed, resolution, and so on. Fig. 8.2 contains an example of how to find all printers in the forest. As you can see in the **Server Name** column, the printers come from various domains. A user can point to an applicable printer and select the necessary operation from the context menu.

Users can carry out the following actions on the found shared folder: open, search the folder, map a network drive, and others.

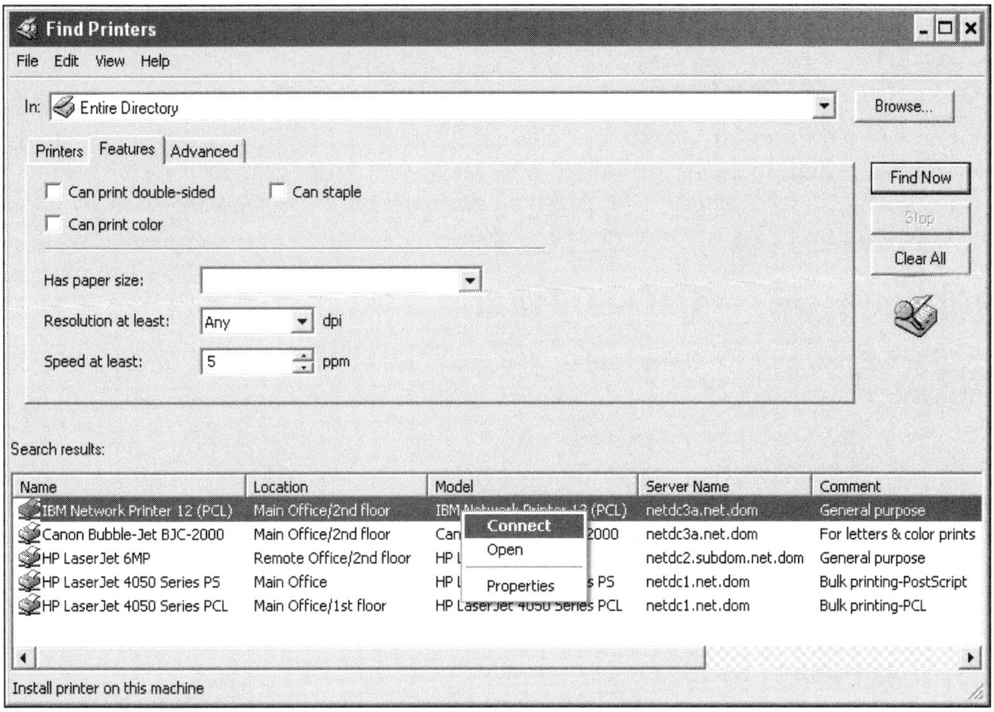

Fig. 8.2. Search for all printers in the enterprise (forest)

Managing FSMO Roles in the Forest

Because the location of the *Flexible Single Master Operation* (FSMO) roles' masters is very important for the proper functioning of a multi-domain forest, an administrator must know which domain controllers possess a specific role(s) at any moment of the entire network's lifetime. Therefore, he or she must have the facilities to find the role masters easily and to transfer a role from one DC to another. Moreover, it is necessary to have a way to *forcibly* transfer a role from a defunct DC. This is referred to as the *"seizing of role"* process.

Finding FSMO Role Owners

To find the owners of FSMO roles (operation masters), an administrator can use the "standard" administrative tools (see the previous chapter):

- The **Active Directory Users and Computers** snap-in displays the RID, PDC, and Infrastructure masters.

- The **Active Directory Domains and Trusts** snap-in displays the Domain Naming master.
- The **Active Directory Schema** snap-in displays the Schema master.

This approach is, however, time-consuming, and it makes sense to use some command-line tools or scripts. Some such tools are described below; for more information, see *Chapter 17, "Scripting Administrative Tasks"* (the "*How to Find an FSMO Master?*" section and *Listing 17.20*).

Windows .NET — DsQuery Utility

A brand-new command-line utility, DsQuery.exe, will help you to find a specific role master, for example:

```
C:\>dsquery server -hasfsmo rid
"CN=NETDC1,CN=Servers,CN=NET-Site,CN=Sites,CN=Configuration,
↳DC=net,DC=dom"
```

You can also specify other roles: `pdc`, `infr`, `name`, `schema`.

Windows Domain Manager (NetDom.exe) (ST)

NetDom.exe (see *Chapter 12, "Manipulating Active Directory Objects"*) can display all operation masters known to a specified DC. Use the following command syntax:

```
C:\>netdom QUERY /Domain:net.dom FSMO
```

DumpFSMOs.cmd (RK)

This command file is, in fact, a chain of instructions to the NTDSutil tool. (These instructions can also be entered manually.) The main command in that file is the following:

```
ntdsutil roles Connections "Connect to server %1" Quit
↳ "select Operation Target" "List roles for connected server"
↳ Quit Quit Quit
```

The only mandatory parameter is the name of the DC from which the information is retrieved. A sample screen output is shown below (the utility's prompt is in bold):

```
C:\>dumpfsmos.cmd netdc1
ntdsutil: roles
fsmo maintenance: Connections
server connections: Connect to server netdc1
```

```
Binding to netdc1 ...
Connected to netdc1 using credentials of locally logged on user.
server connections: Quit
fsmo maintenance: select Operation Target
select operation target: List roles for connected server
Server "netdc1" knows about 5 roles
Schema - CN=NTDS Settings,CN=NETDC1,CN=Servers,
↳CN=NET-Site,CN=Sites,CN=Configuration,DC=net,DC=dom
Domain - CN=NTDS Settings,CN=NETDC1,CN=Servers,
↳CN=NET-Site,CN=Sites,CN=Configuration,DC=net,DC=dom
PDC - CN=NTDS Settings,CN=NETDC1,CN=Servers,
↳CN=NET-Site,CN=Sites,CN=Configuration,DC=net,DC=dom
RID - CN=NTDS Settings,CN=NETDC1,CN=Servers,
↳CN=NET-Site,CN=Sites,CN=Configuration,DC=net,DC=dom
Infrastructure - CN=NTDS Settings,CN=NETDC3,CN=Servers,
↳CN=NET-Site,CN=Sites,CN=Configuration,DC=net,DC=dom
select operation target: Quit
fsmo maintenance: Quit
ntdsutil: Quit
Disconnecting from netdc1...
```

Active Directory Replication Monitor (ReplMon.exe) (ST)

All operation masters can be displayed with ReplMon.exe. Start the tool and add servers to the **Monitored Servers** list (tree). (In this case, it is enough to add one server only.) Select a DC from the tree pane, open the **Properties** window, and click the **FSMO Roles** tab. Fig. 8.3 shows a sample view of this tab.

From this window, you can test any operation master by clicking **Query**. ReplMon answers with the following message: "Active Directory Replication Monitor was able/unable to resolve, connect, and bind to the server hosting this FSMO role."

Note

In addition, ReplMon can display all Global Catalog servers in the enterprise (select the **Show Global Catalog Servers in Enterprise** command in a monitored server's context menu).

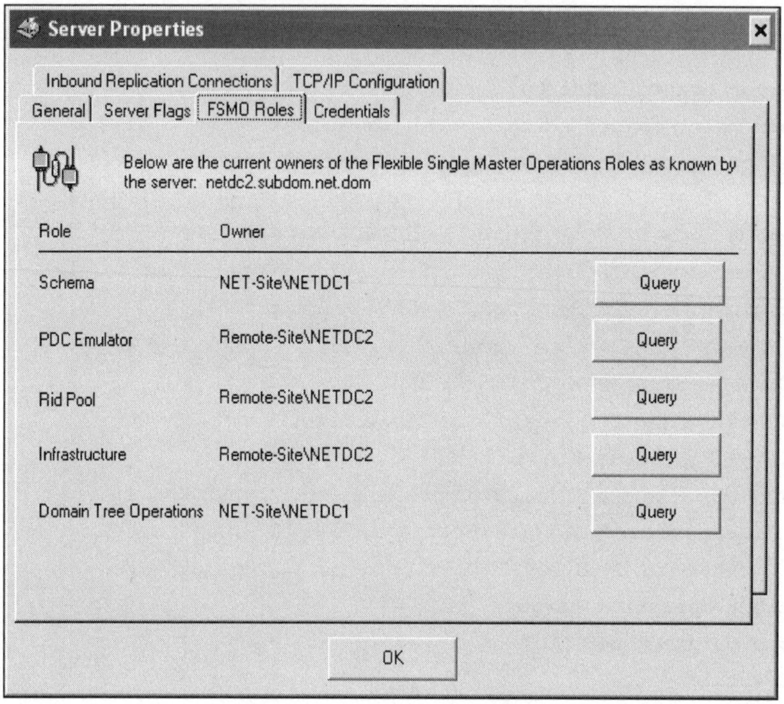

Fig. 8.3. Viewing all operation masters (the owners of FSMO roles) for a domain

Transferring and Seizing FSMO Roles

Usually, to transfer an FSMO role from one DC to another, the administrative snap-ins should be used. To seize a role, you must use the NTDSutil.exe.

Note

For additional information on FSMO roles, you might be interested in Microsoft Knowledge Base articles *Q223787* and *Q223346*.

RID, PDC, and Infrastructure Operation Masters

You might want, for some reason (e.g., before shut downing a DC for maintenance), to transfer a FSMO role from the role's master to another DC in the domain. In the **Active Directory Users and Computers** snap-in window, you must first connect to the DC that is the potential (new) operation master, point to the root node in the tree pane, and select the **Operation Masters** command on either the context or **Action** menus. Click the appropriate tab: **RID**, **PDC**, or **Infrastructure**. You will see the current owner of a FSMO role and the potential master name. Click the **Change** button, and you will get a new operation master.

Be careful when transferring the Infrastructure role. If there are two or more DCs in the domain, make sure that a message similar to the following one has not appeared in the Directory Service log on the new operation master:

```
Event Type:    Error
Event Source: NTDS General
Event Category:   Directory Access
Event ID:  1419
Date:      5/31/2002
Time:      6:07:14 PM
User:      NT AUTHORITY\ANONYMOUS LOGON
Computer:  NETDC1
Description:
The local domain controller is both a global catalog and the
infrastructure operations master. These two roles are not compatible.
If another domain controller exists in the domain, it should be made the
infrastructure operations master. The following domain controller is a
good candidate for this role.
Domain controller:
CN=NTDS Settings,CN=NETDC3,CN=Servers,CN=NET-
Site,CN=Sites,CN=Configuration,DC=net,DC=dom
If all domain controllers in this domain are global catalogs, then there
are no infrastructure update tasks to complete, and this message might
be ignored.
```

Domain Naming Operation Master

The **Active Directory Domains and Trusts** snap-in allows you to transfer the *Domain naming master* FSMO role to any DC in the domain tree. This procedure is simple: connect to the DC that will be the new role's owner, point to the root node in the tree pane, and select the **Operations Master** command from the context menu. Make sure that the names of the current master and future master are correct, click **Change**, and confirm the operation. Remember that only one server in the forest (enterprise) can perform the Domain naming master role, and in addition, that server must be a Global Catalog server.

Schema Operation Master

The **Active Directory Schema** snap-in allows transfer of the *Schema Master* FSMO role to any DC in the forest. You should first connect to the potential master of the role, point to the root node in the tree pane, and select the **Operations Master** command from the context menu. After checking the DC name, click **Change**. Remember that only one server in the forest can perform the Schema Master role.

> ***Attention***
>
> To modify the schema in Windows 2000, you must first enable this operation (see *Chapter 7*, "*Domain Manipulation Tools*"). When you have transferred the Schema Master role to a DC, the flag **The Schema may be modified on this Domain Controller** remains set on the old schema master. This might not be in accordance with your intentions, however.

Using NTDSutil

The NTDSutil can be used for transferring any FSMO role. This is the only tool that allows an administrator to forcibly assign a role to a DC. (It is assumed that the old owner of this role has been destroyed and cannot be repaired.) Using NTDSutil will be discussed in detail in *Chapter 10*, "*Diagnosing and Maintaining Domain Controllers*."

Refreshing Group Policy

When an administrator has changed a GPO, he or she may want to refresh group policy application to verify the effect of the new settings. (Certainly, it is possible to reboot the computer or make the user re-register to the domain. However, this is not always convenient.) On computers running Windows 2000, to perform this task, you can use the *SecEdit.exe* command-line utility. Windows XP/.NET systems offer a new utility (which you should use) — *GPupdate.exe* — for that purpose.

The command syntax is very simple. To refresh user policies, enter either of the following commands (applicable to your system):

```
C:\>secedit /refreshPolicy user_policy   — on Windows 2000
C:\>gpupdate /Target:User                — on Windows .NET
```

The following commands refresh computer policies:

```
C:\>secedit /refreshPolicy machine_policy
C:\>gpupdate /Target:Computer
```

The GPupdate command without parameters updates both user and computer policies.

If you want to re-apply policies (GPOs), even if they have not changed since the last time they were applied, add the `/enforce` parameter to the SecEdit command or the `/Force` parameter to the GPupdate command. (Normally, GPOs are applied only once; unchanged GPOs are skipped.)

> **Note**
>
> You may want to change the default GPO refresh interval (90 minutes for client computers and 5 minutes for domain controllers), as well as the offset (30 minutes for client computers and 0 minutes for domain controllers). For that purpose, use group policies (Computer Configuration | Administrative Templates | System | Group Policy) or modify the system registry. For more information, see *Microsoft Knowledge Base article Q203607*.

Triggering Replication

An administrator has three tools that can be used to trigger Active Directory replication of either all directory partitions (contexts) or just a specified partition between a domain controller and one or all of its direct replication partners:

- The Active Directory Sites and Services snap-in
- RepAdmin command line utility
- ReplMon GUI utility

As is typical for practically any administrative task, you can also use scripts (see example in *Chapter 17, "Scripting Administrative Tasks"*).

> **Note**
>
> Remember that the "source" server (DC) always replicates its changes to the "target" server (DC). Usually, you first select the target, then the source.

The *Active Directory Sites and Services* Snap-in

This snap-in allows an administrator to initiate replication of *all configured* directory partitions from each replication partner *separately*. Select a target DC from the **Servers** container of the applicable site and point to its **NTDS Settings** object. You can trigger replication *from* any server represented by a *Connection* object in the right pane (see example in Fig. 8.4). Select a connection and click **Replicate Now** in the context menu. You must wait until replication completes (with the "Active Directory has replicated the connections" message if successful).

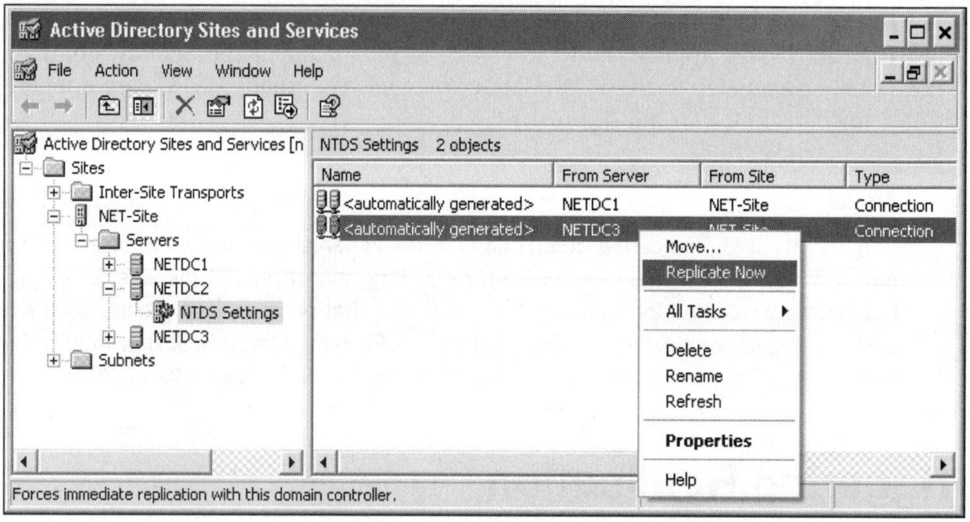

Fig. 8.4. Triggering replication from a direct partner

All directory partitions configured for that partner are replicated. (You can see all their names — including application directory partitions — in a connection's **Properties** window.) You have no options to replicate one partition only.

Replication Diagnostics Tool (RepAdmin.exe) (ST)

With RepAdmin.exe, you replicate each directory partition separately and from one or all sources. (This command-line tool has the same functional capabilities as ReplMon, a GUI tool.) For example, to trigger replication for a destination server, you can use the following command:

```
C:\>repadmin /syncall netdc2.net.dom DC=net,DC=dom,
```

where `netdc2.net.dom` is the server DNS name, and `DC=net,DC=dom` is a partition name (the domain naming partition in this case).

The difference between this command and the operation shown in Fig. 8.4 is the following:

- The command replicates only *one partition*, but from *all partners.*
- In the snap-in window you replicate *all partitions*, but from *one partner* only.

To force replication in the entire domain (forest), you might write similar commands for each DC and all directory partitions to a command file, which will serve to fulfill total replication in the domain.

Caution

- The **repadmin /syncall** *serverName* command replicates only one directory partition (the *Configuration* partition), and performing such a command is not enough to *fully* replicate the server specified.

The Windows .NET version of RepAdmin provides a new flag `/A` for the `/syncall` operations. The following command synchronizes *all partitions* stored on *NETDC1* DC with *all* its replication partners:

```
C:\>repadmin /syncall netdc1.net.dom /A
```

The following command replicates *one partition* from *one partner* (specified by its GUID):

```
C:\>repadmin /sync DC=net,DC=dom netdc1.net.dom
↳ a10bc624-6d04-44e7-adf9-5ef4282efbb1
```

Normally, RepAdmin waits for replication to be completed. You can add the `/async` parameters to the command to start an operation and not wait for its completion.

RepAdmin will be described in detail in *Chapter 11*, "*Verifying Network and Distributed Service*."

Active Directory Replication Monitor (ReplMon.exe) (ST)

A GUI tool, ReplMon.exe, provides an administrator with the following replication modes (from the most "global" to more granular ones) for a server specified:

- Synchronize *each* directory partition with *all* replication partners (there are three additional options available with this mode)
- Synchronize *this* directory partition with *all* replication partners
- Synchronize *this* directory partition with *this* replication partner

You never need wait for a replication operation to complete, and all operation results are written to the log files.

RepAdmin is described in detail in *Chapter 11*, "*Verifying Network and Distributed Service*."

Additional Replication Tools

- To force synchronization of replica sets managed by the **File Replication Service** (FRS), the contents of the SYSVOL volume, for example, use the `ntfrsutl poll` command. See details in *Chapter 11*, *"Verifying Network and Distributed Services."*

To synchronize a Windows 2000- or Windows .NET-based server that owns the PDC Emulator FSMO role with **Backup Domain Controllers** (BDCs) in a mixed-mode domain, use the NLtest.exe tool. See the `/REPL`, `/SYNC`, `/BDC_QUERY`, and other parameters of this tool. The *LBridge.cmd* command file from the *Windows 2000 Server Resource Kit* should be used for copying files from the System Volume (SYSVOL) share to the export directory on a Windows 4.0-based BDC.

You can write **custom scripts** that will initiate replication events in accordance with your own strategy. See, for example, *Listing 17.17* in *Chapter 17*, *"Scripting Administrative Tasks."*

Delegating Administrative Control

One of the most remarkable features that Active Directory realizes is the possibility of delegating all or part of administrative power over an OU or a directory container to a group or a user (in both Windows 2000 and Windows .NET domains). Delegation of control is essentially the same thing as "wizard-aided" granting of permissions on Active Directory objects to a user or group. You can *manually* assign the permissions necessary for performing this administrative task to a user or group, but this process is considerably simplified thanks to the *Delegation of Control Wizard*. Delegating control is quite a simple operation, and problems are only possible when delegated tasks are being revoked from the user or group.

An administrator can delegate control (i.e., use the Delegation of Control Wizard rather than manually assign permissions) for the following Active Directory objects (common administrative tasks are cited in parentheses):

- In the **Active Directory Sites and Services** snap-in (typical permissions are Full Control, Read/Write, Create/Delete All Child Objects, Read/Write All Properties):
  - *Sites* container
  - *Inter-Site Transport* container
  - *Subnets* container
  - A site(s) (only *Manage Group Policy links* task)
  - *Server* container in site(s)
- In the **Active Directory Users and Computers** snap-in (the list of available permissions depends on the type of Active Directory container):
  - Entire domain (Join a computer to the domain; Manage Group Policy links)
  - Organizational unit (Create, delete, and manage user account; Reset passwords on user accounts; Read all user information; Create, delete, and man-

age groups; Modify the membership of a group; and Manage Group Policy links. In Windows .NET, there are a few additional tasks.)

- *Computers* container
- *ForeignSecurityPrincipals* container
- *System* container
- *Users* container

Attention

- Remember that the *Authenticated Users* group (i.e., *any* logged on user) by default has permission to add 10 computers to a domain. This group has permission to *Read All Properties* of a domain object; consequently, the group can read the value of the *ms-DS-MachineAccountQuota* attribute, which by default is equal to 10. (This value can be viewed or modified by using the **ADSI Edit** snap-in.) Draw your own conclusions. (You might want to change this situation.)

To start the process of delegating control, run the appropriate snap-in, point to an Active Directory container, OU, or the domain itself in the tree pane, and select the **Delegate control** command on the context or **Action** menu. Depending on the container type, you can select a *common* task(s) or create a *custom* task. In the first case, you use a pre-defined set of permissions, while in the second case, you select objects and permissions yourself, which allows you to be more specific in delegating the administrative rights.

Although it is very simple to *delegate* control, *revoking* administrative rights from a user or a group requires a bit more effort and clearer understanding of the process. You must turn on the *Advanced Features* mode (see the previous chapter), select the container over which control has been delegated, and open the **Security** tab in the container's **Properties** window. Then, find the permissions and access control settings for the user or the group, and delete them. By doing so, you are editing the ACL entries for a directory object. Delegation of control is done using the same process, but is simplified thanks to the wizard. Understanding this aspect will help you to manipulate directory objects easily and flexibly and, as a result, to tune Active Directory accordingly to fit your tasks.

Look at Fig. 8.5. The Delegation of Control Wizard has been executed twice. First, the permission to join computers to the domain has been delegated to the *Admins* group. (You can see that permission as inherited from the domain context *DC=net,DC=dom.*) Second, the *Admins* group has received the permission to create, delete, and manage user accounts in the *Staff* OU. That right is defined at the OU level and not inherited. As a result, the *Full Control*, *Create/Delete User Objects*, and *Create Computer Objects* permissions have been added to the access control lists (ACL) of the domain container and the Staff OU. (In Fig. 8.5, you can see these permissions in the **Permission entries** pane — the first three lines.) You could add these permissions manually, but the wizard helps you to do this without error and frees you from having to know about all the details of Active Directory object inheritance and permissions.

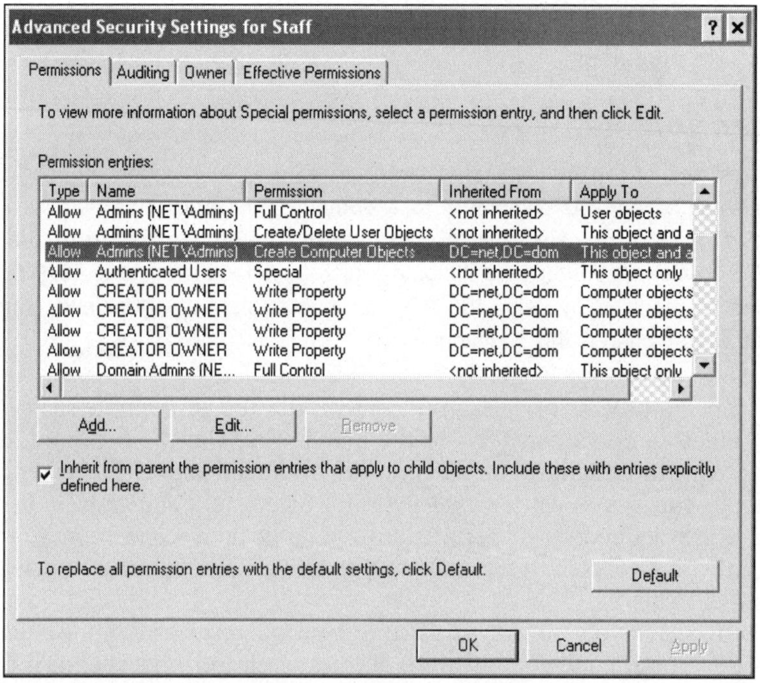

Fig. 8.5. The result of using the Delegation of Control Wizard: the highlighted permission allows the Admins group to join computers to the domain and manage users in the Staff OU

If you want to *revoke all* administrative rights from the Admins group, you should perform the following steps:

1. To revoke control power over the Staff OU, delete the first two lines in the **Permission entries** pane.

   In Windows .NET, you can click the **Default** button, and *all* permissions added for the selected directory object will be deleted. Be careful, since: 1) other users or groups might have administrative rights over the object, and you will delete *all* additional permissions; and, 2) the *inherited* permissions will be restored.
2. To delete the inherited permissions — the Create Computer Objects permission in our case — open the **Security** tab of that object where the permissions have been defined, and delete corresponding line(s) in the **Permission entries** pane.

On the other hand, you might want to allow the Admins group to perform some *additional* tasks (after the Delegation of Control Wizard has been executed once, or in any moment). Click **Edit** on the **Permissions** tab (see Fig. 8.5). The **Permission Entry** window will allow you to define permissions (or delegate/revoke administrative control, which is the same thing) on the selected object with greater granularity then the wizard allows. As you can see in Fig. 8.6, there are a number of operations whose execution by the selected user or group it is possible to allow/forbid.

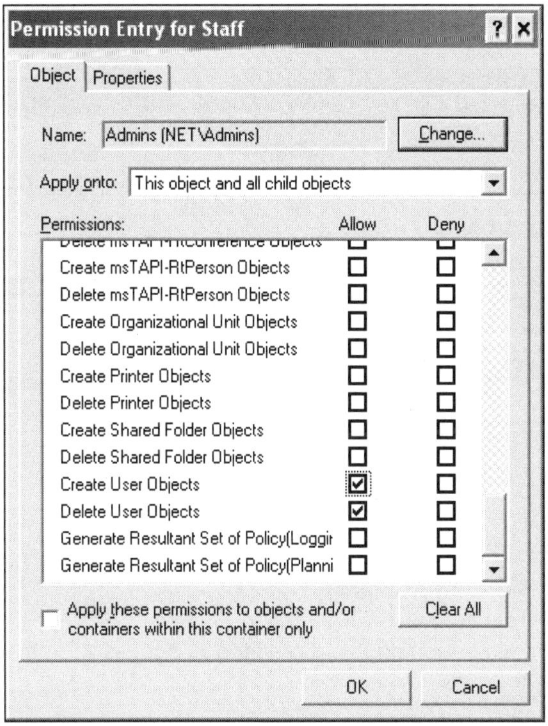

Fig. 8.6. "Fine tuning" of permissions on the selected directory object

Auditing Access to Active Directory Objects

In general, the procedure of enabling audit consists of two steps. To audit access to Active Directory, you must:

1. Enable the appropriate auditing policy.
2. Specify events to audit.

Auditing access to Active Directory objects relates to operations performed on the domain controller. Therefore, the most appropriate place to enable audit is the *Default Domain Controllers Policy* (or another GPO linked to the *Domain Controllers* OU). You may use either the **Group Policy Object Editor** snap-in linked to that GPO or the **Domain Controller Security Policy** snap-in. Select the node **Computer Configuration | Windows Settings | Security Setting | Local Policies | Audit Policy** and click twice on the *Audit directory service access* policy (Fig. 8.7). (Default setting for all audit policies — `No auditing`.) Then set the **Define these policy settings** flag and check the **Success** and/or **Failure** box.

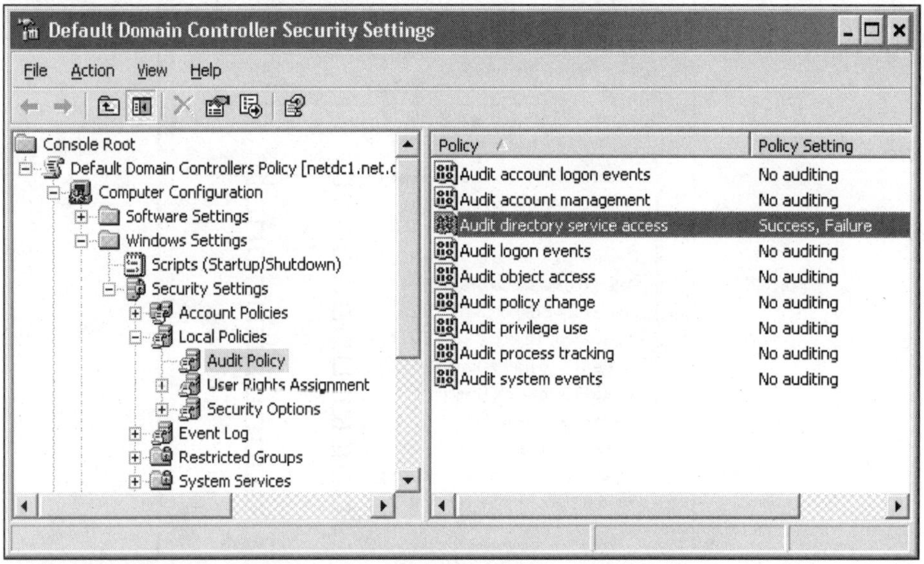

Fig. 8.7. Enabling auditing events related to access to Active Directory objects

Attention

No auditing and *Not defined* are not the same thing. When a policy is *Not defined*, you can define it at any other level. If a policy is set to *No auditing*, it overwrites all possible settings from other levels. The group policies for the Domain Controllers OU are applied the latest and have the highest priority. Therefore, the default audit settings defined by these policies override any parameters assigned at other (lower priority) levels.

After the policy has been set, you can `immediately` apply it with either the `secedit/refreshpolicy machine_policy` or `gpupdate /Target:Computer` command.

For read operations, it is recommended that you audit *failure* events, because a large number of *successful* event entries can quickly overflow the Security log.

The performance of domain controllers can also suffer. For write, create/delete, and other similar operations (that are much less frequent than read operations), it is possible to audit both *success* and *failure* events.

By default, special access (successful and failed events) to all objects in a domain is audited for the *Everyone* group. All domain objects inherit this setting from the root domain container (Fig. 8.8). Some containers have additional audit settings. All settings include auditing for "critical" operations, such as Write, Delete, Modify, and others. (Look up the entire list.)

You can see all audit entries in an object's **Properties** window: open the **Security** tab, click **Advanced,** and open the **Auditing** tab. Then click **Edit** to view or change audit parameters. If you open the **Auditing** tab for a non-root directory object, you will notice that all checked boxes are grayed out. This means that all parameters are inherited from the parent object. They cannot be directly modified, so you may need to address the parent or root object. If you check a free box, the system will create a new auditing entry and *add* it to the list for the selected object only.

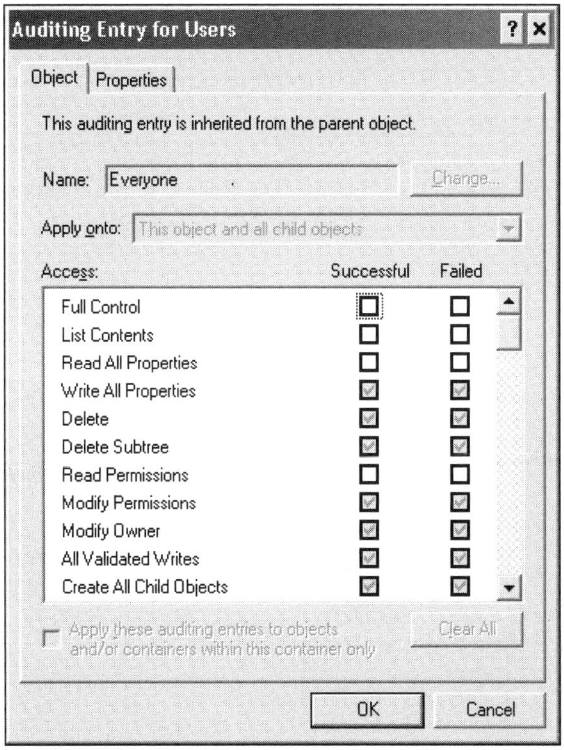

Fig. 8.8. The default audit settings for the Users container

Caution

Because successful events are registered by default, you might get a huge number of entries in the Event Viewer when working with auditing turned on. Therefore, you might want to change the default settings when performing an audit for an extended period of time.

You can view all information on audit events in the Security log of the Event Viewer. The source for these events is "Security", and the category is "Directory Service Access".

Recovering Active Directory

General Considerations

The standard Backup utility (NTBackup.exe) allows you to back up and restore both critical data and Active Directory. Operations with Active Directory can only be done *locally* for each domain controller. A backup operation is performed while a DC is online. To restore Active Directory on a DC, you must boot this DC into *Directory Service Restore Mode* (press <F8> at the computer startup).

System State

Backing up Active Directory is a part of the process of saving the *System State* data of a DC. You cannot back up (or restore) individual items of the System State. On a member server or a workstation, the System State includes the following:

- Boot Files
- COM+ Class Registration Database
- Registry

On a domain controller, two other items are added (Fig. 8.9):

- Active Directory (the ntds.dit, edb.chk, edb*.log, and res1.log and res2.log files)
- SYSVOL (System Volume) (by default, the *%SystemRoot%*\SYSVOL\sysvol folder)

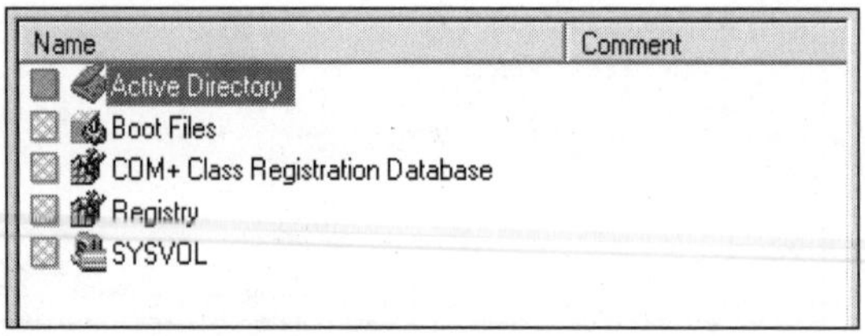

Fig. 8.9. Components of a domain controller's System State

If the Certificate Services are installed on a server or DC, there is one more item:

- Certificate Server

Important

- From the foregoing, it is possible to draw two very important conclusions:
  - You cannot backup the System State on a DC and restore it to another DC, since the System State comprises such important information as Registry, COM+ Class Registration Database, TCP/IP configuration, etc. If you restore backup media on another computer, you will get the same system parameters as the original DC has, which results in fatal conflict.
  - There is no means to save/restore Active Directory configuration "itself", i.e., independently of the domain controllers' configuration. During each restoration of the System State you will reconstruct a *specific* DC. That is why the export/import tools, such as LDIFDE and CSVDE, could be very useful, since they allow you to save/restore the custom Active Directory information only.

Schema

Modifications of the schema are irreversible, so you cannot restore an older version of the schema. Created attributes and classes cannot be deleted, and it is only possible to *deactivate* them. When restoring Active Directory, you cannot mark the *Schema* partition as authoritative.

Tombstones

A recovery plan should take into account the lifetime of the Active Directory *tombstones* (60 days, by default; minimal value is 2 days). This parameter is stored (if it is defined) in the *tombstoneLifetime* attribute of a directory object named *N=Directory Service,CN=Windows NT,CN=Services,CN=Configuration,DC=<ForestRoot>*. Tombstone is a deleted object that is maintained in Active Directory during its lifetime, before the system eventually destroys it. The age of the backup tape should not exceed this period of time, otherwise the outdated data will be rejected.

Using Backup Media to Install Additional Domain Controllers

To reduce the amount of replicated data while promoting a Windows .NET-based server to additional domain controller, you can use a backup file that contains the System State of an existing DC. Therefore, you first need to save current Active

Directory information. This operation will be the same the System State backup discussed below. *Chapter 5, "Installing Active Directory,"* covers information on how to restore a backup file and use it for the promotion of a server.

Backing up Active Directory

To back up the System State:

1. Run the Backup utility: click **Start** | **All Programs** | **Accessories** | **System Tools** | **Backup** or enter `ntbackup` in the **Run** window.
2. Click the **Backup** tab and check the **System State** box in the tree pane. (You can include some files in the backup as well.)
3. Enter the name of the backup file in the Backup media or file name field (keep the file extension BKF) and click **Start Backup**.
4. In the **Backup Job Information** window (Fig. 8.10), enter the necessary data and click **Advanced**.

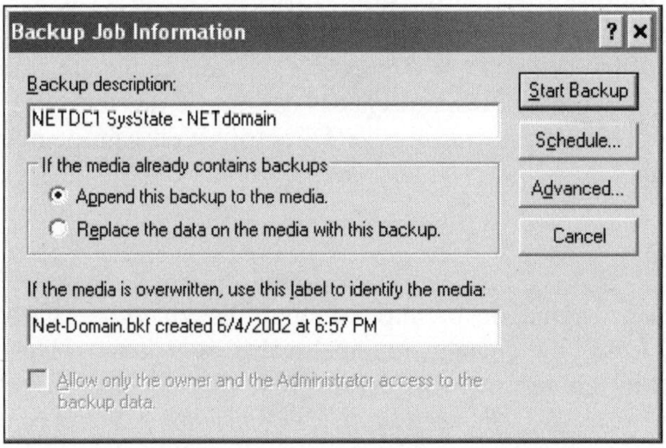

Fig. 8.10. Configuring a backup operation

5. The next window (Fig. 8.11) will allow you to set backup options. The System State should always be saved as a *normal backup*. You might want to clear the **Automatically backup System Protected Files with the System State** box set by default if you need a compact backup file without all system files. Usually, it is enough to have such a compact file (40–50 MB for small domains) for many operations related to saving/restoring Active Directory. A full backup of the System State will be about 300 MB in size.

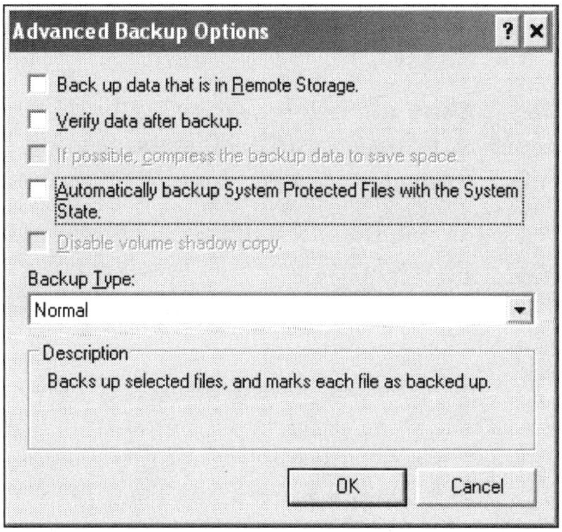

Fig. 8.11. Defining additional backup parameters

6. Close the **Advanced Backup Options** window and click **Start Backup** — the backup process will begin.

Note

Only the *full* backup will allow you to safely restore a crashed DC. It is possible to repair the system from scratch in about 30–40 minutes. Restore a domain controller image from a CD or network drive by using an image-duplicating tool like *Norton Ghost*. Boot the server, and restore the full backup file. You will get a fully operational DC retaining its SID, GUID, and other mandatory Active Directory parameters.

Restoring Active Directory

Restore is a more complicated process than back up. Generally, you have two options:

- Reinstall the system on the damaged computer, promote it to a domain controller, and copy Active Directory information from other DCs through replication. You will get an entirely new DC, and, therefore, need to delete any references to the old DC from Active Directory.
- Restore Active Directory from backup media, retaining the DC identity (SID, GUID, etc.).

There are three different methods of restoring the System State from the backup media:

- Perform a **primary restore** when you have the only DC in the domain and want to rebuild this domain. A primary restore builds a new FRS database; therefore, the restored data will be replicated to other controllers in the domain.
- If there is at least one operational DC in the domain, perform a **non-authoritative (normal) restore**. The repaired DC will receive current data *from* other DCs through normal replication. The restored data will never be replicated *to* other DCs. This is the most used type of restore.
- If you want to restore inadvertently deleted Active Directory data and to replicate these data *to* the other DCs, perform an **authoritative restore**. You cannot perform a "true" rollback, since authoritative restore does not affect changes made in the directory after the backup was created. These new data will be replicated to the restored DC.

Important

It is possible to authoritatively restore any directory partitions ***excluding*** the Schema partition.

Remember that, in any case, Active Directory can be restored only when a DC has been booted into the Directory Service Restore Mode.

Primary Restore

To restore a standalone domain controller:

1. Run the Backup utility and open the **Restore and Manage Media** tab (Fig. 8.12).
2. Select the necessary media and check the **System State** box. Files should be restored to the **Original location**.
3. Click **Start Restore** and confirm overwriting current System State in the **Warning** pop-up window.
4. Click **Advanced** in the **Confirm Restore** window.
5. Set the checkbox shown in Fig. 8.13. Close the window, and begin restore.
6. When the Backup utility will finish and propose you to reboot the computer, answer positively — reboot the computer into normal mode.

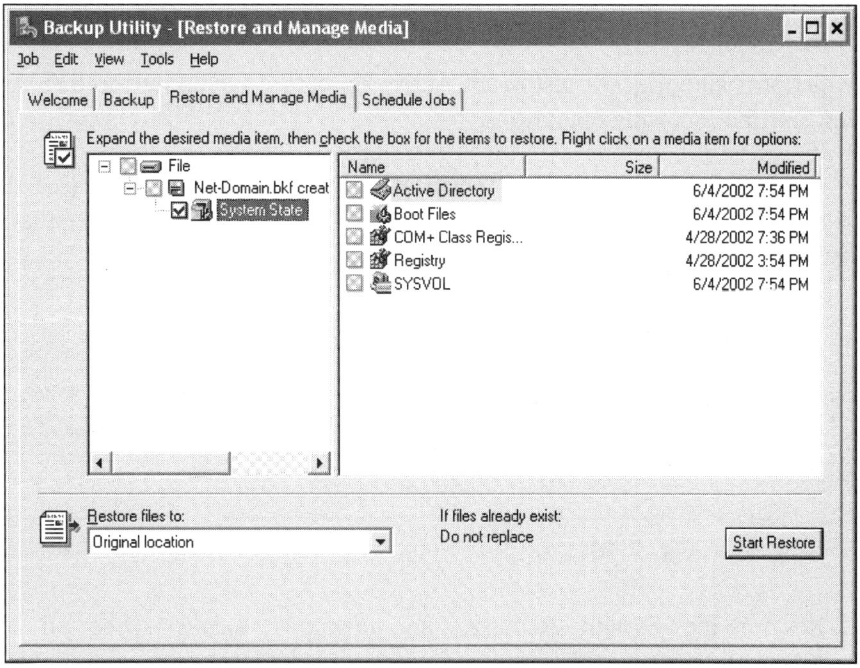

Fig. 8.12. Restoring the System State from a backup media

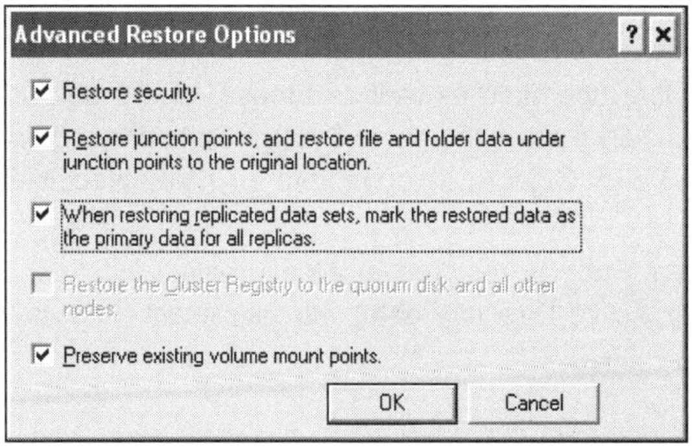

Fig. 8.13. This checkbox is only set for a primary restore

Non-Authoritative (Normal) Restore

A non-authoritative restore is performed as a primary restore; the difference is that you should keep default settings of all options, i.e., the checkbox shown in Fig. 8.13 must be cleared. The restored DC will receive all changes from its replication partners.

Authoritative Restore

To perform authoritative restore of Active Directory including the SYSVOL volume, carry out the following operations:

1. Run the Backup utility and perform non-authoritative restore (see the previous section). When the Backup utility completes its work, it proposes that you restart the computer (Fig. 8.14). ***You must click*** **No**.

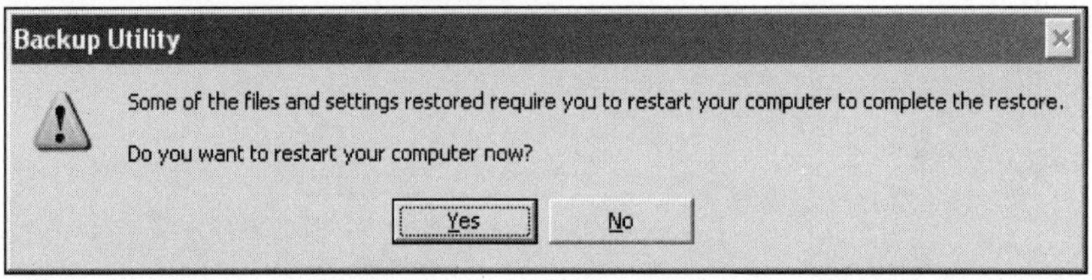

Fig. 8.14. Click **No** if you perform an authoritative restore

2. Restore the System State to an *alternative location*. See an example in Fig. 8.15.

Important

This second restore operation as well as Steps 5 and 6 below are only necessary if you need to authoritatively restore the entire System State or directory objects along with corresponding Group Policy Objects. If you restore a single object, skip this step and go directly to Step 3.

When the System State is restored to an alternative location, the current System State (e.g., Registry or Active Directory data) will stay intact. That is why you should carry out restore twice.

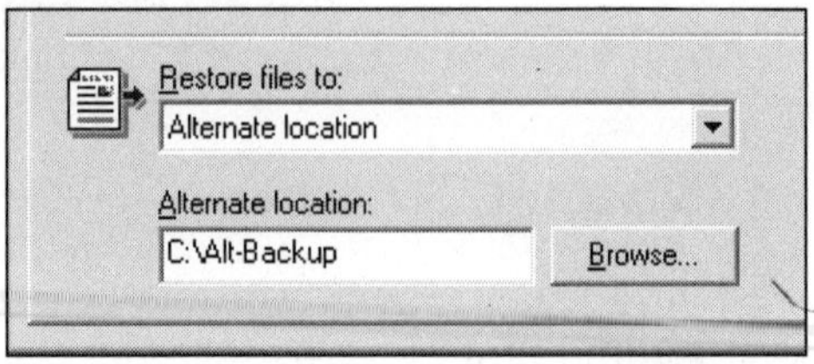

Fig. 8.15. Selecting an alternative location for a restore operation

3. On Windows .NET-based servers, the following folders will appear in the specified folder or on the disk (Fig. 8.16):

   - Active Directory (ntds.dit, edb*.log; these files can be used later to promote a server to additional DC)
   - Boot Files
   - COM+ Class Registration Database (ComReg.Db.bak)
   - Registry (default, SAM, SECURITY, software, system)
   - SYSVOL (this folder reflects the structure of the SYSVOL volume)

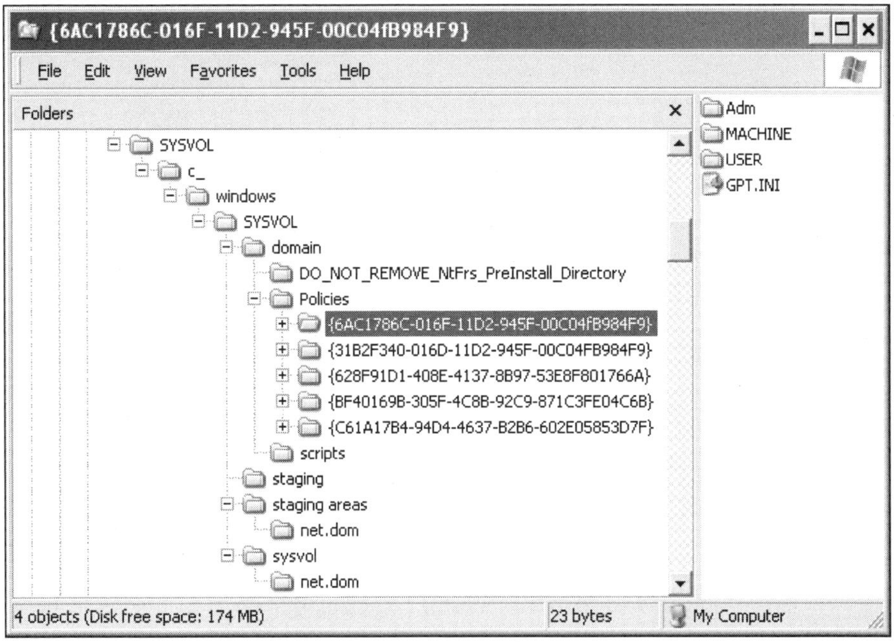

Fig. 8.16. Structure of the SYSVOL folder in alternative location (for domain *net.dom*)

4. When you restore data to an alternative location, the program does not offer to reboot the computer. Close the Backup program.
5. Run *NTDSutil.exe* from the command prompt. A sample dialog for the *authoritative restore* command is placed below (a subtree is restored in this example):

```
C:\>ntdsutil
ntdsutil: Authoritative restore
authoritative restore: Restore subtree OU=Staff,DC=net,DC=dom
[Confirm the restore operation — click Yes in the pop-up window.}
```

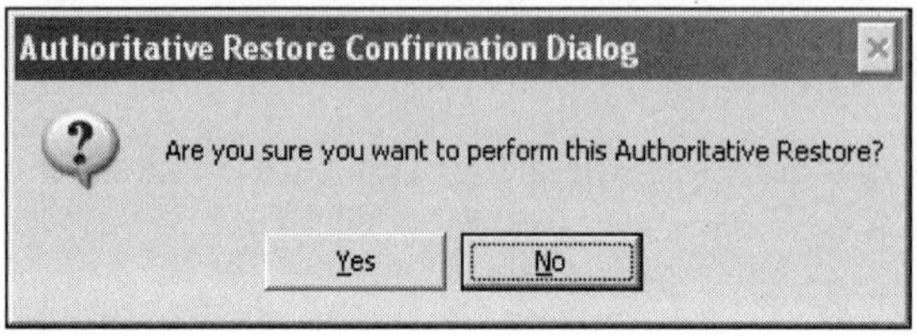


```
Opening DIT database... Done.

The current time is 06-04-02 20:41.05.
Most recent database update occured at 06-03-02 17:52.23.
Increasing attribute version numbers by 200000.

Counting records that need updating...
Records found: 0000000038
Done.

Found 38 records to update.
Updating records...
Records remaining: 0000000000
Done.

Successfully updated 38 records.

Authoritative Restore completed successfully.
authoritative restore: Quit
ntdsutil: Quit
```

6. Reboot the computer into normal mode and ***wait until the SYSVOL volume will be published*** (look for event ID 13516 in the File Replication Service log and use the `net share` command to monitor when the process will be completed).
7. Copy contents of the SYSVOL volume from the alternative location to an existing one. These changes of the SYSVOL volume will be the most recent and, therefore, will be replicated to other DCs as the authoritative data.

In the example shown, an OU object has been restored. You can mark an individual object (in the Windows .NET environment), subtree, or entire directory partition as authoritative. This, however, does not extend to the *Schema* partition.

Caution

- Use authoritative restore with necessary directory objects only. Be very selective and do not restore excessive objects. Be especially careful with the *Configuration* partition. Do not use the `restore database` command unless you completely understand how restore operations work.

Notice the line in bold that indicates an increment of the attribute version numbers, and two previous lines. The version numbers increase by 100,000 for each day after the original backup has been performed. You can view changes of metadata by using *ReplMon.exe*. In our case, for example, the following command will be used:

```
repadmin /showmeta OU=Staff,DC=net,DC=dom netdc4.net.dom
```

By using this command on different DCs, you can verify whether the authoritative restore was successful, and trace the replication's propagation.

If objects in your Active Directory installation have very low volatility, you might wish to override the default value of the version increment. Use a command similar to the following:

```
restore subtree OU=Staff,DC=net,DC=dom verinc 1000
```

PART IV

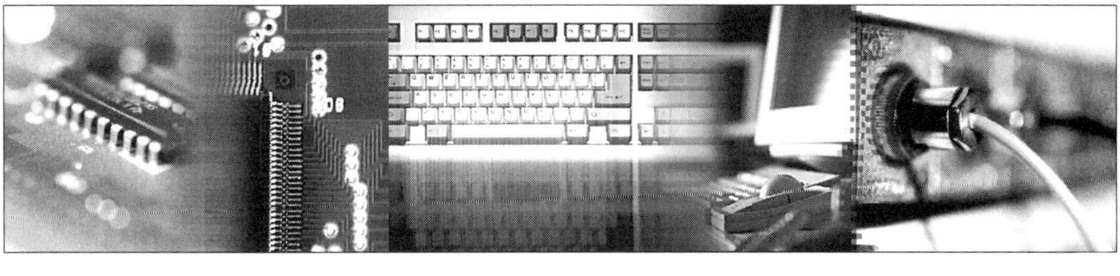

Using System Utilities and Support Tools

Chapter 9: General Characteristics and Purpose of System Tools

Long, long ago, in the time of mainframes and mini-computers, every system programmer knew that if the system was in a faulty state, it was time to run a test. Now, in the epoch of the PC and various GUI tools, system administrators have somewhat forgotten that certain handy and powerful diagnostics facilities still exist. Thanks to them, you need not rack your brains over the sources of these problems (i.e., you do not have to try to find the error source logically). You can get useful and extensive diagnostic information (that can be used for further analysis) quickly and easily, or often even get a ready answer — the reason for the error — right away.

Since Windows 2000 systems came into the world the importance of these facilities has just been confirmed; since many problems that occur during Windows 2000 deployment and maintenance require the use of various command-line or GUI diagnostic tools. The new server platform — Windows .NET — does not change the situation a bit. Sometimes, you need to even better understand how to use these tools for performing routine operations, since there are no other means to accomplish one's goal.

In this chapter, let us try to classify and characterize various system tools provided by Microsoft that help administrators manage and troubleshoot Active Directory services. This chapter should help you to quickly find an appropriate tool for a specific task. In the following chapters, most of these tools are described in more detail. My aim is not to provide comprehensive information on each parameter or option. (You can easily use the built-in help messages or Help files, and obtain a list of all available keys.) We will focus on the most interesting, useful, or non-evident features as well as examples of how to use these tools in real life.

Where Can You Find All These Tools?

Windows .NET Support Tools

Sometimes, administrators forget or simply do not know that each Windows 2000 or Windows .NET (as well as Windows XP) installation CD contains a pack of powerful tools named *Windows Support Tools*. (This pack is the same for both Professional and Server versions of Windows 2000. Windows .NET servers have more recent versions of the Support Tools then Windows XP.) This pack must be installed separately from the operation system itself. Run the Setup.exe or Suptools.msi file from the \SUPPORT\TOOLS folder, and install the pack on the hard disk. (The Windows .NET Support Tools require about 20 MB of the hard disk space.) Then you will be able to start the tools from the **Start** menu or the command prompt.

Windows Resource Kit

The Windows Support Tools can be regarded as a subset of the *Windows Resource Kit*, a separately purchased product that contains hundreds of various utilities as well as comprehensive printed documentation. (There are two versions of the Kit: Server and Professional. Many of the tools described below are present in both versions.) The Windows 2000 Resource Kit requires about 60 MB of the hard disk.

The good news is that the Windows 2000 Resource Kits (both Professional and Server versions including the *Windows 2000 Server Deployment Planning Guide*) and Windows XP Professional Resource Kit are freely accessible on the Microsoft TechNet website (see links in *Appendix A*). Moreover, some very useful tools from these kits can be also downloaded for free from the Microsoft website (see *Appendix A*).

At this time, the Windows .NET Server Resource Kit has not yet been released, so some of the tools (as well as various administrative scripts) from Windows 2000 Server Resource Kit have been tested in the Windows .NET environment. They appear to work properly.

The Windows 2000 Server Resource Kit contains a collection of Visual Basic (VB) scripts called *Remote Administration Scripts*. Several scripts from this collection are mentioned in the tables in this chapter. (These scripts can safely run on Windows .NET servers, too.) If you are going to write your own scripts or applications, pay close attention to these scripts, since they will help you speed up the process of studying scripting basics (including ADSI programming concepts).

Classification by Purpose

First, you should become generally acquainted with the existing tools and the administrative tasks for which they are used. Look at Table 9.1. The tools from the *Windows 2000 Server Resource Kit* and *Windows .NET Support Tools* packs listed in this table are divided into categories depending on the basic purpose of a tool. In some cases, the grouping of tools is rather voluntary, since some utilities can be used for different purposes.

Active Directory Migration Tool (ADMT) and *AdsVw.exe* (from the *ADSI SDK*) can be downloaded for free from the Microsoft website (see links in *Appendix A*). They are also included in the table. Every tool mentioned here is characterized in Table 9.2.

Table 9.1. Windows 2000 Tools Sorted by the Purpose They Serve

Administrative task	Tools to be used
Browsing and editing Active Directory objects	ADSIEdit.msc, Ldp.exe, DsMod.exe, DsMove.exe, DsRm.exe, AdsVw.exe, ModifyUsers.vbs
Querying Active Directory	DsQuery.exe, DsGet.exe, Ldp.exe, Search.vbs, UserAccount.vbs, EnumProp.exe
Migration and restructure; manipulating Active Directory objects	ADMT, MoveTree.exe, NetDom.exe, ClonePrincipal, DsAdd.exe, AddUsers.exe, GrpCpy.exe

continues

Table 9.1 Continued

Administrative task	Tools to be used
Bulk import/export	CSVDE.exe, LDIFDE.exe, AddUsers.exe, CreateUsers.vbs
Active Directory database diagnostics and maintenance	NTDSutil.exe
Diagnosis	NetDiag.exe, NSlookup.exe, DCdiag.exe, NLtest.exe, DNSCmd.exe, RPCPing
Replication	RepAdmin.exe, ReplMon.exe, DsaStat.exe, NTFRSutl.exe
Active Directory security	ACLDiag.exe, DsACLs.exe, SDCheck.exe, KerbTray.exe, KList.exe
System objects (files, shares, registry, etc.) security	SIDWalker, SubInACL.exe, ADMT
Group Policies	GPOTool.exe, GPResult.exe

Note

Windows 2000 servers provide a few "traditional" utilities for administering Windows NT 4.0 domains: *Server Manager* (srvmgr.exe), *User Manager* (usrmgr.exe), and *System Policy Editor* (poledit.exe). These tools have not been included in the current version of Windows .NET servers. The Windows 2000 Server Resource Kit also contains the *Domain Monitor* (dommon.exe). All named tools are the updated versions that differ from their Windows NT 4.0 counterparts. This may be important in some cases. Windows .NET servers do not and, most likely, will not contain the utilities listed, but all of them can safely run on Windows .NET-based computers within AD-based domains.

Description of the Selected Tools

Table 9.2 lists the file names of the tools as well as their "official" names; a short description of each tool's characteristics is also given. The table is sorted by the names of the files, because it is the *filename* of a tool that you will use most often. In addition, the name of the pack that contains the tool is specified, along with the chapter of this book that contains the most complete information about using the tool. ("ST" stands for the *Windows .NET Support Tools*, "RK" means the *Windows 2000 Server Resource Kit*, and "RAS" is the abbreviation for *Remote Administration Scripts*. "Sys" means that the tool is a standard system tool. These marks are also present in the subtitles of the following chapters.)

Important

- Most of the selected tools are contained in both Windows 2000 and Windows .NET systems and can safely run on both Windows 2000- and Windows XP/.NET-based computers. The Windows .NET versions of the tools, as a rule, cannot run on Windows 2000-based computers, so you need to take into account the limitations specific for each tool. See the detailed information in the chapter specified.

  A few brand-new tools are marked by an asterisk (*).

Table 9.2. Purpose of the Selected Windows 2000 and Windows .NET Tools

Tool name	Contained in	Purpose	See chapter
ACLDiag.exe (ACL Diagnostics)	ST	View permissions (ACLs) on a directory object. Verify delegation of administrative control, and whether the object security settings correspond to the schema defaults.	14
AddUsers.exe (Add Users)	RK	Output, create, and delete multiple user accounts. Add users to groups.	8
ADSIEdit.msc (ADSI Edit snap-in) (GUI tool)	ST	View and modify Active Directory objects (including application, schema, and configuration directory partitions). Set objects' ACLs.	7
AdsVw.exe (Active Directory Browser) (GUI tool)	ADSI SDK	Same as above, for both Active Directory-based (Windows 2000 and Windows .NET) and Windows NT domains (SAM database).	12
ClonePrincipal	ST	Create a copy of a user or group account in a different forest and retain user or group access rights to directory objects or shared resources. (Includes Clonepr.dll, Clonepr.vbs, Clonelg.vbs, Clonegg.vbs, Cloneggu.vbs, SIDHist.vbs tools.)	13
CreateUsers.vbs	RK (RAS)	Create multiple user accounts in default or specified containers.	8
CSVDE.exe (CSV Directory Exchange)	Sys	Export and import multiple directory objects using a file in CSV format.	12
DCdiag.exe (Domain Controller Diagnostic Tool)	ST	Diagnose domain controller issues: connectivity, availability of the directory and other services, replication, etc.	10
DHCPloc.exe (DHCP Server Locator Utility)	ST	Display active DHCP servers and detect any unauthorized servers. Find DHCP servers available to a DHCP client.	4

continues

Table 9.2 Continued

Tool name	Contained in	Purpose	See chapter
DNScmd.exe (DNS Server Troubleshooting Tool)	ST	Check and/or modify zones and resource records on a Windows 2000/.NET DNS server. Manage the zones and the DNS server configuration. For the Windows .NET version only: Create/delete an application directory partition, control partition replication scope, move a zone to another directory partition.	4
DsACLs.exe	ST	View and/or modify permissions (ACLs) on directory objects. Restore default permissions.	14
DsAdd.exe*	Sys	Add to the directory a computer, contact, group, OU, or user object.	8
DsaStat.exe (DSA Statistics)	ST	Compare directory partitions on two different domain controllers and display statistics or comparisons of attributes. Global Catalog servers can also be checked.	11
DsGet.exe*	Sys	Retrieve the attributes of a specific object type from the directory.	12
DsMod.exe*	Sys	Modify attributes of a specific object type (computer, contact, group, OU, server, or user).	12
DsMove.exe*	Sys	Rename a directory object or move it to another container.	12
DsQuery.exe*	Sys	Search the directory for objects of any type and display any attributes of found objects. The most flexible command-line search tool.	12
DsRm.exe*	Sys	Delete a directory object or an entire subtree.	12
DumpFSMOs.cmd	RK	Display the FSMO roles known to the specified domain controller.	8
EnumProp.exe	RK	Display some or all attributes (including GUIDs, SIDs, and security descriptor) of an Active Directory object specified by its distinguished name. (The LDAP provider is used.)	—
GPOTool.exe (Group Policy Verification Tool)	RK	Test consistency of GPOs and check their replication in a domain.	15

continues

Table 9.2 Continued

Tool name	Contained in	Purpose	See chapter
GPResult.exe (Group Policy Results)	RK (Windows 2000) Sys (Windows .NET)	View group policy settings applied to a user and/or computer	15
GPUpdate.exe*	Sys	Re-apply computer and/or user group policy settings	8
GrpCpy.exe (GUI Tool)	RK	Copy users from one group to another in the same or another domain	—
KerbTray.exe (Kerberos Tray) (GUI tool)	RK	Display and purge all cached Kerberos tickets for authenticated services	14
KList.exe (Kerberos List)	RK	Same as above. Can purge only specified tickets	14
Ksetup.exe (Kerberos Setup)	ST	Configure Windows 2000 clients to use an MIT Kerberos server instead of a Windows 2000 domain	—
KTPass.exe (Kerberos Keytab Setup)	ST	Configure a non-Windows 2000 (UNIX) Kerberos service as a security principal in the Windows 2000 Active Directory	—
LDIFDE.exe	Sys	Export and import one or more directory objects using a file in LDIF format. Modify attributes of object(s)	12
Ldp.exe (Active Directory Administration Tool) (GUI tool)	ST	Perform LDAP operations against any LDAP-compliant directory such as Active Directory	12
ModifyUsers.vbs	RK (RAS)	Modify specified attributes of multiple domain users. An input text file with defined values can be used	—
MoveTree.exe (Active Directory Object Manager)	ST	Move directory objects, such as user accounts, OUs, and universal groups from one domain to another in the same forest	13
NetDiag.exe (Network Connectivity Tester)	ST	Test various networking and connectivity issues (protocols, binding, DNS, WINS, and many others) on client computers	11
NetDom.exe (Windows Domain Manager)	ST	Manage and verify trusts and secure channels; join, move, and remove computer accounts	12

continues

Table 9.2 Continued

Tool name	Contained in	Purpose	See chapter
NLtest.exe (NLTest)	ST	List domain controllers for a domain, query for trusted domains, query and reset secure channels between domain computers, force replication to Windows NT 4.0 BDCs	11
NTDSutil.exe (Active Directory Diagnostic Tool)	Sys	Manage Active Directory database files, operations masters, orphaned domains and controllers. Perform authoritative restore	10
NTFRSutl.exe	RK	Manage the File Replication Service (including SYSVOL and DFS roots replication)	11
RepAdmin.exe (Replication Diagnostics Tool)	ST	Display replication partners, metadata and connections, force replication of directory partitions, trigger KCC	11
ReplMon.exe (Active Directory Replication Monitor) (GUI tool)	ST	Monitor and force replication, display replication metadata, topology, and domain controller information	11
RPingc.exe (GUI tool) and RPings.exe (RPC Ping: Connectivity Verification Tool)	RK	Test RPC connectivity between clients and RPC servers	11
SDCheck.exe (Security Descriptor Check Utility)	ST	Verify a directory object's ACL inheritance and replication of the security descriptor from one domain controller to another	14
Search.vbs	ST	Search for a object against an LDAP server	12
Security Administration tools (SIDWalker)	ST	Modify SIDs specified in the ACLs of files, shares, and registry keys. Grant access rights on objects to specified users and groups. (Include ShowAccs.exe, SIDWalk.exe, and SIDWalk.msc tools.)	–
SubInACL.exe	RK	Display security descriptors for files, registry keys, or services. Change security information such as owner of an object, domain name, or SID	–
UserAccount.vbs	RK (RAS)	Displays information on normal, locked out, and disabled user accounts in a domain	–

Chapter 10: Diagnosing and Maintaining Domain Controllers

The two system tools described in this chapter treat domain controllers as components that represent Active Directory as a *distributed* network service. In order for Active Directory to function properly as a whole, all of its elements — *Directory System Agents* (DSA) disposed on domain controllers — must be in good operational condition. Therefore, an administrator must have tools that can help him or her to test the actual state of every DC. Moreover, an administrator must have repair tools for those emergency cases when the Active Directory database needs restoring, cleaning up, or other "low-level" operations.

Domain Controller Diagnostic Tool (DCdiag.exe) (ST)

This utility, as a matter of fact, is a complex test (or more precisely — a set of specialized tests) that allows an administrator to give a DC a quick "check up" and locate any possible problems. DCdiag verifies the serviceability of a DC as well as its relations (connectivity, trusts, replication issues, etc.) with other DCs that are the replication partners of the selected DC. Thus, the utility primarily checks up parts of Active Directory at a functional rather than a logical level (i.e., aspects such as data consistency, semantic contents, etc., are not affected).

It would be a good idea to run DCdiag after and even before (see the description of the `DcPromo` and `RegisterInDns` tests in *Chapter 5*, "*Installing Active Directory*") installation of domain controllers. It is fairly typical — especially in small networks — for an administrator to successfully (in his or her opinion) install Active Directory on the first DC and consequently believe that the domain will automatically work correctly since no faults were detected or error messages received. Problems usually begin when the administrator adds clients to the domain or installs a second DC (in the same or a different domain). Apparently, the first (root forest) DC was configured incorrectly; very often this concerns DNS service (on a Windows 2000/.NET Server or a third-party server). In such a situation, DCdiag (especially in conjunction with NetDiag.exe) could locate many potential problems from the beginning.

The DCdiag utility can generate a very generous output — most of all, with enterprise-wide tests, and you should therefore use log files for subsequent analysis of the results. The diagnostic messages are quite informative and very often plainly specify a problem, so you need only eliminate it without any further analysis.

The Windows .NET version of DCdiag is sufficiently documented. You can use the built-in Help (`dcdiag /?`) as a quick reference on all parameters. (The built-in Help seems to be more accurate than *Support Tools Help*.) The *Windows 2000 Server Resource Kit* contains a great deal more information on how to use this utility. We shall discuss some of the most interesting features of DCdiag and examples of their use.

Note

For the Windows 2000 environment, it is recommended that you download the updated version of DCdiag from **http://www.microsoft.com/downloads/release.asp?ReleaseID=22939**.

You can run DCdiag from any network computer and test any DC in the forest. Some tests can be performed under a normal user account (`Replications`, `NetLogons`, and `ObjectsReplicated` cannot), but to get the full functionality of DCdiag, you must either be logged on as an administrator (or even as an enterprise administrator) or provide an administrator's credentials with the command.

The New Version of DCdiag

In comparison with Windows 2000, the Windows .NET version of DCdiag provides a few new tests:

- CrossRefValidation
- CheckSDRefDom
- VerifyReplicas
- VerifyReferences
- VerifyEnterpriseReferences

These tests are especially informative when used with `/a` and `/e` parameters that force the testing of all DCs in the current site or in the forest, respectively. Using these tests, you can quickly locate fault elements of the replication infrastructure — invalid cross-references, improper security descriptors, directory partitions that are not fully instantiated, etc. — particularly when there are many application directory partitions deployed in your enterprise.

Standard Full Test

First, let us look at what happens if DCdiag is passed successfully. You will see from this output how the tests are structured and which tests the DCdiag tool contains. The `Topology`, `CutoffServers`, and `OutboundSecureChannels` tests are omitted by default, so you must run them explicitly or use the `/c` (comprehensive) parameter.

In the Windows 2000 environment, DCdiag runs faster if you specify the DC's DNS name rather than its NetBIOS name. (If the DC name is omitted, your current logon server is implied.) The `/a` or `/e` parameters specified in a command allow you to run a selected test on every DC in a site or in the forest.

If you want to retrieve the maximum possible amount of information from DCdiag, use the `/v` (verbose) parameter with any test. As well, the `/d` parameter is equal to `/v`, and, in addition, produces plenty of information (`pDsInfo`) on your forest configuration. With these parameters, use the `more` pipe or redirect the output to a file in the current or another folder with the `/f` parameter. (The `pDsInfo` section of tests is never redirected to a file: use the pipe to save that information.)

Here is a typical command for testing a DC:

```
C:\>dcdiag /s:netdc3.net.dom [| more]
```

The command's output will be similar to:

```
Domain Controller Diagnosis

Performing initial setup:
   Done gathering initial info.

Doing initial required tests

   Testing server: NET-Site\NETDC3
      Starting test: Connectivity
         ......................... NETDC3 passed test Connectivity

Doing primary tests

   Testing server: NET-Site\NETDC3
      Starting test: Replications
         ......................... NETDC3 passed test Replications
      Starting test: NCSecDesc
         ......................... NETDC3 passed test NCSecDesc
      Starting test: NetLogons
         ......................... NETDC3 passed test NetLogons
      Starting test: Advertising
         ......................... NETDC3 passed test Advertising
      Starting test: KnowsOfRoleHolders
         ......................... NETDC3 passed test KnowsOfRoleHolders
      Starting test: RidManager
         ......................... NETDC3 passed test RidManager
      Starting test: MachineAccount
         ......................... NETDC3 passed test MachineAccount
      Starting test: Services
         ......................... NETDC3 passed test Services
      Starting test: ObjectsReplicated
         ......................... NETDC3 passed test ObjectsReplicated
      Starting test: frssysvol
         ......................... NETDC3 passed test frssysvol
```

```
      Starting test: kccevent
         ......................... NETDC3 passed test kccevent
      Starting test: systemlog
         ......................... NETDC3 passed test systemlog
      Starting test: VerifyReferences
         ......................... NETDC3 passed test VerifyReferences

   Running partition tests on : Schema
      Starting test: CrossRefValidation
         ......................... Schema passed test CrossRefValidation
      Starting test: CheckSDRefDom
         ......................... Schema passed test CheckSDRefDom

   Running partition tests on : Configuration
      Starting test: CrossRefValidation
         ......................... Configuration passed test CrossRefValidation
      Starting test: CheckSDRefDom
         ......................... Configuration passed test CheckSDRefDom

   Running partition tests on : net
      Starting test: CrossRefValidation
         ......................... net passed test CrossRefValidation
      Starting test: CheckSDRefDom
         ......................... net passed test CheckSDRefDom

   Running enterprise tests on : net.dom
      Starting test: Intersite
         ......................... net.dom passed test Intersite
      Starting test: FsmoCheck
         ......................... net.dom passed test FsmoCheck
```

The first two sections — `Initial setup` and `Initial required tests` — are always executed, even if you specify only one test. You may first run the full test to find any problems, which may exist. Then, it's advisable to run tests selectively in verbose mode to get a detailed diagnosis.

In practice, it is handy to run DCdiag with the `/q` parameter. If the DC is working properly, DCdiag will not display any messages at all, so you do not need to worry about anything. Otherwise, only the failed tests will be reported.

Error and diagnostic messages (in verbose mode) are very descriptive, so it is unnecessary to give many examples.

Testing DNS Registration and Accessibility of DCs

The mandatory `Connectivity` test is executed on every DCdiag test run. This test verifies the most important functionalities of a domain controller: whether all DNS resource records are registered on the preferred DNS server, and whether DCs are pingable and have LDAP/RPC accessibility. For example, using `/a` or `/e` parameters, you can quickly find all DCs that are not responsible. The following output will be displayed:

```
C:\>dcdiag /test:connectivity /e
...
   Testing server: NET-Site\NETDC2
      Starting test: Connectivity
         Server NETDC2 resolved to this IP address 192.168.0.2,
         but the address couldn't be reached(pinged), so check the
         network.
         The error returned was: Win32 Error 11010
         This error more often means that the targeted server is
         shutdown or disconnected from the network
         ......................... NETDC2 failed test Connectivity
...
```

The next output sample illustrates errors with DNS registration of the selected DC:

```
...
Doing initial required tests

   Testing server: NET-Site\NETDC1
      Starting test: Connectivity
         The host 02c2b1f6-e9b6-4e64-91f6-3a54b087bacc._msdcs.net.dom
         could not be resolved to an IP address.  Check the DNS server,
         DHCP, server name, etc. Although the Guid DNS name (02c2b1f6-
         e9b6-4e64-91f6-3a54b087bacc._msdcs.net.dom) couldn't be
         resolved, the server name (netdc1.net.dom) resolved to the IP
         address (192.168.0.1) and was pingable.  Check that the IP
         address is registered correctly with the DNS server.
         ......................... NETDC1 failed test Connectivity

Doing primary tests

   Testing server: NET-Site\NETDC1
      Skipping all tests, because server NETDC1 is
      not responding to directory service requests
...
```

As you can see from the foregoing messages, none of the other tests will even be started if there are any errors in the `Connectivity` section of DCdiag. You should first eliminate any existing issues before you continue the diagnosis. To locate the problem shown, use the `netdiag /test:DNS` command, and check all warnings in the "DNS test" section of the output data.

Verifying Replication

DCdiag allows an administrator to resolve replication problems quite well. Let us suppose that a site contains three domain controllers, one of which is refusing to replicate with its partners. The following command will test all DCs and check replication issues on each DC:

```
C:\>dcdiag /test:Replications /a /v
```

Only failed replication events will be included in the resulting report. The output of this command is the following:

```
Domain Controller Diagnosis

Performing initial setup:
   * Verifying that the local machine netdc1, is a DC.
   * Connecting to directory service on server netdc1.
   * Collecting site info.
   * Identifying all servers.
   * Identifying all NC cross-refs.
   * Found 3 DC(s). Testing 3 of them.
   Done gathering initial info.

Doing initial required tests

   Testing server: NET-Site\NETDC1
      Starting test: Connectivity
         * Active Directory LDAP Services Check
         * Active Directory RPC Services Check
         ......................... NETDC1 passed test Connectivity

   Testing server: NET-Site\NETDC3
...
  Testing server: NET-Site\NETDC2
```

```
...
Doing primary tests

   Testing server: NET-Site\NETDC1
      Starting test: Replications
         * Replications Check
         [Replications Check,NETDC1] A recent replication attempt failed:
            From NETDC3 to NETDC1
            Naming Context: DC=net,DC=dom
            The replication generated an error (8456):
            Win32 Error 8456
            The failure occurred at 2002-05-11 20:50:59.
            The last success occurred at 2002-05-11 19:48:32.
            6 failures have occurred since the last success.
            Replication has been explicitly disabled through the server options.
         [Replications Check,NETDC1] A recent replication attempt failed:
            From NETDC3 to NETDC1
            Naming Context: CN=Configuration,DC=net,DC=dom
...
         [Replications Check,NETDC1] A recent replication attempt failed:
            From NETDC3 to NETDC1
            Naming Context: CN=Schema,CN=Configuration,DC=net,DC=dom
...
         *Replication Latency Check
[Information on all directory partitions stored on that DC is reported here.]
            DC=ForestDnsZones,DC=net,DC=dom
               Latency information for 1 entries in the vector were
                ignored. 0 were retired Invocations.  1 were either:
                read-only replicas and are not verifiably latent, or dc's
                no longer replicating this nc.  0 had no latency
                information (Win2K DC).
            DC=DomainDnsZones,DC=net,DC=dom
...
            CN=Schema,CN=Configuration,DC=net,DC=dom
...
            CN=Configuration,DC=net,DC=dom
...
            DC=net,DC=dom
...
            DC=subdom,DC=net,DC=dom
```

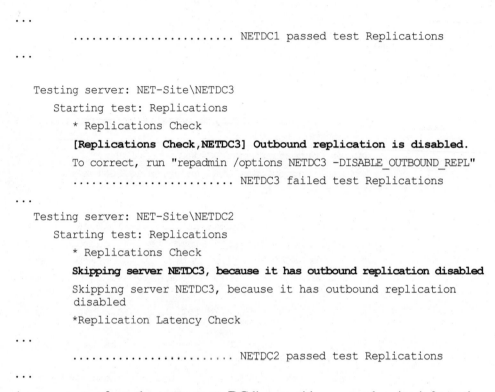

```
...
         ......................... NETDC1 passed test Replications
...

   Testing server: NET-Site\NETDC3
      Starting test: Replications
         * Replications Check
         [Replications Check,NETDC3] Outbound replication is disabled.
         To correct, run "repadmin /options NETDC3 -DISABLE_OUTBOUND_REPL"
         ......................... NETDC3 failed test Replications
...
   Testing server: NET-Site\NETDC2
      Starting test: Replications
         * Replications Check
         Skipping server NETDC3, because it has outbound replication disabled
         Skipping server NETDC3, because it has outbound replication
         disabled
         *Replication Latency Check
...
         ......................... NETDC2 passed test Replications
...
```

As you can see from the test output, DCdiag provides comprehensive information about failed connections for each DC in the site and on each directory partition.

If the local DC has not received replication information from a number of DCs within the configured latency interval (24 hours by default; see *Appendix B*), messages similar to the following ones will be included in the output:

```
         REPLICATION-RECEIVED LATENCY WARNING
         NETDC1:  Current time is 2002-05-10 19:24:28.
            CN=Schema,CN=Configuration,DC=net,DC=dom
               Last replication recieved from NETDC3 at 2002-05-09
19:16:55.
            CN=Configuration,DC=net,DC=dom
               Last replication recieved from NETDC2 at 2002-05-09
19:48:56.
...
```

To obtain additional information on replication topology, you can also use the `repadmin /showconn` command that verifies whether all required connections between DCs were created.

Testing Application Directory Partitions

Application directory partitions that appeared in Windows .NET can generate specific replication problems, and the Windows .NET version of DCdiag offers new tests for troubleshooting similar issues. The following example illustrates the `VerifyReplicas` test that checks on whether all application partitions have replicas stored on the DCs specified as replica servers for these partitions. The problem presented here was caused by missing permissions for the Enterprise Domain Controllers group on the `DC=ForestDnsZones, DC=net, DC=dom` partition, and could be easily detected by the `NCSecDesc` test. When the proper permissions are missed, the NETDC2 and NETDC3 domain controllers could not create the replicas of that partition and, therefore, generate the appropriate replication connections.

```
C:\>dcdiag /test:VerifyReplicas /a


Domain Controller Diagnosis
...
Doing initial required tests
...
Doing primary tests


   Testing server: NET-Site\NETDC1
      Starting test: VerifyReplicas
         ......................... NETDC1 passed test VerifyReplicas


   Testing server: NET-Site\NETDC3
      Starting test: VerifyReplicas
         This NC (DC=ForestDnsZones,DC=net,DC=dom) is supposed to be
         replicated to this server, but has not been replicated yet. This
         could be because the replica set changes haven't replicated here
         yet. If this problem persists, check replication of the
         Configuration Partition to this server.
         ......................... NETDC3 failed test VerifyReplicas

   Testing server: NET-Site\NETDC2
      Starting test: VerifyReplicas
...
         ......................... NETDC2 failed test VerifyReplicas
...
```

Enterprise Wide Tests

Enterprise tests check on many elements that are vitally necessary in order for an enterprise (forest) to work: intersite links, bridgehead servers, FSMO role owners and their accessibility, etc.

It is not a good idea to run the `Intersite` test on one DC only, so you must include the `/a` (current site) or `/e` (entire enterprise) parameters.

Here is a snippet of the test output for two sites (`NET-Site` and `Remote-Site`) in the forest `net.dom` (some lines are in bold for clarity):

```
C:\>dcdiag /test:Intersite /e /v

...

   Running enterprise tests on : net.dom

      Starting test: Intersite

         Doing intersite inbound replication test on site NET-Site:

            Locating & Contacting Intersite Topology Generator (ISTG) ...

               The ISTG for site NET-Site is: NETDC3.

            Checking for down bridgeheads ...

               Bridghead Remote-Site\NETDC2 is up and replicating fine.

               Bridghead NET-Site\NETDC1 is up and replicating fine.

            Doing in depth site analysis ...

               All expected sites and bridgeheads are replicating into
               site NET-Site.

         Doing intersite inbound replication test on site Remote-Site:

            Locating & Contacting Intersite Topology Generator (ISTG) ...

               The ISTG for site Remote-Site is: NETDC2.

            Checking for down bridgeheads ...

               Bridghead NET-Site\NETDC1 is up and replicating fine.

               Bridghead Remote-Site\NETDC2 is up and replicating fine.

            Doing in depth site analysis ...

               All expected sites and bridgeheads are replicating into
               site Remote-Site.

         ......................... net.dom passed test Intersite
```

Active Directory Diagnostic Tool (NTDSutil.exe) (Sys)

This utility is automatically installed into every domain controller (in the *%System-Roor%*\system32 folder). One could hardly say that this tool is for everyday use, but every administrator must be familiar with its features since it is used in certain operations that are very important for Active Directory functioning, such as Active Directory restore, offline defragmentation, FSMO role manipulating, and so on. However, NTDSutil has become one of the major tools for deploying and maintaining application directory partitions introduced in Windows .NET.

Some commands on the NTDSutil's main menu can only be performed when the system is booted in the *Directory Services Restore Mode* (press <F8> at system startup). (If, nevertheless, you wish to enable them, set the environmental variable `SAFEBOOT_OPTION=DSREPAIR`, and restart the utility. This is, however, not advisable, because conflicts with the running processes will not permit you to execute most of the available operations.) The following commands are prohibited when the Active Directory services are online:

- Authoritative restore
- Files
- Semantic database analysis

Windows .NET version of NTDSutil has two new commands:

- Configurable Settings
- Set DSRM Password

The `IP Deny List` command, available in Windows 2000 version, might not be included in Windows .NET.

Commands used in NTDSutil are quite long, but the utility accepts truncated syntax (or you can easily copy-and-paste commands from the built-in help messages). For example, the command

```
connect to server xxx
```

could be shortened to

```
co t s xxx
```

NTDSutil can be called from command files. An example of the invocation method is the DumpFSMOs.cmd file described in the *Chapter 8*, "*Common Administrative Tasks*".

Let's discuss the purpose and use of all NTDSutil's commands in the order in which the corresponding menus appear in the built-in Help.

Note

For presentation purposes, the command's prompts in the given dialogs are shown in bold.

In the Windows 2000 environment, the utility connects to DCs faster if you use the DNS rather than NetBIOS names of domain controllers.

Authoritative Restore

This menu contains commands that allow an administrator to perform an authoritative restore of the entire Active Directory database, a selected subtree, or an object. The commands' syntax is very simple, and it is much more difficult to understand how *to use* these simple commands. Since using commands from the `Authoritative Restore` menu as well as selecting the proper values for the `verinc` parameter is closely related to the entire process of backing up and restoring Active Directory, all of these commands are described in detail in *Chapter 8, "Common Administrative Tasks."*

Here, we will only look at the command that lists all cross-reference objects associated with domain partitions instantiated on the local domain controller. You cannot restore a partition if the corresponding cross-references is absent or has not been created. The following example shows two application partitions and three basic partitions:

```
ntdsutil: Authoritative restore
authoritative restore: List NC CRs

Opening DIT database... Done.

Listing locally instantiated writeable partitions and associated cross-refs:

1) Partition: DC=DomainDnsZones,DC=net,DC=dom
        cross-ref: CN=352cf7f5-327d-4316-9cb7-31c922273752,
CN=Partitions,CN=Configuration,DC=net,DC=dom
2) Partition: DC=ForestDnsZones,DC=net,DC=dom
        cross-ref: CN=3d9c5cba-34b5-4692-b43a-fa7a17161785,
CN=Partitions,CN=Configuration,DC=net,DC=dom
3) Partition: CN=Configuration,DC=net,DC=dom
        cross-ref: CN=Enterprise Configuration,
CN=Partitions,CN=Configuration,DC=net,DC=dom
4) Partition: CN=Schema,CN=Configuration,DC=net,DC=dom
        cross-ref: CN=Enterprise Schema,
CN=Partitions,CN=Configuration,DC=net,DC=dom
```

```
5) Partition: DC=net,DC=dom
        cross-ref: CN=NET,CN=Partitions,CN=Configuration,DC=net,DC=dom
Done.
authoritative restore: ...
```

Configurable Settings

NTDSutil allows you to tune some parameters Active Directory functioning is affected by. In the current version, this concerns only two settings that control *TTL* (Time-To-Live) values for *dynamic objects* (see details in *Chapter 2*, "*Active Directory Terminology and Concepts*" and *Appendix B*).

The following dialog illustrates how to view the current values of these parameters (first, you must be connected to a DC) and increase the value of *DynamicObjectMinTTL*:

```
configurable setting: Show Values

Setting                           Current(New) Seconds

DynamicObjectDefaultTTL           86400      [=1 day]
DynamicObjectMinTTL               900        [=15 minutes]

configurable setting: Set DynamicObjectMinTTL to 1800
configurable setting: Commit Changes
configurable setting: ...
```

Domain Management

The Windows .NET version of NTDSutil contains a lot of new commands in the `Domain Management` menu, since NTDSutil is the main tool for manipulating application directory partitions (see *Chapter 2*, "*Active Directory Terminology and Concepts*").

Essentially, the process of deploying application partitions is not too complicated: you can create and remove partitions, and add and remove the replicas of these partitions. To verify all similar operations, use the DCdiag tool and `repadmin /showconn` command.

Important

See also the description of the Dnscmd.exe utility in *Chapter 4, "Windows .NET DNS Server,"* since only this utility can perform some important operations with application directory partitions.

List Directory Partitions and Application Partition Replicas

First, you may wish to view *all* directory partitions stored on the selected DC. As you can see from the following sample output, the partitions list contains two built-in application partitions (`DC=ForestDnsZones,DC=net,DC=dom` and `DC=DomainDnsZones,DC=net,DC=dom`) created by default on the first DC in the forest if the DNS server is running on the same DC. These partitions are not specifically marked in the list.

```
domain management: List
Note: Directory partition names with International/Unicode characters
will only display correctly if appropriate fonts and language support
are loaded
Found 6 Naming Context(s)
0 - CN=Configuration,DC=net,DC=dom
1 - DC=net,DC=dom
2 - CN=Schema,CN=Configuration,DC=net,DC=dom
3 - DC=ForestDnsZones,DC=net,DC=dom
4 - DC=DomainDnsZones,DC=net,DC=dom
5 - DC=subdom,DC=net,DC=dom
domain management: ...
```

The following command lists all replicas for the specified partition (the command is applicable to *application partitions* only):

```
domain management: List NC Replicas DC=ForestDnsZones,DC=net,DC=dom
```

Creating and Deleting Naming Contexts (Partitions)

The following command creates a new application partition (`app-part.net.dom`) on the currently connected DC (`NULL` is specified instead of the domain controller's DNS name):

```
domain management: Create NC DC=App-Part,DC=net,DC=dom NULL
adding object DC=App-Part,DC=net,DC=dom
domain management: List
...
```

When you create a new partition, the appropriate DNS entries are automatically registered on the preferred DNS server. The distinguished name (DN) of the new partition is added to the *namingContexts* attribute of the *RootDSE* object on each DC that stores a replica of that partition. So you can test creation or deleting naming contexts with Ldp.exe tool.

To delete an application partition, use the following command:

```
domain management: Delete NC DC=App-Part,DC=net,DC=dom
```

```
The operation was successful. The partition has been marked for removal
from the enterprise. It will be removed over time in the background.

Note: Please do not create another partition with the same name until
the servers which hold this partition have had an opportunity to remove
it. This will occur when knowledge of the deletion of this partition has
replicated throughout the forest, and the servers which held the
partition have removed all the objects within that partition. Complete
removal of the partition can be verified by consulting the Directory
event log on each server.
domain management: ...
```

Adding and Removing Partition Replicas

To provide fault tolerance or increase the performance of an application partition, you should create a copy of that partition on several domain controllers, i.e., add them as *partition replicas*. The following command designates the `NETDC2` domain controller as a replica of the `app-part.net.dom` application partition:

```
domain management: Add NC Replica DC=App-Part,DC=net,
DC=dom netdc2.subdom.net.dom
domain management: List NC Replicas DC=App-Part,DC=net,DC=dom
The application directory partition DC=App-Part,DC=net,DC=dom's Replicas
are:
        CN=NTDS Settings,CN=NETDC2,CN=Servers,
CN=NET-Site,CN=Sites,CN=Configuration,DC=net,DC=dom
        CN=NTDS Settings,CN=NETDC1,CN=Servers,
CN=NET-Site,CN=Sites,CN=Configuration,DC=net,DC=dom
The *'ed items are currently uninstantiated replicas.
domain management: ...
```

If the replica has been successfully created, the new context is added to the replication connection with the specified DC. You can verify this with the `repadmin /showconn` command or the **Active Directory Sites and Services** snap-in. The appropriate KCC and NTDS Replication messages should appear in the Directory Service log:

```
Event Type:   Information
Event Source: NTDS KCC
Event Category:   Knowledge Consistency Checker
Event ID:  1903
...
User:       NT AUTHORITY\ANONYMOUS LOGON
Computer:  NETDC1
```

```
Description:
A replication link for the writable partition DC=App-Part,DC=net,
DC=dom from server CN=NTDS Settings,CN=NETDC2,CN=Servers,
CN=NET-Site,CN=Sites,CN=Configuration,DC=net,DC=dom has been added.
```

To remove a partition replica, use a command similar to the following one:

```
domain management: Remove NC Replica DC=ForestDnsZones,DC=net,
DC=dom netdc3.net.dom
```

Verify the operation result with the `List` command and **Event Viewer** snap-in (Event Source: NTDS KCC; Event ID: 1482):

```
...
The following directory partition is no longer available on the domain
controller at the following network address.
Directory partition:
DC=App-Part,DC=net,DC=dom
Domain controller:
CN=NTDS Settings,CN=NETDC2,CN=Servers,CN=NET-Site,CN=Sites,
CN=Configuration,DC=net,DC=dom
...
```

Creating Cross-Reference Objects

Creating a new domain or application directory partition (both represented by a cross-reference object in the *Configuration* partition of the forest) requires more administrative power than does promoting a server to domain controller or instantiating a partition on a domain controller. You may wish to divvy up the tasks of preparing a cross-reference and completing partition creation among employees with different administrative rights and not grant them full administrative power. The NTDSutil command allows you to preliminarily create a cross-reference object (in the existing forest), which could then be used by subordinate administrators.

The following dialog shows how to create a new domain (`intra.subdom.net.dom`) in an existing forest (`net.dom`):

```
C:\>ntdsutil
ntdsutil: Domain management
domain management: Connections
server connections: Connect to server netdc1
Binding to netdc1 ...
Connected to netdc1 using credentials of locally logged on user.
server connections: Quit
domain management: Precreate DC=intra,DC=subdom,DC=net,
DC=dom netdc4.intra.subdom.net.dom
```

```
adding object CN=intra,cn=Partitions,CN=Configuration,DC=net,DC=dom
domain management: List
Note: Directory partition names with International/Unicode characters
will only display correctly if appropriate fonts and language support
are loaded
Found 7 Naming Context(s)
0 - CN=Configuration,DC=net,DC=dom
...
6 - DC=intra,DC=subdom,DC=net,DC=dom
domain management: ...
```

As you can see from the dialog, a new domain context appears after the command has been executed. Also, note that the *NETDC4* domain controller specified in the command does not yet exist in the forest and must be promoted in future.

Files: Managing Active Directory Database Files

The commands in the `Files` menu allow you to perform the following operations:

- Retrieve information on the state of the Active Directory (Jet) database (the ntds.dit file) as well as the log files
- Move database and/or log files to another location
- Re-define paths for Active Directory files
- Check up the Active Directory integrity
- Perform database recovery

Attention

- You can move an already installed Active Directory database and/or log files to another location (folder or disk), but it is ***not possible*** to change the SYSVOL's location without re-installing Active Directory on a domain controller.

Retrieving Information on Active Directory Files

The following command informs you about the size and location of all Active Directory database files. It is advisable that you use the command (and thus verify the presence of the log files) after you have restored Active Directory or done maintenance operations (offline defragmentation, moving files, etc.).

```
file maintenance: info

Drive Information:

        C:\ FAT (Fixed Drive  ) free(551.4 Mb) total(995.9 Mb)
```

```
...
        E:\ NTFS (Fixed Drive  ) free(1.5 Gb) total(9.7 Gb)

DS Path Information:

        Database    : D:\WINDOWS\NTDS\ntds.dit - 12.1 Mb
        Backup dir  : D:\WINDOWS\NTDS\dsadata.bak
        Working dir: D:\WINDOWS\NTDS
        Log dir     : D:\WINDOWS\NTDS - 40.0 Mb total
                        res2.log - 10.0 Mb
                        res1.log - 10.0 Mb
                        edb00001.log - 10.0 Mb
                        edb.log - 10.0 Mb
file maintenance: ...
```

Compressing the Database — Offline Defragmentation

Online defragmentation of the Active Directory database performed automatically at predefined intervals (by default, every 12 hours; see *Appendix B*) does not reduce the physical size of the database file (ntds.dit). To compact this file, you need to perform *offline* defragmentation (in the *Directory Services Restore Mode*). Offline defragmentation may be required when you delete a particularly large number of objects from a DC. For example, this is the case when a GC server loses this function and becomes a regular DC. The disk space saved in such a case may appear to be rather significant.

In general, the procedure of offline defragmentation is as follows:

1. Boot the DC in restore mode.
2. Start the defragmentation process — the new, compact version of the Active Directory database file will be stored in any alternative (specified) location.
3. If defragmentation is successful, copy the compacted file to its original location and delete old log files in that location.

This entire procedure is shown below. In this scenario, the database file is packed to a temporary C:\AD\CompactDB folder, and all log files are stored in the default location — D:\ WINDOWS \NTDS.

```
file maintenance: Compact to C:\AD\CompactDB
Opening database [Current].
Creating dir: C:\AD
Creating dir: C:\AD\CompactDB
Executing Command: D:\WINDOWS\system32\esentutl.exe
/d"D:\WINDOWS\NTDS\ntds.dit" /t"C:\AD\CompactDB\ntds.dit"
```

```
/p /o

Initiating DEFRAGMENTATION mode...
            Database: D:\WINDOWS\NTDS\ntds.dit
      Temp. Database: C:\AD\CompactDB\ntds.dit

                  Defragmentation Status (% complete)

          0    10   20   30   40   50   60   70   80   90  100
          |----|----|----|----|----|----|----|----|----|----|
          ...................................................

Note:
  It is recommended that you immediately perform a full backup
  of this database. If you restore a backup made before the
  defragmentation, the database will be rolled back to the state
  it was in at the time of that backup.

Operation completed successfully in 6.69 seconds.

Spawned Process Exit code 0x0(0)

If compaction was successful you need to:
   copy "C:\AD\CompactDB\ntds.dit" "D:\WINDOWS\NTDS\ntds.dit"
and delete the old log files:
   del D:\WINDOWS\NTDS\*.log

file maintenance: ...
```

Moving the Active Directory Database

You may wish to move Active Directory database files to another location due to disk space limitations or disk volume reconfiguration. The procedure for moving the database file requires the following steps:

1. Backup Active Directory.
2. Restart the DC and press <F8> at startup.
3. Select *Directory Services Restore Mode* and boot the DC.
4. Start NTDSutil from the command prompt and select the `Files` command. You may run `Info` to determine the current locations of the Active Directory database files.

5. Enter `move DB to [drive]:\[new folder]`. Run `Info` to verify the new configuration.
6. Quit NTDSutil and restart the DC in normal mode.

The procedure for moving log files is similar to the one described above.

Active Directory Folder Security

Security of the folder where the Active Directory database files are stored (by default — *%SystemRoot%*\NTDS) is very important for proper Active Directory functioning. The `Set default folder security` command resets mistakenly changed permissions on that folder to default values.

Database Integrity

The `Files` menu also contains two commands — `Recover` and `Integrity` — that can be used to detect corruption of the Active Directory database (with respect to the ESENT database semantics) and to perform some operations for its recovery. The Windows 2000 version of NTDSutil also contains the `Repair` command in the `Files` menu. (All of these commands may require a lot of time to run; this primarily depends on the actual size of the database.) The `Repair` command should not be run without first consulting with service personnel, since it can result in data losses. The `Recover` command should be run first, prior to the `Integrity` command. This command scans the log files and ensures that all transactions are committed. The `Integrity` command can then check the database file for low-level corruption. The command's output will be similar to the following:

```
file maintenance: Integrity
Opening database [Current].
Executing Command: D:\WINDOWS\system32\esentutl.exe
/g"D:\WINDOWS\NTDS\ntds.dit" /o

Initiating INTEGRITY mode...
        Database: D:\WINDOWS\NTDS\ntds.dit
  Temp. Database: TEMPINTEG1696.EDB

Checking database integrity.

                     Scanning Status (% complete)

          0    10   20   30   40   50   60   70   80   90  100
          |----|----|----|----|----|----|----|----|----|----|
```

```
..................................................

Integrity check successful.

Operation completed successfully in 4.156 seconds.

Spawned Process Exit code 0x0(0)

If integrity was successful, it is recommended
 you run semantic database analysis to ensure
 semantic database consistency as well.

file maintenance: ...
```

IP Deny List

The `IP Deny List` command is available in the Windows 2000 version of NTDSutil, but may not be in the Windows .NET version. If it is not, you can manually configure the list of IP addresses using the **ADSI Edit** snap-in (see *Appendix B*).

To increase the security of a DC, an administrator can use the `IP Deny List` command that is applied only to the *Default-Query Policy* object (see also the next section). This list contains IP addresses, from which a domain controller will not accept LDAP queries. A list entry can represent a single host or a subnet. For example, the command

```
Add 192.168.1.1 NODE
```

prevents a DC from accepting queries from the host with the address 192.168.1.1. The following command denies access from all hosts in a subnet with the address 192.168.1.0:

```
Add 192.168.1.0 255.255.255.0
```

LDAP Policies

Using the following example, let us discuss how NTDSutil allows an administrator to work with the *Default-Query Policy* object (see *Chapter 1, "Active Directory Concepts and Terminology"*). A dialog is shown that changes the `Initial Receive Timeout` from the default value of `120` to `30` (the changed value is put in bold italics).

```
ntdsutil: Ldap policies
ldap policy: Connections
server connections: Connect to server netdc1.net.dom
```

```
Binding to netdc1.net.dom ...
Connected to netdc1.net.dom using credentials of locally logged on user.
server connections: Quit
ldap policy: List
Supported Policies:
        MaxPoolThreads
        MaxDatagramRecv
        MaxReceiveBuffer
        InitRecvTimeout
        MaxConnections
        MaxConnIdleTime
        MaxPageSize
        MaxQueryDuration
        MaxTempTableSize
        MaxResultSetSize
        MaxNotificationPerConn
ldap policy: Set InitRecvTimeout to 30
ldap policy: Show values

Policy                          Current(New)

MaxPoolThreads                  4
MaxDatagramRecv                 1024
MaxReceiveBuffer                        10485760
InitRecvTimeout                 120(30)
MaxConnections                  5000
MaxConnIdleTime                 900
MaxPageSize                     1000
MaxQueryDuration                        120
MaxTempTableSize                        10000
MaxResultSetSize                        262144
MaxNotificationPerConn                  5

ldap policy: Commit changes
ldap policy: Quit
```

The *Windows 2000 Server Resource Kit* contains the ModifyLDAP.vbs script (which is included in the *Remote Administration Scripts*). This script allows an administrator to display policy settings, create new policies, and modify existing ones, as well as assign policies to a DC or site. Here is the screen output for the LDAP

Administrative limits of the `Default Query Policy`, which is installed and used (even if not selected) by default on all DCs:

```
C:\modifyldap /P /O:"Default Query Policy"

LDAP Settings for Default Query Policy
InitRecvTimeout=30
MaxReceiveBuffer=10485760
MaxDatagramRecv=1024
MaxPoolThreads=4
MaxResultSetSize=262144
MaxTempTableSize=10000
MaxQueryDuration=120
MaxPageSize=1000
MaxNotificationPerConn=5
MaxConnIdleTime=900
MaxConnections=5000
```

Note

To select an existing LDAP policy, use the **Active Directory Sites and Services** snap-in. Point to the *NTDS Settings* object of the necessary DC and open the **Properties** window. Select a policy in the **Query Policy** list and click **Apply**.

Metadata Cleanup: Removing Defunct Domains or Domain Controllers

Normally, the process of demoting a DC involves deleting the computer account and cleaning up all metadata related to that DC from Active Directory. When the last DC in a domain is deleted, all cross-references (and other information about that domain) are also removed. There are, however, situations when a domain controller is decommissioned incorrectly (or failed and destroyed), and orphaned metadata remains in the directory. In such a case, you can remove information about the retired DC and/or domains by using NTDSutil. (You must not delete any information for *existing* domains and DCs!) In general, the procedure requires the following steps:

1. Connect to a working DC that holds the information about orphaned metadata.
2. Select an operation target (site, naming context, domain, and server). You may select one or more of these targets.
3. Remove the necessary metadata.

The following dialog illustrates how you can remove a retired domain controller (NETDC2) and a child domain (subdom.net.dom) from the forest (net.dom). (In this example, the shortened command syntax is used; comments are in bold square brackets. You can also learn how to select an operation target, which is used in many commands.)

```
C:\>ntdsutil
ntdsutil: m c
metadata cleanup: c
[First, we must be connected to a DC:]
server connections: co t s netdc1
Binding to netdc1 ...
Connected to netdc1 using credentials of locally logged on user.
server connections: q
metadata cleanup: s o t
[Second, we must select an object to delete:]
select operation target: l si
Found 1 site(s)
0 - CN=NET-Site,CN=Sites,CN=Configuration,DC=net,DC=dom
select operation target: s si 0
Site - CN=NET-Site,CN=Sites,CN=Configuration,DC=net,DC=dom
No current domain
No current server
No current Naming Context
select operation target: l d
Found 3 domain(s)
0 - DC=net,DC=dom
1 - DC=subdom,DC=net,DC=dom
2 - DC=dotnet,DC=dom
select operation target: s d 1
Site - CN=NET-Site,CN=Sites,CN=Configuration,DC=net,DC=dom
Domain - DC=subdom,DC=net,DC=dom
No current server
No current Naming Context
select operation target: l se f d i s
Found 1 server(s)
0 - CN=NETDC2,CN=Servers,CN=NET-
Site,CN=Sites,CN=Configuration,DC=net,DC=dom
select operation target: s se 0
Site - CN=NET-Site,CN=Sites,CN=Configuration,DC=net,DC=dom
```

```
Domain - DC=subdom,DC=net,DC=dom
Server - CN=NETDC2,CN=Servers,CN=NET-Site,CN=Sites,CN=Configuration,
DC=net,DC=dom
        DSA object - CN=NTDS Settings,CN=NETDC2,CN=Servers,
CN=NET-Site,CN=Sites,CN=Configuration,
DC=net,DC=dom
        DNS host name - netdc2.subdom.net.dom
        Computer object - CN=NETDC2,OU=Domain
Controllers,DC=subdom,DC=net,DC=dom
No current Naming Context
```

[Now, we have selected the NETDC2 server from the subdom.net.dom domain for subsequent operations:]

select operation target: q

metadata cleanup: r s s

[The following Server Remove Confirmation Dialog **may appear — you must click** Yes.**]**

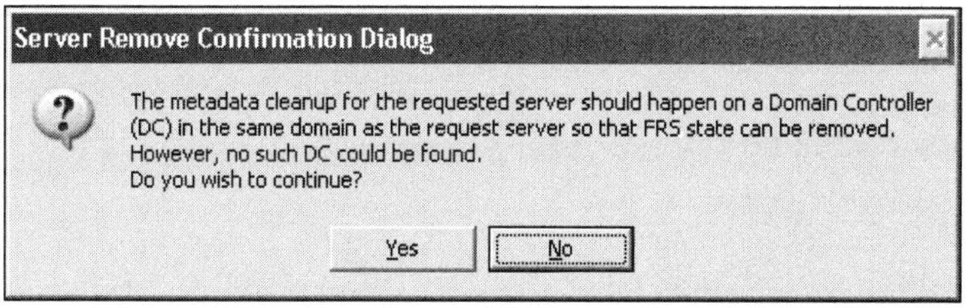

[The Server Remove Confirmation Dialog **will appear — you must click** Yes.**]**

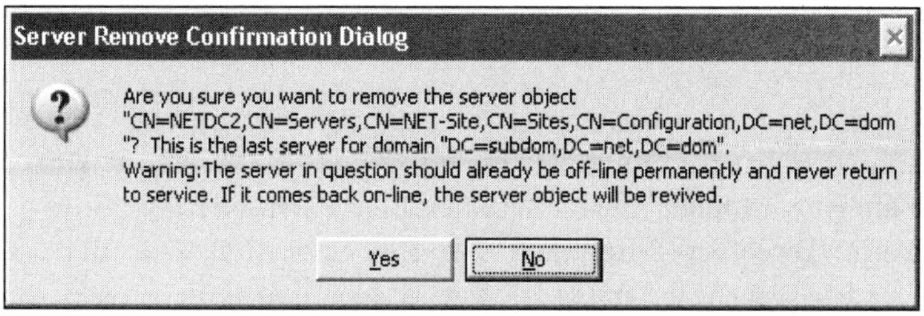


```
"CN=NETDC2,CN=Servers,CN=NET-Site,CN=Sites,CN=Configuration,
DC=net,DC=dom" removed from server "netdc1"
```

[Now, we will delete the entire child domain:]

metadata cleanup: r s d

[The Domain Remove Confirmation Dialog **will appear — you must click** Yes.**]**

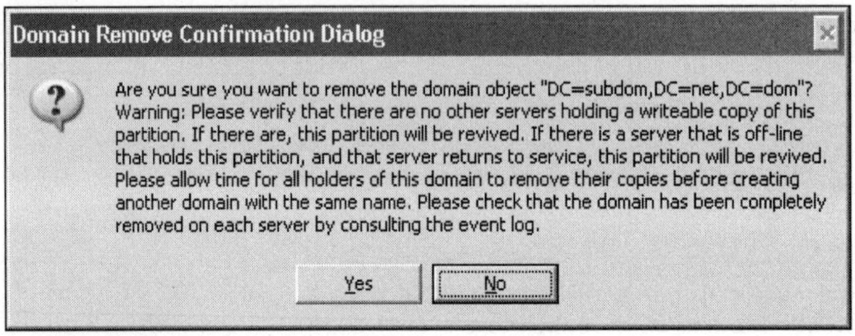


```
"DC=subdom,DC=net,DC=dom" removed from server "netdc1"
[Verifying that the operation has been done correctly:]
metadata cleanup: s o t
select operation target: l d
Found 1 domain(s)
0 - DC=net,DC=dom
[Terminating NTDSutil]
select operation target: q
metadata cleanup: q
ntdsutil: q
Disconnecting from netdc1...
```

Now the `subdom.net.dom` domain has been deleted, and you can verify this by using the **Event Viewer** snap-in. There are many information messages (from NTDS KCC and NTDS Replication sources: ID 1123, 1104, 1270, 1658, 1746, etc.) that appear in the Directory Service log (the source is NTDS KCC) and accompany removing domain controllers, naming contexts, and replication connections. There is no need to explain them specifically.

To verify that the operation was carried off successfully, you may also check the domain configuration by using the following tools: **Active Directory Domains and Trusts**, **ADSI Edit** (the **Configuration** container: the **Partitions** and **Sites | Servers** nodes), and **Active Directory Sites and Services** snap-ins. You may also run DCdiag.exe (as well as `repadmin /showreps`) to ensure that there are no replication problems.

Attention

- When deleting child domains, you must also manually delete the corresponding entries from the DNS server.

Roles: Managing FSMO Roles

NTDSutil allows an administrator to manipulate FSMO roles: to view and transfer them. See *Chapter 7, "Common Administrative Tasks,"* to learn how to dump names of all FSMO role owners. In this section, we'll discuss how to designate a DC as a role owner by using NTDSutil. You can choose either of the following options:

- *Seize role* — this command designates the connected server as the specified role master. The command must be used only when the DC — the current master — has severely crashed and cannot be repaired.
- *Transfer role* — this command "moves" the specified role from the current role holder to the connected server (DC). You can perform the same operation by using various administrative snap-ins (see *Chapter 7*). The NTDSutil.exe also allows you to carry out the operation in batch mode (see DumpFSMOs.cmd).

Transferring a Role

If for some reason you cannot (or do not want to) use the standard administrative snap-ins, you may use NTDSutil to transfer a role from its current owner to another DC. The most common steps are the following:

1. Connect to the potential role owner.
2. Transfer a necessary role from the current owner to the selected server.

Note

It is not advisable to *seize* a FSMO role if you can *transfer* this role. Seizing is used only when a FSMO role owner has failed and is unrecoverable.

In the following dialog, the Schema Master role is transferred to the `netdc2.subdom.net.dom` server. (This is only an example! It is neither practical nor advisable to move the schema master role to a child domain.)

```
C:\>ntdsutil
ntdsutil: Roles
fsmo maintenance: Connections
server connections: connect to server netdc2.subdom.net.dom
Binding to netdc2.subdom.net.dom ...
Connected to netdc2.subdom.net.dom using credentials of locally logged on user
server connections: Quit
fsmo maintenance: Transfer schema master
```

```
[The Role Transfer Confirmation Dialog will appear — click Yes.]
```

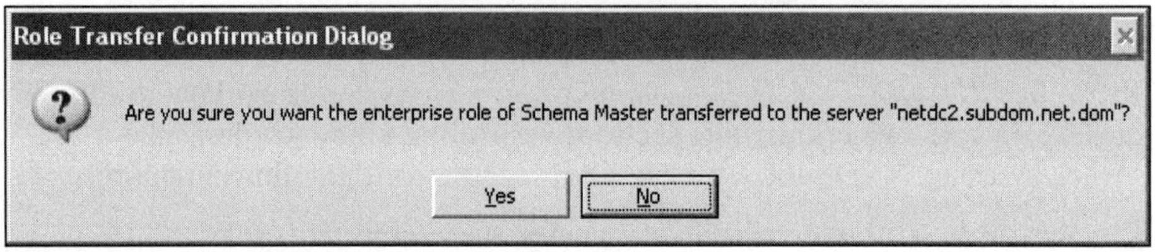


```
Server "netdc2.subdom.net.dom" knows about 5 roles
Schema - CN=NTDS Settings,CN=NETDC2,CN=Servers,CN=NET-
Site,CN=Sites,CN=Configuration,DC=net,DC=dom
Domain - CN=NTDS Settings,CN=NETDC1,CN=Servers,CN=NET-
Site,CN=Sites,CN=Configuration,DC=net,DC=dom
PDC - CN=NTDS Settings,CN=NETDC2,CN=Servers,CN=Remote-
Site,CN=Sites,CN=Configuration,DC=net,DC=dom
RID - CN=NTDS Settings,CN=NETDC2,CN=Servers,CN=Remote-
Site,CN=Sites,CN=Configuration,DC=net,DC=dom
Infrastructure - CN=NTDS Settings,CN=NETDC2,CN=Servers,CN=Remote-
Site,CN=Sites,CN=Configuration,DC=net,DC=dom
fsmo maintenance: ...
```

Note

Notice that the same Configuration partition contains information about servers that may belong to different domains and sites.

Even if the connected DC already possesses the specified role, the command dialog remains the same as shown above. You can verify the requested operation with the Directory Service log. A message similar to the following one should appear (Event Source: NTDS Replication; Event ID: 1458):

```
The operations master role represented by the following object has been
transferred to the following domain controller at the request of a user.
...
```

Seizing a Role

Suppose a DC that holds the Infrastructure FSMO role was destroyed, and you want this role to be designated to another DC. The following dialog shows how to forcibly transfer the role to a new candidate (server `netdc1.net.dom`) (comments are in bold square brackets):

```
C:\>ntdsutil
ntdsutil: Roles
```

```
fsmo maintenance: Connections
server connections: Connect to server netdc1.net.dom
Binding to netdc1.net.dom ...
Connected to netdc1.net.dom using credentials of locally logged on user.
server connections: Quit
fsmo maintenance: Seize infrastructure master
[The Role Seizure Confirmation Dialog will appear — click Yes.]
```

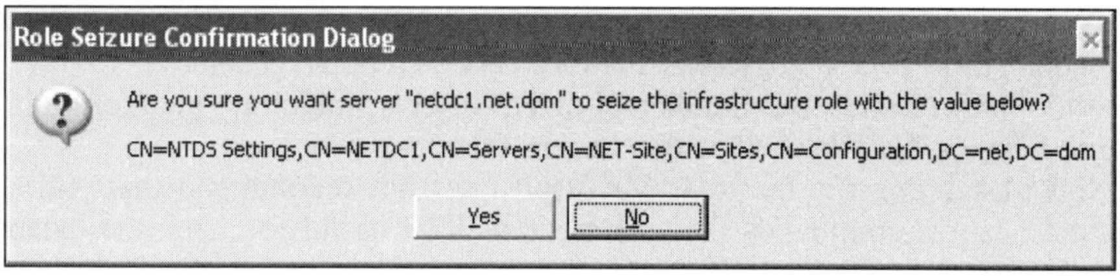


```
[First, the server tries to carry out the standard role transfer
operation and fails. The same error message will appear every time you
want to perform a role transfer operation while the current master is
not operational.]
Attempting safe transfer of infrastructure FSMO before seizure.
ldap_modify_sW error 0x34(52 (Unavailable).
Ldap extended error message is 000020AF: SvcErr: DSID-03210260, problem
5002 (UNAVAILABLE), data 1753
Win32 error returned is 0x20af(The requested FSMO operation failed. The
current FSMO holder could not be contacted.)
)
Depending on the error code this may indicate a connection,
ldap, or role transfer error.
Transfer of infrastructure FSMO failed, proceeding with seizure ...
Server "netdc1.net.dom" knows about 5 roles
...
Infrastructure - CN=NTDS Settings,CN=NETDC1,CN=Servers,
CN=NET-Site,CN=Sites,CN=Configuration,DC=net,DC=dom
fsmo maintenance: ...
```

When a FSMO role is seized, the following message will appear in the Directory Service log (Event Source: NTDS Replication; Event ID: 1837):

```
...
An attempt to transfer the operations master role represented by the
following object failed.
...
```

Security Account Management

Since duplicated SIDs appear, though rarely (due to problems with the RID Master role owners), you may wish to verify a domain for conflicting SIDs. The commands in the `Security Account Management` menu will help you to solve this problem.

Semantic Database Analysis

The commands in this menu test the directory database with respect to Active Directory (not ESENT database!) semantics. The report generated (a file named dsdit.dmp.*nnn*) displays the number of active objects, including phantom and deleted records. The log file is placed in the current folder.

Notwithstanding the fact that Microsoft does not recommend that end users run semantic analysis commands themselves, it may be useful to check the database's integrity in some situations, and fix possible errors. (Be careful with the `Go Fixup` command — your data face a risk here!) For example, the following two consecutive commands have detected and fixed an error with deleted reference objects:

```
ntdsutil: Semantic database analysis
semantic checker: Go
Fixup mode is turned off
Opening database [Current].......Done.

Getting record count...3112 records
Getting security descriptor count...105 security descriptors

Writing summary into log file dsdit.dmp.0
SDs scanned:             105
Records scanned:        3112
Processing records..
Error: Missing subrefs detected.        [Errors are detected!]
Done.

semantic checker: Verbose on
Verbose mode enabled.
semantic checker: Go Fixup
Fixup mode is turned on

Opening DIT database... Done.

Done.

Opening database [Current].......Done.
```

```
Getting record count...3112 records
Getting security descriptor count...105 security descriptors

Writing summary into log file dsdit.dmp.1
SDs scanned:              105
Records scanned:         3112
Processing records..
Error: Missing subrefs detected.

Error: Inconsistent refcounts detected.
Done.

semantic checker: Go
Fixup mode is turned off
...
Processing records..Done.                    [No errors now.]

semantic checker: ...
```

Chapter 11: Verifying Network and Distributed Services

All tools described in this chapter consider Active Directory to be a *distributed* database that along with serving clients must support its own integrity and consistency. This global system task has different aspects, or problem areas, the most important of which are the following:

- Connectivity (including RPC connectivity) between domain controllers, and between a DC and a client
- Proper name resolving
- Mutual authentication (existence of secure channels, or trusts, between domains, domain controllers, and between a client and a DC)
- Synchronizing Active Directory replicas (all directory partitions including Global Catalog) stored on different domain controllers

As you can conclude from the list of problem areas, there are many sources of possible faults, which can prevent Active Directory services from working and responding to client queries properly. The tools described below help administrators to test Active Directory's network infrastructure and monitor its state on different domain controllers.

NLTest (NLtest.exe) (ST)

The *NLTest* tool helps administrators to manage both Windows 2000 native and mixed mode (with Windows NT 4.0 BDCs) domains as well as *Windows .NET (version 2002)* mode domains. The tool has a number of options including the following:

- Verifying and resetting secure channels (trusts)
- Getting information on network topology (a list of DCs, sites, domain trusts, etc.)
- Forcing synchronization with BDCs
- Forcing shutdown on a computer, and other options

NLTest is a very useful tool for troubleshooting authentication problems, since it allows you to test the trust relationships between pairs of specific computers (e.g., between a DC from one domain and a DC located in another domain, or a DC and a domain client) for which these trusts were established.

Note

With most commands of the Windows 2000 version of the NLTest, it is preferable to specify *DNS* rather than NetBIOS names of computers.

Some options of NLTest are similar to the options realized in the NetDom tool. (See *Chapter 12, "Manipulating Active Directory Objects."*) You may choose the tool that is the most appropriate for your specific tasks.

Verifying Secure Channels

First of all, you should not confuse *transitive* Kerberos trust relationships (established in Windows 2000 and Windows .NET domains) with *non-transitive* secure channels (trust links). Although you can, for example, log on to a domain that belongs to one forest tree on a computer that has a machine account in another forest tree, this does not mean that domain controllers from the corresponding domains have *direct* trust relationships. (You *can*, however, manually establish such a relationship named a *shortcut trust*. See *Chapter 5, "Deploying Active Directory."*) That is why you can only verify secure channels directly between a child and its parent domain, or between tree root domains.

Normally, you should get the following result on every domain computer:

```
C:\>nltest /query
Flags: 0
Connection Status = 0 0x0 NERR_Success
The command completed successfully
```

This output means that the computer has been authenticated by a domain controller, and a secure channel exists between the client computer and the domain controller. If a user has been logged on locally, or for some reason a network logon has not been performed (e.g., the DC has not been found, and so on), you will see the following message:

```
Connection Status = 1311 0x51f ERROR_NO_LOGON_SERVERS
```

The following message indicates that the Netlogon service failed to start or is not running on the computer (since it is stopped or disabled):

```
I_NetLogonControl failed: Status = 1717 0x6b5 RPC_S_UNKNOWN_IF
```

In that case, you should open the **Services** snap-in and check the status of the service.

If the domain computer account has been reset, NLTest will respond with the message:

```
Connection Status = 5 0x5 ERROR_ACCESS_DENIED
```

If an administrator has disabled the domain computer account, NLTest reports:

```
Connection Status = 1787 0x6fb ERROR_NO_TRUST_SAM_ACCOUNT
```

If the account is re-enabled, restart the Netlogon service on the computer or run the `nltest /sc_reset` command (see below).

To verify a secure channel or find the logon server, use the `nltest /sc_query` command, for example:

```
C:\>nltest /sc_query:net.dom
Flags: 30 HAS_IP  HAS_TIMESERV
```

```
Trusted DC Name \\netdc1.net.dom
Trusted DC Connection Status Status = 0 0x0 NERR_Success
The command completed successfully
```

If the command responds

```
Connection Status = 1311 0x51f ERROR_NO_LOGON_SERVERS
```

you may try to log off and log on to the system, or to reset (re-establish) a secure channel by using the following command:

```
C:\>nltest /sc_reset:net.dom
```

If there are multiple DCs in the domain, the client computer will establish a secure channel with the DC that responds first.

Note

For verifying and resetting secure channels, it is also possible to use the `netdom /VERIFY` and `netdom /RESET` commands.

Now let us consider a specific scenario. Suppose you have two domains in the forest — a child and a parent — and want to test whether the domain controller `netdc1.net.dom` from the parent domain will be authenticated by the child domain `subdom.net.dom`, i.e., whether the trusts between domains is in the proper state (the child must trust the parent and vice versa). You use the following command, and for some reason it fails:

```
C:\>nltest /sc_query:subdom.net.dom /server:netdc1.net.dom
Flags: 0
Trusted DC Name
Trusted DC Connection Status Status = 1311 0x51f ERROR_NO_LOGON_SERVERS
The command completed successfully
```

You could check this trust in another way. Run the **Active Directory Domain and Trusts** snap-in, open the **Properties** window for the domain `net.dom`, and click the **Trusts** tab. Select the child domain `subdom.net.dom` in the **Domains that trust this domain (incoming trusts)** list and click **Properties**, and then **Validate**[1]**.** (For an alternate way to start verification, you can: run the **Active Directory Users and Computers** snap-in on a DC located in the *child domain*, point to the **System** container, and open the **Properties** window for the object `net.dom` of the *Trusted Domain* type. Then click **Validate**.) The system will display a window shown in Fig. 11.1. (In Windows 2000, the window, though similar, has a different design; however, the sequence of operations will be same.)

---

[1] In Windows 2000, the buttons have other names; however, the procedure, in general, is the same.

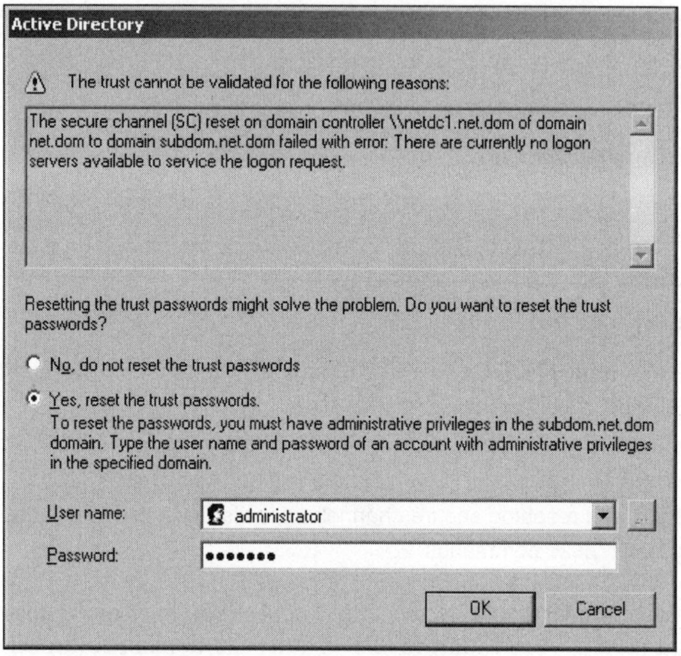

Fig. 11.1. This window informs you that the secure channel between two DCs in related domains is broken, but you can reset it

If you select **Yes, reset the trust passwords**, provide the administrator's credentials, and click **OK**. The system will try to reset the secure channel that failed.

The following command will help you to repair the secure channel from the command prompt:

```
C:\>nltest /sc_reset:subdom.net.dom /server:netdc1.net.dom
Flags: 30 HAS_IP  HAS_TIMESERV
Trusted DC Name \\netdc2.subdom.net.dom
Trusted DC Connection Status Status = 0 0x0 NERR_Success
The command completed successfully
```

To troubleshoot authentication issues, you can test necessary domain controllers and clients in a similar manner and locate the source of the problems.

Viewing Trusted Domains

Using NLTest, you can display all trust relationships that have been established between the current domain and other domains in the same or another forest. Verbose mode allows you to view domain SIDs and GUIDs. Look at a sample output:

```
C:\>nltest /trusted_domains /v
List of domain trusts:
    0: SUBDOM subdom.net.dom (NT 5) (Forest: 2) (Direct Outbound)
(Direct Inbound) ( Attr: 0x20 )
       Dom Guid: 5bcbeeb3-e619-40a6-86b9-4e3d3d9647b2
       Dom Sid: S-1-5-21-1193178465-209799049-3125462871
    1: W2K w2k.dom (NT 5) (Direct Inbound)
       Dom Sid: S-1-5-21-2025429265-113007714-1060284298
    2: NET net.dom (NT 5) (Forest Tree Root) (Primary Domain) (Native)
       Dom Guid: 941fecfd-d067-472b-9253-a3ce94f43b3e
       Dom Sid: S-1-5-21-2033051489-2658513307-2223184096
The command completed successfully
```

How should you analyze the displayed information? From these output lines, you can conclude the following:

- A Windows 2000-based domain `w2k.dom` has an explicit, one-way incoming trust with the current domain (i.e., users from the current domain can access resource in the domain `w2k.dom`).
- A Windows .NET-based domain `subdom.net.dom` is in mixed mode, and belongs to the same forest (`Forest: 2`) as the current domain.
- The current (`Primary`) domain `net.dom` is in Windows .NET (Windows 2002) mode, and is the forest root domain.

Note

This command does not distinguish Windows 2000 domains from Windows .NET domains and marks them both as `NT 5`. Also, the command cannot discern *Windows 2000 native* mode from *Windows .NET (Windows 2002)* mode (functional level).

Viewing Information on Network Topology

Information about the site (in a multiple site network) a client computer is connected to is not configured on that computer in any way. (The site is selected on the basis of client and subnet IP address data.) The following command will help you to find the site to which the local or remote computer has been connected after it has been booted and logged on to the domain:

```
C:\>nltest /dsGetSite
NET-Site
The command completed successfully
```

(Add `/server:<computerName>` for a remote computer.)

Sometimes, a domain controller can serve more than one site. (If a new site has been created but you did not move a DC to that site, some DC from an existing site will be selected to serve the new site. To increase network fault-tolerance, you can also intentionally configure a DC to serve a site when the domain controllers of that site are unavailable.) The following command lists all sites, which the DC can serve:

```
C:\>nltest /dsGetSiteCov /server:netdc1.net.dom
NET-Site
Remote-Site
The command completed successfully
```

(The `/server` parameter is not required if the command is performed on a domain controller.)

Quite often, it is necessary to see the list of controllers located in a domain. A command similar to the following allows you to view all DCs in an AD-based domain:

```
C:\>nltest /DClist:net.dom
Get list of DCs in domain 'net.dom' from '\\netdc1.net.dom'.
    netdc1.net.dom [PDC] [DS] Site: NET-Site
    netdc4.net.dom       [DS] Site: NET-Site
           nt4bdc5
The command completed successfully
```

Servers present in this list may be offline! (Notice that the PDC is marked. To find the PDC, you can also use the `nltest /DCname:<NetBIOSDomainName>` command.) Notice also that a Windows 4.0-based BDC `nt4bdc5` has no directory service and is not connected to the site topology.

To search a domain for a DC performing a specific role (PDC, Global Catalog, writable replica, etc.), use a command similar to the following (search for the PDC Emulator):

```
C:\>nltest /dsGetDC:subdom.net.dom /PDC
           DC: \\netdc2.subdom.net.dom
      Address: \\192.168.0.2
     Dom Guid: 5bcbeeb3-e619-40a6-86b9-4e3d3d9647b2
     Dom Name: subdom.net.dom
  Forest Name: net.dom
 Dc Site Name: Remote-Site
        Flags: PDC DS LDAP KDC WRITABLE DNS_DC DNS_DOMAIN DNS_FOREST
CLOSE_SITE
The command completed successfully
```

You can add the `/FORCE` parameter, and the command will try to find *another* (different) DC with a specified property (if this is possible).

The Windows .NET version of NLTest offers a new option that performs the same actions as the `/dsGetDC` parameter provides (this option uses another system call — *DsGetDcOpen*):

```
C:\>nltest /dnsGetDc:subdom.net.dom /PDC
List of DCs in pseudo-random order taking into account SRV priorities
and weights:
Non-Site specific:
   netdc2.subdom.net.dom  192.168.0.2:389
The command completed successfully
```

Note that the command displays the TCP/IP port number (389) used for access to the service specified.

Note

To find all GC servers in the forest, use ReplMon or query the DNS server for records in the `gc._msdcs.`*`<forestDNSname>`* subdomain, e.g.:

```
C:\>nslookup gc._msdcs.net.dom
Server:  netdc1.net.dom
Address:  192.168.0.1

Name:    gc._msdcs.net.dom
Addresses:  192.168.0.1, 192.168.0.2
```

Note that all GC servers register their IP addresses in the same DNS subdomain regardless of which domain they belong to, and you should always search for a GC server by specifying the DNS name of the forest root domain.

Note

For discovering domain controllers you can also use the `netdiag /test:DcList` and `netdiag /test:DsGetDc /v` commands.

Miscellaneous Options

Forcing Shutdown on a Remote Computer

You can use NLTest as an analog to the *Shutdown.exe* command (from the *Resource Kit*). The following command issues a warning message to the computer `netdc4.net.dom` and shuts it down in 60 seconds:

```
C:\>nltest /shutdown:"Administrative request for shutdown" 60
↳ /server:netdc4.net.dom
```

Note

In contrast to Shutdown.exe, NLTest cannot reboot the computer after shutdown.

Directory Time Conversion

Some attributes, e.g., *pwdLastSet*, *lastLogon*, or *badPasswordTime*, are stored in Active Directory as *Large Integers* (INTEGER8 format). NLTest can convert these values to a human-readable format. The conversion procedure is rather cumbersome, so you may prefer to use the `repadmin /showtime` or `w32tm /ntte` commands (see later in this chapter). Let us, for example, consider converting a time value *126679218485309520* obtained with the **ADSI Edit** snap-in. Copy and paste the value in the *Calculator*, and convert it to a hexadecimal format. The result will be *1C20E13FA3DB050.* Enter `nltest /time:` at the command prompt and paste in the hexadecimal value. Then you must highlight the eight rightmost digits and place them *before* the other digits. You should get the following result:

```
C:\>nltest /time:FA3DB050 1C20E13
fa3db050 01c20e13 = 6/7/2002 15:10:48
The command completed successfully
```

Notice that the command converts the entered value into *local time* rather than UTC.

Network Connectivity Tester (NetDiag.exe) (ST)

NetDiag is a powerful tool that can be used for diagnosing practically any network problem — from physical connectivity to name resolving and authentication. To see a complete list of NetDiag's options (tests), enter `netdiag /?` at the command prompt. You can run all tests, a selected test, or all tests except those specified. The test diagnosis messages are quite explanatory (especially in verbose and debug modes). You should pay particular attention to the lines with `[FATAL]` and `[WARNING]` tags. All fatal problems must be fixed, or the system will not be able to work properly. You need to analyze the warnings and find (and maybe repair) their causes. The warnings, however, can sometimes be safely ignored.

Two options of NetDiag have already been discussed in *Chapter 5, "Installing Active Directory."* These tests (*DcList* and *DsGetDc*) can be useful for running before promoting a server to a DC or joining a client computer (workstation or server) to a domain. In this chapter, we will consider a successful test run (the result output that you need to get for every domain computer to work properly) and fixing DNS issues.

Caution

- The original Windows 2000 version of NetDiag does not run on Windows XP/.NET systems. The Windows .NET version of NetDiag will not run on Windows 2000-based computers.

Note

For the Windows 2000 environment, it is recommended that you download the updated version (from July 5, 2001) of NetDiag from **http://www.microsoft.com/downloads/release.asp?ReleaseID=31169**.

Running Tests

Let us look at a sample test output that has been obtained by a domain administrator on a domain controller (`netdc1.net.dom`). (If a domain user runs NetDiag on his or her computer, the results will be slightly different since a normal user does not have all administrative rights.) Notice that the computer has no WINS settings. You may wish to compare this output with results obtained on domain client computers and analyze the differences. (Comments are given in bold brackets.)

```
C:\>netdiag
....................................
    Computer Name: NETDC1
    DNS Host Name: netdc1.net.dom
    System info : Windows 2000 Server (Build 3621)
    Processor : x86 Family 6 Model 8 Stepping 3, GenuineIntel
    List of installed hotfixes :
        Q147222

Netcard queries test . . . . . . . : Passed

Per interface results:          [All installed network adapters
                                 will be listed below.]

    Adapter : Local Area Connection

        Netcard queries test . . . : Passed

        Host Name. . . . . . . . . : netdc1
        IP Address . . . . . . . . : 192.168.1.2  [Multiple IP
        addresses and other settings can be assigned to the same
        adapter. All of them will be displayed here.]
```

```
        Subnet Mask. . . . . . . . . : 255.255.255.0
        Default Gateway. . . . . . . : 192.168.1.1
        Dns Servers. . . . . . . . . : 192.168.1.2

        AutoConfiguration results. . . . . . : Passed

        Default gateway test . . . : Passed  [This test can fail if
        there is no connectivity with other subnets and if the default
        gateway has not been configured.]

        NetBT name test. . . . . . : Passed
        [WARNING] At least one of the <00> 'WorkStation Service', <03>
        'Messenger Service', <20> 'WINS' names is missing.

        WINS service test. . . . . : Skipped
            There are no WINS servers configured for this interface.

Global results:

Domain membership test . . . . . . : Passed

NetBT transports test. . . . . . . : Passed
    List of NetBt transports currently configured:
        NetBT_Tcpip_{6D657D29-CED0-4322-954B-6B0167289E52}
    1 NetBt transport currently configured. [This test will be
    skipped if NetBIOS over TCP/IP is disabled.]

Autonet address test . . . . . . . : Passed

IP loopback ping test. . . . . . . : Passed

Default gateway test . . . . . . . : Passed

NetBT name test. . . . . . . . . . : Passed  [This test will be
skipped if NetBIOS over TCP/IP is disabled.]
    [WARNING] You don't have a single interface with the <00>
'WorkStation Service', <03> 'Messenger Service', <20> 'WINS' names
defined.

Winsock test . . . . . . . . . . . : Passed
```

```
DNS test . . . . . . . . . . . . . : Passed  [On client computers,
this test only reports 'Passed' or 'Failed'.]
    PASS - All the DNS entries for DC are registered on DNS server
'192.168.1.2' and other DCs also have some of the names registered.
[All warnings in this section must be carefully analyzed, since in fact,
they can represent fatal errors. See also the note below.]

Redir and Browser test . . . . . . : Passed
    List of NetBt transports currently bound to the Redir
        NetBT_Tcpip_{6D657D29-CED0-4322-954B-6B0167289E52}
    The redir is bound to 1 NetBt transport.

    List of NetBt transports currently bound to the browser
        NetBT_Tcpip_{6D657D29-CED0-4322-954B-6B0167289E52}
    The browser is bound to 1 NetBt transport.  [This test will be
    skipped if NetBIOS over TCP/IP is disabled.]

DC discovery test. . . . . . . . . : Passed

DC list test . . . . . . . . . . . : Passed

Trust relationship test. . . . . . : Skipped  [This test is skipped on
the PDC Emulator. Otherwise, if it is 'Passed', it must report the
following:
Secure channel for domain 'NET' is to '\\netdc1.net.dom'.]

Kerberos test. . . . . . . . . . . : Passed   [This test will be skipped
if the user has been logged on to the computer locally.]

LDAP test. . . . . . . . . . . . . : Passed
[You can locate any problems with LDAP by using
 the netdiag /test:LDAP /v command.]

Bindings test. . . . . . . . . . . : Passed

WAN configuration test . . . . . . : Skipped
    No active remote access connections.

Modem diagnostics test . . . . . . : Passed
```

```
IP Security test . . . . . . . . . : Passed
    Service status  is: Started
    Service startup is: Automatic
    IPSec service is available, but no policy is assigned or active
    Note: run "ipseccmd /?" for more detailed information

The command completed successfully
```

Attention

- On domain client computers, if the **Register this connection's addresses in DNS** box is not checked on the **DNS** tab in the **Advanced TCP/IP Settings** window, the DNS test can *pass*, even if there is no corresponding host record for a client on the DNS server. You can test the DNS settings separately with the `netdiag /test:DNS /v` command.

Refreshing DNS Resource Records Registration (*/fix*)

If NetDiag detects that registration of some SRV records has failed for a domain controller, you can try to fix the problem automatically. Executing the `netdiag /fix` command yields the same result as restart of the Netlogon service would. The command looks up all DNS records in the *%SystemRoot%*\system32\config\netlogon.dns file and updates the corresponding records on the DNS server. When the command runs, strings similar to the following will appear in the 'DNS test' section:

```
[FIX] re-register DC DNS entry '_ldap._tcp.36622959-3372-43e6-bbba-
8d77caa1fc46.domains._msdcs.net.dom.' on DNS server '192.168.1.2'
succeed.
```

The following message completes the fixing process:

```
FIX PASS - netdiag re-registered missing DNS entries for this DC
successfully on DNS server '192.168.1.2'.
```

You can analyze the command output to see which records were incorrect or absent. After NetDiag has tried to fix the DNS issues, run it once more to be sure that all the problems have been solved.

Attention

- Remember that only the `ipconfig /registerdns` command re-registers the computer's A (host) record on the DNS server in both forward and reverse zones. (On Windows XP/.NET-based computers, you can refresh DNS registration as well as clear the DNS requestor's cache, if you open the **Local Area Connection Status** window, and click **Repair** on the **Support** tab.) Run it before NetDiag, since the `netdiag /fix` command only affects SRV records.

Attention

Do not forget to clear the cache on the DNS server specified as primary after executing the `netdiag /fix` or `ipconfig /registerdns` commands! (If you don't, you must at least manually delete the records re-registered by these commands from the cache.) Even though the commands may have already updated the information in dynamic zones on the authoritative DNS server, the cache may still contain the old data for some records. As a result, it might seem that the problems still exist, since while testing, the commands use the cached responses from the primary DNS server. You may also need to clear the requester's (local) cache by using the `ipconfig /flushdns` command.

RPC Ping: RPC Connectivity Verification Tool (RK)

The *RPC Ping* tool verifies *remote procedure call* (RPC) connectivity on a network. The tool consists of the following components:

- A server, which echoes to clients and produces statistics
- A client, which connects, binds, and sends requests to the specific destination RPC server

The filenames of these components and the supported systems are listed in the table below.

Utility filename	Platforms supported
	Server component
Rpings.exe	Windows .NET, Windows 2000, and Windows NT
	Client component
Rpingc.exe (32-bit version)	Windows .NET, Windows XP, Windows 2000, Windows NT, Windows 9*x*/ME
Rpingc16.exe (16-bit version)	Windows 3.1*x*

Server Component (RPings.exe)

The server component performs only two RPC functions: *Echo* and *Stats*. You can run it with all available protocols or select only one protocol (`-p` parameter). If, for instance, only the TCP/IP protocol is installed on the server computer, RPings.exe displays the following messages while starting (the names of endpoints are shown in bold; these names will be displayed by clients later — see Fig. 11.2):

```
C:\>rpings
+endpoint \pipe\rping on protocol sequence ncacn_np is set for use.
 -protocol Sequence ncacn_nb_nb not supported on this host
+endpoint rping on protocol sequence ncalrpc is set for use.
+endpoint 2256 on protocol sequence ncacn_ip_tcp is set for use.
 -protocol Sequence ncacn_nb_tcp not supported on this host
 -protocol Sequence ncacn_spx not supported on this host
+endpoint 2256 on protocol sequence ncadg_ip_udp is set for use.
 -protocol Sequence ncadg_ipx not supported on this host
 -protocol Sequence ncacn_vns_spp not supported on this host

Enter '@q' to exit rpings.
```

Now the server is ready to respond to RPC requests (until you stop it), and can serve as many clients as you want.

Client Component (RPingc.exe)

The client component displays all information about the established RPC connection. It has two modes of operation:

- **Ping Only** (default) — can be one step or continuous (until you click **Stop**).
- **Endpoint Search** — a one-time operation that allows you to find all available (responding) endpoints on the RPC server.

Note

Notice that RPingc.exe does not appear on the task pad.

An example of the RPingc's window is shown in Fig. 11.2. (I would recommend that you specify, in turn, both the DNS and NetBIOS names of a RPC server in the **Exchange Server** field. This is because the results may vary depending on the type of specified name and type of the selected operation.)

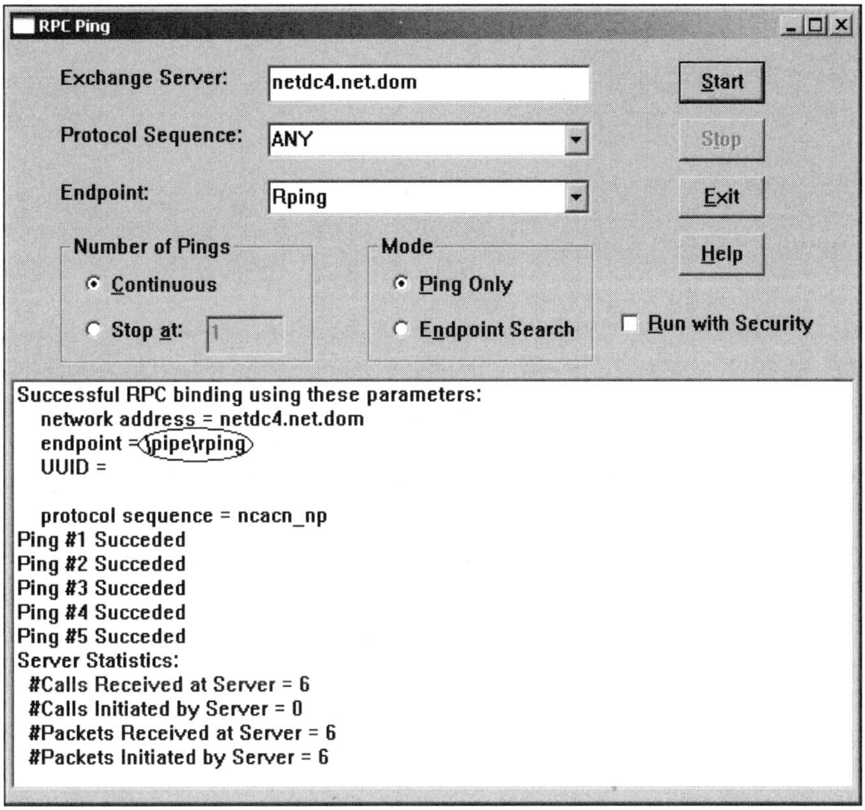

Fig. 11.2. This window contains the result of a few successful pings

A sample result of the *Endpoint Search* operation is shown below. (The settings **Protocol Sequence** = **ANY** and **Endpoint** = **Rping** were selected.)

```
Successful RPC binding using these parameters:
  network address = netdc4.net.dom
  endpoint = \pipe\rping
  UUID =

  protocol sequence = ncacn_np
...searching for uuids and endpoints...
FOUND: uuid for _Rping_ on netdc4.net.dom's protocol sequence: ncacn_np
FOUND: endpoint for _Rping_ on netdc4.net.dom's protocol sequence:
ncacn_np
...
Endpoint Search done.
```

The displayed "FOUND:" strings depend on the types and number of endpoints created on the target computer by RPings.exe.

If a RPC Ping client cannot find the specified server or bind to it using the selected protocol sequence, the following string will appear after all diagnostic messages:

```
Endpoint Search failed to find anything.
```

Some problems will cause the appearance of pop-up error windows, which may contain the return code and the "Unknown exception" message.

To verify authenticated RPCs, check the **Run with Security** box. Normally, this should not affect the results of any operations.

NTFRSutl.exe (RK)

This command-line tool is practically undocumented. You can enter its name at the command prompt and get a list of parameters. This is all the information you have at your disposal. NTFRSutl produces a lot of rather cryptic data. Nevertheless, this tool may be very useful for monitoring, troubleshooting, and — to some extent — managing the *File Replication Service* (FRS) that replicates the *System Volume* (SYSVOL) information and *Distributed File System* (DFS) data. The tool can be run on a local as well as a remote DC.

Note

NTFRSutl has been included in the Windows 2000 Service Resource Kit. Some Beta versions of Windows .NET server family have also comprised this tool.

Let us consider some of the NTFRSutl's parameters and their usage.

- `ntfrsutl ds` and `ntfrsutl sets` — these commands display the FRS configuration (replication partners, file filters, schedules, etc.). This information can be partially viewed in the **Active Directory Users and Computers** snap-in (see the **File Replication Service** node in the **System** container, and the objects of *FRS Subscriptions* type, which every domain controller has).
- `ntfrsutl stage` — this command displays the disk space currently being used by replicated objects. Normally, when the configuration is stable, this space is 0 KB. Allocated space means some data have not yet been replicated. The following two commands allow you to see which specific data are to be replicated.
- `ntfrsutl outlog` and `ntfrsutl inlog` — these commands usually display no data. If there are objects to be replicated, the logs contain information that can be useful to an administrator, such as an object file name, and date and time of changes.
- `ntfrsutl poll /now` — this command can override the current schedule and trigger replication of staging data between the current or any specified DC and its partners. Then, you can check logs or staging areas to make sure that all data have been replicated.

Directory Services Utility (DsaStat.exe) (ST)

This tool is the same as it is in Windows 2000 systems; it allows an administrator to compare full directory replicas stored on different domain controllers, or compare a domain partition with the partial replica stored in Global Catalog. The comparison can be purely statistical or on a per-attribute content basis.

The administrator can test either an entire directory partition or a subtree only. By default, all objects are compared, but it is possible to use a LDAP filter and choose only necessary types of objects. Moreover, you can test either all or only selected attributes, or the attributes replicated to Global Catalog. Thus, DsaStat can serve as an instrument for verifying replication between domain controllers and actual information stored on a DC.

> ***Tip***
>
> In the Windows 2000 environment, use the servers' *DNS* rather than NetBIOS names, and the tool will run faster.

> ***Tip***
>
> The tool may require quite a lot of time to run, and it is difficult to interrupt it. Besides, it produces significant network traffic. Therefore, if you plan to use it, do so carefully.

General Statistical Comparison

Let us first see how DsaStat compares directory replicas and produces statistical data. In this mode, the tool only counts the directory objects and displays totals. In the following example, the *Configuration* partition is verified on DCs from different domains. (It might be necessary to specify a domain administrator's credentials.) If the `-b` parameter has been omitted, all applicable partitions are compared.

```
C:\>dsastat -s:netdc1.net.dom;netdc2.subdom.net.dom
↳ -b:CN=Configuration,DC=net,DC=dom
Stat-Only mode.
Unsorted mode.
Opening connections...
        netdc1.net.dom...success.
Connecting to netdc1.net.dom...
reading...
```

```
 **> ntMixedDomain = 0      [0 - native mode]
reading...
 **> Options = 1            [1 - Global Catalog server]
Setting server as [netdc1.net.dom] as server to read Config Info...
        netdc2.subdom.net.dom...success.
Connecting to netdc2.subdom.net.dom...
reading...
 **> ntMixedDomain = 1      [1 - mixed mode]
reading...
 **> Options = 0            [0 - "normal" server]
[If options have not been defined, you will see the following line:
LocalException <0>: Cannot get Options <2>. ]
Generation Domain List on server netdc1.net.dom...
> Searching server for GC attribute partial set on property attributeId.
> Searching server for GC attribute partial set on property
ldapDisplayName.
Retrieving statistics...
[The command can be cancelled only from this point and afterwards:]
Paged result search...
Paged result search...
  50 entries processed (7 msg queued, 0 obj stored, 0 obj deleted)...
...
2650 entries processed (7 msg queued, 0 obj stored, 0 obj deleted)...
...(Terminated query to netdc1.net.dom. <No result present in message>)
...(Terminated query to netdc2.subdom.net.dom. <No result present in
message>)
2700 entries processed (6 msg queued, 0 obj stored, 0 obj deleted)...
...
2950 entries processed (6 msg queued, 0 obj stored, 0 obj deleted)...

                      -=>>|*** DSA Diagnostics ***|<<=-
Objects per server:

Obj/Svr               netdc1.net.dom  netdc2.subdom.net.dom   Total

configuration                      1        1         2
container                         61       61       122
controlAccessRight                58       58       116
crossRef                           6        6        12
crossRefContainer                  1        1         2
```

```
dSUISettings                         24      24      48
displaySpecifier                   1296    1296    2592
foreignSecurityPrincipal             16      16      32
interSiteTransport                    2       2       4
interSiteTransportContainer           1       1       2
licensingSiteSettings                 1       1       2
lostAndFound                          1       1       2
mSMQEnterpriseSettings                1       1       2
msPKI-Enterprise-Oid                  1       1       2
nTDSConnection                        4       4       8
nTDSDSA                               2       2       4
nTDSService                           1       1       2
nTDSSiteSettings                      1       1       2
physicalLocation                      1       1       2
queryPolicy                           1       1       2
rRASAdministrationDictionary          1       1       2
server                                2       2       4
serversContainer                      1       1       2
site                                  1       1       2
siteLink                              1       1       2
sitesContainer                        1       1       2
subnetContainer                       1       1       2
---
                                   1489    1489    2978
                  . . . . . . . . . . . . . .
Bytes per object:

configuration                   828
container                       18992
controlAccessRight              23564
crossRef                        1952
crossRefContainer               322
dSUISettings                    8400
displaySpecifier                469344
foreignSecurityPrincipal        6056
interSiteTransport              596
interSiteTransportContainer     408
licensingSiteSettings           436
```

```
lostAndFound                    334
mSMQEnterpriseSettings          350
msPKI-Enterprise-Oid            304
nTDSConnection                  1628
nTDSDSA                         660
nTDSService                     324
nTDSSiteSettings                396
physicalLocation                420
queryPolicy                     336
rRASAdministrationDictionary    398
server                          594
serversContainer                304
site                            258
siteLink                        312
sitesContainer                  288
subnetContainer                 300
                            . . . . . . . . . . . . . .
Bytes per server:

netdc1.net.dom                  269052
netdc2.subdom.net.dom           269052
                            . . . . . . . . . . . . . .
Checking for missing replies...
        No missing replies!INFO: Server sizes are equal.
*** Identical Directory Information Trees ***
PASS           -=>> PASS <<=-
closing connections...
        netdc1.net.dom; netdc2.subdom.net.dom;
```

As you can see, the number of objects of each type is displayed, along with the total size of objects of a specific type.

Analyzing Differences between Partitions

Basically, there are three types of inconsistencies between directory replicas which DsaStat can detect. Let us consider these types in the examples given below. In each case, we will compare the results of statistical and full-content comparisons of an OU object's replicas. For compactness, only the most interesting lines from the DsaStat's screen output will be shown.

Different Attribute Values of the Same Object

If the values of one or more attributes of the same object are different on specified domain controllers, *statistical* comparison (similar to the one shown above) only counts total sizes and produces the following result:

```
Checking for missing replies...
     No missing replies!INFO: Server sizes are not equal (min=...,
max=...).
*** Identical Directory Information Trees ***
PASS                -=>> PASS <<=
```

You can only conclude from such an output that the replicas differ, and nothing more.

The following command performs the *full-content* comparison as well as detects both a changed, albeit non-replicated directory object (a GPO) and an attribute name (`versionNumber`) (notice that the `-t:FALSE` parameter is used):

```
C:\>dsastat -s:netdc1.net.dom;netdc4.net.dom -b:DC=net,DC=dom -t:FALSE
Unsorted mode.
...
FAIL  Value [0] of Attr[versionNumber] did not compare on dn
[<GUID=7a8d66e928d2d94c93dd5ca95c7d5ac4>;CN={64C49D93-BBB7-
410E-B999-837B5B90422B},CN=Policies,CN=System,DC=net,DC=dom]
                      Servers [netdc1.net.dom]~[netdc4.net.dom]
FAIL  FAIL[1]: mismatch with current DIT image
...
                      -=>>|*** DSA Diagnostics ***|<<=-
...
Checking for missing replies...
        No missing replies!INFO: Server sizes are equal.
*** Different Directory Information Trees. 1 errors (see above). ***
FAIL                -=>> FAIL <<=-
closing connections...
        netdc1.net.dom; netdc4.net.dom;
```

In this case, a GPO named `{64C49D93-BBB7-410E-B999-837B5B90422B}` has been changed on a domain controller.

Thus, you can see both the number of errors and their location. The sizes of compared trees on the specified servers can be *equal* as well as *not equal*. This depends on the changes made with the directory objects.

Different Number of Defined Attributes of the Same Object

If the replicas of the same object have different numbers of attributes, the statistical comparison, again, reports only that the replicas' sizes are not equal. Let us look at the results produced by a full-content comparison.

```
C:\>dsastat -s:netdc1.net.dom;netdc4.net.dom -b:DC=net,DC=dom -t:FALSE
Unsorted mode.
Opening connections...
...
...(Terminated query to netdc1.net.dom. <No result present in message>)
...(Terminated query to netdc4.net.dom. <No result present in message>)
FAIL  AttrCount mismatch : Attrcount[17]@Server[netdc1.net.dom] !=
Attrcount[16]@Server[netdc4.net.dom]
for Dn
'<GUID=74c87b3d85df0945bab5d2ccd5e31381>;<SID=010500000000000515000000dc
f4dc3ba837d66516c0ea3255040000>;CN=John Smith,OU=Staff,DC=net,DC=dom'
********** Dumping Attribute List **********
---------------> Server [netdc1.net.dom] <--------------
Attr[0] = cn
Attr[1] = description
Attr[2] = displayName
Attr[3] = givenName
Attr[4] = name
Attr[5] = nTSecurityDescriptor
Attr[6] = objectCategory
Attr[7] = objectClass
Attr[8] = objectSid
Attr[9] = primaryGroupID
Attr[10] = replPropertyMetaData
Attr[11] = sAMAccountName
Attr[12] = sAMAccountType
Attr[13] = sn
Attr[14] = userAccountControl
Attr[15] = userPrincipalName
Attr[16] = whenCreated
---------------> Server [netdc4.net.dom] <--------------
Attr[0] = cn
Attr[1] = displayName
Attr[2] = givenName
Attr[3] = name
```

```
Attr[4] = nTSecurityDescriptor
Attr[5] = objectCategory
Attr[6] = objectClass
Attr[7] = objectSid
Attr[8] = primaryGroupID
Attr[9] = replPropertyMetaData
Attr[10] = sAMAccountName
Attr[11] = sAMAccountType
Attr[12] = sn
Attr[13] = userAccountControl
Attr[14] = userPrincipalName
Attr[15] = whenCreated
FAIL  FAIL[1]: mismatch with current DIT image

                    -=>>|*** DSA Diagnostics ***|<<=-
Objects per server:
...
Bytes per object:
...
Checking for missing replies...
        No missing replies!INFO: Server sizes are not equal (min=43841,
max=43830).
*** Different Directory Information Trees. 1 errors (see above). ***
FAIL                -=>> FAIL <<=-
closing connections...
        netdc1.net.dom; netdc4.net.dom;
```

As you can see, the tool displays the number of attributes for each object replica, shows the DN of the object, and then lists the attributes for each replica. The missing attribute can be easily found.

Different Number of Objects

In the following example, a user *mark* and a computer *Comp1* have been deleted from the *Staff* OU on one domain controller, and the changes have not yet been replicated to another DC. In this case, both statistical and full-content comparisons report that the test has failed, and that there has been a "Server total object count mismatch". A full-content test, however, displays specific information about the error: the type and name of the missing object. Look at the following sample output:

```
C:\>dsastat -s:netdc1.net.dom;netdc4.net.dom -b:OU=Staff,DC=net,DC=dom
↳ -t:FALSE
```

```
Unsorted mode.
...
                    -=>>|*** DSA Diagnostics ***|<<=-
Objects per server:

Obj/Svr                  netdc1.net.dom  netdc4.net.dom  Total

computer                              1       2      3
group                                 2       2      4
organizationalUnit                    1       1      2
user                                  4       5      9
volume                                1       1      2
---
                                      9      11     20
FAIL  Server total object count mismatch
...
Checking for missing replies...
Fail [2]: missing 1 replies for
'<GUID=65d29dba5ad79e4e947c4a85bdb2c774>;<SID=01050000000000051500000 0dc
f4dc3ba837d66516
c0ea3264040000>;CN=Compl,OU=Staff,DC=net,DC=dom'
Fail [3]: missing 1 replies for
'<GUID=f8c1c9cf1e919a469821b7ceb67608e2>;<SID=010500000000000515000000dc
f4dc3ba837d66516
c0ea3266040000>;CN=Mark,OU=Staff,DC=net,DC=dom'
INFO: Server sizes are not equal (min=1838, max=2227).
*** Different Directory Information Trees. 3 errors (see above). ***
FAIL            -=>> FAIL <<=-
closing connections...
        netdc1.net.dom; netdc4.net.dom;
```

Replication Diagnostics Tool (RepAdmin.exe) (ST)

Replication Diagnostics Tool is the only facility that allows an administrator to view and manage Active Directory replication topology and events from the command prompt or batch files. This tool, coupled with *DsaStat.exe*, helps to troubleshoot Active Directory consistency problems at a forest-wide level.

The Windows .NET version of RepAdmin provides about a dozen new operations (in contrast with Windows 2000 version) as well as a few new parameters to previously available operations (some of which are discussed below).

We will consider some of the most frequently used options of this tool. Some of these options may seem to be too complicated. However, if you understand the Active Directory replication model well, you will quickly learn how to use the tool in the most effective way.

Note

To use RepAdmin, you should be logged on to the network as a domain administrator. Furthermore, some operations can only be performed on a domain controller rather than on a client computer.

Note

Essentially, the Windows 2000 and Windows .NET versions of RepAdmin work in a similar way and slightly differ in their screen output messages as well as in their usage of some parameters.

Monitoring Replication Topology and Events

Triggering KCC

Normally, the *Knowledge Consistency Checker* (KCC) periodically verifies and automatically rebuilds the replication topology. You might want to forcibly start this process after some topology changes (e.g., after deleting connections). Take a look at the example:

```
C:\>repadmin /kcc netdc1.net.dom
Consistency check on netdc1.net.dom successful.
```

Viewing Replication Partners (*/showreps*)

The first and one of the most important steps for managing replication is to enumerate partners (neighbors) that have connections to the specified DC and to determine the replication topology for each naming context. (This information is used with many other of RepAdmin's parameters.) The following example was obtained for a forest that consists of two domains and two sites. The root domain `net.dom` is located in the `NET-Site` and contains two DCs (`NETDC1` and `NETDC3A`). The child domain `subdom.net.dom` is located in the `Remote-Site` and has a single DC (`NETDC2`). Let's see what kind of information RepAdmin displays for the specified DC. (In-line comments are in bold brackets.)

```
C:\>repadmin /showreps netdc1.net.dom
NET-Site\NETDC1
DC Options: IS_GC       [The specified DC is a Global Catalog server]
Site Options: (none)
DC object GUID: 02c2b1f6-e9b6-4e64-91f6-3a54b087bacc [By using this
GUID, you can bind to the DSA object named CN=NTDS Settings,CN=NETDC1,
CN=Servers,CN=NET-site,CN=Sites,CN=Configuration,DC=net,DC=dom.]
DC invocationID: 02c2b1f6-e9b6-4e64-91f6-3a54b087bacc

==== INBOUND NEIGHBORS ======================================

DC=net,DC=dom    [The Domain partition is only replicated among
DCs that serve the same domain.]
    NET-Site\NETDC3A via RPC
        DC object GUID: a10bc624-6d04-44e7-adf9-5ef4282efbb1
        Last attempt @ 2002-06-02 18:13:57 was successful.
      [The last replication time and the result of this operation is
       displayed for each connection.]

CN=Configuration,DC=net,DC=dom    [The Configuration and Schema
partitions are replicated among all DCs in the forest.]
    Remote-Site\NETDC2 via RPC
        DC object GUID: 8c19c6f6-1821-4ca7-97b5-c23307c5c49c
        Last attempt @ 2002-06-02 16:58:51 was successful.
    NET-Site\NETDC3A via RPC
        DC object GUID: a10bc624-6d04-44e7-adf9-5ef4282efbb1
        Last attempt @ 2002-06-02 17:57:40 was successful.

CN=Schema,CN=Configuration,DC=net,DC=dom
    Remote-Site\NETDC2 via RPC
        DC object GUID: 8c19c6f6-1821-4ca7-97b5-c23307c5c49c
        Last attempt @ 2002-06-02 16:58:51 was successful.
    NET-Site\NETDC3A via RPC
        DC object GUID: a10bc624-6d04-44e7-adf9-5ef4282efbb1
        Last attempt @ 2002-06-02 17:57:40 was successful.

DC=App-Part,DC=net,DC=dom    [The application directory partition
is only replicated among specifically assigned DCs.]
    NET-Site\NETDC3A via RPC
        DC object GUID: a10bc624-6d04-44e7-adf9-5ef4282efbb1
        Last attempt @ 2002-06-02 17:57:40 was successful.

DC=subdom,DC=net,DC=dom     [This domain partition is also partially
replicated to this DC, since it is a GC server.]
```

```
    Remote-Site\NETDC2 via RPC
        DC object GUID: 8c19c6f6-1821-4ca7-97b5-c23307c5c49c
        Last attempt @ 2002-06-02 16:58:51 was successful.
```

To see outbound partners, add the `/repsto` parameter (or `/all`) to the previous command. RepAdmin will append the following lines to the output:

```
==== OUTBOUND NEIGHBORS FOR CHANGE NOTIFICATIONS ============
DC=net,DC=dom
    NET-Site\NETDC3A via RPC
        DC object GUID: a10bc624-6d04-44e7-adf9-5ef4282efbb1

CN=Configuration,DC=net,DC=dom
    NET-Site\NETDC3A via RPC
        DC object GUID: a10bc624-6d04-44e7-adf9-5ef4282efbb1

CN=Schema,CN=Configuration,DC=net,DC=dom
    NET-Site\NETDC3A via RPC
        DC object GUID: a10bc624-6d04-44e7-adf9-5ef4282efbb1

DC=App-Part,DC=net,DC=dom
    NET-Site\NETDC3A via RPC
        DC object GUID: a10bc624-6d04-44e7-adf9-5ef4282efbb1
```

Note

In fact, the `NETDC1` and `NETDC2` domain controllers are connected by the IP transport (since these DCs are related to the different sites). However, both IP and RPC transports are displayed as "via RPC". The `/showconn` operation (see below) displays more detailed information.

To obtain more details, add the `/verbose` parameter to a command. Verbose mode displays additional information; for example:

```
...
 CN=Schema,CN=Configuration,DC=net,DC=dom
     Remote-Site\NETDC2 via RPC
         DC object GUID: 8c19c6f6-1821-4ca7-97b5-c23307c5c49c
         Address: 8c19c6f6-1821-4ca7-97b5-c23307c5c49c._msdcs.net.dom
         DC invocationID: a2043786-1d80-4ea7-b759-c5884ad6085f
         DO_SCHEDULED_SYNCS WRITEABLE COMPRESS_CHANGES
         NO_CHANGE_NOTIFICATIONS
         USNs: 148919/OU, 148919/PU
```

```
        Last attempt @ 2002-06-02 16:58:51 was successful.
    NET-Site\NETDC3A via RPC
        DC object GUID: a10bc624-6d04-44e7-adf9-5ef4282efbb1
        Address: a10bc624-6d04-44e7-adf9-5ef4282efbb1._msdcs.net.dom
        DC invocationID: 15eaa260-364d-469c-b2aa-1fe3c74059df
        SYNC_ON_STARTUP DO_SCHEDULED_SYNCS WRITEABLE
        USNs: 79723/OU, 79723/PU
        Last attempt @ 2002-06-02 18:57:37 was successful.
...
```

Look at the highlighted flags from this output. You can conclude the following from them:

- Both inter- and intra-site replications are scheduled (but these are different schedules!)
- Inter-site replication is compressed.
- There is no *change notification* between DCs related to different sites (this is the default option).
- DCs in the same site are synchronized upon their startup.

Viewing Connections with Replication Partners (*/showconn*)

To display the most comprehensive information on connections that have been established for a DC, use the `/showconn` operation. You can specify:

- The DNS name of the DC that will serve as the source of information
- The GUID (or the NetBIOS name) of the DC you are interested in

(Without the second parameter, you will get all connections for the site where the specified DC is located.) For example, the `NETDC1` domain controller from the sample configuration has two inbound connections:

```
C:\>repadmin /showconn netdc1.net.dom NETDC1
Base DN: CN=NETDC1,CN=Servers,CN=NET-
Site,CN=Sites,CN=Configuration,DC=net,DC=dom
==== KCC CONNECTION OBJECTS ============================================
Connection - [I.]
    Connection name : fcaa1598-8958-40ce-8be7-f585832d086b
    Server DNS name : netdc1.net.dom
    Server DN  name : CN=NTDS Settings,CN=NETDC1,CN=Servers,CN=NET-
Site,CN=Sites,CN=Configuration,DC=net,DC=dom
        Source: NET-Site\NETDC3A                        [From DC...]
                No Failures.
```

```
        TransportType: intrasite RPC
        options:  isGenerated
    [1]     ReplicatesNC: CN=Schema,CN=Configuration,DC=net,DC=dom
        Reason:  RingTopology
                Replica link has been added.
    [2]     ReplicatesNC: DC=App-Part,DC=net,DC=dom
        Reason:  RingTopology
                Replica link has been added.
    [3]     ReplicatesNC: CN=Configuration,DC=net,DC=dom
        Reason:  RingTopology
                Replica link has been added.
    [4]     ReplicatesNC: DC=net,DC=dom
        Reason:  RingTopology
                Replica link has been added.
Connection - [II.]
    Connection name : 8d7bc72b-335c-41c2-82f3-270ce2724c6c
    Server DNS name : netdc1.net.dom
    Server DN  name : CN=NTDS Settings,CN=NETDC1,CN=Servers,CN=NET-
    Site,CN=Sites,CN=Configuration,DC=net,DC=dom
        Source: Remote-Site\NETDC2                  [From DC...]
                No Failures.
        TransportType: IP
        options:  isGenerated
    [1]     ReplicatesNC: CN=Configuration,DC=net,DC=dom
                Replica link has been added.
    [2]     ReplicatesNC: DC=subdom,DC=net,DC=dom
                Replica link has been added.
2 connections found.
```

Notice that two different transport types — one for intra-site (`intrasite RPC`) and one for inter-site replication (`IP`) — are displayed.

The command shown will display all fault connections (that have not been replicated over a period of time) and the possible cause of failure.

Triggering Replication Events

By using RepAdmin, you can initiate replication events very flexibly. For a domain controller, the following replication scenarios are available:

- One directory partition is replicated from another DC.
- One directory partition is replicated from all neighbors.

- All directory partitions are replicated from all neighbors.
- A cross-site replication of a directory partition.
- Replication that will be switched from *pull* mode to *push* mode.

Let us consider them in detail.

Replication between Two Neighbors

To perform the most atomic replication operation, you must specify:

- A directory context (in Windows .NET, you can also specify a single directory object; see below)
- The DNS name of the *target* (destination) server
- The GUID of the *source* server (from which the changes are copied)

For example, to replicate the domain partition between two DCs, use a command similar to:

```
C:\>repadmin /sync DC=net,DC=dom netdc1.net.dom a10bc624-6d04-44e7-adf9-
5ef4282efbb1

Sync from a10bc624-6d04-44e7-adf9-5ef4282efbb1 to netdc1.net.dom
completed successfully.
```

The following command replicates one directory object only, which allows you to avoid excessive network traffic:

```
C:\>repadmin /replsingleobj netdc1.net.dom a10bc624-6d04-44e7-adf9-
5ef4282efbb1 OU=Staff,DC=net,DC=dom
```

You must wait until the operation is completed, or you can start the operation asynchronically and check the replication queue to see whether the operation has completed. To trigger a full replication of a directory context, you can, for example, use the following command:

```
C:\>repadmin /sync DC=net,DC=dom netdc1.net.dom a10bc624-6d04-44e7-adf9-
5ef4282efbb1 /full /async

Successfully enqueued sync from a10bc624-6d04-44e7-adf9-5ef4282efbb1 to
netdc1.net.dom.
```

Then, to monitor the operation, use the command

```
C:\>repadmin /queue
```

Here is a sample output:

```
Queue contains 1 items.

Current task began executing at 2002-06-02 20:01:05.
```

```
Task has been executing for 0 minutes, 7 seconds.


[144] Enqueued 2002-06-02 20:01:05 at priority 250
    SYNC FROM SOURCE
    NC DC=net,DC=dom
    DC NET-Site\NETDC3A
    DC object GUID a10bc624-6d04-44e7-adf9-5ef4282efbb1
    DC transport addr a10bc624-6d04-44e7-adf9-
5ef4282efbb1._msdcs.net.dom
       ASYNCHRONOUS_OPERATION WRITEABLE FULL
```

Replication from All Partners

The `/syncall` parameter can be used to synchronize a directory partition between a DC and *all* its partners. The `/A` parameter available on Windows .NET-based DCs, can initiate replication of *all* partitions stored on a DC.

Sometimes, a command fails. Take a look, for example, at the following output produced by a command:

```
C:\>repadmin /syncall netdc1.net.dom DC=net,DC=dom
Syncing partition: DC=net,DC=dom
CALLBACK MESSAGE: Error contacting server a10bc624-6d04-44e7-adf9-
5ef4282efbb1._msdcs.net.dom (network error):
 1722 (0x6ba):
    The RPC server is unavailable.
CALLBACK MESSAGE: SyncAll Finished.

SyncAll reported the following errors:
Error contacting server a10bc624-6d04-44e7-adf9-
5ef4282efbb1._msdcs.net.dom (network error): 1722 (0x6ba):
    The RPC server is unavailable.
```

(To see a name which corresponds to the GUID shown, use `repadmin /showreps`.)

In Windows 2000, only an error code is displayed. You can get a text description of a message by running RepAdmin with the `/showmsg` parameter and specifying the error code.

When the command runs successfully, it reports all partners' names:

```
C:\>repadmin /syncall netdc1.net.dom DC=net,DC=dom
Syncing partition: DC=net,DC=dom
CALLBACK MESSAGE: The following replication is in progress:
```

```
    From: a10bc624-6d04-44e7-adf9-5ef4282efbb1._msdcs.net.dom
    To  : 02c2b1f6-e9b6-4e64-91f6-3a54b087bacc._msdcs.net.dom
CALLBACK MESSAGE: The following replication completed successfully:
    From: a10bc624-6d04-44e7-adf9-5ef4282efbb1._msdcs.net.dom
    To  : 02c2b1f6-e9b6-4e64-91f6-3a54b087bacc._msdcs.net.dom
CALLBACK MESSAGE: SyncAll Finished.
SyncAll terminated with no errors.
```

Attention

- If you do not specify a naming context in the `repadmin /syncall` command, the *Configuration* partition is only replicated.

Use the `repadmin /syncall /h` command to see help information for additional parameters (flags), some of which are especially important:

- `/A` — replicates all naming contexts stored on the DC. (A new option in the Windows .NET version of RepAdmin.) For example, the following command synchronizes all partitions on NETDC1 DC with all their replicas:

  `repadmin /syncall` `netdc1.net.dom` **`/A`**

- `/d` — changes representation of DCs in output messages, for example, instead of:

  `a10bc624-6d04-44e7-adf9-5ef4282efbb1._msdcs.net.dom`

  you will see

  ```
  CN=NTDS Settings,CN=NETDC3A,CN=Servers,CN=NET-Site,CN=Sites,
  ↳CN=Configuration,DC=net,DC=dom
  ```

- `/e` — enables cross-site replication. You can see the difference if, for example, you try to synchronize the Configuration partition by using a command with this parameter, and then without it.
- `/P` — reverses the direction of replication. When this parameter is used, the changes are propagated *from* the specified server *to* all partners (vice versa by default).

Failed Replications

If a replication partner is not available, or a network connection doesn't work, the scheduled replications periodically fail. The following command allows you to see the statistics on failed replications:

```
C:\>repadmin /failcache netdc1.net.dom
==== KCC CONNECTION FAILURES ==============================
(none)
```

```
==== KCC LINK FAILURES ==================================
    NET-Site\NETDC3A
        DC object GUID: a10bc624-6d04-44e7-adf9-5ef4282efbb1
        No Failures.
    Remote-Site\NETDC2
        DC object GUID: 8c19c6f6-1821-4ca7-97b5-c23307c5c49c
        2 consecutive failures since 2002-06-02 19:57:37.
        Last error: 1722 (0x6ba):
            The RPC server is unavailable.
```

Viewing Directory Changes

RepAdmin has a few options that can be used for monitoring the actual state of domain controllers. You can easily determine whether changes have been made on a DC, and whether directory partitions have been synchronized on different DCs.

Is a Domain Controller up to Date?

Suppose we want to determine whether the domain partition (`DC=net,DC=dom`) is synchronized on two domain controllers — `NETDC1` and `NETDC4`. We need to first find the highest USN on the first DC. Use the following command:

```
C:\>repadmin /showvector DC=net,DC=dom netdc1.net.dom
NET-Site\NETDC1          @ USN     11785 @ Time 2002-06-07 17:11:21
NET-Site\NETDC4          @ USN     18241 @ Time 2002-06-07 17:09:41
```

Then we must check the value known to the second DC. We should specify: the *invocationID* of the first DC (see description of the `/showreps` operation above), the USN found, and the DNS name of either DC:

```
C:\>repadmin /propcheck DC=net,DC=dom b202a2a9-2e6b-4c9f-9c99-
ac00b873e5c2 11785 netdc1.net.dom
NET-Site\NETDC1: yes (USN 11785)
NET-Site\NETDC4: ** NO! ** (USN 11767)  [11767 < 11785]
```

As you can see, the second DC holds an older USN. If we run the command again after replicating changes from NETDC1 to NETDC4, the result should be the following:

```
C:\>repadmin /propcheck DC=net,DC=dom b202a2a9-2e6b-4c9f-9e99-
ac00b873e5c2 11785 netdc1.net.dom
NET-Site\NETDC1: yes (USN 11785)
NET-Site\NETDC4: yes (USN 11785)
```

Displaying Replication Metadata

By viewing replication metadata for a directory object, you can check the consistency between different replicas if you compare attribute versions and USN numbers on different domain controllers. Furthermore, you can see which DC (it is considered to be the *originating DC*) the attributes were last changed on. The following example shows metadata for an OU object. (The output has been compressed horizontally to fit the page.)

```
C:\>repadmin /showmeta OU=Staff,DC=net,DC=dom netdc1.net.dom

13 entries.
Loc.USN   Originating DC   Org.USN Org.Time/Date         Ver Attribute
=======   ==============   ======= =============         === =========
  11826   NET-Site\NETDC1    11826 2002-06-07 17:24:38     1 gPOptions
  11826   NET-Site\NETDC1    11826 2002-06-07 17:24:38     1 gPLink
  11767   NET-Site\NETDC1    11767 2002-06-07 17:09:11     1 objectCategory
  11893   NET-Site\NETDC1    11893 2002-06-07 17:33:59     4 name
  11907   NET-Site\NETDC1    11907 2002-06-07 17:34:49     3 nTSecurityDescriptor
  11767   NET-Site\NETDC1    11767 2002-06-07 17:09:11     1 whenCreated
  11767   NET-Site\NETDC1    11767 2002-06-07 17:09:11     1 instanceType
  11817   NET-Site\NETDC4    18306 2002-06-07 17:24:17     2 description
  11893   NET-Site\NETDC1    11893 2002-06-07 17:33:59     4 ou
  11923   NET-Site\NETDC4    18389 2002-06-07 17:40:59     2 street
  11923   NET-Site\NETDC4    18389 2002-06-07 17:40:59     2 st
  11923   NET-Site\NETDC4    18389 2002-06-07 17:40:59     2 l
  11767   NET-Site\NETDC1    11767 2002-06-07 17:09:11     1 objectClass
```

This output is easier to analyze when compared to the metadata information produced by the Ldp.exe tool (see Fig. 12.17 in *Chapter 12, "Manipulating Active Directory Objects"*). As you can see, the attribute names are displayed here in text format.

Note

If an authoritative restore is performed on a DC, the attribute version numbers will have large values, since by default these numbers increased by a minimum of 100,000 for each "standard" restore operation (i.e., if the `verinc` parameter is not used).

Registering Changes Made on a Specific DC

It is possible to register all of the changes that have been made on a domain controller from a specific time point. The following command analyzes the current state of the domain partition and writes the result to a file:

```
C:\>repadmin /getchanges DC=net,DC=dom netdc1.net.dom /cookie:log1.txt
Using empty cookie (full sync).

==== SOURCE DC: netdc1.net.dom ====

Objects returned: 100
(0) add DC=net,DC=dom
...
Objects returned: ...
...
New cookie written to file log1.txt (132 bytes)
```

The command produces a very large screen output; therefore, you might prefer to add the `/statistics` parameter to this command.

After some time elapses, you can re-run the command:

```
C:\>repadmin /getchanges DC=net,DC=dom netdc1.net.dom /cookie:log1.txt
Using cookie from file log1.txt (132 bytes)

==== SOURCE DC: netdc1.net.dom ====

Objects returned: 3
(0) modify CN=Backup Operators,CN=Builtin,DC=net,DC=dom
        1> objectGUID: c997318b-324a-4fa4-b29d-2b045904e093
        1> member: CN=John Smith,OU=Staff,DC=net,DC=dom
        1> instanceType: 4
(1) delete OU=Marketing\0ADEL:d43d3ee7-861b-4ea1-8b8b-
                        0b51c0db3de1,CN=Deleted Objects,DC=net,DC=dom
        1> parentGUID: eebc28cc-c7b3-4d6f-bd5e-13aef642e30a
        1> objectGUID: d43d3ee7-861b-4ea1-8b8b-0b51c0db3de1
        1> instanceType: 4
        1> isDeleted: TRUE
        1> name: Marketing
DEL:d43d3ee7-861b-4ea1-8b8b-0b51c0db3de1
        1> lastKnownParent: OU=Staff,DC=net,DC=dom
```

```
(2) modify CN=John Smith,OU=Staff,DC=net,DC=dom
        1> objectGUID: 50e649bc-69f8-4313-87a6-765e4a335bdd
        1> description: A test user
        1> instanceType: 4
New cookie written to file log1.txt (132 bytes)
```

As you can see, two objects have been modified, and one object has been deleted. The time stamp is renewed, and only new changes will be registered from that moment.

The same information will be displayed if you run a comparison command:

```
C:\>repadmin /getchanges DC=net,DC=dom netdc4.net.dom b202a2a9-2e6b-
                                4c9f-9e99-ac00b873e5c2
```

Notice that the command contains the domain partition name, the DNS name of a replication partner (in that case, this is a "reference" DC), and the GUID of a tested domain controller (netdc1.net.dom). This command displays changes made on NETDC1 before the replication will be performed and two directory replicas will be synchronized. In comparison to the previous command (with a cookie file), the last command will display the same result (the changes made) repeatedly unless the synchronization of replicas will be carried out. You can choose either command that is the most appropriate for your conditions.

Comparing Information on Different Domain Controllers

A command that compares the partition replicas stored on different servers must contain the DNS name of a "reference" server and the GUID of a "source" (tested) server. All changes made in the source server will be registered. Actually, this command performs the same job as the *DsaStat* tool does. The output shown below was obtained at the time when a great number of user objects on the *NETDC1* domain controller were being removed.

```
C:\>repadmin /getchanges DC=net,DC=dom netdc4.net.dom b202a2a9-2e6b-
4c9f-9e99-ac00b873e5c2 /statistics
Building starting position from destination server netdc4.net.dom

Source Neighbor:
DC=net,DC=dom
    NET-Site\NETDC1 via RPC
        DC object GUID: b202a2a9-2e6b-4c9f-9e99-ac00b873e5c2
        Address: b202a2a9-2e6b-4c9f-9e99-ac00b873e5c2._msdcs.net.dom
        DC invocationID: b202a2a9-2e6b-4c9f-9e99-ac00b873e5c2
        SYNC_ON_STARTUP DO_SCHEDULED_SYNCS WRITEABLE
```

```
        USNs: 12769/OU, 12769/PU
        Last attempt @ 2002-06-07 19:11:29 was successful.

Destination's up-to-date vector:
6a0cdbee-e064-449f-8c09-3f3c45b54fd6 @ USN 20291
b202a2a9-2e6b-4c9f-9e99-ac00b873e5c2 @ USN 12771

==== SOURCE DC: b202a2a9-2e6b-4c9f-9e99-ac00b873e5c2._msdcs.net.dom ====

********* Cumulative packet totals ************
Packets:                1
Objects:                100
Object Additions:       0
Object Modifications: 0
Object Deletions:       100
Object Moves:           0
Attributes:             600
Values:                 600
Dn-valued Attributes: 100
MaxDnVals on any attr:1
ObjectDn with maxattr:C
Attrname with maxattr:1
#dnvals 1-250   251-500 501-750 751-1000 1000+
add     0       0       0       0        0
mod     100     0       0       0        0
**********************************************
...
Packets:                2
...
Packets:                3
...
********* Grand total ************************
Packets:                3
Objects:                230
Object Additions:       0
Object Modifications: 0
Object Deletions:       230
Object Moves:           0
Attributes:             1380
Values:                 1380
```

```
Dn-valued Attributes: 230
MaxDnVals on any attr:1
ObjectDn with maxattr:C
Attrname with maxattr:1
#dnvals 1-250   251-500 501-750 751-1000 1000+
add     0       0       0       0        0
mod     230     0       0       0        0
*************************************************
```

If both replicas are synchronized, the command reports

```
No changes
```

and all totals are equal to zero.

New "Inter-Site" Operations

The Windows .NET version of RepAdmin offers a number of new operations that are especially useful in large multi-site forests. Among them are the following:

- `repadmin /bridgeheads` — lists the bridgehead servers for sites.
- `repadmin /istg` — lists servers that perform the role of the *Inter-site Topology Generator* (ISTG) in sites.
- `repadmin /querysites` — displays the cost of the link between specified sites.
- `repadmin /latency` — displays replication latency between sites; this information allows an administrator to quickly find sites that have not replicated with their partners over a long period of time.

Auxiliary Options

Managing Replication Status (DSA Options)

Each *Directory System Agent* (DSA) is represented in Active Directory by an object of the *nTDSDSA* class named *CN=NTDS Settings* that belongs to the appropriate server object in the *Configuration* partition. (You can view the attributes of DSA objects with the **ADSI Edit** snap-in.) DSA objects have the `options` attribute, which significantly affects their state and behavior. An administrator can set the value of this attribute by using RepAdmin with an undocumented parameter `/options`. Let us discuss a few examples.

The following command detects that the specified domain controller is a Global Catalog server:

```
C:\>repadmin /options netdc1.net.dom
Current DC Options: IS_GC
```

The `options` attribute is equal to 1 in this case. You can set the `IS_GC` flag to promote a DC to GC server. Usually, this operation is performed with the **Active Directory Sites and Services** snap-in.

The following two parameters allow you to "isolate" a DC from its replication partners for troubleshooting or some other purpose. The next example shows that replication *from* the specified DC (outbound replication) is disabled:

```
C:\>repadmin /options netdc4.net.dom
Current DC Options: DISABLE_OUTBOUND_REPL
```

The `options` attribute is equal to 4 (hex) in this case (if the DC is not a GC server!).

The state of inbound replication (from partners *to* a specified DC) is determined by the `DISABLE_INBOUND_REPL` flag. (This flag corresponds to an `options` attribute value equal to 2.) You can set both flags and totally disable replication for the DC.

To set a flag, specify it with a "+" (plus) sign. To clear a flag, use "–" (minus). For example, the following command clears the flag and re-enables outbound replication from the DC:

```
C:\>repadmin /options netdc4.net.dom -DISABLE_OUTBOUND_REPL
Current DC Options: DISABLE_OUTBOUND_REPL
New DC Options: (none)
```

Every "disable replication" operation is registered in the *Directory Service* log (Event ID 1113, 1114, 1115, and 1116). Look at the following two examples:

```
Event Type:   Warning
Event Source: NTDS General
Event Category:  Replication
Event ID:  1115
...
Computer:  NETDC1
Description:
Outbound replication has been disabled by the user.
```

When replication is enabled, an informational event is also registered:

```
Event Type:   Information
Event Source: NTDS General
Event Category:  Replication
Event ID:  1116
...
Computer:  NETDC1
Description:
Outbound replication has been enabled by the user.
```

Converting Directory Time (*/showtime*)

RepAdmin can convert time values stored in Active Directory into a readable format. (See also NLtest description at the beginning of this chapter.) Let us convert the same value *126679218485309520*. Enter `repadmin /showtime` at the command prompt, and paste the value in. Erase the seven rightmost digits and press <Enter>. The result should be the following:

```
C:\>repadmin /showtime 12667921848
12667921848 = 0x2f31125b8 = 02-06-07 11:10.48 UTC = 2002-06-07 15:10:48 local
```

You may notice that both UTC and local time are displayed.

In Windows .NET, you can obtain the same result easier — use the W32tm command:

```
C:\>w32tm /ntte 126679218485309520
146619 11:10:48.5309520 - 6/7/2002 3:10:48 PM (local time)
```

Displaying Error Description (*/showmsg*)

RepAdmin.exe has an option that will help you when you write and debug ADSI scripts and application and analyze event logs, as well as in many other cases. You can use this utility rather than searching the documentation for information on each error. The utility provides many more options than the `net helpmsg` command does. RepAdmin.exe can display error text for both Win32 error codes (including errors for ADSI 2.5) and generic COM error codes.

You can specify an error code in either form: as a long integer (e.g., `-2147016684`) or a hexadecimal value (e.g., `0x80072014`; the `0x` prefix is mandatory, do not forget to add this prefix if you have copied an error's code from the Event Viewer). Short integers, such as `8453`, are also acceptable. Here is an example of how to use this parameter:

```
C:\repadmin /showmsg 0x80072014
-2147016684 = 0x80072014 = "The requested operation did not satisfy one
or more constraints associated with the class of the object."
```

Active Directory Replication Monitor (ReplMon.exe) (ST)

Active Directory Replication Monitor is a GUI tool that is exclusively intended for monitoring and managing all kinds of replication in AD-based domains (Windows 2000 and Windows .NET domains). With this tool, you can monitor and register all replication events, force replication, start generating replication topology, view Global Catalog and bridgehead servers, and view trusts and replication metadata for an Active Directory object. The list of options could be continued. The tool has a simple and friendly user interface.

Preparation Steps and Analysis of Information

After the tool's start-up, you should create a list of monitored servers. This might be a tiresome operation in a large domain, but you only need to perform it once. When all necessary servers have been added to ReplMon, save the current configuration by clicking **Save Monitored List As** in the **File** menu. The next time the tool is running, choose the **Open Script** command and load the necessary configuration. A sample screen of the ReplMon's main window is shown in Fig. 11.3.

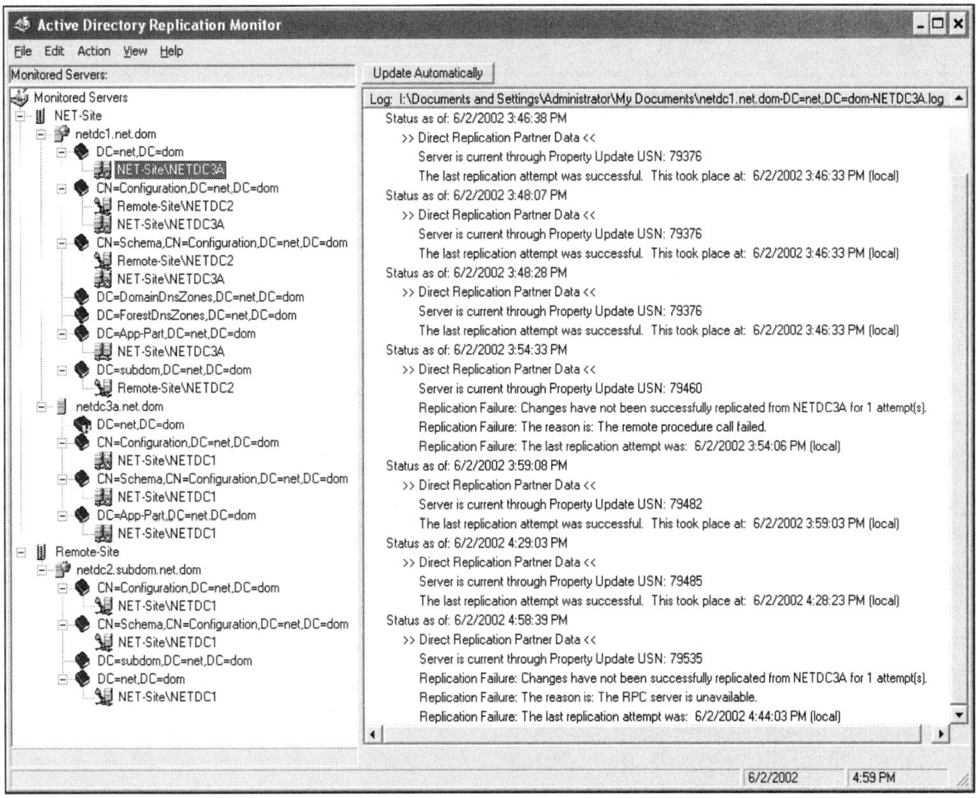

Fig. 11.3. The main window of ReplMon, where you can browse the domain tree and see log files for selected domain partition and replication partner

ReplMon uses various icons to represent monitored servers and their replication partners, which helps an administrator to easily determine replication status. The icons are described in the table below.

Icon	Description
	Directory partition that has replication problems
	Bridgehead server
	Global Catalog server
	Direct replication partner that has encountered replication problems
	Successfully replicated direct replication partner
	Transitive replication partner

Let us consider what replication topology information we can obtain from the screenshot shown in Fig. 11.3:

- The sample forest comprises two domains, two sites, and three domain controllers.
- Each site has a Global Catalog server: *NETDC1* DC receives a partial replica of the *subdom.net.dom* domain, whereas *NETDC2* DC receives partial information about the *DC=net,DC=dom* naming context. In addition, both controllers are the bridgehead servers.
- *NETDC1* DC stores three application directory partitions: *DC=DomainDnsZones, DC=net,DC=dom*, *DC=ForestDnsZones,DC=net,DC=dom*, and *DC=App-Part,DC=net, DC=dom*. Only the last partition has a replica on *NETDC3A* DC.
- *NETDC2* DC stores the domain partition (*DC=subdom,DC=net,DC=dom*) that is not replicating to any other domain controllers.
- Replication events for the selected pair of partners (*NETDC1* and *NETDC3A*) and directory context (*DC=net,DC=dom*) are written into a file named *netdc1.net.dom-DC=net,DC=dom-NETDC3A.log*.
- *NETDC1* DC fails to replicate three directory contexts (domain, schema, and configuration) from *NETDC3A* DC. The log selected contains the reason of failure: "The RPC server is unavailable".
- *NETDC3A* DC has a general problem with replication of the *DC=net,DC=dom* naming context and fails to replicate data from *NETDC1* DC.

As you can see, ReplMon provides an administrator with thorough replication information.

Log Files

By default, ReplMon writes all *Replication Status Logs* to the **My Documents** folder of the currently logged on user. The log name combines the domain controller's DNS name, directory partition name and a replication partner down-level name.

You can assign a different location if you like. Click **Options** in the **View** menu, check the **Default Path for Replication Status Logs** box, and enter the necessary path. (To troubleshoot replication problems, you can also enable debug logging, allowing ReplMon to register every performed operation.)

ReplMon updates the Replication Status Logs at its start-up, and you can specify a time interval for automatic updating. If you do so, all replication activity for monitored servers will be registered in the logs.

Managing Replication

By using ReplMon, you can initiate any replication events possible for the selected domain controller. Most operations are started through the context menu of the selected DC. These operations are quite simple to learn, and all the tool's features are visible in the menu.

ReplMon has a very useful feature that allows you to view performance data usually available through the **Performance** snap-in. (See the *"Monitoring Replication"* section in *Chapter 6*, "*Configuring and Troubleshooting AD-based Domains*".) First, open the **Performance** snap-in and choose the counters you are interested in and write down their names. (You do not need the **Performance** snap-in itself!) To simplify a task, you can add the necessary counters to the **Performance** snap-in's window, click the **Copy Properties** button on the tool bar, and paste the text into a document. This text will contain all counter names (see the `Path` parameter) in addition to other information. Then start ReplMon, click **Options** on the **View** menu, and select the **Status Logging** tab (Fig. 11.4).

Check the **Performance Statistics** box, click **Add,** and enter a counter name (e.g., "\NTDS\DRA Inbound Bytes Compressed (Between Sites, After Compression) Since Boot"). Repeat this step if necessary. If you have already saved the counter names from the **Performance** snap-in into a text document, you can now easily copy-and-paste all names. Now you can select a DC and choose the **Show Current Performance Data** command from the context menu. You will see all current values of counters in the **Performance Data** window. The current data will be also written to the domain controller's logs.

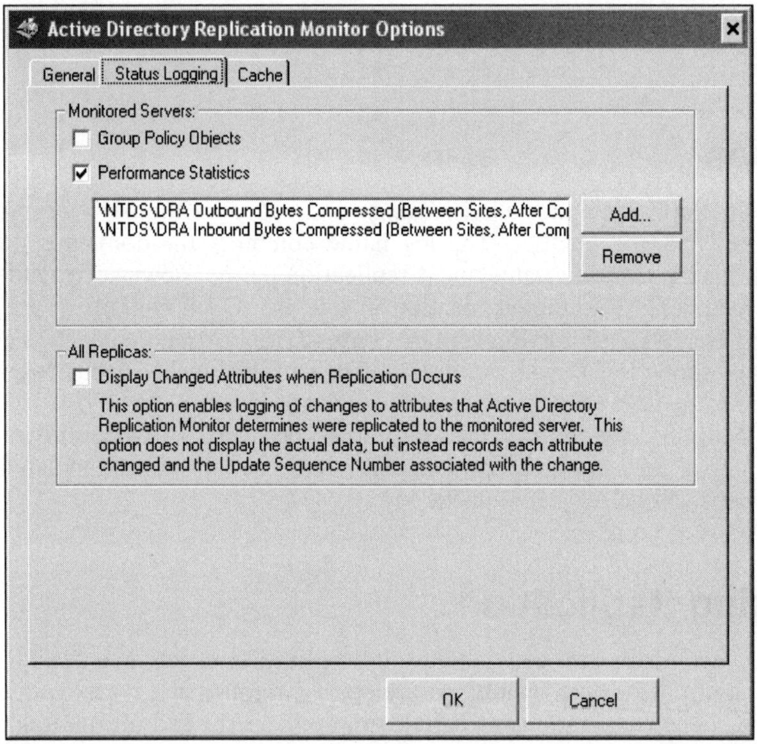

Fig. 11.4. Configuring counters that will comprise current performance data

Also, take note of the **Group Policy Objects** and **Display Changed Attributes when Replication Occurs** checkboxes on the **Status Logging** tab. The former checkbox will allow you to verify consistency of GPOs (AD and SysVol versions) with the **Show Group Policy Object Status** command. The latter checkbox turns on the logging of changed attributes: you will see their names as well as the names of corresponding directory objects in the logs. This will allow you to trace all changes in the directory more precisely.

Chapter 12: Manipulating Active Directory Objects

In this chapter, we will discuss Active Directory modification tools in detail. These tools allow administrators to find necessary directory objects and edit their attribute values; manipulate various domain objects (computer account, domain trusts, secure channels, etc.); export specified objects to a file, and import (create) objects from a file in the same or another domain. All listed operations can be performed with either a single directory object or a number of objects.

Finding Information in Active Directory

Since Active Directory may contain a huge number of directory objects and have a complex domain structure, it is necessary to have the ability to locate, or pick out the necessary objects quickly and view (edit) their attributes. You can use for that purpose the following facilities.

GUI Tools

- The search option of Active Directory client software (built-in features of Windows 2000/XP/.NET, or the Active Directory Client Extension, DSClient). DSClient can be installed on any Windows platform. The **Find** window allows you to look for standard objects (users, groups, computers, etc.) as well as to use the common and custom queries. (See the "*Configuring Search Option on a Client Computer*" section in *Chapter 8*, *"Common Administrative Tasks."*)
- **Active Directory Users and Computers** snap-in — this snap-in has a *Filter* option that allows you to narrow the scope of viewed objects. The *Find* option allows you to locate and select objects for manipulating within a domain as well as in the entire forest (since it is able to work with Global Catalog). Moreover, the Windows .NET version of that snap-in introduces *Saved Queries* that allows the administrator to work with defined sets of selected directory objects. (The snap-in was discussed in *Chapter 7*, *"Domain Manipulation Tools."*)
- AdsVw.exe and Ldp.exe (*ADSI SDK* and *Support Tools*) — these powerful tools allow you to compose complex queries and apply them to a domain as well as to the entire forest. AdsVw.exe can open a number of query windows simultaneously. (Both of these tools are described later in this chapter.)

Command-line Tools

- DsQuery.exe and DsGet.exe — the standard Windows .NET tools (they do not work on Windows 2000 systems!) that use the LDAP protocol (therefore, they can query both Windows 2000- and Windows .NET-based domains) and can find directory objects of various types as well as display their attributes. Search operations can be performed within a single domain or entire forest.

- Search.vbs — a script from the *Support Tools* pack. Can search within a single domain and work with the LDAP provider only.
- Windows Domain Manager (NetDom.exe) (*Support Tools*) — can display specific information about domains (FSMO role owners, trusts, etc.) as well as perform modifications.

Active Directory Search Tool (Search.vbs) (ST)

The *Search.vbs* script is a simple, handy tool that allows you to retrieve the attributes of the specified objects. By default, the script displays the *AdsPaths* of the children of the object specified by its distinguished name. These children objects may be of any type.

Administrators or any other users may use the script on any Windows platform, provided that the Windows Scripting Host (WSH) is installed. This is a unique instrument, since the other search tools require Windows 2000/XP/.NET.

Caution

The *Search.vbs* script does not display certain object attributes, such as *objectGUID*, *objectSID*, *lastLogon* (these are attributes of "complex" types, such as OctetString, LargeInteger, etc.), and some others. What is worse, the script has an internal bug, which sometimes produces an erroneous output when such attributes are included in the returned parameters list (for instance, search for a user's *objectSID*, *lastLogon*, and *cn* attributes).

Analyzing the listing of the script will help you to better understand the methods of retrieving data of various types (see also *Chapter 16, "Active Directory Service Interfaces (ADSI)"*) while composing your own scripts.

Output Data Format

The script outputs the data found as a sequence of lines in the following format:

```
attributeName object# [=] propertyValue
```

If the script cannot *display* a property value, it outputs only the first two components, e.g., `objectSID 1`. If a property has an *empty* value or is *not defined*, the "=" character is added, e.g., `description 1 =`.

A few examples of using Search.vbs are presented below.

Example 1. Searching for an Object Using Its GUID

Suppose you want to verify whether a known GUID really belongs to a directory object, or you want to check the name of this object. You may use the following command:

```
C:\>search "LDAP://<GUID=075f1790071a854d82ee5556c3a11d64>" /S:base
```

The resulting output will be similar to:

```
<LDAP://<GUID=075f1790071a854d82ee5556c3a11d64>>;(ObjectCategory=*);ADsPath;base
Finished the query.
Found 1 objects.
ADsPath 1 = LDAP://OU=Staff,DC=net,DC=dom
```

You may also widen the scope of the search (i.e., use the `/S:oneLevel` or `/S:subTree` parameter and get the base object's children names), or specify output of additional attributes.

Note

If the object's name is all you want to know, you may also use the *Guid2obj.exe* utility from the *Windows 2000 Resource Kit*. You should provide the object GUID as a parameter, and the tool will retrieve the distinguished name of the object from the nearest global catalog server.

Example 2. Finding All Policies in a Domain

Sometimes, it is necessary to know what policies (GPOs) exist in a domain, and which names they go by in administrative snap-ins. You could look up the value of the *displayName* attribute for each policy object in the *CN=Policies,CN=System* subtree of a domain container. However, it is much faster to use Search.vbs. The query might look like this:

```
search "LDAP://DC=net,DC=dom" /C:(objectClass=GroupPolicyContainer)
↳ /S:subtree /P:cn,displayName
```

Possible resulting output:

```
<LDAP://DC=net,DC=dom>;((objectClass=GroupPolicyContainer));cn,
↳ displayName;subtree
Finished the query.
Found 5 objects.
cn 1 = {31B2F340-016D-11D2-945F-00C04FB984F9}
displayName 1 = Default Domain Policy
cn 2 = {6AC1786C-016F-11D2-945F-00C04fB984F9}
displayName 2 = Default Domain Controllers Policy
cn 3 = {9EFADC61-8833-4970-9CE3-AF705E197908}
displayName 3 = NET-Site GPO
cn 4 = {3DE99CCC-C0F6-4F21-BE9C-E6D3F7EB6370}
displayName 4 = ADMINs OU's GPO
cn 5 = {55EAC8BC-D3C7-4B11-AA00-ECB7620A7FB9}
displayName 5 = COMPs OU's GPO
```

As you can see, there are three additional GPOs (one for the site and 2 for OUs) in the domain, besides the default ones.

The same operation could be done using the following command:

```
dsquery * -filter objectClass=GroupPolicyContainer -attr cn displayName
```

Browsing and Editing Active Directory Objects

There are three basic "standard" tools that can be used for browsing Active Directory and editing the properties of directory objects.

- **ADSI Edit** snap-in — from the *Support Tools* or *Windows Administration Tools* packs. This snap-in was discussed in *Chapter 7*, *"Domain Manipulation Tools"*. It does not display all directory objects and attributes, but has a simple user interface and a flexible mechanism of custom query views. It provides you with access to all Active Directory partitions (including application partitions) as well as Global Catalog and offers a standard way of working with permissions on objects. Works with the LDAP protocol only.
- Active Directory Browser (AdsVw.exe) — from the *Active Directory Service Interfaces Software Development Kit* (ADSI SDK). The only tool that is able to work with both the LDAP and WinNT protocols. It therefore allows you to work with AD- and Windows NT-based domains simultaneously. It is not well-documented and requires a solid understanding of Active Directory. Works with security descriptors.
- Active Directory Administration Tool (Ldp.exe) — from the *Support Tools*. The most sophisticated tool for manipulating directory objects with the LDAP protocol. It requires extensive knowledge of LDAP basics (naming, queries, etc.) as well as Active Directory architecture. Works with security descriptors and Active Directory replication metadata.

These utilities can be regarded as "mandatory" tools set for troubleshooting various directory problems, and especially for composing your own administrative scripts or designing Active Directory-oriented applications.

In addition, Windows .NET-based domain controllers offer two powerful command-line utilities — DsGet.exe and DsMod.exe — that are useful for batch modifications of directory objects.

Note

Unfortunately, among the above-mentioned tools, only the **ADSI Edit** snap-in works with non-Latin Unicode names of objects without any problems. The limitations of the other two tools are discussed in the appropriate sections.

If you need to work with objects' GUIDs (the *objectGUID* attribute), use Ldp.exe or DsQuery.exe, since the other two tools (AdsVw.exe and ADSI Edit) display a GUID as a binary value (octet string), which cannot be used for binding, referring, etc.

Active Directory Browser (AdsVw.exe) (ADSI SDK)

The *Active Directory Browser* is included in the *ADSI SDK* (also known as *Active Directory SDK*) that you can download from the Microsoft website (see links in *Appendix A*).

The main peculiarity of the Active Directory Browser is its ability to work with both Windows NT 4.0 and AD-based (Windows 2000 and Windows .NET) domains (see Figs. 12.1 and 12.2). Moreover, this is the only browsing tool that has multiple-document interface (MDI), which allows you to open separate windows for different objects or queries, organize them in the main window, and, therefore, simultaneously work with many directory objects, either in the same domain or in a few domains.

Unfortunately, this tool is not documented. That is why we will consider some basic features in detail, since many of the tool's options are not obvious.

Note

When AdsVw.exe runs on Windows 2000-based computers, it displays a non-Latin Unicode name as a sequence of the question (?) characters. If the LDAP provider is used, distinguished names as well as RDNs with non-Latin coding are also displayed as strings made up of "?". On Windows .NET-based computers, AdsVw.exe works properly within both Windows 2000 and Windows .NET domains.

The tool provides child windows of two types.

- **ObjectViewer** — a two-pane window, in which you can navigate the object tree and view/edit their values (see Figs. 12.1 and 12.2). If the current user doesn't have permissions to access a property, the "???" string is displayed instead of the property's value.
- **Query** — a table form (see Fig. 12.5) that consists of the selected attributes for the objects found in accordance with the specified query string (an LDAP filter or SQL query).

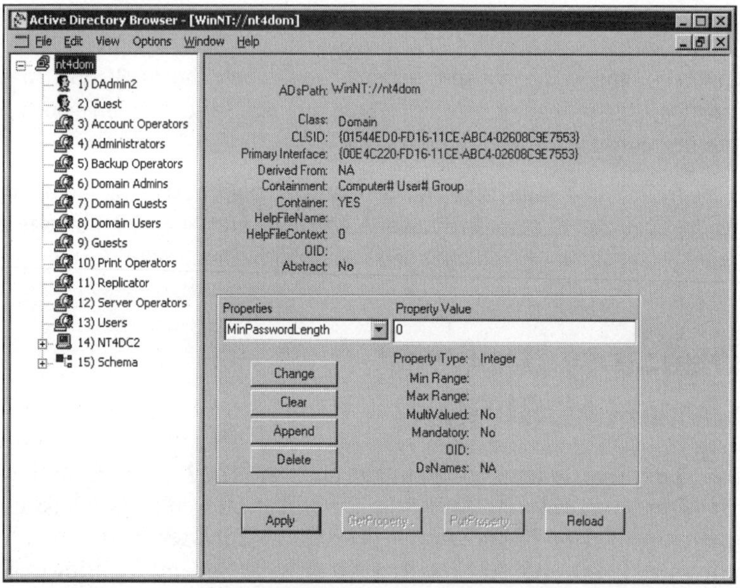

Fig. 12.1. Browsing the flat directory object namespace of a Windows NT 4.0 domain

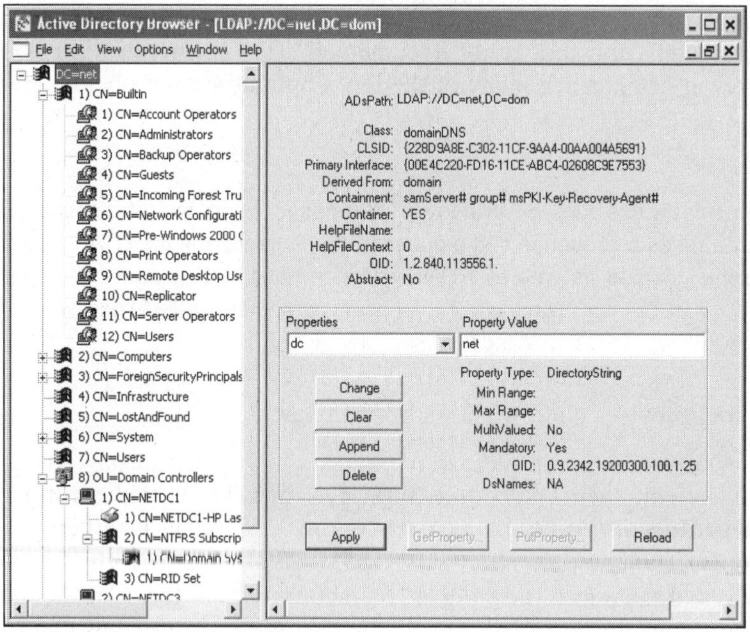

Fig. 12.2. Browsing the object tree of a AD-based domain

To open a new *browsing window*, press the <Ctrl>+<N> keys, select **ObjectViewer** in the opened window, and fill in the **Enter ADs path** field (Fig. 12.3). (Remember that you can include the name of a specific server in the directory path.)

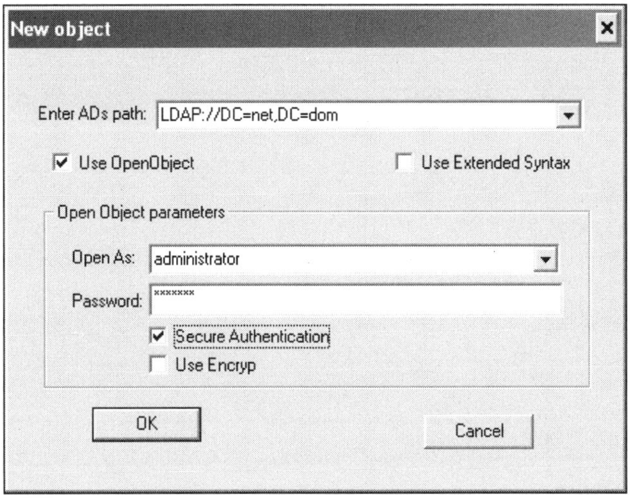

Fig. 12.3. Basic information for a new browsing session

To use credentials different from those of the last connected user, check the **Use OpenObject** and **Secure Authentication** boxes, and fill in the **Open As** and **Password** fields.

Some attributes, such as *primaryGroupToken*, can be viewed only if you have checked the **Use Extended Syntax** box.

Note

The *mandatory* attributes of an object are shown first in the **Properties** list (see Figs. 12.1 and 12.2) and are followed by the *optional* attributes in alphabetical order.

The results of a sample *query* are shown in Fig. 12.5. To start a query, press the <Ctrl>+<N> keys, select **Query** in the opened window, and fill in *all* fields in the **Edit Query** window (Fig. 12.4). All attribute names must be explicitly specified. Click **OK**. You may leave all fields in the next window (**Set Search Preferences**) empty. (You will understand the meaning of the parameters presented in this window better if you read the section about the Ldp.exe tool later in this chapter, and about searching Active Directory in *Chapter 16, "Active Directory Service Interfaces (ADSI)."*)

Note

You may use the privileges of the currently logged user when browsing directory objects (using either protocol), but you must *always* provide valid credentials while creating a new query. Otherwise the query will be unauthenticated (and therefore *very* restricted), and the result set will most probably be empty.

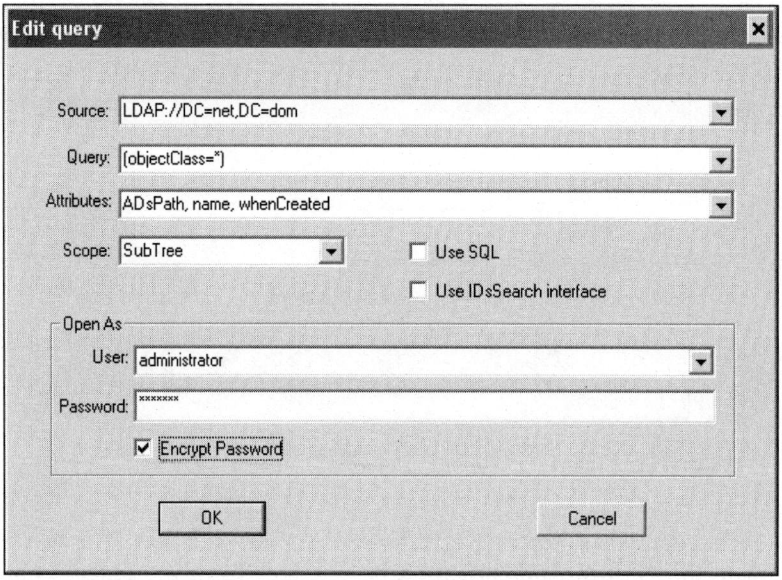

Fig. 12.4. Preparing a sample query: finding all OUs in the domain

The window with the result set for the sample query is shown in Fig. 12.5.

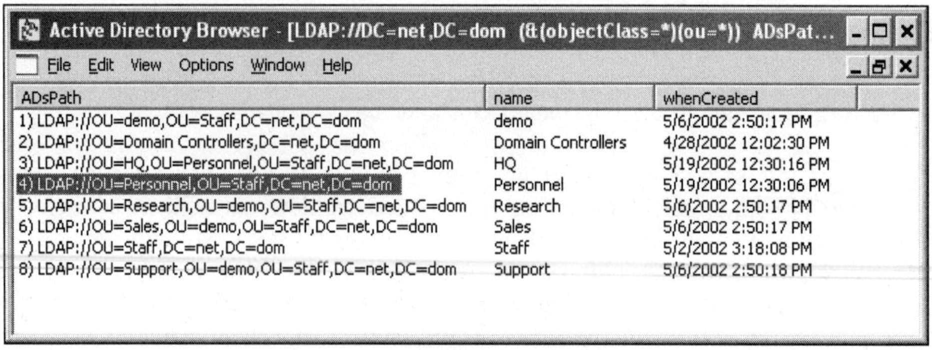

Fig. 12.5. A sample query

If the result set does not fit the window, you must scroll down all lines (using the down arrow button) to see the entire set for the first time.

Active Directory Administration Tool (Ldp.exe) (ST)

Active Directory Administration Tool (Ldp.exe) is a GUI tool, which allows you to query, browse, and modify LDAP-compliant directories (servers) via the LDAP protocol. The tool allows an administrator to access information that cannot be derived with the help of other tools, as well as to compose sophisticated and powerful queries with various scopes.

Note

The Windows .NET version of Ldp.exe works properly within both Windows 2000- and Windows .NET-based domains, but cannot run on Windows 2000 systems. The Windows 2000 version of Ldp.exe fails to display Unicode names in non-Latin coding and the contents of directory containers with similar names. Both in tree-browsing mode and when search operations are performed, Ldp.exe always displays all non-Latin Unicode values of attributes in string format in the form of <ldp: Binary blob>.

Connecting and Binding

To work with an LDAP server, the user must perform two primary operations — connecting and binding. (Connectionless operations and operations without binding (authenticating) are extremely restricted.) The information necessary for both operations is shown in Fig. 12.6.

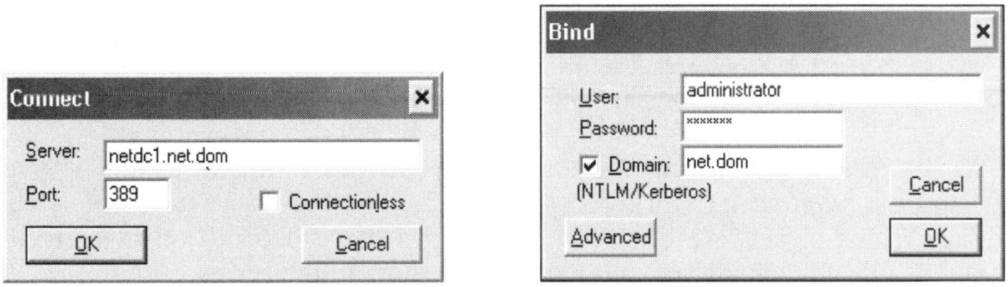

Fig. 12.6. Connecting and binding to a LDAP server

The **Server** field in the **Connect** window can contain a server's DNS name or IP address as well as a domain DNS name. By default, port 389 is used for the LDAP protocol, and port 3268 is designated for Global Catalog. If you leave the **Server** field blank when working on an AD-based domain client computer, a connection is made to your logon DC (LOGONSERVER). (To work with Ldp.exe in an AD-based environment, you must be logged onto a forest.) If the **User** and **Password** fields in the **Bind** window are left blank, the credentials of the user who is currently logged on are used.

If the connection is successful, the information about the *RootDSE* object — base DSA information — is displayed. After binding, you can make queries and/or browse the object tree (click **Tree** in the **View** menu) (Fig. 12.7).

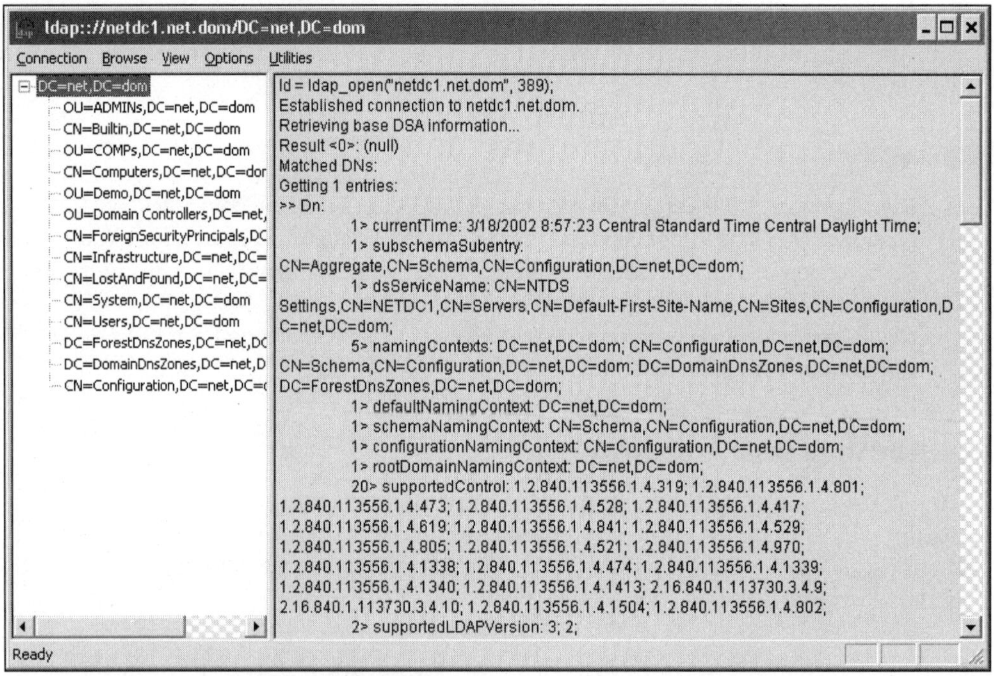

Fig. 12.7. Connecting to an Active Directory server (Windows 2000- or Windows .NET-based domain controller) and viewing the object tree of the domain

As shown in Fig. 12.7, the tool's window is divided into two panes: the *tree pane* (left) and the *result pane* (right). To explode a node in the object tree, simply click on it twice. Which objects are displayed in the result pane depends on the privileges of the user whose credentials you entered while binding to the server.

General Options

The tool's basic options are defined in the **General Options** window. To open it, click **General** in the **Options** menu (Fig. 12.8).

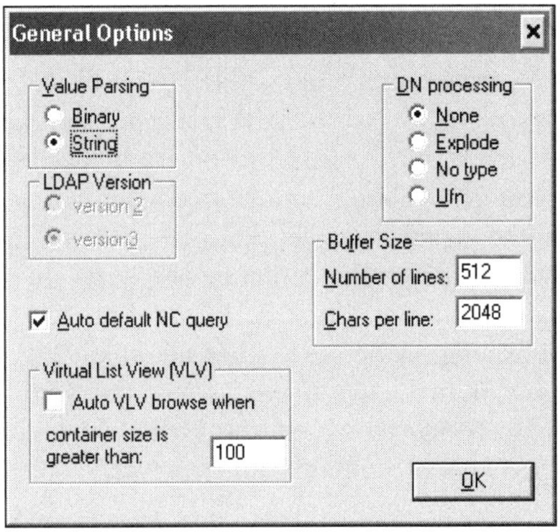

Fig. 12.8. Default general options

Value Parsing

In some specific cases, you may want the values of found attributes to be displayed in binary format. Select the **Binary** switch and, instead of the default string representation of an attribute, you will get its "low-level" value. For instance, the string format may look like:

```
1> whenCreated: 3/15/2002 8:38:45 Central Standard Time Central Daylight Time;
```

The binary format will be:

```
1> whenCreated:
32 30 30 32 30 33 31 35 31 34 33 38 34 35 2e 30   20020315143845.0
5a                                                Z
```

LDAP Version

You can select the version of LDAP protocol only before the connection is made. After this, both switches in the **LDAP Version** group are grayed.

Auto Default NC Query

Checking this box enables the display of the RootDSE information when connecting to a LDAP server. Besides, if this box is checked, the current domain context name is automatically used as the base DN when the tree view is selected. Otherwise, you must always specify a DN of a container.

Virtual List View (VLV)

Virtual List View is a new feature of Windows .NET systems that support a pair of appropriate LDAP controls (namely, 2.16.840.1.113730.3.4.9 and 2.16.840.1.113730.3.4.10). The feature is designed for retrieving information from queries that produce very large result sets. The user can only obtain a predefined number of sorted rows produced by a query rather than the entire result set that can count thousands of rows. Depending on the data received, the user can re-define the query and repeat the search until the necessary information will be obtained. In the Ldp tool, this feature is realized as a special window that can be opened either automatically (if you check the **Auto VLV browse when** box) or manually (if you select the **Virtual List View** command in the **Browse** menu). In the former case, the **Virtual List View** window opens when you try to view (in tree mode) contents of a directory object that comprises more child objects than is specified (by default, 100). The methods of working with this window do not depend on how it is opened. An example of the window is shown in Fig. 12.9.

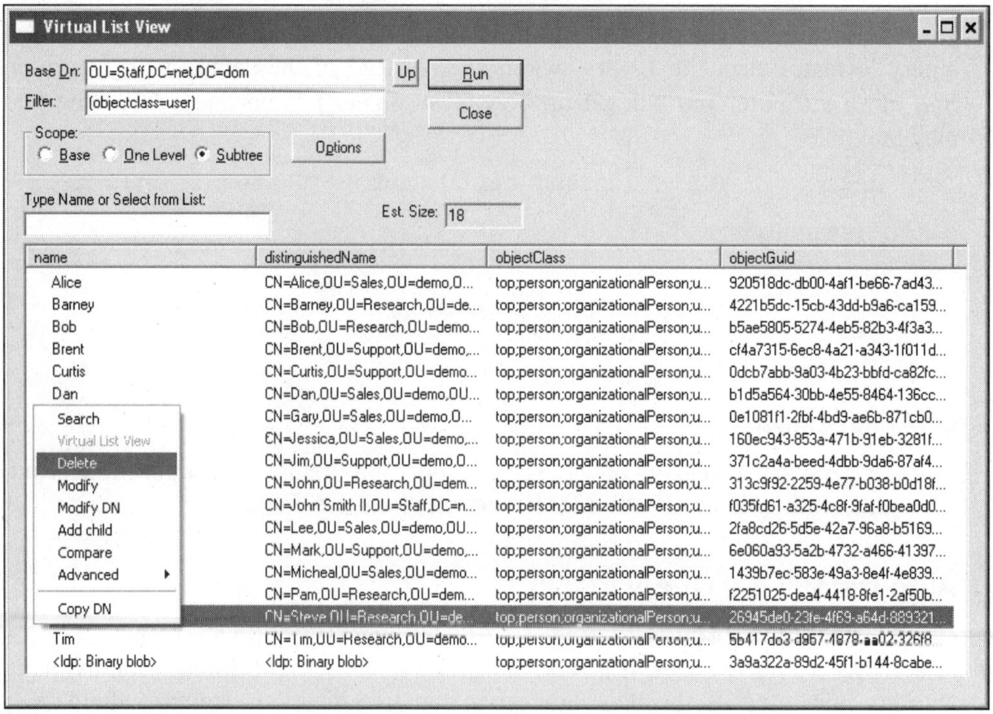

Fig. 12.9. An example view of the **Virtual List View** window

The **Virtual List View** window resembles the **Search** window except for the data pane that displays specified attributes of found objects in a tabular form. The new portions of data will be requested as you scroll down the table rows. The **Type Name or Select from List** field allows you to enter an object name, which the requested server will try to find within the defined query. A few rows before that object and a few rows after that object will only be sent to the client and displayed in the table. To see the children of a found object, click twice on the corresponding row. You can right click on an object and select for it a standard LDAP operation in the context menu (see Fig. 12.9).

DN Processing

In the **DN Processing** group you can indicate how the tool will display the distinguished names of the objects found. All options are listed below with sample strings.

- **None** (default)

  ```
  >> Dn: CN=Administrator,OU=ADMINs,DC=net,DC=dom
  >> Dn: CN=Certificate Templates,CN=Public Key Services,
  CN=Services,CN=Configuration,DC=net,DC=dom
  ```

- Explode

  ```
  >> Dn: CN=Administrator; OU=ADMINs; DC=net; DC=dom;
  >> Dn: CN=Certificate Templates; CN=Public Key Services; CN=Services;
  CN=Configuration; DC=net; DC=dom;
  ```

- No type

  ```
  >> Dn: Administrator; ADMINs; net; dom;
  >> Dn: Certificate Templates; Public Key Services; Services;
  Configration; net; dom;
  ```

- Ufn

  ```
  >> Dn: CN=Administrator, OU=ADMINs, DC=net, DC=dom
  >> Dn: CN=CertificateTemplates, CN=PublicKeyServices, CN=Services,
  CN=Configuration, DC=net, DC=dom
  ```

  Notice that in the last case there are no spaces in RDNs.

Buffer Size

The **Number of lines** parameter sets the number of rows displayed in the result pane before wrapping begins. Do not forget that you cannot obtain more rows in a query than the *MaxPageSize* value in the query policy permits.

The **Chars per line** parameter sets the maximum number of characters displayed in a line. Lines whose length exceeds this value are truncated!

Referrals and Their Effect on Search Results

In practice, referrals are very important in search operations, as they may greatly influence the results. The **Chase referrals** box in the **Search Options** window (see Fig. 12.12, left) determines whether or not the server generates LDAP referrals when trying to find objects. (By default, the box is not checked, since this improves the performance of the search.) However, in some cases, if this box is checked, an error can occur:

```
Error: Search: Referral. <10>
Result <10>: 0000202B: RefErr: ...
```

Some other scenarios in which you may get an unexpected result are also possible. Therefore, it is necessary to select the status of this checkbox carefully. Let us discuss this issue using two examples.

Suppose you are logged onto a computer joined to a child domain, and want to search the parent domain (or a domain from another domain tree) by entering its DN as the base of the search. You must either make an LDAP connection to a DC in the parent domain or enable *chasing referrals.* (Otherwise, the referral error will be reported.) Why referrals should help in such a situation will become clear a bit later. (Maybe you already understand what happens.)

Let us go to the second example. Suppose, for instance, you are searching your own domain for referrals objects or DSA objects. The `(objectClass=crossRef)` or `(cn=NTDS Settings)` filter strings, respectively, can be used for this purpose. The domain DN is specified as the base of the search.

Without the **Chase referrals** box checked, you will get an empty result set. Maybe you have forgotten, or did not initially know, that required objects are stored in the *Configuration* namespace (directory partition). Furthermore, remember that the search is performed in one namespace only unless you enable generating referrals. The above-described search operation will be successful if you have done one of the following: either directly specified the appropriate name context as the base of the search or enabled generation of referrals.

If the **Chase referrals** box is checked, the search is performed:

- Within *all* partitions stored on a server
- Within the domain partitions of *all child* domains, to which the referrals are directed

(There are also other search options, but it is more difficult to configure them. You can find additional information in the *MSDN Library* — look for "Extended Controls".)

Turning to the first example, it is clear now that if a server finds an object that refers to another domain and cannot (is not allowed to) connect to the server that stores the corresponding partition, it will generate a referral error message.

Note

The problem of cross-domain (cross-partition, and cross-tree) searching can also be resolved by using a connection over the Global Catalog (3268) port. This might even be a more appropriate way. Do not forget, however, that not all attributes are replicated to GC.

Paged Search

Sometimes, a requested server can return a number of rows that exceed the *MaxPageSize* value. (Do not confuse the number of rows returned by a server on a request and the number of rows that the tool can display in the result pane — the **Number of lines** parameter.) The following error will be reported:

```
Error: Search: Size Limit Exceeded. <4>
Result <4>: [null]
```

In such a case, it is necessary to use *paging* search results. You can request the results in pages of a specific size. Open the **Search Options** window (see Fig. 12.12; left) and select the **Paged** switch in the **Search Call Type** group. The **Page size** value defines the length of the page. Now you will get the results of a search operation in 16-row pages (by default):

```
Result <0>:
Matched DNs:
Getting 16 entries:
...
 -=>> 'Run' for more, 'Close' to abandon <<=-
```

You can continue searching by clicking **Run,** or you can terminate the operation at any moment. When paging is used, you need not worry about how long the result of a search is.

Retrieving Information about Errors

The Windows .NET version of Ldp.exe has a new option that allows you to obtain additional information about some LDAP operation errors. Suppose you try to connect to a DC and see the following messages:

```
ld = ldap_open("netdc2.net.dom", 389);
Error <0x51>: Fail to connect to netdc2.net.dom.
```

If you select the GetLastError command in the Browse menu, the tool will display the message:

```
0x51=LdapGetLastError() Server Down
```

Sometimes this additional information can be valuable for understanding an error that has occurred.

Saving Results

To clear the result pane before a new operation, click **New** on the **Connection** menu or press <Ctrl>+<N> keys. Any information displayed in this pane can be copied-and-pasted.

At any moment, you may save the contents of the result pane by selecting **Save** or **Save As** from the **Connection** menu. (You need not close the **Search** window.) The latter option always asks you for a file name. The former option allows you to save information in the current output file, and asks for a file name only after the tool starts or a **New** command has been performed.

The Forest View

You may look up all domains and DCs in the forest in tree form. Click **Enterprise Configuration** in the **View** menu. Click **Refresh** in the window that is open. After some time, the actual configuration of your enterprise will be displayed in the window (Fig. 12.10). You can get the configuration only after binding to a DC.

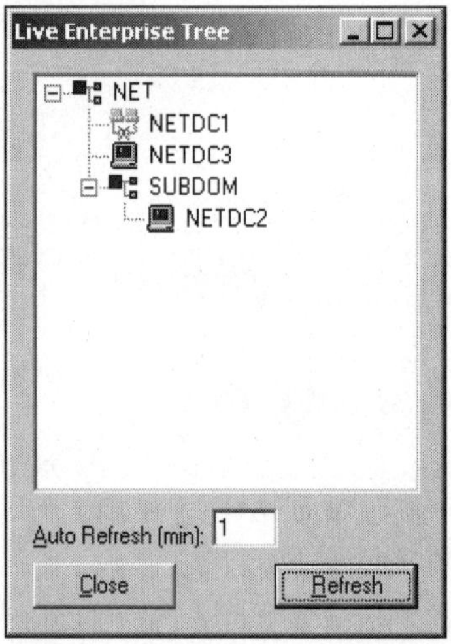

Fig. 12.10. In this window, you can see the entire domain structure (the forest) and the state of all DCs

As Fig. 12.10 shows, two DCs (NETDC2, NETDC3) in the forest are online, and one DC (NETDC1) is offline. Knowledge of the network's real state will help you to select servers for connecting and making queries.

Searching Directory

For clarity and simplicity, we will discuss the procedure involved in finding objects in Active Directory (or any other LDAP-compatible directory) using a few specific scenarios.

Note

Remember that every DC in a domain stores, at minimum, three Active Directory partitions (see the *RootDSE* object's information when a connection is established). Although these partitions (including application partitions) have contiguous DNS names — and this may seem a little confusing — they are absolutely different namespaces when it comes to performing a search.

Example 1. Finding Deleted Objects

Deleted Active Directory objects (so called *tombstones*) are stored in a hidden *Deleted Objects* container for a pre-configured period of time, and then permanently purged during garbage collection. This container cannot be accessed by using standard snap-ins. The *Show Deleted Object* control (controlType = 1.2.840.113556.1.4.417) and search command allow you to retrieve the tombstones. (You must have administrative privileges.)

Start Ldp.exe and carry out the following operations:

1. Connect to a DC, and bind to it using the credentials of an administrator.
2. Click **Search** in the **Browse** menu, and enter the distinguished name of the domain and the filter string `(isDeleted=*)`. Select the **Subtree** switch and click **Options** (Fig. 12.11).

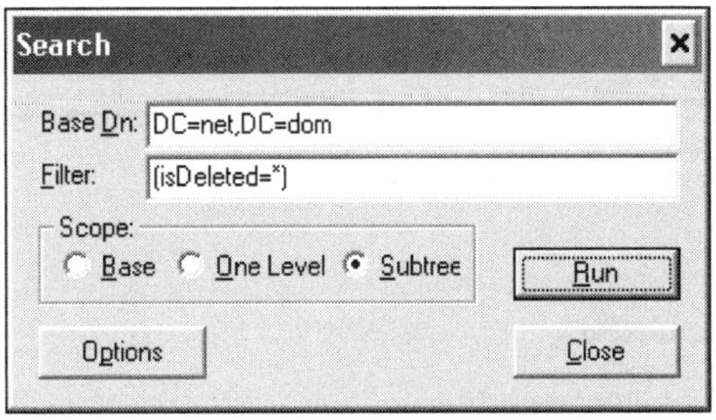

Fig. 12.11. Primary search parameters

3. Click **Extended** in the **Search Call Type** group, and enter the attributes of the deleted objects that you wish to view (see Fig. 12.12, left). (You may also need to

increase the default **Timeout (s)** from zero to a bigger number. The value can be determined by experimenting.) Click **Controls**.

Note

If you receive the following error message, increase the timeout value:

```
Error: Search: Timeout. <85>
Error<94>: ldap_parse_result failed: No result present in message
Getting 0 entries:
```

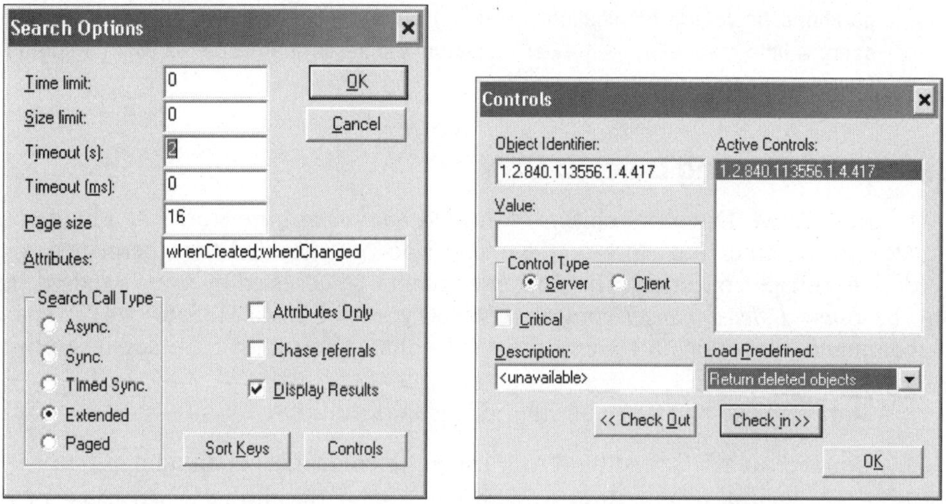

Fig. 12.12. Configuring the search options for deleted objects

4. You can enter the type of the control directly into the **Object Identifier** field and click **Check in** (make sure that the **Server** switch in the **Control Type** group is selected), or simply select the **Return deleted objects** option in the **Load Predefined** list (see Fig. 12.12, right). To delete (deactivate) a control, select it in the **Active Controls** window and click **Check Out**.

Note

You can combine a number of various controls in the same query.

To view and activate/deactivate the controls, you can open the **Controls** window at any moment by clicking **Controls** in the **Options** menu.

5. Close the **Controls** and **Search Options** windows.
6. Click **Run** and execute the search.

Example 2. Searching for Object GUIDs

As you know, the name (e.g., the *cn* attribute) of a directory object can be changed by a *rename object* operation. If, for instance, an application uses the name for referring to the object, it will "lose" this object after its renaming. A more appropriate way would be to use the object GUID, which remains the same throughout the entire lifetime of the object.

The question is thus how to find the object GUID. You might search the directory for the object and specify the *objectGUID* attribute in the **Search Options** window. However, it is possible to get the GUID of each object found in a search operation immediately or to get it while browsing the directory tree. You need to activate the *Return Extended Distinguished Names* LDAP control (controlType = = 1.2.840.113556.1.4.529).

Note

It is also possible to get the GUID of an object by using the **ADSI Edit** snap-in. However, that may be inconvenient, since the *objectGUID* attribute (as well as *objectSID*) is in *Octet-String* format (e.g., "0x73 0xa5 0xe1 0x0d ..." — 16 bytes in all). You cannot directly substitute such a string in a search or bind command. The Dsquery.exe utility would be a better choice.

The GUID search preparation steps are similar to those for deleted objects described above. Let us find the GUIDs of the OUs that are contained in a domain. Enter the following information:

- **Base DN** — domain DN
- **Filter** — `(ou=*)`
- **Subtree** scope
- Search Call Type — **Extended**
- **Attributes** — `ADsPath`
- **Active Controls** — 1.2.840.113556.1.4.529 (the **Extended DN** option in the **Load Predefined** list)

You will get a list of OUs in a format similar to the following:

```
Dn: <GUID=079760441fb9d948afdeacab994997cb>;OU=Domain Controllers,
↳DC=net,DC=dom
```

The new component (marked here in bold) appears in the distinguished name. The found GUID can be verified by using Search.vbs (see *"Searching for an Object using its GUID"* at the beginning of this chapter), or you may use the entire string (between and including the angle brackets) in a script in a bind operation.

For directory objects that represent security principals (user, group, and computer accounts) output strings also contain object SIDs, for example:

```
Dn: <GUID=a6ead32063e11a40924e57f9107a14ec>;
↳<SID=010500000000000515000000 2fd5ec6ddde8e41c8aa7323feb030000>;
↳CN=NETDC1,OU=Domain Controllers,DC=net,DC=dom
```

Example 3. Sorting Search Results

You might notice that the result sets of search operations contain rows in a quite random order. To obtain sorted results, you can use the *Return Sorted Results* LDAP control (controlType = 1.2.840.113556.1.4.473). To obtain sorted results in any search operations, perform the following steps:

1. Add the "1.2.840.113556.1.4.473" value to the **Active Controls** list (see Fig. 12.12; right).
2. Click **Options** | **Sort Keys**.
3. In the **Sort Keys** window (Fig. 12.13), enter OID of a sort key in the **Attribute Type** field and click **Check In** and **OK**. You can obtain the attribute's OID using the **Active Directory Schema Manager** snap-in. The name attribute (1.2.840.113556.1.4.1) has been selected in our example.
4. Select all search parameters and click **Extended** in the **Search Call Type** group in the Search Options window (see Fig. 12.12; left).

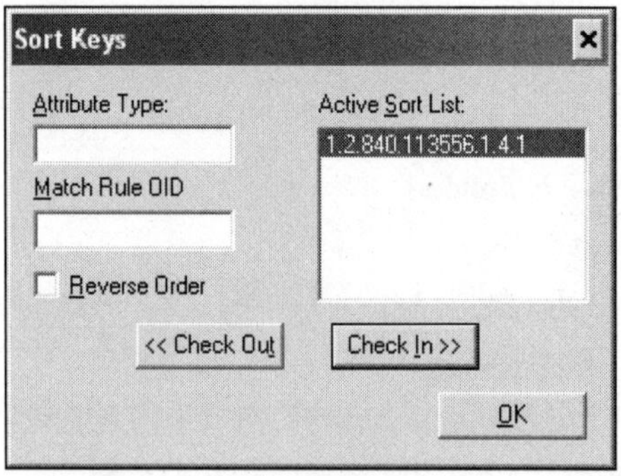

Fig. 12.13. Sorting search results on the name attribute

After all this, any search operations will produce sorted result sets unless the select **Sync** in the **Search Call Type** group or delete the *Return Sorted Results* control from the list of LDAP controls.

Updating Attributes

The LDAP update operations include the following: Add, Modify, Modify RDN, and Delete. On the one hand (regarding the user interface), they are quite simple and obvious; on the other hand, they require a rather keen understanding of Active Directory architecture (particularly the schema, classes, and attributes). That is why other tools, such as administrative snap-ins (**ADSI Edit**, **Active Directory Users and Computers**, and so on), are more suitable for modifying Active Directory objects. In an example below, we will discuss the most common steps involved in using Ldp.exe for this purpose.

Note

The *Modify RDN* operation is equivalent to renaming or moving an object. The *Cross Domain Move* LDAP control (1.2.840.113556.1.4.521) enables you to perform move operations over domain boundaries.

Modifying an Attribute

Let us change a user's UPN. First, click **Modify** in the **Browse** menu. In the opened window, enter the user's DN, the attribute name, and its new value. Then select **Replace** from the **Operation** group (because the attribute already exists), and click **Enter** to add the data to the **Entry List**. No checks are performed at this time, so be careful. You may correct the entered data by clicking **Edit** (and then editing the information) or **Remove**. A sample window is shown in Fig. 12.14.

When everything is ready, click **Run**. The server will verify all entered data (syntax rules, acceptable values, etc.), and perform the operation if all requirements have been met. The result message may be similar to the following:

```
***Call Modify...
ldap_modify_s(ld, 'CN=John Smith,OU=Staff,DC=net,DC=dom',[1] attrs);
Modified "CN=John Smith,OU=Staff,DC=net,DC=dom".
```

If an error occurs while at some step of executing an operation, the tool reports an error message, which is determined by the kind of error (such as a syntax error in the entered data, or an error with the directory database, etc.). The message contains a description of the error.

For example:

```
***Call Modify...
ldap_modify_s(ld, 'CN=John Smith,OU=Staff,DC=net,DC=dom',[1] attrs);
Error: Modify: No Such Object. <32>
```

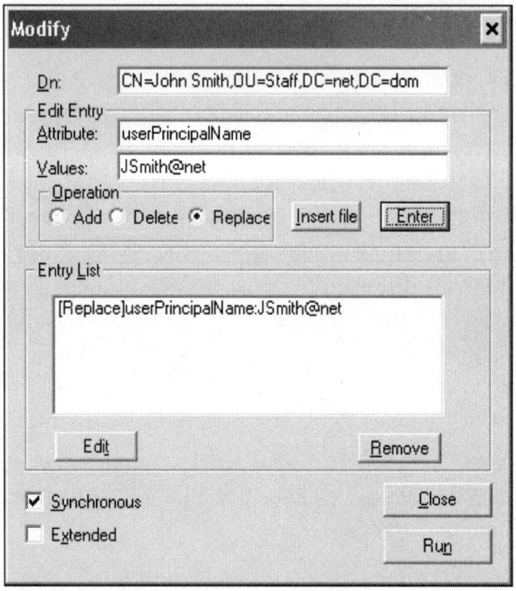

Fig. 12.14. The information necessary to change the UPN of a user

Deleting Objects

The delete operation is also fairly obvious and simple. However, a problem may arise when you want to delete an object that has one or more child objects, for example, an OU with user accounts. The following error may be reported:

```
Error: Delete: Not allowed on Non-leaf. <66>
```

To perform such an operation, you must use the *Tree Delete* LDAP control (controlType = 1.2.840.113556.1.4.805). This control allows you to delete an entire subtree, if you have sufficient permissions.

To delete a non-leaf object (i.e., a container), perform the following operations:

1. Add the *Tree Delete* control to the list of active controls (select the **Subtree Delete** option in the **Load Predefined** list — see Fig. 12.12; right).
2. Click **Delete** in the **Browse** menu.
3. In the **Delete** window, enter the distinguished name of the container and check the **Extended** box. (An example window is shown in Fig. 12.15.)
4. Click **OK**.

Caution

- Be extremely careful when deleting an entire container! No warnings are generated.

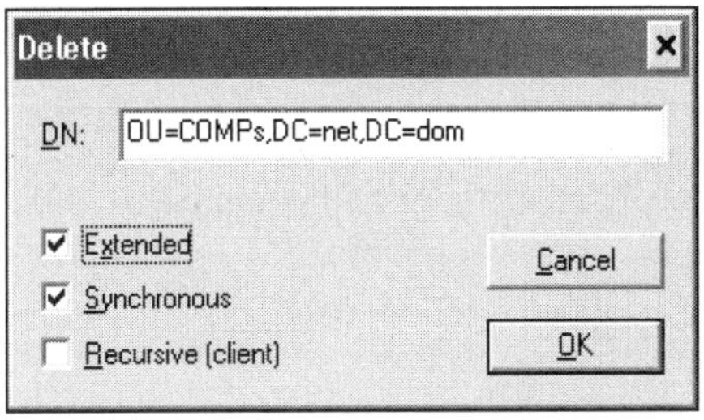

Fig. 12.15. Deleting a *non-empty* container (an OU in this case)

Viewing the Security Descriptors

Ldp.exe allows you to view the security descriptor of any directory object. This feature is intended for solving problems related to the accounts' permissions on directory objects (e.g., when moving the security principals to another domain) and can be especially useful when you are debugging scripts or applications that work with security descriptors (see *Chapter 17, "Scripting Administrative Tasks"*). Using this feature requires a sound understanding of the Active Directory security model (access control lists (ACL) and access control elements (ACE), their inheritance, etc.).

To view the security descriptor for a directory object, select the **Security | Security Descriptor** command from the **Browse** menu and specify the distinguished name of the object. If you want to see the directly specified or inherited audit settings (the system ACLs) of this object, check the **SACL** box. A sample output produced by this command is shown in Fig. 12.16. The command also displays the descriptor in the SDDL (Security Descriptor Definition Language) string format (not shown in the figure). As Fig. 12.16 shows, you can see all the information about the descriptor (some of its elements are circled in the figure). That information includes, in particular, control flags, the owner of the object, the number of ACEs, and elements of each ACE, such as the ACE's type, the access mask, and the name and SID of the security principal that was granted this right. You can retrieve all described information from a descriptor by using a script (*Chapter 17, "Scripting Administrative Tasks"*, contains an example of such a script). You can also programmatically manipulate the ACEs, i.e., grant or revoke permissions on directory objects.

Viewing Replication Metadata

Ldp.exe can display the directory object's metadata information (the *replPropertyMetaData* attribute) that is used in replication. You can also view this information by using the RepAdmin.exe command with the `/showmeta` parameter (see *Chapter 11, "Verifying Network and Distributed Services"*).

To view the metadata for an object, select the **Replication | View Metadata** command from the **Browse** menu and enter the object's distinguished name. A sample output is presented in Fig. 12.17.

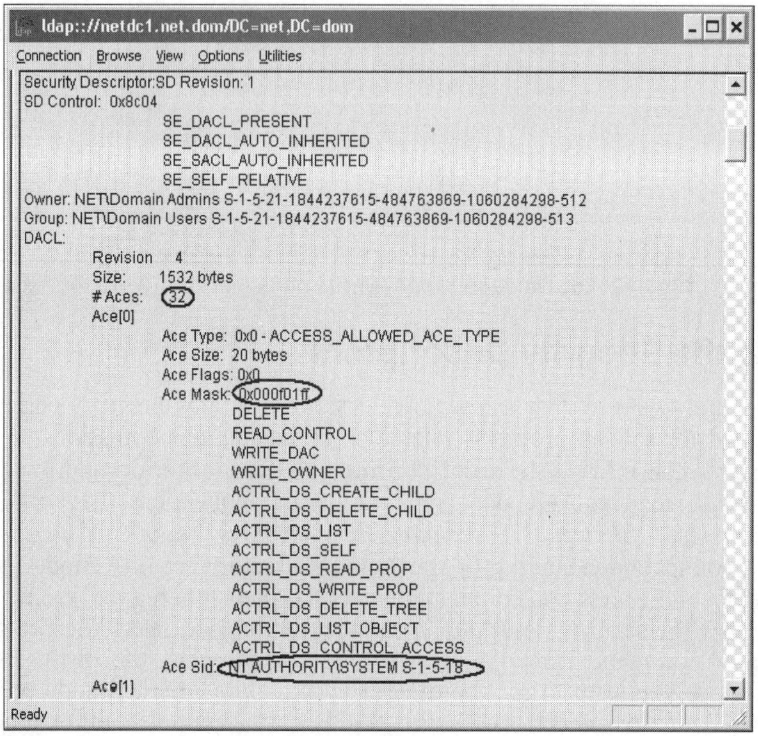

Fig. 12.16. A fragment of a security descriptor shown by using Ldp.exe

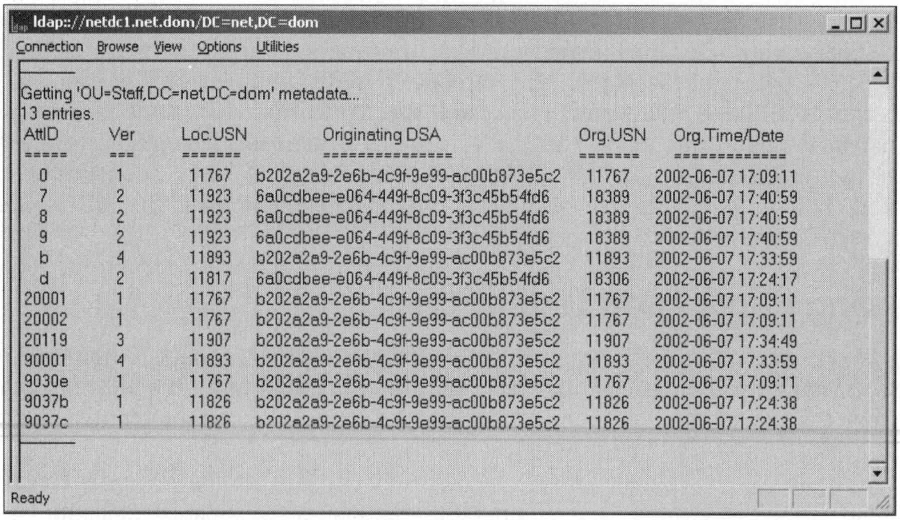

Fig. 12.17. Viewing the replication metadata for a directory object

When troubleshooting replication issues, you can connect to various domain controllers and compare the metadata for the stored replicas of the desired object.

Windows .NET Search and Modification Tools

Windows .NET-based domain controllers have a set of very useful and powerful utilities that help administrators perform a number of operations with Active Directory objects from the command prompt. In addition, these utilities can be used for batch operations. For that purpose the results from a query command can be piped as input to one of the other commands.

All these utilities (listed below) use the LDAP protocol and can query both Windows 2000 and Windows .NET domains. However, they can run on Windows XP/.NET-based computers only.

There are a huge number of parameters of every utility, and you can view their description in the *Help and Support Center* or in the built-in help feature. Do not forget to use quotation marks around a parameter's string value.

DsQuery and *DsGet*

The *DsQuery.exe* utility can find directory objects of any type or objects of a specific type. The *DsGet.exe* utility displays the specified attributes (a limited set of attributes) of specific type objects. These specific types are:

computer	contact	subnet
group	OU	site
server	user	

For example, the following command displays *ADsPaths* and *GUIDs* of the user accounts in the *User* container:

```
C:\>dsquery * CN=Users,DC=net,DC=dom -filter objectClass=user
-attr ADsPath objectGUID
```

The most universal `dsquery *` command can find objects of any type and display any attributes of these objects.

To find all users in the domain, use the command:

```
C:\>dsquery user
```

The following two commands display the first and last names of all users in the domain:

```
C:>dsquery user | dsget user -fn -ln
```

The base and scope of search operations can be specified as `domainroot` (default option), `forestroot` (search in entire forest via Global Catalog), or any distinguished name.

DsMod

The *DsMod.exe* utility can modify attributes of specific object types: computer, contact, group, OU, server, and user. The set of attributes permitted for modification is limited and specific for each object type.

The following command, for example, can find all user accounts in the *Staff* OU, enable them, and modify their description and profile. Notice the special token $USERNAME$. This token will be replaced by the user SAM account name.

```
C:\>dsquery user OU=Staff,DC=net,DC=dom | dsmod user -desc "A test user"
-profile \\NETDC1\Profiles\$USERNAME$ -disabled NO
```

DsMove

The *DsMove.exe* utility allows administrators to rename or move a directory object of any type.

Moving of an object:

```
C:\>dsmove CN=Bob,OU=Staff,DC=net,DC=dom
↳ -newparent OU=Personnel,DC=net,DC=dom
dsmove succeeded:CN=Bob,OU=Staff,DC=net,DC=dom
```

Renaming of an object:

```
C:\>dsmove CN=Sam,OU=Staff,DC=net,DC=dom
↳ -newname Samuel
dsmove succeeded:CN=Sam,OU=Staff,DC=net,DC=dom
```

DsRm

The *DsRm.exe* utility deletes one or more directory objects. You can also delete an entire object subtree.

The following command immediately (without any prompt) removes all child objects in the *Staff* OU, but keeps (do not delete) the OU object itself:

```
C:\>dsrm OU=Staff,DC=net,DC=dom -noprompt -subtree -exclude
dsrm succeeded:OU=Staff,DC=net,DC=dom
```

Importing and Exporting Modifying Directory Objects

By default, every Windows 2000- or Windows .NET-based domain controller contains two utilities installed — LDIF Directory Exchange (LDIFDE.exe) and CSV Directory

Exchange (CSVDE.exe) — that are primarily intended for bulk operations. Unlike *Ds** family tools (DsQuery.exe, DsAdd.exe, DsMod.exe, etc.), these utilities can save results in a file for consequent operations and read data from a file. You can use these utilities to:

- Export Active Directory information to a text file (in LDIF or CSV format) that can be easily viewed or/and edited. The retrieved information can be used for:
  - Composing documentation on directory objects
  - Performing bulk editing operations that cannot be carried out using the standard administrative snap-ins
  - Creating templates for new users (if the standard option of copying user accounts is not convenient for you)
  - Migrating directory objects between domains into the same or another domain forest
  - Backing up the existing domain configuration (for safety or for re-installation of domain controllers)
- Import Active Directory information from a file. This means creating new objects or modifying the attributes of existing ones in batch mode. Besides the already mentioned export operations that imply import — bulk editing, migrating, backing up, and creating user templates — the import into Active Directory can be carried out for:
  - Deploying a pre-configured domain configuration (by the way, import is performed when a domain controller is promoted — the CSVDE utility is used for creating the "default" Active Directory structure)
  - Deploying Active Directory-based applications (extending the schema is also possible)

Note

Normally, the standard *Backup* utility is used for backing up and restoring Active Directory. However, in some cases, export/import may be a preferable choice for preserving domain configuration.

You can select *either* of these utilities for your tasks so long as you keep in mind the two main differences between LDIFDE and CSVDE for a user.

- Data format — LDIFDE uses files that respond to the LDIF standard, whereas CSVDE supports the CSV format (see the appropriate section on each tool).
- Possible operations — CSVDE can only export and import (create) data; LDIFDE also allows you to modify attributes and delete objects.

The book contains a few examples of how to use LDIFDE and CSVDE. These examples can be tested with either utility, depending on your specific requirements.

All of the tasks listed can also be fulfilled (and often, more effectively!) with custom ADSI scripts. Knowing the possibilities and restrictions of all the tools permits you to save time and select the appropriate tool for a specific task.

Basic information on the LDIFDE and CSVDE utilities is contained in the Help and Support Center (search for "LDIFDE CSVDE"). (The `-u` parameter is missing in the Help!) You can also run the utilities without parameters and get help information.

Error Logs

Both utilities create an error log file (csvde.err or ldif.err) and a log for completed operations (csvde.log or ldif.log). By default, these files are stored in the current folder, and the logs' location is configured.

Parameters

Table 12.1 lists some of the most frequently used parameters of both utilities — LDIFDE and CSVDE.

Table 12.1. Some Parameters of the LDIFDE and CSVDE Utilities

Parameter	Description and comments	Meaning (or value) if the parameter is omitted (default)
	Common parameters	
`-f`	Input or output filename. "`-f con`" can be used for output to the console. Required parameter	No
`-s`	DC name	The name of the DC the user is currently logged on to
`-t`	Port number. The Global Catalog port (3268) can also be used	389 (LDAP)
`-u`	Use Unicode format	ANSI format is used
	Parameters for export operations	
`-d`	Search base	Domain naming context
`-c`	Replace all occurrences `of string 1` with `string 2`. Very helpful for copying data from one domain to another	No

continues

Table 12.1 Continued

Parameter	Description and comments	Meaning (or value) if the parameter is omitted (default)
`-r`	Search filter	`(objectClass=*)`
`-p`	Search scope	Subtree
`-l`	Selection. A list of attributes. `"1.1"` or empty string can be used with the meaning of "no attributes returned" (if you need only a list of objects)	All attributes
`-o`	The list of attributes omitted during an export operation	No
	Parameters for import operations	
`-i`	Specifies import mode	Export mode
`-k`	Skip errors. If some objects were successfully imported to the directory and others weren't, you may correct errors in the import file and continue its processing	No

Note

Do not forget about the omitted parameters (which *have* default values), or you may obtain an undesirable or unpredictable result. Compare, for example, cases when you only want to export OU objects and when you need to export an entire OU subtree (default).

Exporting and Re-Importing Objects

Export operations are usually successful. (The worst-case scenario is when an export file does not contain all the objects you expect it to contain.) You need only take into consideration the following: when you specify a list of attributes (by using the `-l` parameter) in the export command, LDIFDE and CSVDE do not include any information about non-defined attributes in the output file. Therefore, you might need to manually include the attributes' names (if you need them) in the *import* file and assign the appropriate values.

Note

It is not possible to export security descriptors (or group policies — for domains and/or OUs). You must also be careful about built-in and default groups, such as *Domain Users*.

In the exported file, you may see a list of members different from the one that the **Active Directory Users and Computers** snap-in displays.

The `(givenName=*)` filter allows you to choose only accounts of newly created users, with the exception of built-in accounts. Built-in users (administrator, guest, etc.) do not have *given names*.

While exporting information from Global Catalog (using the 3268 port), do not forget that GC contains a restricted set of attributes. For example, 40-50 attributes (a very modest value, since the minimum is about 30 attributes and maximum is about two hundred) are exported for a user object by default. When GC is used, only 20-30 attributes are exported.

The number and type of the objects exported depend on a combination of the search base and the LDAP filter (described in detail in *Chapter 1, "LDAP Basics"*). You can export either a single directory object or all Active Directory objects. The choice of the appropriate search base and filter is not a challenge unless you do not use both or you have forgotten about the default values. The following two commands might seem equivalent since either can export a computer account (provided that the computer's *cn* attribute has a unique value in the domain):

```
ldifde -f Export.ldf -d "CN=Comp1,OU=Staff,DC=net,DC=dom"
ldifde -f Export.ldf -r "(&(objectCategory=computer)(cn=Comp1))"
```

In fact, the first command can export a few objects, and the second exports strictly one object. In both cases, the omitted `-p` parameter (the scope of the search) means that the search will be conducted in the subtree. Since the computer object is a container and can have child objects, the first command exports the entire "family". The second command finds the specified computer in the domain and exports it alone (since there is no computer with such a name in the domain).

After a little practice with search base and filters, you will learn how select only the necessary objects from Active Directory in the most effective and precise way. (See more examples of command string in this chapter.)

Note

I prefer to specify *objectCategory* in filters rather than *objectClass*. Both attributes are replicated in Global Catalog. However, the former attribute is indexed, and the latter is not. As a result, filters with *objectCategory* are more effective.

There is, however, a pitfall to such an approach. `(objectCategory=Person)` defines users as well as contacts. Consequently, you need to add the *objectClass* attribute in the filter. Test your filters carefully before using them in real conditions.

Errors are more frequent when import operations are performed. There are three main sources of errors.

- *Read-only attributes, which only the system can change.* A typical error message: 'Unwilling To Perform. The server side error is "Access to the attribute is not permitted because the attribute is owned by the Security Accounts Manager (SAM)."' You cannot include such attributes as *objectSID*, *objectGUID*, etc., in the import files and must always use the `-m` parameter while exporting objects if a consequent import is planned. When the `-m` parameter is specified, all of the SAM attributes are ignored (see also "*Working with User Objects*" later in this chapter).
- *Missed mandatory attributes.* Refer to Table 12.2 to see which attributes must be defined in import files when new directory objects are created. The *objectSID* attribute is shown in bold to remind you that, notwithstanding the fact that it is a mandatory attribute, it must not be used in import.

Table 12.2. Some Important Object Classes and Their Mandatory Attributes

Object class (category)	Mandatory attributes
computer (Computer)	cn, instanceType, objectCategory, objectClass, ***objectSID***, sAMAccountName
group (Group)	cn, groupType, instanceType, objectCategory, objectClass, ***objectSID***, sAMAccountName
organizationalUnit (Organizational-Unit)	instanceType, objectCategory, objectClass, ou
printQueue (Print-Queue)	cn, instanceType, objectCategory, objectClass, printerName, serverName, shortServerName, uNCName, versionNumber
user (Person)	cn, instanceType, objectCategory, objectClass, ***objectSID***, sAMAccountName
volume (Volume)	cn, instanceType, objectCategory, objectClass, uNCName

- *Violations of syntax rules, inconsistency of attribute values, values of wrong types, or values out of range.* For example, using the `-c` parameter may result in incorrect values of naming attributes (see later in the chapter). If you are creating new objects from scratch, carefully verify attribute types and values, and refer to the abstract schema and schema container if needed (see also the schema description in *Chapter 16, "Active Directory Service Interfaces (ADSI)"*).

When directory objects are copied (exported and imported) from one domain to another, it is helpful to use the `-c` parameter.

Unicode Support

LDFIDE and CSVDE have some problems with support of Unicode (namely, with non-Latin localized string values). You should take this into consideration if non-Latin values are stored in your Active Directory. Test your installation before starting the bulk import/export operations. Since such values aren't written in the output file in plain text format, it is hard to edit them. Encoding restrictions of the utilities are listed below.

LDIFDE

- Unless the `-u` parameter is specified, LDIFDE exports non-Latin Unicode values as Base64-encoded (e.g., `cn:: 0JLQsNGB0Y8=`). (Notice that the colon character is doubled in such lines. Binary values are always encoded.) If non-Latin characters are included in the distinguished name of a directory object, the entire line (`dn`) name is coded. You can safely reimport all these values.
- LDIFDE correctly imports non-Latin string values in an input file if only this file is saved as Unicode-encoded. Use common format with *one* colon!

CSVDE

- Regardless of the presence of the `-u` parameter, CSVDE exports non-Latin Unicode (and binary) values (except for `dn`) in the following format: `X'8c39...c3bc'`. You can safely reimport these values. CSVDE fails to export directory objects that have non-Latin characters in their names if the `-u` parameter has been omitted.
- CSVDE imports the non-Latin string values in an input file (in usual format) if this file is saved both as Unicode- and ANSI-encoded. Windows 2000-version of CSVDE accepts only Unicode-encoded files.

LDIF Directory Exchange Utility (LDIFDE) (Sys)

LDIFDE, a command-line utility that is installed by default on every DC, can be used for adding, modifying, renaming, and deleting directory objects. This utility uses *LDAP Data Interchange Format* (LDIF) — an Internet standard that defines a file format to perform batch operations for LDAP-accessible directories. LDIFDE is also a preferred tool for extending the Active Directory schema.

Examples of LDIF files are shown below. LDIFDE can be run on any Windows 2000/XP/.NET-based client, provided you have supplied appropriate domain credentials.

Working with User Objects

Table 12.3 is a snippet of an export file and lists all attributes of an exported user object in LDIF format. Notice attributes in bold face, which are *not exported* when the -m parameter is specified, and should not be imported. Notice also that the *objectGUID* and *objectSID* are exported as binary values (this is marked with a double colon). A few additional remarks are placed at the end of the table. These are not *all* of the possible attributes, only a typical minimal set. The names of some attributes as they are presented in the **Active Directory Users and Computers** snap-in's UI are specified in bold square brackets. The relative DN (RDN) is also specified, although it is not presented in the UI and cannot be directly modified. The mandatory attributes are show in italics.

Table 12.3. Influence of *-m* Parameter on the Resulting Attribute List

Exported attributes and their values
dn: CN=John Smith,OU=Staff,DC=net,DC=dom
changetype: add
accountExpires: 9223372036854775807
badPasswordTime: 0
badPwdCount: 0
***cn*: John Smith
codePage: 0
countryCode: 0
displayName: John Smith **[Display name]**
distinguishedName: CN=John Smith,OU=Staff,DC=net,DC=dom
givenName: John **[First name]**
homeDirectory: \\netdc1\UsersData\jsmith
homeDrive: W:
***instanceType*: 4
lastLogoff: 0
lastLogon: 0
logonCount: 0
memberOf: CN=Account Operators,CN=Builtin,DC=net,DC=dom
memberOf: CN=Server Operators,CN=Builtin,DC=net,DC=dom
name: John Smith
***objectCategory*: CN=Person,CN=Schema,CN=Configuration,DC=net,DC=dom
**objectClass*: organizationalPerson
**objectClass*: person
**objectClass*: top

continues

Table 12.3 Continued

Exported attributes and their values	
**objectClass*: user	
objectGUID:: pME9k/0HNk+lz9/kJBpp3g==	
***objectSid*:: AQUAAAAAAAUVAAAAL9Xsbd3o5ByKpzI/UgQAAA==	
primaryGroupID: 513	
profilePath: \\netdc1\Profiles\jsmith	
pwdLastSet: 126609470367623296	
**sAMAccountName*: JSmith	**[User logon name(pre-Windows 2000]**
sAMAccountType: 805306368	
scriptPath: Users\Logons.vbs	
sn: Smith	**[Last name]**
***userAccountControl: 512	
userPrincipalName: JSmith@net	**[User logon name]**
†uSNChanged: 5950	
†uSNCreated: 4194	
†whenChanged: 20020320164127.0Z	
†whenCreated: 20020318174356.0Z	

* — these attributes *are required* for importing (creating) objects. To create a new user, it is sufficient to specify the *objectClass* and *sAMAccountName* attributes. Other objects will require some additional attributes (see Table 12.2).

** — these attributes are mandatory for a user object, but are *not* required for an import operation since the system itself creates the corresponding values.

*** — if this string is included in an import file, the new user will have to change his or her password at first logon; otherwise the new account will be disabled.

† — these attributes are exported, too, with the -m parameter, but it makes absolutely no sense to *import* them.

Here is a sample command string that allows you to export the specified attributes of all users (except for built-in accounts) from your current domain:

```
ldifde -f ExportedUSERs.ldf
↳ -r "(&(objectCategory=Person)(objectClass=user)(givenName=*))"
↳ -l "cn,givenName,objectClass,sAMAccountName"
```

Working with Container Objects (Domains and OUs)

When working with container objects, you must always remember that the combination of the search base and the LDAP filter defines the result of the operation: either you export only container objects of the specified type, or you export an entire container.

Compare, for example, the following two commands. The first command exports all *OU objects* from the current domain (remember the default values for the omitted `-l`, `-d`, and `-p` parameters):

```
ldifde -f ExportedOUs.ldf -r "objectCategory=OrganizationalUnit" -v
```

The second command exports an *entire* subtree, i.e., all objects (of any type), from the specified OU:

```
ldifde -f ExportedOU.ldf -d "OU=Staff,DC=net,DC=dom" -v
```

Extending the Schema

LDIFDE is the tool recommended by Microsoft for extending the schema (however, using CSVDE is also possible). (The requirements of the schema extension are described in *Chapter 16, "Active Directory Service Interfaces (ADSI)."*) Remember that you must generate the base OID for your own attributes and classes before executing a similar command. The following is an example of an LDIF import file, which creates a string attribute with *stringAttribute* LDAP display name:

```
dn: CN=String Attribute,CN=Schema,CN=Configuration,DC=net,DC=dom
changetype: add
attributeID: 1.2.840.113556.1.4. ... .1
attributeSyntax: 2.5.5.12
cn: String Attribute
isSingleValued: TRUE
objectCategory: CN=Attribute-Schema,CN=Schema,CN=Configuration,
↳DC=net,DC=dom
objectClass: attributeSchema
oMSyntax: 64
```

A successful command output is similar to the following (`netdc1.net.dom` is the name of the DC that is the schema master):

```
C:\>ldifde -i -f AddStrAttr.ldf
Connecting to "netdc1.net.dom"
Logging in as current user using SSPI
```

```
Importing directory from file "AddStrAttr.ldf"
Loading entries..
1 entry modified successfully.

The command has completed successfully
```

Modifying Attribute Values. Deleting Objects

Only the LDIFDE utility can be used for batch *modifying* Active Directory objects from a command file. (Remember also the *DsMod.exe* utility!) To change (or set) one or more attribute values of an object (or a number of objects) use the following procedure:

1. Export the necessary object(s) to a file. Use the appropriate filters. You may export all attributes or specific ones only. This step is optional — you may create the import file manually from scratch.
2. Edit the export file. Delete the entries for unnecessary (unchanged) attributes. Change *changetype* from `add` to `modify`. Replace each attribute entry with the following lines:

```
replace: <attributeName>
<attributeName>: <newValue>
```

If the second line is omitted, the attribute value will be cleared. The "–" (minus) character must follow the lines for *each* attribute (including the last one). An empty line must precede *each* attribute's distinguished name (excluding the first one). Let us illustrate these requirements with an example. The sample import file is used for modifying attributes of two user objects (the comments in bold square brackets are not really included in the file!).

```
dn: CN=user3,OU=Staff,DC=net,DC=dom
changetype: modify
replace: description
description: A test user
-
replace: scriptPath
scriptPath: Users\Logons.vbs
-
   [This empty line is mandatory]
dn: CN=user4,OU=Staff,DC=net,DC=dom
changetype: modify
```

```
replace: description
description: A user
-   [All "-" characters are mandatory]
```

3. Import the edited file. The import is performed until the first error, but you can safely repeat it as many times as you wish while correcting errors.

By modifying attribute values, you can also change membership in a group(s). To add a user to a group, use lines similar to the following:

```
dn: CN=GroupName,OU=Staff,DC=net,DC=dom
changetype: modify
replace: member
member: CN=user2,OU=Staff,DC=net,DC=dom
```

Note

If LDIFDE.exe does not meet your specific needs, write a custom script (see *Chapter 17*, "*Scripting Administrative Tasks*"). This (if you are familiar with ADSI scripting) will not take more time than editing a file. In addition, the scripts are much more flexible as well as reusable. For example, you need to re-do the export and/or edit the export-import file each time a user is added (deleted), whereas the *same* script can modify the specified attributes for any number of users in a container.

To delete a *leaf* object, it is sufficient to include the following two lines into the import file:

```
dn: CN=user2,OU=Staff,DC=net,DC=dom
changetype: delete
```

You *cannot* delete a container if it has child objects. The LDAP protocol, actually, allows you to delete a subtree (see the Ldp.exe tool description earlier in this chapter), but LDIFDE does not permit one to perform such an operation.

CSV Directory Exchange Utility (Sys)

CSVDE uses the *Comma-Separated Value* (CSV) file format (with a .csv extension). Files in this format can easily be viewed (imported) or prepared (edited and exported) by using various applications, including Microsoft Excel. The first line in such files contains the names of attributes, separated by a comma. The next lines contain the values of attributes, one line per object. An example of such a file is shown in the next section.

Working with Unicode String Values

Let us discuss the problem of Unicode support in an example with the CSVDE utility. The following command exports the minimal set of OUs' attributes that allow you to import the OU structure to another domain:

```
csvde -f ExportedOUs.csv -r "(objectCategory=OrganizationalUnit)"
↳ -l "objectClass,ou" -v -u
```

Note

If *all* attributes are to be exported (no `-l` parameter used), add the `-m` parameter to the command.

On the screen, the command produces an output (thanks to the verbose mode) similar to the following:

```
Connecting to "(null)"
Logging in as current user using SSPI
Exporting directory to file ExportedOUs.csv
Searching for entries...
Writing out entries
Exporting entry: "OU=Domain Controllers,DC=net,DC=dom"
...
Exporting entry: "OU=Персонал,DC=net,DC=dom"

Export Completed. Post-processing in progress...
7 entries exported
The command has completed successfully
```

Notice the non-Latin string in an OU's name (`OU=Персонал,...`). If the `-u` parameter has not been specified, the command results in an error (which is also written to the csv.err file):

```
Error writing to file. This error happens when the entry cannot be
written, it can be caused by writing a Unicode value to a non-unicode
file. An error has occurred in the program
```

Here is the exported CSV-file produced by the command (the first line contains the attributes' names):

```
DN,objectClass,ou
"OU=Domain Controllers,DC=net,DC=dom",organizationalUnit,Domain
↳ Controllers
...
```

```
"OU=Персонал,DC=net,DC=dom",organizationalUnit,X'd09fd0b5d180d18
↳1d0bed0bdd0b0d0bb'
```

Notice that the last line contains a coded value for the *ou* attribute.

Caution

- If you create an import file with non-Latin Unicode values from scratch, do not forget to save it in Unicode format (not in ANSI) and use the `-u` parameter when importing the file.

Exporting Information for Successive Import

As mentioned before, some attributes that are present or incorrectly (inconsistently) specified in an import file may cause an error. Here are two frequently encountered errors that are reported on in import operations:

```
Add error on line 2: Unwilling To Perform
The server side error is "The modification was not permitted for
security reasons."
0 entries modified successfully.
An error has occurred in the program
```

The following error specifies that you want to import an attribute(s) that only the system can change:

```
Add error on line 3: Constraint Violation
The server side error is "Access to the attribute is not permitted
because the attribute is owned by the Security Accounts Manager (SAM)."
```

If you encounter such an error, use the `-m` parameter for export, and if the error still exists, check the import file for consistency. Try to get rid of "unnecessary" attributes when doing export. Let us look at a situation where you yourself produce a critical error by using the `-c` parameter.

The scenario is the following. Suppose that you want to copy an entire OU from one domain (*net.dom*) to another (*subdom.net.dom*) and rename the OU at the same time. You use the `-c OU=Personnel OU=Staff,DC=subdom` parameter to change the source DN *OU=Personnel,DC=net,DC=dom* to the destination DN *OU=Staff, DC=subdom,DC=net,DC=dom*. The problem is that the *ou* attribute will not be changed by such a replace operation, and will remain the same. As a result, an inconsistency in the *dn* and *ou* attributes has occured. You can only solve the problem by omitting the *ou* attribute when exporting. The *sIDHistory* attribute presented in the import file will also prevent you from successfully importing. The following command meets all requirements and may perform the desired action:

```
csvde -f Subtree.csv -d OU=Personnel,DC=net,DC=dom
↳ -c OU=Personnel OU=Staff,DC=subdom -o ou,sidhistory -m -v
```

If the OU being copied contains computer accounts, you can copy them by using the following command (or add the *primaryGroupID* attribute in the list of omitted attributes in the previous command):

```
csvde -f Comp.csv -d OU=Personnel,DC=net,DC=dom
↳ -r "objectCategory=Computer" -c OU=Personnel OU=Staff,DC=subdom
↳ -o primaryGroupID -m -v
```

Caution

Note that the *memberOf* attribute is not exported, so you may need to verify (and reestablish) all group memberships of the imported accounts. To add users to a group(s), you can use the *AddUsers.exe* command from *Windows 2000 Resource Kit* or Windows .NET system utility *DsMod.exe* (see *Chapter 8, "Common Administrative Tasks"*).

Windows Domain Manager (NetDom.exe) (ST)

Windows Domain Manager is a command-line tool that has some unique features, such as moving computer accounts between domains, as well as joining computers to a domain and renaming domain controllers or computer accounts. The tool allows you to:

- Retrieve diverse information about domains
- Add, join, and move computers to a domain (these operations are "OU-aware"), as well as remove computers from a domain
- Rename domain controllers and computers
- Reset and verify computer secure channels
- Verify, establish, reset, break, and change domain trusts (including Kerberos trusts)

Caution

Be careful, the documentation on this tool is slightly inconsistent. There are quite a few divergences between parameters' description in the *Support Tools Help* and the built-in help feature.

Windows .NET version of NetDom.exe cannot run on Windows 2000 systems.

Let us discuss some interesting features of NetDom.exe with some examples. To see detailed information on how an operation is performed, you may use the `/Verbose` parameter with any command. Many tool's commands accept the DNS name of computers and domains, but sometimes the NetBIOS names are preferable.

Querying Domains

NetDom.exe is one of the tools that allow you to view FSMO roles' owners in the forest. For example, the following command shows that the server *NETDC2* holds all roles in its domain, whereas all forest-wide roles are owned by the server *NETDC4* in the root domain:

```
C:\>netdom QUERY /D:subdom.net.dom FSMO
Schema owner                netdc1.net.dom
Domain role owner           netdc1.net.dom
PDC role                    netdc2.subdom.net.dom
RID pool manager            netdc2.subdom.net.dom
Infrastructure owner        netdc2.subdom.net.dom
The command completed successfully.
```

The following command displays all domains that have direct trusts with the specified domain (the trusts may be also verified by using the `netdom TRUST` command; see later); notice that the *net.dom* and *NT4DOM* domains are connected with a one-way trust:

```
C:\>netdom QUERY /D:net.dom TRUST /Direct
Direction Trusted\Trusting domain                          Trust type
========= =======================                          ==========
<->       subdom.net.dom                                   Direct
<-        NT4DOM                                           Direct
<->       dotnet.dom                                       Direct
```

The `netdom QUERY` command can also verify and/or reset (the `/Reset` parameter) domain trusts. The following command checks trusts between the parent (current) domain and a child (the command is executed in the parent domain; the credentials of the child's administrator must be provided):

```
C:\>netdom QUERY /D:subdom.net.dom TRUST /UD:administrator /PD:* /Verify
Type the password associated with the domain user:
Direction Trusted\Trusting domain                        Trust type  Status
========= =======================                        ==========  ======
<->       net.dom                                        Direct      Verified
The command completed successfully.
```

When you delegate control over some OUs to a user (`jsmith` is our example), you might want to quickly verify administrative power of that user (you must know the user password). The following command may help you to do this task:

```
C:\>netdom QUERY /D:net.dom OU /UD:jsmith /PD:*
Type the password associated with the domain user:
List of Organizational Units within which the specified user can create
a
machine account:
OU=Staff,DC=net,DC=dom
OU=Sales,OU=Marketing,DC=net,DC=dom
The command completed successfully.
```

Compare this output with the results received for an administrative account.

Managing Computer Accounts

The command shown below creates a computer account in the domain (but doesn't *join* a computer to the domain). Note that you can specify a target OU for that account. Remember that if you are working on a computer and join it to a domain using a newly created account, this account by default is added to the *Computer* container. You may use the command for pre-creating accounts in the necessary OUs (domains) before actually joining the computers to the forest.

```
C:\>netdom ADD compName /D:net.dom /OU:OU=Staff,DC=net,DC=dom
The command completed successfully.
```

NetDom.exe can be used for migrating computer accounts from Windows NT resource domains to an AD-based domain or between AD-based domains. All commands — ADD, JOIN, MOVE, and REMOVE — are "OU-aware", so you can manipulate accounts according to the OU structure of your domains.

To move a computer (`compName` in the example) from the current domain to a destination domain (you must be logged on to the current domain as an administrator and provide an administrator's credentials in the destination domain), use a command similar to:

```
C:\>netdom MOVE compName /D:subdom.net.dom
↳ /OU:OU=Personnel,DC=subdom,DC=net,DC=dom /UD:administrator /PD:*
```

Caution

- The computer being moved must be online and accessible, otherwise the command generates the "The network path was not found" error.

Verifying and Resetting Secure Channels

NetDom.exe can verify and reset the secure channels that exist between each computer in a domain and a domain controller. To verify that the computer *COMP3* has an actual secure channel with its *net.dom* domain, it is possible to use the following command (the command's output is also shown):

```
C:\>netdom VERIFY comp3.net.dom /D:net.dom
The secure channel from COMP3.NET.DOM to the domain NET.DOM has been
verified.  The connection is with the machine \\NETDC1.NET.DOM.
The command completed successfully
```

The same operation can also be performed using the NLtest tool:

```
C:\>nltest /sc_query:net.dom /server:comp3.net.dom
Flags: 30 HAS_IP  HAS_TIMESERV
Trusted DC Name \\netdc1.net.dom
Trusted DC Connection Status Status = 0 0x0 NERR_Success
The command completed successfully
```

To reset the broken secure channel, use the following command

```
C:\>netdom RESET comp3.net.dom /D:net.dom
The secure channel from COMP3.NET.DOM to the domain NET.DOM has been
reset.  The connection is with the machine \\NETDC1.NET.DOM.
The command completed successfully
```

The NLtest tool can also be used for that purpose:

```
C:\>nltest /sc_reset:net.dom /server:comp3.net.dom
Flags: 30 HAS_IP  HAS_TIMESERV
Trusted DC Name \\netdc1.net.dom
Trusted DC Connection Status Status = 0 0x0 NERR_Success
The command completed successfully
```

Managing Domain Trusts

NetDom.exe allows you to verify domain trusts issues (including those that use Kerberos v5 authentication protocol). For example, the following command checks the Kerberos trusts between two domains in the forest (both domain administrators' credentials must be specified!):

```
C:\>netdom TRUST subdom.net.dom /D:net.dom /Kerberos /UD:administrator
/PD:* /UO:administrator /PO:* /Verify
```

```
Type the password associated with the domain user:
Type the password associated with the object user:
The trust between subdom.net.dom and net.dom has been successfully verified
The command completed successfully
```

To reset domain trusts, enter the command:

```
C:\>netdom TRUST subdom.net.dom /D:net.dom /UD:administrator /PD:*
/UO:administrator /PO:* /Reset
```

Successful output should be similar to:

```
Resetting the trust passwords between subdom.net.dom and net.dom
The trust between subdom.net.dom and net.dom
has been successfully reset and verified
The command completed successfully
```

If trust relationship issues exist, you can try to isolate the problem and use the `netdom VERIFY` or `nltest /sc_query` commands to check trusts between pairs of domain controllers.

Note

For verifying and resetting trusts, the **Active Directory Domains and Trusts** snap-in (see *Chapter 7*, "*Domain Manipulation Tools*") can also be used.

NetDom.exe allows you to remove information (including cross reference and trusted domain objects) about a non-existing (defunct) domain, which doesn't contain domain controllers, from Active Directory. The `netdom TRUST /Remove /Force` command can be used for that purpose, for example:

```
netdom TRUST dotnet.dom /D:net.dom /Remove /Force
```

Chapter 13: Migration and Directory Reorganization Tools

Moving Active Directory objects *within* a domain is a rather simple operation. You only need to open the **Active Directory Users and Computers** snap-in, point to the object, and select a target container for the Move operation. Moving objects *between* domains is a more complicated task, requiring specific tools. When the domains belong to different forests, then you should talk about *migrating* rather than *moving* objects.

This chapter describes utilities that allow an administrator to reconfigure domains as well as to migrate (copy) the user, group, and other directory objects from one AD-based forest (or a Windows NT 4.0-based domain) to another forest:

- MoveTree.exe moves the user, group, and OU objects within an AD-based forest (intra-forest migration); the user accounts retain their passwords after moving.
- ClonePrincipal duplicates (clones) the user and group objects between different AD-based forests or from an Windows NT 4.0 domain to an AD-based domain (inter-forest migration); does not maintain users' passwords.
- Active Directory Migration Tool version 2.0 (ADMT) can work as both MoveTree (within AD-based forests) and ClonePrincipal (between forests or Windows NT 4.0 domains and AD-based forest); creates new passwords or migrates existing passwords.

The first two utilities have been included in the *Support Tools* pack, whereas ADMT can be downloaded freely from the Microsoft website (see *Appendix A*).

The main difference between these utilities is that MoveTree operates only in intra-forest scenarios, and ClonePrincipal only provides inter-forest operations. Besides, MoveTree destroys the source object (assigning its GUID to the new object), and ClonePrincipal creates a copy of the object, leaving the source intact. ADMT 2.0 can provide both migration scenarios. All of the utilities add the original objects' SIDs to the *sIDHistory* attribute of target objects.

Adventures of the *ObjectSID* Attribute

Alteration of an Active Directory object's domain membership results in the changing of the object *security identifier* (SID). Windows 2000-based *native mode* domains as well as Windows .NET-based *Windows 2000 native* and *Windows .NET (version 2002)* functional level domains have a mechanism permitting users and other security principals to retain access to network resources after they have been moved to another location in the domain structure. Let us discuss this mechanism in an example using ClonePrincipal.

Every security principal object in non-*Windows 2000 mixed* mode domains has a multi-valued *sIDHistory* attribute. This attribute, as well as the object SID (the *objectSid* attribute), is used in an object's *access token* for granting access to network resources. If any SID value is presented in the ACL of a network resource, the object is granted access to this resource (provided that the granted access permission is *Allow* rather than *Deny*). This process is outlined in Fig. 13.1.

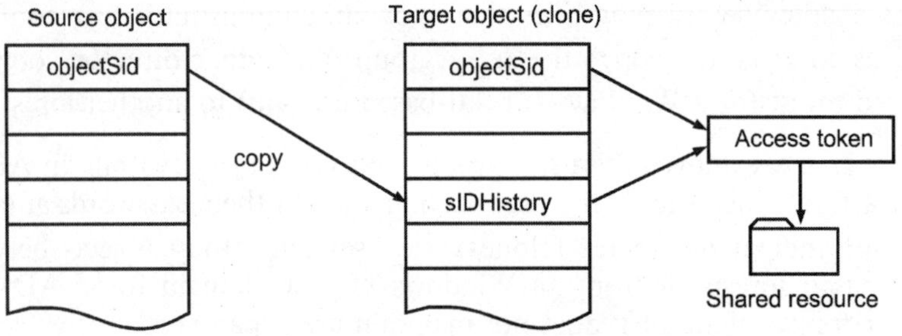

Fig. 13.1. The *sIDHistory* attribute allows a new object to retain the access permissions granted to the source object

After either ClonePrincipal or MoveTree creates a new object, it adds the source object's SID value to the new object's *sIDHistory* list. As a result, the new object will have access to all resources available to the source object (Fig. 13.2).

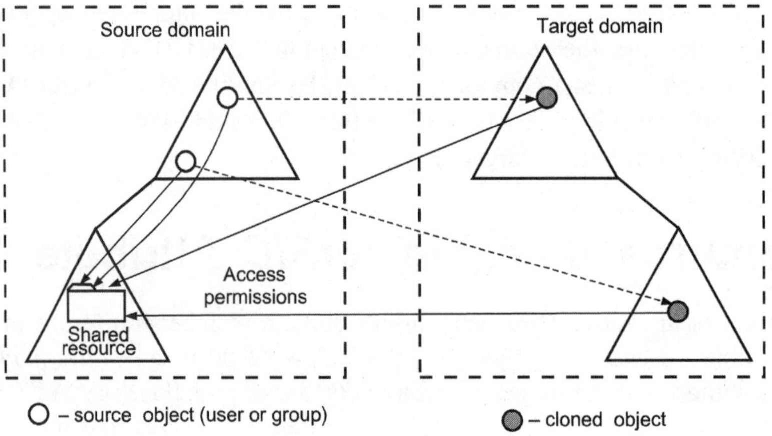

Fig. 13.2. The cloned (or moved) object inherits the access rights of the source object

In addition, the *sIDHistory* list of the source object — if the list is not empty — is added to the *sIDHistory* of the target object.

Active Directory Object Manager (MoveTree.exe) (ST)

MoveTree is the main tool (and the only standard one, if you exclude the Active Directory Migration Tool) that allows administrators to reconstruct AD-based domains which belong to the same forest. This tool can move both single Active Directory objects and entire containers (OU) from one domain to another. The following objects are supported:

- Users (the passwords are preserved)
- *Empty* domain local and global groups
- Universal groups (all members are preserved)
- Organizational units (with or without contents)

You cannot use MoveTree to move computer accounts, system objects, or domain controllers.

Note

If you prefer GUI tools, try the Active Directory Migration Tool (ADMT), which has many additional options when compared to MoveTree. ADMT version 2.0 can be controlled from scripts.

Important

The documentation on MoveTree in the *Support Tools Help* fails to mention the most important restriction of the tool: the target domain must be in *native* mode. Only native-mode domains support the *sIDHistory* attribute (updateable by the tool) for the security principals. You may not consider this fact to be a limitation, but do not forget about it while working with mixed mode domains!

Revise data (such as user profiles, logon scripts, etc.) associated with user objects being moved. These data are not moved, although the user objects preserve all settings. You might need to re-create shared volumes or copy user data, such as logon scripts, before users will be able to successfully log on to the new domain.

The syntax of MoveTree is quite simple: you must specify the source and destination of an operation, as well as the operation's type. Practically all parameters are mandatory. MoveTree has two "modes":

- The *test mode* that checks many conditions without really moving any object
- The *working mode* that initiates or continues a move operation

Moving an OU Subtree

Moving OUs with all their child objects is arguably the most attractive feature of MoveTree. You must take into consideration the fact that when an OU is moved, it retains all links with Group Policy Objects (GPOs) assigned to this OU. It is necessary to re-create these GPOs in the new domain, and break the links with GPOs from the old domain.

Suppose, for example, we would like to move the *Personnel* OU from the *net.dom* domain to the *subdom.net.dom* domain and rename it *Staff*. You must have appropriate privileges in both source and target domains. The following "test mode" command checks whether this operation is carried out correctly (you might also need to provide administrative credentials for the destination domain):

```
C:\>movetree /check /s netdc1.net.dom /d netdc2.subdom.net.dom
↳ /sdn OU=Personnel,DC=net,DC=dom
↳ /ddn OU=Staff,DC=subdom,D=net,DC=dom
```

Notice that the destination OU name differs from the source OU name. Suppose you got the following messages:

```
MOVETREE PRE-CHECK FINISHED.
MOVETREE DETECTED THERE ARE SOME OBJECTS CAN NOT BE MOVED.
PLEASE CLEAN THEM UP FIRST BEFORE TRYING TO START THE MOVE TREE OPERATION.
READ movetree.chk FOR DETAILS.
```

The *movetree.chk* file (in the same folder where the command has been executed) always contains diagnostics messages for each step of the command execution (successful operations have the "0x0" code). This file is generated for each check or successful move operation. (You may also specify the `/verbose` parameter with the command, and all detailed diagnostics will be displayed on the console.) You can easily locate the problem and source of an error (marked here in bold), for example:

```
ReturnCode: 0x0 The operation completed successfully.MoveTree check
destination RDN conflict for object: OU=Personnel,DC=net,DC=dom
ReturnCode: 0x0 The operation completed successfully.MoveTree cross
domain move check for object: OU=Personnel,DC=net,DC=dom
...
ReturnCode: 0x212d Can't move objects with memberships across domain
boundaries as once moved, this would violate the membership conditions
of the account group.  Remove the object from any account group
memberships and retry.MoveTree cross domain move check for object:
CN=Dan,OU=Personnel,DC=net,DC=dom
...
```

Note

With the Windows 2000 version of MoveTree, you will get the *0x212d* error if you try to move a computer account (a single account or an account included in an OU). The Windows .NET version of MoveTree reports the 0x2081 error just when a move operation is really performed. Use NetDom or ADMT for moving computers.

If you delete the reported user object (`cn=Dan`) from any domain local or global security group (excluding universal groups and the primary group — *Domain Users*) and repeat the command, you will get the following result:

```
MOVETREE PRE-CHECK FINISHED.
MOVETREE IS READY TO START THE MOVE OPERATION.
```

The *movetree.err* file will be empty in this case.

This means that the command has found no errors, and the move operation has a chance to succeed. Now you can complete the move operation by replacing the `/check` parameter with either the `/startnocheck` or `/start` parameter. All diagnostic messages are always written to the *movetree.log* file located in the current folder.

Attention

- The "test mode" (with the `/check` parameter) does not guarantee that the operation will not fail. For example, the following error ("Insufficient access rights to perform the operation") may appear only in the "working mode":

```
MOVETREE FAILED. 0x2098
READ movetree.err FOR DETAILS.
```

Note

After directory objects have been moved, force replication or wait until replication is completed. The *Infrastructure* operations master and *Global Catalog* must be updated. Otherwise, some changes in the domains may not be "understood" in the forest.

If for some reason a move operation fails to complete, any remaining objects are placed to the *LostAndFound* container in the source domain. For example, in the Windows .NET environment, such a situation can occur if you try to move an OU containing computer accounts. To solve this problem, view the operation log, delete or move conflicting objects from the LostAndFound container, and restart the operation using the `/continue` parameter. When the move operation is successfully completed, this container will be empty (if there are no failed operations that move other directory objects).

Moving User and Group Accounts

The destination container must already exist before a user or group account is moved. The object can be renamed when moving; you only need to specify the appropriate distinguished names along with the `/sdn` and `/ddn` parameters.

Local and global groups must be empty when moved. (Only universal groups retain all their members when moved.) Otherwise, a message similar to the following will appear in the movetree.chk file:

```
ERROR: 0x2132 Cross-domain move of non-empty account groups is not
allowed. MoveTree object CN=GlobalGroup,OU=Staff,DC=net,DC=dom failed
the Cross Domain Move Check
```

or

```
ERROR: 0x2133 Cross-domain move of non-empty resource groups is not
allowed. MoveTree object CN=LocalGroup,OU=Staff,DC=net,DC=dom failed
the Cross Domain Move Check
```

Cloning Security Principals (ClonePrincipal) (ST)

ClonePrincipal is not really a utility or command, but a set of scripts that allows administrators to perform *inter-forest* migration, primarily to incrementally migrate (copy) accounts from an existing Windows NT 4.0-based domain to a new Active Directory domain (based on domain controllers running Windows 2000 or Windows .NET). (In contrast to MoveTree, ClonePrincipal does not affect the source objects.) ClonePrincipal can also be used for reorganizing AD-based forests. This tool and its GUI counterpart — the Active Directory Migration Tool (ADMT) — are the only facilities used for upgrading existing Windows NT 4.0-based domains in cases when users can preserve continuous access to network shared resources and administrators can fulfill fallback in case of an emergency.

Note

ADMT is a more powerful and user-friendly tool than ClonePrincipal. ADMT has many additional features, for example, it also supports *intra-forest* operations, and can migrate user profiles, computers, and trusts. ClonePrincipal and ADMT have quite a few similar features. However, they differ internally, and Microsoft does not recommend that you mix these tools for migration operations. If you learn ClonePrincipal's basics (especially the environmental requirements and mechanism of SID migration), you will be able to master ADMT without any problems.

Well-Known SIDs and RIDs

Let us first clarify some terms used below.

A unique *Security Identifier* (SID) of a security principal (i.e., user, computer, or group account) is used to grant access rights to shared network resources to a principal. The SID is composed of two parts: a unique "domain part", which is the same for all principals within the domain where they reside, and a *Relative Identifier* (RID), which uniquely identifies the principal in the domain.

Note

Windows .NET domains offer a new security principle — class *inetOrgPerson*. You can use objects of that class in the same way as the user objects and assign them permissions on shared resources and directory objects.

An account with a *well-known RID* has an SID composed of an RID that is identical in every domain, and a "domain part" that is unique for each domain. Such an account can only be cloned onto an account with the same RID. Here are accounts with well-known RIDs:

- Administrator
- Domain Admins
- Domain Guests
- Domain Users
- Guest

An account with a *well-known SID* cannot be cloned, since its SID is identical in every domain. (Therefore, it doesn't make sense to copy an account whose SID already exists in the target domain.) Here are accounts with well-known SIDs:

- Account Operators
- Administrators
- Backup Operators
- Guests
- Power Users
- Print Operators
- Replicator
- Server Operators
- Users

Supported Object Types

With ClonePrincipal, you can clone the following objects:

- User accounts
- Security group accounts:
    - Local groups (from Windows NT 4.0 or Windows 2000 mixed mode domains)
    - Global groups
    - Domain local groups (from at least Windows 2000 native mode Active Directory domains)
    - Universal groups (from at least Windows 2000 *native* mode Active Directory domains)

ClonePrincipal *does not* support the following objects:

- Computer accounts (workstations or domain controllers)
- Inter-domain trusts
- Accounts with well-known SIDs (for example, Administrators or Users local groups)

ClonePrincipal Components

ClonePrincipal consists of the following files:

- Clonepr.dll — a COM server that implements all functions.
- Clonepr.vbs — the script that clones a *single* security principal (user account; global, universal, or domain local group), creating the target principal if necessary.
- Clonelg.vbs — the script that clones *all* local (except built-in) or domain local groups in a domain.
- Clonegg.vbs — the script that clones *all* global and universal groups in a domain.
- Cloneggu.vbs — this script clones *all* users and global groups (user, global group, and universal group accounts) in a domain, including well-known global groups such as Domain Admins, Domain Users, and Domain Guests.
- SIDHist.vbs — the script that copies (adds) the value of the *objectSID* attribute of a source principal to the *sIDHistory* attribute of a target principal.

Use of these scripts is discussed in the following sections.

Configuring Migration Environment

One of the most important requirements for ClonePrincipal (as well as for ADMT) to work well is the proper configuration of both source and target domains. If you are also planning to use ADMT, see also the *additional* requirements below. ClonePrincipal will fail if any of the requirements have not been met.

Here are some general considerations:

- If ClonePrincipal was installed separately from the *Support Tools*, make sure that the Clonepr.dll has been registered on the target DC.
- All ClonePrincipal scripts must be run on the PDC Emulator (the FSMO role master) of the target domain.
- You must log on to the DC as a member of the *Domain Admins* group of the target domain.

Registry Settings (*TcpipClientSupport*)

In the source domain running Windows NT 4.0 (with Service Pack 4 or later) or Windows 2000/.NET, create the registry REG_DWORD:0x1 value named `TcpipClientSupport` on the PDC (or the PDC Emulator) under the following subkey:

```
HKEY_LOCAL_MACHINE\SYSTEM\CurrentControlSet\Control\Lsa
```

Reboot the PDC.

This setting is not necessary if you use ADMT for intra-forest migration.

Audit Settings

It is necessary to set auditing, both in the source and target domains. Use the procedure described below.

For Windows 2000 and Windows .NET domains (both the source and target):

1. Open the Group Policy Object (GPO) for the *Domain Controller* OU. (Use either the **Domain Controller Security Policy** or the **Active Directory Users and Computers** snap-in.)
2. Open the Security Settings | Local Policies | Audit Policy node.
3. Double-click the **Audit account management** policy and check both the **Success** and **Failure** boxes. Click **OK**. A sample screen is shown in Fig. 13.3. Refresh the computer policy or wait for the updates to take place.

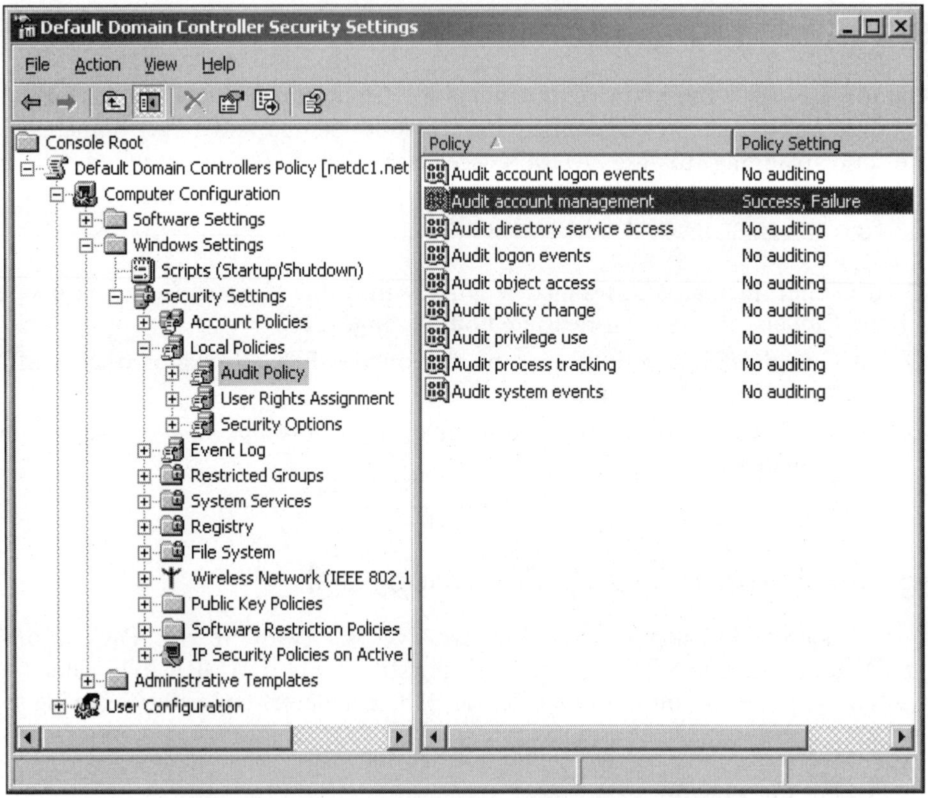

Fig. 13.3. Setting audit on the Windows 2000-based domain controllers

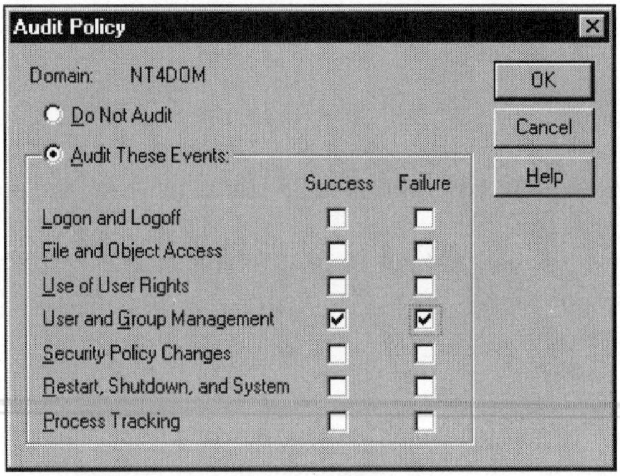

Fig. 13.4. Setting audit on a Windows NT 4.0-based domain controller

For a Windows NT 4.0-based source domain:

1. In User Manager for Domains, click **Audit** in the **Policies** menu.
2. Select **Audit These Events** and check the **Success** and **Failure** boxes for **User and Group Management** (Fig. 13.4).

Creating the Audit Group

In either a Windows NT 4.0- or AD-based *source* domain, you must create a special domain ***local*** group that is used for auditing cloning operations. The name of the group is composed of the source domain NetBIOS (pre-Windows 2000) name appended with three dollar signs, for example, *NT4DOM$$$*. The group must be empty. Without this group, you will not be able to transfer SIDs between forests and update the *sIDHistory* attribute of target objects.

This group is not required if you use ADMT for intra-forest migration.

Trusts

Establish a *bidirectional* trust between the source and target domains (i.e., the source domain must trust the target domain, and vice versa). (For details, see *"Establishing Trusts"* in *Chapter 5, "Installing Active Directory."*) Before that, make sure that name resolving is working properly in your configuration. You must be able to successfully ping the target DC from the source DC by the NetBIOS (pre-Windows 2000) name, and vice versa.

Configuring Groups

To run ClonePrincipal successfully, you must have the appropriate administrative privileges: add the *Domain Admins* global group from the target domain to the *Administrators* local group in the source domain.

Additional Requirements for ADMT

In *addition* to the considerations and necessary procedures described above, you must carry out the following operations:

- Add the *Domain Admins* global group from the source domain to the *Administrators* local group in the target domain.
- Add the *Domain Admins* global group from the source domain to each migrated computer's *Administrators* local group. The same is applicable to each computer on which security will be translated.
- Make sure that administrative shares exist on the target DC as well as on each computer you migrate.

Cloning Users

Even if the source domain is AD-based, ClonePrincipal does not address Active Directory's user properties. (ADMT 2.0 is free of that disadvantage.) Only the following Windows NT 4.0 properties are copied from the source object to the target object:

- General properties:
  - Full name
  - Description
  - Account flags (such as Account Expires, Logon Hours, Logon To, and others)
- Profile properties:
  - User profile (Profile path and Logon script)
  - Home directory (Local path, Connect drive and location)
- Dial-in properties
- File and Print for NetWare properties
- Terminal Server Properties

The following flags are set for the existing or cloned (newly created) user account:

- User must change password at next logon
- Account is disabled

The following flags will be cleared:

- User cannot change password
- Password never expires

The user password is set to empty (null).

By default, the cloned user becomes a member of the *Domain Users* group. The user's group memberships are retained in the target domain if the target global and/or universal groups are clones of the source groups in which the source user is a member. That is, if both user and global (universal) group accounts are copied (Cloneggu.vbs is used), the groups can retain all their members (if *all* of them are cloned).

Cloning Groups

When cloning global groups, you must consider the fact that the Cloneggu.vbs and Clonegg.vbs scripts copy accounts with well-known RIDs, and will fail if you specify a target container (the `/dstOU` parameter) different from the default *Users* container where these accounts reside. For example, you cannot perform such a command without a fatal error:

```
cloneggu /srcDC:nt4dc5 /srcDom:nt4dom
↳ /dstDC:netdc1 /dstDom:net.dom /dstOU:OU=Staff,DC=net,DC=dom
```

In this case, you have the three following options:

1. Specify the *Users* container as the target OU, for example, `/dstOU:CN=Users,DC=net,DC=dom`.
2. In the destination domain, move (temporally) all accounts with well-known RIDs (Administrator, Guest, Domain Admins, etc.) to the target OU.
3. Do not clone (i.e., ignore) the accounts with well-known RIDs. Open the Cloneggu.vbs or Clonegg.vbs script in a text editor, find the code shown below, and uncomment the specified statements:

```
'To Stop Cloning Well Known Sids[1] Uncomment 4 lines below
' if HasWellKnownRid(sidString) then
'   ShouldCloneObject = False
'   exit function
' end if
```

In this case, the target "well-known" accounts will lose access to those network resources which contain the source "well-known" accounts in their ACLs (since the *sIDHistory* attribute of these target accounts will not be updated). You may manually update the ACLs of the appropriate shared resources, or copy the SIDs from the source accounts to the target ones by using SIDHist.vbs.

ClonePrincipal Samples

Let us now consider some examples of how to use ClonePrincipal. Each parameter of every ClonePrincipal script is mandatory. You can view the parameter list for each script by entering the script name and a question mark at the command prompt.

Note

You might wish to set the "command-line" mode of Windows Script Host (WSH), since by default, it outputs all messages in pop-up windows, which is not convenient when you are working with ClonePrincipal scripts. Enter `cscript //H:CScript` at the command prompt.

---

[1] This is a typo in the scripts; should be "RIDs".

Cloning SID (*SIDHist.vbs*)

Usually, the SIDHist.vbs is executed by other ClonePrincipal scripts. However, you might want to run it manually to accomplish some specific tasks (for example, if you have disabled cloning groups with well-known RIDs). You may want to, for example, grant the Domain Admins group in the target domain the right to access network resources available to the same group from the source domain.

Note

You can monitor all changes of the *sIDHistory* attribute with Ldp.exe. (Use the same version of Ldp on both domains!) AdsVw.exe allows you to view the *objectSid* attribute (in hexadecimal byte format) on the source Windows NT-based DC. To see this attribute in the same format on the destination DC, you can also use the **ADSI Edit** snap-in.

The following script adds the *objectSid* attribute of the *Mark-W2K* user object from the *w2000* domain to the *sIDHistory* attribute of the *Mark-NET* user object located in the *net.dom* domain:

```
C:\>sidhist /srcDC:w2kdc3 /srcDom:w2000 /srcSAM:Mark-W2K
↳ /dstDC:netdc1 /dstDom:net.dom /dstSAM:Mark-NET
```

As a result, the Mark-NET user will have the same resource access rights as the Mark-W2K user.

You can perform this operation only for *one* selected account in the target domain. Otherwise, the script will fail with the following error:

```
Connected
 Error 0x8007215B occurred.
 Error Description: Failed to add the source SID to the destination
 object's SID history. The error was: "The source object's SID already
 exists in destination forest."
 Error HelpContext: 0
 Error HelpFile    :
 Error Source      : DSUtils.ClonePrincipal.1
```

If the operation is successful, the resulting output is very simple:

```
C:\>sidhist /srcDC:w2kdc3 /srcDom:w2000 /srcSAM:Mark-W2K
↳ /dstDC:netdc1 /dstDom:net.dom /dstSAM:Mark-NET

Connected
Success
```

After the above-mentioned command has been executed, the following message appears in the Security Log on the destination DC:

```
Event Type:   Success Audit
Event Source: Security
Event Category:  Account Management
Event ID: 669
...
User:      NET\Administrator
Computer: NETDC1
Description:
Add SID History:
    Source Account Name: w2000.dom\Mark-W2K
    Source Account ID:   NET\Mark-NET
    Target Account Name: Mark-NET
    Target Domain:   NET
    Target Account ID:   NET\Mark-NET
    Caller User Name:    Administrator
    Caller Domain:   NET
    Caller Logon ID: (0x0,0x115EB)
    Privileges:   -
```

Cloning a User (*ClonePr.vbs*)

The following script clones a user from a Windows 2000 domain to a Windows .NET domain, where the user is placed into a specified organizational unit. This container must exist before the script is executed. (Note that the user can already exist on the target DC.)

```
C:\>clonepr /srcDC:w2kdc3 /srcDom:w2000 /srcSAM:Mark
↳ /dstDC:netdc1 /dstDom:net.dom /dstSAM:Mark
↳ /dstDN:CN=Mark,OU=Migrated,DC=net,DC=dom
...
Connected to source and destination domain controllers
Bound to source User Mark
Destination object Mark not found (by SAM name) path used: WinNT://
net.dom/netdc1/Mark
Destination object CN=Mark,OU=Migrated,DC=net,DC=dom not found (by DN)
path used: LDAP://netdc1/CN=Mark,OU=Migrated,DC=n
et,DC=dom
Creating CN=Mark,OU=Migrated,DC=net,DC=dom
```

```
Created CN=Mark,OU=Migrated,DC=net,DC=dom
Setting properties for target User CN=Mark
Downlevel properties set.
Fixing group memberships for User CN=Mark
  Found global group WinNT://w2000/w2kdc3/Domain Users
  Skipping WinNT://w2000/w2kdc3/Domain Users -- not cloned yet
User's Group memberships restored.
User changes commited.
Adding SID for source User Mark to SID history of target User CN=Mark
SID history set successfully.
Mark cloned successfully.
```

Two events will be registered in the Security log on the target DC: Event ID 624 (User Account Created) and Event ID 669 (Add SID History). Thus, you can trace all clone operations performed in the domain.

Note

When a user object is cloned, the source account remains active, and the new account will be disabled.

Finding Groups of a Specific Type

When cloning groups, you may need to view the list of already copied groups and monitor the process of migration. There is a trick described below that allows you to find *only* the groups of a specific type located in any container in the object tree.

You need to use a LDAP search operation and the *LDAP_MATCHING_RULE_BIT_AND* (1.2.840.113556.1.4.803) matching rule control in the search filter. (For details, search for the "query filter" string in the *ADSI SDK*.) For example, the following command displays the *ADsPath* property of all universal groups that exist in the domain:

```
C:\>search "LDAP://DC=net,DC=dom"
↳ /C:"groupType:1.2.840.113556.1.4.803:=2147483656" /S:subtree
```

With the DsQuery utility, the command is even shorter:

```
C:\>dsquery * -filter groupType:1.2.840.113556.1.4.803:=2147483656
```

This search filter can also be used in other tools, such as Ldp.exe (specify it in the **Filter** field). The filter's values for various group types are listed in the table below. (Only the decimal values can be used. Notice also the minus sign in the last row of the table.)

Group type	Hexadecimal value	Decimal filter value
Built-in and Domain local	0x80000004	2147483652
Global	0x80000002	2147483650
Universal	0x80000008	2147483656
Built-in only	0x7FFFFFFB	-2147483643

Active Directory Migration Tool (ADMT)

Active Directory Migration Tool is the most powerful utility among migration facilities supported on Windows 2000 and Windows .NET systems. Besides that, ADMT is the only GUI tool among them. You can download it freely from the Microsoft website (see *Appendix A*).

ADMT is easy to use if you are acquainted with such migration tools as MoveTree and ClonePrincipal. In addition, all operations in ADMT are performed with the help of various wizards that significantly decrease the probability of errors in entered parameters.

ADMT can migrate all objects, which ClonePrincipal supports, as well as computer accounts (not domain controllers) and domain trusts. In addition, ADMT helps administrators to merge groups and "transfer" access rights from source domain accounts to migrated ones.

Note

Some options described below only relate to ADMT version 2.0. This primarily concerns intra-forest migration, scripting the tool operations, and password migration.

Note

The **Active Directory Migration Tool** snap-in can be added to any custom MMC console.

Note

Some ADMT operations, such as Security Translation, Reporting, or Group Mapping and Merging, "remember" and use results of previous operations. Therefore, you should perform all migration operations according to a considered plan and avoid un-necessary tool runs.

Note

The computer accounts in the source domain will not be deleted or disabled after the computer migration has been performed. Keep in mind that fact.

The main window of the tool (Fig. 13.5) only displays various reports if you have generated them. All operations are started from the **Action** menu, and their results are displayed in special pop-up windows and log files. This menu illustrates all general features of ADMT.

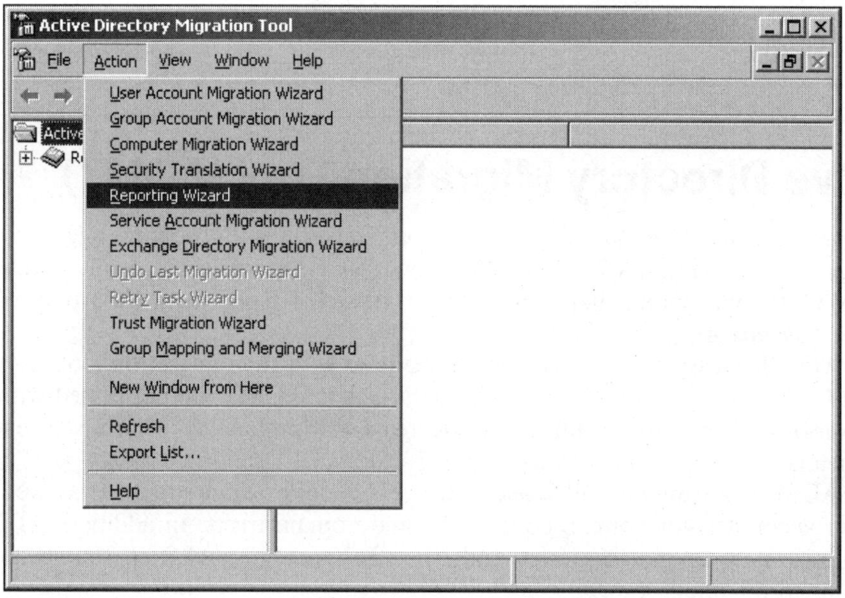

Fig. 13.5. The main window of ADMT

We will not discuss how to use ADMT 2.0 from the command prompt or batch files. This is not a difficult topic if you have mastered ADMT as a GUI tool and know all the environmental requirements. To view ADMT 2.0 command-line operation parameters, enter `admt` at the command prompt or find the "ADMT Command-line Reference" section in the ADMT Help file. You can also view a sample script, *TemplateScript.vbs*, which is located in the ADMT installation folder.

To demonstrate ADMT features and methods of preparation of migration operations, we will consider a user migration operation in explicit detail. All other operations are performed in a similar way, and a specific wizard will be used for each operation.

General Considerations

ADMT should be installed in a target domain only. Most of migration environment requirements for using ADMT are the same as for ClonePrincipal (see the *"Configuring Migration Environment"* section). You must fully comply with all the requirements described (without any exceptions); otherwise, migration operations will fail. The requirements are only slightly less strict when you perform intra-forest migration. In that case, `TcpipClientSupport` registry setting and audit local group are not necessary.

Important

Make sure that the domain controller acting as the Infrastructure Master is accessible, since it is responsible for updating the group-to-user references. Otherwise, you can get problems with the accounts names.

When performing inter-forest migration, you must run ADMT on a domain controller that belongs to the target domain. When intra-forest migration is performed, run ADMT on the RID Master in the target domain.

Before running ADMT, you should break any existing connections (like mapped network drives, etc.) between the source DC and the target DC. Otherwise, a migration operation fails due to a "credentials conflict" error.

ADMT agent (used when the computer accounts are migrated or security translation is performed) can operate on any Windows NT systems from Windows NT 3.51 to Windows .NET Server family. It ***automatically*** uploads to migrated computer(s) and performs necessary operations (including system rebooting).

ADMT supports a log file for each operation. These files are located in the *Logs* folder residing in the ADMT installation folder. If a migration operation fails, you should look through one of the logs, and correct your actions or rearrange domain objects in some way.

Migrating Users

1. Start ADMT and select the **User Account Migration Wizard** command from the **Action** menu. Click **Next** in the welcome wizard's window.
2. Select the operation mode; you have two options here:
   - Test the migration settings and migrate later
   - Migrate now

   Choose the necessary option and click **Next**.
3. In the next window, specify the source and target domain names (Fig. 13.6). You can enter domain names in the corresponding fields; however, it is better to choose them from the lists because these lists should already contain the names of all domains "visible" to the target domain. Therefore, you will select only valid names. Click **Next**.
4. On the "User Selection" wizard page, click **Add**. You can enter user names directly in the **Select Users** window; however, you can also choose them from a source container, and this is a more convenient way. To do so, click **Advanced**.

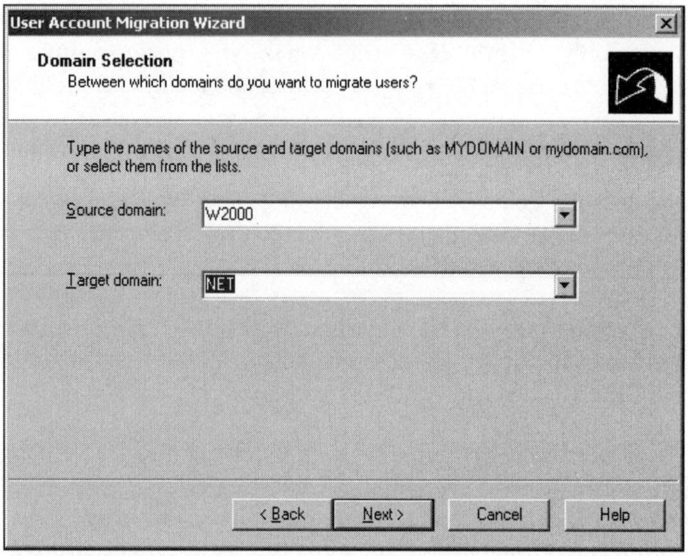

Fig. 13.6. Select the source and target domains

5. In the advanced **Select Users** window (Fig. 13.7), click **Locations** and select an applicable container (OU) in a object tree browse window. In our example, we have chosen the *Sales* OU. To find users, you can use common queries or simply click **Find Now** and view all users in the specified OU. Select necessary users or all of them, and click **OK**. To continue the operation, click **OK** in the initial **Select Users** window and **Next** on the "User Selection" page.
6. In the next window, enter the distinguished name of the target OU, or click **Browse** and select it in the target domain's object tree. Click **Next**.
7. In Fig. 13.8, you can see three options that ADMT supports for user passwords. If ADMT creates new passwords, it saves them in a specified file. Select the necessary option and click **Next**.

Important

- To migrate passwords between domains, you should ensure that the 128-bit high-encryption pack has been installed on both source and target domains. This requirement implies that you have the following systems: Windows NT 4.0 with Service Pack 5 or later; Windows 2000 with the 128-bit high-encryption pack installed (SP 2 or later is acceptable); and Windows .NET Server family.

  To enable password migration, you must carry out all operations described in the "Password migration" section in the ADMT Help file. These operations cover both the source and target domains. Keep in mind that you must add the Everyone group from the command prompt rather than by using the **Active Directory Users and Group** snap-in!

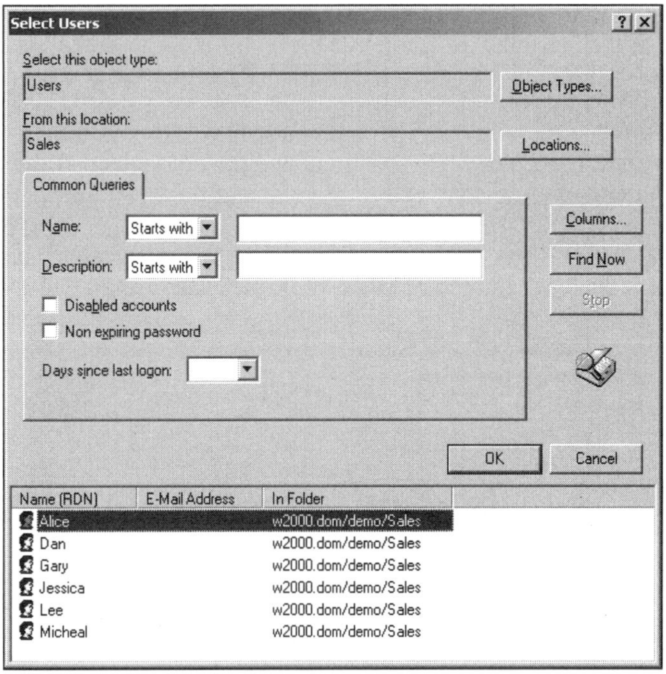

Fig. 13.7. In this window, you can easily select necessary user objects in a source container or in the entire domain

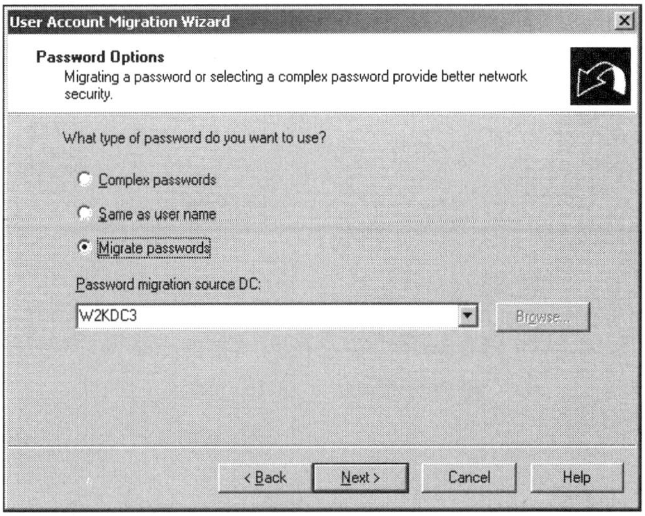

Fig. 13.8. With ADMT, you can either create new passwords for user accounts or migrate the existing passwords

8. In the next window (Fig. 13.9), you can select the state of both source and target accounts, as well as enable/disable SID migration. (The default settings are shown; they do not require any special comments.) If you have chosen to migrate SIDs to the target domain, you must provide credentials of a user with appropriate privileges in the following window. This user must have Administrator's rights in both domains. Be careful, since the credentials entered are not verified at the current step!
9. On the next wizard page (Fig. 13.10), you can specify which user options are to be migrated and how ADMT should treat migrating account names. You can enable migration of the groups whose members are involved in the current operation. By default, this option is disabled, and the **Migrate associated user groups** flag is cleared.

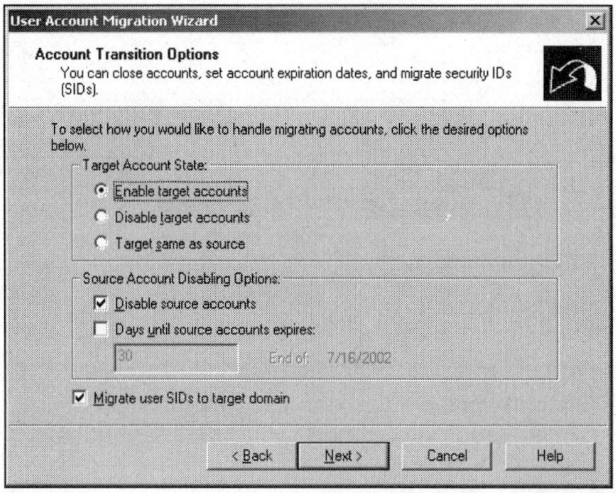

Fig. 13.9. Selecting state of accounts and enabling SID migration

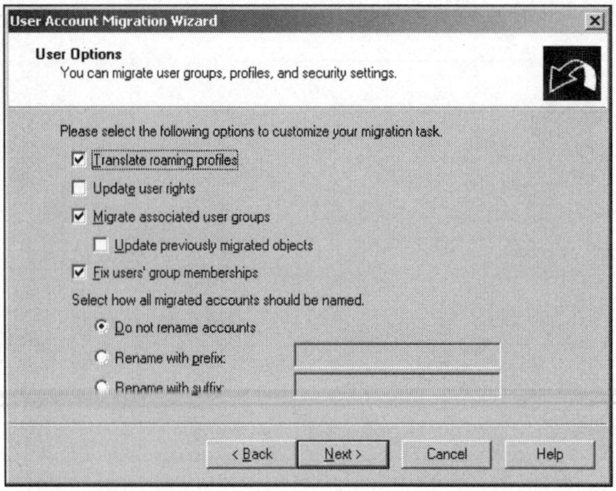

Fig. 13.10. Defining options for migrating accounts

10. In contrast to ClonePrincipal, ADMT 2.0 can migrate *all* Active Directory properties of user, group, and InetOrgPerson objects. Such behavior is defined by default. You can control this process and exclude some properties. Edit the property list on the "Object Property Exclusion" page (Fig. 13.11), or skip this step.
11. In the next window (Fig. 13.12), you should specify what ADMT will do if account name conflicts will occur. In the example shown, a rename option has been selected: if a migrating account name conflicts with an existing name, the new name will be prefixed with "net-" token.

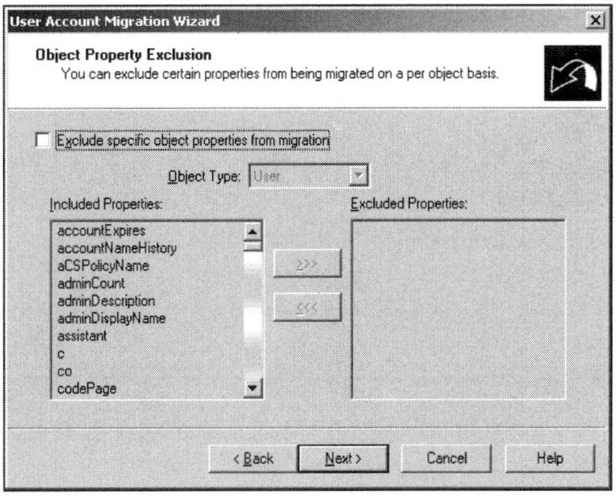

Fig. 13.11. You can exclude some object properties from migration process

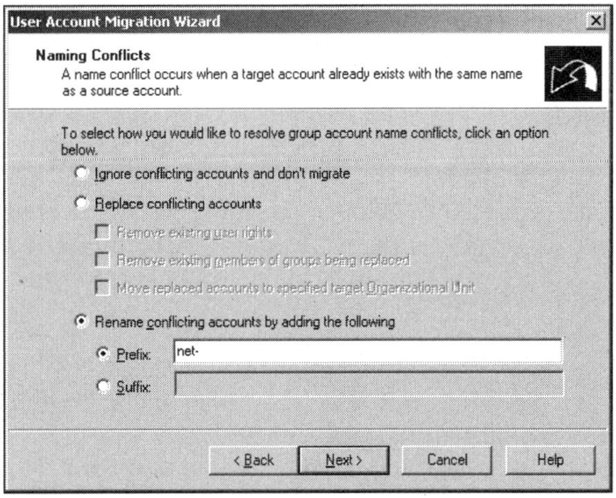

Fig. 13.12. Define ADMT's behavior in the case of name conflicts

12. On the final wizard page, you can review the requested task, revise it (by clicking **Back** and changing settings), and confirm it if all parameters have been set properly. To start the operation, click **Finish**.
13. The migration process is monitored in the **Migration Progress** window (Fig. 13.13). In our example, the operation was completed with non-critical errors. To view all migration events, click **View Log**. The current operation results are written into the *Migration.log* file. The "Migration XXXX.log" files contain the results of previous migration operations.
14. Click **Close** and return to the main ADMT window.

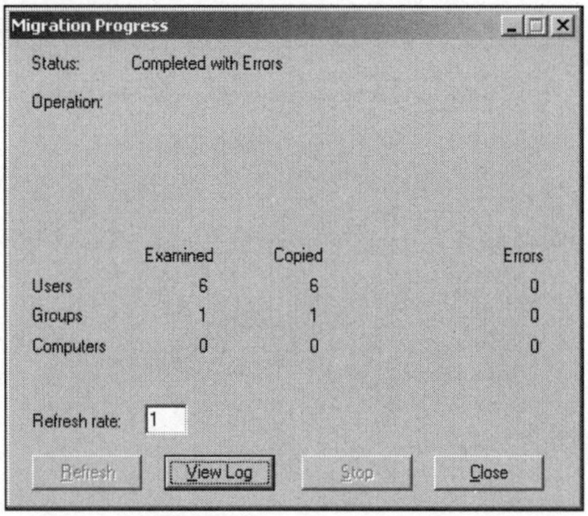

Fig. 13.13. In this window, you can monitor events occurred during migration as well as view the operation results

Security Translation

The Security Translation option will allow you to modify access permissions on various system objects (files and folders, shares, registry, etc.) assigned to the migrated users and groups. These objects reside on computers (including domain controllers) that belong to the source domain.

Let us consider a scenario. Suppose some users and groups have access rights to folders and files located on computers in the source domain. You have migrated these user accounts and want for new users to have the same rights to the source domain resources. Start Security Translation Wizard and select a translation of access rights for just migrated accounts. There are three options:

- **Replace** — new accounts will have the same rights as the accounts in the source domain that lose their access rights.
- **Add** — both accounts from the source domain and their clones (accounts migrated to the target domain) will have the same access rights to a resource on the computers specified.

- **Remove** — neither original accounts nor their clones will have access rights granted earlier to the source domain accounts.

You should specify the computers where the resources are located, and the ADMT agents will be dispatched to them. All agents' activity can be monitored in the **Active Directory Migration Tool Agent Monitor** window (Fig. 13.14) that is opened automatically. On the **Summary** tab, you can watch how the agents start on remote computers.

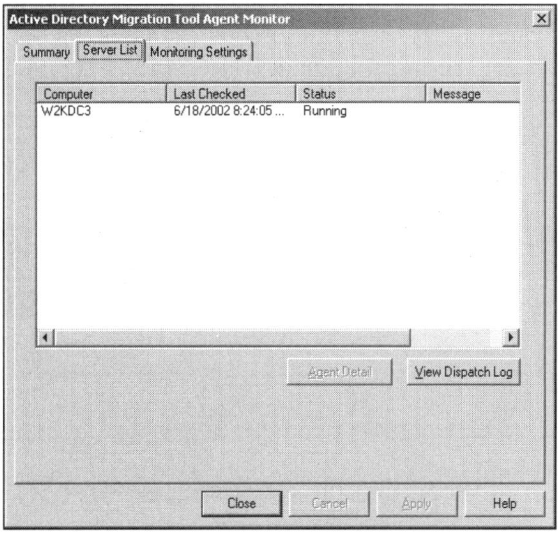

Fig. 13.14. In this window, you can monitor the activity of all agents dispatched to remote computers

When security translation is completed, you can migrate groups and repeat the translation operation for group accounts.

As a result, all migrated users and groups will have the same access rights to all system resources defined for them earlier within the source domain.

Group Mapping and Merging

The Group Mapping and Merging Wizard helps administrators to reorganize groups and can perform the following operations:

- Assign group members' rights to a target group.
- Copy SIDs of selected groups from different source domains to a target group (you can perform this operation manually by using the SIDHist.vbs script).
- Add all users that are members of source groups to a target group.

The last operation should be performed only after migration of all member accounts.

Migrating Domain Trusts

Let us now discuss, with an example, what domain trust migration is. Suppose the NT4DOM domain trusts the W2000 domain. We want to copy this trust relationship to the target domain NET. This means that the NT4DOM domain will also trust the NET domain. (We are considering one-way trusts; however, two-way trust can also be migrated.)

Start the Trust Migration Wizard, and select the source and target domains. Fig. 13.15 shows an ADMT window for our example. As you can see, the selected trust does not exist for the target domain ("No" in the last column).

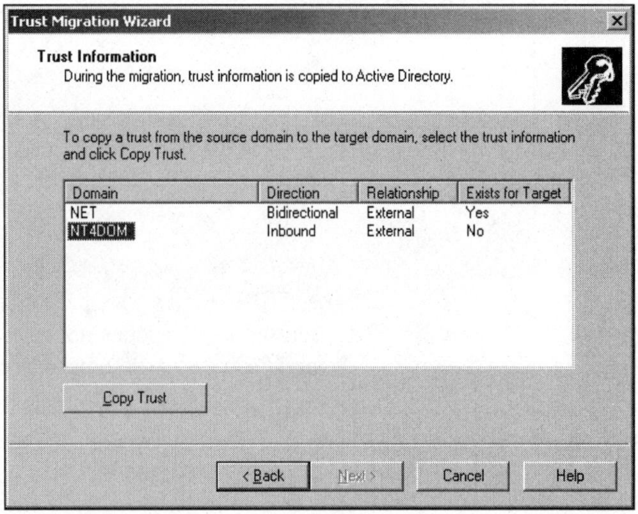

Fig. 13.15. Migrating domain trusts

Click **Copy Trust**. In the following window, enter an administrator's credentials for the trusting domain (NT4DOM) and click **OK**. The new trust will be created, and you will see "Yes" in the **Exists for Target** column.

Overall, this operation is simple and helpful. The operation results (whether or not they are successful) are written into the *trust.log* file.

Chapter 14: Security Tools

This chapter describes the tools related to Active Directory security, and primarily, permissions on directory objects. These tools allow an administrator to perform the following tasks:

- View and/or modify permissions (the ACL lists) on directory objects (ACLDiag, DsACLs) and verify delegation of administrative tasks
- Verify inheritance of ACLs at different levels of the directory object hierarchy and replication of ACLs between domain controllers (SDCheck)
- Verify Kerberos authentication (KerbTray, KList)

ACL Diagnostics (ACLDiag.exe) (ST)

Most often, an administrator views and modifies the security settings (an *Access Control List*, ACL) on an Active Directory object by using the **Security** tab of the object's **Properties** window. This window can be opened from an appropriate administrative snap-in. Sometimes, however, it is more convenient to analyze the ACL lists in a "plain text" form. The *ACLDiag* tool will allow an administrator to view all the information about a directory object's security settings. Any user can run ACLDiag, but the tool's output will depend on the user's rights to view that object (or some other objects).

The ACLDiag's options will be discussed in examples of the following section. (You might prefer to use the DsACLs tool discussed later; it does not have some of the features that ACLDiag does, but it allows ACL modifications and seems to be more reliable.)

Note

It is necessary to note that this tool requires quite a long time to run, especially when the `/geteffective` parameter is specified and produces an output that should usually be redirected to a file.

Viewing All Permissions

ACLDiag can display (in a readable or tab-delimited form) all directly defined or inherited permissions on an Active Directory object, as well as the audit settings. The tool's output is structured to help an administrator to analyze information. Essentially, the tool has two subtests: *Security Diagnosis* (you may skip this by using the `/skip` parameter) and *Effective Rights Diagnosis*. Let us see, for example, in which form ACLDiag displays permissions for an OU. (For clarity, the output section's titles are in bold.)

```
C:\>acldiag "OU=Staff,DC=net,DC=dom"


Security Diagnosis for OU=Staff,DC=net,DC=dom
```

```
Description

          Owner: NET\Domain Admins

          Permissions effective on the object:
                    Allow NT AUTHORITY\Authenticated Users  Read all properties
                    Allow NT AUTHORITY\Authenticated Users  List contents
                    Allow NT AUTHORITY\Authenticated Users  List object
                    Allow NET\Domain Admins Create all subobjects
                    Allow NET\Domain Admins Delete all subobjects
...
Permissions inherited by subobjects:
          Inherit to All Subobjects:
                    Allow BUILTIN\Administrators    Create all subobjects
                    (Inherited permission from DC=net,DC=dom)
                    Allow BUILTIN\Administrators    Read all properties
                    (Inherited permission from DC=net,DC=dom)
...
          Inherit to Group objects only:
...
          Inherit to User objects only:
...
          Inherit to InetOrgPerson objects only:
...

Auditing effective on this object:
                    Audit Successful and Failed Create all subobjects
attempts by \Everyone
                    Audit Successful and Failed Delete all subobjects
attempts by \Everyone
...
Auditing inherited to subobjects:
          Inherit to All Subobjects:
                    Audit Successful and Failed Create all subobjects
attempts by \Everyone
                    Audit Successful and Failed Delete all subobjects
attempts by \Everyone
...
```

Note

As you can see from above, there is a new security principle in Windows .NET — an object type named *inetOrgPerson*. Naturally, you can create objects of that type and assign permissions to them.

Viewing Effective Rights

To view the effective rights for all or some users or groups, use the `/geteffective` parameter. For example, the following command displays rights on an OU for all users and groups. If the rights are not defined directly for a user or group, the corresponding output section will be empty. As you can see, detailed information on each object's permissions is given.

```
C:\>acldiag "OU=Staff,DC=net,DC=dom" /geteffective:* /skip
Security Diagnosis for OU=Staff,DC=net,DC=dom

Effective Rights Diagnosis

NET\Domain Admins:
                Can Modify Membership (via NET\Domain Admins membership)
                All control accesses for class Organizational Unit (via
NET\Domain Admins membership)
                Can List object (via NET\Domain Admins membership)
                Can List contents (via NET\Domain Admins membership)
                Write all properties for class Organizational Unit (via
NET\Domain Admins membership)
                Read all properties for class Organizational Unit (via
NET\Domain Admins membership)
                Delete all subobjects of class Organizational Unit (via
NET\Domain Admins membership)
                Create all subobjects of class Organizational Unit (via
NET\Domain Admins membership)

JSmith@net.dom:
                Can List contents
                Read all properties for class Organizational Unit

NET\Staff-Admins:
                Delete all subobjects of class Organizational Unit (via
NET\Staff-Admins membership)
                Create all subobjects of class Organizational Unit (via
NET\Staff-Admins membership)

NET\Enterprise Admins:
                Can Modify Membership
                All control accesses for class Organizational Unit
```

```
Can List object
Can List contents
Write all properties for class Organizational Unit
Read all properties for class Organizational Unit
Delete all subobjects of class Organizational Unit (via
NET\Enterprise Admins membership)
Create all subobjects of class Organizational Unit
```

Verifying Delegation of Control

ACLDiag allows an administrator to check whether the *Delegation of Control Wizard* has been run for an object, and whether or not this wizard has been run successfully. Let us consider an example. In the following scenario, a user `jsmith@net.dom` and a group `Staff-Admins@net.dom` have received specific administrative rights over the *Staff* OU. (Remember that in Windows .NET, there are 11 common administrative tasks for OU objects; in Windows 2000 — only six tasks.) By using a command similar to the following, you can easily determine who has the delegated rights and which rights these are:

```
C:\>acldiag "OU=Staff,DC=net,DC=dom" /chkdeleg /skip
Security Diagnosis for OU=Staff,DC=net,DC=dom

Delegation Template Diagnosis:

        Create, delete, and manage user accounts allowed to NET\Staff-Admins
                Status: OK
                Applies on this object: YES
                Inherited from parent: NO

        Reset user passwords and force password change at next logon
        allowed to JSmith@net.dom
                Status: OK
                Applies on this object: YES
                Inherited from parent: NO

        Read all user information allowed to JSmith@net.dom
                Status: OK
                Applies on this object: YES
                Inherited from parent: NO

        Create, delete and manage groups allowed to NET\Staff-Admins
```

```
        Status: MISCONFIGURED
        Applies on this object: YES
        Inherited from parent: NO

Modify the membership of a group
        Status: NOT PRESENT

Manage Group Policy links allowed to NET\Staff-Admins
        Status: OK
        Applies on this object: YES
        Inherited from parent: NO

Generate Resultant Set of Policy (Planning)
        Status: NOT PRESENT

Generate Resultant Set of Policy (Logging)
        Status: NOT PRESENT

Create, delete, and manage inetOrgPerson accounts
        Status: NOT PRESENT

Reset inetOrgPerson passwords and force password change at next
logon allowed to JSmith@net.dom
        Status: OK
        Applies on this object: YES
        Inherited from parent: NO

Read all inetOrgPerson information
        Status: NOT PRESENT
```

Notice that if a common task has not been delegated, the tool reports `Status` as `NOT PRESENT`. As you can see, one task's status is `MISCONFIGURED`. (In this case, one of the ACEs composing that administrative task has been deleted.) If the `/fixdeleg` parameter cannot fix the problem, you should run the Delegation of Control Wizard again. You may also run the DsACLs.exe utility with the `/S` parameter, which resets all permissions on the object to schema defaults. (Use this option with caution! See the *"Restoring Security Settings"* section in this chapter.)

To fix delegated control settings, use the following command:

```
C:\>acldiag "OU=Staff,DC=net,DC=dom" /chkdeleg /fixdeleg /skip
```

The command verifies all permissions, and if some permission is missed, the program asks if you want to fix the problem; for example:

```
Create, delete and manage groups allowed to NET\Staff-Admins
        Status: MISCONFIGURED
        Applies on this object: YES
        Inherited from parent: NO

        Do you want to fix this delegation? (y/n) y
```

Comparisons with Schema Default Permissions

To verify whether an Active Directory object retains all the permissions that were set at the moment of its creation, use a command similar the following:

```
C:\>acldiag "OU=Staff,DC=net,DC=dom" /schema /skip

Security Diagnosis for OU=Staff,DC=net,DC=dom

Schema Defaults Diagnosis
        Schema defaults: Present
        Obtained            : At CREATION
```

In the case shown, the tool reports that the object kept all permissions assigned upon its creation. If some permission has been removed, the tool displays the message

```
Schema defaults: Partial
```

To see the default (schema) permissions on a directory object, you should refer to the Schema partition. For an OU object, use a command similar to the following:

```
C:\>acldiag "CN=Organizational-Unit,CN=Schema,CN=Configuration,
 ↳ DC=net,DC=dom"
```

DsACLs (DsACLs.exe) (ST)

In contrast to ACLDiag, the *DsACLs* command-line tool allows an administrator to both view and modify the ACL lists of directory objects, i.e., to carry out all operations available on the **Security** tab in the object's **Properties** window. (For directory objects, DsACLs does a job similar to what the CACLs.exe utility does for file system objects.) Modifying security descriptors may require a good understanding of Active Directory objects' security model, especially inheritance of permissions.

DsACLs is quite well documented, so we will only consider a few examples.

Note

The DsACLs' parameters are case-sensitive and all letters must be upper case.

Viewing Security Settings

You can analyze the following screen output and decide what tool — DsACLs or ACLDiag — is more convenient for you to use when viewing security descriptors of directory objects. (The former command works faster, but it is not as comprehensive as the latter. Notice, for example, the lines related to the *Domain Admins* group in both commands' output. Perhaps, you yourself want to select an object and compare the *complete* outputs.) When the `/A` parameter is specified, the owner and auditing information is also displayed. In the audit list, "All" means that an audit is performed for both *Successful* and *Failed* events.

```
C:\>dsacls OU=Staff,DC=net,DC=dom /A
Owner: NET\Domain Admins
Group: NET\Domain Users

Audit list:
Effective Permissions on this object are:
All     Everyone  SPECIAL ACCESS   <Inherited from parent>
                  DELETE
                  WRITE PERMISSIONS
...
Permissions inherited to subobjects are:
Inherited to all subobjects
All     Everyone  SPECIAL ACCESS   <Inherited from parent>
                  DELETE
                  WRITE PERMISSIONS
...
Access list:
Effective Permissions on this object are:
Allow NT AUTHORITY\Authenticated Users          SPECIAL ACCESS
                                                READ PERMISSONS
...
Allow NET\Domain Admins                         FULL CONTROL
Allow NT AUTHORITY\ENTERPRISE DOMAIN CONTROLLERS SPECIAL ACCESS
                                                READ PERMISSONS
```

```
...
Allow NT AUTHORITY\SYSTEM                    FULL CONTROL
Allow BUILTIN\Administrators                 SPECIAL ACCESS
<Inherited from parent>
                                             DELETE
                                             READ PERMISSONS
...
Permissions inherited to subobjects are:
Inherited to all subobjects
Allow BUILTIN\Administrators                 SPECIAL ACCESS
<Inherited from parent>
                                             DELETE
                                             READ PERMISSONS
...
Inherited to computer
...
Inherited to group
...
Inherited to user
...
Inherited to inetOrgPerson
...
The command completed successfully
```

Granting and Removing Permissions

Let us now consider a couple of examples of how to modify security descriptors. The first command grants the user `jsmith@net.dom` the *Generic Read* right (List Contents, Read All Properties, and Read Permissions) for all objects in (and including) the `Staff` OU:

```
C:\>dsacls OU=Staff,DC=net,DC=dom /G jsmith@net.dom:GR /I:T
```

You may verify the result of the operation with all possible (and already mentioned) means.

The second command prevents the user from reading two properties of the OU object:

```
C:\>dsacls OU=Staff,DC=net,DC=dom /D jsmith@net.dom:RP;gPLink
↳ jsmith@net.dom:RP;gPOptions
```

Attention

- The attribute names in the last command are case-sensitive. You can specify any applicable number of attributes in the same command.

Restoring Security Settings

For various reasons, you may want to return an object's security settings to their initial (default) state. The default settings for an object class are defined in the Active Directory schema. (In addition, the settings inherited from the parents are also applied to the object.) For example, the following command restores defaults for an OU object:

```
C:\>dsacls OU=Staff,DC=net,DC=dom /S
```

(You can also use the `/T` parameter and restore the defaults on the entire tree of objects.)

If the operation was successful, the `acldiag <objectName> /schema /skip` command will report the following:

```
Schema Defaults Diagnosis
        Schema defaults: Present
        Obtained            : At CREATION
```

Be cautious; the `dsacls /S` command deletes the audit settings from the object. The command

```
C:\>dsacls OU=Staff,DC=net,DC=dom /A
```

will display the following message:

```
Audit list:
{This object is protected from inheriting permissions from the parent}
THERE ARE NO ACCESS CONTROL ENTRIES
...
```

To restore the default audit settings, open the object's **Properties** window (in the **Active Directory Users and Computers** or **ADSI Edit** snap-in), click the **Security** tab, and then **Advanced**. In the **Auditing** tab in the **Access Control Settings** window, check the **Allow inheritable auditing entries from parent to propagate to this object** box, and click **Apply**. Click **OK** in the warning pop-up window and close all opened windows.

Caution

- If you do not restore the audit settings after the `dsacls /S` command, the Windows 2000 version of ACLDiag command with the `/chkdeleg` or `/schema` parameters will fail. The Windows .NET version works properly.

Kerberos Tray (KerbTray.exe) (RK)

The *Kerberos Tray* tool lists all cached Kerberos tickets and allows you to view the tickets' properties as well as to purge tickets. This information may help in resolving problems with authentication and access to network resources. (If an AD-based computer has not obtained the initial ticket-granting-ticket (TGT) from a *Kerberos Distribution Center* (KCC) during the first logging on to the domain, or if the cached tickets have expired and haven't been renewed, the computer won't be authenticated to access the resources.) For Kerberos authentication to be performed successfully, you should ensure that all computers have time settings synchronized with a common time service (within five minutes of delta).

The tool starts in minimized mode, and you can find its icon on the system tray (in the right bottom corner of the screen). If you move the mouse cursor over the icon, the time left on the initial TGT will be displayed (Fig. 14.1; left).

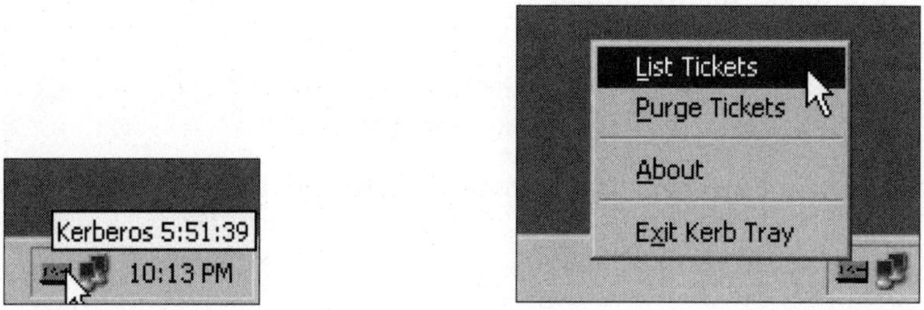

Fig. 14.1. The Kerberos Tray tool displays the time left on the initial TGT before it expires (left); the tool's context menu (right) allows you to select an operation

If you double-click the icon or select the **List Tickets** command from the context menu (Fig. 14.1; right), the main tool's window will appear (Fig. 14.2). It displays all cached Kerberos tickets acquired upon/since the first user's logon.

The **Purge Tickets** command clears the entire ticket cache (thus, KerbTray differs from the *Kerberos List* tool, which is able to delete tickets selectively). No warnings are issued before clearing the cache, so be cautious! While the cache is empty, you may be prevented from being authenticated to resources, and a logoff/logon operation will be required.

Note

The utility's window is not updateable. Therefore, if you believe that new tickets might appear (while connecting to a new resource or new services), close the window and open it again.

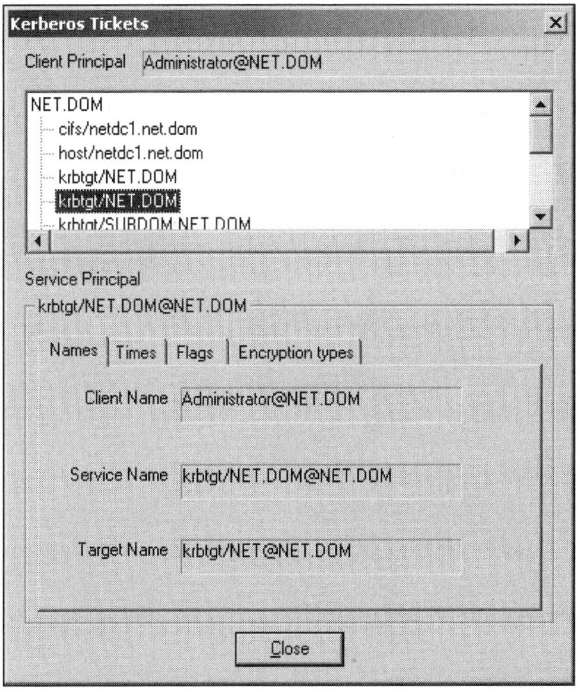

Fig. 14.2. In this window, you can see the information about all cached tickets and their properties

Let us discuss the main ticket's properties, which are displayed by the tool.

- The **Client Principal** field contains the name of the current logon account. If the ticket cache is empty, this field displays the "No network credentials" message.
- All tickets obtained since logon are listed in the scrolling window. The properties of the selected ticket are displayed on the tabs below.
- The strings below the scrolling list contain the name of a security principal for the selected ticket. If the ticket time is over, the "Expired" string is displayed and no properties are shown on the tabs.
- The **Names** tab contains:
  - **Client Name** — requestor of the ticket. In most cases (while accessing resources in the current domain) this is the same name that is displayed in the **Client Principal** field.
  - **Service Name** — the security principal (account) name for the service. The *samAccountName* attribute of the account's directory object stores this name.

- **Target Name** — one of the service names contained in the multi-valued *servicePrincipalName* attribute of the computer's directory object. This is the service name the ticket has been obtained for.

- The time when the ticket was obtained (**Start time**) and its expiration time (**End time**) are shown on the **Times** tab. Interpretation of the **Flags** tab requires a more profound understanding of Kerberos protocol. The **Initial** flag is set only for the ticket that was obtained without the TGT.

Kerberos List (KList.exe) (RK)

This command-line tool has practically the same possibilities and features as the *Kerberos Tray* tool described earlier. This tool has the following commands:

- `klist tgt` displays the initial TGT.
- `klist tickets` lists all cached tickets.
- `klist purge` allows you to delete a specific ticket in a dialog.

Here is an example of such a dialog:

```
C:\>klist purge
Cached Tickets: (10)

   Server: krbtgt/SUBDOM.NET.DOM@NET.DOM
      KerbTicket Encryption Type: RSADSI RC4-HMAC(NT)
      End Time: 6/12/2002 1:33:40
      Renew Time: 6/18/2002 15:33:40

Purge? (y/n) : y
        Deleting ticket:
           ServerName = krbtgt/SUBDOM.NET.DOM (cb=42)
           RealmName  = NET.DOM (cb=14)
Submit Buffer size = 84
        Ticket purged!
```

You must answer "yes" or "no" for each ticket.

If the client has no cached tickets, the tool returns the "Cached Tickets: (0)" message.

Security Descriptor Check Utility (SDCheck.exe) (ST)

The *SDCheck* command-line tool is primarily intended to help administrators verify and monitor the following issues related to directory objects' security descriptors:

- Propagation of inherited ACLs for a specified directory object
- Replication of ACLs between different domain controllers

Let us consider how to fulfill these tasks using the following sample output. In this scenario, we will test the ACLs of a user object (`Alice@net.dom`) that belongs to a nested OU. (A domain controller must also be specified in the command.) Some lines, as well as the comments placed in the text below these lines, are shown in bold.

```
C:\>sdcheck netdc1.net.dom Alice@net.dom
Security Descriptor Check Utility - build(3621)

Input:  Alice@net.dom
Object: CN=Alice,OU=Marketing,OU=Staff,DC=net,DC=dom
Domain: net.dom
Domain: DC=net,DC=dom
Server: netdc1.net.dom

*** Warning: No values returned for dSCorePropagationData on
DC=net,DC=dom

Object:   CN=Alice,OU=Marketing,OU=Staff,DC=net,DC=dom
Classes:  top person organizationalPerson user
SD:       2060 bytes
Metadata: 06/13/2002 20:26:22 @ netdc4.net.dom ver: 3
History:  06/13/2002 20:28:43 flags(0x1) SD propagation
          06/13/2002 20:36:08 flags(0x1) SD propagation
          06/13/2002 20:49:29 flags(0x1) SD propagation
          06/13/2002 20:51:06 flags(0x1) SD propagation
[By viewing metadata on different DCs, an administrator can monitor the
replication of the changed security descriptor. For example, you can
note that the version number on another DC differs from the version
shown, and that another DC has originated the changes. To view the
replication metadata, you can also use the repadmin /showmeta command.]

  Object:   OU=Marketing,OU=Staff,DC=net,DC=dom
  Classes:  top organizationalUnit
```

```
SD:       1332 bytes
Metadata: 06/13/2002 20:20:41 @ netdc1.net.dom ver: 3
History:  06/13/2002 20:28:43 flags(0x1) SD propagation
          06/13/2002 20:36:08 flags(0x1) SD propagation
          06/13/2002 20:49:29 flags(0x1) SD propagation
          06/13/2002 20:51:06 flags(0x1) SD propagation

  Object:   OU=Staff,DC=net,DC=dom
  Classes:  top organizationalUnit
  SD:       1332 bytes
  Metadata: 06/13/2002 20:51:06 @ netdc1.net.dom ver: 6
  History:  06/13/2002 20:22:10 flags(0x1) SD propagation
            06/13/2002 20:49:29 flags(0x1) SD propagation
```

[Take note of the lines within the object's history. This information helps an administrator to trace changes and determine their originating container. For example, the changes made at the Staff OU level at 30:51:06 have been successfully propagated to all child objects including Alice's user object. At 20:49:29, the domain security descriptor has been changed, and the changes have been extended through the entire domain. If the time values are different at some levels, the inheritance might be blocked and this fact should be tested.]

```
    Object:   DC=net,DC=dom
    Classes:  top domain domainDNS
    SD:       1400 bytes
    Metadata: 06/13/2002 20:49:29 @ netdc1.net.dom ver: 4
```

Checking ACL inheritance ... **[This test will display the ACL inheritance errors at any level if such an error has been found.]**

```
        Parent: 3 - DC=net,DC=dom
        Child:  2 - OU=Staff,DC=net,DC=dom
*** OK

Checking ACL inheritance ...
        Parent: 2 - OU=Staff,DC=net,DC=dom
        Child:  1 - OU=Marketing,OU=Staff,DC=net,DC=dom
*** OK

Checking ACL inheritance ...
        Parent: 1 - OU=Marketing,OU=Staff,DC=net,DC=dom
        Child:  0 - CN=Alice,OU=Marketing,OU=Staff,DC=net,DC=dom
*** OK
```

The output shown is an example of a successful test.

To verify the "continuity" of the inherited ACLs, use the `-debug` parameter. Suppose, in our example, that propagation of ACLs is blocked at the Marketing OU level. This means that the **Inherit from parent the permission entries that apply to child objects** checkbox on the **Permissions** tab in the **Advanced Security Settings** window has been cleared. To see this window, open the Marketing's **Properties** window and click **Advanced** on the **Security** tab. (In Windows 2000, the **Allow inheritable permissions from parent to propagate to this object** checkbox on the **Security** tab is used for that purpose.)

In our case, you can quickly diagnose whether an inheritance is blocked or not by using the command:

```
C:\>sdcheck netdc1.net.dom Alice@net.dom -debug
```

At a specific moment, the tool outputs a warning:

```
...
Checking ACL inheritance ...
        Parent: 2 - OU=Staff,DC=net,DC=dom
        Child:  1 - OU=Marketing,OU=Staff,DC=net,DC=dom
*** Warning: Child has SE_DACL_PROTECTED set, therefore doesn't inherit
- skipping test
*** OK
...
```

If the ACL inheritance is not blocked, the test will run without any warnings.

Chapter 15: Group Policy Tools

On Windows 2000 systems, an administrator has only two tools — GPResult and GPOTool — that can help him or her to troubleshoot group policies by analyzing the effect that a group policy object (GPO) produces on a computer and/or user as well as by verifying the "health" of GPOs and their replication between domain controllers in a domain. These tools are included in the *Windows 2000 Server Resource Kit* or can be downloaded through the Internet.

Windows XP and Windows .NET systems offer GPResult as a standard built-in tool that fulfills some options of the *Resultant Set of Policy* (RSoP) technology. In addition, these systems include a GUI tool with similar functions — the **Resultant Set of Policy** snap-in that allows administrators to analyze group policy settings for existing users and computers as well as to simulate (plan) these settings for any user and computer objects stored in Active Directory.

Group Policy Results (GPResult.exe) (SYS)

GPResult is a very powerful, and at the same time, a rather simple instrument that allows an administrator to manage and troubleshoot issues related to *Change and Configuration Management* and implemented through group policies (registry and software settings, disk quotas, folder redirection, IP security, and scripts). The tool's screen output may be enormous and laden with details. (As a rule, you should redirect it to a file for successive analysis, or use the `more` pipe.) This shouldn't frighten you too much, since the tool is pretty well documented, and its results are, in fact, quite simple to interpret.

The Windows 2000 version of GPResult can only be run on the current computer for the currently logged-on user. (You cannot use the *RunAs* command with GPResult.) You can also run GPResult on a remote computer by using a *telnet* session.

The Windows XP/.NET version of GPResult (v2.0) can be targeted to any domain client computer and any domain user. (GPResult works in the *logging mode* only. This means that the user must log on to the target computer at least once before GPResult will be executed and the computer must be online!). See, for example, the following command:

```
C:\>gpresult /S xp-pro3.net.dom /SCOPE USER /USER JSmith /V
```

This command displays detailed information on the group policy settings that are applied (or will be applied) to the user *JSmith* on the *xp-pro3.net.dom* computer.

In this chapter, we will discuss GPResult v2.0 — the most powerful and flexible version; however, both versions (Windows 2000 and Windows .NET) are rather similar if one compares their output information.

Note

If a GPO is created and linked to a container, but not yet configured (i.e., has the version 0:0; see the *GPOTool*'s description below), it will be "invisible" to GPResult, even if the group policies linked to that container must affect (directly or by inheritance) the user or computer.

Note

For Windows 2000 systems, you can download a free copy of GPResult.exe from the Microsoft website (see links in *Appendix A*).

Note

You can run the Windows 2000 version of GPResult on Windows XP/.NET-based computers.

Note

Keep in mind that Windows XP and Windows .NET systems have *different* versions of GPResult, though they have the same options.

General Structure of the Tests

The best way to get acquainted with GPResult is to view a brief description of sample output from the tool. Let us first look at the general structure of the full test. GPResult displays the following information:

- Date and time when the test was run
- Information on the operating system where the test was run
- Information on the *computer* for which the RSoP data is displayed (this information is omitted if the `/SCOPE USER` parameter is specified)
  - Date and time when the computer policy was last applied
  - Settings received by the computer
  - Computer's security group membership
- Information on the *user* for which the RSoP data is displayed (this information is omitted if the `/SCOPE COMPUTER` parameter is specified)
  - Date and time when the user policy was last applied
  - Settings received by the user
  - User's security group membership

The tool has three operational modes:

- **Normal** — displays general information only (described above). You may use this mode to verify whether or not the user or computer has received settings from a particular GPO that you are interested in, or to find out which GPOs affect the user or computer.

- **Verbose** — the basic mode to view detailed information (for example, exact policy settings assigned in a specific GPO).
- **Super-verbose** — a special mode for thorough analysis (for example, this mode allows you to see whether the same policy was assigned at several levels in the GPO hierarchy; if a policy was assigned in two or more GPOs, then other modes will display only the name of a GPO with the highest precedence).

Description of Tests

Let us discuss a sample output, which GPResult has produced in verbose mode. The comments divide the output into logical sections. For presentation purposes, some lines and words are shown in bold. Comments in bold square brackets have also been inserted.

Since the computer account is in another domain, an administrator's credentials are provided in the command.

```
C:\>gpresult /S xp-pro3.subdom.net.dom /USER JSmith
↳ /U SUBDOM\administrator /P admPsw /Z
Microsoft (R) Windows (R) Operating System Group Policy Result tool v2.0
Copyright (C) Microsoft Corp. 1981-2001
```

The date when the test was run:

```
Created On 6/20/2002 at 7:27:21 PM
```

The target system information:

```
RSOP data for NET\jsmith on XP-PRO3 : Logging Mode
--------------------------------------------------
OS Type:                     Microsoft Windows XP Professional
OS Configuration:            Member Workstation
OS Version:                  5.1.2600
Terminal Server Mode:        Remote Administration
Site Name:                   NET-Site
Roaming Profile:             \\NETDC1\Profiles\JSmith
Local Profile:               I:\Documents and Settings\jsmith.NET
Connected over a slow link?: No
```

The general information on the computer account:

```
COMPUTER SETTINGS
------------------
    CN=XP-PRO3,OU=Staff,DC=subdom,DC=net,DC=dom
```

```
Last time Group Policy was applied: 6/20/2002 at 7:24:48 PM
Group Policy was applied from:      netdc2.subdom.net.dom
Group Policy slow link threshold:   500 kbps
Domain Name:                        SUBDOM
Domain Type:                        Windows 2000
```

Group policies from the following GPOs have been applied to the computer:

```
Applied Group Policy Objects
-----------------------------
    Default Domain Policy
    NET-Site's GPO
```

The following GPO does not contain any settings for computer accounts, therefore it has not been applied:

```
The following GPOs were not applied because they were filtered out
-------------------------------------------------------------------
    Local Group Policy
        Filtering:  Not Applied (Empty)
```

The computer account's group membership:

```
The computer is a part of the following security groups:
---------------------------------------------------------
    BUILTIN\Administrators
    Everyone
    BUILTIN\Users
    XP-PRO3$
    Domain Computers
    NT AUTHORITY\NETWORK
    NT AUTHORITY\Authenticated Users
```

Exact policies applied to the computer account:

```
Resultant Set Of Policies for Computer:
----------------------------------------
    Software Installations
    ----------------------
        N/A  [this means that the GPOs that affect this computer
             account do not contain policy settings of that kind]
    Startup Scripts
  ---------------
      GPO: Default Domain Policy
          Name:          Up.vbs
```

```
        Parameters:
        LastExecuted: 2:28:49 PM
Shutdown Scripts
----------------
    N/A
Account Policies
----------------
    GPO: Default Domain Policy  [account policies can be defined
                                 at the domain level only]
        Policy:             MinimumPasswordAge
        Computer Setting:   N/A
    GPO: Default Domain Policy
        Policy:             PasswordHistorySize
        Computer Setting:   3
    GPO: Default Domain Policy
        Policy:             MinimumPasswordLength
        Computer Setting:   N/A
    GPO: Default Domain Policy
        Policy:             LockoutBadCount
        Computer Setting:   N/A
    GPO: Default Domain Policy
        Policy:             MaximumPasswordAge
        Computer Setting:   42
Audit Policy
------------
    N/A
User Rights
-----------
    N/A
Security Options
----------------
    GPO: Default Domain Policy
        Policy:             RequireLogonToChangePassword
        Computer Setting:   Not Enabled
    GPO: Default Domain Policy
        Policy:             PasswordComplexity
        Computer Setting:   Not Enabled
    GPO: Default Domain Policy
        Policy:             ForceLogoffWhenHourExpire
        Computer Setting:   Not Enabled
```

```
    GPO: Default Domain Policy
        Policy:              ClearTextPassword
        Computer Setting:    Not Enabled
Event Log Settings
------------------
    N/A
Restricted Groups
-----------------
    N/A
System Services
---------------
    N/A
Registry Settings
-----------------
    N/A
File System Settings
--------------------
    N/A
Public Key Policies
-------------------
    N/A
```

Registry-based policies applied to the computer; as you can see, these policies come from different GPOs. All such policies are located in the `HKEY_LOCAL_MACHINE` registry branch.

```
Administrative Templates
------------------------
    GPO: Default Domain Policy
        KeyName:      Software\Policies\Microsoft\Windows NT\
                      ➥Printers\PublishPrinters
        Value:        1, 0, 0, 0
        State:        Enabled
    GPO: NET-Site's GPO
        KeyName:      Software\Policies\Microsoft\Windows\
                      ➥System\DeleteRoamingCache
        Value:        1, 0, 0, 0
        State:        Enabled
    GPO: NET-Site's GPO
        KeyName:      Software\Policies\Microsoft\Netlogon\
                      ➥Parameters\SiteName
```

```
        Value:          78, 0, 69, 0, 84, 0, 45, 0, 83, 0, 105, 0,
                        ↳116, 0, 101, 0, 0, 0
        State:          Enabled
    GPO: Default Domain Policy
        KeyName:        Software\Policies\Microsoft\Windows NT\
                        ↳Reliability\ShutdownReasonUI
        State:          disabled
```

The information for the user account is structured in the same way as for the computer; general information for the user account:

```
USER SETTINGS
--------------
    Last time Group Policy was applied: 6/20/2002 at 6:45:00 PM
    Group Policy was applied from:      N/A
    Group Policy slow link threshold:   500 kbps
    Domain Name:                        NET
    Domain Type:                        Windows 2000
```

Notice that the user account is located in one domain (*NET*), whereas the computer account belongs to another domain (*SUBDOM*). Therefore, the user and computer get policies from different domain controllers. However, since both domains are placed in the same site (*NET-Site*), both the user and computer receive the settings from a GPO linked to that site.

The list of applied and non-applied GPOs:

```
    Applied Group Policy Objects
    -----------------------------
        Marketing's GPO
        Staff's GPO
        Default Domain Policy
        NET-Site's GPO

    The following GPOs were not applied because they were filtered out
    -------------------------------------------------------------------
        Local Group Policy
            Filtering:  Not Applied (Empty)

    The user is a part of the following security groups:
    ----------------------------------------------------
        Everyone
        BUILTIN\Users
        GlobalGroup
        LOCAL
        NT AUTHORITY\INTERACTIVE
```

```
        NT AUTHORITY\Authenticated Users

    The user has the following security privileges:
    ------------------------------------------------
        Bypass traverse checking
        Shut down the system
        Remove computer from docking station
```

Below, all settings (divided by type) that the user has been received are listed in detail.

```
    Resultant Set Of Policies for User:
    ------------------------------------
        Software Installations
        ----------------------
            N/A
```

The scripts defined are followed below. Notice that if the script is located in the default folder (...*policyGUIDName*\USER\Scripts\Logon), only the script's name is displayed. However, if a script is stored in a shared folder, you can specify a UNC name for that script.

```
        Logon Scripts
        -------------
            GPO: Default Domain Policy
                Name:         Welcome.vbs
                Parameters:
                LastExecuted: 3:26:45 PM

        Logoff Scripts
        --------------
        Public Key Policies
        -------------------
            N/A
```

For each policy applied, a corresponding registry value and data are specified. You can see all these values by using Regedit.exe; they are placed in the `HKEY_CURRENT_USER` branch.

```
        Administrative Templates
        ------------------------
            GPO: NET-Site's GPO
                KeyName:      Software\Policies\Microsoft\Windows NT\
                              ↪SharedFolders\PublishSharedFolders
                Value:        1, 0, 0, 0
```

```
        State:       Enabled
    GPO: Marketing's GPO
        KeyName:     Software\Microsoft\Windows\CurrentVersion\
                     ↳Policies\Explorer\NoSMMyDocs
        Value:       1, 0, 0, 0
        State:       Enabled
    GPO: Default Domain Policy
        KeyName:     Software\Microsoft\Windows\CurrentVersion\
                     ↳Policies\Explorer\NoRun
        Value:       1, 0, 0, 0
        State:       Enabled
    GPO: Marketing's GPO
        KeyName:     Software\Microsoft\Windows\CurrentVersion\
                     ↳Policies\Explorer\NoWindowsUpdate
        Value:       1, 0, 0, 0
        State:       Enabled
    GPO: Staff's GPO
        KeyName:     Software\Microsoft\Windows\CurrentVersion\
                     ↳Policies\Explorer\NoDesktop
        Value:       1, 0, 0, 0
        State:       Enabled
    GPO: Marketing's GPO
        KeyName:     Software\Microsoft\Windows\CurrentVersion\
                     ↳Policies\Explorer\NoStartMenuSubFolders
        Value:       1, 0, 0, 0
        State:       Enabled
Folder Redirection
------------------
    N/A
Internet Explorer Browser User Interface
----------------------------------------
    N/A
Internet Explorer Connection
----------------------------
    N/A
Internet Explorer URLs
----------------------
    N/A
Internet Explorer Security
--------------------------
    N/A
```

```
Internet Explorer Programs
--------------------------
    N/A
```

In order to find policies' names settled in the **Group Policy** snap-in that correspond registry settings displayed in GPResult output data, an administrator can use the *Group Policy Reference* from the *Windows 2000 Server Resource Kit* documentation or follow the web link **http://msdn.microsoft.com/library/default.asp?url=/library/en-us/gp/GPRef.asp?frame=true**.

You can find additional information on GPResult in the *Help and Support Center* or in the *Windows 2000 Resource Kit Tools* documentation.

Group Policy Verification Tool (GPOTool.exe) (RK)

Group Policy Verification Tool allows you to:

- Check the internal consistency of the specified or all group policy objects that are stored on the selected domain controller or all DCs. These DCs can be located in the current or specified domain. The tool verifies both the directory service and SYSVOL parts of each GPO.
- Check replication of GPOs by comparing replicas (instances) of each GPO on different domain controllers.

The tool can be run with any credentials on any domain computer.

Note

The *policy* and *group policy object* (GPO) terms are used as synonyms in this section. Remember that each GPO has a *directory service part* that is stored in Active Directory and a *SYSVOL part* that is stored in the system volume (SYSVOL) on the disk.

Note

The `/new` and `/del` parameters described in the *Windows 2000 Resource Kit Tools* help file are not realized in the released version of the tool.

Note

You can download a free copy of GPOTool.exe from the Microsoft website (see links in *Appendix A*).

General Tests

By default, *all* policies on *all* domain controllers in the current user's domain are tested. If some DCs are offline, their names will not be listed in the "Available DCs" section (they will be shown as "down" only in verbose mode). Here is an example of the tool's resulting output:

```
C:\>gpotool
Validating DCs...
Available DCs:
netdc1.net.dom
netdc4.net.dom
Searching for policies...
Found 5 policies
============================================================
Policy {31B2F340-016D-11D2-945F-00C04FB984F9}
Policy OK
============================================================
Policy {64C49D93-BBB7-410E-B999-837B5B90422B}
Policy OK
...

Policies OK
```

If a corrupted policy is found, it is displayed in *verbose* mode (see below) and the "Errors found" line appears at the end of the tool's output.

Note

A unique name (e.g., `{31B2F340-016D-11D2-945F-00C04FB984F9}`) is displayed for each policy (and extension) in the tool's output. This name is the policy's *cn* attribute rather than the *GUID of the object* that stores the directory part of the policy in Active Directory. (The braces are included in the policy name.) Remember that you can bind to a directory object only by using its GUID or distinguished name, not a "naming" attribute (*cn*, *displayName*, etc.).

It is possible to specify a testing domain different from the user's logon domain by using the `/domain` parameter. Also, you can specify one or more domain controllers that will be tested with the `/dc` parameter. To test only one or a certain set of policies, use the `/gpo` parameter with the policies' unique names (*cn*) or *friendly* names. Note that all names must be separated with comma (,) and specified without spaces.

Detailed Information about the Policies

More detailed information can be obtained from the tool by using the `/verbose` parameter. Since the output can be very large, redirect it into a file for subsequent lookup. An example of the resulting output in verbose mode is shown below (the comments are in bold square brackets).

```
C:\>gpotool /verbose
Domain: net.dom
Validating DCs...
netdc1.net.dom: OK
netdc4.net.dom: down                    [one DC in the domain is down]
Available DCs:
netdc1.net.dom
Searching for policies...
Found 6 policies
============================================================
Policy {31B2F340-016D-11D2-945F-00C04FB984F9}
Policy OK
Details:
------------------------------------------------------------
DC: netdc1.net.dom       [information on the policy is displayed
individually for each DC that stores this policy (GPO)]
Friendly name: Default Domain Policy    [this is the value of the
displayName attribute of the policy's object in Active Directory]
Created: 5/12/2002 1:22:08 PM
Changed: 6/15/2002 6:09:41 PM
DS version:      15(user) 28(machine)
Sysvol version: 15(user) 28(machine)   [SYSVOL version must correspond to
directory service (DS) version]
Flags: 0                               [see Notes below]
User extensions: [{3060E8D0-7020-11D2-842D-00C04FA372D4}{3060E8CE-7020-
11D2-842D-00C04FA372D4}]
Machine extensions: [{35378EAC-683F-11D2-A89A-00C04FBBCFA2}{0F6B957D-
509E-11D1-A7CC-0000F87571E3}{53D6AB1B-2488-11D1-A28C-
00C04FB94F17}][{827D319E-6EAC-11D2-A4EA-00C04F79F83A}{803E14A0-B4FB-
11D0-A0D0-00A0C90F574B}][{B1BE8D72-6EAC-11D2-A4EA-
00C04F79F83A}{53D6AB1B-2488-11D1-A28C-00C04FB94F17}]     [The extension
name is enclosed in square brackets. Here are three extension names
displayed]
```

```
Functionality version: 2                      [must be 2 or higher]
------------------------------------------------------------
------------------------------------------------------------
DC: netdc4.net.dom
Friendly name: Default Domain Policy     [the same GPO stored on another DC]
...
============================================================
...
...
============================================================
Policy {D6ECB136-92B4-484C-AF84-5697050BA978}
Policy OK
Details:
------------------------------------------------------------
DC: netdc1.net.dom
Friendly name: NET-Site's GPO
Created: 5/19/2002 12:53:31 PM
Changed: 6/19/2002 12:54:22 PM
DS version:     0(user) 2(machine)              [see Notes below]
Sysvol version: 0(user) 2(machine)
Flags: 0
User extensions: not found          [this means that user policies has
not been set in that GPO]
Machine extensions: [{35378EAC-683F-11D2-A89A-00C04FBBCFA2}{0F6B957D-
509E-11D1-A7CC-0000F87571E3}]
Functionality version: 2
------------------------------------------------------------
...
------------------------------------------------------------

Policies OK
```

Note

You can disable the unused parts of a GPO — Computer Configuration and User Configuration — in its **Properties** window. `Flags: 1` corresponds to a disabled User Configuration, and `Flags: 2` corresponds to a disabled Computer Configuration.

Note

Version numbers `0:0` correspond to a new GPO that may even be linked to a container, but is not configured yet.

Note

GUIDs for client-side extensions are listed in the article Q216357 in the *Microsoft Knowledge Base*. For example, GUID 35378EAC-683F-11D2-A89A-00C04FBBCFA2 belongs to the *Registry Settings* component, and GUID 25537BA6-77A8-11D2-9B6C-0000F8080861 is assigned to the *Folder Redirection* component. These and other GUIDs are the same in each Windows 2000 system.

Notice that this output does not contain any information on policies' options (whether a policy is disabled or not) and on the state of inheritance (blocking and overriding). Also, you cannot see whether the policy is linked to a container or not.

To obtain information on one or more policies, use the `/gpo` parameter. You can specify either a unique policy name or a friendly name. Several policy names — if specified — must be separated by a comma; spaces between names are not allowed. For example:

```
C:\>gpotool /gpo:{31B2F340-016D-11D2-945F-00C04FB984F9},{64C49D93-BBB7-410E-B999-837B5B90422B}
```

or

```
C:\>gpotool /gpo:"Staff's GPO","Marketing's GPO"
```

Corrupted Policies

The tool returns quite informative messages on the corrupted GPOs; therefore, you can locate a problem and find the missed components of the failed GPO. Look below at a few examples of error messages.

The following message indicates that a replication problem existed, and that two replicas of a GPO on different domain controllers are not consistent:

```
Error: netdc1.net.dom - netdc4.net.dom sysvol mismatch
```

This means that the GPO has been corrupted on a DC and has not been repaired by the *File Replication Service* (FRS) that should have copied correct information from another domain controller but did not.

The message shown below indicates that the SYSVOL part of a GPO is not complete (the gpt.ini file is missing):

```
Error: Cannot access \\netdc1.net.dom\sysvol\net.dom\policies\{64C49D93-BBB7-410E-B999-837B5B90422B}\gpt.ini, error 2
```

In this case, again, check the FRS replication between domain controllers.

Here is an example of a GPO's problem related to the information stored in Active Directory (notice the comments in bold):

```
C:\>gpotool /gpo:"Marketing's GPO"
Validating DCs...
```

```
Available DCs:
netdc1.net.dom
netdc4.net.dom
Searching for policies...
Found 1 policies
============================================================
Policy {E327A07E-0482-4223-BB50-4BFAD097E406}
Error: Version mismatch on netdc4.net.dom, DS=65540, sysvol=131076
Details:
------------------------------------------------------------
DC: netdc1.net.dom
Friendly name: Marketing's GPO
...
Changed: 6/19/2002 1:35:55 PM
DS version:     2(user) 4(machine)  [versions are not coincided]
Sysvol version: 2(user) 4(machine)
...
------------------------------------------------------------
------------------------------------------------------------
DC: netdc4.net.dom
Friendly name: Marketing's GPO
...
Changed: 6/19/2002 12:55:54 PM    [time stamps are not coincided]
DS version:     1(user) 4(machine)
Sysvol version: 2(user) 4(machine)
...
------------------------------------------------------------

Errors found
```

This means that the GPO has been changed on the *netdc1.net.dom* DC and these changes were not copied to the *netdc4.net.dom* DC due to some problems with Active Directory replication (as you can see, the SYSVOL information is correct on both DCs). In such a case, you should verify directory object replication from the first DC to the second DC.

Resultant Set of Policy (RSoP)

Resultant Set of Policy is a technology of gathering group policy settings applied to the user and computer objects located at various levels (including local GPOs) in the Active Directory object hierarchy — from site to organizational unit. It uses *Windows*

Management Instrumentation (WMI) to retrieve data from the *Common Information Management Object Model* (CIMOM) database.

Administrators can use this technology through the following features:

- The GPResult command-line tool (described above)
- The built-in HTML report generator
- **The Resultant Set of Policy** snap-in

Planning and Logging Modes

The Resultant Set of Policy (RSoP) data can be obtained in one of the following modes:

- The *planning mode* allows administrators to simulate use of group policies applied to the user and computers objects through different GPOs, even if the target users and computers have not been specified. For example, this mode can answer the question: "What policy settings will be applied to those users whose accounts are located in the OU named *AllUsers* if they are logged on to computers located in the *AllComputers* OU?"
- The *logging mode* can only be used to determine already existing policy settings for a user logged on to a computer.

Note

In both modes, the target users and computers can belong to different domains, even to different forests.

The planning mode is permitted for any applicable directory object: domain, OU, user, and computer. It is obvious that the logging mode can only be used with user and computer objects (only a *user* can be logged on to a *computer*). See additional explications in the *"Analyzing RSoP Data in Domain"* section.

HTML Report on Group Policy Settings

On Windows XP- and Windows .NET-based computers, you can quickly determine group policy settings and save them to a file. Here are the steps necessary on a computer running Windows .NET (on Windows XP systems, the steps will be similar):

1. Open the *Help and Support Center* and click **Tools** in the **Support Tasks** group.
2. Click **Advanced System Information**.
3. Click **View Group Policy settings applied**.

An updatable report will be generated, containing RSoP data for the local computer and currently logged on user. You can save current data as a HTML file. It is possible to run the **Resultant Set of Policy** snap-in directly from that report and obtain more detailed information.

Using the *Resultant Set of Policy* Snap-in

The **Resultant Set of Policy** (RSoP) snap-in can be started as a standalone snap-in from an MMC console or be configured from either the **Active Directory Users and Computers** or **Active Directory Sites and Services** snap-in. Let us first discuss the former option.

You can run the **RSoP** snap-in on any domain client computer running Windows XP or Windows .NET. Necessary steps will be the same on both systems; the only difference is how the snap-in is configured:

- On Windows XP, the snap-in is configured (targeted) *before* it is added to an MMC console. Therefore, the snap-in's settings cannot be changed afterwards. It runs in the logging mode only, and operates best of all for the local computer and the currently logged on user. The RSoP data are updated at the snap-in's startup.
- On Windows .NET, the snap-in is configured *after* it has been added to an MMC console, and the RSoP data query can be changed after the MMC console has been saved. The snap-in operates in both the logging and planning modes, and the RSoP data can be updated directly from the console.

To start the **RSoP** snap-in on a computer running Windows .NET:

1. Start an MMC console (empty or custom) and add the **Resultant Set of Policy** snap-in to it.
2. In the tree pane, right click the snap-in name and select the **Generate RSoP Data** command from the context menu. The Resultant Set of Policy Wizard will be started; it will help you to prepare an RSoP query. Click **Next**.
3. On the "Mode Selection" wizard page, choose either **Logging mode** or **Planning mode**. Suppose you want to determine the policy settings for a user that is currently logged on to a domain client computer.
4. On the "Computer Selection" page, click **Another computer**, then **Browse**. The standard **Select Computer** window will help you to find a computer in the forest object tree. Enter or select a computer name, and click **Next**.
5. On the "User Selection" page, you will see the list of users that already have the RSoP data on the selected computer. You may select a user from that list only. Select a user name and click **Next**.

6. On the next wizard page (Fig. 15.1), you can verify all settings made. To start a query, click **Next**.
7. When the wizard collects all the required data, click **Finish**.

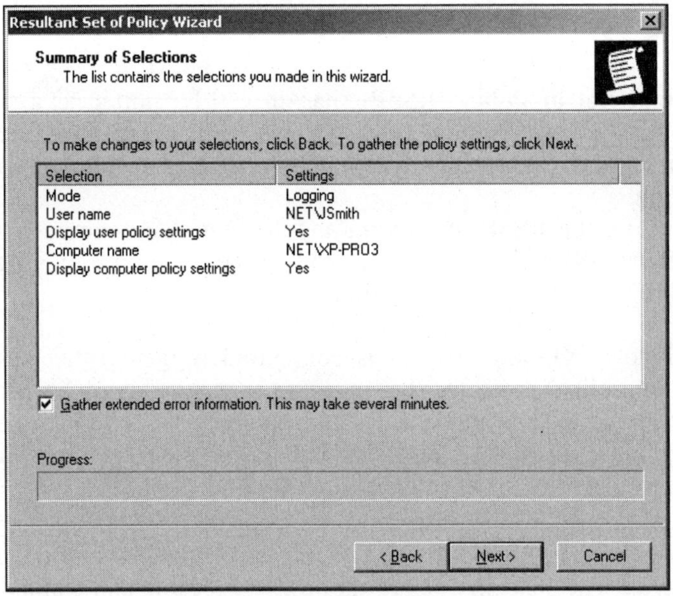

Fig. 15.1. An RSoP query will be executed for the selected user and computer

In a MMC console, you will see an **RSoP** snap-in window that contains all group policy settings applied to the selected computer and user.

The main snap-in's window (Fig. 15.2) resembles the main window of the **Group Policy Object Editor** snap-in and contains all standard GPO nodes. Right click the snap-in name (it is composed from the user and computer names) and notice the first two commands on the context menu. At any moment, you can click **Change Query** and re-define the snap-in's configuration with the help of the Resultant Set of Policy Wizard. The **Refresh Query** command allows you to regenerate RSoP data if the domain or other GPOs have been changed. Just do not forget to update new group policies applied to a computer or a user with the GPupdate command!

Now you can analyze the obtained data in the **RSoP** snap-in's window. You can expand any tree node and view group policies applied to the computer or user. If some policies have not been defined, the corresponding node will be empty or absent. It is not possible to change policies from that window.

In our example, you could obtain the same results that the RSoP snap-in displays with the help of the following command:

```
C:\>gpresult /S xp-pro3.net.dom /USER JSmith /Z
```

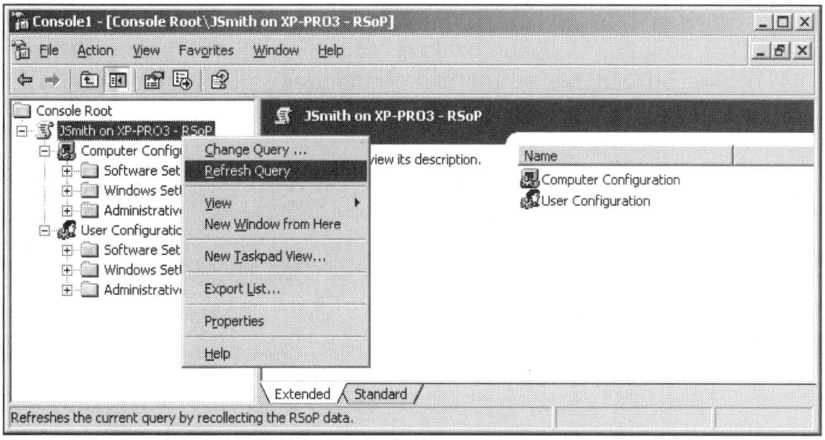

Fig. 15.2. The main window of the **Resultant Set of Policy** snap-in

You can compare results produced by both tools and select a tool that is the most convenient for your needs.

Fig. 15.3 contains an example view of various group policies. As you can see, these policies come from different GPOs linked to nested organizational units. Only GPOs with the highest priority are shown in this window. These GPO define the resulting settings of the listed policies.

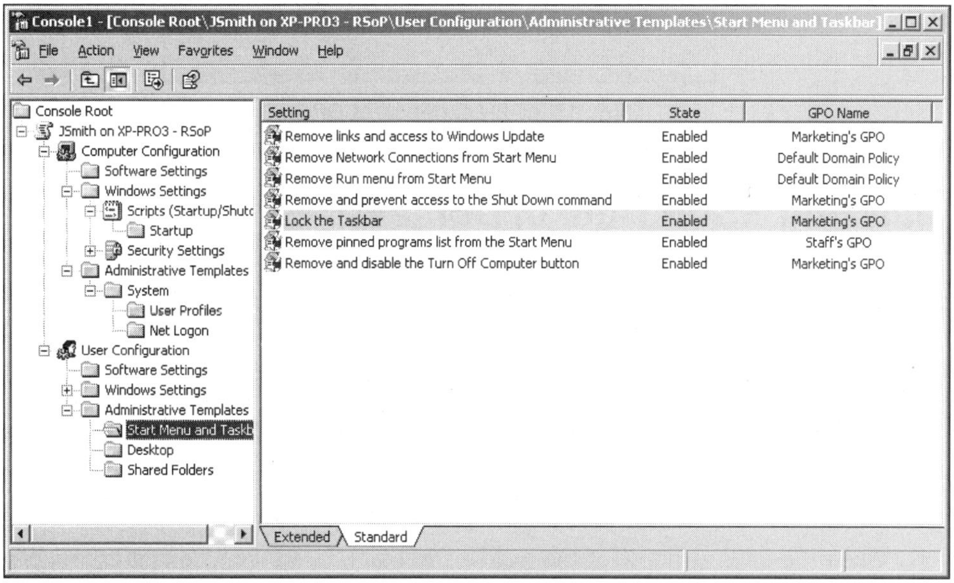

Fig. 15.3. Viewing policy settings defined in different GPOs affecting the selected computer or user

To see whether a policy has been defined on other levels in the GPO hierarchy, double click a policy and open the **Precedence** tab in the policy **Properties** window (Fig. 15.4). As you can see in the sample window, the selected policy is defined at every GPO affecting the selected user, and the resulting state is "Enabled".

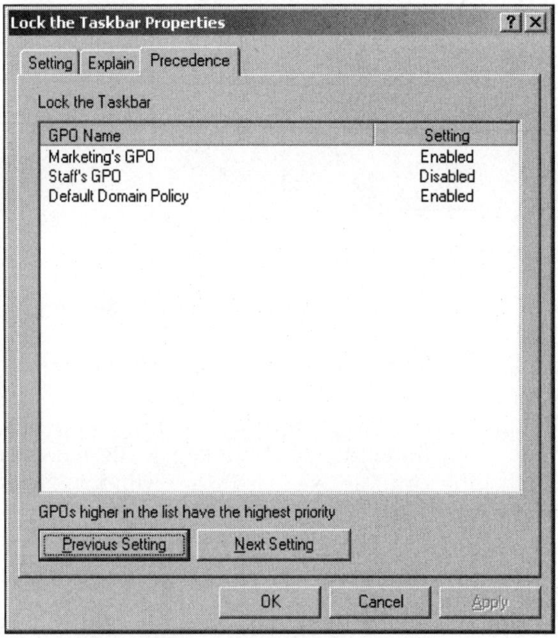

Fig. 15.4. Precedence of GPOs

Analyzing RSoP Data in Domain

From the **Active Directory Users and Computers** snap-in, you can obtain the RSoP data for any user, computer, and OU. The **Active Directory Sites and Services** snap-in will help you to run an RSoP query on a site. In all cases, the *Resultant Set of Policy Wizard* is used to prepare a query. There is nothing difficult in testing groups policy settings, and you will see this yourself if you run the wizard two or three times.

Using an example, let us discuss how to prepare an RSoP query for a domain or an OU object (this is the most generic type among RSoP queries.) The preparation procedure is the same for any other query types.

1. Open the main window of the **Active Directory Users and Computers** snap-in and right click an OU object in the tree pane. Select the **All Tasks | Resultant Set of Policy (Planning)** command from the context menu.

2. On the first page of the Resultant Set of Policy Wizard (Fig. 15.5), you should specify user and computer objects. In fact, you have four options here — you can simulate policy settings for the following objects:
   - Any user and any computer in the specified containers
   - Any user in the specified container logged on to a selected computer
   - A selected user logged on to any computer in the specified container
   - A selected user logged on to a specified computer

   If you select a specific user and/or computer object, you may also specify a container (OU) *different* from the container where the user and/or computer are really located. Therefore, you can determine what policy settings (directly defined and inherited) would be applied to the user and/or computer if they were placed into the specified container(s). At the same time, it is not necessary to *really* move the selected objects to the target container(s). This opportunity is essentially what the words "planning mode" imply. Thus, it is possible to plan and test various combinations of placement of the user and computer objects at once.

   All other wizard pages are optional, and you may set the **Skip to the final page...** flag. Do not use this flag unless you are familiar with how the wizard works.

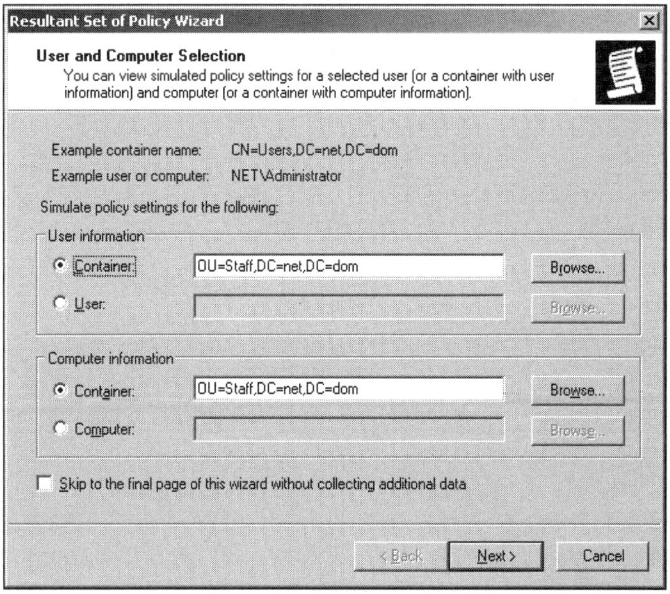

Fig. 15.5. Selecting user and computer objects for which policy settings will be simulated

3. Suppose you want to test a specific user's policy settings when he or she is logged on to the computers located in the selected OU. Set the **User** switch in the **User**

information group and enter the user name in the "Domain\User" format; otherwise, click **Browse** and select the user from the domain object tree. Click **Next**.

4. As a rule, you can skip settings show on the **Advanced Simulation Options** wizard page; however, you should select a site if there are GPOs linked to the site object.
5. The wizard page shown in Fig. 15.6 will only be displayed if you have selected a specific user and/or computer objects. The **User location** field contains the name of the container where the selected user is currently located. You can choose any other container and test the user policy settings for a target container (OU). The **Restore to Defaults** button restores the real paths to the user and/or computer objects.

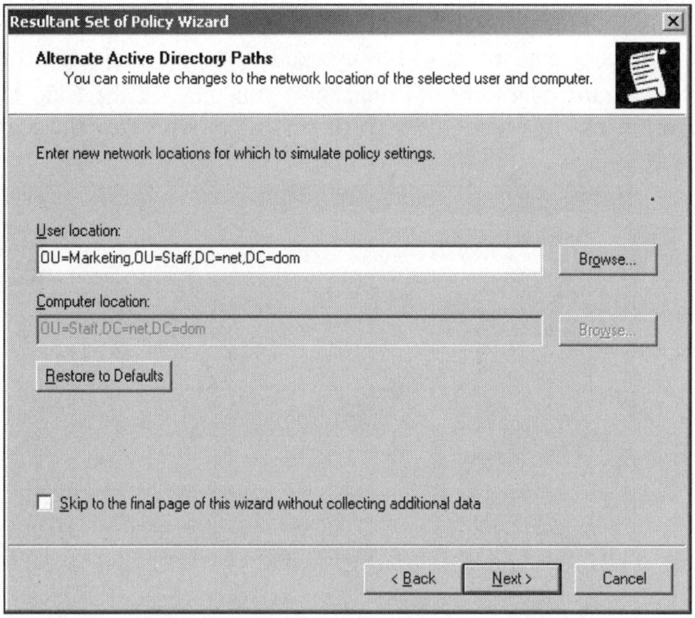

Fig. 15.6. This page initially displays existing paths to the selected user and/or computer objects; you can change these paths

6. The next wizard page (Fig. 15.7) displays all security groups where the selected user is a member. This is important if group filtering is used for one or more GPOs, since filtering affects the resulting policy settings applied to the user object. You may add groups to that list and simulate another group membership for the selected user. Otherwise, simply click **Next**. A similar page will be displayed for computer objects.

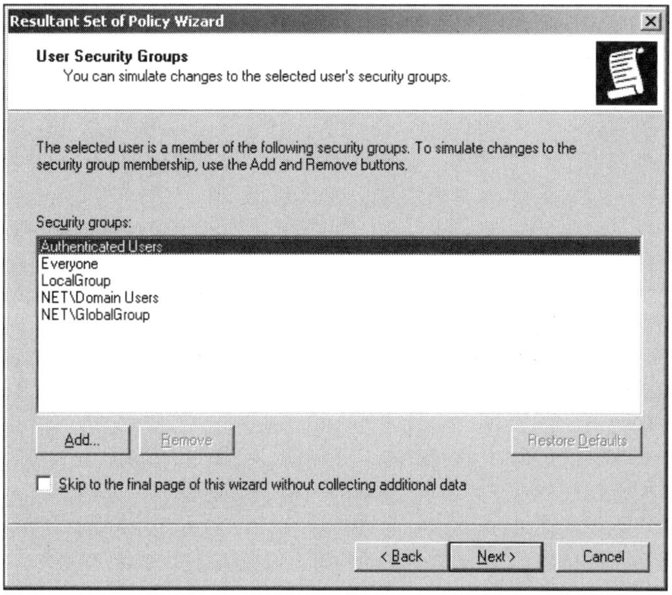

Fig. 15.7. Current group membership of the selected user

7. The next two wizard pages allow you to specify WMI filters linked to GPOs. Either skip them or make the necessary selections.
8. The "Summary of Selections" wizard page contains all options you have selected. Verify them and click **Next** to start the process of gathering the RSoP information.
9. Close the wizard window by clicking **Finish**.

You will see the standard window of the **Resultant Set of Policy** snap-in; in that window (see example in Fig. 15.2), it is possible to view policy settings for the objects selected. All features of this snap-in have been discussed earlier in the *"Using the Resultant Set of Policy Snap-in"* section. Now, you can:

- Close window
- Save the window as a custom MMC console for subsequent use
- Change the query and test the other settings

Preparation steps and results for the *logging mode* will be the same as described above; the only difference is that the target computer must be online and the user selected should have the RSoP data on that computer (i.e., it must be logged on to that computer at least once).

PART V

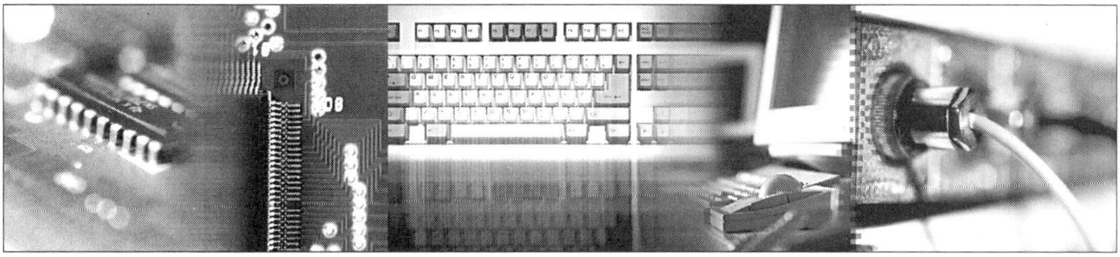

Program Access to Active Directory

Chapter 16: Active Directory Service Interfaces (ADSI)

The last two chapters of this book are intended for those administrators who want to learn how to use scripting methods for managing various directories, primarily Windows NT 4.0 and Active Directory-based domains (Windows 2000 and Windows .NET). Two of Microsoft's program products — *Active Directory Service Interfaces* (ADSI) and *Windows Script Host* (WSH) — allow administrators to implement a uniform approach to managing various platforms and program products. We will consider only a small part of this challenging problem area, and try to describe how to use ADSI for managing Windows NT 4.0- and AD-based directories (i.e., NT Directory Service, or NTDS, and Active Directory). The Visual Basic and VBScript are the programming languages selected for the examples provided, since Basic is a popular, simple, and compact language for illustrating ADSI programming. I do not want to overload the book with reference information nor overburden you with documentation that you can find elsewhere. (You can find and print out the necessary help files yourself.) Rather, I would like to consider some ADSI essentials and pitfalls that can be dangerous for beginners, and illustrate basic programming methods with simple but practical scripts and programs. (Most of them illustrate several methods at the same time.) I would strongly recommend that you download the *ADSI SDK* (also known as Active Directory SDK) from the Microsoft website, or use the online MSDN library (see links in *Appendix A*). You will need to have on hand many reference tables, definitions of interfaces and their methods and properties, constants, error codes, etc. You can print out the necessary documents as required.

ADSI as an Administrative Tool

ADSI is a very valuable facility for administrators, since ADSI is quite easy to learn and use, and can significantly help in performing bulk or routine operations. For example, you can write an export/import tool specific to your domain configuration, or a specialized migration utility. Although Windows .NET systems provide administrators with a new option of multiple selection of directory objects, scripting is a much more flexible way to manipulate various objects.

For an administrator, ADSI has two distinct advantages:

- ADSI can communicate with a number of platforms and products, including the following:
  - LDAP-compliant servers, such as Active Directory servers based on Windows 2000/.NET, and Exchange 5.*x*
  - Windows NT 4.0 Primary and Backup Domain Controllers
  - Internet Information Services (IIS)
  - Novell Directory Services (NDS) servers (4.*x* and higher)
  - Novell NetWare Servers (3.*x*)

- ADSI supports many languages like Visual Basic, VBScript or JScript, and Perl that are automation-aware (certainly, "full-fledged" languages, such as C/C++ are also supported), and uses the same component object model (COM). Scripting languages do not require a lot of preliminary study. You can combine or modify a few existing scripts, and quickly construct a working, individual tool.

To work with ADSI, it is very helpful to have some administrative tools on hand, such as the Ldp.exe and AdsVw.exe utilities, and the **ADSI Edit** and **Active Directory Schema Manager** snap-ins. These tools will allow you to control the results obtained from the developed scripts or applications, monitor Active Directory's state and values of object attributes, and do a lot of work, without which your programming efforts would be ineffective.

Remote Administration Scripts

The *Windows 2000 Server Resource Kit* contains a collection of scripts called *Remote Administration Scripts.* (Windows .NET Server Resource Kit will most likely include them, too. "Professional" versions of the Resource Kits also contain many useful scripts.) You can use these scripts not only for performing various administrative tasks, but as a "cookbook", too, while learning ADSI basics and creating your own scripts. All scripts are located in the Ras.cab file on the *Windows 2000 Resource Kit* CD and installed into the same folder as all other Resource Kit tools.

Windows Script Host (WSH)

Windows Script Host is a framework to run scripts written in VBScript or JScript. WSH is a standard component of Windows 2000/XP/.NET and Windows 98/ME, and can be installed into Windows 95 and Windows NT 4.0 systems. Therefore, administrators can run the *same* scripts on *all* of the mentioned platforms. The latest WSH version (current version is 5.6) can be downloaded free from the Microsoft website (see links in *Appendix A*).

Do not forget that WSH can be used for managing various system components, not only Active Directory (however, these topics are beyond the scope of this book). Such program interface as *Windows Management Instrumentation* (WMI) provides scriptable access to many system services and modules. We shall discuss an example that uses WMI via ADSI for retrieving information about domain computers.

Informal View on the ADSI Architecture

For a beginner, the main challenge in studying ADSI is arguably the great number of exposed interfaces (over 50) which in turn have many methods and properties. If, however, one understands the ADSI essentials and certain restrictions, it is easy to begin using ADSI, and then gradually learn new interfaces and advanced programming topics.

Attributes and Properties

Let us outline the problem in general words. All you need to do is to *select* a directory object — a user, group, computer, or some other item — and *perform* some action over its properties.

Hereafter, the terms *attribute* and *property* will be used as synonyms. *Attribute* is an element of an object stored in Active Directory, whereas *property* relates to an ADSI object represented programmatically. You can find mapping between ADSI properties and Active Directory attributes in the ADSI SDK.

ADSI System Providers

Any directory object exists in a *namespace* that is specific to each directory type. (The hierarchical structure of Active Directory evidently differs from the flat namespace of Windows NT domains.) Besides, a user in a Windows NT 4.0 domain has a set of attributes different from the attribute set available for a user in Active Directory. Therefore, ADSI has a specific *system provider* (or simply *provider*) for every supported directory type. Here are four main ADSI providers:

Provider name	Directory	DLL name(s)
`WinNT:`	Windows NT 4.0 domains	adsnt.dll
`LDAP:`	LDAP servers (Exchange 5.*x* and Active Directory)	adsldp.dll, adsldpc.dll, and adsmsext.dll
`NDS:`	Novell Directory Services (NDS)	adsnds.dll
`NWCOMPAT:`	Novell NetWare bindary (3.*x*)	adsnw.dll

(Provider names are case-sensitive!) The following script lists all providers installed in a system:

```
'Dim objRoot, objChild As IADs
Set objRoot = GetObject("ADs:")
For Each objChild In objRoot
  WScript.Echo objChild.Name
Next
```

When selecting a system provider, you define both the naming conventions for a directory object and the ADSI program representation of this object (i.e., the set of exposed properties and methods).

ADSI also supports so called *IIS Admin Objects* that provide programmatic access to Internet Information Services (IIS). Using scripts for administering IIS metabase is a vast and specific subject, so we shall not discuss it in the book.

Interfaces and Methods

A programmer can access the ADSI objects that correspond to the directory objects via COM *interfaces*, or, more precisely, through *methods* and *properties* of these interfaces. Therefore, the selected interface determines what operations can be performed with the object, or which information can be retrieved/set. Compare, for instance, the lists of methods and properties of the *IADs* and *IADsUser* interfaces. Some interfaces are supported by each provider, whereas some interfaces can be supported by only one provider. For example, Table 16.1 lists some basic ADSI objects for the LDAP provider, together with the ADSI interfaces, which the provider supports. (You can also find a similar table for the WinNT provider and other providers.)

Table 16.1. Basic ADSI Objects and Corresponding Interfaces Supported by the LDAP Provider

ADSI object	Supported interfaces
General object (generic features of user, computer, group objects, etc.)	IADs
	IADsContainer
	IDirectoryObject
	IDirectorySearch
	IADsPropertyList
	IADsObjectOptions
	IADsDeleteOps
Group account	IADsGroup
Organizational unit	IADsOU
Print queue	IADsPrintQueue
	IADsPrintQueueOperations
RootDSE	IADs
	IADsPropertyList
Schema	IADs
	IADsContainer
User account	IADsUser

In Table 16.1, you can see that many ADSI objects implement two or more interfaces. This means that you can call *any method of any implemented interface*, and the object exposes *all properties defined in these interfaces.* This table must serve as a starting point for selecting a suitable interface, or for understanding methods and properties that ADSI provides for a directory object. You need not learn all or most of the interfaces (especially in the beginning). Quite a few interfaces, called *core interfaces*, can cover most of your needs. (See the table in *Appendix C.* These interfaces are shown in bold.) The *IADs* and *IADsContainer* interfaces provide access to practically any directory object, and allow you to perform a number of manipulations with objects — create, delete, rename, enumerate, and so on. The *IADsOpenDSObject* interface allows users to specify alternative credentials when binding to an object. (See *Chapter 17, "Scripting Administrative Tasks,"* for examples.)

As you can see from the table of the supported interfaces (*Appendix C*), the WinNT provider does not support, for example, OU objects, and the LDAP provider does not support file shares or services. Therefore, you should not be under the impression that either the LDAP or WinNT provider is better. Certainly, only the LDAP protocol can provide full value access to Active Directory. Nevertheless, there are operations that can only be performed via the WinNT provider and situations where this provider produces a more compact code (for example, when filtering objects of a given type in an entire domain regardless of organizational units and other containers). You can use it effectively even in a pure Windows 2000/.NET environment.

For a programmer, selecting a provider and interface for a directory object is, therefore, a crucial operation that determines the methods and properties that will be accessible later. The ADSI SDK help file contains lists of interfaces and properties supported by each provider, and you can print out the necessary tables. If you have a solid understanding of all the stated considerations, you will have no problems when declaring variables or calling an object's methods.

The *IADsADSystemInfo* Interface

There is a very useful interface available only under Windows 2000/XP/.NET and not mentioned in the basic ADSI SDK documentation (see the updated documentation in the *Platform SDK*). It allows you to retrieve current domain information for a client computer. To use this interface, you must first explicitly create an instance of the *ADsSystemInfo* object. Look at the following code snippet — it illustrates how to use some methods of the *IADsADSystemInfo* interface.

```
Dim objSysInfo
Set objSysInfo = CreateObject("ADSystemInfo")
' In a VB program the next statement is sufficient:
'    Dim objSysInfo As New ADSystemInfo

WScript.Echo objSysInfo.ComputerName
```

```
WScript.Echo objSysInfo.DomainDNSName
WScript.Echo objSysInfo.ForestDNSName
WScript.Echo objSysInfo.IsNativeMode
WScript.Echo objSysInfo.PDCRoleOwner
WScript.Echo objSysInfo.SiteName
WScript.Echo objSysInfo.GetAnyDCName
WScript.Echo objSysInfo.UserName
```

The last statement displays the DN name of the currently logged on user.

Such a script can be useful for determining which domain, site, and DC a client is currently connected to.

Basic ADSI Programming

In every script or application, the programmer needs to select an object and perform some action over it. To implement these general tasks, ADSI provides operations of the following types.

- *Binding* to an object and *authenticating* in Active Directory. Before any operation begins, the programmer selects an object, or *binds* to the object using either *current* user credentials (recommended choice) or the *specified* (alternative) ones.
- *Accessing the object's attributes.* Depending on the ADSI object's declaration and methods implemented by the object, you can retrieve different values of an object's attributes.
- *Enumerating objects.* There are a few programming methods that allow you to obtain a set (group) of objects (users, computers, groups, etc.) — or to *enumerate* objects — selected on a specific criterion. You will not know the number of objects beforehand. (You can see a few examples of enumerating in the next chapter.) It is possible to enumerate:
  - Child objects in a container (*Listings 17.6 and 17.7*)
  - All objects of a specific type in a container (this is also called *filtering*)
  - Members of a group (section *"Manipulating Group Memberships"*)
- *Manipulating objects.* An object can be created, moved to another container or domain, or deleted.
- *Querying a Directory.* ADSI provides search access via the ADO *read-only* interface.
- *Managing security descriptors.* ADSI can manipulate permissions on various objects, including Active Directory objects, files, etc.
- *Managing the schema.* The schema can be changed or extended via ADSI. Schema extension is the process of adding new attributes or classes to the schema.

The next chapter contains examples that illustrate all the listed operations.

Accessing Object Properties

The Active Directory objects have three types of properties that are stored and accessed differently. Beginners sometimes ignore this fact, which often results in program errors.

Replicated properties stored in Active Directory

Most properties are stored in Active Directory (such as *cn*, *description*, *objectGUID*, etc.) and replicated between all domain controllers within a domain. Some of them are indexed, and some are replicated to Global Catalog. (Including an indexed property in a query improves the performance of the query.)

To read these properties, use the obj.*Get* method or the methods of *IADsProperty** interfaces (*IADsProperty*, *IADsPropertyEntry*, etc.). Use the obj.*Put* method for updating these properties.

To read and set *multi-valued* properties, use the obj.*GetEx* and obj.*PutEx* methods, respectively.

Non-replicated properties stored locally on a DC

Some properties (*lastLogon*, *lastLogoff*, *badPwdCount*, etc.) are not replicated between domain controllers. To determine the last logon time of a user, you need to read the *lastLogon* property for the user object on *every* domain controller in the domain, and compare the values. These properties can be retrieved the way they usually would be.

Operational (constructed) properties

There are properties (such as *primaryGroupToken*, *distinguishedName*, *canonicalName*, etc.) that Active Directory uses for its own administrative purposes. These properties are not stored in the directory, but calculated by a domain controller. (Note that the *primaryGroupToken* or *distinguishedName* attributes are not even defined as optional attributes of the *user* class.) These properties require the obj.*GetInfoEx* method to retrieve them (use the obj.*PutInfoEx* method for updating such properties), for example:

```
obj.GetInfoEx Array("canonicalName"), 0
WScript.Echo obj.Get("canonicalName")  'for a single value property
```

Searching Active Directory

ADSI provides search operations via *ActiveX Data Objects* (ADO). There are two syntaxes used by ADSI in query statements.

- LDAP dialect consists of the base DN, search filter (according to RFC 2254), list of attributes, and search scope:

```
<LDAP://DC=net,DC=dom>;(objectCategory=group);ADsPath;subtree
```

- SQL dialect is similar to the SELECT statement from standard SQL language. The following search string performs the same operation as the preceding string, but in addition, produces a sorted result:

```
SELECT ALL ADsPath FROM 'LDAP://DC=net,DC=dom'
↳ WHERE objectCategory='group' ORDER BY name
```

Attention

- ADSI provides *read-only* access to OLE DB interfaces. If you need to *change* a found object after a search operation, bind *directly* to that object and modify its attributes.

The following program finds all groups in the domain and displays their *ADsPath*. Both LDAP and SQL dialects can be used in this example. The program also illustrates how to navigate the resulting record set.

Listing 16.1. ADOQuery.bas — Searching for Groups in an Entire Domain (*net.dom*)

```
Option Explicit
Sub Main()

Dim objConnection As Connection
Dim objCommand As Command
Dim objRSet As Recordset
Dim i As Integer

' Open a connection:
Set objConnection = CreateObject("ADODB.Connection")
objConnection.Provider = "ADsDSOObject"

' Prepare the command:
Set objCommand = CreateObject("ADODB.Command")
objConnection.Open "Active Directory Provider"
Set objCommand.ActiveConnection = objConnection

' To find all groups (or any objects) in the forest, you must specify
' "GC:" instead of "LDAP:" for both dialects, for example:
'   <GC://DC=net,DC=dom>...
' The LDAP dialect:
```

```
objCommand.CommandText = _
"<LDAP://DC=net,DC=dom>;(objectCategory=group);ADsPath"
' The search scope could be defined directly in the command string:
'   objCommand.CommandText = _
'   "<LDAP://DC=net,DC=dom>;(objectCategory=group);ADsPath;subtree"

' The SQL dialect allows you to sort (notice the ORDER BY clause)
' the record set by some attribute:
'objCommand.CommandText = "SELECT ALL ADsPath" + _
'" FROM 'LDAP://DC=net,DC=dom' WHERE objectCategory='group'" + _
'" ORDER BY name"

' The search scope can be defined here or directly in the string
' assigned to the CommandText property (above):
objCommand.Properties("SearchScope") = ADS_SCOPE_SUBTREE  '=2
        'This constant is defined in the ADS_SCOPEENUM enumeration
objCommand.Properties("Page Size") = 1000
' Many other command properties can be set here. For details, search
' for the "Searching Properties" string in the ADSI SDK documentation:
'objCommand.Properties("Timeout") = 30     'seconds
'objCommand.Properties("Chase referrals") = 0x20
      '=ADS_CHASE_REFERRALS_SUBORDINATE - chase only referrals
      ' which are subordinate naming contexts

' Execute the prepared query:
Set objRSet = objCommand.Execute
Debug.Print "Ready... (Total) " + CStr(objRSet.RecordCount)

If objRSet.RecordCount = 0 Then
  Debug.Print "No records found!"
  Exit Sub
End If

' Display the record set
objRSet.MoveFirst
While Not objRSet.EOF
  ' The following lines must be modified to accept
  ' multi-valued properties!
  For i = 0 To objRSet.Fields.Count - 1
    Debug.Print objRSet.Fields(i).Name + " = " + _
```

```
                    objRSet.Fields(i).Value
    Next
    objRSet.MoveNext
  Wend

  Set objConnection = Nothing
  Set objCommand = Nothing
  Set objRSet = Nothing
  Debug.Print "End."

  End Sub
```

Note

To compile the shown program, do not forget to add the reference to the *Microsoft ActiveX Data Objects Library* (besides common for all ADSI projects reference to the *Active DS Type Library*) to a VB project.

Important

The number of rows returned from a normal (non-paged) search operation is limited by the *MaxPageSize* parameter (by default, 1,000) of *Default Query Policy* (see *Index* for details). (This is also applicable to other search tools, such as Ldp.exe or Search.vbs.) If you *explicitly* specify the `Page Size` parameter in your script or program, the paged search is performed, and you can retrieve any number of rows.

Active Directory Schema

Even if you are an administrator rather than a professional programmer, you might still need to know the basics of the *Active Directory schema*. For example, using various administrative tools (such as Ldp.exe or **ADSI Edit**) for troubleshooting or tuning Active Directory may require some knowledge about attribute syntax, the values range, etc. Among many other things, the schema indicates whether an attribute is indexed or replicated to Global Catalog. Understandably, if you want to *modify* or *extend* the schema, knowing its essentials is very important. Extending the schema is the same operation as creating new attributes and classes. It is not a very sophisticated process, and even a non-programmer can manage it. You need to know only some basic rules and requirements.

Note

You can obtain a lot of information about the schema (both Windows 2000 and Windows .NET versions are covered), including descriptions of all attributes and classes, on the web page **http://msdn.microsoft.com/certification/schema/**.

The Abstract Schema

All definitions of a forest's classes and attributes (the *classSchema* and *attributeSchema* objects) are located in the *Schema* partition. This partition also contains an object of the *subSchema* class. This object, named *Aggregate*, is known as the *abstract schema.*

The abstract schema contains an "extract" from class and attribute definitions. It provides a simple and efficient mechanism for retrieving frequently used information about classes and attributes, such as the optional and mandatory attributes of an object class, or the value range of a numeric attribute.

Listing 17.1 in the next chapter presents a script that reads the abstract schema. The listing also contains some samples of information that can be obtained.

Extending the Schema

When extending the schema, you must specify a unique *Object Identifier* (OID) for every new attribute or class. A *base OID* for your organization can be requested from an International Standards Organization (ISO) Name Registration Authority, or obtained by using a command-line utility, *OID Generator* (OidGen.exe), that is included in the *Windows 2000 Server Resource Kit.* This utility generates two base OIDs: one for attributes and one for classes. You must run it *only once.* (Do not use different root OIDs in the same Active Directory installation.) New OIDs for your attributes and classes are generated by adding "suffixes" (i.e., the unique numbers separated by a period from the base part) to the appropriate base OID. It is your responsibility to manage these suffixes.

See examples of creating a new attribute and class in the next chapter (*Listings 17.25* and *17.26*).

Caution

- It is not possible to delete an attribute or class. You can only *deactivate* it in the **Active Directory Schema Manager** snap-in. The status of deactivated objects is indicated as `Defunct`. In Windows .NET you can also redefine attribute or class and activate it again.

Note

You may wonder how to create a UI for custom classes and attributes, or how to add new tabs to existing administrative snap-ins for editing new attributes. This is a rather sophisticated topic, which requires, in addition, using non-scripting programming languages, such as C/C++. See the "*Extending the User Interface for Directory Objects*" section in the ADSI SDK Help, or search for the "display specifier" string on the Microsoft website. You may also wish to look up one of the "Step-by-Step" articles related to this topic.

Creating a New Attribute

When creating an attribute, you must define the following properties of a new *attributeSchema* object:

- *attributeID* (OID)
- Naming properties — *cn, lDAPDisplayName*
- Syntax properties — *attributeSyntax*, *oMSyntax* (see *Table 16.2*)
- *isSingleValued*

If omitted, the *schemaIDGUID* and *adminDisplayName* properties are generated by the system (the last one is copied from the *cn* property). If the *searchFlags* and *isMemberOfPartialAttributeSet* properties are not defined, the new attribute is neither indexed nor replicated to Global Catalog.

Optional properties: *rangeLower*, *rangeUpper*, *linkID*, *adminDescription*. (It is a good idea to always define the last property, since this is very useful information for browsing the schema.)

Creating a New Class

When creating a class, you must define the following properties of a new *classSchema* object:

- *governsID* (OID)
- Classes from which the new class inherits — *subClassOf*
- *objectClassCategory* (Structural, Auxiliary, or Abstract; remember that only structural classes can be instantiated in the directory)
- Naming properties — *cn, lDAPDisplayName*
- Mandatory and/or optional attributes of the new class — *mustContain*, *systemMustContain*, *mayContain*, *systemMayContain*
- Possible parents (if, for example, you specify `organizationalUnit`, the instances of the new class will only be created in OUs) — *possSuperiors*, *systemPossSuperiors*

If omitted, the *schemaIDGUID* and *adminDisplayName* properties are generated by the system (the last one is copied from the *cn* property). By default, the naming attribute for the new class is CN. The *rDnAttId* property allows one to define a different value (but this is discouraged).

Optional properties: *auxiliaryClass, systemAuxiliaryClass, defaultSecurityDescriptor, adminDescription.* (It is advisable that you always define the last property.) The *defaultHidingValue* property of the new class (TRUE, by default) specifies that new instances of this class will be hidden from the **Active Directory Users and Computers** snap-in (and the **My Network Places** folder — on Windows 2000). This means that the *showInAdvancedViewOnly* attribute of new instances will be set to TRUE.

Naming Attributes and Classes

Microsoft recommends that you use some naming conventions for new Active Directory attributes and classes. You should also explicitly specify the *lDAPDisplayName* for all custom attributes and classes. Meeting these conventions ensures the consistency of names used by different software vendors, convenient browsing of the schema, and the possibility of using documentation programs (see later).

According to these recommendations, the *Common-Name* must consist of the following parts:

- DNS domain name of the company
- Four-digit year indicating when the DNS name was registered
- Company's product name
- Attribute or class description

Each part in the name begins with an uppercase letter and is separated by a hyphen.

To derive the *LDAP-Display-Name* from the *Common-Name*, use the following rules:

- Make the first character lowercase.
- Capitalize the first character immediately following each hyphen.
- Remove all hyphens except those immediately following the company and product components of the name.

Here are a few examples of names:

Common-Name (*cn*)	**LDAP-Display-Name (*lDAPDisplayName*)**
Microsoft-Com-1999-DS-Consistency-GUID	microsoftCom1999-DS-ConsistencyGUID
Microsoft-Com-1999-RRAS-Attribute	microsoftCom1999-RRAS-Attribute
MyCorp-Com-2002-TEST-User-ID	myCorpCom2002-TEST-UserID

For development or testing purposes, you may also add a version suffix to the *cn* and *lDAPDisplayName* attributes.

Syntaxes of Active Directory Attributes

Table 16.2 contains a list of some frequently used attribute syntaxes. This vital information is used for creating attributes (either programmatically or by using such tools as LDIFDE, CSVDE). The *Name* column of the table contains two syntax names: the first name is used in the **Active Directory Schema Manager** snap-in, the second one (in parentheses) is used in the Windows 2000-version **ADSI Edit** snap-in. The *Description* column also contains examples of Active Directory attributes that have the given syntax.

Table 16.2. Some Basic Syntaxes of Active Directory Attributes

Name	*oMSyntax*	*attributeSyntax*	Description
Boolean (Boolean)	1	2.5.5.8	Boolean (*isDeleted, isMemberOfPartialAttributeSet*).
Integer (Integer)	2	2.5.5.9	32-bit integer (*flags, groupType, primaryGroupID, rangeLower, rangeUpper, userAccountControl*).
Large Integer/Interval (INTEGER8)	65	2.5.5.16	64-bit integer (*accountExpires, lastLogon, maxPwdAge, uSNCreated, uSNChanged*).
Octet String (OctetString)	4	2.5.5.10	Array of bytes (*objectGuid*). Use OctetString to store binary data.
NT Security Descriptor (ObjectSecurityDescriptor)	66	2.5.5.15	Octet string containing a security descriptor (*nTSecurityDescriptor*).
Distinguished Name (DN)	127	2.5.5.1	String containing a distinguished name (DN) (*member, memberOf, objectCategory*). Active Directory automatically keeps up-to-date distinguished names stored in strings of this syntax, i.e., if the object referenced by the distinguished name is renamed or moved, Active Directory tracks all changes. Consider, for example, the relationships of a group and its members. If a user is renamed, it does not lose group membership.
Unicode String (DirectoryString)	64	2.5.5.12	String: Unicode, case-insensitive (*description, displayName, name, sn, location*).
Generalized Time (GeneralizedTime)	24	2.5.5.11	Time string format (*whenCreated, whenChanged*). For example: 01/11/2002 10:34:28 AM.

continues

Table 16.2 Continued

Name	*oMSyntax*	*attributeSyntax*	Description
Object Identifier (OID)	6	2.5.5.2	String containing OIDs (*objectClass*). The OID is a string containing digits (0-9) and decimal points (.).
SID (Sid)	4	2.5.5.17	Octet string containing a security identifier (SID) (*objectSid*, *sIDHistory*). Use this syntax to store SID values only.

Useful Tools for Working with the Schema

SchemaDiff.vbs Script

The *Windows 2000 Server Resource Kit* (the *Remote Administration Scripts* section) contains the *SchemaDiff.vbs* script, which allows an administrator to compare the schema of two different forests. This script checks the schema version number, the number of classes, the mandatory and optional attributes for each class, and the syntax and range for each attribute. You can also use the script as an example of manipulations with schema objects when composing your own scripts or learning ADSI programming basics.

SchemaDoc Program

The *Schema Documentation Program* (SchemaDoc.exe) is used to document the schema extensions made in your Active Directory installation. The program copies the information from the classes and attributes into an XML-file. To use SchemaDoc, it is necessary to comply with Microsoft recommendations on attribute and class names, i.e., use the same prefix on all created names. SchemaDoc will search Active Directory based on this prefix.

You can see the program's documentation on the web page **http://www.microsoft.com/TechNet/win2000/schema.asp**.

IADsTools ActiveX DLL

The *Windows .NET Support Tools* pack (see *Chapter 9*, "*General Characteristics and Purpose of System Tools*") contains a COM object named *IADsTools* that is used, in particular, by *Active Directory Replication Monitor* (ReplMon.exe). You can call the IADsTools functions from a custom script or application. IADsTools can be regarded as a high-level framework of basic ADSI interfaces. The supplied iadstools.doc file provides a description of all function calls. *Appendix D* contains the complete list of these functions. A few examples of using IADsTools will be discussed in the next chapter.

The IADsTools DLL is installed as a part of the Support Tools, but can be distributed separately. Copy the iadstools.dll file from the \Program Files\Support Tools folder to the *%SystemRoot%* folder on a target computer, and run the regsvr32 iadstools.dll command from the command prompt on that computer.

By default, all the IADsTools' errors are recorded in the Application log (Source: IADsTools; Category: None; Event ID: 1).

Using Visual Basic and VBScript

Visual Basic is a powerful interactive environment that can be used for developing both applications and scripts. You can first design and debug Visual Basic applications, and then transform them into VBScript scripts. These language versions have some differences, but they can be easily bypassed.

You need to add references to the appropriate Active Directory libraries to Visual Basic projects. Click **References** in the **Project** menu and check the **Active DS Type Library** box in the **Available References** list. If you use the *ADSI Resource Kit*, you also need to add the appropriate DLLs (such as ADsSecurity.dll or ADsError.dll) to the project's references. (Don't forget to register these DLLs: enter regsvr32 <DLLName>.dll at the command prompt.) To use ADSI search via ADO, add the *Microsoft ActiveX Data Objects Library* to the references as well.

The standard Visual Basic feature — *Code Completion Assistant* — significantly simplifies ADSI for beginners. You need not remember all of the methods and properties of an ADSI interface, since the assistant will display them for each declared variable (Fig. 16.1).

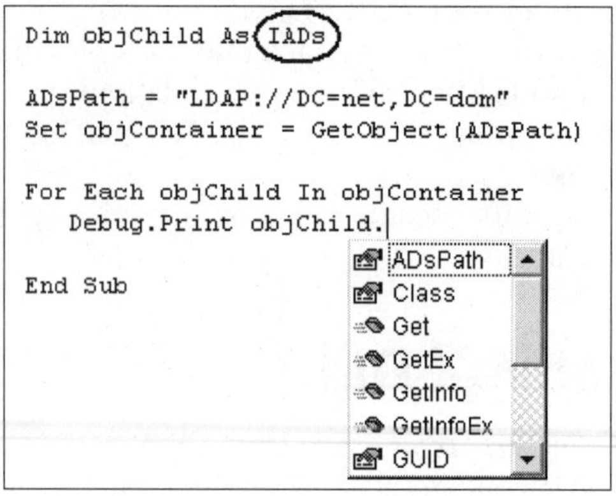

Fig. 16.1. Code Completion Assistant will help you to correctly select a method according to the object's definition

There is, however, a pitfall here. You remember that an ADSI object can implement several interfaces at once, so you can call methods of *all* these interfaces and access *all* their properties. Code Completion Assistant, however, only displays information about the interface that was used in a variable declaration. Therefore, the other interfaces will be accessible, but not "visible".

In Visual Basic, you should carefully select variable declarations. Consider, for example, the following program that enumerates all child objects in an OU:

```
Dim ADsPath As String
Dim objContainer As IADsContainer
Dim objChild As IADs

ADsPath = "LDAP://OU=Staff,DC=net,DC=dom"
Set objContainer = GetObject(ADsPath)

For Each objChild In objContainer
   Debug.Print objChild.Name + " ---> " + objChild.Class
Next
```

Suppose you wish to view all users in this OU and use the following declaration

```
Dim objChild As IADsUser
```

instead of

```
Dim objChild As IADs
```

The program will work fine if the OU contains user objects only. However, you will get the error "Type mismatch" if there are objects of other types in this OU. In this case you must use a more "universal" interface — *IADs*. VBScript would not impose such a problem, since all its variables always have one fundamental data type, *Variant*.

Converting a Visual Basic Program to a Script

To transform a Visual Basic program into a script in VBScript, it is sufficient to perform the following operations over the program code:

- Delete the `Sub` and `End Sub` statements
- In variable declarations (the `Dim` statements), delete all substrings, beginning with (and including) the `As` keyword
- Replace the `Debug.Print` statement (or a similar one) with `WScript.Echo`

Certainly, a reverse conversion is also possible.

Debugging Scripts

The simplest tool for debugging scripts written on VBScript or JScript is the *Microsoft Script Debugger*. You can download Script Debugger from the Microsoft website (see *Appendix A*). To start a debug session, use a command similar to the following (the script name must include the extension):

```
cscript Enumerating.vbs //X
```

The debugger starts and the script code is displayed in the debugger window. Then you can perform the following operations.

1. Start the script by pressing the <F5> key.
2. Point to the code line(s), toggle breakpoint(s) (<F9> key), and run the code between them.
3. View and modify the values of variables. Select the **Command Window** from the **View** menu.
4. Stop debugging. The debugging session terminates, and you can only save the modified text or immediately exit the debugger.

Note

You cannot actually change the script code in the debugger window. All changes to the code require that you restart the debug session.

A sample debugging session is shown in Fig. 16.2. The presenting code is used for enumerating objects in a specified container, i.e., the code has a loop. Let us discuss some details of working with the command window.

The first request for a value for the object (*objContainer*) was unsuccessful in this example, since the debugger cannot display the entire object. Step 1 shows that we can view the current value of *any* valid property of the specified object. In successive loops, we can trace the same property or select others (Step N). Note that the character case in the names of objects and properties does not matter. It is possible at any moment to view and modify all objects already created. For instance, while debugging the presented code, we can use the `? objContainer.Parent` command and get the parent name of the specified container.

To change a value, enter an assignment statement in the command window. In our example, we could enter the following string after executing the first line of the code:

```
ADsPath = "LDAP://DC=net,DC=dom"
```

After this modification, we will get a list of child objects that relate to the domain container rather than to the *Staff* OU, as was initially specified.

Certainly, debugging in such an environment as Visual Basic offers many more possibilities and features in comparison to the Script Debugger.

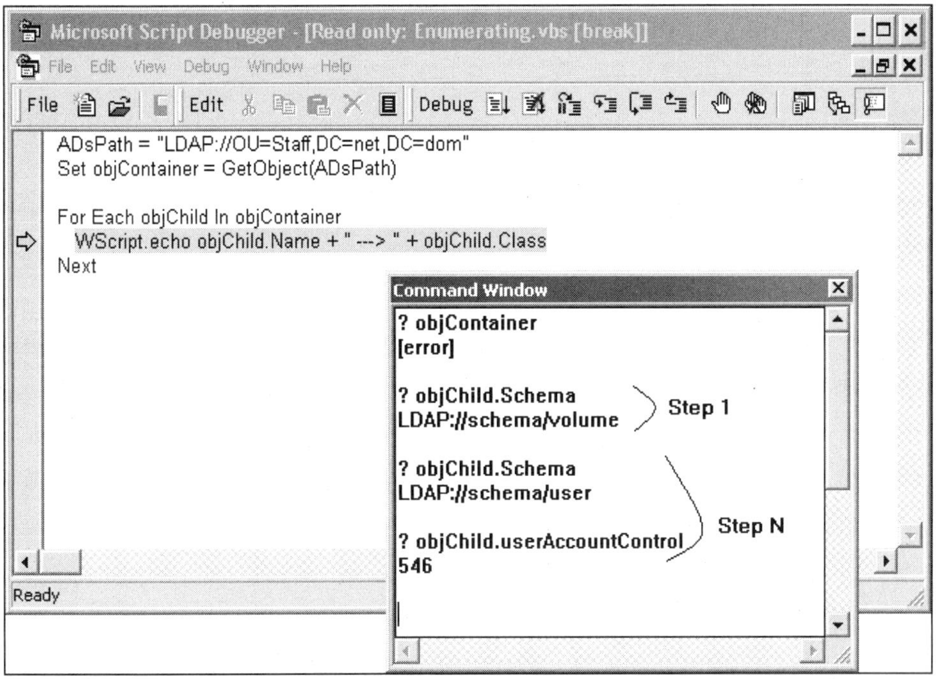

Fig. 16.2. Viewing the current values of variables in a script debugging session

ADSI Error Codes

You have two options for interpreting error in ADSI scripts or applications.

- Find "Win32 Error Codes for ADSI 2.5" in ADSI SDK or MSDN (see links in *Appendix A*).
- Use the `repadmin /showmsg <errCode>` command (see detailed information in *Chapter 11*, "*Verifying Network and Distributed Services*").

Chapter 17: Scripting Administrative Tasks

This chapter contains many examples that will illustrate some basic ADSI programming principles and that at the same time will be useful to an administrator. You can easily extend functions of every script to meet your specific tasks. As well, you can look up all examples given, since many scripts illustrate programming methods useful in various scenarios that are different from the main purpose of these scripts. You can combine elements of the scripts and thus quickly start composing your own scripts or applications without an extensive familiarity with all ADSI interfaces and techniques.

All proposed examples are written in either VBScript or Visual Basic languages. You can easily translate them into another language, for example, JavaScript or Perl. The rules of converting a VBScript script into a Visual Basic application (and vice versa) were stated in the previous chapter.

This chapter covers how to use ADSI with Active Directory only (plus one example illustrates WMI). Remember, however, that you can also use scripts for managing many other components of Windows systems (including Windows NT and Windows 9*x*/ME) — via WSH objects or WMI — and the WinNT provider can be used for managing both Windows NT and Active Directory-based domains (Windows 2000 and Windows .NET).

Object Names Used in This Chapter

All scripts and programs discussed below have been debugged in a test environment. You must replace the string values in the listings with values relevant to your network environment. Here are some "tunable" parameters:

- `DC=net,DC=dom` — the distinguished name of the forest root domain *net.dom* (which has the child domain *subdom.net.dom*)
- `NET` — the NetBIOS (pre-Windows 2000) name of the domain
- `NET-site` — name of the site where domain *net.dom* is located
- `NETDC1` — the NetBIOS (pre-Windows 2000) name of the domain controller *netdc1.net.dom*
- `Staff` — a sample organizational unit (OU)
- `administrator` — a SAM account name with administrative privileges
- `psw, newPsw` — a password

Note

If two or more lines in the scripts or programs presented in this chapter are split with this symbol ↳ (due to limitations of the page width), they must be treated as a single line (statement).

Reading Information from Active Directory

Retrieving information from Active Directory is perhaps one of the most important and frequently used operations. (Writing data into Active Directory or modifying attributes of Active Directory objects is not a challenge if you know the type of these data, i.e., attribute syntax rules, and are familiar with methods of access to data of that type.) Certainly, you can use any standard tools and administrative snap-ins discussed earlier in this book to get information; however, custom scripts allow you to save a lot of time on routine operations or combine results in a way that is most convenient for you. Here are topics that the following scripts aim to demonstrate:

- Which data and operations can be valuable for administrators
- Where these data are located
- How to retrieve data of frequently used types

Saving Results to a Disk File and Reading the Abstract Schema

Before we begin discussing various ADSI scripts, let us consider how to save results for subsequent analysis. As an example, we will use a script that produces more than two thousand lines in total. The following script reads all information about attributes and classes represented in the Active Directory schema (in a particular installation), simultaneously displays results on the screen and writes them to a file. You can insert statements (only four in all!) similar to the bold ones into any script, and save the obtained results if necessary.

All attributes of the abstract schema used — *attributeTypes*, *extendedAttributeInfo*, *objectClasses*, and *extendedClassInfo* — are multi-valued. Thus, this script is also an example of reading properties that may have more than one value. Note that in Windows .NET these attributes are only accessible with the *GetInfoEx* method, whereas on Windows 2000 servers you can use the usual *GetInfo* method.

The following table shows the total number of attributes and classes in Windows 2000 (schema version 13) and Windows .NET (build 3663, schema version 29):

	Windows 2000 (schema version 13)	**Windows .NET (build 3663, schema version 29)**
Attributes	1035	1063
Classes	180	189

Listing 17.1. AbstrSchema.vbs — Writing the Definitions of Active Directory Attributes and Classes to a File

```
Dim objSchema 'As IADsContainer
Dim attr
Dim x 'As Variant
Dim i 'As Integer
Dim myFile 'As Variant
Dim objFSO 'As Variant

Set objSchema = _
  GetObject("LDAP://CN=Aggregate,CN=Schema,CN=Configuration," + _
            "DC=net,DC=dom")
objSchema.GetInfo
Set objFSO = CreateObject("Scripting.FileSystemObject")
' Specify your own file name. An existing file will be re-written!
Set myFile = objFSO.CreateTextFile("C:\Abstract Schema.txt", True)

i = 1
' ***** Read attributes represented in the schema. *****
' Here is a sample output string (parentheses are included):
'   ( 2.5.4.3 NAME 'cn' SYNTAX '1.3.6.1.4.1.1466.115.121.1.15'
'   ↳SINGLE-VALUE )
' All Microsoft attribute IDs begin with the prefix "1.2.840.113556.1".
objSchema.GetInfoEx Array("attributeTypes"), 0
attr = objSchema.Get("attributeTypes")
myFile.WriteLine "Attributes" + vbCrLf
For Each x In attr
  'WScript.Echo CStr(i) + ". " + x
  myFile.WriteLine CStr(i) + ". " + x
  i = i + 1
Next
WScript.Echo " Attributes (TOTAL) " + CStr(i - 1)

i = 1
' ***** Read additional information about attributes. *****
' Here is a sample output string:
'   ( 2.5.4.3 NAME 'cn' RANGE-LOWER '1' RANGE-UPPER '64'
'   ↳PROPERTY-GUID '3F7996BFE60DD011A28500AA003049E2'
```

```
'    ↳PROPERTY-SET-GUID '54018DE4F8BCD111870200C04FB96050' INDEXED )
objSchema.GetInfoEx Array("extendedAttributeInfo"), 0
attr = objSchema.Get("extendedAttributeInfo")
myFile.WriteLine vbCrLf + "Attributes - Extended information" + vbCrLf
For Each x In attr
  'WScript.Echo CStr(i) + ". " + x
  myFile.WriteLine CStr(i) + ". " + x
  i = i + 1
Next

i = 1
' ***** Read classes represented in the schema. ******
' Output strings are similar to the following:
'   ( 2.5.20.1 NAME 'subSchema' SUP top STRUCTURAL MAY
'   ↳(extendedClassInfo $ extendedAttributeInfo $ dITContentRules
'   ↳ $ attributeTypes $ objectClasses $ modifyTimeStamp ) )
' Keep in mind that each class also inherits the attribute list of its
' parent class!
objSchema.GetInfoEx Array("objectClasses"), 0
attr = objSchema.Get("objectClasses")
myFile.WriteLine vbCrLf + "Classes" + vbCrLf
For Each x In attr
  'WScript.Echo CStr(i) + ". " + x
  myFile.WriteLine CStr(i) + ". " + x
  i = i + 1
Next
WScript.Echo " Classes (TOTAL) " + CStr(i - 1)

i = 1
' ***** Read additional information about classes, for example:
'   ( 2.5.20.1 NAME 'subSchema'
'   ↳CLASS-GUID '61328B5A8DC3D111BBC90080C76670C0' )
objSchema.GetInfoEx Array("extendedClassInfo"), 0
attr = objSchema.Get("extendedClassInfo")
myFile.WriteLine vbCrLf + "Classes - Extended information" + vbCrLf
For Each x In attr
  'WScript.Echo CStr(i) + ". " + x
  myFile.WriteLine CStr(i) + ". " + x
  i = i + 1
Next
```

```
WScript.Echo "End."
myFile.Close

Set objSchema = Nothing
Set attr = Nothing
Set x = Nothing
Set objFSO = Nothing
Set myFile = Nothing
```

Retrieving Information from a RootDSE

From the following script, you can learn how to access the *RootDSE* object and use two popular interfaces, namely, *IADsPropertyList* and *IADsPropertyEntry*. RootDSE is the main source of information about names of Active Directory partitions and Directory Service Agents. (See *Chapter 2*, "*Active Directory Terminology and Concepts,*" for detailed information on RootDSE.)

This script can also serve as an example of handling ADSI errors.

Listing 17.2. getRootDSE.vbs — Reading the Attributes of a RootDSE Object

```
Dim objRootDSE 'As IADsPropertyList
Dim objProperty 'As IADsPropertyEntry
Dim i 'As Integer
Dim intCount 'As Integer

On Error Resume Next
' Serverless binding is preferable.
Set objRootDSE = GetObject("LDAP://RootDSE")
' Yet in some cases, you may need to bind to a specific DC:
'    Set objRootDSE = _
'       GetObject("LDAP://netdc2.subdom.net.dom/RootDSE")
' Catch possible errors:
If Hex(Err.Number) = "8007203A" Then
   WScript.Echo "ERROR_DS_SERVER_DOWN (" & Hex(Err.Number) & ")"
   WScript.Quit
ElseIf Hex(Err.Number) <> 0 Then
```

```
   WScript.Echo "Error", Hex(Err.Number)
   WScript.Quit
End If

objRootDSE.GetInfo
WScript.Echo "*** RootDSE object on " + objRootDSE.Get("dnsHostName") _
           + " ***" + vbCrLf
intCount = objRootDSE.PropertyCount
For i = 0 To intCount - 1
   Set objProperty = objRootDSE.Item(i)
   WScript.Echo CStr(i + 1) + ") " + objProperty.Name
Next
WScript.Echo "------------------------------------"

WScript.Echo " DSA name: " + objRootDSE.dsServiceName
' Names of Active Directory partitions must be always obtained
' from the RootDSE object only:
WScript.Echo " Domain partition:        " + _
             objRootDSE.Get("defaultNamingContext")
WScript.Echo " Schema partition:        " + _
             objRootDSE.Get("schemaNamingContext")
WScript.Echo " Configuration partition: " + _
             objRootDSE.Get("configurationNamingContext")

WScript.Echo " Highest USN: " + objRootDSE.Get("highestCommittedUSN")
WScript.Echo " Is synchronized?     " + _
             objRootDSE.Get("isSynchronized")
WScript.Echo " Is a Global Catalog? " + _
             objRootDSE.Get("isGlobalCatalogReady")

Set objRootDSE = Nothing
Set objProperty = Nothing
```

The highest *USN* committed by the server is one of the basic parameters used for troubleshooting Active Directory replication. Besides, if you write down the USN at a specific moment, you'll be able to determine which objects have been modified since then, for instance, by using a simple command similar to the following one:

```
search "LDAP://DC=net,DC=dom" /C:"uSNChanged>=123456" /S:subtree
```

The *isSynchronized* attribute indicates whether the DC has replicated all directory partitions after its promotion. Do not confuse this initial replication with a normally scheduled one.

Remember that the *isGlobalCatalogReady* attribute is TRUE only when the DC has successfully completed its promotion to a GC server. Do not expect that it will be *immediately* set once you have designated (manually or programmatically) that DC as a GC server.

Reading the Property List

Here is another example of using the *IADsPropertyList* and *IADsPropertyEntry* interfaces with various providers as well as with Global Catalog. By using this code, you can compare a directory object's attribute lists received from different providers or see the attributes replicated to Global Catalog. Only defined attributes (i.e., those that have values) are included in the list. (To see *all* possible attributes, you must refer to the schema; see *Listing 17.4*.) You can also view the type of each attribute as it defined in the *ADSTYPE* enumeration.

The program also illustrates how to use one more important (core) interface — *IADsOpenDSObject*. This interface is used when you want to explicitly specify the credentials, which the program will use for binding to the directory object. Authentication flags used to define the binding options are listed in the *ADS_AUTHENTICATION_ENUM* enumeration.

Listing 17.3. Prop-of-Obj.bas — Retrieving the Property List of a Directory Object

```
Option Explicit
Sub Main()

Dim objContext As IADsOpenDSObject
Dim objAD As IADsPropertyList
Dim objProp As IADsPropertyEntry
Dim iCount As Integer
Dim i As Integer

Set objContext = GetObject("LDAP:")
' Set objAD = objContext.OpenDSObject _
'             ("LDAP://CN=John Smith,OU=Staff,DC=net,DC=dom", _
'              vbNullString, vbNullString, _
'              ADS_SECURE_AUTHENTICATION)
' The preceding statement is equal to
```

```
'     Set objAD = GetObject("LDAP://...")
' i.e. you bind to the object using the credentials
' of the caller (currently logged on user)

On Error Resume Next
' Bind using the specified credentials:
Set objAD = objContext.OpenDSObject _
            ("LDAP://CN=John Smith,OU=Staff,DC=net,DC=dom", _
             "administrator", "psw", _
             ADS_SECURE_AUTHENTICATION)

If Hex(Err.Number) = "80072030" Then
   Debug.Print "LDAP_NO_SUCH_OBJECT (" + Hex(Err.Number) + ")"
   Exit Sub
ElseIf Hex(Err.Number) <> 0 Then
   ' You may or may not be authenticated:
   Debug.Print "Error (" + Str(Err.Number) + ") Hex: " + Hex(Err.Number)
   Exit Sub
End If

' As an alternative, you can use the security context of the currently
' logged on user. Instead of all preceding statements choose one
' of the following applicable binding strings:
' * Binding to a user object:
'   Set objAD = GetObject("LDAP://CN=John Smith,OU=Staff,DC=net,DC=dom")
' * Binding through Global Catalog:
'   Set objAD = GetObject("GC://CN=John Smith,OU=Staff,DC=net,DC=dom")
' * Binding to a user or group object with use of the WinNT provider:
'   Set objAD = GetObject("WinNT://NET/jsmith,user")
'   Set objAD = GetObject("WinNT://NET/Domain Users,group")
' * Binding to the domain object:
'   Set objAD = GetObject("WinNT://NET,domain")
objAD.GetInfo

Debug.Print "Attributes of", objAD.ADsPath
iCount = objAD.PropertyCount
Debug.Print "  Total # " + CStr(iCount)
For i = 0 To iCount - 1
   Set objProp = objAD.Item(i)
```

```
    Debug.Print CStr(i + 1) + ") " + objProp.Name + _
                " (type " + CStr(objProp.ADsType) + ")"
Next

Set objAD = Nothing
Set objProp = Nothing
End Sub
```

Retrieving Characteristics of an Object Class from the Schema

You might want to retrieve the complete information about a directory object derived from an object class. These data are stored in the *Schema* partition, and there is a special interface named *IADsClass* that allows you to access these data. A few methods of this interface as well as the *Schema* and *Class* methods of the *IADs* interface are represented in the following program.

Listing 17.4. Attrs-of-Class.bas — Obtaining Common Information and a List of Possible Attributes for a Directory Class

```
Option ExplicitSub Main()

Dim strPath As String
Dim objAD As IADs
Dim objClass As IADsClass
Dim varAttr As Variant
Dim arr As Variant
Dim n As Integer

' A user account has been specified here;
' you can specify any directory object:
strPath = "LDAP://CN=John Smith,OU=Staff,DC=net,DC=dom"

' Connect to the directory object specified in the path
Set objAD = GetObject(strPath)
Debug.Print "Schema path: '" + objAD.Schema & "' for " + strPath
Debug.Print "Object class: '" + objAD.Class + "'" + vbCrLf
Debug.Print "=== The properties of the class ==="
```

```
' Retrieve the information about the class - bind to the schema.
' You could omit the previous statements and directly specify the name
' of the necessary object class, for example "LDAP://schema/user".
Set objClass = GetObject(objAD.Schema)
Debug.Print "Is abstract class? " + CStr(objClass.Abstract)
Debug.Print "ADsPath: " + objClass.ADsPath
Debug.Print "Is container? " + CStr(objClass.Container)
If objClass.Container Then
  Debug.Print "  May contain:"
  ' The list of object classes that the selected class can contain:
  arr = objClass.Containment
  On Error Resume Next
  If Len(arr) = 0 Then
    For Each varAttr In arr
      Debug.Print "    - " + varAttr
    Next
  Else
    Debug.Print "    - " + objClass.Containment
  End If
End If
Debug.Print "Derived from: " + objClass.DerivedFrom
Debug.Print "Naming: " + objClass.NamingProperties
Debug.Print "Class OID: " + objClass.OID
Debug.Print "Possible superiors:"
arr = objClass.PossibleSuperiors
On Error Resume Next
If Len(arr) = 0 Then
  For Each varAttr In arr
    Debug.Print " - " + varAttr
  Next
Else
  Debug.Print " - " + objClass.PossibleSuperiors
End If
Debug.Print vbCrLf + "=== Attributes ==="
Debug.Print "MUST have:"      ' The list of mandatory attributes
n = 0
For Each varAttr In objClass.MandatoryProperties
  Debug.Print " :: " + varAttr
  n = n + 1
Next
```

```
Debug.Print "(TOTAL): " + CStr(n)
Debug.Print

Debug.Print "MAY have:"      ' The list of optional attributes
n = 0
For
  Each varAttr In objClass.OptionalProperties
  Debug.Print " :: " + varAttr
  n = n + 1
Next
Debug.Print "(TOTAL): " + CStr(n)

Set objAD = Nothing
Set objClass = Nothing
End Sub
```

Reading Property Values of Different Types

Some problems may arise when you attempt to display the values of certain properties. This is often due to selection of an inappropriate format. The following example program displays some property types. Some types, such as *Large Integer*, *NT Security Descriptor*, or *Octet String* (for example, the *objectSid* property), require special conversion procedures. Take note of the obj.*Guid* method inherited from the *IADs* interface. It produces a string that can be used for binding to the object (in the format `"LDAP://<GUID=xxxx...>"`); however, this string cannot be used with the Search.vbs script or Guid2obj.exe tool.

Data types are defined in the *ADSTYPE* enumeration.

Listing 17.5. getProps.vbs — Retrieving the Property Values for a User Object

```
Option Explicit
Sub Main()

Dim objPropList As IADsPropertyList
Dim objPropEntry As IADsPropertyEntry
Dim objVar As IADsPropertyValue
Dim v As Variant
Dim i As Integer
Dim iCount As Integer

' You can select any directory object; a user account, for example:
```

```
Set objPropList = _
        GetObject("LDAP://CN=John Smith,OU=Staff,DC=net,DC=dom")
objPropList.GetInfo

iCount = objPropList.PropertyCount
Debug.Print "***** Total " + CStr(iCount) + _
            " attributes have values for " + _
            objPropList.ADsPath; " *****"
Debug.Print "GUID: " + objPropList.Guid

For i = 0 To iCount - 1
  Set objPropEntry = objPropList.Item(i) 'or = objPropList.Next
  Debug.Print objPropEntry.Name + " (" + _
              CStr(objPropEntry.ADsType) + ")"

  Select Case objPropEntry.ADsType
    Case 1  'ADSTYPE_DN_STRING
      For Each v In objPropEntry.Values
        Set objVar = v
        Debug.Print "    Value: " + objVar.DNString
      Next

    Case 3  'ADSTYPE_CASE_IGNORE_STRING
      For Each v In objPropEntry.Values
        Set objVar = v
        Debug.Print "    Value: " + objVar.CaseIgnoreString
      Next

    Case 7  'ADSTYPE_INTEGER
      For Each v In objPropEntry.Values
        Set objVar = v
        Debug.Print "    Value: " + CStr(objVar.Integer)
      Next

    Case 8  'ADSTYPE_OCTET_STRING
      Debug.Print "    .OctetString"

    Case 9  'ADSTYPE_UTC_TIME
      For Each v In objPropEntry.Values
        Set objVar = v
```

```
        Debug.Print "   Value: " + CStr(objVar.UTCTime)
      Next

    Case 10  'ADSTYPE_LARGE_INTEGER
      Debug.Print "   .LargeInteger"   ' Object doesn't support this
                                       ' property or method

    Case 25  'ADSTYPE_NT_SECURITY_DESCRIPTOR
      Debug.Print "   .SecurityDescriptor"   ' Object doesn't
                          'support this property or method

    Case Else
      Debug.Print "   The value hasn't been converted."
  End Select
Next

Set objPropList = Nothing
Set objPropEntry = Nothing
Set objVar = Nothing
End Sub
```

Searching Active Directory for Objects

There are several ways of treating directory objects of the same type (enumerating objects). Generally, the most preferable way is the following one:

1. Use ActiveX Data Objects (ADO) for searching Active Directory, and obtain a set of necessary objects. (Remember that access through ADO is read-only!)
2. Bind directly to an object found.
3. Carry out modifications.
4. Repeat Steps 2 and 3 for the next object found.

Nevertheless, it is also possible to *filter out*, or *enumerate* child objects located in containers. This approach spreads over one selected domain only. Let us discuss some facts that you must take into consideration.

Note

It is clear that the members of a group are not child objects of that group, so you cannot use filtering. There is a special way to enumerate group members (see the *"Manipulating Group Memberships"* sections).

The flat WinNT namespace can have advantages if you need to find similar objects in an entire domain. However, you will not be able to determine locations of found objects in the OU structure.

Caution

- If the filter is not set, is set to empty, or is not correct, all objects of all classes will be retrieved. In the case of the LDAP provider, an incorrect filter will produce an empty result.

The following program (Listing 17.6) finds all groups in a domain.

Listing 17.6. Filtering.bas — Using Filters with Different Providers

```
Option Explicit
Sub Main()

Dim objAD As IADsContainer
Dim obj As IADs
Dim i As Integer

Set objAD = GetObject("WinNT://NET,domain")
' Or, you can bind to a computer object:
'    Set objAD = GetObject("WinNT://netdc1,computer")

' Using the LDAP provider is not effective, since you cannot filter
' objects in the nested containers. WinNT namespace is flat,
' so all objects are "visible" at the same level.
' The following string will allow you to find objects
' at one level only:
'    Set objAD = GetObject("LDAP://DC=net,DC=dom")

objAD.Filter = Array("group")
' "user" and "computer" are also acceptable for domain objects.
' You can specify two or more object types in the same filter:
'    objAD.Filter = Array("group", "user")
' "printQueue" and "service" can be specified for computer objects
' and the WinNT provider.

' With the LDAP provider, you can also select the following object
' classes:
```

```
' printQueue, builtinDomain, container, organizationalUnit, volume.

i = 1
For Each obj In objAD
  Debug.Print i; obj.Name; " ("; obj.ADsPath; ")"
  i = i + 1
Next

Set objAD = Nothing
Set obj = Nothing
End Sub
```

The following program (Listing 17.7) enumerates all children of both the domain object and nested containers. Thus, all objects of a specified type can be found, and the directory path to each object reflects its location in the entire domain namespace (taking into account the OU structure). This script, however, runs slower than the previous one.

Listing 17.7. EnumeratingInLDAP.bas — Using Recursion and the LDAP Provider

```
Option Explicit
Sub Main()

Dim objAD As IADsContainer
Dim strClass As String
Dim i As Integer

  i = 1
  strClass = "group"  'or obj.Class = "user", etc.

  Sct objAD = GetObject("LDAP://DC=net,DC=dom")
  Call getGroups(objAD, strClass, i)

End Sub

Sub getGroups(objRoot, strType, i)
  Dim obj As IADs

  For Each obj In objRoot
    If obj.Class = strType Then
```

```
      Debug.Print i; obj.Name + " ..... " + obj.ADsPath
      i = i + 1
    End If
    If obj.Class = "organizationalUnit" _
       Or obj.Class = "builtinDomain" _
       Or obj.Class = "container" Then
         Call getGroups(obj, strType, i)
    End If
  Next
End Sub
```

Manipulating User Objects

This section describes some typical manipulations with the most frequently used directory objects — user accounts. I would once again recommend that you print out all documentation on the user object (methods and properties supported by various system providers, relevant enumerations, etc.) to keep on hand.

Note

Refer *Listing 17.13* for information on moving and renaming user accounts.

Creating a User Account

Creating a user account is basically a very simple operation. You need only to consider a few details, which different providers will determine. In general, the procedure is the same for both WinNT and LDAP providers: you bind to a container object and use the *IADsContainer.Create* method for creating a new object of a specified type. However, if the WinNT provider is used, you must bind to a domain, and the new account will appear in the default container — *Users*. By using the LDAP provider, you can bind to any container or OU and create an account within it. Look at the following code snippets:

WinNT provider:

```
Set objDomain = GetObject("WinNT://NET")
Set objUser = objDomain.Create("user", "JSmith")
objUser.SetInfo
```

LDAP provider:

```
Set objOU = GetObject("LDAP://OU=Staff,DC=net,DC=dom")
Set objUser = objOU.Create("user", "cn=John Smith")
```

```
objUser.Put "samAccountName", "JSmith"
' Additional (optional) property definitions go here, e.g.:
'   objUser.FirstName = "John"
'   objUser.LastName = "Smith"
'   objUser.UserPrincipalName = "JSmith@net.dom"
' You can set the password only after creating the user account!
objUser.SetInfo
```

In both cases, a user account with the *minimal* number of defined attributes is created. (See also the *"Creating Multiple Objects"* section.) Table 17.1 shows the differences between these cases.

Table 17.1. The Default Values of User Object Attributes

Property (AD attribute)	Value	
	LDAP provider	WinNT provider
Account Disabled	**TRUE**	**FALSE**
Account Never Expires	TRUE	TRUE
Common Name (cn)	**Must be specified explicitly**	**SAM Account Name**
First Name (givenName)	Empty	Empty
Full Name (displayName)	**Empty**	**SAM Account Name**
Group	Domain User	Domain User
Last Name (sn)	Empty	Empty
Password	Empty	Empty
Password Never Expires	FALSE	FALSE
Profile	Empty	Empty
SamAccountName	Must be specified explicitly	Must be specified explicitly
User Cannot Change Password	FALSE	FALSE
User Must Change Password	TRUE	TRUE
User Principal Name (UPN)	Empty	Empty

Resetting the Password

To set or change the password of a user account, you need to use the special methods — *SetPassword* and *ChangePassword* — of the *IADsUser* interface. The following script (Listing 17.8) sets a new password for a user and forces him or her to change it at the first logon to the system.

Listing 17.8. setPassword.vbs — Resetting User Password

```
Dim strPath 'As String
Dim objUser 'As IADsUser

strPath = "WinNT://netdc1/JSmith"
'strPath = "LDAP://CN=John Smith,OU=Staff,DC=net,DC=dom"

' Connect to the directory object specified in the path:
Set objUser = GetObject(strPath)

' The following statements are used with the LDAP provider:
'   objUser.SetPassword "newPsw"
' User must change the password:
'   objUser.Put "pwdLastSet", 0

' The following statements are used with the WinNT provider:
objUser.SetPassword "newPsw"
' User must change the password:
objUser.Put "PasswordExpired", CLng(1)

On Error Resume Next
objUser.SetInfo
WScript.Echo "Error: " + Hex(Err.Number)

Set objUser = Nothing
```

Disabling Accounts

You can disable or enable a user or computer account by binding to an object and using the *AccountDisabled* method of the *IADsUser* interface. Take a look at the following example script:

Listing 17.9. disableAccount.vbs — Disabling an Account

```
Dim objAccount 'As IADsUser

'   Set objAccount = GetObject("WinNT://NET/JSmith") - for users only
' The LDAP provider allows you to disable both user and computer
' accounts, for example:
'   Set objAccount = _
'           GetObject("LDAP://CN=John Smith,OU=Staff,DC=net,DC=dom")

' Disable a computer account:
Set objAccount = _
       GetObject("LDAP://CN=W2KPRO3,CN=Computers,DC=net,DC=dom")
objAccount.AccountDisabled = True  'False - to enable
objAccount.SetInfo
Set objAccount = Nothing
```

Manipulating Groups

The *IADsUser* and *IADsGroup* interfaces have a few useful methods that are designated for enumerating groups and users.You could certainly directly access the appropriate properties — *memberOf* for user objects, and *member* for group objects — that are responsible for membership information. However, it is much more convenient to use the special access methods, especially when modifying memberships.

Note

Refer *Listing 17.13* for information on moving and renaming group accounts.

Which Groups Does a User Belong to?

The *Groups* method of the *IADsUser* interface allows you to enumerate all groups that a user belongs to. Here is a script that displays the names of the groups for a specified user account:

Listing 17.10. listOfGroups.vbs — Enumerating Groups

```
Dim objUser 'As IADsUser
Dim x 'As Variant

Set objUser = GetObject("LDAP://CN=John Smith,OU=Staff,DC=net,DC=dom")
For Each x In objUser.Groups
   WScript.Echo x.ADsPath
   WScript.Echo x.Name
   WScript.Echo x.distinguishedName, vbCrLf
Next
```

(The `ADsPath` value can be used for subsequent direct binding to a group object.)

Otherwise, you can directly read the value of the *memberOf* property and use the following statements, instead of the last five statements shown above:

```
'Dim arrGroups As Variant
arrGroups = objUser.Get("memberOf")
For Each x In arrGroups
  WScript.Echo x
Next
```

Caution

- Neither by using the *Groups* method nor by reading the *memberOf* property can you display a user's primary group, i. e. the *Domain Users* group (default for user accounts). (By default, the primary group for computer accounts is *Domain Computers*, and for DCs — *Domain Controllers*.) To see an account's primary group, bind to that account and use the *Get* method: `object.Get("primaryGroupID")`.

Who Are the Members of a Group?

By using the *Members* method of the *IADsGroup* interface, you can list all members — users or another groups — of the specified group. Here is a sample script:

Listing 17.11. listOfUsers.vbs — Enumerating Users

```
Dim objGroup 'As IADsGroup
Dim x 'As Variant

Set objGroup = GetObject("LDAP://CN=LocalGrp,OU=Staff,DC=net,DC=dom")
For Each x In objGroup.Members
   WScript.Echo x.Class
   WScript.Echo x.Name
   WScript.Echo x.ADsPath
   WScript.Echo x.distinguishedName + vbCrLf
Next
```

How Can One Add a Member to a Group?

Only one statement (shown in bold) is sufficient to add an account (user, computer, or group) to an existing group. Look at the following code snippet:

```
Dim objGroup As IADsGroup

Set objGroup = GetObject("LDAP://CN=LocalGrp,OU=Staff,DC=net,DC=dom")
objGroup.Add ("LDAP://CN=John Smith,OU=Staff,DC=net,DC=dom")
objGroup.SetInfo
```

Creating Multiple Objects

For experimental purposes, or to evaluate the query performance of your server configuration under stress, you may want to create a large number of directory objects of some type (usually user, computer, or group accounts). The following program will help you to perform this task. You can easily modify it to fit your domain environment as well as to meet your requirements of number and type of objects.

Listing 17.12. new1000.bas — Creating Multiple Objects in Active Directory

```
Option Explicit
Sub Main()

Dim strPath As String
Dim objAD As IADs
Dim objContainer As IADsContainer
Dim n As Integer
Dim nMax As Integer
Dim strName As String

nMax = 1000  ' The number of new objects
strPath = "LDAP://OU=Staff,DC=net,DC=dom"   ' any container you want
'***** For the WinNT provider:
'   strPath = "WinNT://NET,domain"
' The accounts will be created in the Users container.

Debug.Print "Connecting to " + strPath
Set objContainer = GetObject(strPath)

For n = 1 To nMax
  strName = "user" + String(4 - Len(CStr(n)), "0") + CStr(n)

  '********** For the LDAP provider **********
  Set objAD = objContainer.Create("user", CStr("CN=" & strName))
  ' or Set objAD = objContainer.Create("group", CStr("CN=" & strName))
  objAD.Put CStr("sAMAccountName"), CStr(strName)
  ' Statements for defining other properties can be placed here.

  ' The following four statements are necessary in order to immediately
  ' enable the new account:
  '    objAD.SetInfo
  '    strPath = objAD.ADsPath   'bind to the user object
  '    Set objAD = GetObject(strPath)
  '    objAD.AccountDisabled = False
  ' Now, you can also set a password:
  '    objAD.SetPassword "psw"

  '********** For the WinNT provider **********
  '    Set objAD = objContainer.Create("user", strName)
  ' The account will be enabled after creation, and you can
```

```
    ' immediately set the password:
    '    objAD.SetPassword "psw"
    ' The WinNT provider only makes a very restricted set of user
    ' properties available, including PasswordAge, PasswordExpired,
    ' UserFlags, and a few others.
    objAD.SetInfo

    Debug.Print "User " + strName
  Next

  Debug.Print CStr(nMax) + " objects have been created."
  Set objAD = Nothing
  Set objContainer = Nothing
  End Sub
```

Reconstructing an Object Tree

By using ADSI, you can programmatically reconfigure your domain structure: i.e., move, delete, and rename objects. Do not forget that this opportunity does not extend to built-in and system objects.

Moving and Renaming Objects

Moving and renaming an object are essentially the same LDAP operations ("Modify DN"). (***This means that you cannot move or rename objects using the WinNT provider!***) You simply specify *different* source and target containers for a move operation, and the *same* container for a rename operation. While moving, the object can retain or change its name. The following script moves a user from one OU to another. The *MoveHere* method of the *IADsContainer* interface is used.

Important

- The source and destination containers can be located in *different* domains in the same forest. Thus, it is possible to perform inter-domain move operations, but you must take into account possible authentication issues.

Caution

- Changing the distinguished name of a user object does not affect values of such properties as the user's first name, last name, display name, or logon name. Most probably, you will need to renew them, too. Also, make sure to change the value of the *sAMAccountName* attribute (pre-Windows 2000 name) for either user or group accounts. You can do this by binding to the object and using calls to the *Get* and *Put* methods.

Listing 17.13. moveRenameObject.vbs — Moving or Renaming a Directory Object

```
Dim strOldContainerPath, strNewContainerPath, strOldObjName, _
  strNewObjName 'As String
Dim objCont 'As IADsContainer
Dim objObject 'As IADs

' If strNewContainerPath is equal to strOldContainerPath,
' then a renaming operation is performed,
' if not, a moving one is performed.
strOldContainerPath = "OU=HQ,OU=Personnel,DC=net,DC=dom"
strNewContainerPath = "OU=Staff,DC=net,DC=dom"

' If strNewObjName is equal to strOldObjName, the object is moved
' to a new container, retaining its name.
' You can move and rename an entire OU, a group or user object
' as well as directory objects of other types.
strOldObjName = "CN=John Smith"
strNewObjName = "CN=John Smith II"

Set objCont = GetObject("LDAP://" + strNewContainerPath)
Set objObject = objCont.MoveHere("LDAP://" + _
            strOldObjName + "," + strOldContainerPath, strNewObjName)

Set objCont = Nothing
Set objObject = Nothing
```

Deleting Objects

There are two ways to delete a directory object: use the *Delete* method of the *IADsContainer* interface, or use a special interface named *IADsDeleteOps*.

To delete an object using the former method, you need to bind to the object's parent container and call the *Delete* method. This method is applicable to leaf objects only (i.e., the object must not have any child objects). If you try to delete a non-leaf object, you will get the error 2147016683 (0x80072015), which means "The directory service can perform the requested operation only on a leaf object".

By using the *IADsDeleteOps* interface, you can delete an *entire* container with all child objects. (Be careful, since this is a crucial operation. You may want to verify first whether an object has children.) Take a look at the following two scripts.

Listing 17.14. deleteObject.vbs — Deleting a User (a Leaf Object)

```
Dim objCont 'As IADsContainer

Set objCont = GetObject("LDAP://OU=Staff,DC=net,DC=dom")
Call objCont.Delete("user", "CN=Manager")

Set objCont = Nothing
```

Listing 17.15. deleteContainer.vbs — Deleting an Entire Container

```
Dim objCont 'As IADsDeleteOps

Set objCont = GetObject("LDAP://OU=Personnel,DC=net,DC=dom")
Call objCont.DeleteObject(0)

Set objCont = Nothing
```

Designating a Global Catalog Server

The following program checks whether the specified DC is a GC server and if it is so instructed, changes the status of the DC.

Listing 17.16. SetGC.bas — Designating a DC as a Global Catalog Server

```
Option Explicit
Sub Main()

Dim strDSSettings, strServerDN As String
Dim objRootDSE As IADs
Dim objDsService As IADs
```

```
Dim objComp As IADs
Dim iFlag As Integer

' Bind to the RootDSE on a specific server
Set objRootDSE = GetObject("LDAP://netdc2.subdom.net.dom/RootDSE")

' *** Get the Directory Service Settings ***
strDSSettings = objRootDSE.Get("dsServiceName")
Debug.Print "NTDS Settings: " + strDSSettings
Set objDsService = GetObject("LDAP://" & strDSSettings)

' *** Get the distinguished name of the server ***
strServerDN = objRootDSE.Get("serverName")
Debug.Print "Server Name: " + strServerDN
Set objComp = GetObject("LDAP://" & strServerDN)

On Error Resume Next
iFlag = objDsService.Get("options")
If Hex(Err.Number) = "8000500D" Then
  Debug.Print "PROPERTY_NOT_FOUND"
  iFlag = 0
End If

Debug.Print "Current flag value is " + CStr(iFlag)
' Remove comment marks (') from necessary statements to toggle the status
' of the server
If (iFlag And 1) Then
  Debug.Print objComp.Get("name") + " IS a GC server"
  ' Revoke the GC server role:
  '     objDsService.Put "options", iFlag Xor 1   'clear the flag
  '     objDsService.SetInfo
  '     Debug.Print objComp.Get("name") + " is no longer a GC server"
Else
  Debug.Print objComp.Get("name") + " is NOT a GC server"
  ' Assign the GC server role:
  '     Debug.Print objComp.Get("name") + _
                      " will be advertised as a GC server"
  '     objDsService.Put "options", iFlag Xor 1   'set the flag
```

```
'     objDsService.SetInfo
End If

Set objRootDSE = Nothing
Set objDsService = Nothing
Set objComp = Nothing
End Sub
```

How Can the User Find an FSMO Master?

Basically, in Active Directory-based domains (Windows 2000 and Windows .NET), there are five FSMO roles, and every forest contains at least five Active Directory objects, which "know" the names of these operations' masters. Windows .NET domains support *application directory partitions*, and each created partition has its own *Infrastructure Master*. Thus, the total number of operation masters in a single domain forest can exceed five. In addition, every new domain in the forest introduces three operation masters within that domain, since the *PDC*, *RID*, and *Infrastructure* FSMO roles are specific to each domain.

You can easily find all operation masters in a forest by using Ldp.exe. Make a synchronous search with the following parameters:

- **Base DN** — the forest root distinguished name
- **Filter** — `fSMORoleOwner=*`
- **Scope** — `Subtree`
- **Attributes** — `objectClass`
- Chase referrals — `On`

The results — the distinguished names of the objects as well as their types — must be similar to those shown in Table 17.2. The table contains an example of application partition — *forestDnsZones.net.dom.*

Note

It is possible to use other tools, or to retrieve this information programmatically, for example, by making a search using ADO queries. (Specify the filter and an object class shown in Table 17.2.) You can simply display data on the screen or use them in your scripts or programs.

Table 17.2. Active Directory Objects that Hold Information about the FSMO Masters

Object's distinguished name	objectClass
PDC FSMO master	
DC=net,DC=dom	domainDNS
RID FSMO master	
CN=RID Manager$,CN=System,DC=net,DC=dom	rIDManager
Infrastructure FSMO master	
CN=Infrastructure,DC=net,DC=dom	infrastructureUpdate
CN=Infrastructure,DC=ForestDnsZones,DC=net,DC=dom	infrastructureUpdate
Domain Naming FSMO master	
CN=Partitions,CN=Configuration,DC=net,DC=dom	crossRefContainer
Schema FSMO master	
CN=Schema,CN=Configuration,DC=net,DC=dom	DMD

The *fSMORoleOwner* attribute (syntax *DN*) of each found object holds the distinguished name of the DSA (an object of the *nTDSDSA* class) that possesses the appropriate FSMO role. Here is an example of such a name (the elements that will retain their names in all Active Directory installations are in bold):

```
CN=NTDS Settings,CN=NETDC1,CN=Servers,CN=NET-Site,CN=Sites,
↳CN=Configuration,DC=net,DC=dom
```

You can bind to a specific DSA and ask for its parent object (by using the *Parent* method) — this will be the ADsPath of the server that holds the appropriate FSMO role (see *Listing 17.25*).

Using IADsTools

The IADsTools DLL contains over 180 functions (see the full list in *Appendix D*), which administrators can use when performing various tasks — from retrieving some domain configuration data to triggering replication of a directory partition. This facility is not supported, so you may refrain from using a function if you encounter problems.

We will consider only a few examples of using IADsTools for scripting administrative tasks. You can easily expand their basic approach to other functions.

Initiating Replication

To force replication that meets specific requirements, it is possible to write a command file that uses the RepAdmin utility. IADsTools allow you to write a more customizable script that will perform the same task and maybe, some others. The following example illustrates how to initiate replication of a directory partition (shown in bold) between two domain controllers.

Listing 17.17. initReplication.vbs — Replicating the *Configuration* Partition from One DC to Another

```
Dim objDLL 'As Object
Dim intResult 'As Long
Dim strDestDC, strSrcDC 'As String

strDestDC = "netdc2.subdom.net.dom"
strSrcDC = "netdc1.net.dom"

Set objDLL = CreateObject("IADsTools.DCFunctions")
' Initiate inter-domain replication of the configuration container
intResult = objDLL.ReplicaSync(CStr(strDestDC), _
            CStr("CN=Configuration,DC=net,DC=dom"), CStr(strSrcDC))
If intResult = 0 Then
  MsgBox "Replication" + vbCrLf + " FROM " + strSrcDC + vbCrLf + _
         " TO " + strDestDC + vbCrLf + _
         "has been completed SUCCESSFULLY."
Else
  MsgBox "Replication FAILED!"
End If
```

Note that the script waits until the replication process has been completed.

Triggering Knowledge Consistency Checker (KCC)

To manually start the topology generation on a specific DC, you can start the **Active Directory Sites and Services** snap-in, select the **NTDS Settings** object for the DC, open the context menu, and click **Check Replication Topology** in the **All Tasks** submenu. The following script will accomplish the same operation:

Listing 17.18. TriggerKCC.vbs — Manually Triggering the Knowledge Consistency Checker (KCC)

```
Set comDLL=CreateObject("IADsTools.DCFunctions")
intResult=comDLL.TriggerKCC("NETDC1")
If intResult=0 then MsgBox "KCC has been triggered successfully." _
   else MsgBox "Failed"
```

Viewing the Flags of a Domain Controller

IADsTools have many functions that allow administrators to gather information about the configuration of Active Directory. For example, here is a script that displays the flags, i.e., the functional roles, for a specified DC. You can get the same information by entering `nltest /dsGetDC:<domainName>` at the command prompt. (For additional information on Nltest, see *Chapter 11, "Verifying Network and Distributed Services."*)

Listing 17.19. getDcInfo.vbs — Getting a Domain Controller's Flags

```
Dim strDomainName 'As String
Dim strDCName 'As String
Dim objDLL 'As Object
Dim intReturn 'As Long
Dim strFlags 'As String

strDomainName = InputBox("Domain:", "Enter the name of a domain", _
                         "net.dom")
strDCName = InputBox("Domain controller:", "Enter the name of a DC", _
                                     "netdc1.net.dom")
Set objDLL = CreateObject("IADsTools.DCFunctions")
On Error Resume Next
intReturn = objDLL.DsGetDcName(CStr(strDomainName), CStr(strDCName))
If intReturn <> 0 Then
  WScript.Echo "Error # " + Hex(Err.Number)
```

```
Else
  strFlags = Replace(objDLL.ReturnedFlags, vbCr, vbCrLf + vbTab)

  WScript.Echo "Flags for server " + objDLL.DCName + ":"
  WScript.Echo vbTab + strFlags
    End If
```

Here is a sample output of this script:

```
Flags for server netdc1.net.dom:
        DS_PDC_FLAG
        DS_GC_FLAG
        DS_DS_FLAG
        DS_KDC_FLAG
        DS_TIMESERV_FLAG
        DS_CLOSEST_FLAG
        DS_WRITABLE_FLAG
        DS_GOOD_TIMESERV_FLAG
        DS_PING_FLAGS
        DS_DNS_CONTROLLER_FLAG
        DS_DNS_DOMAIN_FLAG
        DS_DNS_FOREST_FLAG
```

Finding FSMO Role Owners

IADsTools have specific methods that return the names of FSMO masters. You need only one statement per FSMO master. In the following script, the domain and DC names are "hardwired" into the script, but you may want to enter them interactively (as in the previous example).

Listing 17.20. getFSMOs.vbs — Asking a DC for the Known FSMO Role Owners

```
Dim strDomainName 'As String
Dim strDcName 'As String
Dim objDLL 'As Object

strDcName = "netdc1.net.dom"        'any DC name
strDomainName = "subdom.net.dom"    'requested domain
Set objDLL = CreateObject("IADsTools.DCFunctions")
```

```
WScript.Echo "Schema Master:          ", _
                         objDLL.GetSchemaFSMO(CStr(strDcName))
WScript.Echo "Domain naming Master: ", _
                         objDLL.GetDomainNamingFSMO(CStr(strDcName))

WScript.Echo "PDC Master:             ", _
    objDLL.GetPdcFSMO(CStr(strDcName), CStr(strDomainName))
WScript.Echo "Infrastructure Master:", _
    objDLL.GetInfrastructureFSMO(CStr(strDcName), CStr(strDomainName))
WScript.Echo "RID Master:             ", _
    objDLL.GetRidPoolFSMO(CStr(strDcName), CStr(strDomainName))
```

This script produces an output similar to the following (the "Site\Server" format is used):

```
Schema Master:          NET-Site\NETDC1
Domain naming Master:   NET-Site\NETDC1
PDC Master:             Remote-Site\NETDC2
Infrastructure Master:  Remote-Site\NETDC2
RID Master:             Remote-Site\NETDC2
```

From this output you can see that the server *NETDC2* (*Remote-Site*) owns three FSMO roles in its own domain, while the server *NETDC1* (*NET-site*) owns two forest-wide FSMO roles.

Various Operations

The following script contains a few more quite different examples of using IADsTools functions. Some screen outputs are placed below.

Listing 17.21. iADsTools.vbs — Various Examples of Using the IADsTools ActiveX Object

```
Dim comDLL 'As Object
Dim i, intResult 'As Integer

Set comDLL = CreateObject("IADsTools.DCFunctions")

'***** Displaying some metadata information for a directory object
```

```
'      stored on the specified DC:
intResult = comDLL.GetMetaData("netdc1.net.dom", _
                         "CN=Sites,CN=Configuration,DC=net,DC=dom")
WScript.Echo "Attribute  *  Local USN  *  Version"
For i = 1 To intResult
  WScript.Echo comDLL.MetaDataName(i) + ": " + _
             CStr(comDLL.MetaDataLocalUSN(i)) + " " + _
             CStr(comDLL.MetaDataVersionNumber(i))
Next

'***** Sending a message to a network computer (xp-pro3.net.dom):
intResult = comDLL.NetSendMessage("xp-pro3.net.dom", _
        "Domain Administrator", "XP-PRO3 will be rebooted in 30 sec!")

'***** Enumerating all GC servers advertised in the forest:
intResult = comDLL.GetGCList("netdc1.net.dom")
WScript.Echo "GC servers (total): " + CStr(intResult)
For i = 1 To intResult
   WScript.Echo comDLL.GCName(i)
Next
```

Here is a sample output of metadata for a directory object:

```
Attribute  *  Local USN  *  Version
objectClass: 1165 1
cn: 150104 2
instanceType: 150105 100001
whenCreated: 150105 100001
showInAdvancedViewOnly: 150105 100001
nTSecurityDescriptor: 150105 100001
name: 150104 100001
systemFlags: 150105 100001
objectCategory: 150105 100001
```

You can obtain the same data by using the Ldp.exe tool and the `repadmin / showmeta` command.

IADsTools provide a very easy way to find all GC servers in the enterprise. The example script produces a result similar to the following:

```
GC servers (total): 2
NETDC1
NETDC2
```

Manipulating Security Descriptors

Working with security descriptors of Active Directory objects is an advanced programming topic that requires a solid understanding of the Active Directory access-control model. However, administrators can easily use some operations that deal with reading and/or settings permissions on Active Directory and other objects. ADSI 2.5 contains three interfaces that help to perform these tasks:

- *IADsSecurityDescriptor* provides access to the common properties of a directory object's security descriptor, such as the owner of the object, the meaning of the descriptor, etc.
- *IADsAccessControlList* allows you to manage the object's Discretionary Access Control List (DACL) that contains the Access Control Entries (ACEs). System ACL (SACL), which controls audit settings, is also supported.
- *IADsAccessControlEntry* manages individual ACEs.

When programmatically setting permissions, you should reference the enumerations shown in the table below. These enumerations contain all necessary constants that must be set in the new Access Control Element (ACE).

Property	Enumeration
AccessMask	ADS_RIGHTS_ENUM
AceFlags	ADS_ACEFLAG_ENUM
AceType	ADS_ACETYPE_ENUM

The following program adds a new ACE that allows the user *NET\Jessica* to read properties (permissions *List Contents*, *Read All Properties*, and *Read Permissions*) of the *Staff* OU directory object. The program also displays all permissions set on this object.

Listing 17.22. addSecDescr.bas — Viewing and Modifying the Security Descriptor of an Object

```
Option Explicit
Sub Main()

Dim objObject As IADs
Dim objSD As IADsSecurityDescriptor
Dim objPropEntry As IADsAccessControlEntry
Dim objDACL As IADsAccessControlList
```

```
'Dim objSACL As IADsAccessControlList     'System ACL
Dim i As Integer

'***** Bind to an Active Directory object:
Set objObject = GetObject("LDAP://OU=Staff,DC=net,DC=dom")
objObject.GetInfo

'***** Retrieve the security descriptor and some its properties:
Set objSD = objObject.Get("ntSecurityDescriptor")

Debug.Print "======================================================="
Debug.Print "Control", objSD.Control, Hex(objSD.Control) + "(Hex)"
Debug.Print "Group", objSD.Group
Debug.Print "Owner", objSD.Owner
Set objDACL = objSD.DiscretionaryAcl
'Set objSACL = objSD.SystemAcl

'***** Create a new ACE:
Set objPropEntry = CreateObject("AccessControlEntry")

'***** Define properties of the ACE *****
' The permissions are granted to the user...
objPropEntry.Trustee = "NET\Jessica"
' Which permissions are granted (0xF01FF = Full control):
objPropEntry.AccessMask = ADS_RIGHT_GENERIC_READ 'ADS_RIGHTS_ENUM

' Define objects the permissions are applied to:
'   ADS_ACEFLAG_NO_PROPAGATE_INHERIT_ACE = This object only (Default)
'   ADS_ACEFLAG_INHERIT_ACE = This object and all child objects
objPropEntry.AceFlags = ADS_ACEFLAG_INHERIT_ACE 'ADS_ACEFLAG_ENUM

' Grant or deny (ADS_ACETYPE_ACCESS_DENIED) access rights:
objPropEntry.AceType = ADS_ACETYPE_ACCESS_ALLOWED 'ADS_ACETYPE_ENUM

'***** Modify the ACL and assign it to the security descriptor:
objDACL.AddAce objPropEntry
objSD.DiscretionaryAcl = objDACL
On Error Resume Next
objObject.Put "ntSecurityDescriptor", Array(objSD)
```

```
objObject.SetInfo
If Err.Number = 0 Then
  MsgBox "ACE has been successfully added!", , "Permissions"
Else
  MsgBox "Error (Hex): " + Hex(Err.Number), , "Permissions"
  Exit Sub
End If

'***** Read current ACL:
objObject.GetInfo
Debug.Print objDACL.AceCount   'Total number of the ACEs

i = 1
For Each objPropEntry In objDACL   'Display some ACE's properties
   Debug.Print CStr(i) + ") "; objPropEntry.Trustee
   Debug.Print "   Mask (Hex)   " + Hex(objPropEntry.AccessMask)
   Debug.Print "   Flags (Hex) " + Hex(objPropEntry.AceFlags)
   Debug.Print "   Type", objPropEntry.AceType
   i = i + 1
Next

Set objObject = Nothing
Set objPropEntry = Nothing
Set objSD = Nothing
Set objDACL = Nothing
End Sub
```

The program presented will display the permissions on the directory object in the following form:

```
1) NT AUTHORITY\SYSTEM
   Mask (Hex)  F01FF
   Flags (Hex) 0
   Type        0
2) NET\Domain Admins
   Mask (Hex)  F01FF
   Flags (Hex) 0
   Type        0
3) NT AUTHORITY\Authenticated Users
   Mask (Hex)  20094
```

```
   Flags (Hex) 0
   Type        0
...
33) NET\Jessica
   Mask (Hex)  80000000
   Flags (Hex) 2
   Type        0
```

With minimal changes, you can use this program with the NTFS File, Registry, Exchange Directory, or Active Directory objects, if you install the *ADsSecurity* DLL from the *ADSI SDK Resource Kit.* (You may also want to go over the examples located in the \ResourceKit\ADsSecurity\File folder.) The following listing illustrates how the same code can be used with both AD objects and files. Notice the statements marked in bold.

Listing 17.23. addSecDescr.bas — Using ADsSecurity for Viewing and Modifying Security Descriptors

```
Option Explicit
Sub Main()

Dim objObject As New ADsSecurity
Dim objSD As IADsSecurityDescriptor
Dim objPropEntry As IADsAccessControlEntry
Dim objDACL As IADsAccessControlList
'Dim objSACL As IADsAccessControlList     'System ACL
Dim i As Integer

' In VBScript you must also add the following statement:
'    objObject = CreateObject("ADsSecurity")

' Read the object's security descriptor directly:
' - from an Active Directory object
Set objSD = _
   objObject.GetSecurityDescriptor("LDAP://OU=Staff,DC=net,DC=dom")
' - from a file (BE SURE THAT THE FILE EXISTS!)
' Set objSD = _
'            objObject.GetSecurityDescriptor("FILE://D:\text.txt")

' Retrieve some properties of the security descriptor:
```

```
Debug.Print "========================================================"
Debug.Print "Control", objSD.Control, Hex(objSD.Control) + "(Hex)"
Debug.Print "Group", objSD.Group
Debug.Print "Owner", objSD.Owner
Set objDACL = objSD.DiscretionaryAcl
'Set objSACL = objSD.SystemAcl

'***** Create a new ACE *****
Set objPropEntry = CreateObject("AccessControlEntry")

'***** Define properties of the ACE *****
' The permissions are granted to the user:
objPropEntry.Trustee = "NET\Jessica"
' Which permissions are granted (0xF01FF = Full control):
objPropEntry.AccessMask = ADS_RIGHT_GENERIC_READ 'ADS_RIGHTS_ENUM

' Define objects the permissions are applied to:
'   ADS_ACEFLAG_NO_PROPAGATE_INHERIT_ACE = This object only (Default)
'   ADS_ACEFLAG_INHERIT_ACE = This object and all child objects
objPropEntry.AceFlags = ADS_ACEFLAG_INHERIT_ACE 'ADS_ACEFLAG_ENUM

' Grant or deny (ADS_ACETYPE_ACCESS_DENIED) access rights:
objPropEntry.AceType = ADS_ACETYPE_ACCESS_ALLOWED 'ADS_ACETYPE_ENUM

'***** Modify the ACL and assign it to the security descriptor **
objDACL.AddAce objPropEntry
objSD.DiscretionaryAcl = objDACL
On Error Resume Next
objObject.SetSecurityDescriptor objSD
If Err.Number = 0 Then
  MsgBox "ACE has been successfully added!", , "Permissions"
Else
  MsgBox "Error (Hex): " + Hex(Err.Number), , "Permissions"
  Exit Sub
End If

'***** Read the current ACL *****
objObject.GetInfo
```

```
Debug.Print objDACL.AceCount   'Total number of the ACEs

i = 1
For Each objPropEntry In objDACL   'Displaying some ACE's properties
   Debug.Print CStr(i) + ") "; objPropEntry.Trustee
   Debug.Print "   Mask (Hex)   " + Hex(objPropEntry.AccessMask)
   Debug.Print "   Flags (Hex) " + Hex(objPropEntry.AceFlags)
   Debug.Print "   Type", objPropEntry.AceType
   i = i + 1
Next

Set objObject = Nothing
Set objPropEntry = Nothing
Set objSD = Nothing
Set objDACL = Nothing
End Sub
```

Caution

- If you are going to use ADsSecurity.dll from a Visual Basic application, do not forget to register the DLL and add a reference to the *ADsSecurity 2.5 Type Library* to the project.

Important

- By using ADsSecurity.dll, you can manipulate permissions on the file system as well as other objects. However, in the current version of ADSI, it is not possible to control access to file or print *shares*.

Using WMI via LDAP

Windows Management Instrumentation (WMI) contains the *WMIExtension* interface that allows an administrator to use WMI for managing computer objects returned from the LDAP namespace. WMI provides the user with a great deal of power over computer components (including OS, services, file systems, event logs, etc.), and description of all its possibilities requires of a separate book. We will only consider the use of methods (*GetWMIObject*, *GetWMIServices*) and property (*WMIObjectPath*) of the *WMIExtension* interface for retrieving some information, which usual ADSI interfaces cannot supply. You can find WMI SDK documentation yourself and easily expand the examples proposed to cover your own needs.

The following program comprises a few samples of information, which you can retrieve using WMI ADSI Extension. To get a list of other properties that can be obtained, see the definition of the class specified in the `"select ... from ..."` string when the *ExecQuery* method is called.

Caution

- To compile the program presented, you must add a reference to the *WMI Extension to DS 1.0 Type Library* and *Microsoft WMI Scripting V1.2 Library* to your VB project.

Listing 17.24. WMI-ADSI.vbs — Using WMI ADSI Extension

```
Option Explicit
Sub Main()

Dim objAD As IADsContainer
Dim obj As IADs
Dim ADSObject As WMIExtension
Dim WMIServices As SWbemServices
Dim WMIObject As SWbemObject
Dim recSet As SWbemObjectSet
Dim LogFile As SWbemObject
Dim i As Integer

' Obtain a list of computers and query each of them:
Set objAD = GetObject("LDAP://CN=Computers,DC=net,DC=dom")
objAD.Filter = Array("computer")
i = 1
For Each obj In objAD
  Debug.Print "#"; i; obj.Name; " ("; obj.ADsPath; ")"
  ' Get a computer object from the LDAP namespace:
  Set ADSObject = GetObject(obj.ADsPath)
  Debug.Print "WMI Object Path: " + ADSObject.WMIObjectPath
  Set WMIObject = ADSObject.GetWMIObject
  Debug.Print vbCrLf

  ' Now you can use any properties or methods of the WMI object.
  ' For the list of properties, see the Win32_ComputerSystem
  ' WMI class definition.
```

```
' Display some system information about the currently
' selected computer:
Debug.Print "Status = " + WMIObject.Status
Debug.Print "Boot state = " + WMIObject.BootUpState
Debug.Print "Computer name = " + WMIObject.Caption
Debug.Print "Role within domain = " + CStr(WMIObject.DomainRole)
Debug.Print "Total memory (bytes) = " + WMIObject.TotalPhysicalMemory
Debug.Print "User registered = " + WMIObject.UserName
Debug.Print vbCrLf

' Get a WMI services object for the "root\cimv2" namespace:
Set WMIServices = ADSObject.GetWMIServices

' Get some information about the OS installed:
Set recSet = WMIServices.ExecQuery _
             ("select * from Win32_OperatingSystem")
' Use GetWMIObject to retrieve a WMI object:
For Each WMIObject In recSet
  Debug.Print WMIObject.Name
Next
Debug.Print vbCrLf

' List all running services:
Set recSet = WMIServices.ExecQuery _
       ("select * from Win32_Service where State<>'Stopped'")
' The following statement allows you to get a list of services that
' have failed to start on the selected computer:
' Set recSet = WMIServices.ExecQuery("select * from Win32_Service
'↳ where State='Stopped' and StartMode='Auto'")
Debug.Print "Services (TOTAL)"; recSet.Count
For Each WMIObject In recSet
  Debug.Print WMIObject.Name
Next
Debug.Print vbCrLf

' List all processes running on the target computer:
Set recSet = WMIServices.ExecQuery("select * from Win32_Process")
Debug.Print "Processes (TOTAL)"; recSet.Count
For Each WMIObject In recSet
```

```
    Debug.Print WMIObject.Name
  Next
  Debug.Print vbCrLf

  ' Enumerate event logs:
  Set recSet = WMIServices.ExecQuery _
             ("select * from Win32_NTEventLogFile")
  Debug.Print "Event logs (TOTAL)"; recSet.Count
  For Each LogFile In recSet
    Debug.Print LogFile.Name
    ' The following statement saves a log to a file
    ' on the target computer;
    ' you need only to form a unique file name:
    '    LogFile.BackupEventlog ("C:\net.evt")
  Next
  Debug.Print vbCrLf

  ' Display all events in the specified log (Application,
  ' Security, System, etc.):
  Set recSet = WMIServices.ExecQuery _
         ("select * from Win32_NTLogEvent WHERE LogFile='Security'")
  Debug.Print "Events (TOTAL)"; recSet.Count
  For Each LogFile In recSet
    ' The latest event will go first.
    ' For a list of properties, see the Win32_NTEventlog
    ' WMI class definition.
    ' You can redirect this information to a file
    ' on the local computer (where the program is running):
    Debug.Print LogFile.CategoryString, LogFile.SourceName, _
           LogFile.EventCode, LogFile.LogFile, LogFile.TimeGenerated
  Next
  Debug.Print vbCrLf

  ' Go to the next computer
  i = i + 1
Next

Set objAD = Nothing
Set obj = Nothing
Set ADSObject = Nothing
```

```
Set WMIServices = Nothing
Set WMIObject = Nothing
Set recSet = Nothing
Set LogFile = Nothing
End Sub
```

Windows 2000 and Windows .NET systems contain the so-called *Windows Management Instrumentation Tester* (wbemtest.exe). If you become particularly interested in using WMI and are not afraid to spend some time learning this powerful technology, you can use that GUI tool for browsing WMI objects and testing queries used in your ADSI scripts.

Note

WMI Query Language (WQL) is used to compose queries that retrieve information about WMI objects. WMI filters written in WQL are also used with Group Policy Objects (GPO). For additional information, start the *Help and Support Center* and search for "WQL."

To start the Windows Management Instrumentation Tester, enter `wbemtest.exe` in the **Run** window. Then, you must connect to a WMI namespace. Click **Connect** and enter `root\cimv2` in the **Namespace** field. In Fig. 17.1, you can see the main window of the tool and the **Query** window that allows you to execute WQL requests.

Caution

- Do not try *to change* anything using that tool until you become familiar with WMI basics and understand the results you can get from using it.

There is another relatively "safe" operation — you can obtain a list of WMI classes and properties of those classes. Click **Enum Classes**. In the **Superclass Info** window (Fig. 17.2), select **Recursive** and click **OK**.

In the class list, you can double click a class name and view the properties and methods exposed by that class. The **Instances** button will allow you to see all objects of the class selected that exist on the computer. All that information might be useful for you to learn WMI objects and debug WQL queries.

Extending the Schema

You can verify the accuracy of the created attributes and classes by using either the **Active Directory Schema Manager** or **ADSI Edit** snap-ins. Make sure that the tools are connected to the Schema Master. Do not forget to reload or refresh the schema if these tools have been opened before a creation operation.

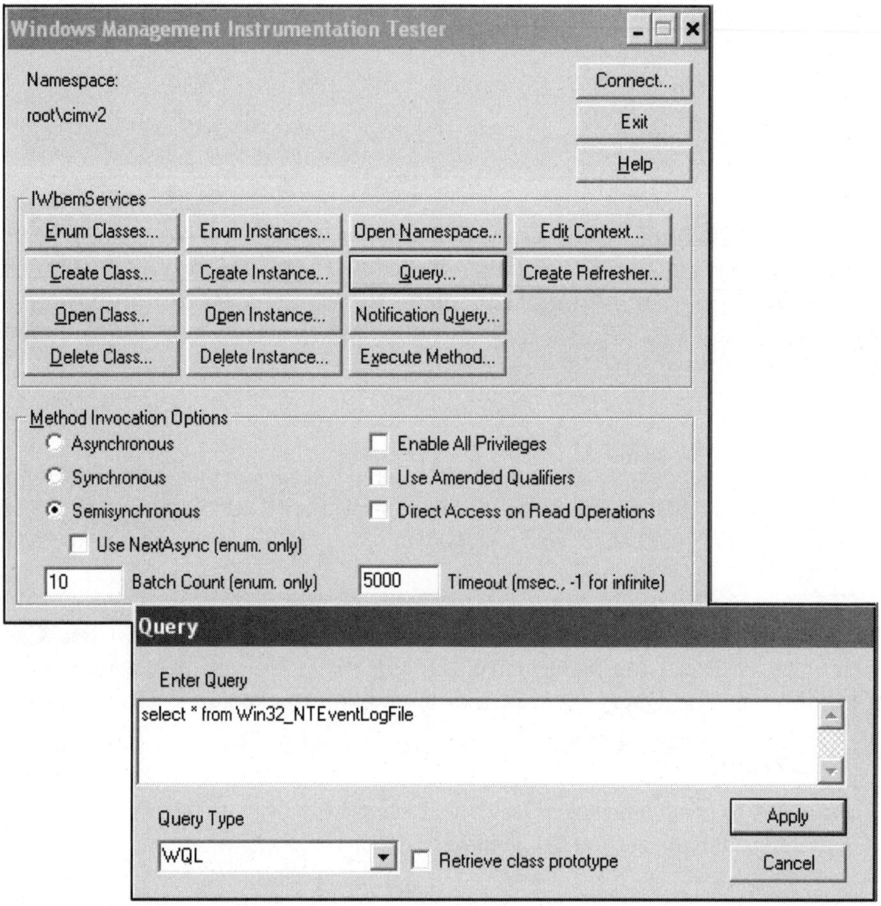

Fig. 17.1. Performing interactive WMI queries using the Windows Management Instrumentation Tester

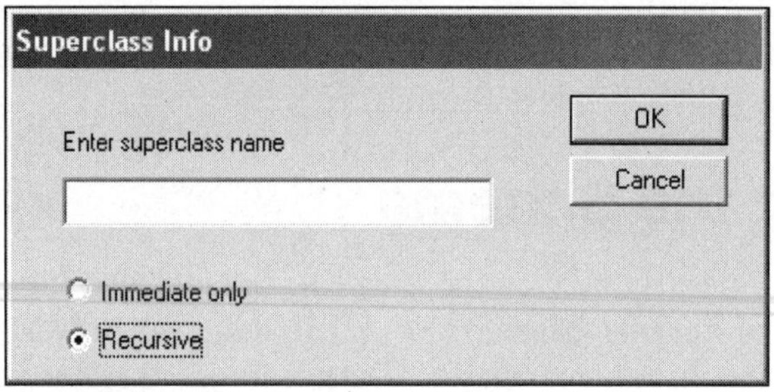

Fig. 17.2. Enumerating all WMI classes

Note

Remember that the **Active Directory Schema Manager** snap-in, when it starts, always connects to the Schema FSMO operation master.

To understand the entire procedure of extending the schema and its requirements and restrictions better, you may first create a sample attribute or class interactively by using the features of the **Active Directory Schema Manager** snap-in (see *Chapter 7, "Domain Manipulation Tools"*). It is possible also to use the **ADSI Edit** snap-in, but this tool is not as straightforward as the aforementioned snap-in.

Creating a New Attribute

The following script creates a new string attribute. All defined properties except *adminDescription* are mandatory. Notice that this script always connects to the Schema Master!

Listing 17.25. newAttribute.vbs — Creating a New String Attribute in the Schema

```
Dim objSchema 'As IADsContainer
Dim objRoot 'As IADs
Dim objNewAttr 'As IADs
Dim str1 'As String
Dim strSchema 'As String

' Retrieve the Schema context:
Set objRoot = GetObject("LDAP://RootDSE")
strSchema = objRoot.Get("schemaNamingContext")
' Bind to the Schema context:
Set objSchema = GetObject("LDAP://" + strSchema)

' Find the Schema Master:
str1 = objSchema.Get("fSMORoleOwner")
Set objRoot = GetObject("LDAP://" + str1)
str1 = objRoot.Parent
Set objRoot = GetObject(str1)
' Get the DNS name of the Schema Master:
str1 = objRoot.Get("dNSHostName")

' Bind to the Schema context on the Schema Master:
```

```
Set objSchema = GetObject("LDAP://" + str1 + "/" + strSchema)
objSchema.GetInfo

' Create the attribute object:
Set objNewAttr = objSchema.Create("attributeSchema", _
                                  "cn=My-Corp-TEST-String-Attribute")
objNewAttr.Put "cn", "My-Corp-TEST-String-Attribute"
objNewAttr.Put "lDAPDisplayName", "myCorp-TEST-StringAttribute"
objNewAttr.Put "attributeID", "1.2.840.113556.1.4.7000. ... .1"
objNewAttr.Put "attributeSyntax", "2.5.5.12"
objNewAttr.Put "oMSyntax", 64
objNewAttr.Put "isSingleValued", True
objNewAttr.Put "adminDescription", "My test attribute"

On Error Resume Next
' Commit the changes:
objNewAttr.SetInfo
If Hex(Err.Number) = 0 Then
  WScript.Echo "The attribute has been successfully created!"
ElseIf Hex(Err.Number) = "80072035" Then
  WScript.Echo "Error (LDAP_UNWILLING_TO_PERFORM)"
ElseIf Hex(Err.Number) = "80071392" Then
  WScript.Echo "Error (LDAP_ALREADY_EXIST)"
Else
  WScript.Echo "Error:" + Hex(Err.Number)
End If

Set objSchema = Nothing
Set objRoot = Nothing
Set objNewAttr = Nothing
```

Using the Created Attribute

When a new attribute has been created, how will you use it? In order to do so, you must perform one more step in extending the schema: add the new attribute to an existing class. (It either can be a standard or newly created class.) The **Active Directory Schema Manger** snap-in is the best tool for this purpose.

1. Open the **Class** folder in the snap-in's window and find the class you want to extend. Suppose we choose the *user* class.
2. Open the **Properties** window and select the **Attributes** tab (Fig. 17.3).

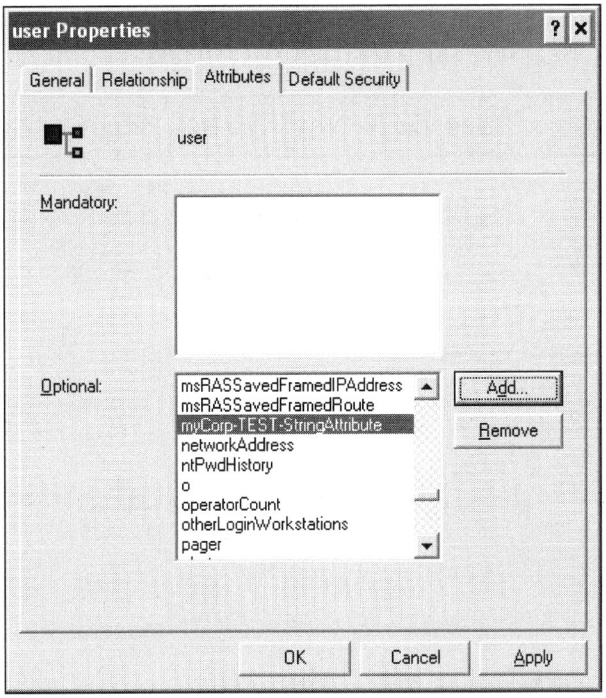

Fig. 17.3. In this window, you can view mandatory and view/add optional attributes of an object class

3. Click **Add** and choose a new attribute in the **Select Schema Object** window (multiple selection is not possible). Click **OK**.
4. Until you click **Apply**, you can remove the attributes that have been added incorrectly. When the selection is done, click **Apply** and close the window.
5. Point to the root in the tree pane and select **Reload the Schema** to write the changes from the memory cache to disk.

Now you can open the **Properties** window for a user in the **ADSI Edit** snap-in and verify whether the new attribute(s) has appeared in the list of optional properties. Either this snap-in or a custom script can be used for setting the values of that attribute.

Creating a New Class

The script presented below creates a structural class inherited from — and *is a subclass of* — the *Person* abstract class. Objects of a new class can be created (instantiated) in organizational units (the *possible superiors*). The *mustContain*, *defaultSecurityDescriptor*, and *adminDescription* properties are not mandatory in this case. (Remember that an object of a class always inherits all attributes of both its own class and parent classes.)

Listing 17.26. newClass.vbs — Creating a New Structural Class

```
Dim objSchema 'As IADsContainer
Dim objRoot 'As IADs
Dim objNewAttr 'As IADs
Dim str1 'As String
Dim strSchema 'As String

' Retrieve the Schema context:
Set objRoot = GetObject("LDAP://RootDSE")
strSchema = objRoot.Get("schemaNamingContext")
' Bind to the Schema context:
Set objSchema = GetObject("LDAP://" + strSchema)

' Find the Schema Master:
str1 = objSchema.Get("fSMORoleOwner")
Set objRoot = GetObject("LDAP://" + str1)
str1 = objRoot.Parent
Set objRoot = GetObject(str1)
' Get the DNS name of the Schema Master:
str1 = objRoot.Get("dNSHostName")

' Bind to the Schema context on the Schema Master:
Set objSchema = GetObject("LDAP://" + str1 + "/" + strSchema)
objSchema.GetInfo

' Create a class object:
Set objNewClass = objSchema.Create("classSchema", _
                                   "CN=MyCorp-TEST-My-Class")
objNewClass.Put "cn", "MyCorp-TEST-My-Class"
objNewClass.Put "lDAPDisplayName", "myCorp-TEST-MyClass"
objNewClass.Put "governsID", "1.2.840.113556.1.5.7000. ... .1"
' 1 = ADS_CLASS_CATEGORY_STRUCTURAL
objNewClass.Put "objectClassCategory", 1
```

```
' 3 = ADS_PROPERTY_APPEND
objNewClass.PutEx 3, "possSuperiors", Array("organizationalUnit")
objNewClass.Put "subClassOf", "2.5.6.6" 'Person
objNewClass.PutEx 3, "mustContain", Array("name", "description")
objNewClass.Put "defaultSecurityDescriptor", _
                "D:(A;;RPWPCRCCDCLCLOLORCWOWDSDDTDTSW;;;DA)" + _
"(A;;RPWPCRCCDCLCLORCWOWDSDDTSW;;;SY)(A;;RPLCLORC;;;AU)"
objNewClass.Put "adminDescription", "My test class"

' Commit the changes:
On Error Resume Next
objNewClass.SetInfo
If Hex(Err.Number) = 0 Then
  WScript.Echo "The class has been successfully created!"
ElseIf Hex(Err.Number) = "80072035" Then
  WScript.Echo "Error (LDAP_UNWILLING_TO_PERFORM)"
ElseIf Hex(Err.Number) = "80072032" Then
  WScript.Echo "Error (LDAP_INVALID_DN_SYNTAX)"
ElseIf Hex(Err.Number) = "80071392" Then
  WScript.Echo "Error (LDAP_ALREADY_EXIST)"
Else
  WScript.Echo "Error:" + Hex(Err.Number)
End If

Set objSchema = Nothing
Set objRootDSE = Nothing
Set objNewClass = Nothing
```

To configure the *defaultSecurityDescriptor* property, use the *Security Descriptor Definition Language* (SDDL) (see the Platform SDK) or use the default value shown in the listing. This security descriptor provides the following default (i.e., directly defined, not inherited) permissions on objects of the new class:

- Authenticated Users — **Read**
- Domain Admins — **Full Control**
- System — Full Control

Using the Created Class

Usually, you can only create objects of a custom class by using either the **ADSI Edit** snap-in or a script. For our sample class, the procedure will be the following:

1. Open the **ADSI Edit** snap-in and select an OU (since the only superior of the sample class is `organizationalUnit`), where the new object will be created.
2. Click **New | Object** on the context or **Action** menu. Select the class from the list (Fig. 17.4).

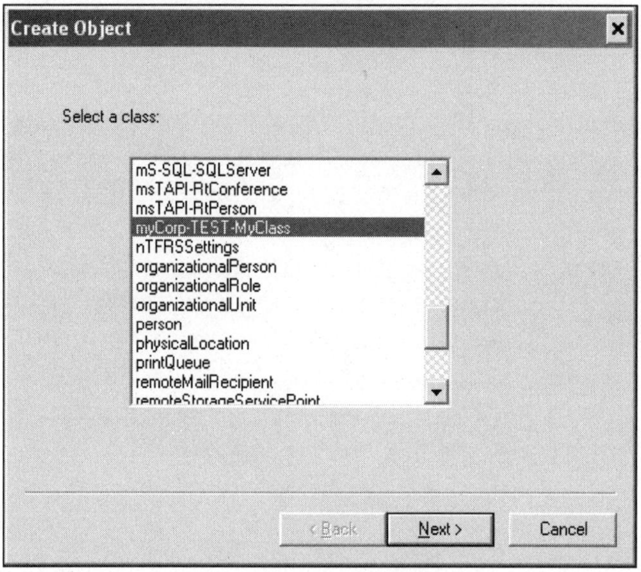

Fig. 17.4. You can create objects of any class listed in this window

3. Enter the name of the new object and the values of all mandatory attributes (directly defined or inherited). You may also click **More Attributes** and define the values of necessary optional attributes.
4. Click **Finish**. The new object of the selected class will be created. Check its type (*myCorp-TEST-MyClass*) in the **Class** column.

You can also make possible adding objects of a custom class through the UI of the **Active Directory Users and Computers** snap-in. See details in the *"ADSI Edit Snap-in"* section (Example 2) of *Chapter 7, "Domain Manipulation Tools."* (You might need to restart administrative snap-ins if you have made any schema changes concerning appearance of objects in the UI.)

PART VI

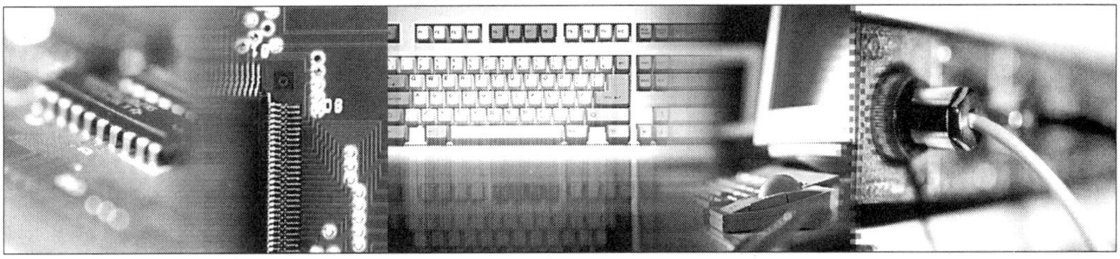

Appendixes

Appendix A: Web Links

Sometimes, the links on the Microsoft website are changed due to site reconstruction. If this occurs, you can search the site contents for the appropriate key words (for example, for a utility's name or document's title).

Do not be confused about the fact that there are many links on Windows 2000; a lot of its information is still relevant for Windows .NET.

General

- Microsoft Help and Support

  The main support resource and the starting point for searching the *Microsoft Knowledge Base* — you can find an article by its number, e.g. *Q265706.* In the Windows .NET environment, you can search for KB articles directly from the *Help and Support Center* (provided that connectivity exists with the Internet):

  http://support.microsoft.com/

- Windows Resource Kits (include Windows XP Professional Resource Kit Documentation and Windows 2000 Resource Kits):

  http://www.microsoft.com/windows/reskits/default.asp
  http://www.microsoft.com/windows2000/techinfo/reskit/en-us/default.asp

- Windows 2000 Server Resource Kits documentation:

  http://www.microsoft.com/technet/treeview/default.asp?url=/technet/prodtechnol/windows2000serv/reskit/default.asp?frame=true

- Windows 2000 Resource Kit Sample Chapters:

  http://www.microsoft.com/windows2000/library/resources/reskit/samplechapters/default.asp

- Windows 2000 Server Home page:

  http://www.microsoft.com/windows2000/server/default.asp

- Deployment Planning Guide:

  http://www.microsoft.com/windows2000/techinfo/reskit/dpg/default.asp

- Active Directory Branch Office Planning Guide:

  http://www.microsoft.com/windows2000/techinfo/planning/activedirectory/branchoffice/default.asp

- Windows Resource Kits — Web Resources (a number of links on various topics):

  http://www.microsoft.com/windows/reskits/webresources/default.asp

- Technical Resources (links to sets of technical information sorted into the phases you will pass through as you use Windows 2000 — Planning and Deployment; Step-by-Step Guides; How it Works, and so on):
  http://www.microsoft.com/windows2000/techinfo/default.asp
- TechNet Online (one of the main web links for a Windows administrator):
  http://www.microsoft.com/technet
- Windows 2000 page on TechNet:
  http://www.microsoft.com/technet/treeview/default.asp?url=/technet/prodtechnol/windows2000serv/Default.asp?frame=true
- Windows 2000 Downloads (Service Packs; Updates; Tools and Utilities, and so on):
  http://www.microsoft.com/windows2000/downloads/default.asp
- Microsoft Download Center (from here, you can find any utility, for example, DCdiag.exe, NetDiag.exe, schemadoc.exe, etc.):
  http://www.microsoft.com/downloads/search.asp
- Active Directory Client Extensions for Windows 95, Windows 98, and Windows NT Workstation 4.0:
  http://www.microsoft.com/windows2000/server/evaluation/news/bulletins/adextension.asp
- Active Directory Client Extensions for NT Workstation 4.0:
  http://www.microsoft.com/ntworkstation/downloads/Other/adclient.asp
- ADMT 1.0 (2,543 Kb):
  http://www.microsoft.com/downloads/release.asp?releaseid=19183
- Domain Rename Tool (with documentation; for Windows .NET only):
  http://www.microsoft.com/windows2000/downloads/tools/domainrename/
- Group Policy Registry Table (the table that displays the Group Policy settings in the Administrative Templates folder and the registry entries that they change):
  http://msdn.microsoft.com/library/default.asp?url=/library/en-us/gp/GPRef.asp?frame=true
- Free Tool Downloads (from the *Windows 2000 Resource Kit*; include GPOTool.exe, GPResult.exe, DumpFSMOs.cmd, KerbTray.exe, etc.):
  http://www.microsoft.com/windows2000/techinfo/reskit/tools/default.asp
  - Windows 2000 Support Tools: DCdiag.exe Utility Update:
    http://www.microsoft.com/downloads/release.asp?ReleaseID=22939

- Windows 2000 Support Tools: NetDiag.exe Update:
  http://www.microsoft.com/downloads/release.asp?ReleaseID=22938

- Windows 2000 Server Resource Kits' documentation:
  http://www.microsoft.com/technet/treeview/default.asp?url=/technet/prodtechnol/windows2000serv/reskit/default.asp?frame=true
- Public newsgroups (on msnews.microsoft.com):
  microsoft.public.win2000.active_directory

Active Directory Service Interfaces (ADSI)

- MSDN Library (Platform SDK, ADSI, and other technical programming information):

  http://msdn.microsoft.com/library/
- Active Directory Service Interfaces Overview (links to resources and downloads):
  http://www.microsoft.com/adsi

  It is advisable to download the *updated version* from the Microsoft Platform SDK page. You can only select and download the necessary files:

  http://www.microsoft.com/msdownload/platformsdk/setuplauncher.asp
- Microsoft Active Directory Services Interfaces 2.5 and SDK (or Active Directory SDK; code and documentation):

  http://www.microsoft.com/ntserver/nts/downloads/other/ADSI25/default.asp
- MSDN Online Windows Development Center:
  http://msdn.microsoft.com/windows2000

  Online documentation — click Networking and Directory Services | Active Directory, ADSI, and Directory Services | SDK Documentation | Directory Services.
- System Administration Scripting Guide Series ("Disclaimer: The article(s) for this guide series is derived from the *System Administration Scripting Guide*, a new book that will ship as part of the Windows .NET Server Resource Kit"):

  http://www.microsoft.com/technet/treeview/default.asp?url=/technet/prodtechnol/windows2000serv/maintain/optimize/script/NETScrgd.asp?frame=true
- Windows Scripting Solutions (a new resource for administrators):
  http://www.winscriptingsolutions.com/

Windows Management Instrumentation (WMI)

- Windows Management Instrumentation Scripting for Beginners (an introduction to WMI scripting for administrators):
  http://www.winscriptingsolutions.com/articles/index.cfm?articleid=20376

VBScript

- Microsoft Scripting Technologies (JScript, VBScript, WSH, etc.):
  http://msdn.microsoft.com/scripting
- Script Debugger 1.0 (description and download; versions for Windows 98/ME and Windows NT/2000/XP):
  http://msdn.microsoft.com/scripting/debugger

Windows Script Host (WSH)

- WSH 5.6 for Windows 98/ME, Windows NT 4.0, and Windows 2000 (description; for download, see http://msdn.microsoft.com/scripting):
  http://msdn.microsoft.com/scripting/windowshost

Appendix B: AD Attributes and Registry Settings Affecting Active Directory Operations

This appendix summarizes some registry settings and Active Directory objects that can be useful for administrators when managing and tuning Active Directory. Be careful, since direct editing of the registry and Active Directory objects is an advanced technique!

Keep in mind that some registry values may be absent on domain controllers, especially on those that are running on Windows .NET (in such cases, the default values are used). Therefore, you need to first create a value and then give it a specified setting. To edit attributes of directory objects, use the **ADSI Edit** snap-in.

General

DNS Resolver Cache

To disable caching of *positively* answered lookup queries on the DNS client, set the REG_DWORD `MaxCacheEntryTtlLimit` value to zero (default is 86,400 seconds, or a day) under the registry key `HKLM\System\CurrentControlSet\Services\DnsCache\Parameters\`.

To disable caching of *negatively* answered lookup queries, set the REG_DWORD `NegativeCacheTime` value to zero under the key `HKLM\SYSTEM\CurrentControlSet\Services\Dnscache\Parameters` (the default value is 300 seconds).

Advertising Global Catalog

When a domain controller is ready to operate as a Global Catalog server, the `Global Catalog Promotion Complete` registry value under the `HKLM\SYSTEM\CurrentControlSet\Services\NTDS\Parameters` key must be equal to `1` (you cannot change it, nor do you need to); at the same time, the *isGlobalCatalogReady* attribute of the RootDSE object is set to `1`.

Advertising Domain Controller

When a server has been successfully promoted to a domain controller, the `HKLM\SYSTEM\CurrentControlSet\Services` registry key must contain the `NTDS` subkey. When the DC has performed a full synchronization of all directory partitions, the *isSynchronized* attribute of the RootDSE object is set to `TRUE`.

Active Directory Diagnostic Levels

To troubleshoot Active Directory problems, you raise the diagnostic levels (up to 5) for necessary event types and then view them in the Directory Service log. All level values are stored under the `HKLM\SYSTEM\CurrentControlSet\Services\NTDS\`

`Diagnostics` key. For example, to track all changes in Active Directory on a specific DC, set the `8 Directory Access` value to 4.

Time-To-Live (TTL) Limits (for Dynamic Objects)

All created dynamic objects live for one day. When a dynamic object is updated, its existence is determined by a minimal lifetime. Both control values are stored in the *msDS-Other-Settings* attribute of the CN=Directory Service,CN=Windows NT, CN=Services,CN=Configuration,DC=*ForestDnsName* directory object:

`DynamicObjectDefaultTTL=86400 sec` (1 day)
`DynamicObjectMinTTL=900 sec` (15 minutes)

IP Deny List

You can prevent a domain controller from answering the LDAP queries from specific IP address(es). To do so, edit the *lDAPIPDenyList* attribute of the CN=Default Query Policy,CN=Query-Policies,CN=Directory Service,CN=Windows NT,CN=Services, CN=Configuration,DC=*ForestDnsName* directory object. Follow two examples: the string of ASCII codes "31 39 32 2E 31 36 38 2E 31 2E 31 32 33 20 32 35 35 2E 32 35 35 2E 32 35 35 2E 32 35 35" defines a single node "192.168.1.123 255.255.255.255"; and the string "31 39 32 2E 31 36 38 2E 31 2E 30 20 32 35 35 2E 32 35 35 2E 32 35 35 2E 30" defines a subnet "192.168.1.0 255.255.255.0".

LDAP Default Query Policy

By default, the Default Query Policy is used (albeit not set!) on every domain controller. It is stored in the CN=Default Query Policy,CN=Query-Policies,CN=Directory Service,CN=Windows NT,CN=Services,CN=Configuration,DC=*ForestDnsName* object. The *lDAPAdminLimits* attribute contains all LDAP administrative limits.

To assign a query policy to a site, create a query policy object and specify its distinguished name in the *queryPolicyObject* attribute of the *NTDS Site Settings* object (of the *nTDSSiteSettings* object class). Every site has a similar object; see childs of the CN=Sites,CN=Configuration,DC=*ForestDnsName* object.

Enumerating Replicas of an Application Directory Partition

To see which DCs store the replicas of an application partition, find the corresponding *crossRef* object in the CN=Partitions,CN=Configuration,DC=*ForestDnsName* container. The multi-valued attribute *msDS-NC-Replica-Locations* (syntax *DN*) contains distinguished names (DN) of all *nTDSDSA* objects that represent the domain controllers (Active Directory servers) that hold replicas of that partition; here is an example of such a name: CN=NTDS Settings,CN=NETDC1,CN=Servers, CN=NET-Site,CN=Sites,CN=Configuration,DC=net,DC=dom.

You can also search the *Sites* container of the *Configuration* partition for *nTDSDSA* objects whose *hasMasterNCs* attribute contains the DN of the application partition. For example, for the *ForestDnsZones.net.dom* application partition, you can use the following search filter:

```
(&(objectClass=nTDSDSA)(hasMasterNCs=DC=ForestDnsZones,DC=net,DC=dom)).
```

Active Directory Backup

When the Active Directory database is restored from backup media, it is not in a valid format. The Backup utility automatically adds the `RestoreInProgress` value to the `HKLM\SYSTEM\CurrentControlSet\Services\NTDS` key when restore is successful. Active Directory reads this value after the system reboot, and performs a consistency check and re-index of the database files. Then, the `RestoreInProgress` value is automatically deleted. You must not add, delete, or change this value; however, you can check it to be sure that the restore has been successfully completed and that Active Directory is in operational condition.

Show Directory Objects in the Advanced View Only

To disable browsing of Active Directory containers and OUs as well as specific directory objects in the **My Network Places** folder or in the **Active Directory Users and Groups** snap-in (in normal node), you can modify the *showInAdvancedViewOnly* attribute of the corresponding object and set it to `TRUE` (default setting for usual objects, such as users, groups, as so on, is <Not Set>, i.e., `FALSE`).

Garbage Collection, Online Active Directory Database Defragmentation, and Tombstone Lifetime

When a directory object is deleted, it is moved to the Deleted Objects container and is marked as a *tombstone*. By default, the tombstone lifetime is 60 days (minimum setting is 2 days). When a tombstone is deleted during a period that exceeds the lifetime value, a special *garbage collection* process will completely remove the directory object. This process runs at regular intervals (by default, 12 hours; minimum setting is 1 hour); it also *defragments* the Active Directory database. Two attributes, *tombstoneLifetime* and *garbageCollPeriod*, of the cn=Directory Service,cn=Windows NT, cn=Services,cn=Configuration,dc=*ForestDnsName* object control both parameters.

Removing Lingering Objects

When a DC has been offline for a period that exceeds the tombstone lifetime, the tombstones stored on it cannot be completely removed and replicated to/from other

DCs (since the other DCs do not store such deleted objects at this point). The following sample command will help you to remove tombstones and repair replication:

```
C:\>repadmin /removelingeringobjects netdc4.net.dom df69f38c-c924-492d-a7e6-3b0b1bc7dcc5 DC=net,DC=dom
RemoveLingeringObjects sucessfull on netdc4.net.dom.
```

The target DC is specified by its DNS name, and a "reference" DC is represented by its GUID name (use the `repadmin /showreps` command to view DC object GUIDs).

Replication Issues

Replication Events

To see when replication starts and finishes, increase the `5 Replication Events` value under the `HKLM\SYSTEM\CurrentControlSet\Services\NTDS\Diagnostics` key to value 2, and use Event Viewer. If you set this value to 4 or 5, you can see the names of attributes that have been replicated.

Replication Latency Interval

By default, a DC waits for replication with its partners during a latency interval equal to 24 hours. If a DC does not respond during that period of time, a replication error event will be registered. To change the default latency interval, modify the `HKLM\System\CurrentControlSet\Services\NTDS\Parameters\Replicator latency error interval (hours)` registry value.

Normal Intra-Site Replication Intervals

If a DC updates an object attribute, it will send a notification message to its first replication partner within a specified time interval (5 minutes by default). To change the default setting (300 seconds), modify the `Replicator notify pause after modify (secs)` value under the `HKLM\SYSTEM\CurrentControlSet\Services\NTDS\Parameters` key. The originating DC will notify the next replication partner within the time specified by the `Replicator notify pause between DSAs (secs)` registry value (30 seconds by default). These values affect replication of all partitions.

To change settings for a specific partition (e.g., for an application directory partition), use the corresponding *crossRef* object in the CN=Partitions,CN=Configuration, DC=*ForestDnsName* container:

- The *msDS-Replication-Notify-First-DSA-Delay* attribute specifies when the DC will notify the first replication partner (5 minutes by default).

- The *msDS-Replication-Notify-Subsequent-DSA-Delay* attribute specifies when the DC will send subsequent notifications to the second, third, and any other replication partners (30 seconds by default).

Replication to Global Catalog

To enable/disable an attribute to be replicated to Global Catalog, find the corresponding attribute object in the *Schema* partition and set the value of its *isMemberOfPartialAttributeSet* attribute to `TRUE` or `FALSE` (default settings is <Not set>, i.e., `FALSE`).

Intervals at Which the Knowledge Consistency Checker (KCC) Runs

The KCC evaluates the replication topology every 15 minutes (900 seconds) and makes changes as necessary. To change this interval, modify the REG_DWORD `Repl topology update period` value under the `HKLM\SYSTEM\CurrentControlSet\Services\NTDS\Parameters` key and set a new number of seconds.

Disabling the Knowledge Consistency Checker (KCC)

To disable automatic generation of replication topology for a site, you can modify the *options* attribute of the CN=NTDS Site Settings,CN=Default-First-Site-Name, CN=Sites,CN=Configuration,DC=*ForestDnsName* object:

- To disable intra-site topology generation, set the attribute to 1 (0 × 1)
- To disable inter-site topology generation, set the attribute to 16 (0 × 10)
- To disable both intra-site and inter-site topology generation, set the attribute to 17 (0 × 11)

In a Windows .NET environment, you can also use the `repadmin /siteoptions` command (to see the command parameters, enter `repadmin /experthelp` at the command prompt).

To verify replication topology, use the *ReplMon.exe* utility and generate a report on the site configuration.

Appendix C: ADSI Interfaces Supported by the LDAP and WinNT Providers

The following table lists all interfaces (42 in total) supported by either the LDAP or WinNT provider, or by both of them. The last column indicates one of 10 categories to which an interface belongs. First of all, get acquainted with the *core* interfaces.

Interface name	LDAP	WinNT	Category
IADs	**Yes**	**Yes**	**Core**
IADsAccessControlEntry	Yes	No	Security
IADsAccessControlList	Yes	No	Security
IADsClass	Yes	Yes	Schema
IADsCollection	No	Yes	Persistent object
IADsComputer	No	Yes	Persistent object
IADsComputerOperations	No	Yes	Dynamic object
IADsContainer	**Yes**	**Yes**	**Core**
IADsDeleteOps	Yes	No	Utility
IADsDomain	No	Yes	Persistent object
IADsExtension	Yes	Yes	Extension
IADsFileService	No	Yes	Persistent object
IADsFileServiceOperations	No	Yes	Dynamic object
IADsFileShare	No	Yes	Persistent object
IADsGroup	Yes	Yes	Persistent object
IADsLargeInteger	Yes	No	Data Type
IADsLocality	Yes	No	Persistent object
IADsMembers	Yes	Yes	Persistent object
IADsNamespaces	**Yes**	**Yes**	**Core**
IADsO	Yes	No	Persistent object
IADsObjectOptions	Yes	No	Utility
IADsOpenDSObject	**Yes**	**Yes**	**Core**
IADsOU	Yes	No	Persistent object
IADsPathname	Yes	Yes	Utility

continues

Continued

Interface name	LDAP	WinNT	Category
IADsPrintJob	No	Yes	Persistent object
IADsPrintJobOperations	No	Yes	Dynamic object
IADsPrintQueue	Yes	Yes	Persistent object
IADsPrintQueueOperations	Yes	Yes	Dynamic object
IADsProperty	Yes	Yes	Schema
IADsPropertyEntry	Yes	Yes	Property Cache
IADsPropertyList	Yes	Yes	Property Cache
IADsPropertyValue	Yes	Yes	Property Cache
IADsPropertyValue2	Yes	Yes	Property Cache
IADsResource	No	Yes	Dynamic object
IADsSecurityDescriptor	Yes	No	Security
IADsService	No	Yes	Persistent object
IADsServiceOperations	No	Yes	Dynamic object
IADsSession	No	Yes	Dynamic object
IADsSyntax	Yes	Yes	Schema
IADsUser	Yes	Yes	Persistent object
IDirectoryObject*	Yes	No	Core/Non automation
IDirectorySearch*	Yes	No	Core/Non automation

* — Non-automation clients only!

Appendix D: IADsTools Functions

The complete list of the functions (183 in total) that are implemented in the IADsTools DLL has been placed below. Use a context search to find the description of a function in the iadstools.doc file.

AddPerformanceCounter()
ADSPNMappings()
ADStayOfExecution()
BridgeHeadName()
CheckDNForSpecialChars()
ClearPerformanceCounters()
ClearUserCredentials()
ClientSiteName()
ClosePerformanceData()
ConvertDNSToLDAP()
ConvertErrorMsg()
ConvertLDAPToDNS()
DCAddress()
DCAddressType()
DCListEntryComputerObject()
DCListEntryDnsHostName()
DCListEntryHasDS()
DCListEntryIsPDC()
DCListEntryNetBiosName()
DCListEntryServerObject()
DCListEntrySiteName()
DCName()
DCSiteName()
DirectPartnerFailReason()
DirectPartnerFailReasonText()
DirectPartnerGuid()
DirectPartnerHighOU()
DirectPartnerHighPU()
DirectPartnerInConflict()
DirectPartnerLastAttemptTime()
DirectPartnerLastSuccessTime()
DirectPartnerName()
DirectPartnerNumberFailures()c
DirectPartnerObjectGuid()
DirectPartnerSyncFlags()
DirectPartnerTransportDN()
DirectPartnerTransportGuid()
DSABridgeHeadTransport()
DSABridgeHeadTransportCount()
DSAComputerPath()
DSAConnectionAdminGenerated()
DSAConnectionEnabled()
DSAConnectionName()
DSAConnectionNotify()
DSAConnectionNotifyOverride()
DSAConnectionReasonCode()
DSAConnectionReasonCount()
DSAConnectionReasonPartition()
DSAConnectionServerName()
DSAConnectionTwoWay()
DSADNSHostName()
DSAInvocationID()
DSAMailAddress()
DSAObjectGUID()
DSAOptions()
DSASchemaLocation()
DsGetDcList()
DsGetDcName()
DsGetSiteName()
EnableDebugLogging()
GCName()
GetActiveDirectoryProperties()
GetBridgeHeadsInSite()
GetChangeNotifications()
GetConfigurationNamingContext()
GetDefaultNamingContext()
GetDirectPartners()
GetDirectPartnersEx()
GetDomainNamingFSMO()
GetDSAConnections()

GetDSAProperties()
GetGCList()
GetGPOs()
GetGPOSysVolVersion()
GetGPOVersion()
GetGuidForServer()
GetHighestCommittedUSN()
GetInfrastructureFSMO()
GetInterSiteTopologyGenerator()
GetInterSiteTransports()
GetIPConfiguration()
GetMetaData()
GetMetaDataDifferences()
GetNamingContexts()
GetObjectFromGuid()
GetObjectGuidForServer()
GetPartialNamingContexts()
GetPDCFSMO()
GetPerformanceData()
GetRDNForObject()
GetRegistryData()
GetReplicationUSNState()
GetReplicationUSNStateEx()
GetRidPoolFSMO()
GetSchemaFSMO()
GetServerFromGuid()
GetServersInSite()
GetServersInSiteWithWritableNC()
GetSiteForServer()
GetSiteLinkBridgeProperties()
GetSiteLinkBridges()
GetSiteLinkProperties()
GetSiteLinks()
GetSiteList()
GetSiteProperties()
GetSubnets()
GetTrustRelationships()
GetWritableNCsForServer()
GPOGuid()
GPOName()
GPOSysVolVersion()
GPOVersion()
InitPerformanceData()
LastCallResult()
LastErrorText()
MetaDataDifferencesAttribute()
MetaDataDifferencesCount()
MetaDataDifferencesLastWriteTime()
MetaDataDifferencesObjectDN()
MetaDataDifferencesOrigServer()
MetaDataDifferencesOrigUSN()
MetaDataLastWriteTime()
MetaDataLocalUSN()
MetaDataName()
MetaDataServerName()
MetaDataSourceUSN()
MetaDataVersionNumber()
NamingContextName()
NetSendMessage()
NotificationPartnerAddedTime()
NotificationPartnerName()
NotificationPartnerObjectGuid()
NotificationPartnerSyncFlags()
NotificationPartnerTransport()
PerfCounterName()
PerfCounterValue()
ReplicaSync()
ReplicaSyncAll()
ReplPartnerGuid()
ReplPartnerInConflict()
ReplPartnerName()
ReplPartnerUSN()
ReturnedFlags()
ServerInSiteEntryName()
ServerInSiteEntryUUID()
SetDsGetDcNameFlags()
SetReplicaSyncAllFlags()
SetReplicaSyncFlags()
SetUserCredentials()
SiteEntryName()

SiteLinkBridgeEntryDN()
SiteLinkBridgeEntryName()
SiteLinkBridgeSiteCount()
SiteLinkBridgeSiteList()
SiteLinkBridgeTransport()
SiteLinkCost()
SiteLinkEntryDN()
SiteLinkEntryName()
SiteLinkEntryType()
SiteLinkName()
SiteLinkOptions()
SiteLinkReplInterval()
SiteLinkSiteCount()
SiteLinkSiteList()
SiteOptions()
SiteTopologyFailover()
SiteTopologyGenerator()
SiteTopologyRenew()
SubnetName()
SubnetSiteObject()
TestBind()
TranslateDNToNT4()
TranslateNT4ToDN()
TransportAddress()
TransportAddress()
TransportDLLName()
TransportName()
TreeName()
TriggerKCC()
TrustDirection()
TrustDomainName()
TrustNetBIOSName()
TrustType()

GLOSSARY

Application directory partition — a user or application created partition; this partition type is only available on domain controllers running Windows .NET. Can store any type of object (including *dynamic objects*) except for security principals. Data from application partitions are not replicated to Global Catalog. The replication scope of an application partition is defined by administrators and can include any set of domain controllers in the forest. By default, built-in application partitions `ForestDnsZones` and `DomainDnsZones` with different replication scopes are used to store DNS information when the Windows .NET DNS Server is installed automatically on the first domain controller in a forest. See also *Directory partition*.

Authoritative restore — a type of restore operation in Active Directory domains in which objects of the restored directory subtree are treated as authoritative, replacing all copies of these objects that exist in a domain or in the forest. To make a normal restore the authoritative restore, use the NTDSutil tool. See also *Non-authoritative restore*.

Authoritative server — a DNS server that registers resource records for a domain and is allowed to resolve queries about the names stored in the appropriate zone. The authoritative server is specified in SOA and NS records for this zone.

Authoritative zone — a DNS zone that contains resource records related to a domain name. The right to resolve this domain's names is delegated to that zone.

Backup Domain Controller (BDC) — in a Windows NT 4.0 or earlier domain, domain controllers that store a read-only copy of the directory database that is replicated from the PDC. They are used for fault tolerance and distributing logon attempts.

BDC — see *Backup Domain Controller*.

Caching name server — does not contain any zone files and is only used for improving DNS performance in local networks. The caching server can store a resolved query and quickly respond to subsequent queries from clients by using cached information without addressing the remote authoritative servers.

Cross-reference object — the Active Directory object that stores information about "external" directory objects and services, e.g., about an object that belongs to another domain (and, therefore, is stored in another directory partition).

Delegation (DNS) — a method for distributing the workload among several name servers within the Internet or a domain. A name server may itself have the right to resolve queries for domain names, or can delegate some of the authority to other servers. This right is stated in the appropriate authoritative zones (with SOA and NS records).

Directory partition — a unit of replication in Active Directory, a part of directory namespace. There are at least three directory partitions: schema, configuration, and domain. Every domain controller holds two former partitions and its own domain partition. So, the forest of 5 domains will contain 7 directory partitions: one schema, one configuration, and 5 domains. The domain partition is replicated only within a given domain. The schema and configuration partitions are replicated through the whole forest. Global Catalog contains a subset of attributes of all domain objects. See also *Application directory partition.*

Directory System Agent (DSA) — a core Active Directory service that manages the directory information stored on a hard disk. Runs on Active Directory domain controllers only.

Distinguished Name (DN) — the name that uniquely identifies an object within Active Directory. DN consists of the *relative distinguished name* (RDN) of the object and a set of parent objects' RDNs, e.g., `CN=dc1,OU=Domain Controllers, DC=domain,DC=com`.

DN — see *Distinguished Name.*

DNS — see *Domain Name System.*

Domain — 1. **DNS domain** — any tree or subtree that is a part of DNS namespace. DNS naming starts with the *root domain* represented as "." (period). 2. **Active Directory domain** (Windows 2000 or Windows .NET) — a group of computers and other network resources that can be administered as a whole. The security parameters (i.e., policies) of one domain do not affect other domains and are not affected by them.

Domain local group — a security or distribution group that can be granted rights and permissions on resources that only reside in the same domain where this group is located. Groups with that scope can contain universal, global, and other domain local groups from their own domain, as well as accounts from any domain in the forest.

Domain Name System (DNS) — de facto Internet standard used for registering a computer's friendly names and IP addresses. DNS has a hierarchical structure of names that form a single namespace called the domain tree. DNS is, by nature, a static service, but later realizations (RFC 2136) describe a dynamic method of updating DNS information (recourse records). In Active Directory domains, DNS is a *must-have* service, and if configured incorrectly, can generate many problems with authentication, administering, etc.

DSA — see *Directory System Agent.*

Dynamic object — an Active Directory object which has an associated Time-To-Live (TTL) value that is set when the object is created; when TTL expires, a dynamic object disappears. Therefore, clients that store dynamic information will need to periodically refresh that information. This object type is only supported on Windows .NET.

File Replication Service (FRS) — a standard Windows 2000/.NET Server service used for replicating system policies and logon scripts stored in System Volume (SYSVOL). FRS also replicates data sets defined by the Distributed File System (DFS).

Forest — Active Directory domains that are linked with automatically established two-way, transitive trusts. They share the same schema, replication information, and Global Catalog.

Forwarder — a DNS server that can continue resolving the client query if the client's preferred server could not answer the query. A typical example is the ISP's DNS server configured as a forwarder on a local DNS server.

FQDN — see *Fully Qualified Domain Name.*

FRS — see *File Replication Service.*

Fully Qualified Domain Name (FQDN) — a DNS name that uniquely identifies a computer on the network and consists of the computer (host) name plus all names in the domain tree starting with the root domain. An FQDN name reflects the hierarchy of all host's parent domains. For example, the FQDN for a `host1` that is a member of the `department` in the `company` will be `host1.department.company.com`.

Global Catalog — a directory that contains a partial replica of every object in the forest. Clients can use it to quickly locate any object that can belong to any domain. Global Catalog is hosted on one or more domain controllers called Global Catalog servers. A forest should contain at least one Global Catalog server.

Globally Unique Identifier (GUID) — a 128-bit (8-byte) number that is automatically generated for referencing objects in the Active Directory. Here is an example of GUID: `7050f604-9f15-4536-a592-76d5af2e3487` (32 hex digit).

GUID — see *Globally Unique Identifier.*

Host — a computer or other TCP/IP network resource with a unique name and IP address. Hosts can communicate one with another in a network using their IP addresses or some name resolving system (such as DNS or WINS).

InetOrgPerson — an object class that is defined in RFC 2798 and supported by Active Directory on Windows .NET servers. The InetOrgPerson object is derived from the user class and can be used as a security principal. Support for InetOrgPerson makes easier migration from other LDAP directories to Active Directory.

Master server — same as *Authoritative server*. Master servers will either be primary or secondary; this depends on the method of obtaining zone data.

Name server (NS) or **service** — a service that resolves friendly names (DNS or WINS) to IP address(es). Name servers store all information about the namespace. In Active Directory domains, name services are widely used for locating sites, domain controllers, Global Catalog servers, and many other network resources.

Namespace — a list of available named objects that forms a hierarchical tree. An example of a namespace might be the folder structure on a hard disk. For name services, the DNS namespace is hierarchical, while the WINS namespace is flat.

Non-authoritative restore — the normal restore operation in Active Directory domains. The objects restored from backup media can be updated with new object copies stored on other domain controllers. See also *Authoritative restore*.

PDC — see *Primary Domain Controller*.

Primary Domain Controller (PDC) — in a Windows NT 4.0 or earlier domain, a singular domain controller that holds the master read-write copy of the directory database for the domain; authenticates domain logon attempts, and updates user, computer, and group accounts in the domain. In an Active Directory domain, the PDC Emulator provides PDC functionality for pre-Windows 2000 client computers.

Primary master server — the master server that can be used for direct updating of zone information. The primary master is the source for replicating the zone file to other (secondary) DNS servers.

Primary zone — a directly updatable store for DNS resource records that belong to that zone. Can be considered to be an analog of the PDC's database, replicated to all other replicas (BDCs).

RDN — see *Relative Distinguished Name*.

Recursive query — one of two methods used by DNS servers to resolve queries (see also *Iterative query*). If a DNS server cannot answer the query itself, in recursive mode it becomes a resolver of another DNS server, retrieves its answer, and passes it to the waiting client. In this mode, the DNS server performs all the work in finding the final answer.

Relative Distinguished Name (RDN) — the name that uniquely identifies an object within a directory container. In a sense, SAM account names can be regarded as RDNs in the domain container. The same RDN may be repeated in a naming tree (in a domain or in a forest), but must be unique in a particular chain of parent names, i.e., distinguished names cannot be repeated.

Resolver — a DNS client that submits queries to name servers and receives IP address(es) that correspond(s) to a requested name. Windows 2000/XP/.NET resolver also performs the caching and some other "intellectual" functions.

Resolving — in DNS or WINS, the process (and mechanism) of finding a host IP address using its name, or vice versa. This process has two participants: a client issues a request to a name server, and this server returns the appropriate information.

Resource record (RR) — an element of the DNS database. A group of RRs make up a DNS zone. Depending on their purpose, resource records vary by type: there are A, PTR, CNAME, SRV, MX, and other records.

Secondary master server — a master that cannot perform zone updates on its own and renews its data only as a result of zone replication from primary masters.

Secondary zone — a read-only copy of the primary zone, updated from it with zone transfers. It is used for DNS load distribution and fault tolerance. Can be considered to be an analog of a BDC's database that contains the information replicated from the master store (PDC).

Security principal — a user, security group, or computer account. In Windows .NET, a new security principal, *InetOrgPerson*, has been introduced.

SOA — see *Start of Authority*.

SRV record — a resource record type used for registering and locating well-known TCP/IP services. Vitally important for Active Directory domains, because such records are used to locate domain controllers, sites, Global Catalog servers, and other resource.

Start of Authority (SOA) — for DNS, a resource record that specifies the domain's authoritative name server. The required first record in all forward and reverse zone files.

System state — system state is used for backing up and restoring system-specific information including Active Directory. On domain controllers, it consists of the registry, class registration database, system boot files, Active Directory database files, and SYSVOL volume.

Time-To-Live (TTL) — a time interval of caching a resource record on a client side (in the resolver) or on a name server. In Windows .NET, this term is also applicable to *dynamic objects*, too.

Tombstone — a "hidden" Active Directory object that is removed from the directory but not yet entirely deleted. Tombstones are necessary to replicate deleted objects trough the entire forest.

TTL — see *Time-To-Live.*

Update Sequence Number (USN) — a 64-bit counter that is used for tracing replication changes between Active Directory domain controllers. Each domain controller increments its current (highest committed) USN at the start of each object update transaction.

UPN — see *User Principal Name.*

User Principal Name (UPN) — the standard naming format for logging on to Windows 2000 domains: `user@domain.com`. Consists of a user logon name and a *UPN suffix* that by default is equal to the domain name where the user account is registered. To simplify logging on, additional UPN suffixes can be used for *any* users in the domain tree. These suffixes are not required to be valid DNS domain names, e.g., such UPNs as `user@corpName` or `user@local` are valid.

USN — see *Update Sequence Number.*

Windows Name System (WINS) — a naming service that permits clients to get the IP address(es) corresponding to the requested NetBIOS name. Since clients can register or release their own names, WINS is a dynamic service in contrast to *standard* DNS. In Active Directory domains, WINS can be used in conjunction with a Windows 2000/.NET DNS Server to allow pre-Windows 2000 clients to update their names.

WINS — see *Windows Name System.*

Zone — a part of DNS database stored on a name server. Zone is an element of DNS domain namespace and DNS database.

Zone transfer — the process of copying a DNS zone file from the primary master to the secondary master(s).

"How to...?"

This index, divided into themes, will help you to find where the answer to a specific, practical question is located. It is often difficult to locate the information you need in a certain situation, even if this information is contained in the book.

General Issues

Active Directory Installation and Configuration

Active Directory Domain Administration

Active Directory Maintenance

Active Directory Replication

Active Directory Security and Group Policies

Program Access to Active Directory

...import, export, or modify AD objects in batch mode, 320
...modify (extend) the Active Directory schema, 149, 329, 417, 469
...modify an attribute of an Active Directory object, 298, 323, 437
...modify attributes of a number of directory objects, 132, 330
...modify directory objects from the command prompt or a command file, 320
...move a directory object to another container, 449
...move directory objects from one domain to another domain within the same forest, 342
...move or rename a directory object from the command prompt, 320
...promote a DC to a Global Catalog server from the command prompt, 289, 451
...rename a directory object (user, group, OU, etc.), 449

Index

G

H

I

T

U

V

W

X

Z